ARAFAT:
THE BIOGRAPHY

Tony Walker and
Andrew Gowers

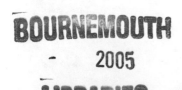

Virgin
BOOKS

For Nicolas, Jessica and Nathaniel,
Daniel and Madeleine

This edition published in 2003 by
Virgin Books
Thames Wharf Studios
Rainville Road
London W6 9HA

A version of this book was first published in Great Britain in
1990 as *Behind the Myth: Yasser Arafat and the Palestinian
Revolution* by W.H. Allen.

www.virgin.com/books

Typeset by TW Typesetting, Plymouth, Devon

Printed and bound by CPD Wales

ISBN 0 7535 0888 5

A catalogue record for this book is available from the
British Library.

CONTENTS

PREFACE AND ACKNOWLEDGEMENTS

This is the second – more extensive – revision since this work was first published by W.H. Allen in 1990 as *Behind the Myth: Yasser Arafat and the Palestinian Revolution*. A comprehensive revision, *Arafat: The Biography* published by Virgin Books followed the signing of the Oslo Accords in September 1993. In 1991, Corgi published a paperback version of *Behind the Myth*. Much has happened since 1993 to justify a substantial reworking of the original: the stuttering Oslo process, the failure of Camp David 2, the impact of 11 September 2001, terrorist bombings in the Middle East, and the contagion of Palestinian suicide attacks against Israeli targets mean that circumstances are vastly different today compared with a decade ago. Views of Arafat have fluctuated wildly in the intervening period – from a willingness by the international community to accord him the benefit of the doubt, even embrace him, to a pervasive view today that he has squandered his opportunities. Whatever the validity of these judgements, this deeply flawed individual remains leader of the Palestinians in the absence of a realistic alternative. Thus, for better or worse, he remains significant to future developments. More to the point, it is impossible to comprehend the Middle East predicament without reference to Arafat's role over four decades since he launched his Fatah movement, and subsequently assumed chairmanship of the Palestine Liberation Organisation in 1969. This most recent work, which encompasses the latest crisis period in Middle East peacemaking, tracks Arafat from his early life as a student leader in Cairo and underground activist in the Gulf to his present bleak circumstances, shunned by friend and foe.

A number of those who were interviewed for the first and subsequent versions have fallen by the wayside. But except where death is relevant to the ebb and flow of events we have not complicated the text by reference to the passing away of less prominent individuals.

Between 1989, when the initial research was undertaken, and the present we cast our net wide in seeking to establish facts of what has been – continues to be – a murky story. The book is based on many hundreds of hours of interviews with the principals most intimately involved in the Palestinian struggle, many of whom are no longer with us and whose first-hand testimony would otherwise have been lost.

In Cairo, Jerusalem and Gaza, we interviewed members of his family; in Egypt and the Gulf, we tracked down Palestinians who were involved in the national movement during its early years; in Syria and Jordan, we spoke to allies and opponents of the PLO leader; in Tunis, we lost count of the hours we spent with senior Arafat lieutenants; in Israel, Europe and the US, we quizzed officials for whom Arafat had been the enemy. Some of these individuals asked us not to use their names; many others are named in the text and notes; all gave more generously of their time and attention than we could have reasonably expected, and for this we are most grateful.

Above and beyond all others there are two Palestinians in particular without whom this book would not have been possible. The late Salah Khalaf, Arafat's number two until his assassination in January 1991, and Nabil Shaath, a longstanding Arafat confidant, devoted many painstaking hours to discussing the evolution of the movement from their respective vantage points. For their help, and for the frankness with which they expressed their views, we offer special thanks. Shaath was again unstinting with his time in early 2002 in hours of conversation conducted at his home and in his office in the Gaza Strip. As always his insights and his anecdotes helped illuminate the story, as did Arafat's special adviser, Bassam Abu Sharif. The authors also drew on the personal observations in this most recent period of Ziad Abu Amr, Marwan Kanafani, Eyad el Serraj and Raja Sourani in Gaza; in Jerusalem Mehdi Abdul Hadi and Hanna Seniora; and in Ramallah Hanan Ashrawi. Albert Aghazarian, a true friend of this project for more than a decade, made his usual invaluable contribution. Other Palestinians, notably those in the business community, provided insights on the basis of anonymity.

Other Palestinian figures who were unsparing with their time over the years included Farouk Kaddoumi, George Habash, Khaled al-Hassan, Hani al-Hassan, Yasser Abed-Rabbo, Bassel Akel, Munib al-Masri, Gamal Sourani, Jaweed al-Ghussein, Ibrahim Bakr, Fathi Arafat and other relatives including cousin Umm Mohammed, Jamil Hilal, Suleiman Najab, Abdullah Hourani, Abdel Latif Abu Hijleh, Zoheir al-Alami, Mohammed Milhem, Faisal al-Husseini, Sari Nusseibeh, Hanna Seniora, Saeb Erakat, Bashir Barghouti, Mohammed Sobhieh, Ahmed Kora'i, Emad Shakur, Mohammed al-Natour, Rafik al-Natshe, Asad Abdelrahman, Ibrahim Abu Ayyash, Mamdouh Nofal, Ahmed Sidki Dajani, Mohammed Abu Mayzar, Mohammed Said Musa Maragha, Mohammed Hamza, Leila Shaheed, Maghoub Omar, Khaled Fahoum, Sakher Abu Nizar, Abbas Zeki, Bahjat Abu Gharbiyya, Intissar al-Wazir, Ahmed Abdelrahman, Sami Musallam, Ilan Halevy, Yaacoub Diwani, Qais al-Samarai, Abu Ali Moustafa, Abu Daoud Mohammed Awdah, Abdullah Franji, Said Kamal, Afif Safieh, Abdulmajeed Shoman, Selim Zaanoun, Awni Battash, Zakaria Abderrahim, Ahmed Khalidi, Professors Edward Said and Walid Khalidi and the military historian Yezid Sayigh.

On the Israeli side, Generals Aharon Yariv and Avraham Tamir and David Kimche among many others provided special guidance, while Uri Avnery, Uri Milstein, Shlomo Avineri and David Tal were generous with time and counsel.

In the recent research Dan Yatom, Ron Pundak, Nahum Barnea, David Hartman and Tom Segev were particularly helpful in Tel Aviv and in Jerusalem, as was Terje Roed Larsen, the United Nations special envoy and midwife to Oslo 1. In Washington, William Quandt and Judith Kipper, as always, provided wise counsel, as did Richard Murphy in New York. In Egypt, at different times, Tahseen Bashir, Esmat Abdel Meguid, Mahmoud Riad, Ahmed Baha el-Dine, Ihsan Bakr, Selim Issa, Sir James Adams and Mohammed Hassanein Heikal were invaluable sources of information and advice; as were, in Jordan, Taher al-Masri, Marwan Qasem, Zeid Rifai, Jamal Sha'er and Mashour Haditha al-Jazy. In Washington and New York, the late Cyrus Vance, Alfred Atherton, Joe Sisco, Talcott Seelye, John Edwin Mroz, Nicholas Veliotes, Richard Viets, Brian Urquhart, Geoffrey Kemp and Rita Hauser provided many useful insights, and so, in Europe, did the late General Vernon Walters, Anders Bjurner and Lakhdar Brahimi. In Tunis, Robert Pelletreau and Stephen Day were always helpful and hospitable.

The book also drew heavily on the efforts of our researchers, Jihan el-Tahri, Shahira Idris and Efrat Shvilly, who put in much hard work on our behalf in Tunis, Cairo and Jerusalem. Suleiman Khalidi offered valuable help in Kuwait. A special thank you is in order to Lamis Andoni, who conducted several interviews for us and otherwise provided wise counsel.

Over the years we owe a debt of gratitude to our editors: Sir Geoffrey Owen and Richard Lambert of the *Financial Times*; Creighton Burns and Michael Smith of *The Age*; and more recently Michael Gill, Colleen Ryan and Glenn Burge of *The Australian Financial Review*. We have also been fortunate with our publishers and book editors, first, Gill Gibbins, our editor at W.H. Allen, and most recently Paul Copperwaite of Virgin Books. Professional colleagues too numerous to mention have rendered assistance, but it would be remiss not to single out Walter Helfer of German television ARD, and his wife Randa, whose help was invaluable in many different ways, not least in unravelling what transpired at Munich in 1972. Walter also deserves mention for his excellent translation for the German edition. Thanks also to the respective families of the authors who were obliged to endure lengthy absences as this project was born, and then reborn. This work sets out to be one without prejudice, but if perceived otherwise the judgements made and conclusions reached are those of the authors and the authors alone.

T.W. and A.G.
New York, November 2002

GLOSSARY OF TERMS

Amal ('Hope'). Pro-Syrian militia unit in Lebanon.

Arab National Movement. Founded by George Hasbash and others in the 1950s; after the 1967 Arab–Israeli war, transformed itself into the Popular Front for the Liberation of Palestine (q.v.).

Al-Asifa ('The Storm'). The name under which Fatah (q.v.) conducted military operations; now no longer in use.

Baath ('Renaissance'). Pan-Arab political movement that took power in Syria and Iraq in the 1960s.

Black September. The Palestinians' name for their defeat in the Jordanian civil war, September 1970.

Black September Organisation. Fatah's terrorist arm, disbanded in 1974.

Camp David Accords. Agreements signed in September 1978 by Israel, Egypt and the US, leading to the Israeli–Egyptian peace treaty.

Central Council. The PLO's 'mini-parliament', midway between the Executive Committee and the Palestine National Council.

Democratic Front for the Liberation of Palestine. Marxist PLO faction, led by Nayef Hawatmeh.

Executive Committee. The PLO 'cabinet', chaired by Arafat.

Fatah ('Conquest'). The Palestine Liberation Movement, the largest faction in the Palestine Liberation Organisation (q.v.), founded by Arafat and others in 1958. It is headed by a Politburo, or General Secretariat, under Arafat's leadership, and has its own quasi-democratic institutions of which the largest and most representative is the 1,200-member Fatah Congress.

Fedayeen ('Those who sacrifice themselves'). Palestinian guerrillas.

Force 17. Arafat's personal security force.

Haganah. The Jewish regular force in Palestine before the establishment of the state of Israel.

Hizbollah ('Party of God'). Fundamentalist party in Lebanon.

Ikhwan al-Muslimun. The Moslem Brotherhood, a fundamentalist political movement.

Intifada ('The Shaking'). The Palestinian uprising in the Israeli-occupied territories, December 1987–present.

Irgun. Jewish terrorist group in the 1940s, led by Menachem Begin.

Jihad. Holy war.

Occupied Territories. The West Bank and Gaza Strip, captured by Israel in 1967.

October War (or Yom Kippur War). The 1973 war between Israel and Arab states which led eventually to the peace treaty with Egypt.

Oslo Accords. Declaration of Principles reached by Israeli and Palestinian negotiators in 1993 laying out blueprint for steps towards peace.

Palestine Liberation Front. PLO faction notorious for the hijacking of the cruise liner *Achille Lauro*, 1985.

Palestine Liberation Organisation. Body founded by Arab states in 1964 to represent the Palestinians, taken over by Fatah and other guerrilla groups in 1969.

Palestine National Council. The PLO 'parliament'.

Palestine National Fund. The PLO's 'finance ministry', in charge of raising and administering the organisation's money.

Palestinian. An Arab who originates from, or whose family originates from, the area formerly known as Palestine, between the Jordan river and the Mediterranean. The Palestinians are estimated to number between five and six million today, of whom around 2.3 million are registered as refugees in Arab countries and the Israeli-occupied territories.

Palestinian National Covenant. The PLO Charter, setting out the organisation's aims and strategy, adapted by the Palestine National Council in July 1968. It calls for the liberation of all Palestine through armed struggle and declares the establishment of Israel 'fundamentally null and void'. Western governments have long urged the PLO to repeal the covenant, and Arafat maintains that it is now outdated.

Palestinian Resistance. Generic term for guerrilla groups.

Popular Front for the Liberation of Palestine. Marxist PLO faction, led by George Habash.

Resolution 242. The 1967 UN Security Council resolution that has been a touchstone for efforts to foster Middle East peace negotiations ever since. The Resolution calls for: '1) withdrawal of Israeli armed forces from territories of recent conflict. 2) termination of all claims or states of belligerency and respect for and acknowledgement of the sovereignty, territorial integrity and political independence of every state in the area and their right to live in peace within secure and recognised boundaries free from threats or acts of force.' Its sole reference to the Palestinians consists of a call for 'a just settlement of the refugee problem'.

Six-Day War. The June 1967 war between Israel and Arab states in which Israel captured the West Bank, the Gaza Strip, the Sinai Peninsula and the Golan Heights.

Stern Gang. Jewish terrorist group in the 1940s, led by Yitzhak Shamir.

Western Sector. Section of Fatah devoted to attacks on Israel, commanded until his death by Khalil al-Wazir.

Zionism. The creed of the Jewish national movement which established the State of Israel in 1948.

CHRONOLOGY

November 1947. United Nations General Assembly votes to partition Palestine, then under British rule, into two states, one Jewish, one Arab.

1948. Britain pulls out of Palestine. With Palestianian inhabitants and neighbouring Arab states refusing to implement the partition plan, Jewish leaders establish the State of Israel and defeat the Arabs in the War of Independence. By the end of the fighting, hundreds of thousands of Palestinians have fled.

1950. Jordan, which controls the West Bank of the Jordan river after the 1948 war, formally annexes it, bringing the remaining inhabitants of Palestine under Hashemite control.

1952. Gamal Abdel Nasser comes to power in Egypt; Yasser Arafat is elected president of Palestinian Students' League in Cairo.

1956. Together with Britain and France, Israel attacks Egypt, occupies most of the Sinai Peninsula and the Gaza Strip before withdrawing under US pressure. Palestinian unrest in Gaza on the increase.

July–December 1958. Arafat and other Palestinians agree to establish the Fatah movement in Kuwait.

July 1962. Algeria gains independence from France after an eight-year colonial war. Fatah allowed to establish its first office in Algiers.

January–June 1964. Arab states agree to establish the Palestine Liberation Organisation; first session of the Palestine National Council in Jerusalem.

January 1965. Fatah launches armed raids into Israel.

January–May 1966. Arafat arrested and imprisoned twice in Syria.

June 1967. Israel attacks Egypt, Syria and Jordan; captures the West Bank, the Gaza Strip, the Golan Heights and the Sinai Peninsula.

March 1968. Israel attacks Palestinian guerrilla bases in the Jordan Valley, in the Battle of Karameh.

February 1969. Arafat elected chairman of the executive committee of the Palestine Liberation Organisation.

September 1970. King Hussein's army moves against PLO guerrillas in Jordan; after fierce fighting, the Palestinians are saved by intervention of Arab states.

July 1971. The last PLO guerrillas are ejected from Jordan and take refuge in Syria and Lebanon.

September 1972. The Black September Organisation seizes Israeli athletes at Munich Olympic Games. Nine Israelis die in airport shoot-out.

October 1973. Egypt and Syria launch surprise attack on Israeli forces occupying the Sinai Peninsula and the Golan Heights.

October 1974. Arab leaders, meeting in Rabat, declare the PLO the 'sole legitimate representative' of the Palestinian people.

November 1974. Arafat addresses the United Nations General Assembly in New York.

April 1975. Civil war breaks out in Lebanon, with Palestinian guerrillas fighting alongside Lebanese leftists and Muslims against Maronite Christians.

October 1976. After Syrian intervention in the Lebanese war on the side of the Maronite Christians, Arab leaders agree a ceasefire.

November 1977. Egyptian President Anwar Sadat goes to Jerusalem and in a Knesset address offers peace.

March 1978. Israel invades south Lebanon and attacks PLO guerrillas.

September 1978. Camp David Accords signed by Israel, Egypt and the US.

February 1979. Ayatollah Khomeini returns to Iran at the climax of the Iranian revolution.

March 1979. Egypt and Israel sign peace treaty.

July 1981. 'Katyusha War' between Israel and PLO guerrillas in southern Lebanon.

June 1982. Israel invades Lebanon again in an all-out offensive against the PLO, and its forces reach the outskirts of Beirut.

August 1982. After an 88-day siege, the PLO withdraws its forces and staff from Beirut under a US-brokered agreement, establishing a headquarters in Tunis, and scatters its fighters to seven Arab countries.

September 1982. Hundreds of Palestianian refugees massacred by Lebanese Maronite Christian gunmen in Beirut.

June–November 1983. Fatah commanders in Lebanon stage a mutiny against Arafat's leadership; Arafat returns to the Lebanese port of Tripoli, where he is again besieged.

December 1983. After being evacuated from Tripoli, Arafat provokes controversy by visiting Egypt.

February 1985. Arafat, on a visit to Amman, signs a political co-operation accord with King Hussein with the aim of taking part in an international Middle East peace conference.

October 1985. Israeli planes attack PLO headquarters in Tunis. Guerrillas from the Palestine Liberation Front hijack the cruise liner *Achille Lauro* in the Mediterranean.

February 1986. The Arafat–Hussein accord collapses.

December 1987. The Palestinian uprising begins in the Israeli-occupied Gaza Strip and spreads to the West Bank.

April 1988. Khalil al-Wazir slain by Israeli commandos in Tunis.

November 1988. The Palestine National Council declares an independent Palestinian state and implicitly recognises Israel by accepting UN Security Council Resolution 242.

December 1988. Arafat addresses the UN General Assembly in Geneva, explicitly recognises Israel and renounces terrorism. The US agrees to open dialogue.

November–December 1989. Mass emigration of Soviet Jews to Israel begins.

May 1990. An Arab League emergency summit convenes in Baghdad at the PLO's behest to debate the Jewish immigration issue.

August 1990. Iraq invades Kuwait. Saddam Hussein links withdrawal from Kuwait with settlement of the Palestine question.

January 1991. Salah Khalaf and two colleagues slain by renegade Palestinian.

January 1991. War breaks out in the Gulf. Allied bombing campaign continues for more than a month.

February 1991. President Bush announces suspension of hostilities and the return to the Middle East of Secretary of State Baker to seek a 'durable' peace.

October 1991. Middle East Peace Conference in Madrid. Israel begins direct talks with its neighbours.

November 1991. Arafat marries Suha Tawil secretly in Tunis.

April 1992. Arafat survives plane crash in Libyan desert, pilot and co-pilot killed.

June 1992. Yitzhak Rabin's Labour Party wins Israeli election and moves to engage PLO in dialogue.

September 1993. Israel–PLO mutual recognition. Interim self-rule agreement initialled for Gaza and Jericho.

May 1994. Arafat and Rabin initial Cairo Agreement giving effect to Oslo Declaration of Principles on Interim Self-Government Arrangements, effectively blueprint for the peace process.

July 1994. Arafat returns to the occupied territories after an absence of nearly three decades.

October 1994. Israel and Jordan sign peace treaty.

December 1994. Arafat, Rabin and Shimon Peres receive Nobel Peace Prize.

September 1995. Arafat and Rabin sign 'Oslo 2' Interim Agreement on the West Bank and Gaza.

November 1995. Rabin assassinated at a Peace Now rally in Tel Aviv. Peres sworn in as Prime Minister pending fresh elections.

January 1996. Arafat elected Prime Minister of the Palestinian National Authority. Fatah wins majority in Legislative Council.

May 1996. Benjamin Netanyahu of Likud defeats Peres. Opposes Oslo.

January 1997. Israel and Palestinians conclude Hebron Accords paving way for further redeployment of Israeli forces in the occupied territories.

October 1998. Wye River Agreement on further implementation of Oslo.

May 1999. Ehud Barak prevails over Netanyahu in elections for Prime Minister.

July 2000. Camp David 2 ends in failure. Arafat blamed.

September 2000. Ariel Sharon visits Temple Mount/Haram al-Sharif prompting widespread rioting among Palestinians.

December 2000. George W. Bush prevails over Al Gore for Presidency. Clinton makes last ditch 'lame duck' attempt to ignite peace process.

February 2001. Sharon defeats Barak in elections for Prime Minister.

September 2001. Islamic terrorists fly planes into World Trade Center towers, precipitating war between the West and terrorist gangs.

June 2002. Bush announces support for 'two-state solution' to the Arab–Israel conflict, but provides no timetable.

March 2003. Mahmoud Abbas named Prime Minister.

March 2003. War in Iraq.

PROLOGUE

'It's unbelievable, unbelievable, unbelievable.' Yasser Arafat, 11
September 2001.

The time was 5.56 p.m. in Gaza (10.56 a.m. in New York), two
hours after American Airlines Flight 11 had slammed into the
World Trade Center. Yasser Arafat was lost for words, falling back
on one of his pet phrases in times of stress. Indeed, much had
happened that was scarcely believable in Arafat's turbulent career
as leader of the Palestinians between his first tentative steps on to
a world stage in the late 1960s as Chairman of the Palestine
Liberation Organisation and 11 September 2001. The Palestinians
themselves had been responsible for acts of terror which had made
an indelible impression on world history, such as their assault on
the Israeli team headquarters at the Munich Olympics in 1972.
But even Munich paled into relative insignificance compared with
9/11, as it came to be known. As Arafat, flicking from one news
channel to another in his Gaza headquarters, digested the
implications of the most brazen terrorist assault on Western
interests in the name of militant Islam, he knew that he needed to
move quickly to condemn the attack and in the process quell
whatever triumphalism might be felt among Palestinians living
under Israeli occupation. As it happened, Arafat was huddled with
Miguel Moratinos, the European envoy to the Middle East,
discussing yet another faltering peace initiative. Moratinos, according to those present, advised, indeed urged, Arafat to waste no
time at all in voicing his outrage. There must be no repeat of the
equivocation which Arafat had shown over Iraq's grab for Kuwait
ten years previously. He must demonstrate leadership in dis-
couraging the sort of scenes which had reflected so badly on the
Palestinians, namely people of the territories on their rooftops
cheering on the Iraqi Scud missile attacks against Israel. So it was
that an hour and sixteen minutes after the attack on the Pentagon
– the third of three aircraft suicide bombings that day – Arafat

appeared before a media scrum: 'I send my condolences, and the condolences of the Palestinian people, to American President Bush and his government and to the American people for this terrible act. We completely condemn this serious operation . . . We were completely shocked . . . It's unbelievable, unbelievable, unbelievable.'[1]

Unbelievable or not, it was clear that 9/11 would have implications for the Palestinians and Arafat in particular that stretched well beyond the shocking events they had witnessed on their television screens. Not only were the Palestinians obliged to deal with a first-term US President who had to that point evinced little interest in – and even less knowledge of – Middle East issues, but they would also now have to contend with a terror-obsessed and vengeful US administration. Circumstances were bleak enough for the Palestinian leadership anyway, following the election of Ariel Sharon as Israel's Prime Minister just a few months previously, an event which coincided with an intensification of armed conflict in the West Bank and Gaza. The use of guns and the increasing resort to suicide bombings as a means of protest meant that trust between Palestinians and Israelis had all but dissipated by the time the World Trade Center towers collapsed. Arafat himself was bearing the scars of all the years of politicking and manoeuvring in a Middle East bazaar. At the age of 72, his voice was weakening, his lips trembled, his hands shook and his imperfect English required more conspicuous prompting from close aides when he appeared in public. At an age when he might have expected respite from his travails, Arafat was finding the going rough, to say the least. After the euphoria of his handshake with Yitzhak Rabin on the White House lawn on 13 September 1993, circumstances virtually eight years later to the day could hardly have been less propitious. All the promise of the early Oslo process, even the anticipation surrounding Camp David in 2000, had dissipated and, worse, Arafat was again face to face with his nemesis, General Sharon who, as Defence Minister in the Begin Government, had tried to kill him during the siege of Beirut in 1982. Sharon, ever the opportunist, certainly saw opportunity in 9/11 to exert further pressure on the Palestinians, especially in the court of American opinion rubbed raw by the trauma of seeing one of the country's architectural icons demolished and so many of its citizens tragically killed. But not for the first time would Sharon overplay his hand, describing Arafat as the 'bin Laden of the Middle East'. He also sought to draw parallels between Arafat's Palestinian Authority and bin Laden's terrorist network, al- Qaeda. Sharon also seized the moment to crack down harder on the territories, sending tanks into the Arab towns of Jenin and Jericho to quell unrest, while resisting pressure from Washington to resume meaningful peace negotiations. It was to be a pattern which would continue over the next weeks and months as the US, preoccupied first with its war in Afghanistan and subsequently with preparation for an attack on Iraq, exerted little meaningful endeavour in the cause of Middle East peace.

Emphasising the Palestinian predicament in the days after the World Trade Center attacks was an unhelpful message from Osama bin Laden in which he sought to link his own *jihad* against the West with the Palestinian cause: 'When these (holy warriors) defended their oppressed sons, brothers and sisters in Palestine and in many other countries, the world at large shouted, followed by hypocrites. (But) Israeli tanks and tracked vehicles also enter to wreak havoc in Palestine, in Jenin, Ramallah, Rafah, Beit Jala and other Islamic areas and we hear no voices raised or moves made. But if the sword falls on the United States after 80 years, hypocrisy raises it head, lamenting the death of these killers who tampered with the blood, honour and holy places of the Muslims. The least that one can describe these people (*sic*) is that they are morally depraved. They champion falsehood, support the butcher against the victim, the oppressor against the innocent child. May God mete out to them the punishment they deserve.'

Needless to say bin Laden's words were swiftly rejected by the Palestinian leadership who observed – correctly – that the Saudi renegade had never evinced much interest in the Palestinian cause before. The last thing Arafat and his colleagues needed was to be identified in any way shape or form with bin-Ladenism. In their efforts to neutralise any hint of sympathy for what happened in New York, the Palestinian leadership went to almost comical lengths, including Arafat's own theatrical gesture of donating a pint of his own blood for the New York victims. At the American consulate in Jerusalem Palestinians laid flowers, carrying placards which read: 'Terror is our common enemy', and, 'We are victims too'. In the remorseless struggle for victimhood between Israelis and Palestinians, 9/11 was hardly the issue. It was much closer to home – in the towns and hamlets of the West Bank and Gaza – where the Israeli military fought daily battles with stone-throwing Palestinian youths and fought occasional armed skirmishes with militants.

Observing all this from either Ramallah – where he spent much time in 2001–2 cooped up under virtual house arrest – or from his headquarters in Gaza, an ageing Arafat could not but have chafed that time was passing, that dreams he had harboured as a student in Cairo more than half a century before would not be realised. For an old man apparently nearing the end of his public career these were bleak moments, for which he himself was responsible in no small measure indeed. It would have been no consolation for him to reflect on opportunities lost, most recently at Camp David in mid-2000 where the prospect of a 'peace of the brave' had been proffered, but had not been taken.

His words, uttered in 1993 at the signing of the Declaration of Principles negotiated in Oslo, seemed more than a little ironic, in view of all that had happened in the meantime. 'It is on our shoulders that everyone should accept this agreement, but there is little time. This is an experiment that has to succeed. We have no time to waste'.

Part One

1. MR PALESTINE

'I am a refugee for I have nothing, for I was banished and dispossessed of my homeland.' Yasser Arafat, interview with *Al-Sayyad*, Beirut, 1969.

The young engineering student with thinning hair and slim features took more than usual care with his appearance. Peering in the mirror in his family's five-room ground-floor apartment at 24 Baron Empain Street in Cairo's respectable suburb of Heliopolis, he noted with approval his clean white shirt, sober tie and the cut of his modish double-breasted suit, with its exaggerated lapels. At the age of 23, the man who would become known to the world as 'Yasser' Arafat was about to take his first tentative steps on to an international stage.

With the inventiveness that had helped secure his election as President of the Palestinian Students' League the previous year, he had dreamed up an idea to engage the attention of Egypt's Prime Minister, Mohammed Naguib – and, more importantly, of the local press. Five years after the Arabs' humiliating defeat in the first of many wars with Israel, he had, together with comrades in the leadership of the League, drawn up a petition written in blood to General Neguib, head of the Revolutionary Command Council, the military junta that ruled Egypt following the 1952 revolution. The thousands of Palestinian students who had gathered in Cairo had a simple plea for the Egyptian leadership: Don't Forget Palestine. The date was 12 January 1953.

The petition in blood produced instant and quite gratifying results. Page eight of *Al-Ahram*, Egypt's daily newspaper, carried a photograph the next day of an earnest-looking Arafat presenting his petition to General Neguib, one of the few Arab commanders to have distinguished himself in the 1948–9 war for Palestine. The Prime Minister's ornate offices in an Ottoman palace near the city's busy Tahrir Square may have witnessed more momentous events, but it can have seen few debut appearances that would lead to such a lengthy and melodramatic career. Never mind that *Al-Ahram* misspelt Arafat's name at the first attempt, referring to him as 'Mr Farhat'. He was on his way and had even managed to persuade Egypt's premier to become patron of the Palestinian Students' League, thus guaranteeing it semi-official status.

In reality, Arafat's emergence as leader of a band of embittered and dispossessed students hardly caused a ripple in the Egypt of the early 1950s, much preoccupied, as it was, with its own internal upheavals; but it was no accident that Cairo, turbulent centre of the Arab world, hotbed of revolutionary ideas and ideals, had proved a crucible for the birth of a new Palestinianism. There was no shortage there of willing converts to *the cause*.

The leaders of the Palestinian revolution-to-be were the sons and daughters of the men and women driven from their homes in Israel's War of Independence. In the exodus of 1948 and 1949, between 650,000 and 750,000 people out of a total Palestinian population of 1.3 million had been displaced. More than half the Arab inhabitants of what had been the British-ruled territory of Palestine fled, mostly to the West Bank of the Jordan river, but also to Jordan itself, to Lebanon, to Syria, or to the Gaza Strip.[1]

In squalid refugee settlements that gradually became permanent shanty towns, the desire for revenge festered. Haltingly, the new nationalism was born of the memories of Jaffa, of Lydda and of Ramleh, to name just a few of the Arab towns forcibly evacuated as Jewish forces swept aside corrupt, chaotic and, at times, non-existent, Arab resistance. Albert Hourani, the Middle East scholar, observed acutely many years later that it was the 'shock of exile' that had created a Palestinian Arab nation.[2]

For Salah Khalaf, later known as Abu Iyad, godfather of the PLO's notorious Black September terrorist group, the date of 13 May 1948 was etched in his memory. As a 14-year-old, Khalaf found himself in an open boat with dozens of other sobbing residents, fleeing the bombardment of Jaffa, the large Arab coastal town adjacent to Tel Aviv. Families had gathered the few belongings they could carry and rushed towards the sea to escape the shells that were falling thick and fast as the Jewish forces laid siege to Jaffa. Khalaf was 'overwhelmed by the sight of this huge mass of men, women, old people and children, struggling under the weight of suitcases or bundles, making their way painfully down to the wharfs of Jaffa . . . Cries mingled with moaning and sobs, all punctuated by deafening explosions.'[3]

It was an exodus that had few parallels in history, and it was spurred on partly by fears of massacre. On 9 April, the Irgun – a Jewish underground group – had slaughtered as many as 250 inhabitants of Deir Yassin, an Arab village near Jerusalem. Arab radio broadcasts, from Baghdad to Cairo, did their bit to spread word of Deir Yassin to a panic-stricken populace. The Irgun leader, Menachem Begin, Israel's Prime Minister from 1977–83, always denied stories of massacre but later he would say that, 'Out of evil : . . good came.' This Arab propaganda spread a legend of terror amongst Arabs and Arab troops, who were seized with panic at the mention of Irgun soldiers. The legend was worth half a dozen battalions to the forces of Israel.[5]

For a quietly determined 12-year-old named Khalil al-Wazir, 12 July 1948 turned out to be a most fateful day. It was the day on which Prime Minister David Ben-Gurion issued orders to expel the Arabs from the towns of Ramleh and Lydda in what is now the centre of Israel.[6] Wazir, later to emerge as a key figure in the Palestinian underground, joined his mother, brothers and sisters in a pathetic retreat by road from the besieged Arab town of Ramleh, towards Ramallah. Before long the family found itself in the Gaza Strip – destination for about one-quarter of the Palestinians dispersed by the fighting of 1948 and 1949 – and the breeding ground for violent opposition to the Jewish state.[7]

For George Habash, a handsome medical student with a volatile temperament, 13 July was a day of truth. The day after Ramleh was emptied of its Arab inhabitants, Lydda succumbed following a fierce bombardment. Habash, later to become founder of one of the PLO's most radical factions, had rushed home from his medical studies in Beirut to work as a hospital orderly. He had witnessed the casualties of war first-hand and had been seized and beaten by soldiers determined to rid the town of its population. It had been a shocking experience. 'From 1948 I was definite about it,' he said. 'When I was expelled and treated in that way, from that time I felt that I had to sacrifice all my life for my just cause.'[8]

What of Arafat himself? While Khalaf, Wazir and Habash were experiencing the shock of exile, Arafat was completing secondary school in Cairo and did not stray far from the Egyptian capital during the great catastrophe, in spite of his own myth-making about having been, at 18, the 'youngest officer' in the Palestine Army of Abdel Kader al-Husseini, the Palestinian hero, who died in the battle of Qastal near Jerusalem on 8 April 1948.[9]

As student friends tell it, Arafat's main activity during the war of 1948 was to act as a go-between in efforts to procure arms for Husseini's ill-equipped Jihad al Muqqadis irregulars as they fought their losing battle. By all accounts, Arafat helped to establish a supply line to Bedu tribesmen in the Western desert who were trafficking in arms left strewn on the Second World War battlefields of Benghazi, Tobruk and El Alamein.

Mohammed Abdel-Raouf Arafat al-Qudwa al-Husseini was, according to his university record, born in Cairo on 4 August 1929, sixth child of Abdel-Raouf al-Qudwa al-Husseini, a stern, bespectacled merchant, and of Zahwa, a member of the prominent Abu Saoud family of Jerusalem. The al-Qudwas had arrived in Cairo from Jerusalem late in 1927 and had settled in a large apartment in the Sakakini district not far from the city centre. They did not attract much attention. Sakakini was one of Cairo's more cosmopolitan areas; Palestinians, Lebanese, Jews, Armenians and Greeks all gravitated to the comfortable residential district with its attractive villas, well-regarded schools and wide, tree-lined streets.

The infant Arafat first saw the light of day in a city very different from today's dusty, traffic-clogged metropolis. Cairo in the 1920s had a population of about one million, housed in an eclectic mixture of the old and decaying, and the modernistic. French architectural influence was strong in the business centre and in some of the grander dwellings on the Nile. The country was in the throes of political ferment. The first of a series of nationalist governments had come to power, demanding complete independence from Britain. Between 1919 and 1936 there were no fewer than twenty governments and eight sets of negotiations in which the Egyptians ceaselessly tried to whittle away British privilege in the face of obstinate resistance. But in spite of this turbulence, war and revolution seemed very far away.

A certain mystery surrounds Abdel-Raouf's departure from Jerusalem, where he had been a moderately successful small trader and before that a policeman in the Ottoman police force, but it seems that he had removed himself and his family to Cairo to pursue an inheritance claim. Arafat himself says that his father fought a long, expensive legal battle to secure title to a large parcel of land in an area that is now dominated by Ain Shams University in the east of the city.[10] Abdel-Raouf claimed ownership of the land through his Egyptian mother, who was a member of the prominent al-Radwan clan. Years of legal machinations were unsuccessful, however, when laws were arbitrarily changed, after Egypt's 1952 revolution, to restrict transfer of property from one generation to another. It was a crushing disappointment for the elder Arafat who had spent more than two decades fighting the Egyptian courts and bureaucracy.

When Arafat was born his industrious father was already well established in business as a trader in groceries, spices and incense, a well-known figure in Sakakini with the fez he habitually wore. But in 1933, when Arafat was 4, his mother Zahwa, a pleasant-looking, open-faced woman, died suddenly of kidney failure, leaving Abdel-Raouf with seven children on his hands. It was an impossible burden, so Arafat and his infant brother, Fathi, were packed off to Jerusalem to stay with their uncle, Selim Abu Saoud, in the large, comfortable family house in the Fakhriyya area of the Old City.

The Abu Saoud house adjoined the 'Wailing Wall', most sacred site to the Jews. It also lay virtually in the shadow of the Haram al-Sharif, home of Islam's third holiest shrine after Mecca and Medina. The relatively well-to-do Abu Saouds had lived in the area since the middle of the sixteenth century in a collection of fine Mamluk buildings. By chance and at a young age, Arafat found himself in the front line of the increasing conflict between Arab and Jew. Thus, he saw trouble between Muslims and Jews in the narrow streets of Old Jerusalem during the 1936–9 Arab Revolt; he observed the detention of relatives by the British authorities, whose rule was becoming steadily more oppressive; and he was present during anguished family debates about the future of Palestine.[11]

Despite his youth, he left a strong impression on his relatives. 'He always wanted to be the boss,' recalls his first cousin, the daughter of his father's sister and one of his early playmates in the tangled pathways of the Old City. He also exhibited, in his cousin's words, an early gift for 'showmanship'.[12] He was part of an extended and very traditional Palestinian family. Amira Musa Arafat, his maternal grandmother, was the daughter of Musa Arafat, an important Gazan merchant. Her marriage to an Abu Saoud was referred to with satisfaction in family circles as the 'union of the aristocracy and merchant classes'.[13] While not in the front rank of status-conscious Palestinian society, Arafat was nevertheless well connected, especially on his mother's side. The Abu Saouds were regarded as minor aristocracy.

One story frequently told about his family can be firmly laid to rest. Arafat was not related, as has often been reported, to Haj Amin al-Husseini, the Mufti of Jerusalem and later the exiled leader of the Palestinians. His first cousin in Jerusalem said emphatically that the al-Qudwa (Arafat's father's family) are 'the Husseinis of Gaza. They are nothing to do with the Husseinis of Jerusalem.'[14] Arafat's contacts with the Mufti, who lived in exile in Cairo in the late 1940s, had probably come, she thought, through his uncle, Sheikh Hassan Abu Saoud, who was very close to Haj Amin.[15]

Arafat's sojourn in Jerusalem came to an end in 1937 soon after his father's remarriage to an Egyptian woman. Summoned home to Cairo, he reluctantly left a city that he would later, with a canny eye for its political significance, claim as his birthplace. The Arafat brothers returned to a country already being buffeted by the storms of the Second World War breaking over Europe, to continue their education at private school in the Abbasiyya district. King Farouk had ascended the throne the previous year, ill educated and ill prepared to deal with the internal unrest and strikes that were the order of the day.

Arafat settled into a relatively comfortable middle-class existence with his six brothers and sisters and a disciplinarian father then beginning his second family. He attended Farouk college and earned the nickname 'Yasser', meaning carefree or easy-going. By all accounts, he was a hyperactive child. Inam, his elder sister by about ten years, recalls that even at that relatively young age Arafat showed a compulsive need to organise and mobilise others, marshalling children in the street into military formations and marching them up and down with metal plates on their heads, tapping them with a stick if they got out of line.[16]

War in the desert between Rommel and the Allies provided distraction from the looming conflict between Arabs and Jews, but not for long. As Arafat – he had spent the war years in Cairo observing the comings and goings of an odd collection of Allied troops – approached young adulthood in the post-war period, the Palestine question re-emerged with a vengeance.

Shame over the Holocaust had strengthened the hands of those who agreed with the Jewish nationalist, or Zionist, movement in advocating a separate and secure homeland in Palestine for the Jews. The result – adopted amid great controversy by the United Nations in 1947 – was a plan to partition Palestine into two states, one Jewish, one Arab. Arab states, grouped in the Arab League since 1945, proved powerless to prevent what became the Palestinian catastrophe. As a guest in the houses of prominent Palestinians in Cairo and therefore privy to their discussions, Arafat could not but have been affected by the gloom.

The two-stage war for Palestine – first civil resistance and then open warfare – ended in total humiliation for the Arabs. Weak and divided, their armies were no match for the superior organisation and firepower of the Zionist military machine. The Palestinians on the ground had been hamstrung by their own internal feuds and, after the war, efforts to build an all-Palestine Government under the leadership of Hai Amin al-Husseini were almost universally regarded as an irrelevance. The name of Palestine was gradually being erased from the map.

Like many other young Palestinians, Arafat's first inclination in 1949 was to flee the Middle East for a new life elsewhere. He had been appalled by the Palestinian refugee exodus and sickened by the futile Arab response. At 19, he applied for admission to a university in Texas. 'I was a very desperate Palestinian, so I decided to leave the whole area like many Palestinians,' he recalled. 'Some of them went to continue their studies in Canada and others in the US and Latin America. I decided to continue my studies in the States.'[17]

But Arafat never followed up his application because, in his own words, 'I became completely involved in the atmosphere all around me.'[18] It is not hard to understand why. Cairo in the late 1940s was seething with political activity. A weak and corrupt constitutional government had all but collapsed; the continued presence of British troops on Egyptian soil provoked constant protest and agitation; and the playboy King Farouk, last in a faltering line of discredited rulers, exerted minimal influence over events that were moving inexorably towards revolution. In their Nile-side salons, members of the *ancien régime* were about to be dispossessed of much of their inherited wealth. The rebellious Muslim Brotherhood, the *Ikhwan al-Muslimun*, founded in 1928 by the charismatic Sheikh Hassan al-Banna, was a surging influence in the streets and on the campuses. Attempts by the authorities in 1948 to suppress Muslim militants came too late. Entrenched in the army, the *Ikhwan* had even managed to penetrate the Communist Party. It was the most conspicuous among all Egypt's political groups in championing the cause of Palestine, and had backed that up by committing forces to the battle of 1948, as it had supported the Palestinians in their 1930s revolt against Jewish immigration and British mandatory rule.

Inevitably, Arafat was drawn to the Brotherhood's militant doctrines of anti-imperialism and national revival through Islam. It remains moot whether Arafat was actually a member or merely a sympathiser – he insists now that he was never a member – but he drew heavily on *Ikhwan* support in student elections at King Fouad I University (later Cairo University) and subsequently in elections for the Palestinian Students' League. Arafat had entered university in the late summer of 1949 when riots and demonstrations against the despised British were an almost daily occurrence. The rule of law had all but broken down. 'Disorder, destruction, violence and bloodshed, inspired by any and all groups wielding a minimum of power, official or unofficial, were the costly accompaniment of that breakdown,' according to one account of that period.[20]

In this highly charged atmosphere, a distracted Arafat began what can only be described as a mediocre university career. His record shows that he completed his preparatory year in the faculty of civil engineering in 1949–50 with a *maqboul* or pass, but he had to repeat two of his subsequent years. Mathematics was not his strong point; he failed the subject in years two and three, and again when he repeated his third year. Zoheir al-Alami, Arafat's best student friend and an early Fatah activist, recalled a colleague consumed by politics. 'His only activity was politics,' Alami remembered. 'Very seldom would he come to the School of Engineering.'[22]

In the beginning, Arafat did not restrict himself exclusively to Palestinian student politics. An Egyptian contemporary, who recalls Arafat as being 'very thin' and 'rather quiet', said that his election as one of the two representatives of the engineering faculty to the students' union was an error, as those places were strictly reserved for Egyptians.[25] It is possible that Arafat had passed himself off as a local.

Throughout 1950 and 1951 agitation against the continued British military presence in the canal zone grew, *Ikhwan* agents stirred anti-imperialist hostility up and down the country, and particularly on university campuses until, responding to over-whelming public pressure, the Egyptian parliament on 16 October 1951 unilaterally abrogated the 1936 Anglo–Egyptian Agreement under which British bases were permitted on Egyptian soil. It was the signal for all-out resistance to the British presence in Egypt.

Egyptians were exultant, one newspaper crowing that 'The helpless and hungry Egyptian horse tied to the British chariot and whipped by a relentless and cruel driver has been freed.'[26] Whether they wished it or not, the authorities were helpless to prevent the beginning of 'armed struggle' against the British. Thanks to the campaign initiated on university campuses, Arafat was about to get his first rudimentary military training.

As the Egyptian revolution got into full swing in the summer of 1951, a young, strongly built Palestinian with an unforgiving nature arrived in Cairo from the Gaza Strip. His name was Salah Khalaf, one of thousands of Gazan students, most of them refugees, who flooded Egyptian universities and other institutes of higher learning in the 1950s and early 1960s, and who were to provide more than a few recruits to the hard core of the PLO.

Embittered by his experiences as a refugee – a constant series of humiliations and hardships – and itching to join the fray, Khalaf was about to begin a relationship with Arafat that spanned more than thirty years. Stormy at times, it was, nevertheless, a partnership that served the interests of the two of them well as they rose through the ranks of the nationalist movement. Khalaf later observed that 'The Cairo years were extremely important in forming our personal relationships and helping us to resolve our differences later on. This is why we never split.'[27]

Elsewhere in the Arab world, Palestinian students of a new and more militant generation were stirring after the initial shock of exile. In Beirut, George Habash, who graduated in 1951 near the top of his class from the American University Medical School, had begun discussing nationalist ideas with a small group of fellow intellectuals at a waterfront coffee shop. Influenced by Baathism, a pan-Arab version of socialism taking root in Syria and Iraq, and by the revolutionary tide beginning to sweep the Third World, Habash and his associates decided to form a nationalist movement wedded to the idea of reclaiming Palestine in a united Arab struggle.

The decision to form the Arab National Movement, Habash said, was taken with 'six or seven associates' in 1951 before he left to set up medical practice in Amman the following year.[28] Among these associates was Dr Wadi Haddad, who went on to master-mind a bloody rash of Palestinian terrorism in the late 1960s. Habash says that in these formative years, he and Haddad were 'much more than brothers'.[29]

Things went from bad to worse for the foreign presence in Egypt. On Black Saturday, 26 January 1952, in an orgy of burning and looting, 750 buildings in Cairo were damaged or destroyed. An attack on the Turf Club, a popular British watering hole, left ten Britons dead. The British Embassy in Cairo accused the Egyptian Government of 'connivance' in the attack in which a 'savage mob under organised leadership broke into the premises'.[30]

There is no suggestion Arafat himself was involved in any of the destruction or killing, but nor is there any question where his sympathies lay. 'I considered this as one movement, one battle and one target,' he said. 'I held the British as the main people responsible for the Palestinian tragedy. Up to now I believe that the main culprits are the British. We were under their mandate and instead of giving us independence we became refugees and stateless. Hence I found it was my duty to participate with the Egyptians against the British troops.'[31]

In Cairo, Black Saturday marked the beginning of the end for the monarchical regime. Within six months, in fact, on the night of 22–3 July, a tall army colonel named Garnal Abdel Nasser seized power in a bloodless coup. Time had run out for King Farouk.

Within a few weeks of the Nasser revolution, Arafat and Khalaf, who had by then become firm friends, mounted their own 'coup', taking control of the Palestinian Students' League on a slate they called the 'Student Union'. The tireless organiser became chairman of the League, and Khalaf, the angry young man of the Palestinian student fraternity, joined him on the nine-member executive committee.

While Palestinian mythology has invested much historical importance in the activities of the Students' League under Arafat, in reality the union functioned mostly as a non-ideological self-help body, dealing with the grievances and everyday financial problems of Palestinian students. Money worries were ever-present. Students, who eked out an existence on a miserable stipend they received from the Arab League or from the United Nations Relief and Works Agency (UNRWA), were invariably in financial difficulties, since in most cases their impoverished families were in no position to support them. The League also functioned as a social club. Students would arrange picnics and other get-togethers; early photographs show the young men of the Palestinian movement boating on the Nile, and eating snacks at Cairo Zoo.

As a student politician, Arafat was also learning some of the stagecraft that would become his stock-in-trade in later years. Associates from the time remember emotion-laden and little-varying Arafat speeches in which he would shed tears, as if on cue, after reading the same four-line poem about Palestine. He would also make liberal use of a small selection of Koranic sayings.[32]

A picture emerges of Arafat in those years as an extraordinarily energetic student leader whose dominance of almost all facets of the League's activities got on his colleagues' nerves. He was a compulsive doer, and fellow students would often find that tasks they had been allotted had already been performed by Arafat. Other characteristics that emerged early included a volatile temperament, and chronic unpunctuality. Arafat had no 'concept of time', recalled Salah Khalaf. 'He was always late.'[33] One Arafat characteristic evident then was his elusiveness. He would simply disappear without explanation.

Arafat's other role was to act as something of an ombudsman at large for the Palestinian community in Egypt. By all accounts he was quite adept at it.

During this time Arafat began to take an increasing interest in developments in Gaza, where his father died in 1953, and where Arafat himself still owns property in a street that bears the family name, al-Qudwa. A frequent visitor to the Gaza Strip after the Egyptian revolution, especially to see one of his sisters, Youssra, living there after her marriage to a high school teacher, he was not at all disappointed by what he found. Palestinian nationalism was flourishing in the narrow strip of land that would prove so troublesome for its Israeli occupiers. Just 45 kilometres long and an average of six kilometres wide, it had absorbed a huge number of refugees, trebling its population after the war of 1948. By the mid-1950s, it had become the nursery of the most committed Palestinian nationalists and a focus of resistance activity. It was a place of great significance for the men who went on to lead the PLO.

In those days, Gaza enjoyed a special quasi-independent status under a loose, if corrupt, Egyptian administration. Fortunately for the Palestinian resistance, it was spared the same rigid control that applied in the West Bank after Jordan's King Abdullah annexed it in 1950. Gamal Sourani, a veteran PLO official and native Gazan, said that, unlike refugees elsewhere in the Arab world, Palestinians in Gaza were at liberty to 'shout out loud, I am a Palestinian. Egypt had no ambition to annex Gaza or erase the Palestinian identity,' he recalled. 'Palestinians in Gaza were the first to organise themselves for the liberation of Palestine.'[34]

Into the liberation struggle plunged Khalil al-Wazir, then in his late teens. In 1954 he became, in a word, a *fedai*, which means literally one who offers up his life. He was one of the earliest students of an Egyptian intelligence officer by the name of Mustapha Hafez, who had been authorised by Nasser to organise an underground resistance movement in Gaza. Under Hafez's direction, Wazir and other young men began cross-border raids into Israel, a niggling use of the Gaza Strip which was to explode into something infinitely more lethal years later.

'We managed to conduct several operations behind the armistice line at the time,' Wazir wrote in a fragmentary account of his early years. 'We also used to send groups to the Negev desert to plant anti-tank mines and other groups to destroy the water pipes in the [Jewish] settlements.'[35]

Arafat himself was not involved in these activities, nor, it seems, did he actually meet Wazir, who was to become his closest lieutenant, until early in 1955. According to Wazir's own account, their first meeting occurred during Palestinian demonstrations following an Israeli attack on Gaza, in February 1955, in retaliation for guerrilla activities in which Wazir himself had been involved.[36]

It was after this Israeli attack that Palestinian students started talking seriously about armed struggle. 'Then we felt we were helpless, nothing was being done,' recalled Zoheir al-Alami, who was elected to the League's executive committee in 1955. 'The Egyptians were there in Gaza, but they didn't defend us.'[37] The pot was simmering.

While Palestinian nationalism was stirring in Gaza, Egypt was still far from stable in the face of the restless challenge of the *Ikhwan*. Nasser himself was lucky to survive an assassination attempt in the late afternoon of 26 October 1954. As he addressed a large crowd in Alexandria's main square, pistol shots rang out and a lightbulb above his head shattered. Enraged, Nasser ordered a sweep against his political opponents. Among those caught in the net, according to his own account, was Yasser Arafat.[38] As an associate, if not a member, of the *Ikhwan*, his name was almost certainly recorded in the voluminous files of Nasser's secret police.

For Arafat and his closest colleagues in the League, 1956 was an important year and not only because of the cataclysmic events that briefly raised the spectre of superpower confrontation over the control of the Suez Canal. In August 1956, Arafat and his two fellow executive committee members, Zoheir al-Alami and Salah Khalaf, journeyed to Prague for a meeting of the International Students' Congress. They were to gain full membership for Palestine – a small diplomatic victory, but a victory nevertheless. Short of funds, the three travelled deck cargo to Italy and then by plane to Prague, returning the same way. Snapshots show the three of them sitting in deck chairs in the stern of the ferry from Alexandria, earnestly studying documents.

Ever the showman, Arafat had a surprise for his colleagues when they arrived in Prague. From his luggage, he produced a *keffiyeh*, or headdress, that would become his political trademark and distinguish him in later years from all his PLO contemporaries. His amused companions had not known that he had planned to dress up for the Prague conference, but after witnessing the attention a *keffiyeh*-clad Arafat attracted to the Palestine delegation, they followed his example at a similar student gathering the following year.[39]

Arafat's first *keffiyeh* was white. For many years, he has worn a carefully starched black and white version folded in such a way as to match the dagger-like shape of Palestine. Apart from sensing the *keffiyeh's* theatrical possibilities, Arafat also wanted to make an historical point, it seems: those engaged in resistance against British troops and the Zionists in Palestine in the 1936–9 revolt had worn the *keffiyeh* as part of their battledress.

After the congress, the three received invitations to visit surrounding East Bloc countries. Al-Alami went to Moscow and Khalaf to East Germany. Arafat succumbed to a debilitating virus that laid low many of the student delegates, and was taken to hospital to await his friends' return.[40] But even on his sick bed, Arafat made an impact on those around him. Peter Ruehmkorf, a German student activist and later one of his country's better-known poets, had a colourfully vivid recollection of his own hospital encounter with the PLO leader-to-be. According to Ruehmkorf, he shared a ward in the Central Hospital with two Indians, two Algerians, one Venezuelan, one Madagascan, one Cuban and one 'Mr Palestine'. When Mr Palestine had recovered sufficiently to engage Ruehmkorf, in the next bed, in conversation, it was to mount an imaginary and full-scale assault on the Jews. 'With extravagant gestures,' Ruehmkorf wrote in his autobiography, 'he began to drive the Jews (that was me) into an imaginary sea (to the right of my bed) in the process of which he absentmindedly turned my bed cover into a map with already occupied towns here, high points still to be captured there, and my dressing gown as the centre of resistance.'[41]

So enthusiastic was Mr Palestine's assault on his imaginary Jewish adversaries that Ruehmkorf, who was afraid of being driven into a make-believe sea himself, put his neighbour in a fraternal arm-lock until Arafat was liberated by hospital orderlies.[42]

Arafat, Khalaf and al-Alami returned to Nasser's Egypt on the eve of one of the great military and diplomatic dramas of the twentieth century. Sir Anthony Eden, Britain's Prime Minister, appalled by Nasser's abrupt nationalisation of the Suez Canal on 26 July, determined to have his revenge. On 29 October, under a secret agreement with France and Britain, Israeli troops crossed into the Sinai. They faced little resistance and within two days had reached the east bank of the Suez Canal. On 5 November, British and French paratroopers parachuted into Port Said at the entrance to the Suez Canal, supported a day later by British troops brought in by sea. Street-to-street fighting over the next few days left 2,700 Egyptian civilians and soldiers killed or wounded and some 150 casualties among the British and French. The canal itself was blocked with sunken vessels.[43]

Qualified as a reserve officer in the Egyptian Army from his university training, Arafat was called up to serve as a bomb disposal expert. He served, he says, in the headquarters of General (later Field Marshal) Abdel Hakim Amer, commander-in-chief of the Egyptian forces.[44] It is not exactly clear what role he played in the hostilities, which in any case turned out to be short-lived.

International pressure forced a ceasefire at midnight on 6 November and Nasser emerged a towering hero in the Arab world.

He had defied the might of Britain and France, not to mention Israel. It was a 'victory' that seemed to Arafat and his colleagues to augur well for the Palestinian cause but as they discovered, nothing could have been further from the truth. In full cry after his triumph over the tripartite aggression, Nasser cracked down even harder on the *Ikhwan* and anyone else he considered a threat to public order. Student activists who had flirted with the *Ikhwan* were among those kept under close surveillance. The ubiquitous Egyptian secret police had, in any case, long been taking a close interest in Arafat's activities.

His time in the country of his birth was coming to an end. Cairo had ceased to be fertile territory for aspiring revolutionaries whose views did not correspond with Nasser's pan-Arabism. 'The atmosphere in Cairo for the Palestinian movement was very difficult,' Arafat recalled. 'The interests of the Egyptians lost touch with the Palestinian movement, and became more involved in Arab unity and pan-Arabism. After the Suez Canal War, Nasser began to move on the other side.'[45] What Arafat meant was that the Egyptian President had begun to support a Palestinian pan-Arabist tendency that was in opposition to his (Arafat's) own robustly independent views of where the Palestinian movement should be heading. One of the immediate beneficiaries was the Arab National Movement of George Habash. Much to Arafat's chagrin, Habash and his followers began receiving material support from Nasser in the mid-1950s, whereas it would be many years before Arafat himself would receive Egyptian assistance.

Mohammed Abdel-Raoul Arafat al-Qudwa al-Husseini graduated from Cairo University in 1956, seven years after entering the faculty of engineering. His graduation project was a study of local sanitation. His first job as an engineer was with the Egyptian Cement Company, then engaged in a project at Mahallah Kubra, a stiflingly dull industrial town about two hours' drive north of Cairo. It was clear from the start that Arafat's heart was not in his new career. Restlessly, he sought alternatives, establishing a union of Palestinian graduates so that he could continue to have a forum for political activities, taking part in demonstrations in the Gaza Strip after the Suez Canal War, visiting Iraq immediately after the mid-1958 coup in which the monarchy was overthrown.[46] But none of this satisfied his craving for action. Besides he was under unwelcome pressure from his eldest sister, Inam, to get married to one of his Abu Saoud cousins and settle down.

Bored and unfulfilled, Arafat left the oppressive atmosphere of Nasser's Egypt soon after his return from Baghdad. Seeking an antidote for the *ennui* that had settled over him since the 1956 Suez crisis – and, just as important, seeking money – he headed for the relative political freedom of Kuwait. In Arafat's words, he left for the Gulf state because 'I really wanted to work and I wanted money, to speak frankly, and besides the atmosphere around me in Egypt was not an active one and not healthy.'[47]

2. STRUGGLE

'Let the imperialists and Zionists know that the people of Palestine are still in the field of battle and shall never be swept away.' Al-Asifa communiqué No. 1, 1 January 1965.

One evening in the second half of 1958, five young Palestinian professionals gathered in a house inhabited by one of their number in Kuwait. Talking into the night, they lamented the loss of Palestine a decade before. They spoke of their disenchantment with the Arab regimes and political parties of the day. And they talked about organising themselves for action.

Of the five young men present, two were already firm friends: Yasser Arafat and Khalil al-Wazir. In their earlier meetings in Cairo and Gaza they had reached two simple conclusions. Arab states, they reasoned, were not going to recover Palestine by force of arms. The Palestinians would therefore have to take their future into their own hands.[1]

Now, in conditions of great secrecy, Arafat and Wazir had decided to share their thoughts with a few select contemporaries. A revolutionary movement had begun, and it would soon have a name: Fatah.

Kuwait in the late 1950s was not exactly the sort of place where you would expect to find armed revolution being plotted. A backwater still under a British protectorate, the emirate had been largely sheltered from the political turbulence then sweeping through other parts of the Middle East, but it could not remain immune. As the Gulf states woke up to their oil riches and the need for hospitals, schools and roads, they attracted increasing numbers of young, educated Palestinians in search of work. Arafat and his friends from student days, anxious to earn money in order to pursue their political activities, were no exception. Wazir took a teaching job in Saudi Arabia for six months before landing up in a secondary school in Kuwait. Arafat used his degree to obtain a post as a junior site engineer in the road-building and sewage section of the Kuwaiti Public Works Department.

Arafat found himself living in purpose-built staff quarters with doctors, civil servants and other professionals in Suleibikhat, fifteen miles outside Kuwait City. His office was a prefabricated shed, but the road-building job meant that he was often out in the open, exposed to temperatures of up to 120° Fahrenheit. At first, he did not find the work easy, partly because the chief engineer was British and Arafat's command of English was distinctly shaky.

Kuwait had other attractions, though, which helped to make up for the appalling humidity, the lack of air conditioning and the rusty-coloured water that trickled out of the taps. For one thing the political atmosphere was relatively relaxed. Palestinians who had come from countries like Syria sensed the difference immediately: so long as they stayed out of Kuwaiti affairs, they were left to their own devices and enjoyed freedom of expression and assembly. If there were problems, there were Palestinians in positions of influence who could help to sort them out: men such as Talat al-Ghussein, a Palestinian civil servant who later became Kuwait's ambassador to Washington; and Hani al-Kaddoumi, who as director of the Interior Minister's office offered much assistance with visas, sponsorships and introductions to the right people. Above all, there was sufficient money around to give the young Palestinian professionals who had gravitated to the Gulf their first genuine taste of financial independence.

Freedom, money and powerful friends: these three elements turned Kuwait into fertile soil in which the seeds of political activism sown in Cairo began to germinate. There was little else for these bachelors so far from home to do after work in the evenings but talk, and the late-night talk was all about politics and Palestine.

A host of Palestinian groups – by one count, as many as forty in Kuwait alone – sprang up around this time.[2] Most were just informal debating forums with a few members. Some had more serious intentions.

Arafat and Wazir – better known in later years by his *nom de guerre*, Abu Jihad – were in no doubt about what was to be done. They were intent on uniting Palestinians in a violent struggle against Israel. To say this was an ambitious task would be an understatement. Since the 1930s, Palestinian society had been notoriously fractious; indeed, a breakdown of society amid feuding between rival clans had been one reason for the great exodus of Palestinians from their land in 1947–8. In exile the

divisions had widened, exacerbated by the conflicting ideologies –
from secular Arab nationalism to militant Islamic fundamentalism
– then swirling about the Arab world. Arafat and Wazir, members
of a generation that had grown up in exile, were determined to
leave all this behind. Their movement, they decided, should
embrace all Palestinians, regardless of previous political affiliations. And they began to put across this simple message – liberate
Palestine – in a crudely produced magazine that started to appear
sporadically in 1958, *Filastinuna: Nida Al Hayat* (Our Palestine:
The Call of Life).

Filastinuna was essentially the handiwork of Wazir, who had
always wanted to be a journalist and indeed displayed a facility
for words as well as for organisation. Printed at first on a stencil
machine, it was filled with crude sketches and simply written
poetry and prose. Anonymous articles – a rare exception being one
in the first issue carrying the initials Y.A. – discussed the plight of
the Palestinians, expounded their right to return to their homeland, criticised Arab regimes for their failure to act, and called on
the Palestinians to unite and take up arms against Israel.

But the magazine was more than just an outlet for rhetoric and
rudimentary analysis; its young editors meant it as a channel of
communication and organisation throughout the Palestinian Diaspora. They had, by definition, to be discreet, because they were
treading on sensitive political ground. The Arab states, in
particular, were most unlikely to approve of their activities. The
insecure heirs to Arab rulers who were significantly responsible
for the original displacement of the Palestinians in the 1948 war
were now trying to appropriate the Palestinian cause for themselves in an effort to cover their embarrassment. Posing as
standard-bearers for the sacred struggle, Arab governments would
not brook rivals – and certainly would not tolerate anything
resembling an independent Palestinian organisation. Arab countries neighbouring Israel kept the Palestinian refugees to whom
they were reluctantly playing host on a tight leash.[3] If the
Palestinians were to do something for themselves, they would have
to operate underground.

During a visit to Lebanon in 1959, Arafat and Wazir persuaded
an influential friend, Tawfik Houri, to seek the authorities'

permission to publish *Filastinuna* from Beirut, then the hub of an Arab publishing industry and a centre for political activity of all kinds. From that point, between 5,000 and 10,000 copies of the magazine were distributed regularly to Palestinians all over the Middle East and beyond. Every edition carried a Beirut P.O. box number (1684) through which readers could get in touch, creating a network of contacts which proved extremely useful to Arafat and Wazir as they set out to recruit like-minded Palestinians to the cause.[4]

As *Filastinuna* took shape, so did the movement known as Fatah. Arafat and Wazir had already drawn up general guidelines which they now elaborated into a formal political programme and organisational structure, circulated secretly by hand among trusted friends and acquaintances. One of the main issues for debate was what to call the new organisation. 'We first agreed that we were neither a party nor an association but a movement with all its dynamic implications,' explained Wazir. 'And the movement was for the liberation of Palestine.'[5] The name Fatah was, according to some accounts, the brainchild of one Adel Abdelkarim, a clever young mathematics teacher who had been present at that first meeting with Arafat and Wazir in 1958 and who thought it up by taking the Arabic words for Palestine Liberation Movement (*Harakat Tahrir Filastin*) and reversing their initials. Spelled forwards, the initials meant 'Death' (*Hataf*); backwards, they spelled the altogether more appropriate word 'Conquest.'[6]

Having laid the foundations, the young activists now faced the task of building up structures that extended beyond Kuwait. According to Salah Khalaf, who had by now joined his friends, this effort began at another discreet meeting in a private house in Kuwait on 10 October 1959. It was a small affair, involving fewer than twenty politically active Palestinians – many of whom had contacted the founders through the all-important P.O. box 1684 – but it marked the real beginning of Fatah as an organisation.[7] Members were still engaged in talk rather than in action, but it was clearly understood by all that the eventual goal was to take up arms.

At that stage, their preoccupation was secrecy, a concern inculcated by restrictions on Palestinian activism in other Arab countries and by a desire to insulate the movement from

infiltration by Arab intelligence services. It was this which
determined the tightly knit cell structure that Fatah began to
construct in different locations, the caution its leaders displayed
in vetting potential recruits, and the care they took in concealing
their movements outside Kuwait.

'At the start we would not talk about our plans to anybody,' said
Salah Khalaf. 'We kept our secret so close that the word Fatah
would not be mentioned except to a member. Only Fatah
members could see our two basic documents, the organisational
structure and the political programme.'[8]

Would-be recruits had to be recommended by two or three
existing cells and to demonstrate that they had severed all links
with Arab political parties. They were then interviewed at length
by a member of the inner circle to ensure they could be trusted,
and required to take a solemn oath of allegiance which has not
changed to this day:

I swear by God the Almighty,
I swear by my honour and my conviction,
I swear that I will be truly devoted to Palestine,
That I will work actively for the liberation of Palestine,
That I will do everything that lies within my capabilities,
That I will not give away Fatah's secrets,
That this is a voluntary oath, and God is my witness.[9]

Members would operate strictly on a 'need-to-know' basis in a cell
consisting of only two or three people, often members of the same
profession in the same place. They were strictly prohibited from
communicating by telephone, and messages from the leadership
were delivered in person or via hand-picked emissaries.

All this cloak-and-dagger activity had undoubted theatrical
possibilities, which Arafat was quick to exploit. To disguise their
identities, Fatah leaders adopted *noms de guerre* based on the
Arabic for 'father of', Abu, and often carrying religious or mythical
connotations. Arafat chose the name 'Abu Ammar', a reference to
the legendary Muslim warrior and close companion to the Prophet
Mohammed. Wazir became Abu Jihad – *jihad* being the Arabic for
holy war.

So insistent were members of the movement on covering their tracks that close relatives often did not know of one another's involvement; legend has it that one married couple only discovered that they both belonged when the wife asked her husband for fifty dinars to give to the cause.

Arafat and Wazir were especially close. Apart from the fact that they thought the same about the need to move from theory to practice, their personalities complemented each other to a striking degree: Arafat impetuous, hot-tempered and hyperactive; Wazir cool-headed, rational and deliberate. There was no doubt, even then, as to who the principal activists were. Arafat, in particular, was already developing a reputation among his peers as compulsive; contemporaries recall him as an intense, single-minded, even obsessive, young man. Inclined neither towards reading books nor towards socialising, awkward in the company of women, he seems to have had no real interests apart from Palestine. In pursuit of that cause, he and Wazir were without equal for perseverance. There was something distinctive and personal about Arafat's monomania; indeed, it contained an echo of his father's ill-destined attempts to claim his own inheritance back in the 1940s.

It was now that the freedom and financial autonomy the Palestinians enjoyed in Kuwait proved invaluable. Wazir spent the long school holidays travelling extensively, and without telling anyone but his closest friends where he was going. Arafat likewise used his vacations to slip off to other Arab countries to build up useful Palestinian contacts. The trips and other expenses were financed entirely from the pockets of Fatah's inner circle, several of whom are said to have devoted half their salaries or more to the cause.

Fatah's need for funds prompted Arafat, within a couple of years of arriving in Kuwait, to supplement his government job with a business career. For him, as for many other expatriates in Kuwait, the oil-fuelled construction boom presented opportunity. In 1959, he decided to cash in on the flow of contracts by setting up a private construction venture. By day, he continued to work on the roads; by night, he collaborated with an Egyptian engineer by the name of Abdel Muaz in building up a contracting business specialising in residential property. His government connections enabled him to channel a sizeable quantity of business to Muaz, who managed their joint venture. Palestinian contemporaries report that Arafat personally supervised the construction of six apartment blocks for the sons of a leading Kuwaiti merchant.[10]

With the passage of time, Arafat took to exaggerating the scale of his business career and of the wealth it generated. He told various interviewers that he set up three contracting companies as well as an engineering consultancy; that he owned four cars – two Chevrolets, a Thunderbird and a Volkswagen; and that by the time he eventually left Kuwait he had become a 'small millionaire' with sufficient savings to ensure that he would never have to draw a salary from the Palestinian liberation movement. 'I was very rich . . . I was well on the way to being a millionaire,' he told *Playboy* magazine in 1988.[11] 'I was a contractor. We built roads, highways, bridges. Large construction projects.' To *Time* magazine, the same year, he added, 'Let us say I have enough. Until now I have not taken any money from the PLO or the Fatah organisation. I still spend my own money.'[12]

The truth was somewhat different. Palestinian contemporaries agree that he had a penchant for flashy cars and fast driving, but they reckon the sort of sum he stood to make out of his joint venture was in the tens rather than hundreds of thousands of Kuwaiti dinars.

Whatever the state of Arafat's own finances, he and his friends did manage to scrape together enough money to finance a considerable amount of travel for recruitment purposes. The main aim at this stage was to establish a network of influential contacts. Meeting Palestinians around the Gulf and further afield, Arafat and Wazir put the emphasis on quality rather than on quantity. Arafat's principal targets were professionals, especially members of the Palestinian elite who had turned to education as a means of self-advancement – the teachers, doctors, engineers and civil servants who had emerged from the universities of Cairo, Beirut and Damascus and were beginning to dominate the bureaucracies of the Arab oil states. Desperate to give their still tiny movement credibility, Arafat and Wazir had few scruples about exaggerating its size and resources, regularly telling potential recruits that they had thousands of fighters and an array of armaments including tanks and helicopters at their disposal. For Arafat, then as throughout his career, the wish was father to the fact.

One important early trip took Arafat down the Gulf to Qatar, another rapidly developing city-state. Qatar, like Kuwait, had enlisted large numbers of Palestinians to staff its schools, oilfields and ministries, and here too they enjoyed unaccustomed personal freedom. 'There had been no censorship since 1956, and we used to hold big rallies, under the auspices of the Ministry of Education, which allowed us to address the students about Palestine,' said Rafik al-Natshe, a Palestinian activist who ran the office of the Qatari Education Minister and built up close ties with the emirate's ruling al-Thany family.[13] In parallel with Arafat and his friends in Kuwait, the Palestinians of Qatar had independently begun to organise themselves into secret cells. Several of them were Cairo graduates who remembered Arafat's 'Mr Palestine' exploits and had similar fundamentalist leanings; others knew Wazir from Gaza. During a visit to the emirate in 1961, Arafat persuaded the Qatari group to join forces with Fatah. It was an important step, since the Qatari group had extensive contacts of its own elsewhere in the Gulf and several of the activists involved there later became prominent figures in the Palestinian guerrilla movement.

Another significant excursion was to distant Libya, still ruled by a traditional monarchy but in the first stages of its own oil boom. Libya in the early 1960s was home to around 5,000 Palestinians. Arafat and Wazir – as ever looking for an influential foothold – sought to recruit the Palestinian deputy director of state security, a man named Abu Nabil, who, as it happened, was a distant relative of Wazir from Gaza. 'They came to me and asked me to join them in Fatah,' he recalled. 'I said I couldn't because I was working for the Libyan security forces, and Palestinian political activity was forbidden under the monarchy. They stayed for three days to try to convince me, and on the fourth day I agreed.'[14] Their recruitment of Abu Nabil paid dividends in the mid-1960s; as the country's oil revenues rose, wealthy and influential Libyans contributed generously to Fatah's coffers.

There was one other, unexpected area where Fatah's recruitment activities bore quick results: among young Palestinians living in Europe, notably the 3,500 strong contingent of Palestinian students in West Germany. From the late 1950s, Palestinian student activists had begun to organise themselves in the German industrial heartland. At the centre was a civil engineering student and former *Ikhwani* named Hani al-Hassan, whose career had parallels with that of Arafat himself.

At the Technical University of Darmstadt, south of Frankfurt, he linked up with like-minded contemporaries to publish a crude magazine by the name of *Al-Awda* (The Return). His group joined forces with the body that Arafat had helped to found some years before, the General Union of Palestinian Students, and at a student congress in Gaza in 1963, Hani al-Hassan's radical views – like Arafat, he called on Palestinians to take the liberation of Palestine into their own hands – brought him to the attention of the Fatah leadership. Several weeks later, Hassan was recruited into the movement by Wazir.

The link thus established between the activists in Kuwait and those in Germany proved a vital source of support for Arafat in the next few years, generating much-needed funds for Fatah's early guerrilla activities and providing numerous trainee commandos. At its peak, the European group had branches in twenty-six German and three Austrian towns, and enlisted Palestinians as far afield as France, Italy, Spain and Sweden. Several of its members later became key Arafat associates, including Hani al-Hassan himself. Contacts built up in Europe, notably among revolutionary socialists in Germany, would also be of importance when Fatah turned to international terrorism in the early 1970s.[15]

Such early successes were the exception rather than the rule, however. In general, recruitment was slow, for in its first, clandestine efforts to win broader support among Palestinians, Fatah was swimming against a powerful political tide. Egypt's President Nasser was at the height of his powers and popularity: the hopes of millions had been aroused by his drive to unify the 'Arab nation' and in particular by his country's union with Syria in 1958, which many Palestinians naively saw as a prelude to military action to recover their land. Fatah's 'narrower view', emphasising the liberation of Palestine before the mystical goal of

Arab unity, struck many contemporaries as heresy. By 1963, when Fatah – now operating from Wazir's house in the Hawalli district of Kuwait – had contrived to weld together a collection of groups that shared its 'Palestine first' views, the membership still totalled only a few hundred, and the inner circle numbered fewer than twenty.

But in the early 1960s, two events occurred which began to reverse the political tide. First, the Egyptian union with Syria broke up acrimoniously only three years after it had begun, swiftly deflating hopes that the Arab regimes were in the process of burying their differences. Nasser, discreetly putting out word that he had 'no plan to liberate Palestine', initiated instead plans to set up a separate body under his control to represent the Palestinians. Second, in July 1962 the Algerian revolutionaries of the Front de Libération National (FLN) gained independence from France after a bloody, eight-year colonial war. Suddenly, the arguments put forward by Fatah – that guerrilla warfare was the way forwards and that Palestinians should take it upon themselves to fight the Israelis – began to make more sense.

These developments presented Fatah's leaders with both an opportunity and a challenge. On the one hand, they calculated, the FLN's triumph in Algeria – in a war led both from outside and inside the country by an organisation relying principally on its own resources – could serve as a useful model. On the other, Nasser's proposal that the Arab governments set up what was rather vaguely called a 'Palestinian entity' – an idea first put forward at a meeting of Arab League foreign ministers in the Lebanese town of Chtaura in March 1959 – threatened to fill the same political vacuum that Fatah itself was trying to exploit.

Aware that they were now in a race with the Arab regimes, Arafat and Wazir redoubled their organising efforts outside Kuwait. In Beirut, Arafat re-established contact with his old friend Zoheir al-Alami, who had arrived back in Lebanon from the US in September 1962 to teach at the American University. Through him, he got to know some of the leading political figures in what was then the cultural capital of the Arab world. Arafat would show up regularly at Alami's apartment near the Riviera Hotel without so much as a change of clothes. 'In the old days, he never took much care of his appearance,' recalls his friend, who would take Arafat shopping before they embarked on the political round.[16]

Arafat also made a beeline for Syria. A radical new leadership had seized power in March 1963 in the latest of many coups, and Arafat sensed that influential figures in the new regime might be persuaded to lend support. His main target was the military. He struck gold by making the acquaintance of a Palestinian soldier, Colonel Khaled Hussein, then serving with the Syrian air force. Hussein was the personal bodyguard of an air force general who had played a key role in the March coup, and who was already developing a reputation for cunning and ruthlessness in equal measure. The general's name was Hafez al-Assad; this first meeting with Arafat during 1963 marked the beginning of a long and chequered relationship.[17]

But perhaps Arafat's most valuable entrée had come in Algeria, while the FLN nationalists were celebrating their 'liberation' from France. He and his friends had long admired the Algerian independence movement, and some Palestinians had actually sought to join the FLN's war. Indeed, the link between Fatah and Algeria's revolutionaries had been cemented in Cairo. Arafat's elder brother Gamal had befriended an exiled Algerian freedom fighter named Mohammed Khider and that relationship had yielded an invitation to Yasser Arafat to attend Algeria's independence celebrations, and to Fatah to establish a mission of its own in Algiers.

This was a breakthrough for the Palestinian group, still operating underground and without support from any Arab government. Not only did opening a first office give Fatah the chance to venture cautiously on to the surface of Middle Eastern politics. More than that, Algiers, now becoming a self-styled centre for the world's liberation movements, enabled Arafat and his associates to establish a wide range of new friendships that were to prove vital as they prepared to embark on their 'armed struggle'.[18]

The man chosen to head the new Bureau de la Palestine (after Gamal had made a start but was withdrawn owing to inadequate command of French) was Khalil al-Wazir. In 1963, Wazir became the first Fatah member to leave his job and devote himself to the struggle full time. Together with his teacher wife Intissar, a young baby and a 'family' of office employees, he established himself in penurious circumstances at No. 15 avenue Victor Hugo, Algiers. Living in an attic above the office, he set about increasing the number of Palestinians in Algeria by arranging student scholarships and teaching jobs. He had articles published in Algerian newspapers extolling the virtues of Fatah and armed struggle, much to the puzzlement of the local intelligentsia. And he also worked to consolidate Fatah's ties with the ruling FLN. The latter was no easy task at first, since the new regime was gripped by a power struggle between the charismatic post-independence leader, Ahmed Ben Bella, and the military man who eventually ousted him, Colonel Houari Boumedienne. At one point the authorities were being so obstructive that Wazir was ready to quit in defeat. But when Boumedienne took power a period of fruitful co-operation began. Algeria became Fatah's most solid and constant supporter amid the otherwise shifting sands of Arab politics and, to this day, its friendship remains more dependable than any of Arafat's other alliances.[19]

In Algiers, more than 2,000 miles from Palestine, Wazir was able in 1964 to establish the first summer training camp for around one hundred fighters, and to arrange instruction in rudimentary guerrilla techniques for a further twenty at the newly opened Cherchel Military Academy. He laid the groundwork for some of Fatah's earliest supplies of arms and funds. Most important of all were the contacts he made with sympathetic foreign governments and liberation movements. Working the diplomatic circuit, Wazir got to know a junior official at the Chinese embassy in Algiers, and managed to obtain an invitation for himself and Arafat to visit Peking as guests of the Chinese Committee for Afro-Asian Solidarity. They arrived on 17 March 1964, travelling on false passports under the respective pseudonyms of Galal Mohammed and Mohammed Rifaat.

Back in Algiers, Wazir and his deputy, Mohammed Abu Mayzar, had the Palestinians' first and only encounter with that guerrilla icon, Che Guevara. It took place in the summer of 1964 – ironically enough, in the headquarters of the former French governorate, an edifice the Algerian revolutionaries had turned into the Hotel Aletti and were using to host a conference of liberation movements from around the world. 'I remember Guevara with his fatigues, his beret and his cigar,' recalled Abu Mayzar. 'It was the first time he had heard about Palestine. He was astonished that we had not begun our revolution already, but said that if we did begin we would immediately obtain Cuban solidarity.'[20]

Guevara touched a sensitive nerve, for he obliquely alluded to the central difficulty that had afflicted Fatah since its foundation. For years, as they had put the building blocks of Fatah in place, Arafat and the others had spoken in general terms about launching an 'armed struggle' to wrest Palestine back from the Zionists, but in their preoccupation with organisational tasks, they had been unable to agree on what form the struggle might take, or when it might be mounted; all they had managed to do thus far was send a few score Palestinians for basic weapons training in Algeria. Arafat himself was impatient to begin, but he was still very much one among equals in the movement. Now their debate was coming to a head as a result of political moves beyond the Palestinians' control.

On 13 January 1964, President Nasser had summoned his fellow Arab leaders to a summit meeting in Cairo. Top of the agenda was a project that was causing immense unhappiness in the Arab world: Israel's diversion of water from the River Jordan, through its National Water Carrier, to the Negev desert. Nasser feared that Israel's plan would strengthen its capacity to absorb large numbers of new immigrants and in the process erase the Palestinian issue once and for all. But the project bad also become an emblem of Arab impotence. Powerless to do more than expostulate, the summit covered its own confusion by agreeing on Nasser's long-nurtured plan for the creation of an institution to represent the Palestinians. The assembled leaders mandated a middle-aged Palestinian lawyer and diplomat named Ahmed Shukairy to explore ways of setting up a representative body for all Palestinians, a body that became known as the Palestine Liberation Organisation.

Shukairy, a florid speaker, was well known on the diplomatic circuit, having served the Arab League and represented Saudi

Arabia and Syria at the United Nations. In the West, he later gained notoriety for what was taken as a crude threat to throw the Jews into the sea. As he toured the Arab world in the first half of 1964, consulting Palestinians whose views had long been ignored, he was received with enthusiasm. Palestinians in Kuwait, Syria and elsewhere leaped at his proposal that they take part in elections to a national assembly to be convened in east Jerusalem, then under Jordanian control, and rallied behind the idea of a Palestine liberation army to give the new organisation military muscle. The assembly itself, held in Jerusalem's Ambassador Hotel at the end of May, was a grand occasion: a gathering of the clans from all parts of the Diaspora at a time when Palestinians were subject to strict travel restrictions, it seemed to many of them to herald a new start in the battle to return to Palestine.

'For me personally, going to Jerusalem was something extra-ordinary. It was full of hope,' recalled Ahmed Sidki al-Dajani, a leading Palestinian intellectual and writer who had founded his own political movement in Libya in 1958.[21]

To the clandestine leadership of Fatah, however, the advent of Shukairy, a standard-bearer of the older generation, was disturbing news. A body like the PLO, dependent on – and subservient to – the Arab regimes, was not at all what they had in mind. Worse still, Shukairy's army – albeit a puppet force under Arab command – threatened to divert potential recruits from the 'revolutionary' struggle.

Fatah sent a handful of its militants to that first Palestine National Council in Jerusalem, led by Khalil al-Wazir, the sole publicly identified member of the movement, rather than the then invisible Arafat. Describing themselves as 'independents', they roamed the corridors of the hotel preaching the need for a 'people's war' and telling anyone who would listen that they had a fighting force of 300 to 400 men waiting to be unleashed against Israel through Jordan.[22]

Arafat and his colleagues also sought to open channels to Shukairy himself. In a series of meetings, they proposed that the PLO should give secret support to Fatah in a sabotage campaign against Israel, a relationship similar to that in pre-1948 Palestine between the Jewish Agency's mainstream Haganah forces and irregular terrorist groups such as Menachem Begin's Irgun and Yitzhak Shamir's more extreme Stern Gang. Shukairy, who was infuriated by the disrespect he was receiving from young Palestinian militants, worried that such underhand dealings risked undermining his connections with the Arab regimes. Rejecting the idea, he tried instead to co-opt Fatah members into the PLO. Relations between him and Arafat soured.

Fatah was thus brought face to face with the question of how to seize the initiative. The process of answering it threatened to split the movement at that early stage. On one side were Arafat, Wazir and a few impetuous supporters who became known as 'the adventurers' or 'the mad ones', arguing that Fatah should embark on military action without further delay. On the other, a group of more cautious colleagues in Kuwait – 'the sane ones' – insisted that the movement should wait until it had adequate supplies of arms, ammunition, manpower and money.[23]

The advocates of caution, led by an articulate Palestinian named Abdullah Danaan, later a professor of linguistics at Kuwait University, certainly had logic on their side. For all its rhetoric about 'revolutionary violence', Fatah was starved of weapons and funds, it had yet to build significant popular support, it had very few powerful friends and could field only a handful of fighters. The idea that such a force could set out to take on Israel was simply laughable.

Arafat pretended not to be consumed by such doubts. In his view, to wait any longer would be to risk being outflanked by Shukairy's 'official' PLO and portrayed as just one more Palestinian talking shop. Now was the time for action, not words. By initiating attacks on Israel – whatever the odds – Fatah's guerrillas would at least be making waves. The fact that something was being done would trigger off a flow to provoke reprisals that might draw neighbouring Arab states into the fight. Eventually, by a drawn-out process of action and reaction, the movement might succeed in igniting an all-out conflict with the Zionist enemy, with the Palestinians in the vanguard. Such was the theory of 'popular liberation war', although for Arafat, theory and strategy have always been less important than the compulsive need to be active.

* * *

By 1964, Fatah had become virtually a full-time occupation for Arafat. He was away from his road-building job for months at a stretch, and to justify his prolonged absences pleaded sickness, supporting his claim with forged medical certificates provided by a sympathetic Palestinian doctor. Above all, Arafat was driven by a sense of urgency. 'I had already made a pledge to God and myself,' he said, 'that 1964 would see the launching of our armed struggle.'[24]

The problem preventing his private vow from being fulfilled was that his 'sane' opponents were still refusing to sanction military action. Apart from worrying that armed struggle might turn out to be a failure, they hesitated to give the impetuous Arafat too much of a free hand. He was already attracting criticism for maverick tendencies and for not consulting sufficiently with his colleagues. To win them over, in the autumn of 1964 Arafat offered a compromise: Fatah would start its attacks but under another name – Al-Asifa, meaning The Storm, a title dreamed up one night on a Kuwaiti beach. 'If Al-Asifa succeeded, Fatah would then endorse the armed struggle,' Arafat explained. 'If Al-Asifa did not succeed, then Al-Asifa would take responsibility for the failure, and not Fatah.'[25] To provide additional assurance for the counsellors of caution, military activities would be under the command not of the volatile Arafat but of Mohammed Yousef al-Najjar, a tough Gazan militant then living in Qatar.

Still the argument festered on. As late as December, the 'sane ones' were continuing to set conditions for the commencement of military action, including a demand that a large reserve of cash be set aside to finance the first operations. Against this background, and with time running out for Arafat's pledge, a young Fatah member named Selim Zaanoun was dispatched to Jordan on 26 December to assess whether conditions were ripe for armed struggle. After visiting Amman, Nablus and Jerusalem, Zaanoun reported back to Kuwait that it was time to make a start, and the Fatah central committee duly agreed that attacks on Israel should begin.[26]

It was the cue Arafat had been waiting for. He gave up his job and left Kuwait.

From then on, life was lived perpetually on the move: between Beirut; a military camp in Damascus, where Fatah established its first base; and the supposedly 'forbidden kingdom' of Jordan, where restrictions on Palestinian political activity were in force.

As Fatah leaders took stock of their resources that winter, the picture was not exactly encouraging. Their ranks were divided, with some of those who disapproved of the decision to start fighting now peeling away from the movement. Fatah had a bank account in the Ras Beirut branch of the Palestinian-owned Arab Bank, opened by Zoheir al-Alami with himself and Arafat as co-signatories, but it contained very little money. Indeed, Alami had to finance the first guerrilla operations with an overdraft of between 6,000 and 7,000 Lebanese pounds.[27] On the ground, Fatah had a total of 26 fighters armed with an array of creaking old weapons.[28]

Preparing for the first actions in December 1964, one of the commando units discovered that five men were supposed to share three firearms, including a hunting rifle and a rusty machine-gun that would disgorge three bullets in a burst and required persistent thumps to function at all.

Starting from such meagre origins, the 'Palestinian revolution' was, above all, a revolution of symbols. Fatah lore traces it to New Year's Day, 1965, when a typed statement entitled 'Al-Asifa Communiqué Number One' was dropped into Beirut newspaper offices. It was a piece of bombast that vastly exaggerated the modest dimensions of the first *fedayeen* raids. 'From among our steadfast people, waiting at the borders, our revolutionary vanguard has issued forth, in the belief that armed revolution is our only path to Palestine and freedom', it grandly proclaimed.[29] There was one problem. The action this portentous statement was supposed to be announcing, a raid into northern Israel from Lebanon on New Year's Eve, had not taken place. Embarrassingly, the first Fatah *fedayeen* action was stillborn. The Lebanese authorities had arrested the raiding parties before they set out.

Indeed, most of the Arab states bordering Israel showed no inclination to encourage the *fedayeen*; only a few days into January 1965, Jordanian troops shot a Palestinian guerrilla as he returned from a raid into Israel. It was significant that Fatah's first 'martyr', Ahmed Musa, died from an Arab bullet. When Al-Asifa operations did get under way, a few days later, they turned out mostly to be pinprick affairs. Planned in co-operation with Syrian military intelligence, they were aimed at symbolic targets such as Israel's National Water Carrier – the scheme that had been the subject of much hand-wringing by the Arab states – and caused few Israeli casualties. The Israeli authorities, who captured their first *fedayeen* prisoner near Jerusalem on 7 January 1965, had little trouble dealing with the small numbers of guerrillas involved. 'The first terrorist raids were a nuisance, not a strategic threat – not politically, nor militarily,' remarked General Aharon Yariv, at the time Israel's head of military intelligence.[30]

If this was the puny reality of Fatah's early military efforts, its leadership set out in the first few months of 1965 to create a quite different impression. Boastful communiqués would arrive at media organisations in Beirut and Damascus, typed by Khalil al-Wazir in an apartment in west Beirut, copied on a stencil machine and distributed by Arafat in his VW Beetle. Invariably they claimed that Al-Asifa units had inflicted heavy casualties on Israeli military patrols or had blown up parts of the Zionist infrastructure before returning safely to base.

In the Arab world, word of Fatah's attacks set off a variety of conflicting political responses. In terms of money and arms, the decision to launch armed struggle began to pay dividends, as Arafat had predicted it would. Early in 1965, three Kuwaiti citizens came up with a contribution of between seven and eight thousand Kuwaiti dinars, more than adequate to clear al-Alami's overdraft. Members of the Qatari ruling family also began to provide money – enough to help the guerrillas buy weapons on the open market to augment their rudimentary arsenal – and other items, such as Racal communications equipment and a pair of night binoculars. Then came a windfall way beyond the leadership's dreams: a donation of 22,000 riyals from a wealthy Saudi. The amount was less important than the identity of the benefactor, Sheikh Ahmed Zaki Yamani, a close confidant of King Faisal and later Saudi Arabia's high profile oil minister. The connection was to be of critical importance for Fatah. It was also useful to the Saudis, who approved of the new Palestinian group's *Ikhwan* background and were keen to back any movement likely to be disapproved of by their old rival, Egypt. Arafat was already developing an aptitude for manoeuvring amid the perpetual squabbles that divide the Arab world.

In 1965 and 1966, Yamani arranged for members of the leadership to meet the Saudi monarch secretly, and the Saudis began discreetly supplying Fatah with arms, a liaison conducted through an official in their embassy in Ankara who would bring weapons via Syria to Lebanon in his diplomatic car.[31]

From other Arab countries, however, the reaction to the guerrilla movement's activities was much more circumspect, not to say hostile. Since nobody could pinpoint exactly who was behind the mysterious Al-Asifa, everybody leaped to his own self-serving conclusions, conservative Arab states depicting the Palestinian militants as agents of international communism and Shukairy's PLO calling them enemies of the Palestinian liberation movement. President Nasser suspected Arafat and his comrades of being a front for the *Ikhwan*. Egyptian intelligence inserted smears in the Cairo and Beirut press, denouncing Fatah as the tool of a plot by the Western powers and Zionism, aimed at providing Israel with a pretext to attack its Arab neighbours.[32] And Nasser's aides belittled Al-Asifa as 'a group of enthusiastic young Palestinians who think that the operations they undertake inside Palestine will lead to instability within Israel'.[33]

So it was that Nasser's men put out word that Fatah cross-border attacks should be restrained. Palestinian guerrillas were arrested in the Egyptian-controlled Gaza Strip. Reports about Al-Asifa's activities were censored, so much so that the oxygen of publicity sustaining Fatah through these early years came mainly from Israeli news reports. Even within Fatah, opinion was still divided about guerrilla actions.

In Kuwait, unease persisted about the commando activities. Concern intensified when Mohammed Yousef al-Najjar, the group's first military commander, handed over to Arafat himself – the leader of the 'mad ones'. Najjar, who had six children, found he had neither the time nor the money to devote to the struggle. The unmarried Arafat, by contrast, had all the time in the world and used it to burnish his credentials as an active guerrilla fighter. Arafat's participation in raids on Israel brought him much respect, but his autocratic behaviour as leader caused mounting unease among the armchair revolutionaries still working in the Gulf. They tried to rein him in by cutting back the supply of funds for the guerrillas, but to no avail. By early 1966, tensions within the leadership had reached such a pitch that a split seemed probable.

On 2 May, the Fatah central committee decided to suspend Arafat as military commander on charges that would become familiar in later years. He was accused by his colleagues of dispensing money 'in an irresponsible manner', of 'failing to carry out collective decisions', of taking 'unauthorised trips', and of sending 'false reports', especially 'in the military field'.[34]

To make matters worse, problems were also looming for the guerrilla movement in Syria, Fatah's frontline base. Behind the scenes in Damascus, a power struggle was unfolding between radicals who believed in promoting guerrilla warfare and a posse of more conventionally minded military men. In 1966, this produced frictions between Arafat and his Syrian sponsors. The more Arafat battled to assert his own leadership of the *fedayeen*, the more the Syrians – who supported and had given army training to a rival guerrilla commander named Ahmed Jibril – worked to bring the Palestinians under tighter control.

Even then, it was becoming clear that some of Fatah's biggest problems would come not in its confrontation with Israel but in its dealings with Arab regimes intent on trying to hold sway over the Palestinian cause.

In Arafat's eyes, however, these difficulties conveyed a perversely encouraging message. They showed that despite its modest beginnings and its often ludicrously inflated claims, Fatah had become a factor to be reckoned with in the Middle East equation. Its continuing raids on Israel were being aped by a smattering of other small Palestinian groups, with grandiloquent names like the Heroes of Return and the Vengeance Youth. What is more, they were provoking Israeli retaliation, as Arafat had hoped they would. The Israelis clashed repeatedly with Syrian forces throughout 1966, and on 13 November launched their biggest action to date, an attack on the village of Samu in the Jordanian-ruled West Bank, supposedly a reprisal for guerrilla raids.

Deeply divided among themselves, Arab states responded by outbidding each other rhetorically against the enemy. Inexorably, they were being dragged towards war, and the fulminations from Egypt, Syria and Jordan and from the head of the 'official' PLO, Ahmed Shukairy, ignored the fact that they were hopelessly ill equipped to fight it. At the end of May 1967, on the eve of what was to become known as the Six-Day War, Shukairy was to be found in a suite at Amman's Intercontinental Hotel predicting with typical braggadocio that the Arab states would crush Israel if fighting should break out. Of the Israelis he said, 'I don't expect any of them to stay alive.'[35] He did not have long to wait to discover how wrong he was.

3. TAKING CONTROL

'Not only we but the whole world senses that the Palestinian people have risen to champion their own cause by themselves.' President Gamal Abdel Nasser of Egypt, Revolution Day speech, 23 July 1968.

On 9 June 1967, as the dust began to clear after one of the quickest and most decisive military campaigns in history, a small group of Palestinians huddled round a radio set in a military camp outside Damascus. At the controls was Khalil al-Wazir. The others – fellow members of the full-time Fatah leadership, together with a group of militants who had hastened to Syria from Kuwait when they heard of the outbreak of war – simply listened in stunned silence as Wazir twiddled the dial.

The Arab news blackout that had replaced early, confident trumpetings about the destruction of the Israeli air force had already made it clear that the fighting was not exactly going the Arabs' way. But only now did the Fatah leaders begin to comprehend the scale of the defeat. Here, live on Cairo Radio, was the voice of the great Arab nationalist hero, Nasser himself, speaking of the 'grave setback' he had suffered, admitting his responsibility for serious miscalculations and vowing 'completely and finally' to resign.[1] There, on the enemy channel, were the sounds of Israel's jubilation at the victory that, within the space of a couple of days, had more than doubled the territory under its control and created a sense of invincibility in the Jewish state.[2]

Nobody in that small, gloomy gathering in the Syrian camp had the slightest doubt as to what Israel's walkover meant for the Palestinians. Ironically, a war that the Arabs had blundered into, telling themselves that they were about to restore Palestinian rights, had enabled Israel to swallow up all that was left of Palestine. The Israelis, having knocked out the entire Egyptian air force on the ground, had snatched the Gaza Strip from Egypt; they were in full control of the West Bank. Worst of all, the holy city of Jerusalem – Palestine's centre of gravity – had fallen to the Jews.

The news meant much, much more than military defeat, a loss of Arab territory and a displacement of more Palestinians. It marked a comprehensive overturning of all the hopes that the Palestinians and other Arabs had pinned on their leaders for much of the previous decade. Ever since the mid-1950s Nasser and his generation had lulled the masses into a belief in inevitable victory once the Arab states pooled their resources in a conventional war against Israel. In the first few months of 1967, the bravado had reached a new pitch as Egypt and Syria battled to outbid each other in commitment to the Palestinian cause. Yet within a matter of hours it was all exposed as a sham. It was a jolt that every politically aware Palestinian of that era can remember vividly to this day.

'Nineteen sixty-seven was the greatest shock of my life,' says Nabil Shaath, a business consultant who later became one of Yasser Arafat's top advisers. 'I remember I was in Alexandria attending a management conference when I heard about the war on June the fifth. I immediately went with some colleagues on a train back to Cairo. During the seven-hour journey, we tuned in to my transistor radio and kept listening to the number of planes Israel had lost. By the time we arrived in Cairo, Israel had lost its entire air force. And I believed it all. Until I got to Cairo, I thought I would be given instructions to leave for Palestine. This was the illusion that was perpetuated by Egyptian propaganda. But as dusk fell, I reached a Cairo that was under curfew. I had never seen it that way. As I walked to my house in Garden City, I felt that things were not going that well.'[3]

For Palestinians who had placed their faith in the Arab regimes, the falsity of Egyptian official communiqués exacerbated what amounted to a sense of betrayal. But out of their despair sprang new feelings of specifically Palestinian nationalism. The 'official' Palestine Liberation Organisation of Ahmed Shukairy had been exposed as a sham. If the Arab regimes and their stooges were incapable of defending the Palestinian cause, then perhaps the Palestinians would now really have to do something for themselves.

Fatah's leaders were still smarting from the shock of defeat as they assembled a few days later in the living room of Khalil al-Wazir's home in a suburb of Damascus. Many of the twenty or so people present – Palestinians from the Gulf and from as far afield as Europe – were meeting for the first time to consider what, if anything, to do next, and in particular whether to relaunch military raids on Israel. By all accounts it was a contentious affair. Arafat, the compulsive doer, was convinced that the struggle must go on; his more cautious comrades, including his younger brother Fathi, were equally convinced that this was madness.[4]

One by one, the old arguments against precipitate military action that had been endlessly rehearsed during 1964 resurfaced. Leading the attack on this occasion was Mahmoud Mesweida, a Damascus-based Fatah member with leadership ambitions and Syrian support. Mesweida, a man of Islamic fundamentalist sympathies, argued against restarting guerrilla activity on the grounds that it would risk provoking heavy Israeli retaliation and 'destroying the movement with nothing to show for it.'[5] To the 37-year-old Arafat this was defeatist talk. The miserable performance of Arab armies against Israel, he said, merely vindicated what he had been saying all along about the need for the Palestinians to help themselves. The Palestinian revolution must continue in order to revive popular morale. 'The defeat of 1967 is the prelude to a great victory,' predicted Arafat boldly, if rather implausibly, in front of his squabbling comrades.[6]

Once again, the argument was turning into a battle for control of Fatah's military wing, Al-Asifa. Arafat manoeuvred with his usual mixture of skill and theatrics – rushing round the room and getting down on his knees – to fight off trouble. The result was a compromise: the cobbling together of a nine-member interim leadership and the postponement of further discussion.

Arafat, however, was not waiting for the debate to play itself out. Concluding that Fatah had no time to lose if it wanted to capitalise on the state of affairs created by the Six-Day War, he had dreamed up a fresh plan of action: to organise resistance among the million Palestinians living in the territories newly occupied by Israel, the West Bank and the Gaza Strip. As his comrades continued to quarrel in Damascus, he headed south into Jordan and from there, evading Israeli frontier controls, crossed the river into the West Bank. Operating alone for much of the time, he set out to construct a network of terrorist cells in line with the teachings of Mao Tse-Tung's *People's War*.

Many myths surround Arafat's exploits during this period, not least those propagated by the man himself, who still boasts of having been on Palestinian soil at this critical moment. He claims that he made regular visits to the territories to 'lead the resistance movement against the occupation'; that he travelled widely throughout the West Bank, Gaza and the towns of Israel itself; and that his life on the run from the Israeli authorities lasted until early 1968.[7]

This is almost certainly an exaggeration. But, as Israeli officials have since acknowledged, security was lax enough in the early days of the occupation to permit Arafat and his deputy, Abu Ali Shaheen, to slip back and forth from Jordan undetected. As Arafat tells it, they set up a clandestine headquarters in the northern village of Kabatiyeh, near Jenin. From there, they recruited potential guerrillas and smuggled them out for training at Fatah camps in Syria, established arms caches and safe houses, and built a network of sympathisers who would provide the revolutionary 'sea'. Arafat's relatives living in Jerusalem say he even had time to say a clandestine prayer in the Al-Aqsa mosque.

One man Arafat did meet at the time was Faisal al-Husseini, son of the Palestinian hero Abdel Kader al-Husseini, who knew Arafat well from Cairo days. Husseini had been a follower of George Habash's left-wing Arab National Movement, had worked for the 'official' PLO after its initial establishment in Jerusalem, and had subsequently received military training at a Syrian officers' academy. But he switched his sympathies to Fatah when he returned to live in the family house outside the Old City of Jerusalem after the 1967 war. 'We exchanged points of view,' Husseini recalled.[8] Arafat agreed to supply weapons to be stored in Husseini's house, and Husseini undertook to begin training guerrillas in the West Bank.[9] Arafat himself said he recruited many others in the West Bank in 1967, including Fatah's first woman guerrilla commander and a man who would later become PLO ambassador in Romania and Libya.[10]

In most respects, though, Arafat's forays into the territories were failures. The expected armed revolt did not materialise. The inhabitants of the West Bank, a conservative rural society where political activity had been tightly controlled during the previous two decades of Jordanian rule, were simply not ready for it. Local leaders were still looking principally to Jordan to liberate them from Israeli rule, and discouraged collaboration with alien and disruptive revolutionaries. The supply of arms and funds from outside the territories was never more than a trickle.

Not that this deterred Arafat from delivering an enthusiastic report to his comrades in Damascus. Summoned back in late August 1967 for a fresh meeting of the leadership, amid considerable Syrian pressure on Fatah to halt military action, he suggested that the West Bank was a revolutionary tinderbox that merely awaited Fatah's spark. On the strength of his exaggerated account, the decision was taken to defy the Syrians and relaunch 'armed struggle'. The first attack was mounted within the occupied territories a few days later.

Arafat sneaked back across the frontier but, contrary to the wilfully optimistic presentation he had given his friends, he found that organising in the West Bank was an uphill task, not least because the barren terrain was unfriendly to guerrilla activities. Shortly after his return to the territories, Abu Ali Shaheen was arrested in the northern West Bank town of Jenin and held in an Israeli jail. And it was not long before Arafat himself, operating in the same area, was betrayed but made his getaway; amid the many conflicting stories about his escape, his version is that he got out disguised as a married woman carrying a baby. True or not, the close shave gave him another excuse for myth-making, enabling him to boast, as he has done repeatedly ever since, of his uncanny nose for danger.[11]

As time went by and the occupation came to look more and more like a long-term affair, Israel's grip tightened. When Fatah violence started, the authorities – taking advantage of intelligence files left behind by the Jordanians – arrested hundreds of political activists, smashed the embryonic Palestinian cells and dynamited the houses of those suspected of giving them succour. By December 1967, the Israeli Defence Ministry could announce that 60 *fedayeen* had been killed and 300 imprisoned since the June war.[12]

Arafat's underground activities in the West Bank had one unexpected legacy: they gave rise to the nickname by which he has been known to intimates ever since. To avoid identifying him by name, his contacts in the villages simply referred to the balding but still relatively youthful guerrilla leader as 'Al Khityar' – literally, 'The Old Man'.[13]

Quixotic it may have seemed, but Arafat's effort to promote an insurrection in the territories did pay dividends. During the summer of 1967 some 400 Palestinian students and workers left their universities and jobs in Germany to join up. They flew first to Algeria, where they stayed in a military encampment and underwent physical training, and then on to the Hama military base in Syria. Recruits received no more than a week's weapons instruction, and seven bullets to practise with, before being despatched on raids into the West Bank. Poorly qualified and ill equipped, many of them were arrested and some were killed.[14]

Fatah also received the sincerest form of flattery around this time, when a number of Palestinian imitators went into action. Principal among them was the man who was to be Arafat's lifelong rival: George Habash. For much of his early political life, Habash had put his faith in Nasser, arguing that any Palestinian action should be co-ordinated with the acknowledged leader of the Arab world. The defeat of 1967 – bitterly described by Habash at the time as the third occasion on which the Arab armies had failed the Palestinians – changed all that. After the war, the doctor turned further leftwards in his political thinking, opted unequivocally for armed struggle, and tried to join forces with Arafat. The meeting in a Damascus restaurant during the summer of 1967 was their first.

'I think that the first time we saw that they [Fatah] were right was after 1967. Only after that did we feel that the conditions were right for Palestinian armed struggle,' recalled Habash. 'We talked about what happened in June. We agreed that we were facing a new era and that there was no other way but armed struggle . . . At the time we were insistent on starting something together. We knew that in order to have victory there should be unity.'[15]

Yes, said Arafat to himself, but unity under whose leadership? Whatever he may have told Habash that summer, he had no intention of blending anonymously into some kind of cumbersome guerrilla coalition. He wanted to be out in front. Fatah's August decision to relaunch the armed struggle had in effect been a decision to go it alone.

So began a series of parallel races among the Palestinians. Unity talks with other groups collapsed and, later that year, a separate leftist coalition was formed under Habash's leadership: the Popular Front for the Liberation of Palestine. Armed attacks on Israel accelerated, with a profusion of groups under a bewildering variety of names claiming credit in a battle of ludicrously inflated communiqués. Palestinian factions competed for support from rival Arab regimes. The regimes themselves, fearful of the new Palestinian self-assertion, hastened attempts to harness and control it, either by setting up their own guerrilla clients – as did Syria and Iraq in the form of Al-Saiqa and the Arab Liberation Front respectively – or by building bridges to existing factions.

The war of the communiqués often made the guerrillas look ludicrous. On a number of occasions, Arafat's group made claims that turned out to be fiction: when Israeli Defence Minister Moshe Dayan was injured on an archaeological dig, Fatah took responsibility; likewise, it said it had caused an explosion in the garage of former army chief of staff Yitzhak Rabin – although Rabin did not have a garage at the time.[16] If this seemed no more than an immature competition between commando groups to see who could claim to have inflicted the most casualties on the enemy, it had a more serious point: it was also a contest to fill the vacuum that had developed where there should have been a representative body that would make the Palestinians' voice heard. The new generation of activists was determined to give the lie to Israeli propaganda that said, as Prime Minister Golda Meir did of the Palestinians in a 1969 interview with the *Sunday Times*, that 'they did not exist'. Arafat, for his part, had his sights set on assuming the leadership of the resistance movement for himself and for Fatah. It was his good fortune that there were those within the three-year-old 'official' Palestine Liberation Organisation who had similar ideas.

After the Six-Day War, it was obvious that the PLO was as discredited in the eyes of the masses as the Arab regimes that had supported its foundation in 1964. Wracked by internal divisions, the organisation had come to be seen as little more than a platform for the posturings of its chairman Ahmed Shukairy, who was now seeking to establish militant credentials by announcing a 'revolution' of his own. Most Palestinians rejected Shukairy and the old guard of bureaucrats and politicians he represented, scornfully termed by the *fedayeen* 'the generation of defeat'. Shukairy's blustering statements were beginning to cause irritation even among his sponsors. During the second half of 1967, other members of the PLO leadership contacted Arafat to see whether he might be capable of stopping the rot. Events were not long in coming that propelled Arafat into a leading role. In December 1967, seven of Shukairy's colleagues on the Executive Committee demanded that he resign. He refused, prompting a tug of war that was only resolved when the PLO's bankers cut off funds. Increasingly desperate, Shukairy appealed for support to his old mentor, President Nasser, but Nasser declined to intervene. On Christmas Eve Shukairy retired to write his memoirs in Beirut.[17] It was the second time in less than twenty years that a Palestinian leader had been dismissed into lonely exile. Despite Shukairy's undeniable contribution to the Palestinian movement, he had come to be seen as a figure of fun, a man of words rather than of action. The time had come to hand over to a younger, more assertive generation. Shukairy's replacement as PLO Chairman, an ineffectual left-wing lawyer named Yahia Hammouda, was a caretaker with the job of preparing for the guerrillas' takeover. Arafat's opportunity had arrived.

In the autumn of 1967, guerrillas belonging to Fatah and other factions had begun establishing bases for cross-border raids into Israel in a cluster of Palestinian refugee camps near the Jordan river. Below sea level, it was a barren place – blazing hot in summer, freezing cold in winter, surrounded by rocky hills. One of these camps, at a place called Karameh, was the scene of a fierce battle between Israeli forces and the *fedayeen* – a real battle which, once embellished in Fatah propaganda, assumed mythic status for the Palestinian movement.

The build-up to Karameh was well under way by the first weeks of 1968. Palestinian guerrillas, now better armed and trained than before and operating with impunity from Jordanian territory, had become a major nuisance for Israel. Transporting their weapons on makeshift rafts made out of tractor tyres, small groups of commandos would slip across the river by night, plant mines, throw grenades and try to slip back. At the end of February 1968, the Israelis claimed that there had been 91 incidents so far that year. Although 80 per cent of the attacking guerrillas were killed or captured, their attacks – often aimed indiscriminately at civilians – were doing enough damage to cause the government serious concern.

Israel's military leaders knew that they had not devised an effective response. General Aharon Yariv, then head of military intelligence, recalls that in August 1967 he had warned his colleagues on the Israeli general staff that the guerrillas were going to undertake 'massive infiltration' across the Jordanian border, and proposed that Israel should fence off the entire valley. But the authorities – at that stage surprisingly complacent about the terrorist threat – were slow to act, and the fence was not completed for another two years.[18] In the meantime the Israelis found themselves simply improvising. They frequently shelled the *fedayeen* camps and sometimes became embroiled in artillery duels with Jordanian army units providing covering fire for the guerrillas. These actions, together with occasional bombing strikes from the air, may have settled scores, but the ad hoc nature of Israel's retaliation merely served to embolden the guerrillas.

On 18 March 1968, a major showdown with the Palestinians became inevitable when an Israeli school bus ran over a *fedayeen* mine near the Jordanian border. A doctor and a schoolboy were killed and 29 children injured. Israel was stung into action. It resolved to hit the guerrillas, and hit them hard.

Across the river in his Karameh base, Arafat was aware that a large-scale attack was imminent – a senior Jordanian intelligence officer, acting on a tip-off from America's Central Intelligence Agency, had told him as much early in March. On the 18th, Arafat and Salah Khalaf were summoned to Amman by the Jordanian army commander, General Amer Khammash. In a meeting also attended by the head of a 10,000-strong Iraqi army division that had been stationed on Jordanian soil since the 1967 war,

Khammash gave the Fatah leaders a warning. 'Do you not see the massing of Israeli troops?' he said. 'In the next few hours, they will smash you'.[19]

To enable them to avoid the attack, Khammash said he would for the first time allow the Palestinian guerrillas to leave their riverside camps and take refuge in the nearby hills. But Arafat had a quite different idea. 'Our Arab nation has been escaping and fleeing continuously,' he replied. 'No, we have to prove to the Israeli enemy that there are people who will not flee. We are going to confront him in the same way that David confronted Goliath.'[20] It was folly, contrary to the precepts of guerrilla warfare and military good sense. But for Arafat, the impending battle was an irresistible opportunity to put the Palestinian resistance on the map.

What followed was one of his boldest pieces of political theatre. Arafat and Khalaf hastened back to Karameh and rallied the troops, shivering in their unheated shacks. Without mentioning the Jordanian warning, they explained the need for the guerrillas to stand their ground, even if all present ran a heavy risk of ending up either dead or in Israeli hands. 'We will make Karameh the second Leningrad,' Arafat proclaimed. Although he offered anyone who disagreed the opportunity to leave, he boasts that no Fatah member did, apart from the sick and lame. Fighters from Habash's Popular Front decided to take themselves off into the surrounding hills and harass Israeli forces from there.[21]

Contrary to the impression projected in subsequent propaganda, Arafat did not leave everything to fate. He had established links with the Jordanian army commander in charge of the area, General Mashour Haditha al-Jazy, who, unlike his superiors back in Amman, sympathised with the guerrillas. Arafat had also discreetly sought to enlist the Iraqi army, although in the event this came to nothing.

Battle was joined on 21 March at 5.30 a.m., with Israeli aircraft dropping yellow leaflets urging the terrorists to surrender, and landing paratroopers in the hills behind Karameh. Their task: to encircle the bases and block the guerrillas' escape route to the east before the army swept into Karameh itself. But the paratroopers were astonished to encounter a group of PFLP commandos, who engaged them in hand-to-hand fighting. It was the first of a string of surprises for the Israelis that day. As the main body of Israeli tanks, accompanying a force of several thousand men, rolled across the border, confusion spread. The paratroopers having failed to 'clean up' the surrounding hills, Israeli ground forces departed from their battle plan, moved east, and ran straight into unexpected artillery and tank fire from Haditha's Jordanian army division, which had ignored strict orders from Amman to stay out of the fighting. The ensuing duel bogged the Israeli forces down for the rest of the day, distracting them from their main mission of rooting out the guerrilla bases. By the time they were ordered to withdraw, the Israelis had suffered an unanticipated and unacceptable level of casualties: 28 dead, 69 injured and 34 tanks hit. At least one of the tanks remained in the Palestinians' hands together with the charred remains of its driver, and was used by the *fedayeen* to great publicity effect in the next few days.

Not that the guerrillas had escaped unscathed as they battled to stop the Israeli advance. One of the fighters, so the story goes, had wired himself up with explosives and hurled himself at a tank. Seventeen men had dug themselves into trenches along the Jordan river from which they fired rocket-propelled grenades at virtually point-blank range. All but one were killed, but their show of defiance was later immortalised in the name of Arafat's elite security service, Force 17. By the end of the day, 98 of the 400 or so Palestinian fighters at Karameh had been killed, and their base devastated.[22] The survivors were jubilant nonetheless. By the simple act of standing firm against the odds and inflicting casualties on the enemy, they felt they had made an important point. For Arafat (who has always maintained he was present on the battlefield although the Israelis predictably claim he fled east when the fighting commenced) the battle was 'the first victory for our Arab nation after the 1967 war.'[23]

Strictly speaking, it had been the Jordanian army, not the guerrillas, that had done most of the damage and eventually forced the Israelis to withdraw. In the words of General Haditha, 'They [the guerrillas] fought bravely, but they certainly could not have done it alone. If the Jordanian army had stayed out, the *fedayeen* would have been crushed.'[24] That, however, was not the impression that began to ricochet around the Arab world, aided by Fatah's crude but effective propaganda and by the fact that Jordan could not trumpet its own involvement for fear of provoking harsher Israeli reprisals. The battle – bungled by Israel, hushed up by Jordan – was transformed by the *fedayeen* into a model for Arab steadfastness. Arafat's flair for publicity had pressed Karameh (conveniently enough, the Arabic word for dignity) into service as a potent symbol of Fatah's 'revolution'.

The results were more impressive than he could have dared to hope. In Israel, the battle came as a shock which jolted the military bosses out of their post-1967 complacency. 'After Karameh, we understood that we had on our hands a serious movement,' said General Yariv. 'Although it was a military defeat for them, it was a moral victory.'[25] In the Arab world, Karameh detonated an explosion of support for the *fedayeen*. Palestinian and other Arab volunteers flocked to join the resistance, and Fatah, in particular, was overwhelmed: within 48 hours of the battle it received 5,000 applications, many more than it could handle. The columns of Arab newspapers were full of exaggerated tales of Palestinian heroism. Speculation swirled around the role of a shadowy guerrilla leader known only by his *nom de guerre*, Abu Ammar.

Despite its hunger for publicity about its actions, Fatah had long been obsessively secretive about its structure, origins and membership. Journalists' questions concerning the movement received vague and unhelpful replies. Anyone enquiring who was in charge would be referred to a faceless collective leadership. After Karameh it was clear that this would no longer do. The moment was rapidly approaching when Fatah would have to emerge from under ground and present a public face to the world: that of the 38-year-old Yasser Arafat. It is not the smallest irony of Middle Eastern history that a mishandled Israeli military offensive helped to put him on the road to becoming chairman of the PLO.

The first outsider to identify Arafat in public as Fatah's leader was a journalist on Egypt's *Al-Ahram* newspaper, Ihsan Bakr, who stayed with the guerrillas for a week just after the Battle of Karameh. 'At first, they did not tell me their real names. They all said they were called Abu Maher,' Bakr recalled. 'The one exception was Arafat, whom everybody referred to as Abu Ammar, "the father" or "the choice". After two or three meetings with him, I was convinced he was the leader, although when I asked him he said everyone there was leader of the revolution.'[26]

Less than a month later, Arafat was nominated as Fatah's official 'spokesman'. It was typical of the fractious organisation that the move was prompted by yet another leadership struggle. Mahmoud Mesweida, Arafat's post-1967 opponent, had started to issue bogus communiqués claiming credit for actions against Israel in the name of Fatah's military wing, Al-Asifa. Word of the problem reached Salah Khalaf, Fatah's intelligence chief, in Damascus in mid-April when all but one of his colleagues in the Fatah leadership were away. To head off trouble, he took it upon himself to issue a statement naming Arafat as the sole person authorised to speak for Fatah, together with a faked declaration from Arafat himself 'accepting' the nomination.[27]

Some Fatah members were uneasy about the appointment, given the reputation Arafat had already developed for acting as a law unto himself. But those who most strongly disapproved drifted away from the movement and the rest deferred to Arafat's age, his pragmatism and above all to his hyperactive character.[28]

Arafat's nomination as front man was a watershed. Suddenly he was visible on an international stage and the image he had cultivated since the start of the guerrilla struggle was projected to a receptive new audience. Pictured on the front of myriad Arab magazines and newspapers, his stubbly face – adorned with the chequered headdress, the wraparound dark glasses – became an emblem of resistance; carefully mythologised versions of his life story were handed out; and as the mystique seeped through to the Western media, he took his theatrics to new lengths, luring camera crews to staged midnight assignations in the hills outside Amman. He could just as easily have met his interlocutors in a downtown hotel, but being filmed with his fighters in a cave helped to inflate the myth. Arafat's appetite for publicity was boundless, and he made himself available for numerous newspaper interviews with Western reporters, almost invariably talking to them in his idiosyncratic broken English. Before 1968 was out he made the first of several appearances on the cover of *Time* magazine under a headline identifying the *fedayeen* as a powerful new force in the Middle East.

Fatah had already confirmed its status as the largest and most broadly based of the Palestinian guerrilla grouping. Now its members began to parade openly with their weapons on the streets of Lebanese and Jordanian towns and to preach the doctrines of 'popular liberation war'. Money was collected through the sale of specially printed stamps around the Arab world. Military and other supplies poured into the guerrilla bases. By the end of 1968, Fatah alone had at least 2,000 men under arms, a cadre of officers trained at a military academy in the Chinese city of Nanking and a stockpile of Kalashnikovs, AK-47s and other weapons. The Kalashnikov, the 'Klashin', became an object of worship, for which Fatah guerrillas had a special chant:

Klashin makes the blood gush in torrents.
Haifa and Jaffa are calling us.
Commando, go ahead and do not worry:
Open fire and break the silence of the night![29]

Arafat was particularly proud of the measures Fatah was taking to prepare for a long, drawn-out struggle. It set up a special section – known as the Ashbal or 'Cubs' – to train children as young as eight in guerrilla warfare. It also set out to build an array of non-military institutions, responsible for anything from health care (the Palestinian Red Crescent) to vocational training (Samed, Fatah's economic arm). Modelled in part on the organisations that had helped to implant the Jews in Palestine in the 1930s and 1940s, in time they gave the liberation movement many of the characteristics of a Palestinian government in exile.

For their part, Arab governments, faced with a surge of public support for the *fedayeen*, had little choice but to lend support. After long years of restricting Palestinian movements, they opened their borders to the resistance, enabling its growing legions of recruits to travel freely on production of a photo-less Fatah identity card. Wealthy countries, such as Libya and Saudi Arabia, vied to contribute to Palestinian coffers. Commando training was stepped up at bases in Iraq and Syria; one training camp near the

Syrian port of Latakia ran six-week courses in guerrilla warfare for 350 recruits at a time.

It was a stunning vindication for Arafat, less than a year after his ambitions had been ridiculed by many of his colleagues. But it was not enough. What he really wanted was something he valued higher than all the money and arms then pouring in: official recognition of Fatah by the Arab regimes. And that meant prising open a door that had consistently remained closed to him, that of President Nasser of Egypt.

A word of support from Nasser could still bestow tremendous prestige, despite his fall from grace in the wake of 1967. Yet the Egyptian President had always viewed Fatah with suspicion, fuelled by intelligence reports of its leaders' *Ikhwan* connections and ties with Syria. It was only after Nasser's defeat in the Six-Day War and at the urging of his confidant, the journalist Mohammed Hassanein Heikal, that Nasser began to conclude that Arafat and his colleagues might be useful. 'I thought that it was time for us to overcome all these old suspicions because 1967 had changed so much,' recalled Heikal. 'I thought we should give them a chance to prove themselves.'[30]

Nasser, warned at one stage by his intelligence people that the Palestinians were plotting to assassinate him, did not readily drop his guard. When he first met Farouk Kaddoumi and Salah Khalaf, he suggested – in jest – that a green briefcase Kaddoumi was carrying might be packed with explosives. But after sounding them out on Fatah's motives and aims, he agreed in April 1968 to receive Arafat himself. For Nasser, who remained sceptical about what the Palestinian group could achieve, it was a question of expediency. At a time when he was both pursuing a war of attrition with Israel and co-operating with United Nations peace moves, Fatah's continuing armed struggle – however ineffectual – might serve as a useful, if indirect, signal that the Arab regimes had not given up the fight.

'I would be more than glad if you could represent the Palestinian people and the Palestinian will to resist, politically by your presence and militarily by your actions,' he told Arafat when they met at last in his modest residence, not far from the Fatah leader's family home in the Cairo suburb of Heliopolis.[31] Significantly, he advised Fatah to preserve its independence from Arab regimes, but to co-ordinate with them in the same way that Jewish terrorist groups did with the mainstream Zionist movement before the establishment of Israel – just the sort of relationship Arafat had proposed to Shukairy four years before.[32] Nonetheless, Nasser remained puzzled by the impetuous guerrilla leader. At one point in their conversation, he asked Arafat what time limit he was setting for his revolution. 'Mr President, a revolution has no time limit,' was Arafat's reply.[33] Thus began a relationship that was to take Fatah into the highest councils of Arab politics within little more than a year. Arafat came to place more trust in Nasser than in any other Arab leader. Apart from offering frequently forthright advice, Nasser promised to – and did – provide Arafat with arms and his men with training. He arranged instruction courses for the Palestinians at Egyptian military bases, covering such matters as intelligence-gathering and sabotage. Just as important, he allowed Fatah to establish its own broadcasting station in Cairo. Known as 'Voice of Fatah', its signature song soon became familiar across the Arab world:

> The Revolution of Fatah exists,
> It exists here, there and everywhere.
> It is a storm, a storm in every house and village.[34]

Nasser also gave Arafat valuable introductions, not least to his superpower ally, the Soviet Union. In July 1968, he allowed the Fatah leader, travelling on a false Egyptian passport bearing the name Muhsin Amin, to tag along with a presidential delegation on a visit to Moscow. Arafat's talks with relatively junior Soviet officials were not all that satisfactory and certainly did not come up to his ambitious expectations. At the time, the Soviets saw Fatah as a band of 'adventurists'. Arafat was merely allowed the briefest of handshakes with members of the ageing Kremlin leadership before being fobbed off with a modest financial donation.[35] But at least it was a start. Arafat was beginning to learn the tricks of the diplomatic trade. As he had from the outset, he maintained a studied vagueness about his own political views, a fact which not only gave Fatah broad appeal among Palestinians but also helped it win support from powerful patrons.

To Saudi Arabia's conservative King Faisal, who agreed to deduct a seven per cent 'contribution' to Fatah – a 'liberation tax' – from the salaries of Palestinians working in the kingdom, Arafat was a devout Muslim fighting to recover the holy shrines of Jerusalem. To the Communist Chinese, now supplying arms to Fatah, he was an anti-imperialist revolutionary struggling against American hegemony in the Middle East. To 'progressive' and 'reactionary' Arab regimes alike, he cast himself as the keeper of the seals of Arab nationalism: as Fatah put it, the liberation of Palestine was an essential step towards the elusive dream of Arab unity. This last message was one calculated to appeal to the new, more pragmatic generation of Arab leaders coming to power in the wake of the 1967 defeat. For men like Hafez al-Assad in Syria and, later, Anwar Sadat in Egypt – more interested in keeping the peace at home than in going to war abroad in pursuit of some grand Arab design – Fatah had its uses. Arafat has always taken pride in his ability to play the political chameleon. 'What meaning does the left or the right have in the struggle for the liberation of my homeland?' he said in an interview with the Lebanese newspaper *Al-Sayyad* in January 1969. 'I want that homeland even if the devil is the one to liberate it for me. Am I in a position to reject the participation or assistance of any man? Can I be asked, for example, to refuse the financial aid of Saudi Arabia with the claim that it belongs to the right? After all, it is with the Saudis' money that I buy arms from China.'[36]

Uninterested in ideology Arafat may have been, but other Fatah leaders had by now begun to define some political aims for their movement. Their central idea was spelled out by ex-*Ikhwan* member Salah Khalaf, already Fatah's principal ideologue, at a press conference on the premises of a Beirut newspaper. It was one which outsiders found highly implausible: a democratic state in the whole of historic Palestine in which 'Arabs and Jews would live together harmoniously as fully equal citizens'.[37]

The dream was drawn from idealised visions of Palestine that had circulated in the 1930s and 1940s and from a slogan adopted by the Arab League back in 1947[38] but in the Arab world in 1968 it was presented and received as a bold attempt to break with the past. Gone, said Fatah, were the old chauvinistic slogans about revenge and 'throwing the Jews into the sea' that had been the stock-in-trade of Shukairy's generation of leaders – people who, as one Fatah representative put it, saw only 'the Palestine of the past, that is a Palestine without three million Jews'.[39]

Instead, the Palestinians were now proposing to co-operate with those Jews who had been prepared to throw off the shackles of Zionism in building a completely new society. 'In itself this was saying something revolutionary at the time as far as Arabs were concerned: that we were willing to live with the Jews in Palestine,' said Khalaf.[40] Although the proposal initially drew fire both from within Fatah and from other Palestinian Resistance factions, the idea of 'a free and democratic society in Palestine for all Palestinians including Muslims, Christian and Jews', subsequently became official PLO policy.[41]

Some Arafat associates, such as Nabil Shaath, actually went one step further and sought to interest Israelis in the idea. In 1969 and 1970, with Arafat's blessing, he met and sounded out the Israeli mathematics professor Moshe Makhover and, more importantly, Lova Eliav, secretary general of the ruling Labour Party who was well known for his doveish views. 'If you stop thinking about revenge and start thinking about one country for all of us, then logically you would want to see how Jews respond to that idea,' Shaath explained.[42] In these early meetings are to be found the precursors of many similar contacts – initially secret, then increasingly public – between PLO functionaries and Israeli leftists in the mid- to late 1970s.

There was never any chance that this early initiative would make much impact on the Israeli political mainstream, preoccupied as it was with Palestinian attacks on Jewish civilians. But attempts to signal greater flexibility towards the Jews undoubtedly made for good public relations in the West. In 1968, Fatah, with the aid of its Algerian friends, had been allowed by President de Gaulle to set up its first European mission in Paris. There, the group's representative, Mohammed Abu Mayzar, cultivated contacts with members of the European New Left who had supported the Algerian FLN and were beginning to take an interest in the Palestinian cause: academics like Maxime Rodinson and radical chic politicians such as Michel Rocard, later to become Socialist

Prime Minister. De Gaulle's gesture in allowing Fatah to establish a foothold in western Europe is something Arafat has never forgotten. To this day, he wears around his neck a memento the general sent him before he died: La Croix de Lorraine, a symbol of the French Resistance forces de Gaulle commanded. On the wall of one of the safe houses Arafat inhabited in Tunis in his long years in exile was a framed wartime quotation from the French leader: 'Nous avons perdu une bataille mais nous n'avons pas perdu la guerre' (We have lost a battle, but we have not lost the war).

Arafat has always been much less interested in airy political theory than in power. Armed with his new Arab support, the Fatah 'spokesman' had embarked on a bid for overall leadership of the Palestinian movement. With Nasser's assistance, he was to succeed more quickly than anticipated.

During 1968, negotiations began with the aim of reviving the lifeless PLO by bringing in the guerrilla groups that had sprung up since the previous year. This posed a dilemma for Arafat's colleagues, many of whom believed that if Fatah joined the PLO, it would become bogged down in bureaucracy. Their first inclination had been to try to organise a joint military organisation led by Al-Asifa which would serve as an alternative to the PLO. 'The PLO is an organisation of offices and cars,' they would tell middle-aged functionaries sent to negotiate with them in the shabby basements of Damascus. 'We don't want offices; we are fighters and our operations must take place only in the occupied territories.'[44]

But if Arafat harboured reservations about taking over the PLO's existing infrastructure, he swallowed them. He saw that the organisation, with its diplomatic missions, political institutions and money, could be a useful vehicle. In fact, it might provide the key both to consolidating Fatah's influence and to building up support from the Arab states which, after all, had founded the organisation in the first place.

The important question concerned terms. Some of Arafat's new Arab friends – and several members of the Fatah leadership – advised him that it would be better for Fatah to take over the PLO alone and leave the other, smaller Palestinian factions outside. But here again Arafat had firm views, reflecting his stuttering attachment to consensus building. Leaving the other groups out, even if it proved possible, might induce strife such as had occurred among Palestinians in the 1930s – a disaster which Arafat has often said he is determined to prevent. Better to gather as many groups as possible within the PLO and turn the organisation into a broad national front along the lines of the motley coalition of political and guerrilla factions that confronted the Americans in Vietnam.

So it was that after much haggling the commando organisations joined the PLO's legislative body, the Palestine National Council, for the first time in July 1968. Reflecting the influence of its militant new members, the Council rewrote the PLO's National Covenant, its statement of beliefs and objectives, with a ringing endorsement of guerrilla war against Israel: 'Armed struggle is the only way to liberate Palestine. Thus it is the overall strategy and not merely a tactical phase.'[44]

Arafat's ascent to the pinnacle of the PLO very nearly did not happen. In early January 1969, he was involved in the most serious of his several car crashes, on the road between Amman and Baghdad. Arafat had always had a penchant for fast driving, a predilection he would in later years put down to fear of an Israeli helicopter attack. But on that January morning, seated at the wheel of his black Mercedes, he was in a particular hurry. Bowling along the rainy highway at 130 kilometres an hour, he tried to overtake a truck and found himself headed straight for a car coming in the opposite direction. He slammed on the brakes and skidded under the lorry. 'After a few seconds I heard Arafat moaning and I thought he was dying,' recalled guerrilla commander Abu Daoud, one of Arafat's two passengers, 'He was on the floor of the car, his hand was broken and he was hurt in the chest. He also lost his memory for a few days.[45]

Less than a month later, Arafat had recovered sufficiently to make his first appearance at a meeting of the Palestinian 'parliament' in Cairo. On 3 February 1969, a reconvened and restructured PNC, with the *fedayeen* in unchallenged control, duly elected him chairman of the Executive Committee of the Palestine

Liberation Organisation. In the presence of President Nasser and in a capital emblazoned with posters of his Fatah movement, Arafat had been hailed as the paramount Palestinian leader. He hastened to assert his dominance, promising to expand military operations until the movement was engaged in a 'fully-fledged war of liberation', rejecting 'all political settlements' and intervening with gusto in the National Council debates.[46]

To those who did not know Arafat well, his behaviour during the meeting was annoying. 'He would interrupt everybody; he would shout whenever he thought anybody infringed on his prerogatives; he would stand up and insist on being given the floor,' said his latter-day adviser Nabil Shaath. 'At first I thought this was very childish and that if he talked less it would have been better.'[47]

For the mornent, Fatah's triumph seemed almost complete. It had conquered the Palestinian labour union, the writers' and artists' groups, the women's and students' organisations that had grown up in the diaspora. Thanks to Ahmed Shukairy's efforts, it had inherited an organisation with a ready-made infrastructure – a 'finance ministry' of sorts, an army under its nominal control, an executive committee for day-to-day decision-making and an irregular parliament. Most important, Arafat had got his hands on an instrument of power that he was to wield with considerable skill: money. In taking over the PLO, he had tied a knot that supposedly bound the Arab regimes to support his new 'auton-omous' movement as representative of the Palestinian people. Just how far he had travelled was apparent at a summit meeting in the Moroccan capital, Rabat, in December 1969, when he demanded that Arab leaders contribute 44 million US dollars to the cause. History does not relate how much they actually chipped in then, but Arafat succeeded in building the PLO in his years in exile into an organisation as rich as a multinational corporation, and every bit as complex.

The honeymoon with the Arab regimes, however, rested on fragile relationships. Even at the moment of success, the divisions within Palestinian ranks were obvious: the main leftist group, led by George Habash, refused to recognise Fatah's hegemony and boycotted the National Council in protest at a miserly allocation of seats; the commanders of the Palestine Liberation Army protested about the guerrilla takeover. Just as significantly, behind the lip service they paid to the PLO, Arab states were even then plotting to curb its new-found independence. In Lebanon and more particularly in Jordan, the upsurge of raids into Israel and the resulting Israeli reprisals were causing political ructions.

Small wonder that when Arafat's election as PLO chairman was announced, the look on his face spoke more of foreboding than of euphoria. Asked by a colleague what was troubling him, he replied with one word: 'Responsibility'.[48]

4. BLOOD FEUD

'Leadership is not easy in a jungle of guns.' Yasser Arafat, quoted in the *Los Angeles Times*, 21 June 1981.

One crisp morning in mid-October 1968, tens of thousands of Palestinians, many of them armed, took to the streets of the Jordanian capital, Amman. From their refugee camps and commando bases, they snaked their way along the gravelly hillsides and into the town, chanting slogans against the Jordanian Government and in support of the Palestinian Resistance. They heard speeches from Fatah leaders exalting the guerrilla struggle. They swaggered and fired their rifles in the air.

The occasion was ostensibly one of mourning for a top Fatah leader, Abdel Fattah Hamoud, who had been killed in a car crash near the Syrian border several days earlier. But what started out as a funeral turned into a mass political demonstration, with a grieving Yasser Arafat at its head. It was the first time the *fedayeen* had shown up in force in Amman. For King Hussein bin Talal, Jordan's ruler for fifteen years, it was, to say the least, a disturbing sight.

Ever since their showdown with the Israelis at Karameh the previous March, the Palestinians had been flexing their muscles in Hussein's kingdom. Home to the largest number of Arab refugees from the Arab–Israeli wars of 1948 and 1967, Jordan was also the principal recruiting ground for a proliferation of guerrilla groups, and their main launching pad for attacks on Israel. Hussein, his country and army still shattered by the 1967 defeat, was then in no position to stand in their way. The pro-Western monarch's grip on power had always been shaky. But with the *fedayeen* now openly brandishing their Kalashnikovs in Amman and with their raids on Israel attracting inevitable reprisals, Palestinian guerrilla power was beginning to look like a full-scale challenge to his authority. Something would have to be done to bring it under control.

Within days of the October rally, the frictions began to tell. *Fedayeen* leaders complained that Jordanian roadblocks and vehicle searches were hampering them in their armed struggle against Israel; they protested at restrictions on their movements and at attempts by the king's army to control their operations. Violence was the inevitable result. On 2 November 1968, Palestinians stormed the American embassy in Amman during a demonstration to mark the 51st anniversary of the Balfour Declaration – Britain's promise to work for the establishment of a Jewish homeland in Palestine. Security forces dispersed the mob with tear gas and in the ensuing melee arrested the leader of the small but grandly named guerrilla faction that had organised the riot, the Victory Legions. Next day, followers of the arrested man, a former Syrian army officer named Taher Dablaan, retaliated by ambushing a police car and kidnapping and murdering a group of policemen. When the authorities seized an arms cache in one of Amman's Palestinian refugee shanty towns, clashes broke out between Dablaan's group and the Jordanian army, and more than 10,000 people came out on the streets again in a massive anti-government demonstration. Hussein, accusing 'phoney elements' among the commandos of seeking to foment a revolution in Jordan, sent his army in to crush the unrest. Thousands of troops surrounded and shelled the refugee camps for more than three days, while the commandos issued statements accusing Hussein of colluding with Israel in 'a conspiracy to eliminate the resistance'.

All this happened several months before Arafat assumed the chairmanship of the PLO. Thus he found himself pitched into a task that was henceforth to take much of his time: damage limitation. With feelings still running high, he toured Amman in the company of a Jordanian police commander, urging Palestinian refugees not to support the renegade Victory Legions. As the fighting sputtered on, he requested an audience with King Hussein.

It was to be the first of many difficult encounters between the men over the next two years. In some ways they were evenly matched: apart from both being small in stature, they shared a taste for theatrics, volatile temperaments and a capacity for deviousness. King Hussein treated Arafat and a group of other Palestinian leaders to a histrionic display of rage in which he pinned responsibility for the disturbances on the resistance leadership and threatened to take action against the guerrillas. The result, on 16 November, was an agreement between the government and the resistance which banned them from carrying weapons and wearing uniform in the towns and prohibited the shelling of Israeli targets from the East Bank of the Jordan.[1]

It was a victory on points for the regime but although the agreement succeeded in defusing the immediate crisis, the underlying contradictions between the two sides had been more starkly exposed. For Yasser Arafat, what was to prove a long and brutal lesson in Arab politics and the failings of his own movement had begun.

He and his Fatah comrades had long believed that Jordan, not Syria, was the most natural base for their guerrilla operations. Its long and permeable frontier with Israel; its sympathetic, sixty per cent Palestinian population; its weakened government in the aftermath of the Six-Day War – all these things led Arafat to conclude that Jordan was 'safe ground' on which to land his 'revolution on a flying carpet'.[2] In time, the *fedayeen* should be able to transform it into a centre of resistance for the Palestinians, as the Vietnamese had Hanoi. Provided that Fatah promised not to interfere in Jordanian politics, there was no reason why the Jordanian authorities should curb the *fedayeen* in their armed struggle against Israel.[3] That, at least, was the theory. At the outset that is how it worked: deeply unhappy as King Hussein was about the new armed presence on his soil, there was little he could do about it. Two days after the Battle of Karameh a monarch who only a month earlier had threatened to 'act with force and determination' against the guerrillas, had even felt constrained to make his own half-hearted expression of support for them, saying, 'We may well arrive at a stage when we shall all be *fedayeen*.'[4]

Arafat was beginning to feel at home in Jordan. Living with a group of other Fatah leaders in a flat in the Jebel Hussein area of Amman, he spent his time in triumphal tours of his group's guerrilla bases. According to those who were with him, it was a frugal life. Arafat slept little, neither smoked nor drank. His diversions consisted of comics, TV cartoons and the occasional game of ping-pong.

As 1968 progressed, the power of the Palestinian resistance had grown to a point where it began to act as a state within the state. Fatah's military activities had generated enormous enthusiasm among politically active Jordanians as well as the Palestinian refugees. Arafat's followers had managed to penetrate the Jordanian army, secretly recruiting a number of middle-ranking to senior officers. They also obtained extensive assistance from the Iraqi army there. For a while, at least, the *fedayeen* had the pleasurable feeling that there were no limits to their freedom of action. As Khalil al-Wazir nostalgically put it a few years later, 'We were mini-states and institutions. Every sector commander considered himself God . . . everyone set up a state for himself and did whatever he pleased.'[5]

But it was an illusion. In emerging so publicly in Jordan, the guerrillas had unleashed forces that would drag them inexorably into conflict with the established order, and ultimately towards their own downfall. One problem was the increasingly determined Israeli retaliation against Palestinian raids – reprisals that had turned the fertile Jordan Valley into a virtual no-go area. Pushed back from the border, the fighters scattered their bases across an ever wider area, from the steep and rocky hills of western Jordan to the refugee camps of the capital and the forests of the north. As Israel adopted a strategy of what it called 'active self-defence', involving air raids and artillery attacks deep inside Jordan, the local population began to suffer. More problematic still was the behaviour of the *fedayeen*. Placing themselves above the law, they showed scant regard for the sensibilities of ordinary Jordanians or for their government. Self-styled guerrillas were extorting 'donations' at gunpoint from the residents of Amman.

Such indiscipline was a symptom of a more basic flaw. In Jordan, guerrilla groups were proliferating like mushrooms. At one point, the government counted 52 separate Palestinian factions, some of them numbering only a few members, but all answerable only to themselves or to whichever Arab regime had chosen to sponsor them, all with more or less easy access to money and weapons.[6] The result was that, even after Arafat's election as chairman of the PLO in February 1969, his control over the movement – the 'jungle of guns' – was tenuous at best.

The multifarious factions, including Arafat's own Fatah, were still in a battle for publicity, members and funds. More to the point, beyond the common aim of fighting Israel, they could not agree among themselves on what strategy to adopt in Jordan.

At one extreme was George Habash's pseudo-Marxist Popular Front for the Liberation of Palestine. He called for a revolution not only against the Jews in Palestine but also against 'reactionary' Arab leaders, principal among whom he counted King Hussein, who was especially close to the US and Britain. It later emerged, Hussein had been on the payroll of the CIA since 1957. At the other extreme, Arafat and his Fatah colleagues sought, at least in principle, to stay out of Jordanian affairs. Trying to take over Jordan, Arafat argued, would bog the movement down in administrative concerns for which it was neither equipped nor disposed. Better for the Palestinians to keep their powder dry for the fight that mattered – the struggle against Israel. 'Under no circumstances will any Arab regime deter us from our goals and push us into side battles,' said a Fatah statement issued in 1968. 'Our bullets will target only the enemy, but at the same time we will not drop our arms under any threats.'[7] Or as Arafat himself put it later that year, 'One enemy at a time is enough.'[8]

The competition between Arafat and his left-wing rivals took on increasingly dramatic forms. In the summer of 1968, just a few months after Karameh had made Arafat the toast of the Arab world, the Popular Front hit on its own arresting way of grabbing the headlines. On 23 July, three PFLP gunmen seized an Israeli El Al flight en route from Rome to Tel Aviv and diverted it to Algiers, demanding, in exchange for the Israeli passengers and crew, the release of Palestinians held in Israeli jails. Israel issued what was to become a customary disclaimer that it did not negotiate with terrorists, but after more than a month of mediation Algeria released the plane and the last of the passengers and crew. Two days later, Israel freed sixteen convicted Arab infiltrators who had been jailed before the 1967 war.

King Hussein was under mounting pressure to crack down. Especially restive was his loyal Bedu army. As army units skirmished periodically with the *fedayeen*, these troops – and sympathetic officers higher up – found it difficult to understand why the king was hesitating to assert his authority. Nor did they find any respite from their frustrations when off duty. Back in their home villages and towns, soldiers often found themselves humiliated and stripped of their weapons by Palestinian militia-men anxious to show that they were the real power in the land.

'The army was out of the city, but the soldiers would take holidays and were prevented from coming into town carrying their arms. They were very antagonised,' recalled Zeid al-Rafai, a confidant of the king. 'In one incident, the *fedayeen* killed a soldier, beheaded him and played soccer with his head in the area where he used to live. The soldiers would also get reports about their families being attacked. So the army was really antagonised.'[9]

It was clear that Hussein was not going to tolerate the growth of a Palestinian authority in Jordan rivalling his own indefinitely. Ever since the establishment of Israel in 1948, his family had claimed what was left of Palestine for itself and he, like his grandfather before him, had long maintained secret contacts with the Israelis to reinforce that claim. The growth of Arafat's nationalist movement could only be a threat to what had become his number one priority – recovery of the territory lost to Israel in the 1967 war – and ultimately to the continuation of Hashemite rule.

Such was the gulf that divided Hussein and Arafat as they manoeuvred uncertainly around each other during 1969. Hussein repeatedly reshuffled his government and his army command as if groping for a way of coming to grips with the complex political equation on his doorstep. Arafat, struggling to hold his movement together and shaken by an unsuccessful attempt to assassinate him by parcel bomb that summer, negotiated hesitantly a *modus vivendi* with the regime. Although the two men were at one in their indecision, theirs was in every other way an uneasy relationship. Pressed by Hussein to impose some discipline on the movement under his nominal command, Arafat instead chose to temporise. Not only was he a hostage to the divisions within the guerrilla factions that made up the PLO, but he was also labouring under severe delusions of his own.

Among the Palestinians, power bred arrogance. The *fedayeen* ran their own police force and their own courts. They set up roadblocks at random and careered around the rocky hillsides of Amman in their military vehicles. Palestinian factions took their internecine skirmishing on to the streets. Progressively, the rule of law seemed to be succumbing to the rule of the gun. Stories of petty thuggery and crime circulated. Shopkeepers found themselves strong-armed into contributing to the cause. The leftists, from Habash's Popular Front to a host of radical splinter groups, daubed Maoist slogans round the capital, preached Marxism from mosque loudspeakers, and infiltrated the local labour unions, stirring up unrest. A motley crew from the European New Left, some of whom received military training and went on to found terrorist cells in West Germany, installed itself in the Palestinian refugee camps. 'All power to the resistance,' ran the persistent refrain. Many of Arafat's own followers in Fatah now shared the view that the resistance should be working to take power in Jordan. Abu Daoud, who commanded the 15,000-strong Palestinian militia forces from a base in Amman's Wahdat refugee camp, was one of several Fatah leaders arguing for such a course during 1969. 'Until February 1970, it would have been very easy for us to topple the regime if we had wished to do so,' he said.[10] As Salah Khafaf commented ruefully, 'Our problem was that the regime had only one decision, whereas we always had at least twelve.'[11]

Just turned 40, Arafat was enjoying his first taste of what he took to be real power. He was certainly not about to undermine his position by agreeing to controversial restrictions on his own supporters. He was also inexperienced in statecraft, displaying little understanding of the Jordanian scene. As many PLO leaders are today prepared to admit, he devoted insufficient attention to building links with Jordanian activists who could have warned him of impending danger and might have helped to shelter the *fedayeen* from the fallout.

One delusion above all coloured Arafat's interpretation of events. He simply could not believe that Hussein was capable of militarily defeating the *fedayeen*. If the king tried to unleash his army, he reasoned, its Palestinian contingents would surely revolt; if the resistance were in danger, it could surely count on help from the

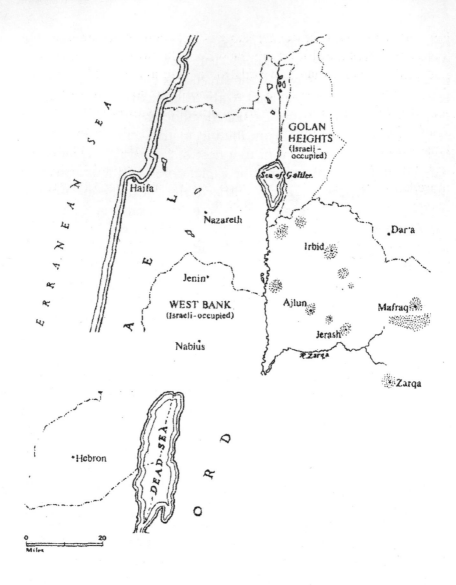

surrounding Arab states, in particular from the Iraqi army division that was strengthening its presence in Jordan. Such was his faith in the appeal of his cause to other Arabs – and in the admittedly wide chasm of distrust between King Hussein and the radical regime next door in Iraq.

At the end of 1969, the political temperature in Jordan rose sharply, thanks partly to American-sponsored Middle East peace moves. In December, Secretary of State William Rogers put forward a plan for peace agreements between Israel on the one hand and Egypt and Jordan on the other. The proposals, which did not address Palestinian demands for a state and would oblige all three parties to halt 'hostile acts originating from their territories',[12] set off protests among the *fedayeen* and their supporters.

For Arafat, the so-called 'Rogers Plan' played on fears that Hussein might make an accommodation with Israel to regain his lost territories at the PLO's expense. A new and inflammable ingredient had been injected into the volatile mix of relations between Jordan and the resistance.

It would not be long before fire broke out. On 10 February 1970, King Hussein signalled his intention to restore authority in the kingdom with an eleven-point decree imposing severe restrictions on the *fedayeen*. The use, carrying or stockpiling of firearms and explosives was to be banned; demonstrations, party political activities and pamphleteering would be prohibited; and guerrillas would henceforth have to carry identity cards and license their vehicles.

Infuriated, *fedayeen* leaders denounced the decree as a provocation to civil war. They demanded that the government revoke it, withdraw army units from the cities and give the guerrillas full freedom of action. They staged demonstrations and meted out more 'revolutionary justice' to Jordanian security forces. But Hussein's move had caught the resistance off guard. Arafat was out of Jordan, cementing his relations with the Soviet leadership in Moscow, which was now showing increased interest in the PLO as a means of winning friends in the Arab world. There, inexplicably, he stayed, as the situation in Jordan continued to deteriorate. It was by no means the last occasion in Arafat's career on which he displayed a perverse sense of priorities. Basking in the international spotlight now trained on his movement, he often seemed to prefer dabbling in diplomacy to dealing with crises in his home base.

As the Jordanians moved to enforce the law, fighting broke out between the police force and the *fedayeen*. Scores of people, mainly Palestinians, were killed or wounded in clashes which continued for three days. To step up the pressure, Hussein's forces shut off water and electricity supplies to the Palestinian refugee camps. The resistance, more deeply divided than ever in Arafat's absence, despite belated moves to set up a 'unified command', was in no position to put up a credible fight. In desperation, those PLO leaders still in the country appealed for support to Iraq and Syria. It was only when both countries responded with threatening noises that the Jordanian Government climbed down.

On 14 February, King Hussein suspended his controversial measures, saying the whole affair had been a 'misunderstanding' and that Jordan would remain the home of the Palestinian resistance. On Arafat's return from Moscow a full week later, he met Hussein and signed an agreement formally declaring the crisis closed. Within 24 hours, the man who had introduced the anti-*fedayeen* decree in the first place, hardline Interior Minister Mohammad Rasul al-Kaylani, had resigned.[13]

The *fedayeen* had won the first of a series of tactical victories over King Hussein's regime. Under fire from his supporters for being absent in their hour of need, Arafat sought to restore his position by seeking further concessions from the government. As negotiations continued throughout the spring, Hussein appeared to be going out of his way to accommodate Arafat's demands. In April, he reshuffled his cabinet yet again and brought in Arafat's old friend from the Battle of Karameh, Mashour Haditha, as army chief of staff. For the resistance, it was richly symbolic. Haditha was an active mediator, taking Arafat in his Volkswagen to regular meetings with the king, and pleading with Hussein to avoid a confrontation.[14]

But such triumphs were temporary. Clashes continued between the army and the guerrillas. It seemed Arafat had neither the capacity nor the inclination to rein in his followers. Although he stepped up his efforts to unify Palestinian ranks under his leadership, he still did not realise how urgent the task had become.

'We in the leadership never concluded that a clash was inevitable,' said Ibrahim Bakr, the tough and sharp-witted lawyer who served under Arafat in 1969 as the PLO's first and last deputy chairman. 'The regime was under internal and Arab constraints not to act against the *fedayeen*. But the leadership interpreted this restraint as weakness. It was under the impression that the regime was not able to defeat them in a military clash. All the time, the Palestinian leadership believed it was in a military and popular position that was stronger than that of the regime. All the time, this was false.'[15]

Yasser Arafat refused to admit having miscalculated in Jordan: 'Fatah and myself did not commit mistakes,' he said. 'The mistakes were made by other factions that held Marxist banners inside the mosques.'[16] Yet the fact is that his own group's confusion about its strategy did contribute at least as much to its problems.

Tension reached a new peak when fighting broke out on 7 June in the town of Zarqa, site of the Jordanian army headquarters and of a large Palestinian refugee camp, and rapidly spread to Amman. As troops moved into the capital on 9 June, King Hussein narrowly escaped death when his motorcade came under fire outside the city.[17] Once again, Hussein and Arafat found themselves face to face at the negotiating table, but the ceasefire agreement they struck was instantly rejected by radical PLO factions. Turning up the heat, the Marxist Popular Front held 68 Westerners hostage in two downtown hotels for 48 hours. King Hussein was pushed to further concessions. On 11 June, he announced the resignation from key army posts of two close relatives, uncle Sharif Nasser bin Jamil and cousin Zeid bin Shaker (whose sister had been killed by Palestinians during that month's fighting). For Hussein this was a humiliation.

In the ensuing weeks, the king went further in appeasing the Palestinians, allowing their leaders to nominate ministers for a new government that was formed towards the end of June. According to Arafat, he even offered the PLO itself the chance of forming a government. Arafat refused, telling the king, 'We are not hungry for power. It is not my dream to rule any other Arab country but only to reach Jerusalem.'[18]

Even if Arafat's account is true, it seems unlikely that Hussein's offer was genuine, for having effectively suffered two defeats at the hands of the *fedayeen*, the king could not afford to contemplate a further erosion of his power. Indeed, his resolve was stiffened by the international concern that events in Jordan were provoking. In Israel, a debate was under way within the military establishment about the Palestinian threat to Hussein. Although some voices argued that Israel should stay out of the conflict and let the *fedayeen* take over, the majority took the opposite view: if the Hashemite throne was in serious danger, Israel might have to intervene.[19] Just as ominous for Arafat, Hussein's difficulties were also attracting attention in Washington. The Americans had been worried for some time about the growing strength of the Palestinians – a fact of which senior State Department officials had had first-hand experience earlier in the year, when they had had to cancel a helicopter trip across the Jordan river for fear of being shot down by guerrillas in the valley. In the eyes of Henry Kissinger, President Nixon's National Security Adviser, who counted the 'Little King' as a personal friend, the rise of the *fedayeen*, backed by radical, pro-Soviet regimes in Syria and Iraq, posed almost as much of a threat to American interests as to those of Jordan. Kissinger concluded that the confrontation in Jordan was a superpower trial of strength in the making, and set out during the summer to encourage Hussein to make a decisive move against the *fedayeen*.[20]

Quietly but deliberately, Hussein began to prepare for the worst. He reshuffled senior military officers under his own command and cancelled army leave. To ensure rank and file loyalty, a heavy propaganda campaign against the *fedayeen* was conducted in the barracks. Desultory negotiations continued throughout the summer of 1970, but when the time came for Hussein to act, the *fedayeen* had managed, by their own mistakes, to ensure that nobody was eager to come to their aid.

Their biggest blunder was to alienate President Nasser. For more than two years, he had acted as the Palestinians' friend and protector, helping Arafat to take over the chairmanship of the PLO, providing his movement with money and persuading numerous Third World and socialist countries to recognise it. But now he was tired and ill, and looking for at least a breathing space in the cycle of Arab–Israeli violence in which his country had been locked for most of his career. The result was increasing strain in his relationship with the Palestinian leaders, who vehemently opposed all talk of a political settlement.

On 23 July 1970, Nasser unexpectedly accepted a revised American peace plan for the Middle East. The move unleashed a storm of protest among the resistance organisations in Jordan. Even Arafat's Fatah group, hitherto anxious to preserve its ties with Egypt, attacked Nasser by name and threatened in a radio broadcast to 'use bullets to quash any attempt to impose a political solution.'[21] Insultingly, Palestinian demonstrators paraded through the streets of Amman displaying a picture of Nasser attached to a donkey.

Incensed, Nasser closed down PLO broadcasting stations in Cairo and expelled radical Palestinian activists from the country. In Amman, Arafat was swiftly brought to realise that his movement was in big trouble. He hurried to Cairo in August, at the head of a senior PLO delegation, to patch things up. Receiving the Palestinian leaders at his holiday retreat outside Alexandria, Nasser was furious. He told them he had been pacing up and down the roof of his house for an hour to get his feelings under control.[22] It was a long and difficult meeting. For seven hours, Nasser sought to explain his position to Arafat and his comrades, and to warn them against trying to topple King Hussein. 'I'm an army officer,' he said. 'Don't give me heroic speeches about resistance. I want to keep Hussein. I'm not asking for your secrets, but I tell you: don't try and do such a thing.'[23]

In late August, Hussein threw down the gauntlet. Returning from a three-day visit to Cairo, he warned the *fedayeen* that he would tolerate no challenge to his 'absolute sovereignty'. It was the cue for intensified street disturbances, more clashes with the army and another attempt on the king's life. Palestinians called for a general strike to protest against Hussein's co-operation with American peace moves, but it was now clear to their enemies in Jordan that few Arab tears would be shed if the resistance were cut down to size. As Jordanian shells rained on PLO headquarters, Arafat appealed to Arab heads of state for immediate intervention. On a visit to Baghdad in early September he was promised the protection of the Iraqi army division stationed in Jordan, and told to 'take any arms you want from our stores'.[24] But from other Arab states, reaction was limp.

Into this highly charged atmosphere, the left wing of the resistance threw a bomb. On 6 September 1970, while their leader George Habash was away in North Korea fraternising with the

Japanese Red Army, members of the Popular Front engaged in a frenzy of air piracy. They brought two hijacked planes – a Swissair DC-8 and a TWA Boeing 707 – to a remote desert airstrip known as Dawsons Field, renamed 'Revolution Airport'. Six days later, after bringing in a hijacked BOAC VC-10 to join the other two and removing the passengers and crews, they blew up all three.

Arafat was furious. Although he had made no conspicuous attempt to stop the two-year wave of PFLP hijackings, he had long made clear his disapproval. Realising the threat that this latest outrage posed to his already flimsy hold over revolutionary events in Jordan, he had been working to defuse the crisis by laying down guidelines for the release of passengers and planes. Now his authority had been flouted. All he could do in response was have the Popular Front suspended from the PLO's policy-making Central Committee. It was a case of too little, too late.

Meanwhile, Arab mediators urged the PLO leadership to 'count to ten' and reach an accommodation with Hussein and yet another compromise agreement, imposing restrictions on the resistance, was hammered out in mid-September.[25] But King Hussein was already busy formulating other plans. In a radio broadcast on 16 September, he declared martial law and announced that he was setting up a military government to restore 'order and security'. Within 24 hours, bloody score-settling had broken out on the hillsides of Amman as the army closed in on the *fedayeen*.

So long in the making, the showdown still caught the Palestinian resistance unprepared. It had no battle plan and had not even prepared hiding places for its leaders. Arafat, named PLO commander-in-chief only hours before the fighting started, wavered between calling for the overthrow of the military government and trying to patch things up with King Hussein by telephone. He could not get through. Hussein and his advisers, he was told, were saying their morning prayers.

But even had he been able to reach the king, it is not clear what he could have said. According to a close adviser of Hussein, the military government had already sent emissaries to Arafat for one last try at salvaging the situation. 'I am sorry,' he is quoted as replying, 'the situation has run out of my hands and all I can do is give the king 24 hours to leave the country.'[26]

The conflict of that September – Black September as it came to be known – was bloody and protracted. Given the disorganised state of the resistance, Hussein had anticipated it would all be over within 48 hours. But the Palestinians, armed with Kalashnikovs, hand grenades and a handful of mortars and rocket-propelled grenades, fought with courage and determination. Hundreds of Palestinian and Jordanian army soldiers defected to them. Around the northern town of Irbid, the *fedayeen* managed to establish a 'liberated zone' which they named the Republic of Palestine. As the army sent tanks into Amman, rounding up any resistance leaders its troops could find and pounding the refugee camps with its artillery, the onslaught began to look like an all-out tribal war. No part of the capital was safe. Dead bodies rotted in the streets as casualties – most of them civilian – climbed into the thousands.

Arafat, in particular, was a marked man. 'It was an attempt to liquidate both the revolution and the PLO,' he said. 'There was a special squad from the Jordanian forces whose sole task was to follow me.'[27] Unlike many of his peers in the Fatah leadership, he evaded capture. Followers, who moved him from house to house to keep him out of harm's way, describe him as active in the front line, co-ordinating the troops by makeshift wireless here, carrying an RPG launcher on his shoulder there.

But the odds against the Palestinians were overwhelming. In response to pleas for help from King Hussein, the United States Sixth Fleet was on the alert in the eastern Mediterranean and Israel was being encouraged to contemplate intervention by air or land to save his regime. Against such an array of forces, Arafat's supposed Arab friends hesitated to come to his aid. Iraq, which had been warned by Washington not to mobilise its Jordanian expeditionary force, meekly pulled back. The radical leaders of Syria did send a contingent of tanks, painted in Palestinian army colours, into northern Jordan, but then thought better of engaging the Jordanian army.

It was not until the sixth day of fighting that Arab efforts to end the fighting were energised. The ailing President Nasser, ordered by his doctors to rest, had been slow to intervene, but on 22 September he convened a summit meeting of Arab leaders at the Nile Hilton Hotel to discuss ways of saving the resistance from destruction. They decided to launch a last-ditch mission: Jaafar Nimeiri, the soldier-president of Sudan, was to lead a small delegation to Amman, secure the freedom of the jailed resistance leaders and negotiate a ceasefire.

The events that followed were a cross between thriller and farce. The mediators managed to hammer out an agreement between Hussein and a group of PLO leaders freed from prison, and to take them back to Cairo, but no sooner was the deal broadcast over Radio Amman than Arafat – from his hiding place elsewhere in the capital – rejected it. The resistance would fight 'until the overthrow of the fascist regime in Jordan', he vowed.[28] Given that the *fedayeen* were running low on ammunition and losing ground to the Jordanian offensive, it was a foolhardy stand, but it prompted the Arab leaders to have one more stab at mediation.

Reluctantly, Nimeiri and his fellow envoys returned to Amman in an attempt to find Arafat before the Jordanian army did.

Speaking from the Egyptian embassy, he made a radio appeal for the PLO leader to meet him. Shortly afterwards Arafat signalled his assent on the PLO's own wireless channel, named Zamzam 105 after the sacred well in Mecca.

Under sporadic shellfire, which the mediators vainly tried to halt by telephoning the king, the two leaders met in a flat in an area of Amman controlled by the resistance. 'You should come with us back to Cairo, because Nasser told us not to return without you,' said Nimeiri.[29] The question was, how was Arafat to escape from a capital where he was in constant danger of being shot? The answer was provided by Sheikh Saad al-Abdullah, Crown Prince of Kuwait, who was a member of the Arab delegation. He provided Arafat with a set of Arab robes, and the Palestinian leader was smuggled out of the country disguised as a Kuwaiti official.[30]

When he arrived at the Nile Hilton, Arafat, armed and on his guard, complained bitterly about King Hussein's 'conspiracy' against the Palestinian revolution.[31] Some of his listeners turned a willing ear. Colonel Gadaffi, the Libyan leader, was for hanging the 'madman' Hussein in Cairo's central Tahrir Square.[32] Finally, a weary President Nasser sought to bring the discussion to a close. 'It seems to me that we are all mad,' he said.[33]

In due course, Hussein did show up, decked out in military fatigues and carrying a bag he said contained tape recordings that would prove the Palestinians had been plotting to overthrow him. The upshot, on 27 September, was a frosty handshake between Arafat and Hussein. They signed a fourteen-point agreement providing for a ceasefire, the withdrawal of all forces from Amman and a regrouping of commandos in agreed areas suitable for guerrilla attacks on Israel, and the drawing-up under an Arab committee of another, more durable accord. A civil war that had cost some 3,000 lives according to Red Cross estimates – and 20,000 according to Arafat's own inflated guess – seemed, for the moment at least, to be over.[34]

One other result of Nasser's peace initiative made news that same night. After spending hours at the airport seeing off his guests, the exhausted President collapsed at home and died of a heart attack. Arafat was grief-stricken on hearing the news – as well he might. With Nasser's death disappeared the last guarantee that the PLO–Jordanian accords he had expended so much effort in putting together would be implemented.

Neither side in any case had much commitment to the agreement to which they had put their names in Cairo. The *fedayeen*, suspecting that Hussein was intent on ejecting them from Jordan altogether rather than allowing them to continue their guerrilla raids, hung on to the sizeable portion of Amman which they still controlled. In secret talks with Israeli Foreign Minister Yigal Allon in October 1970, Hussein promised to do his best to prevent *fedayeen* actions against Israel.[35] In subsequent meetings between the king's men and the PLO to dot the 'i's and cross the 't's, negotiators found themselves back at square one: the follow-up agreement reached in mid-October merely rehearsed all the old contradictions between the two sides without resolving them.[36]

Bit by bit the Jordanians, under a new hardline Prime Minister, Wasfi Tal, closed the net on the resistance. First the heat was stepped up on Palestinian bases in the north and west. Then the regime demanded the evacuation of the *fedayeen* from Amman, as provided for under the initial agreement. Finally, all that was left to the resistance was a couple of pockets of forested territory north of the capital. In the hills around Jerash and Ajlun, around 4,000 fighters entrenched themselves in caves and underground excavations. They were tired, isolated from the majority who had taken refuge in Damascus, and demoralised.

Arafat was holed up with his men in the Ajlun area, negotiating fitfully with officials in Amman to preserve some breathing space for the resistance. But as Jordanian troops moved closer to the guerrilla hideaways and began to lay siege to the area in the spring of 1971, he realised that the end was only a matter of time; in April, he prepared to take his leave of a country where only twelve months earlier his movement had been riding high. From his mountain hideaway, he sent one last urgent appeal for help to Munib al-Masri, a Palestinian friend serving as Minister of Public Works in King Hussein's government. Together with the Saudi ambassador and an officer from the Jordanian army, Masri set off to see what could be done. When they finally found Arafat, he regaled them with tales of Jordanian atrocities. They decided to take him to see King Hussein and try, yet again, to resolve the problem.

On the journey back towards Amman in the Saudi ambassador's car, Arafat sat between the diplomat and the Jordanian officer, nervously fingering his Kalashnikov. 'At every Jordanian checkpoint, they wanted to shoot him,' said Masri.[37]

In fact, Arafat had no intention of going back to Amman. Once they had driven down from the hills, he asked instead to be taken to a town on the Syrian border, where he had an urgent task to perform. And there, after despatching the others into the cold night, he slipped away into Syria. 'I don't want to go as a renegade to Amman,' he told Masri before departing. 'I've had reports that my life is in danger. I want to come back as head of state for the PLO.[38] Arafat would not return to Jordan for another seven years.

The attack on those Palestinians who remained around Ajlun came on 12 July. It was of a ferocity to rival the fighting of the previous September. The guerrillas were rooted out of their bases; many, including the Fatah commander Abu Ali Iyad, were massacred by the king's Bedu soldiers; ninety were so terrified by what they saw that they were authorised by their commanding officer, Abbas Zeki, to seek refuge across the river in Israel rather than allow themselves to fall into the hands of Jordanian troops. The Israelis willingly took the guerrillas in. 'It was a nice, human gesture,' said General Yariv, the former Israeli military intelligence chief. 'And in the history of relations between Israel and the PLO, human gestures are few and far between.'[39]

Deprived of its main launching pad for attacks against Israel, its ranks decimated by the fighting with Jordan, the Palestinian revolution limped away to lick its wounds in the only other frontline states that would still receive it, Syria and Lebanon. In this second exile, the *fedayeen* were confronted with a series of questions about their experience of the past four years. What exactly had gone wrong? How had the resistance movement's internal divisions contributed to the catastrophe? How should they be resolved? Why had the Arab states not done more to assist them? The last question was in a way the most disturbing, for it raised serious doubts about the extent to which the new generation of Arab leaders who had pledged support to Arafat's PLO could deliver. Perhaps men like Hafez al-Assad, by now Syria's President, were less interested in saving the PLO's skin than their own. Perhaps for them Palestine was a political symbol to be manipulated more than a prize to be won.

Above all, the *fedayeen* leaders asked, where were they to go from here? In the bitterness of defeat, it was not surprising that their thoughts turned to revenge against the regime that had so violently ejected them – and against the world. King Hussein had already been warned what to expect. At a meeting early in 1971, Salah Khalaf had told him: 'If you strike the *fedayeen* in their last hold-outs, I'll follow you to the end of the earth, to my dying breath, to give you the punishment you deserve.' Shaken, the king murmured, 'God forbid.'[40]

5. BLACK SEPTEMBER

'A bomb in the White House, a mine in the Vatican, the death of Mao Tse-tung, an earthquake in Paris; none of these could have produced the far-reaching echo to every man in the world like the operation of Black September in Munich.' Commentary in *Al-Sayyad* newspaper, Beirut, 13 September 1972.

In the early morning of 5 September 1972, a tall, slim Palestinian checked out of the Eden-Hotel-Wolff, a cormfortable, family-style hotel on Arnulfstrasse near the centre of Munich. For anyone anxious to make a quick getaway from the city and its environs, the Eden-Hotel-Wolff was perfectly situated. Opposite was the railway station and right outside the front entrance was an airport bus terminal. If staff had been vigilant they would have noticed that their Middle Eastern guest was hastening to leave behind a city that was just awakening to the news that its attempts to stage a trouble-free Olympic Games had been shattered.

The mysterious Palestinian had registered at the hotel On 25 August with a bogus Iraqi passport in the name of Saad el-Din Wali, a 37-year-old journalist. In a city full of foreign journalists, busy hotel staff had no reason to disbelieve him, although had they monitored his movements carefully they would have seen no evidence of bona fide journalistic activity. He spent much of his time in his room in hushed conversation with Arab colleagues. He phoned Beirut, Tripoli and Tunis. 'Wali' was, in fact, one of the chief planners of the Black September Organisation. His mission was to oversee preparations for an assault on the Israeli team headquarters in the Munich Olympic Village.[1]

In the 24 hours following his hasty departure, the world was brought face to face with Palestinian terror at its most extreme. The code-name Black September, the mainstream PLO's terrorist arm forged from anger and despair after the bloody expulsion of Palestinian guerrilla forces from Jordan in July 1971, was emblazoned across newspaper front pages in dozens of languages. The phrase 'the Munich massacre' would find a permanent and sinister place in the lexicon of the Palestinian–Israeli struggle. For

Western intelligence services and for foreign journalists, the name spawned perturbing questions. What was Black September and, more to the point, who was behind it? It was not long before the world heard an unexpectedly frank accounting from one of the terrorist organisation's most senior figures.

On 24 March 1973, six months after Munich, Abu Daoud Mohammed Awdah, a tall man, his dark hair flecked with grey, was brought before a television camera in Amman. Staring into the camera's baleful eye, Awdah uttered words that cannot but have dismayed his masters in Damascus and in Beirut. In a televised confession he stated there was 'no such thing' as Black September. 'Fatah,' he declared, 'announces its operations under this name so that Fatah would not appear as the direct executor of the operations of the intelligence organ which is run by Abu Youssef [Mohammed Youssef al-Najjar] and Abu Hassan [Ali Hassan Salameh] . . . Abu Iyad [Salah Khalaf],' he added, 'carries out big operations like the Munich operation.'[2]

What the television camera did not show was the extent to which Awdah had been tortured by Hussein's secret police. He had been trussed up like a chicken and could barely walk; to this day, he bears the scars of the rope burns on his legs. Awdah said that he has no recollection of the events leading up to his televised 'confession'. The tape, he claims, was 'doctored'.[3] But at the time his words confirmed a widespread assumption: that Fatah was behind Black September. Israeli retribution was swift. Within a few weeks three of the PLO's top operatives were slain by Israeli paratroopers; Salah Khalaf himself was lucky to survive.

Khalaf, Fatah's security and intelligence chief, was for a long time the PLO's deadly pragmatist and in the end before his death in 1991, at the hands of a renegade Palestinian, one of its more moderate voices. But back in July 1971 when the PLO's northern Jordanian bases were smashed by Hussein's Bedu legions, he had been an angry foe of the Hashemites, of Israel and the West. He was not alone. Demand for revenge pushed PLO leaders of all factions into a bidding war.

'Between 1969 and 1972 we were crazy people,' recalled Yasser Abed Rabbo, then a leader of the Marxist Democratic Front, and now one of the PLO's leading moderates. 'We wanted to change the whole world. We wanted to fight Israel, the Americans, even the Soviets, because they were not supportive, King Hussein, the Palestinian bourgeoisie – everybody.'[4]

If Arafat had had any doubts about what course to take, the demands for revenge from his own supporters would have been more than enough to convince him. Some Fatah militants were threatening to defect to more extreme factions, such as Habash's Popular Front. At acrimonious meetings in Damascus in late August and early September 1971 a few select Fatah leaders, including Arafat himself, took the decision to establish a special unit to conduct revenge operations against Hussein's Hashemite regime and other targets. It was a fateful step that would have decidedly mixed consequences for Arafat and his organisation, but after Jordan vengeance was paramount. 'Our whole purpose was how to tell the world we weren't down and that the world will not enjoy full peace without us,' recalled a close Arafat adviser. 'Up to early 1973 Arafat gave his green light [to major terrorist operations], but details were worked out by others. These were not matters that were debated.'[5] At Arafat's insistence, Fatah leaders resolved that every effort be made to disguise its links with the terrorist unit. Just as the founders of the guerrilla organisation had named their military wing Al-Asifa, to obscure its connection with the parent organisation, so they created a new 'front' for terrorist operations. Thus, Black September was born.

As the winter of 1971 approached in the barren hills of the Arqoub region in southern Lebanon, later to be known as Fatahland, preparations were already well under way for a series of stunning terrorist attacks to be carried out in the name of Black September. Recruits came from the embittered ranks of Fatah itself, from Habash's Popular Front, and from splinter factions such as the Syrian-backed Saiqa. Operationally, Fatah and elements of the Popular Front – differences were buried temporarily – came together in the planning and execution of a series of terrorist coups that would in the minds of many in the West associate Arafat and the PLO leadership with violence and mayhem on a grand scale. It was the Arab world, and Jordan in particular, that bore the initial brunt of the Palestinian desire for vengeance.

On 28 November 1971, at around 1.30 p.m., a solidly built Jordanian, exuding confidence and authority, climbed the steps of the Cairo Sheraton on the banks of the Nile. Tailed by a posse of security guards, Wasfi al-Tal, Prime Minister and strongman of Jordan, was meeting his wife after an early lunch with officials of the Arab League. If he had other thoughts in mind, they may well have concerned his secret discussions with Khaled al-Hassan, the Fatah moderate, on a truce between Jordan and the PLO in the wake of Black September. The two men had been talking about an arrangement that would have allowed Palestinian fighters to continue operating from remote bases in Jordan, but Tal did not live to see these delicate negotiations come to fruition. As he approached the hotel lobby, thronged with tourists and other visitors, he was cut down by a youthful gunman. Coolly, Tal's assassin emptied five shots into the man many Palestinian militants held most responsible for their expulsion from Jordan. In an obscene gesture, and one that underscored the hatred behind the attack, the assassin, later identified as Mansur Suleiman Khalifah, kneeled down and lapped up Tal's blood as it oozed from his wounds on to the hotel steps.

Tal was, in a way, an obvious target. In the Palestinian mythology of the time, he was rumoured personally to have tortured and killed Abu Ali Iyad, the leader of the Fatah militia in Jordan, and then to have ordered that his body be dragged through northern Jordanian villages behind a Centurion tank. The four-man terrorist cell responsible for Tal's execution was in fact initially identified as the 'Abu Ali Iyad group'. Little attention was paid at first to the commandos' triumphant cry as they were bundled into a police van outside the Sheraton. 'We are Black September,' they shouted, raising their fingers in an aggressive salute.

Tal's death was greeted jubilantly in the Palestinian Diaspora, with dismay among Jordanians and with grim satisfaction by PLO leaders, with one notable exception. Khaled al-Hassan, the moderate, condemned the slaying, describing it as 'one of the acts of terrorist, fascist thinking which conflicts with the thinking of the revolution'.[6] But his voice was ignored in an organisation bent on revenge.

Although it is inconceivable that Arafat was not aware of the major terrorist operations, this era is not something he has been prepared to discuss. His deputies, however, have been much more forthcoming. Salah Khalaf, for one, offered a clear rationale for the PLO's resort to terror. In his memoir, he explained that because they were unable to wage classic guerrilla warfare across Israel's borders after they had lost their bases in Jordan in 1971, Fatah's young men 'insisted on carrying out a revolutionary violence of another kind, commonly known elsewhere as "terrorism"'.[7] The slaying of Tal, whom he described as 'one of the butchers of the Palestinian people', was a warning to others in the Arab world who might be tempted to 'sacrifice the rights or interests of the Palestinian people'.[8] At the time, Arafat himself was scarcely less forthright. He told PLO Radio in Cairo that before the year 1971 was out 'four of our revolutionaries had overthrown the traitor Wasfi al-Tal, and our revolutionaries will continue to pursue all traitors in the Arab nation.'[9]

The Tal execution was merely the first of a series of attacks on Jordanian officials, including several plots to kill Hussein himself. Khalaf made no secret of his own central role as head of the 'underground apparatus' which the PLO leadership established in September 1971 to 'work for the downfall of the [Jordanian] regime'.[10]

A little more than two weeks after Wasfi al-Tal's death, Black September struck again, this time in Europe. On 16 December, a gunman fired thirty to forty rounds from an automatic weapon into a Daimler carrying Zeid al-Rifai, then Jordan's ambassador in London. Rifai, described by Khalaf as 'one of Hussein's minions' and a 'deadly' adviser to the king,[11] was slightly wounded in the hand. Later enmity between Rifai and the Palestinian leadership is not hard to understand in light of this event.

In their fury, the Jordanian authorities wasted no time in associating Arafat's Fatah mainstream faction with Black September. A broadcast on Amman radio on 17 December charged that the terror front was 'only a mask used by Fatah to hide its treacherous schemes'.[12] But the barrage of words from Amman did nothing to deflect the PLO's hard men from their avowed aim of settling their blood feud with the Hashemites.

Between 1971 and 1973 the PLO made the overthrow of the 'puppet royal regime' of King Hussein its main aim, even it seemed at the expense, at times, of confrontation with Israel. The PLO's Planning Centre in Beirut – the PLO think-tank headed by Arafat's confidant, Nabil Shaath – drew up a blueprint for a Palestinian–Jordanian National Liberation Front with the express purpose of bringing down the Hashemites. The Palestinian 'parliament', the Palestine National Council, in Cairo in April 1972, gave 'legislative' support to these aims when it declared that the 'liberation of Jordan' was as important as removing Israel from Palestine.[13]

Cairo, meanwhile, had witnessed an extraordinary judicial event. On 29 February 1972 after a sham trial, a court had released, on bail provided by the PLO, the four defendants who had admitted their role in the assassination of Wasfi al-Tal three months previously. Leftist Arab lawyers vied with each other to represent the 'defendants'. After their release on bail, the four were quietly spirited out of Egypt to Damascus, and never again came to trial. Not only was justice not done, it was seen not to be done.

As 1972 dawned, the world's intelligence services were buzzing with talk of Palestinian terrorism. America's CIA was devoting much closer attention to the subject. So were its European counterparts, no one more than the West Germans. Ever since 1970, Germany's intelligence services had known that members of the German Red Army Faction were being trained in terrorist tactics in camps in southern Lebanon and South Yemen. 'We knew perfectly well before Munich that the Middle East conflict would take place on European soil, too,' said a German spymaster. 'After Black September 1970, we were convinced that something was going to explode. Arafat switched his operations to Europe, to hit at soft targets with the assistance of the Red Army Faction.'[14]

But nobody foresaw Munich. Israel's intelligence community had concluded that it would face continuing Palestinian terrorism, including the danger of spectacular and eye-catching operations, but none of Israel's three intelligence and security services dreamed that the Palestinians would seek to disrupt the Olympic Games, the world's most sacred sporting occasion. 'We thought at the beginning of 1972 that they [the Palestinians] were sort of stymied. We thought they were going for operations that would have a major impact,. and it was up to our intelligence to see whether we could forestall them. But we didn't see Munich,' said General Yariv.[15] Perhaps surprisingly, there are those among former heads of Israeli intelligence who believe today that the PLO gained ground from Munich. The organisation could not have made a more emphatic statement about the plight of the Palestinians. Munich proved in many ways the great divide, the watershed event in the post-1967 Palestinian struggle. Things would not be the same again.

German intelligence documents reveal that the seeds of Munich had begun to germinate in the minds of Black September commanders in Beirut early in 1972. By mid-year, senior operatives had been despatched to Germany to investigate. They considered several options. One was to kidnap Israeli officials and to hold them hostage against the release of Palestinians in Israeli jails. But it was the attack against the athletes, with its awesome potential to shock, that held most appeal.

On 8 July, as the heat of summer slowed life in Damascus to a crawl, Mohammed Yousef al-Najjar, the tough operational head of Black September, held a series of meetings with counterparts from Habash's Popular Front and from the Syrian-backed PLO faction, Saiqa. The terrorist bosses decided, in principle, to proceed. In early August, the two leaders of the chosen Black September commando unit arrived in Munich to 'acclimatise' themselves, followed in succeeding weeks by the rest of the eight-member team.'[16] None flew to the Federal Republic. They came by a variety of land routes from Rome and from Belgrade. None of them was to carry guns or explosives across national frontiers either. That detail had been taken care of. Syrian diplomats would act as arms couriers.

The stage was set for the invasion of the Olympic Village at 4.30 a.m. on 5 September by the eight commandos who had no difficulty breaching flimsy security. Swiftly, the Palestinians, well briefed about the village layout, entered the Israeli team headquarters. Two team members were killed and nine others were kidnapped in the process. A day of high drama that was to end in tragedy had begun. The world watched transfixed as the television cameras beamed pictures live from the Olympic Village. Throughout a long day of almost unbearable tension one image above all others, that of the hooded gunman on the balcony of the team headquarters, was to be repeated over and over again until it came to represent, in the minds of a generation, Palestinian terrorism at its bloodiest. In jittery negotiations, the guerrillas pressed for the release of dozens of Arab prisoners held in Israel.

The Israeli cabinet, meeting in emergency session with Prime Minister Golda Meir in the chair, was adamant that there could be no dealing with the terrorists, let alone meeting their conditions. As night fell German authorities had decided that a rescue attempt would have to be made. The PLO commandos, who had demanded that they be flown to Cairo together with their hostages, were taken by helicopter to the Fuerstenfeldbrueck military airport on the outskirts of Munich. They had been duped into believing they would be allowed to board a Lufthansa plane for the Egyptian capital, where negotiations would continue. But the Germans had no intention of letting them leave the ground with the Israeli athletes still captive. Nor, needless to say, did the Israeli Government, which had despatched General Zvi Zamir, the gaunt, balding chief of its overseas spy force, Mossad, to monitor developments.

Zamir later told colleagues that he had a 'hollow feeling' as he took the lift to the darkened control tower at Fuerstenfeldbrueck that evening.[17] He was not convinced that German plans to attack the PLO gunmen with sniper fire offered the best chance of freeing the Israeli hostages, but nor did he feel he was in a position to criticise the German tactics. He was reduced to asking questions about the numbers of snipers that would be employed and where they might be deployed.

Zamir's sense of impending disaster deepened as the leaders of the terrorist commandos left their helicopters just before 11 p.m. to inspect the Lufthansa Boeing, sitting some distance away on the tarmac. In an instant, the gunmen realised they had been tricked. The plane was cold and empty. There was no crew on board. It was not going anywhere, certainly not to a safe haven in Cairo. Nervously, they moved back towards the helicopters, but before they could reach them they were cut down by snipers' bullets. In the control tower, the Germans and Israelis watched, appalled as the Arab gunmen traded shots with German police and fired on their hostages. A grenade was thrown into one of the helicopters, blowing it to pieces; the other caught fire. In the end fifteen people died. All nine hostages were killed, five of the eight gunmen and one policeman.

In Damascus and Beirut, PLO leaders congratulated themselves on the Munich operation; in their terms it had been a qualified success. But they must also have realised that there would be penalties. Munich would mark the beginning of a vicious underground war as Israel sought vengeance against Black September's leaders. The question then, as now, was whether the price to the Palestinians in terms of international outrage and the certainty of reprisals was worth paying. Black September chief Salah Khalaf had little doubt that the operation had attained at least some of its objectives. In his memoir, he wrote that 'world opinion was forced to take note of the Palestinian drama, and the Palestinian people imposed their presence on an international gathering that had sought to exclude them.'[18]

Arafat and the PLO leadership did not have to wait long for the first Israeli downpayment. On 8 September, two squadrons of Israeli jets blasted Arab guerrilla targets in Lebanon and Syria. The PLO also came under heavy international censure. George Bush, the US representative at the UN, spoke for the West in condemning the 'senseless and unprovoked terrorist attack in Munich'.[19]

Arafat, for his part, was careful not to comment directly on the Munich episode. The PLO, in an official statement on 14 September, disavowed responsibility, declaring that the 'wave of propaganda' in the Western press was aimed at 'spreading world hatred against the Arabs in general.[20] As condemnation of the PLO ricocheted around the world, Mahmoud Darwish, the Palestinian 'poet laureate', sought to justify what many saw as the unjustifiable:

> The one who has turned me into a refugee has made a bomb
> of me.
> I know that I will die.
> I know that I'm venturing into a lost battle today because it is
> the battle for a future.

I know that Palestine on the map is far away from me.

I know that you have forgotten its name and that you use a
new term for it.
I know all that.
That is why I carry it to your streets, your homes and your
bedrooms.
Palestine is not a land, gentlemen of the jury.
Palestine has become bodies that move, that move to the
streets of the world,
Singing the song of death because the new Christ has given
up his cross . . .
and gone out of Palestine.[21]

A deeply humiliated Germany took immediate action against
Palestinian activists who had made the Federal Republic their
European stronghold, expelling student and worker militants, and
setting up a special anti-terrorist squad. But, unhappily for the
Germans, that was not the end of the story. On 29 October, two
Black Septembrists seized a Lufthansa flight over Turkey and
demanded the release of the three surviving Munich gunmen.
Germany, fearing another disaster, gave in. The three Munich
survivors were flown to Libya to a hero's welcome, and later to
Lebanon. Incensed at what it regarded as weakness by the
Germans, Israel charged that 'every capitulation encourages the
terrorists to continue their criminal acts'.[22]

Within weeks of the Munich massacre, Israeli intelligence had
established to its satisfaction who was responsible. It had no doubt
it was Fatah. It was also certain that the man operationally in
charge had been Ali Hassan Salameh – young, charismatic, a
favourite of Arafat and head of Force 17, the chairman's personal
security detachment.

The conclusions Israeli intelligence drew when it began to
reassess the threat posed by the PLO were not comforting. Since
the Battle of Karameh in March 1968, and the later rash of plane
hijackings and terrorism, Fatah and other guerrilla factions had
been regarded as a nuisance, but one that could he dealt with

militarily. After Munich that all changed, as the realisation dawned that the Palestinian leadership was much more sophisticated politically than it had been given credit for. 'They think in strategic terms much better than we do,' was General Yariv's perhaps surprising assessment. 'They analyse our strategy. They do not always draw the right conclusions, but they understand that the aim of any military operation is political, and that the success of such operations should be measured in political terms.'[23]

Veterans of the Zionists' underground War of Independence in the 1940s began to see parallels between their own earlier struggle and that of Arafat and the Palestinians. But none of this softened attitudes in Israel after Munich. Prime Minister Golda Meir, who has been likened by one of her close associates at the time to a 'fiercely protective mother shielding her children from some sort of ogre', was determined that the war be carried to those deemed by Israeli intelligence to have been behind the Munich massacre, wherever they could be hunted down. One of her first acts after Munich was to appoint General Yariv, the cerebral outgoing chief of military intelligence, as her special assistant in combating terrorism. His task was to help co-ordinate the activities of the three intelligence and security services – Mossad, Shin Bet and military intelligence – as the underground war with the PLO reached a peak in the spring of 1973.

'The policy was to go for the leaders, and also to create circumstances under which it would make it very difficult for them to operate. It was not an easy decision to make, but at the time we believed we had no other choice,' General Yariv recalled. 'There were debates and discussion at the time that maybe there were other defensive ways, and we also understood that it was risky. What we could do, they could do as well.'[24]

Between September 1972 and July 1973, the capitals of Europe witnessed a string of reprisals and counter-reprisals. Arafat estimates that more than sixty of his people were killed or maimed in the ten-month shadow war. Israeli casualties were significantly fewer.

Much has been written about the formation of a special Mossad 'Wrath of God squad' to carry out assassinations, but according to an Israeli official intimately involved in planning and directing the underground war, 'no special unit was established that was not there before. What was there was good enough,' he said grimly.[25]

Israeli gunmen and explosives experts struck repeatedly and lethally in actions reminiscent of a gangland war. Their targets ranged across the spectrum of Palestinians in Europe. On 16 October 1972, just a little more than a month after Munich, Wael Zuwaiter, a Palestinian writer, was gunned down in Rome as he was returning late one evening to his apartment; on 8 December, Mahmoud Hamshari, the PLO's Paris representative, was blown up in his apartment; on 6 April 1973, Bassel Kubeissy, a professor at the University of Baghdad and a PLO supporter, was shot in a Paris street.

These killings seemed, however, like minor tremors compared with a cataclysmic event (for the PLO) that took place less than a week after Kubeissy's death, well away from the European theatre, and much closer to the sliver of land at the heart of the dispute between Arabs and Jews.

Beirut on 10 April 1973 was calm. Its residents, seemingly oblivious to the fact that their country was sliding towards civil war, were enjoying a pleasant eastern Mediterranean spring, the illusion of wellbeing, and the good life. The PLO high command, housed in comfortable apartments in the fashionable Ras Beirut area near the waterfront, was no exception. After its expulsion from Jordan, the guerrilla movement had regrouped surprisingly quickly; within a relatively short time its cadres were engaged, like soldier ants, in building another state within the state.

That April day, Black September chief Salah Khalaf departed from his normal routine of not appearing in public. He enjoyed a leisurely lunch at a fish restaurant on the waterfront with three of his closest friends in the leadership: Mohammed Yousef al-Najjar, the Black September operations chief; Kamal Adwan, in charge of operations in the occupied territories; and Kamal Nasir, the PLO spokesman. It was their last meal together. By early next morning, three of the four were dead, killed by Israeli seaborne commandos who attacked their apartment building in Verdun Street. The fourth – Khalaf himself – was a prime target but he was saved by a stroke of luck. Ironically, as the attack began, he was in a nearby building, debriefing the three survivors of Munich. Arafat was also in the area. Interestingly, the leader of the commandos was Ehud Barak, later Israel's Prime Minister.

By any terms, the slayings were devastating for the PLO. Najjar, the former schoolteacher who had become a powerful PLO orator, and Adwan, the tough, no-nonsense engineer, were key figures in the second tier of Fatah leaders. Their elimination left a gaping hole in the PLO hierarchy. In addition, the Israelis had carried away from Adwan's apartment secret archives that helped identify a number of PLO underground cells in the occupied territories. 'It was a catastrophe, and many men were forced to leave Palestine due to those documents,' said a top PLO intelligence official.[26]

Arafat, who two weeks earlier had warned his colleagues about security lapses, now adopted much stricter safety precautions himself. His Force 17 bodyguard, under Ali Hassan Salameh, was given additional resources and he himself became an even more elusive figure, moving from one safe house to another, rarely spending two consecutive days in the same place. He also turned his wrath against the United States, accusing it of complicity in the Israeli attack. Echoing an Algerian radio broadcast calling on Arabs to attack US embassies, Arafat charged on 13 April 1973 that the Central Intelligence Agency had been behind the Israeli attack. On the same day, the US State Department warned against the anti-American campaign and said such charges could harm the long-range interests of the Palestinian people.[27]

The Israeli assault on the apartment in Verdun Street was not quite the last shot in the underground war's most bloody phase. In Europe, the tit-for-tat conflict continued in fits and starts. On 21 July, it reached the little Norwegian town of Lillehammer. Relentlessly criss-crossing Europe in their efforts to hit Ali Hassan Salameh, Mossad assassins shot the wrong man. Ahmed Bouchiki, a Moroccan waiter, was gunned down as he was strolling home from the cinema late in the evening with his pregnant Norwegian wife. Israeli embarrassment was compounded when six members of the Mossad 'support team' – the two assassins had escaped – were rounded up and put on trial, ensuring maximum publicity for the affair.

Lillehammer marked the end of the all-out underground war in Europe. Mossad scaled down its activities. General Zamir retired.

There was relief on both sides, a sentiment fully shared by Europe's counter-terrorism services. 'The Europeans were not at all happy having their countries as a playground for the Arab–Israel war,' said an Israeli intelligence official who helped direct the hostilities. 'Lillehammer brought about a halt in operations, and that was OK with us.'[28]

Arafat and his senior colleagues had, in any case, been reviewing their options since early 1973, concluding that resort to international terrorism was bringing diminishing returns. What had jolted Arafat and the leadership into a testy debate about the benefits of this bloody phase in the organisation's history was the furore surrounding an event that remains perhaps the PLO's most controversial terrorist escapade, more perhaps even than Munich. It dogs the organisation's top leadership to this day.

At 7 p.m. sharp on 1 March 1973, a four-wheel drive vehicle with four gunmen on board had crashed through the gates of the Saudi embassy compound in Khartoum, torpid capital of Sudan. Within seconds the gunmen, firing indiscriminately, had forced their way into the embassy building where a farewell party for G. Curtis Moore, the departing US *chargé d'affaires*, was in progress. The cream of the Khartoum diplomatic corps was present, including the incoming US ambassador, Cleo A. Noel. The gunmen seized Noel and Moore, along with Sheikh Abdullah al-Malhouk, the ambassador of Saudi Arabia, his wife, and the *chargés d'affaires* of Jordan and Belgium.

Inexplicably, Black September – in the persons of an eight-man commando unit headed by Selim Rizak, the deputy chief of the PLO office in Khartoum – had defiled the premises of the wealthiest Arab state and one that had been the earliest and most consistent financier of Arafat's mainstream Fatah faction.

Holding the diplomats at gunpoint, the guerrillas issued an ultimatum. They would kill their hostages within 24 hours if their demands were not met. Some of their requests were bizarre, to say the least. They included the release of Fatah members imprisoned in Jordan; the freeing of Sirhan Sirhan, the convicted assassin of Robert F. Kennedy; all Arab women detained in Israel; and members of the Baader-Meinhof urban guerrilla group in West Germany 'because they supported the Palestinian cause'.[29]

Angrily, the US, Jordan and West Germany rejected the hostage-takers' demands, while behind the scenes Sudan and Egypt sought to defuse the crisis. Egypt even offered to send a plane to pick up the eight gunmen and their hostages to bring them back to Cairo for further negotiations. But these efforts were in vain.

Just before 8 p.m. on Friday 2 March, as the 24-hour deadline approached, Ambassador Cleo A. Noel made what was to prove the last of several telephone calls to the American embassy in Khartoum. Under the guns of his captors, Noel, who had suffered an ankle wound in the initial attack, enquired about the planned arrival of a senior American official who was expected to take charge of negotiations. When he was told that it would be later that evening, Noel replied tersely, 'That will be too late.'[30]

Soon after 9 p.m., forty equally spaced shots were clearly audible over the sound of a dust storm. Noel, Moore and Guy Eid, the Belgian *chargé d'affaires*, had been put up against a wall in the embassy basement and machine-gunned to death in a cold-blooded slaying. A short time later, the leader of the commandos, Selim Rizak, informed the Sudanese Foreign Ministry by telephone that his gunmen had executed three of their captives.

Incensed, Sudan's ruler, Jaafar Nimeiri, who at some risk to himself had rescued Arafat when he was being hunted down in Jordan in 1970, accused Fatah of a 'criminal rash act devoid of revolutionary spirit and bravery'.[31] Saudi Arabia's King Faisal kept his counsel, but Arafat and his colleagues in Beirut can have been in no doubt about the depths of his displeasure.

The affair continues to haunt Arafat and other top leaders of the PLO but the key question has long since ceased to be whether Fatah was behind the Black September assault. Debate now centres on whether Arafat himself communicated directly on the radio link established between the PLO's Beirut communications centre and the Khartoum gunmen.

Israel still claims that it has a tape recording of Arafat's voice uttering the code-word Nahr el-Bared, which means 'the cold river' in Arabic, to check whether the execution had been carried out. (Nahr el-Bared was a guerrilla training camp in Lebanon attacked by Israeli jets in late February 1973.) Israel has not yet produced the tape and neither has the US: an attempt by a group of Congressmen in 1986 to pressure the Justice Department into bringing an indictment against Arafat for murder on the basis of the alleged tape recording was deflected by the administration.[32]

A senior US military intelligence official, familiar with details of the Khartoum affair, doubted that a recording of Arafat's voice actually giving instructions to the Khartoum gunmen exists: 'Now, if the Israelis have such a recording why haven't they brought it forward?' he asked. 'There's no reason why they should hold it back, after all. Or why don't they fake it? The answer is that there is a question of credibility here. They didn't fake it or leak it even through cut-outs because they know that there are people around – I think from one of the allied services in Beirut – who do know exactly what happened, and who would call their bluff. This is such a central issue that they dare not be exposed over it.'[33]

The US certainly has recordings of the radio traffic that passed between Khartoum and Beirut in the tense hours after a radio link was established between the gunmen and the Black September headquarters. Both the US embassy in Khartoum and the US mission in Beirut monitored every squeak that came out of each location. In fact, in a confidential cable dispatched within days of the slayings, the US embassy in Khartoum reported that it was 'notable that terrorists were apparently under external control from Beirut and did not murder Ambassador Noel and Moore nor surrender to GoS [Government of Sudan] until receiving specific code-word instructions'.[34]

While Arafat has steadfastly refused to discuss Khartoum, his late deputy, Salah Khalaf, had been more forthcoming. In his memoir he stated bluntly that the guerrillas' target was 'the American *chargé d'affaires* [G. Curtis Moore], who had been stationed in Amman prior to the 1970 war and bore a heavy responsibility for its preparation'.[35]

Whatever the extent of Arafat's involvement, he took the threats that the Khartoum affair posed to his moderate Arab support seriously. On 18 March, two weeks after the slayings, he despatched the first of several high-level missions to the Sudan. It was led by Mohammed Abu Mayzar, later head of Fatah's foreign relations department, in an attempt to end the damaging rift with Nimeiri. Several other senior Fatah officials also visited Khartoum.

They were told that if there was a repeat of recent events they would 'give them a whole year of Black Septembers'.[36]

Khartoum may have been, as has been claimed, a dying sputter of Black September but the episode certainly served as a warning to Arafat and his colleagues of the high cost of guerrilla actions that embarrassed friendly Arab states. It also – and not for the first time – brought suspicion of direct, personal involvement in terror activities uncomfortably close to Arafat himself. Not surprisingly, the debacle prompted a rethink of the PLO's strategy. Arafat, who had never publicly evinced as much enthusiasm for the use of the terror weapon outside Israel and the occupied territories as some of his colleagues, resolved to calm the more extreme elements in his own Fatah mainstream. By early 1974, he was telling journalists that 'We must struggle for the liberation of our fatherland, but within the occupied territories, not outside them.'[37]

To their chagrin, however, Fatah leaders would find that turning off the terror tap would prove infinitely more difficult than they imagined. They were to be reminded of this in the months and years ahead as the Fatah renegade, Sabri al-Banna, better known by his *nom de guerre*, Abu Nidal, continued the work of Black September by various other names after splitting openly with Arafat in 1973. Khartoum amply demonstrated to the organisation the danger of being consumed by the monster it had helped to create.[38]

Part Two

6. LOST ILLUSIONS

'This is the insidious theme they are harping on: you have had enough fighting, enough battles. The only solution of the Palestine problem is to establish a Palestinian state in the West Bank and Gaza Strip. This is the most dangerous proposal that could be made,' Yasser Arafat, commenting on a meeting with West Bank leaders, after Black September 1970.

At ten o'clock on a quiet November evening in 1973, a large official-looking car pulled up in a leafy street of the Moroccan capital, Rabat. Two men, one burly and broad-shouldered, the other dapper and slight, climbed out and made their way towards an elegant villa set back from the road. To a casual observer, they might have been members of Morocco's privileged classes pursuing the normal social round. But these were no ordinary visitors, and their business at the house of a senior Moroccan military officer was far from a routine social call, as would have been apparent to anyone noticing the numbers of Moroccan troops surrounding the area in the darkness. The burly man was General Vernon Walters, deputy director of the US Central Intelligence Agency. The other, without his usual entourage, was King Hassan II, Morocco's monarch and a long-standing contact of Walters. More intriguing still, the intelligence man was about to be introduced to two representatives of an organisation which had murdered his friend Cleo Noel, the American ambassador in Khartoum, only nine months before.

Walters' improbable mission was to open a high-level and top-secret channel of communication between the Nixon Administration and the Palestine Liberation Organisation, and to deliver a warning. 'I must tell you quite clearly that this killing of Americans has got to stop – or else it will come to a situation where torrents of blood will flow, and not all of it will be American,' Walters told the Palestinians as they sat alone at a round table for two and a half hours that night.[1]

Walters' message surprised his listeners: Khaled al-Hassan, the veteran Fatah official, and his colleague, Majed Abu Sharar, had not expected to hear such a direct threat from an American official. The Rabat meeting raised other, rather more tantalising questions for the PLO. For, in addition to delivering his warning, Walters had also been authorised by Secretary of State Henry Kissinger to sound out the Palestinians on their political thinking, and to assess whether a dialogue might be set in train between the US and the PLO. What was the organisation's approach to a negotiated settlement of the Arab–Israeli conflict? Was it simply out to cause trouble for Arab states then contemplating negoti-ations, or might it be prepared to set out a realisable political objective of its own? Under what conditions, if any, would it consider recognition of Israel? And what was its real attitude to America's ally, the Hashemite Kingdom of Jordan?

These were the questions round which Walters and Khaled al-Hassan circled warily on 3 November and in another encounter in a government guesthouse in the Moroccan royal city of Fez on 7 March the following year.[2] It is no surprise that the results of both meetings were inconclusive. Such questions had caused the greatest difficulties for the Palestinian movement from the moment Arafat had emerged at its head in Jordan nearly six years before, and had in any case become the subject of a feisty debate among the factions of the PLO itself at exactly the time when Walters asked them.

The issues had begun to come into focus as the Palestinian movement surveyed the catastrophe that had befallen it in Jordan in 1970–1. Black September had been a protracted and painful encounter with reality, nowhere more so than within Fatah, the inner core of the PLO. In the process, many of the assumptions underlying resistance activity had been exposed for what they were: illusions.

It was in the early 1970s that Arafat and his colleagues began to realise that their dreamy notion of a shared Palestinian state with the Jews had a fundamental flaw: it was founded on a quite elementary misconception about Israel. PLO leaders, like many Arabs at the time, tended to assume that the Jewish state was weak and divided and that, confronted with a Palestinian offer of coexistence after the elimination of Israel, significant numbers of Jews would jump ship and join the struggle. Nothing, of course, could have been further from the truth.

For Israelis of most political hues, it had all along been convenient to pretend that the Palestinian problem did not exist; that the Arab inhabitants of what had been Palestine had fled at the behest of neighbouring states in 1948 and should subsequently have been blending in with the people of the Arab world. The idea of abolishing Israel and becoming a minority in an Arab-dominated bi-national state, as the Palestinian 'terrorists' proposed, was simply too bizarre to contemplate.

Innate Israeli suspicion had been fuelled by the PLO's studied vagueness about the implications of the proposal. Arafat and his fellow leaders never even tried to spell out in concrete terms how it might be implemented. Unable to accept the Jews as a people in their own right rather than just as practitioners of the Jewish faith, they deliberately fudged the question of which Jews might be allowed to stay in the new utopia or what rights they might enjoy there. The result was to suggest to many Israelis that the whole idea was merely a new variation on the old theme of mass extermination or, at the very least, eviction. Yehoshafat Harkabi, an Israeli Arabist and later a leading advocate of a dialogue with the PLO, who once headed the country's military intelligence, set the tone at the time by writing of 'the impossibility of destroying Israel as a state without destroying a considerable part of her inhabitants'.[3]

What baffled and at times exasperated the outside world was the Palestinians' refusal to set a more attainable interim goal, to divide their struggle up into realisable stages. After the Six-Day War, President Nasser, among other Arab leaders, had floated the idea of establishing a Palestinian state in just a part of Palestine as a first step. But within the PLO itself, still wedded to total liberation, such ideas took a long time to prompt anything other than violent rejection. When a few intellectuals and traditional Palestinian leaders in the occupied territories began late in 1967 to promote a plan for a Palestinian 'mini-state' in the West Bank and Gaza, the notion was dismissed by Arafat and his colleagues in their Jordanian fastnesses as treason, They had devoted little or no attention to building mass political support in the territories, and had no desire to see locals challenging their own claims to represent the Palestinian people. In Fatah radio broadcasts and sometimes through the mail, advocates of the proposal were branded as 'collaborators' with Israel and threatened with retribution.

In December 1967, the *fedayeen* attempted a bazooka attack on the house of Dr Hamdi al-Taji al-Faruqi, who had published pamphlets presenting the case for a Palestinian state.[4] When the idea surfaced again in October 1970, the PLO decided to establish a 'revolutionary tribunal' to judge 'anyone acting in the name of the Palestinian people outside the framework of the revolution'. Arafat bluntly told West Bank leaders, 'If anybody raises his head and demands an abortive state, we shall behead him.'[5] The West Bankers who had risked their necks with the mini-state proposal prudently piped down; they were simply ahead of their time.

It took a calamity on the scale of that which had unfolded in Jordan from September 1970 to suggest that time might not, after all, be on the side of the Palestinian resistance, and that a fundamental rethink was required. Ironically, the same conditions which had prompted the PLO's lurch into international terrorism also produced the beginnings of a political approach that eventually won Arafat a ticket to the podium of the United Nations.

As they licked their wounds in Damascus in 1971, and even as the terrorist Black September organisation moved into action, Fatah's leaders had begun to talk among themselves about a change of tack. According to Salah Khalaf, they had been heavily influenced in their furtive deliberations by the brutal treatment that the Palestinians had received at the hands of King Hussein's Bedu soldiers.

'The one memory that will always stay with me was the incident when scores of *fedayeen* fled from Jordanian troops and asked for asylum in Israel. It was the most difficult thing I have ever faced,' he said. 'We realised at that point that our problem was not just with Israel but also with the Arabs – and to an extent Israel was not as bad as the Arabs. That's when we realised that we'd have to devise a political strategy for setting up a state on any part of liberated Palestinian soil. We didn't make it public, but there was a private decision of that kind among Fatah leaders quite early on.'[6]

Between this discreet coming to terms with reality and public presentation of the idea lay a long and laborious road. Not the least of the Fatah leadership's difficulties was the fact that a 'policy of stages', in which the Palestinians would settle for less than the whole cake to start with, ran counter to everything they had been saying. Only the previous year, Arafat himself had responded to a similar suggestion from West Bank notables by proclaiming, 'In the name of the Palestinian revolution I hereby declare that we shall oppose the establishment of this state to the last member of the Palestinian people, for if ever such a state is established it will spell the end of the whole Palestinian cause. '[7]

There, in essence, was the central dilemma, of which Arafat and his colleagues were all too frequently reminded by hardline opponents of a phased approach: if they were to settle for a mini-state, as a first step towards the liberation of all Palestine, there was a distinct possibility that it would also be the last step. If so, the refugees that filled the ranks and leadership of the PLO would in effect be abandoning the central aim of their fight: to return to their homes in the land now called Israel. Squaring that particular circle in a way likely to prove palatable to the movement as a whole was to occupy thousands of hours of argument over the next few years.

The problem, on this occasion as on so many others before and since, was that the Palestinians were not in a position to dictate the terms of the debate. Weakened by division and defeat, they were also being buffeted by a host of external pressures. For one thing, the PLO's arch-enemy, King Hussein was advancing designs of his own on the occupied territories with a proposal, announced on 15 March 1972, to establish a United Arab kingdom under Jordanian rule after an eventual Israeli withdrawal from the West Bank and Gaza. For another, Israel was proceeding apace with efforts to demonstrate that the Palestinians in the territories had settled down under occupation by staging municipal elections there. To the PLO leadership, newly ensconced that year in a cluster of offices near the Beirut waterfront, it all looked suspiciously like another 'Israeli–Jordanian plot' against the Palestinians, and one it was powerless to thwart. Despite orders from Arafat for a boycott, and PLO assassination attempts against participants, the polls went ahead as planned and strengthened Jordan's influence at the expense of the PLO.[8] To complicate matters further, Egypt, under its new President, Anwar Sadat, was looking for ways of breaking out of the no-war-no-peace stalemate in which the Arab world had been locked since the 1967 war, and pressing the Palestinians to come up with a more realistic approach. In a speech to the Palestine National Council on 28 September 1972 – just three weeks after the attack on the Munich Olympics – Sadat urged the guerrilla organisation to break with the past and form a government in exile.

It was a suggestion that dismayed his audience. Not only would any attempt to form such a government be guaranteed to spark off a fresh bout of squabbling about leadership responsibilities; it would also require the Palestinians to define their territorial aims, to seek diplomatic recognition – and to distance themselves from terrorist acts.[9]

As Arafat himself had put it in 1970, 'We are not acting to set up just any form of government. We have always said that we are a national liberation movement with the goal of liberation and return and we are not anxious for a new showcase which would be a burden on our national liberation struggle. And a Palestinian government to us means greater "officialisation" and complications.'[10]

To Arafat's ears, Sadat's proposal sounded another alarm. For he remembered a previous occasion on which Palestinians had formed a government in exile: the Government of All Palestine sponsored by the Arab League exactly 24 years before. Set up in Gaza after the defeat of the Arab armies by a newly independent Israel in 1948, it had been doomed to irrelevance and had swiftly disappeared from the map. If there was one fear that haunted and still haunts Arafat above all others, it is the fear of being marginalised in similar fashion.

Yet that was precisely the danger staring the PLO in the face in 1972, despite the international opprobrium generated by Palestinian terrorist outrages. As Salah Khalaf observed that summer, the resistance was threatened with 'total collapse'.[11] Watching Jordan gearing up to reclaim the West Bank and Sadat's Egypt setting a new and unpredictable agenda in the Arab–Israeli conflict, Arafat and his movement knew they risked being left on the sidelines in the admittedly comfortable refuge of Beirut unless they found something new to say. Their quest was brought dramatically into focus by the sudden outbreak, just twelve months later, of another Arab–Israeli war.

The first open sign that something new was astir within the Palestinian movement had been prompted by Israel's audacious raid on Beirut and assassination of three of the top PLO leaders there in April 1973. Spontaneously, protests erupted throughout the West Bank in a mirror image of the demonstration that accompanied the funeral of the murdered men in Lebanon. Palestinian newspapers were filled with death notices and attacks on Israel's leaders and, to give the protests added form, Palestinian flags – red, black, green and white symbols of allegiance to the PLO – began to appear on the streets of Israeli-ruled towns and villages.[12]

More noteworthy still was the political message that the West Bankers and Gazans began to convey to Beirut and to the international community. Quietly at first, then more openly, representatives of Palestinians from the territories were telling the leadership, preoccupied as it was at the time with consolidating its new haven in Lebanon, that they had their own distinctive views concerning the Arab–Israeli conflict that the PLO would do well to take into account. Gradually, beneath the deceptively tranquil surface of the West Bank and the Gaza Strip, a new Palestinian movement was emerging with a vigorous rebuttal of Israel's claims to have pacified the territories.

Unlike many of their exiled brethren, the Palestinians under occupation harboured no illusions about Israel. Many of them had taken jobs in Jewish-owned factories or construction sites; their daily experience taught them that the vision of Israel crumbling to make way for a Palestinian state was a mirage. Some sort of accommodation would eventually have to be found.

In the summer of 1973, more than one hundred prominent figures from all corners of the West Bank political spectrum addressed two memoranda to the United Nations, condemning the Israeli occupation and demanding 'the right to self-determination and to sovereignty on their own land for the inhabitants of the

West Bank and Gaza Strip'.[13] The message for the guerrilla bosses in Beirut was clear: priority should be given to ending the occupation and establishing a mini-state.

This wave of self-assertion on the part of a populace that the PLO had long criticised for its apparent quiescence under occupation was intriguing, and to Arafat himself – ever anxious to guard against alternatives to his leadership – not a little unsettling. Something would have to be done to bring the new forces in the territories under PLO influence. The PLO itself would have to show it was listening. 'It is the duty of all of us together to increase our cohesion and strengthen the strong links that exist between us,' Arafat said in an uneasy message to the Palestinians under occupation at the end of that year. 'We are with you in a single trench.'[14]

To strengthen the relationship between Palestinians inside and the PLO outside, Arafat acquiesced in a move by local activists, led by West Bank communists, to organise themselves along new lines. The so-called Palestinian National Front, established in August 1973, provided the Palestinians under occupation with a novel framework in which to express their defiance of Israel. Significantly, it also gave them an opportunity for concerted lobbying of the exiled leadership in Beirut on behalf of a more feasible approach to the recovery of Palestine.

Within the resistance, the first public airing for such 'treasonous' propositions[15] came not from Arafat or his friends in Fatah's inner circle, who had been nervously keeping their thoughts on the subject to themselves for the previous two years, but from an altogether more unlikely quarter: a left-wing group of intellectuals and fighters known as the Popular Democratic Front for the Liberation of Palestine. Its leader, a young Marxist from Jordan, Nayef Hawatmeh, was already carving out a reputation as one of the more intelligent and realistic Palestinian leaders. He was to become a pioneer of Palestinian contacts with Israeli leftist groups, as well as instigator of some of the bloodiest PLO terror attacks on Israel during the 1970s.

In the first half of August 1973, he and his comrades set out a new proposal designed to take account of the heavy odds then stacked against the Palestinian movement. Achieving the liberation of all pre-1948 Palestine, they concluded in a clinically worded understatement, was 'not realistic in terms of the present balance of forces'. The Palestinians should therefore concentrate on 'the art of the possible', including the more modest aim of forcing Israeli withdrawal from the territories occupied in 1967 and the establishment of what was called a 'national authority' in the West Bank and Gaza.

To the bulk of the guerrilla movement – dominated as it was in Lebanon by refugees from what was now northern Israel, people who had no interest in setting up a 'mini-state' in the West Bank – this was still heresy of the deepest dye. Other leftist and Arab nationalist factions immediately condemned Hawatmeh for voicing unpalatable truths and PDFLP leaders were threatened with assassination. Even within Fatah, a large majority of rank and file members came out against the idea. 'There were differences in Fatah, but Arafat and Khalaf sided with us,' recalled Hawatmeh.

In mid-August 1973, with the controversy over Hawatmeh's statement bubbling, Salah Khalaf and Farouk Kaddoumi were invited to call on Egypt's President Sadat at his out-of-town retreat of Borj al-Arab, on the Mediterranean. What they heard, when he received them breezily on the veranda of his residence, was electrifying. 'He said there will be a war soon, in the coming months – definitely before the end of 1973,' recalled Khalaf. 'He called it the "spark" and said it would be waged jointly with Syria. He asked us to prepare our armies so we could join in the fighting and participate in the settlement that would follow.'[16]

Khalaf and Kaddoumi were so excited by the prospect of the major Arab power launching an offensive against Israel that they scarcely heard Sadat spell out the limit of his aims: simply to break the deadlock in the Arab–Israeli conflict and then proceed to a peace conference. They hastened back to Beirut, where Arafat, too, could hardly believe his ears. He heard Sadat's promise for himself on 9 September, when the President set it out in more detail before an enlarged delegation of Fatah leaders in his residence in Cairo. Promising to inform Arafat of the date of hostilities at the appropriate time, Sadat said he aimed to convene a peace conference involving the two superpowers and the regional parties, including Israel and the PLO. How, he asked, would the movement reply to an invitation to attend? It was a question to which Arafat and his colleagues were in no position to respond immediately; PLO decision-making bodies would have to be consulted first. But it also crystallised in acute form all the political dilemmas over which the Palestinians had been privately agonising for the previous year or more.

Still, most of the leadership had difficulty in believing that Sadat was serious. PLO leaders did not have to wait long to find out just how wrong they were. When Khalaf belatedly complied on 4 October with an urgent summons to Cairo, he found war preparations already at an advanced stage. It was not until the very eve of the offensive that Arafat himself got the news, via a hand-carried message from Cairo purporting, under a pre-arranged code, to contain Khalaf's resignation from the move-ment.[17] For all Sadat's careful efforts to involve the Palestinians – preparations he was later to regret, blaming Salah Khalaf for prematurely leaking news of his plans – the October War seemed to have caught much of the PLO leadership unawares.[18] When Egyptian tanks surged across the Suez Canal on the Israeli holy day of Yom Kippur, the Palestinians found themselves well away from centre stage.

It was not that the resistance was not involved in the war: units of the Palestine Liberation Army fought alongside the Egyptians at the canal and behind Israeli lines in the Golan Heights. PLO guerrillas sought valiantly to open another front in the north by mounting commando raids across the Lebanese–Israeli border. But their activities were little noticed in the midst of what for a while at least seemed to be another full-blown Arab–Israeli war. With Israel caught off guard and under severe pressure, the super-powers coming close to confrontation, Henry Kissinger making frantic efforts to broker a ceasefire, and the Arab states embargoing oil deliveries to the West – amid all this drama, the Palestinians, whose cause was ostensibly at the centre of the trouble, were strangely forgotten.

With foreboding the PLO leadership gradually realised what it all amounted to. By the end of the first day's fighting, it was already dawning on Khalaf and Kaddoumi, who had been invited to join Sadat in the makeshift operations headquarters in his living room, that this was no all-out onslaught on Israel but a more limited endeavour designed to compensate for the defeat of 1967, to pave the way for Arab economic pressure on the US, and to force the door open towards a negotiated settlement. Sadat was playing things just as he had said he would. Far from pressing ahead to liberate the Sinai Peninsula, his tanks went a few kilometres beyond the canal and stopped, leaving a substantial portion of the Egyptian army exposed to an Israeli counter-thrust. After three weeks of bloody conflict, Egypt and the other Arab states involved accepted a UN call for a ceasefire and the immediate start of negotiations aimed at establishing 'a just and durable peace in the Middle East'. By the end of October the war was, to all intents, over.

For Sadat, it was a performance respectable enough to erase the six-year-old stain of his predecessor's defeat and to justify a dignified move towards peace negotiations. For the Palestinians, the benefits seemed more equivocal. To their advantage was the fact that the war had created a momentary impression of solidarity in the Arab world and had unsheathed the Arab oil weapon. In the prospect of concerted economic as well as political pressure on Israel and the West, Arafat and his PLO comrades saw a potential new source of power.

It was this feeling of increased strength that enabled the leadership, in the face of determined internal opposition, to take a preliminary step towards abandoning international terrorism. At a meeting in Damascus in February 1974, Arafat and other Fatah leaders decided in principle to draw a line under this still controversial phase. Salah Khalaf put it as follows: 'The desperation waned because of the change in the situation. The leadership could assert its control.'[19] The Palestinians certainly did not cease terror attacks, but after 1974 the PLO mainstream focused its fire on Israel and the occupied territories.

Sadat's pursuit of a negotiated solution emphasised the deep dilemmas facing the PLO leadership. Would they, as Sadat again asked Khalaf and Kaddourni on 26 October, now be prepared to participate in the proposed Geneva peace conference? The Palestinians could only prevaricate, pointing out that the basis on which it was likely to be held – UN Security Council Resolution

242 of 1967 – had always been rejected by their organisation on the grounds that it treated the Palestinians merely as refugees rather than as a people with national rights. But they did promise to put the idea to PLO policy-making bodies in Beirut without delay.[20]

The question was whether to accept the still hypothetical invitation to Geneva and work for establishment of a state in the West Bank and Gaza, or whether to say no and run the risk of leaving the field open to King Hussein, who was showing interest in using the proposed peace conference to restore his rule over the occupied territories. There was no shortage of external 'advice'. Apart from the pressure exerted by Sadat, there was the position of the Soviet Union, now firmly backing Arafat but demanding a more realistic political strategy in return, to take into account. Even Fatah's old friends in Algeria were cautioning the PLO to formulate a clear and 'responsible' approach.[21]

The ever-impatient Arafat would not wait for the internal debates to play themselves out before drawing his own conclusions. Showing the streak of individualism which has always provoked criticism within the movement – and kept him one jump ahead of his peers – he began to send out signals suggesting that he was ready to play the diplomatic game. As far as Arafat was concerned, at least in his public statements, the October War had been a turning point for the Palestinians, creating opportunities that had to be exploited to the full. 'We have paved the way for it, and taken part in it, and it is still going on for us,' he said in an interview in 1974. 'We must therefore attend to the consequences of this war . . . we must take advantage of them and avoid their negative aspects.'[22] What he meant was that he intended to insert the PLO into the peace negotiations in prospect between Israel and the Arabs, and communicate with the country that had cast itself as principal mediator, the United States.

Even before the war, Arafat had seen encouraging signs. In June 1973, during a visit to the US by President Brezhnev, the two countries had issued a joint statement that referred for the first time to 'the legitimate interests of the Palestinian people'.[23] Arafat took it as a signal that superpower détente was inducing Washington to take more account of Moscow's views on the

Middle East, and wanted to know more. That summer he asked a close associate to approach the US ambassador to Iran, Richard Helms, and to propose PLO talks with Washington, based on two premises: that 'Israel is here to stay' and – more controversially – that Jordan should be the home for a putative Palestinian state.[24] It was the first of several messages the PLO leader sent over the next few months to the Nixon Administration through such intermediaries as Morocco's King Hassan.

On 10 October, just four days into the Arab–Israeli war, came another. According to Henry Kissinger, reading Arafat's communications with a mixture of interest and scepticism, its terse message was that the PLO chairman was '99 per cent sure that the Israelis will rout the Egyptians and Syrians in the next few days. The United States therefore should not intervene or provide any more aid to Israel until after hostilities. The United States should seek a ceasefire soonest without preconditions.'[25] If the Americans did not resupply Israel while the conflict continued, the PLO would undertake no hostile actions against US personnel and installations. And, Arafat implied, while reserving the right to settle scores with King Hussein, the Palestinians would be willing to participate in eventual peace talks with Israel.

Kissinger did not reply immediately but Arafat's messages evidently set him thinking. On 25 October, the Secretary of State signalled back through Morocco that he was prepared to send a representative to meet PLO officials. So it was that General Vernon Walters found himself travelling incognito to Rabat little more than a week later. 'This was to be a very special channel, a private channel from the Secretary of State through a trusted emissary,' said Alfred (Roy) Atherton, who was one of Kissinger's top Middle East aides.'[26]

Walters, who attended the meeting alone, unarmed, said he had been briefed to deliver his warning on terrorism and little else. 'It was all very dramatic,' he said. 'King Hassan introduced us and then left, saying, "We all believe in one God, and may He show you the way to stop the killing." '[27] Kissinger, in his memoirs, lays emphasis on the political discussions and indicates that the Palestinians, not the American, did most of the talking. He stresses, however, that the PLO officials were told that the US would not support any Palestinian manoeuvre aimed at over-throwing King Hussein – a fact, he says, which effectively aborted the talks after the further meeting in March 1974.[28]

The truth, it seems, is somewhat more intriguing, for Kissinger – despite his innate antipathy to the PLO – appears to have come closer to opening a negotiating channel with the PLO in the months after the October War than he subsequently cared to admit. According to a senior diplomat who later served as US ambassador to Beirut and was then in the State Department itself, the Secretary told colleagues at the time that the US would open a dialogue in a matter of weeks. 'The 1973 war had opened up possibilities that had not existed before, and it had become clear that the PLO could not be ignored if we were to solve this problem,' observed this former official. 'Kissinger had become aware of this through his contacts with Arab states. And he was frustrated at having to talk to the PLO through intermediaries.'[29]

For Arafat, such American soundings were a hopeful portent. Already encouraged by a developing relationship with the Soviet Union, he interpreted them as a sign that the views of the superpowers were converging to the point where they would be able to impose a solution in the Middle East. 'In January 1974, he thought that it was going to be possible to have a state before the end of the year,' said Nabil Shaath. 'He was that sure and that anxious.'[30]

But such optimism was hopelessly misplaced. Opposition in Israel to any hint of contacts with an organisation it saw as a threat to its very existence, strangled the American initiative. In any case, Kissinger was preoccupied by the need to deal with the immediate aftermath of the 1973 war. Step by step he gradually prised apart the coalition of Arab states that had fought the October War – a process in which he was actively assisted by Sadat's pressing desire for progress towards a settlement. Arafat and his colleagues, who had not after all been invited to the Geneva peace conference that opened and then swiftly adjourned on 21 December 1973, were left out in the cold.

Arafat's failure to get through to Washington was a bitter disappointment, but the abortive talks in Morocco marked the beginning of what was to become one of his abiding obsessions:

a desire to obtain American support. Like many other Arab leaders, Arafat had become convinced that the US president had the power to 'deliver' Israeli concessions at the negotiating table, if only he could be persuaded to exercise it. The overriding need, therefore, was to persuade the Palestinian movement to accept a more plausible political strategy.

The battle within the resistance on this issue came to a climax in a series of meetings at the American University of Beirut in late 1973 and early 1974. One by one, PLO ideologues trooped to the campus to present their often tortuous arguments before Palestinian audiences. From the left, Nayef Hawatmeh argued for his 'national authority' proposal with a rigorous presentation of the limited options facing the movement. For Fatah, with Arafat, as always, floating above the debate and not showing his hand, Salah Khalaf entered the lists, making a plea for 'new and original decisions' to capitalise on the Arab strength asserted in the October War. 'The question we most ask ourselves,' he said, 'is whether, by our refusal to accept anything less than the full liberation of all Palestine, we are prepared to abandon a portion of our patrimony to a third party.'[31] The Zionists, after all, had obtained their state of Israel in the late 1940s by accepting only a portion of the land they claimed. The Palestinians, by consistently saying no, had ended up with nothing.[32]

What none of the speakers advocated was something that most of them knew in their hearts was the real issue: recognition of Israel. It was a question that the Palestinian movement as a whole – Arafat included – was simply not ready to face. The PLO factions who favoured the national authority idea told themselves that having established control over part of Palestine they could use it as a base for continuing the fight against the 'Zionist entity'. How the Israelis might be persuaded voluntarily to evacuate territory under their control in these circumstances was a conundrum that nobody could answer.

It took Arafat's old rival, George Habash, the Arab nationalist and arch-opponent of any accommodation with Israel, to remind everyone of the reality. To Habash, it was obvious that, under the prevailing balance of power, Israel would extract a heavy price for withdrawing from the occupied territories, including

Arab recognition, demilitarised zones, international guarantees and all the other unacceptable paraphernalia of peacemaking. 'An Israeli withdrawal from the West Bank is only possible in the event of there being established there a reactionary force that is ready to surrender,' he proclaimed. 'Will Israel withdraw from the West Bank and just say goodbye? No, this is impossible.'[33]

So it was from this muddle of ideas that the Palestinians adopted a contradictory strategy at a meeting of the Palestine National Council in Cairo in the first week of June 1974. Refusing to recognise or to make peace with Israel and insisting on the ultimate aim of establishing a democratic state in all of Palestine, they called for the establishment of a 'people's national, independent and fighting authority on every part of Palestinian land that is liberated.'[34] Known subsequently as the PLO's 'transitional programme', it did not long succeed in papering over the cracks. Only weeks after agreeing to the statement, George Habash began publicly to dissociate himself from Arafat's diplomatic manoeuvrings and, by the end of September, Habash's Marxists had pulled out of day-to-day involvement in the PLO and formed a 'Front for the Rejection of Capitulationist Solutions', thus opening a damaging split. Nor did the supposed pragmatism of the PLO's statement impress the leaders of Israel, who – still in shock after the October War – instantly focused on the continuing call for the Jewish state's destruction rather than on the suggestion that the Palestinians might be prepared to settle for something less. 'It was clear,' said Shlomo Avineri, then director of Israel's Foreign Ministry, 'that this was all tactics – that stage one, the establishment of a mini-state, was purely aimed at better enabling them to achieve stage two.'[35]

For the PLO mainstream, however, the June statement, with all its elisions and ambiguities, was in its way an historic document, marking a major step into the real world of Middle East power politics. Above all, it was the first concrete recognition of the gap that existed between the Palestinians' dream and the more practical goals they would ultimately have to accept if they were to get anything at all. The compromise had a host of other consequences for the Palestinian movement, not all of which could have been foreseen. It fostered Arab and international recognition of the PLO as representative of the Palestinian people. It paved the way for clandestine contact between Palestinian representatives and sympathetic Israelis. And it launched Arafat himself onto the carousel of international diplomacy. Within five short months of this decision, and just two years after many outside observers had been inclined to write his movement off, the PLO leader found himself at the centre of international attention in a new and unfamiliar guise.

7. GUERRILLA-DIPLOMAT

'Today I have come bearing an olive branch and a freedom fighter's gun. Do not let the olive branch fall from my hand. I repeat: do not let the olive branch fall from my hand.' Yasser Arafat, addressing the United Nations General Assembly, 13 November 1974.

As the scheduled flight from Paris touched down at New York's John F. Kennedy Airport, the orotund Palestinian professor surveyed his fellow passengers. Could any of them be aware of the sensitive mission on which he was embarked? Could any of them conceivably be out to stop it?

It was early September 1974. Nabil Shaath was headed for the office complex on the bank of the East River that serves as headquarters of the United Nations. A day or so earlier, he had been asked to go to Manhattan and help prepare for Yasser Arafat's debut on the world stage. He had travelled via Tunis, where he had picked up a Tunisian diplomatic passport – a 'flag of convenience' for the trip to New York – and had changed planes in Paris. Now, with his Egyptian wife at his side, Shaath pondered the risks: this was the heart of 'enemy territory'; a city where Arafat was reviled as leader of a terrorist organisation and where Israel's opposition to any form of recognition for the PLO would be powerfully echoed by the local Jewish community.

Yet the Palestinians, too, had influential friends. The Arab states, flushed with partial victory in the fourth Arab–Israeli war and awakened to the power they wielded in the world oil market, now commanded attention among members of the world body. Thanks in part to lobbying, cajoling and threatening by Arafat and his followers, that new muscle was being flexed in support of the Palestinian cause. The result was that for the first time since 1952 the General Assembly had set aside time for a special debate on the question of Palestine. On 14 October 1974 an overwhelming majority of members – no fewer than 115 countries, most of them in the Third World – had voted in favour of inviting the PLO itself to join the discussion as 'representative of the Palestinian people'.

It was an illustration of the way the tables had shifted against Israel and towards the Arabs after the Yom Kippur War. In all previous petitions to the UN, the maximum number of votes the Palestinians had been able to muster was 82. Now, with the Soviet Union and its allies supporting the Palestinians and even the oil-deficit countries of Western Europe voting for the motion or at most abstaining, only the US, Bolivia and the Dominican Republic joined Israel in voting against. In vain did Israel's ambassador, Yosef Tekoah, circulate official documents detailing 'one hundred PLO crimes' or fulminate that the UN was overturning its own principles in order to welcome 'those who have turned the premeditated murder of innocent women, children and men into a profession'. In vain did the chief US delegate warn that a 'dangerous precedent' was being set.[1] By asking Yasser Arafat to become the first non-governmental representative to address the General Assembly, the UN allowed what even the move's most trenchant opponents concede was 'one of the great propaganda coups of the twentieth century'.[2]

For Arafat, the invitation was the most important fruit of a diplomatic offensive that he had been discreetly preparing for over a year. Armed with the PLO's June 1974 decision to pursue the struggle against Israel in stages, he had set out to obtain wider international recognition and to win the Palestinians a say in the peace moves that appeared to be gathering momentum. It was a new role for Arafat, and one that required a new repertoire of manipulative skills. Never mind that his movement's strategy as stated that summer was still riddled with ambiguities: the loopholes merely created greater room for manoeuvre. As translated by the PLO leader to his new international audience, the call for a 'fighting, independent national authority' on liberated land became implicit acceptance of a mini-state after an Israeli withdrawal.[3] The rejection of 'recognition, peace or secure borders' did not mean that the PLO was completely ruling out the idea of joining negotiations, merely that it was waiting for an invitation to the Geneva conference before deciding how to respond.[4]

Arafat's creative reinterpretation of agreed PLO policy swiftly landed him in trouble with his peers, notably with the arch-rejectionist George Habash, who accused Arafat – correctly as it turned out – of engaging in secret contacts through Palestinian intermediaries with the embodiment of Western imperialism, the

United States. But such squalls must have seemed a small price to pay for the plaudits Arafat was winning in the outside world. His more reasonable-sounding pronouncements pleased Egypt's President Sadat. Just as significant they delighted Arafat's friends in the Soviet Union. Invited to Moscow in July 1974 by Foreign Minister, Andrei Gromyko, the Palestinian leader had been rewarded with official recognition and a promise of Soviet anti-aircraft and anti-tank guns.[5]

The Soviet relationship was one to which Arafat the tactician, as ever subordinating ideology to *realpolitik*, attached the highest importance, and not just because it enhanced his personal prestige. Soviet support was a counterweight to the machinations of Henry Kissinger, who had set aside the search for a comprehensive settlement to the Middle East conflict and was then sparing no effort to lure the Arab states singly into peace talks that excluded the PLO. In the words of the capitalist-minded Nabil Shaath, who had many arguments with his boss at the time about this new cosiness with the Communists, 'The chairman definitely felt that he had to secure an alliance with the Soviets for his own protection.'[6]

Before striking out from Beirut for a bigger political stage, Arafat still had to deal with a crucial problem closer to home. As he was only too uncomfortably aware, it was among the Arab rulers who posed as the Palestinians' friends and protectors that he could be least sure of his position. At the earliest opportunity and in the clearest possible terms, the Arab states had to be forced to make a formal pledge of support for the movement. Extracting such a commitment would mean a showdown, and above all a settling of scores with King Hussein of Jordan, still pushing his claim to speak on behalf of the Palestinians. The struggle came to a head at a gathering of Arab heads of state in the Moroccan capital, Rabat, towards the end of October 1974.

In the middle of that month, Morocco's King Hassan, had received a worrying report from his intelligence services that they had uncovered a plot by Palestinian militants for the assassination of several Arab leaders – Hussein of Jordan, King Faisal of Saudi Arabia, President Sadat of Egypt, President Nimeiri of Sudan and himself – at the forthcoming summit.

The operation bore the trademarks of the Black September Organisation. Summoning Arafat, King Hassan blamed Black September's 'spiritual leader', Salah Khalaf, for the plot. Arafat disavowed all knowledge, but was able to identify two of the commandos. Khalaf insisted that the Fatah leadership was blameless. If so, his subsequent account of the operation, which, he surmises, was aimed only at King Hussein and not the other leaders, betrays surprisingly detailed knowledge of its preparation and planning. A few weeks later, he assumed 'full responsibility' for the plot in a speech at the Arab University of Beirut in defence of the imprisoned commandos.[7]

Albeit unsuccessful, the planned attack evidently served its purpose as far as the PLO leadership was concerned. Behind their verbal expressions of support, the autocrats who ruled the Arab world had long been wary of the PLO – of its potential to create trouble, of its subversive appeal to Arab public opinion, of its disturbingly 'democratic' style. But the suggestion, as they gathered for the summit, that a real gun was pointing at their heads served to concentrate minds wonderfully, creating what Khalaf described as 'a climate of terror'.[8]

A few days before the full meeting of heads of state, Arab foreign ministers gathered in Rabat to contemplate the issues, central among them how the Palestinians were to be represented in Middle East peace moves then under way. In essence it amounted to a choice between two men who had been bitterly at odds for more than four years: King Hussein of Jordan and Yasser Arafat. The former, the majority of whose subjects were of Palestinian origin, was looking for a green light to involve himself in American-brokered efforts to restore the West Bank from Israeli to Jordanian rule. The latter, anxious to secure his status as unchallenged spokesman for the Palestinian people, was equally keen on thwarting any such Jordanian involvement.

It was a choice that had caused the Arab states the greatest of difficulty in the past and one that they had always fudged, not least during the savage Jordanian–Palestinian civil war of 1970. Even at their previous summit in Algiers in November 1973, when all but one of them agreed in principle that the PLO was 'sole legitimate representative' of the Palestinians, they respected the dissenting voice – that of King Hussein himself – by keeping their decision secret. In the intervening months, President Sadat had attempted again to engineer an accommodation that would allow representation to be shared, thereby drawing criticism from the PLO. The fact that the argument was almost entirely hypothetical, given Israel's refusal to withdraw its forces from the West Bank, did not lessen its intensity. As ever in the Arab world, form seemed as important as substance. At stake was not only the self-esteem of two protocol-obsessed leaders but also the future shape of the kingdom of Jordan and the prospects for a peaceful settlement on Israel's eastern frontier. Now, with Henry Kissinger pressing ahead in his mediation between Hussein and the new Israeli Prime Minister, Yitzhak Rabin, the choice would wait no longer.

Neither the Jordanians nor the Palestinians were in a mood to compromise. In the Jordanian corner, Prime Minister Zeid al-Rifai, 'left no stone unturned to prevent recognition of the PLO', according to the account of one of those present.[9] For the Palestinians, Farouk Kaddoumi, who had been appointed as PLO 'foreign minister' two years before, responded in kind. Urged on by Arafat, who aimed abuse down the telephone at the Arab leaders, he thumped the table, threatened to inflict public embarrassment on the others by walking out, and ensured that his henchmen in the conference committees did not shift in their insistence on PLO demands. 'In fact I talked too much,' recalled Kaddoumi. 'I heavily attacked the Jordanians and told them to take their hands off the Palestinian cause.'[10] By the next day, thanks also to the lone support of Egypt's Foreign Minister, Kaddoumi's blunderbuss tactics had paid off. The Arab foreign ministers adopted the PLO's proposals without discussion and transmitted them to the summit.

When the Arab leaders gathered, fretting in their robes, expensive lounge suits and military uniforms, Hussein turned in a masterful performance. In a speech stretching over thirty large pages and lasting two hours, he surveyed the history of his kingdom's involvement in the Palestinian issue, testified eloquently about its right to the West Bank, and pointed out truthfully that he offered the only real chance for restoring it to Arab rule, given Israel's refusal to have any truck with the PLO. But it was all to no avail. After his speech, a long silence descended on the ornate conference hall, broken first by a blunt put-down from the Arab leader who had given Arafat's group its first tangible support, Algeria's President Boumedienne. 'Algeria does not recognise anybody to speak for the Palestinians except the PLO,' he said.[11] As other rulers demonstrated their support for Arafat, Hussein had no choice but to concede defeat and agree to a statement effectively barring him from speaking for the Palestinians.

'It was really a joke,' said Mahmoud Riad, the Egyptian who was serving at the time as secretary-general of the Arab League. 'The decision was taken without any real study. It became a competition between the Egyptians and the Syrians to see which of them supported the Palestinian cause more than the other,'[12]

Be that as it may, on 28 October 1974, the Arab world hailed the PLO a 'sole legitimate representative' of the Palestinian people and gave Arafat's movement what purported to be a right of veto over Arab moves towards a settlement with Israel.[13] The high point of the PLO leader's political fortunes to date, it constituted a laying on of hands by a bloc of countries now seen by the outside world as a formidable power in its own right.

'Today is the turning point in the history of the Palestinian people and Arab nation,' Arafat proclaimed exuberantly in the conference's closing session. 'I vow to continue the struggle until we meet together in Jerusalem with the same smiling faces we see here tonight. Victory is close at hand.'[14] It was another case of Arafat hyperbole and as usual bore little relation to the real balance of forces. But the Rabat summit decision did have a number of positive consequences for him. It boosted his standing among the Arabs under Israeli occupation in the West Bank and the Gaza Strip, who showed their support for him in a wave of demonstrations. Almost exactly ten years after Arafat's comrades had set out to attack Israel with a couple of rusty guns, Arab leaders were forced to treat him as an equal. Just as important, it paved the way for an increase in official Arab contributions to his organisation's coffers, with a promise from the assembled Arab leaders of 50 million US dollars a year for the PLO. Arafat was already well on his way to being head of the richest liberation movement the world had ever seen.

From now on, Arafat was virtually guaranteed a hearing abroad; indeed, just one week earlier, France had become the first Western country to open high-level contact with the PLO leader by sending its Foreign Minister, Jean Sauvagnargues, to meet him in Beirut. Now the PLO leader could seek to insert himself into continuing peace moves, or at least to thwart any such moves that might be taking place without him. As he put it in early November 1974, 'Before the Rabat summit we were only a figure in an equation. Now we are at the peak of events.'[15]

Not the smallest source of gratification to Arafat was the dismay the PLO's dramatic gains caused among other diplomatic players. For Henry Kissinger in particular, now Secretary of State to a newly installed President Ford, the Rabat decision doomed the whole effort to promote a peaceful settlement involving Israel and Jordan, as well as Egypt, by depriving the only Arab party to which the Israelis would talk about the future of the West Bank of the right to negotiate. Government officials in Jerusalem concluded that negotiations were 'at an impasse'.[16] Israeli newspapers began warning – like Arafat himself – of another war. Prime Minister Rabin commented dourly, 'There is no one to talk to about peace on the eastern borders. We will not negotiate with the terrorist organisations.'[17]

Arafat had played shrewdly on the insecurities of the assembled Arab leaders. At a time when some of them, principally President Sadat, were contemplating painful compromises with Israel, none could afford to be seen by domestic public opinion to be short-selling the Palestinian cause. Arafat had forced them to translate their lip service to the cause into support for his organisation. It was a conjuring trick of which he was to make frequent use in later efforts to keep the Arab world on what he saw as the straight and narrow.

Disturbed the Americans may have been by the Rabat resolution, but there was little they could do to prevent Arafat going on to reap the propaganda advantage of his new status in his visit to the United Nations General Assembly in New York just over a fortnight later.

Denying him entry – as the vocal pro-Israeli lobby did not hesitate to demand and as a subsequent Secretary of State did fourteen years later – was not an option. The administration did bow to Jewish pressure by confining Arafat's visa to a 25-mile radius of the UN building, thus depriving him of the chance to give a lecture at a prestigious university in New England and to appear on a Washington talk show. But to go further, as the State Department saw it then, would not only have violated the agreement regulating relations between the United Nations and the federal government; it would also have constituted a provocation at a time when America was under continuing pressure from a newly powerful Arab world to pay attention to Arafat. To underline the point, the Arab leaders had agreed to send President Suleiman Franjieh of Lebanon – a man not normally noted for his sympathy for the Palestinians but who had buried his differences with the PLO for the occasion – to speak on their behalf in support of Arafat during the General Assembly debate.

Thus on 13 November 1974, the US authorities found themselves playing reluctant hosts and protectors to a man who had vowed to destroy two of Washington's closest allies in the Middle East and whom they strongly suspected of involvement in terrorist acts against American citizens. Not since Fidel Castro and Nikita Kruschev had visited UN headquarters together in 1960 had New York seen a security operation like it. Against a background of threats from extremist Jewish groups that they would not let the PLO leader out of the city alive, and plans for a massive anti-Arafat demonstration on the day of his appearance, thousands of police and secret service men were mobilised. Over a period of four days, New York's mayor Abraham Beame afterwards revealed, his administration had spent 750,000 dollars to protect Arafat and his entourage, and all this for a visit that lasted less than 24 hours.

Arafat himself left nothing to chance. His own elite security squad comprised Force 17 commander Ali Hassan Salameh and ten commando leaders from southern Lebanon. In the run-up to the trip, his movements were shrouded in mystery. Courtesy of the Egyptian Government, one aircraft was at his disposal in Cairo; another had been chartered in Damascus; then, suddenly, just before he was due to depart for New York, he hastened to Algiers for a meeting with Swedish Prime Minister Olof Palme.

In the end it was a plane specially chartered for him by the Algerians that took him to New York. The purpose of all the evasion was simple: to confuse anybody who might have harboured thoughts of shooting Arafat down before he had even left the Middle East.[18]

Precautions were no less tight in midtown Manhattan. The Waldorf Astoria Hotel, where Arafat, using his adviser Nabil Shaath as food-taster, was to partake of lunch after giving his speech, had been turned into a fortress. Over at UN headquarters, a large swathe of territory along the East River was encircled by police, off-limits to visitors and other unauthorised persons from 24 hours before Arafat's arrival. When they landed at 5 a.m. in a remote corner of Kennedy Airport, Arafat and his 'favoured son' Salameh were whisked to the UN premises not in the usual motorcade, but in a US military helicopter with a State Department security officer and a secret service agent on board. With tens of thousands of protesters in the streets outside chanting 'Arafat go home', he remarked wryly to his aides that it was with this purpose in mind that he had come to New York in the first place.[19]

Every aspect of the PLO chairman's performance that day was stage-managed, with a result poised somewhere between historic occasion and slapstick comedy. His speech had been the subject of hours of haggling, drafting and redrafting by committees of officials and experts in the PLO's Beirut offices. Arafat's appearance itself had subtly changed: he had been persuaded to shave off the familiar stubble as part of his bid for new respectability, leaving a thin moustache.

'The whole thing had a slight Marx Brothers element to it,' recalls Brian Urquhart, a senior UN official later to have many dealings with the PLO leader. 'I say this with great kindness, but it was sort of like everything that Arafat does, with a certain element of farce and a great deal of rushing about.'[20]

Once positioned at the UN lectern, however, Arafat adopted a solemn tone in keeping with what he sensed was an unparalleled opportunity to bring the grievances of the Palestinians to the world's attention. Had not the UN overseen the very origins of his people's problem by endorsing the right of the Zionists to set up a state on part of Palestine? As Israel's world stature grew, had the UN not relegated Palestinian status to that of refugees – issuing limp calls affirming their 'right of return' but otherwise treating them as people to be compensated, cared for and resettled rather than a distinct people deserving of a homeland? Yet, as a growing number of developing countries were granted independence by imperial powers, had not the UN enshrined the right of peoples to self-determination as a cornerstone of its Charter?

Arafat saw his speech that day as a chance to correct the record. In remarks calculated to appeal to the UN Third World majority he equated the 'Jewish invasion of Palestine' and the actions of the Israeli state with colonialism and apartheid. Surveying the history of Palestine and describing himself with some licence as a son of Jerusalem', he sought to compare the Palestinian cause with various anti-colonial liberation struggles, even with America's war of independence. 'I am a rebel and freedom is my cause,' he proclaimed.[21]

Less immediately obvious to Arafat's audience was what kind of vision of the future he was offering. It was not that he failed to adopt conciliatory language: there were soothing remarks about peace, about the olive branch accompanying the freedom fighter's gun and about political struggle as a complement to armed struggle. But for Israel itself, there were accusations – of racism, terrorism and oppression – and a robust denial of Jewish nationhood. As for the Palestinians' ultimate goal, the PLO leader carefully avoided specifics, reverting to the 'dream' which he had first propounded in public more than six years earlier. 'Why therefore should I not dream and hope?' he asked in a passage reminiscent of the words of the American civil rights leader, Martin Luther King. 'For is not revolution the making real of dreams and hopes? So let us work together that my dream may be fulfilled, that I may return with my people out of exile, there in Palestine to live . . . in one democratic state where Christian, Jew and Muslim live in justice, equality, fraternity and progress.'[22]

If there was any hint here of the compromise that the PLO had debated and adopted the previous June – calling for a 'national authority' in the occupied territories – it was buried deep between the lines, much to the private relief of the Israelis, who had feared that a more specific proposal might put them under real pressure in the UN. 'The speech was long and complex, and nobody could really understand what it meant,' recalls one diplomat who was serving in Britain's UN mission at the time. 'It took our Middle East experts two days to work it out. It just went to underline Arafat's imperfect understanding of the international arena.'[23]

In truth, Arafat and his associates had already concluded back in Beirut that the General Assembly debate was not the place to put forward specific peace proposals. Not only would such a move have strained the organisation's fragile unity; they also felt it would, in a curious way, have seemed irrelevant. 'This was supposed to be an historical speech,' said Nabil Shaath, who had a hand in drafting it, along with Khalil al-Wazir, the Palestinian poet Mahmoud Darwish and a lawyer, Salah Dabbagh. 'It was the first opportunity we ever got to present the case of the Palestinian people to the world on record. Arafat was convinced it was not the moment to talk about a compromise.'[24]

In any case, the search for Arafat's real meaning was swiftly overtaken by a media hullabaloo concerning allegations that he had appeared before the UN with a gun on his hip. As he clasped his hands above his head in a triumphal acknowledgement of the General Assembly's tumultuous applause, a holster was spotted poking out beneath his jacket. The fact that the PLO leader was subsequently attested to have been persuaded to leave his Beretta backstage did little to quell Israeli and Jewish objections. Ever-conscious of the significance of symbols, Arafat knew that his supporters still wanted to see the gun at least as much as the hypothetical olive branch.

The next day brought bemused and in some cases negative reactions to Arafat's UN speech in the American press, particularly to his comparison of himself with such US icons as George Washington, Abraham Lincoln and Woodrow Wilson. It was, opined the *New York Times*, 'a distasteful, hypocritical perform-ance', featuring 'tendentious characterisations of Zionism, highly selective accounts of twentieth-century history', and an 'unim-aginative rehash of vaguely Marxist revolutionary ideology'. It was now up to the General Assembly to 'puncture the self-delusions of this shadowy organisation'.[25]

Among the Third World delegates, however, the response was something else entirely. After the PLO leader had spoken, in what Israel's chief delegate colourfully described as a 'homage to bloodshed and bestiality',[26] representatives of a host of African, Asian, socialist and, of course, Arab countries lined up to praise his 'noble', 'inspiring' and 'moving' sentiments; his political realism; his broad-minded tolerance and moderation.[27] At a reception organised by Egypt, Arafat was lionised by senior members of the New York diplomatic corps, with the notable exceptions of its Israeli and American members.

Arafat hardly lingered to savour the moment. In the dead of night, less than a day after arriving in New York, he was on the move again, this time southwards to the safer haven of communist Cuba, leaving his 'foreign minister', Farouk Kaddoumi, to garner the fruits of that day's work. As Kaddoumi discovered the fruits were substantial.[28] Of 81 speakers in a subsequent debate lasting nine days, 61 spoke out against Israel. To cap it all, On 22 November the General Assembly voted overwhelmingly to adopt two resolutions endorsing self-determination for the Palestinians and granting the PLO observer status in UN institutions.

This was a breakthrough by any measure. In one leap, the PLO was admitted to the UN as if it were the government of an existing state – a position identical to that enjoyed by North and South Korea, Switzerland and the Vatican. From then on, the UN would remain a focus of Palestinian political activity. The PLO used the built-in majority it could command in the General Assembly to push through a seemingly endless series of motions supporting its views, including some that caused the world body no end of problems with its American hosts, such as the controversial 1975 resolution stating that 'Zionism is racism'. It also set out to conquer, and in the process politicise, many of the specialised United Nations agencies. Late in 1975 the PLO was invited for the first time to participate in a debate in the UN's highest decision-making body, the Security Council.

The fact that these were entirely 'paper victories' – and of dubious relevance to the Palestine question – was beside the point. For Arafat, they confirmed that the Palestinian voice was being heard in the world. As the PLO leader has put it, recalling the 1974 trip, 'In the UN I felt the return of the soul to the Palestinian body, which the world had been trying to kill.'[29]

The PLO had certainly come a long way from the early, clandestine days of 'armed struggle' in the mid-1960s and from its friendlessness of the early 1970s. Now, headquartered in a sprawl of offices in Beirut, it was developing many of the appurtenances of a government bureaucracy, complete with an army of sorts, a finance ministry and departments to deal with Palestinian internal and external affairs. It built hospitals and schools for Palestinian refugees, and paid pensions to the families of Palestinian 'martyrs'. By 1975 it had some form of diplomatic representation in at least forty countries. A procession of foreign dignitaries lined up to call on the chairman himself as if he were already in charge of a state. All this was a costly business. But then, thanks in large part to Araft's skills at extracting 'conscience money' from the wealthy Arab oil states, principally Saudi Arabia, and at attracting contributions from the Palestinian Diaspora, the PLO and its component factions were already by far the richest irredentist movement the world had ever seen.

After his UN appearance, Arafat plunged into a frenetic diplomatic whirl, hopping between Arab capitals in private jets placed at his disposal by his wealthy sponsors. In a manner he was to make all his own in subsequent years, he took to making fanciful statements as to what sort of settlement the Palestinians would be prepared to accept, like a trader offering an opening bid in some kind of political bazaar. On one occasion, he pronounced himself ready to raise the Palestinian flag, just in the West Bank town of Jericho as a start: on another, he told the Egyptian foreign minister, Ismail Fahmy, that all he wanted at this stage was 'a piece of land wide enough to raise the Palestinian flag, even if it was not more than five kilometres wide'.[30] Strictly speaking, such statements did not contravene the letter of the PLO's June 1974 policy declaration but they stretched its meaning almost beyond recognition and provoked harsh criticism from his internal opponents – people who, Arafat still insists, 'misunderstood, or did not want to understand'.[31]

In the diplomatic arena, however, Arafat's rubbery approach proved an asset, not least in wooing the countries of Western Europe, an increasingly important priority as the 1970s unfolded.

Easily the most controversial, and perhaps the most important, aspect of Arafat's manoeuvring in the mid-1970s was one of which the world was only dimly aware at the time. It involved a series of secret contacts between Arafat associates and left-wing Israelis who professed sympathy for the Palestinian cause, and constituted the first tangible sign that the PLO leader might really be beginning to grope towards some sort of accommodation with the Jewish state. In these early days, it was also a course of action fraught with peril and one that would later cost the lives of two of Arafat's most prominent foreign envoys.

The idea that Palestinians should talk to Israelis was not in itself either new or particularly heretical. But not until the October War forced the Palestinians to think about political options did the concept of initiating talks develop a head of steam. After 1973, articles began to appear in the Palestinian periodical *Shu'un Filastiniya* about the Israeli left, pointing out that not all Israelis were committed to trampling on Palestinian rights. Within the Palestinian movement as a whole, in the words of Ilan Halevy, a Jewish Marxist who had left Israel in 1976 to join the PLO, 'Gradually, the idea that there was at least some tiny minority of Israelis with whom you could talk was becoming current.'[32]

Although they refrained from saying so publicly, it was a conclusion that Arafat and a small group of colleagues had already privately reached. Meeting in Beirut in late November or early December 1973, the Fatah central committee decided to set up a special team to 'keep in touch with events in Israel'.[33] Its chairmen were to be Arafat's deputy, Khalil al-Wazir, and another long-serving Fatah leader, Mahmoud Abbas, who had written a doctoral thesis on Zionism at the University of Moscow and was 'a pioneer of the idea that you have to study your enemy'.[34] The new team included two men who were to play a crucial role in pursuing contacts with the Israelis: Said Hammami and Issam Sartawi. The former, a bright young guerrilla turned diplomat, was the PLO's man in London. The latter, an American-educated heart surgeon, had led his own guerrilla faction in the late 1960s but was now a member of Arafat's Fatah group charged with special missions by the PLO chairman.

Hammami, posted to London in 1972, had already caused a stir among diplomats and journalists with his original views on the Palestinian problem. In late 1973, his name appeared on two articles in *The Times* calling for the establishment of a Palestinian state in the West Bank and Gaza as a means of 'drawing out the poison at the heart of Arab–Israeli enmity' and urging Israeli Jews and Palestinian Arabs to 'recognise one another as peoples'.[35] The articles, while not publicly endorsed by Arafat, were trial balloons for views the PLO leader was keen to convey to the West. In Israel, they attracted the attention of a man who had long been looking for potential interlocutors among the Palestinians: the peace campaigner and maverick parliamentarian, Uri Avnery. Avnery, who himself had fought in a Jewish underground terrorist group before the creation of Israel, contacted Hammami through intermediaries. The result, in January 1975, was the first of many secret meetings between this unlikely pair and the beginning of what later became a semi-public dialogue between like-minded Israelis and senior PLO officials acting on the specific instructions of Yasser Arafat.[36]

Avnery, who in June 1975 formed a group known as the Israeli Council for Israel–Palestine Peace, started from a simple premise: if the Palestinians were to get anywhere in their struggle for statehood, they needed to work to reduce the deep hostility to their organisation in Israeli public opinion. It was a question, as Avnery put it, of 'trying to break down the psychological inhibitions . . . on both sides'.[37]

As it turned out, the inhibitions were simply too immense. Israel's Prime Minister, Yitzhak Rabin, who received periodic reports of the meetings, was unyielding in his refusal to contemplate even indirect communication with the 'terrorist' PLO. On the Palestinian side, the idea of negotiating with the 'enemy' was for the most part ahead of its time. Conciliatory statements from one official would be swiftly disavowed by others, not least by Farouk Kaddoumi, who used his position as PLO 'foreign minister' to pour cold water on Sartawi's efforts. Arafat was left in the middle, as ever appearing to temporise between extremes and laying himself open to accusations of double-talk from his foes.

Although Arafat deserves credit for seeking to open channels to Israelis, the exercise said as much about his personal leadership style as it did about real prospects for Palestinian–Israeli peace at the time. In any case, Israel had already erected a formidable obstacle to the PLO's involvement in American-brokered Middle East peace moves by persuading the US to abstain from talking to the PLO until it had recognised the Jewish state.

Even as the 'dialogue' continued, events closer to home created a formidable distraction for Arafat and his comrades. For in the country that the PLO had now turned into its main base, Lebanon, the organisation was becoming dragged into another Arab conflict with effects as devastating as those of the Jordanian civil war five years earlier.

8. THE LEBANESE QUAGMIRE

'I cannot imagine what the connection is between the fighting of
Palestinians in the highest mountains of Lebanon and the liberation of
Palestine.' President Hafez al-Assad of Syria, Radio Damascus, 20 July
1976.

It was a warm June morning on the wooded slopes above Beirut,
but as they drove up the winding road to Baabda, Yasser Arafat
and Salah Khalaf experienced a sense of chill. Summoned to call
at the hillside palace of Lebanese President Suleiman Franjieh,
neither anticipated an easy encounter. For more than two months,
Lebanon had been sinking steadily deeper into civil war. A testy
exchange with the President five weeks earlier had left Arafat in
no doubt as to whom Franjieh was inclined to blame. Even so, the
reception waiting them caught the Palestinians unprepared.
Ushered into the presence not only of the Maronite Christian
President, a white-haired mountain clan leader, but also of the
Saudi and Egyptian ambassadors and a bevy of Muslim army
officers, they were treated to a stream of accusations and demands.
'Your behaviour is intolerable for the Lebanese population,'
charged the chain-smoking President. 'I am asking you today –
indeed, I am insisting – in the presence of two Arab ambassadors
friendly to your cause, to confine yourselves to the limits of your
camps and sectors.'[1] Arafat, accused of dishonesty in his claims
about the activities of his Lebanese opponents and – more
woundingly – of lacking the courage to discipline his own troops,
was placed well and truly on the defensive. After a four-hour
exchange which resolved little, Franjieh paradoxically insisted that
his visitors stay for lunch. To those not directly involved, it might
just have been one of those set-piece encounters, replete with
posturing, threats and sudden reconciliation, for which Lebanese
politics had long been famous. But to the antagonists, it was in
deadly earnest. This meeting, on 23 June 1975, was Arafat's last
with the Lebanese President. It provided the clearest possible
illustration of the speed with which things had deteriorated for the
Palestinians since their diplomatic triumphs of the previous year,

when Franjieh had led a nineteen-member Arab delegation to the United Nations and delivered a fulsome speech in support of Arafat's quest for international recognition. Now, here he was, lending his full backing to Lebanese factions who were arming themselves to fight the Palestinians.

Gone were the words of Lebanese solidarity with the Palestinian cause that had wafted down from the UN podium in November 1974; vanished were Franjieh's claims for Lebanon as 'that land of tolerance' and 'a human synthesis of peace and brotherhood'.[2] In their place was a reality that had been hidden beneath the febrile surface of Lebanese society for many years and now emerged in all its ugliness: a spectacle of sectarian prejudice and suspicion, of government enfeebled by division and corruption, and of violence on an appalling scale. Within a matter of months, it ensnared the Palestinians in another full-scale armed confrontation with their Arab brethren. Thanks to the machinations of their foes and in no small measure to their own mistakes, it was a fight for survival every bit as serious as the conflict which had led to the PLO's expulsion from Jordan in 1970–1. It also proved a diversion which distracted them for years from the struggle to liberate Palestine.

Ain Rummaneh was a largely Christian district that had sprung up amid the orange groves southeast of Beirut in the 1950s. On 13 April 1975, as the Maronite Christian elder Pierre Gemayel attended the consecration of a new church in a street bearing his name, shots were fired at his entourage from a passing car, killing four men, including a bodyguard and two members of Gemayel's Phalange militia. Precisely who was responsible for the incident was unclear, but members of the Phalange leaped to their own conclusions. Later that same morning in the same suburb, a bus carrying a group of Palestinians back to their nearby refugee camp was ambushed by Christian gunmen: all 28 passengers were shot dead in cold blood.

Within 24 hours of the Ain Rummaneh massacre, as if on cue, mortar and machine-gun battles between Phalangist militiamen and Palestinian commandos erupted all over Beirut, setting a pattern in three days that would become familiar in the following eighteen months. Lebanese Christian forces in the east of the city traded artillery fire with Palestinians in their refugee camps; armed gangs rampaged through the Christian quarters of town, looting shops and homes and blowing up cars; gunmen of various sectarian stripes, and of none, committed all manner of senseless crimes; and political leaders poured fuel on the flames with a plethora of provocative declarations. By the time the Arab League had hastily arranged a ceasefire on 16 April, it was already clear that the truce would be broken almost as soon as agreed.

For Yasser Arafat, who from his headquarters in the tumbledown Fakhani district of west Beirut had urged Arab leaders to intervene on the first day of the fighting, the outbreak of civil war in Lebanon spelled disaster. Its continuation might destroy everything he had worked for since the PLO's expulsion from Jordan four years earlier: the military infrastructure painstakingly constructed in the south for armed raids into Israel; the base for autonomous political and diplomatic action he had managed to establish in Beirut; and the support Arafat had sought to generate for his movement among important segments of the Lebanese political establishment. In effect, the PLO saw Lebanon as its 'last refuge', the only country on the front line with Israel where its presence in force was permitted. All this was now under serious threat. Small wonder that Arafat himself, as ever sensing the work of unseen forces against him, described it all at the outset as 'a conspiracy to disrupt Lebanese–Palestinian relations'.[3]

In truth, he must have known that the root of the trouble went much, much deeper than that. It stretched right back to the foundation both of the Lebanese Republic and of the Palestinian national movement, tapping deep-seated fears and insecurities on both sides. Even without the Palestinians as a focus, the conflict between Lebanon's minority Maronite Christian community and its Muslim and Druze sects over the division of the country's political spoils had a momentum all its own. But undoubtedly it was the Palestinians who were the catalyst for civil war, and it was controversy over the PLO's armed presence that became its principal driving force. In the wake of Israel's War of Independence in 1948, Lebanon had become home to some 180,000 refugees from the towns and villages of what had been northern

Palestine, and by the 1960s – thanks to natural increase and further waves of immigration – Palestinians represented around ten per cent of Lebanon's resident population. Not all of them remained in temporary accommodation by any means, but the ramshackle refugee camps that sprang up along the country's southern coast and in the outer suburbs of Beirut were an ever-present reminder of the dispossessed. A source of cheap labour for Lebanon's growing industries, the Palestinians of the camps had been kept on a tight rein by the authorities for two decades. Just as the country's much-feared military security service, the Deuxieme Bureau, stamped on political activism, so the army sought to suppress early cross-border raids by the underground Fatah movement for fear of Israeli reprisals.

Towards the end of the 1960s, however, when Arafat had taken the helm of a newly awakened national movement, the Palestinians of Lebanon began to emerge as a force in their own right. Their stirrings had an inevitable ripple effect in a country where divisions along sectarian, social and political lines were in any case becoming increasingly exposed.

Inexorably, as in Jordan at about the same time, the authorities were forced by a wave of public (especially Muslim) support for the Palestinians to loosen their control. Armed *fedayeen* appeared in the streets of Beirut, as they had in Amman. Resistance groups implanted themselves among the refugees and turned their settlements into armed camps. An upsurge of cross-border attacks brought heavy Israeli retaliation. As the Lebanese army attempted to halt guerrilla activity in the south, it became embroiled in repeated skirmishes with PLO commandos. Among the Maronite Christians, who held the main levers of power under an unwritten agreement dating back to Lebanon's independence from France in 1943, the new military presence in their midst caused rising alarm.

By October 1969 the situation was rapidly getting out of hand. The Lebanese army was in no position to implement orders to restrain the *fedayeen*. Bloody clashes between the two both created friction within the government and attracted disapproving attention from the Palestinians' friend and protector, President Nasser, whose foreign minister invited Arafat and the Lebanese army commander, General Emile Boustany, to Cairo to try to work out some sort of *modus vivendi*. The result, on 3 November, was the signing of the so-called Cairo Agreement, which aimed to regulate relations between the Palestinians and Lebanese, on the basis of confidence, frankness and co-operation.[4] From now on, in theory, the PLO would confine its military activities to specified areas in the southeast of the country, co-ordinate them with the Lebanese army, and promise not to interfere in Lebanese affairs. In return, the army would 'facilitate' the passage of commandos to border areas.[5]

In practice, the agreement was shot full of holes. For one thing, it was most unlikely that the Palestinian guerrillas would confine themselves to southeastern Lebanon when their main recruiting grounds were in the refugee camps of Beirut and the southwest. For another, there was no mechanism to ensure the smooth working of the accord. As Walid Khalidi, a Palestinian professor who mediated between Arafat and the Lebanese Government in the 1970s and was frequently confronted with breaches of the accord, put it, 'There were so many loopholes in it that it really is difficult to see how it could have been implemented without the most elaborate monitoring system. The idea of confining the military presence of the Palestinians to just a corner of Lebanon at a time when there were hundreds of thousands of refugees along the coast was simply not practical.'[6]

To Arafat, then preoccupied by the worsening crisis in Jordan, this was all beside the point. The important thing for him was that, for the first time, an Arab government had formally recognised the organisation's right to pursue armed struggle from its sovereign territory and had entrusted security in the Palestinian refugee camps to the PLO itself rather than to the hated Lebanese security service. Pocketing these enormous gains, he did not make much effort to enforce the reciprocal limits on PLO activity. Instead, using the Cairo Agreement as one foundation stone and the Lebanese Government's inherent weakness as the other, he set out to build a state within a state that was to put the Palestinian movement on a collision course with Lebanese Christian hardliners. 'There was no real co-ordination between us and the Lebanese authorities,' commented a senior Palestinian military commander. 'Their aim in the agreement was to control us rather than to co-ordinate, so friction was inevitable,'[7]

Nevertheless, by the early 1970s Lebanon had become the only country where the *fedayeen* could operate in relative freedom. It was the Arab world's closest approximation to a parliamentary democracy and the government, unlike those of Jordan and Syria, was too divided between supporters and opponents of the resistance to call the shots. In Syria, where between 3,000 and 4,000 *fedayeen* had fled from King Hussein's vengeful legions in 1970 and 1971, the Palestinians had swiftly found themselves subject to onerous restrictions. Hafez al-Assad, the country's new President, had long before developed a deep suspicion of Arafat and had come to think of himself rather than Arafat or Hussein as the rightful guardian of the Palestinian cause, frequently telling visitors that Palestine was historically part of southern Syria. He forbade armed operations against Israel without his army's permission, impeded PLO troop movements with roadblocks, banned *fedayeen* from carrying weapons in public and subjected Palestinians to all manner of petty harassment. Such measures may have made sense from the standpoint of Syrian stability, but to a liberation movement that was still struggling to assert itself, and to a Palestinian leader for whom independence of action was always the most jealously guarded priority, they amounted to an intolerable interference. 'Assad wanted to freeze the operations of the Palestinian movement in Syria, so we went to Lebanon to escape the freezer,' observed Sakher Abu Nizar, an Arafat aide who took charge of Fatah's organisation in Lebanon from 1973.[8]

Assad, needless to say, had another motive for wanting the Palestinians to enhance their presence in Lebanon rather than on his territory, seeing it as a covert way of increasing his influence in the country on his western borders – as a way, in the words of one senior PLO official, of 'controlling both Lebanon and the Palestinians'.[9]

Thus, with Assad's encouragement, Palestinian fighters began a major infiltration into the barren and hilly Arqoub region of southeastern Lebanon. Defying attempts by the Lebanese Army to halt their progress, and efforts by local Fatah commanders to resist an invasion of what they regarded as their personal fief, the ill-disciplined and fractious PLO forces gradually built up new bases and amassed an array of heavy weaponry in the coastal refugee camps and in the eastern town of Baalbeck. It was only a matter of time before they became a significant military force in the capital itself, further infuriating the hard core Maronite Christians, who saw in the PLO presence a shameful violation of Lebanese sovereignty and feared that Lebanon was in danger of becoming a substitute Palestinian homeland.

It was all too obvious that the rule of law in Lebanon was crumbling. Unchecked by an efficient security service – one of the first acts of President Franjieh's government after his election in 1970, having been to disband the old Deuxieme Bureau – parts of the country, and especially of the capital, slid towards anarchy as armed Palestinian and Lebanese gangs took matters into their own hands. Leftist factions of the PLO, using Beirut as their new revolutionary platform, did not hesitate to confront the authorities. Smuggling and other rackets were on the increase; bank robberies multiplied; and a series of mysterious bomb explosions in Beirut suggested that Arab intelligence services, aided and abetted by the various Palestinian factions in their pay, were using Lebanon as never before for their own nefarious purposes. Although the President himself bore responsibility for the atmosphere of growing disorder through his toleration, indeed encouragement, of corruption on a massive scale, it was more often than not the Palestinians who got the blame for Lebanon's manifest ills. What is more, they were now openly allying themselves with Lebanese radicals dedicated to the overthrow of the existing order.

The turning point came in April 1973, after the daring night-time raid on Beirut and assassination of three PLO leaders by Israeli commandos. News of the Israelis' penetration to the very heart of the city provoked a political outcry, with Muslim leaders voicing strong suspicions of collusion by elements in the Lebanese security forces. Saeb Salam, the Sunni Muslim Prime Minister and a friend of Arafat, resigned when President Franjieh refused his demand for the army commander's dismissal. Palestinians and Lebanese leftists organised mammoth anti-government demonstrations in downtown Beirut.

Within days of the Israeli attack, a series of skirmishes took place between Lebanese security forces and Palestinian commandos, culminating in the arrest of several Lebanese and Palestinian extremists and the kidnapping in return of three Lebanese soldiers by Palestinian leftists. This was the last straw. On 2 May, the army took up positions round Palestinian refugee camps in Beirut's southern suburbs and, when commandos in two of them, Sabra and Shatila, were falsely reported to have shelled the nearby international airport, the Lebanese air force bombarded the camps. 'Franjieh was absolutely shaking with anger,' recalled Walid Khalidi, who was with the President when the reports of Palestinian shelling reached the Baabda palace above Beirut. 'The airport was not being shelled, but he insisted that it was. And he said, "I have ordered the air force to bomb your camps. The raid is going to take place in five minutes, and you're going to come out on to the terrace and witness it." And lo and behold, while we were arguing, two air force planes appeared in the skies of Beirut and dive-bombed the outskirts of Sabra and Shatila.'[10]

It took two and a half weeks of Arab mediation for the clashes to be brought to a halt. A substantial legacy of bitterness remained on all sides. President Franjieh could not forgive the Palestinians for challenging his authority. Christian hardliners spearheaded by the Phalange, a militaristic Maronite movement modelled by its leader, Pierre Gemayel, on the fascist youth organisations that had sprung up in other Mediterranean countries in the 1930s, became more vocal in their calls for an end to the presence of the Palestinians on Lebanese soil. Belatedly, Arafat and his fellow PLO leaders, now bereft of powerful friends in the disintegrating government, began to realise they had a serious problem on their hands in a country where they had thought they could operate with impunity.

In effect, the battle lines had been drawn. As Salah Khalaf later observed, had it not been for the temporary distraction of the October War in 1973, Lebanon would probably have slid all the way to full-scale civil strife a good deal sooner than it did.[11] The respite that followed the war and accompanied by Arafat's first foray into the international diplomatic arena was thus an illusion.

During the lull, the PLO's Lebanese opponents were preparing for a conflict they knew would not be long postponed. The hardcore Maronites in particular, convinced that since the government was too weak to act they would have to do the job themselves, scoured Arab and European countries for arms that would enable them to match the formidable arsenal already amassed by the Palestinians and their Lebanese allies.

For Palestinians in general and Yasser Arafat in particular, the situation evoked memories of their recent experience in Jordan. Well aware of the importance of preserving his movement's new refuge, the PLO leader had in fact worked hard to maintain good relations with the most important players in Lebanese politics, including the principal Maronite chieftains. He had striven to keep mainstream PLO forces out of the trouble that was brewing in the heart of the country around Beirut: he had concentrated these forces in the south and kept their guns pointing towards Israel. But Israel's retaliatory bombing raids had triggered off a chain reaction among the Lebanese, causing thousands of Shia Muslims from the southern border country to flee to the relative safety of Beirut. As in Jordan, Arafat, again unable to control flagrant misbehaviour by rank and file Palestinians, found himself embroiled in another interminable round of mediation and conciliation, this time involving the Phalange.

These were precarious days with the spectre of Black September ever present. For if Arafat had learned one lesson above all from Jordan, it was that simply keeping lines of communication to all the relevant parties open was not enough. Something more was required, something the Palestinians had not had among the Jordanians: a dependable and powerful political ally. It so happened that such a figure was present in Lebanon, in the form of a charismatic politician named Kamal Jumblatt.

Leader of a rapidly growing umbrella organisation of leftist and Muslim groups known as the Lebanese National Movement, Jumblatt is universally acknowledged to have been an extraordinary man. Lanky and dishevelled, with a high piping voice and a dreamy look in his eyes, he was part feudal lord, part socialist visionary, part vaultingly ambitious politician. As the scion of an ancient clan inhabiting the Chouf Mountains of central Lebanon,

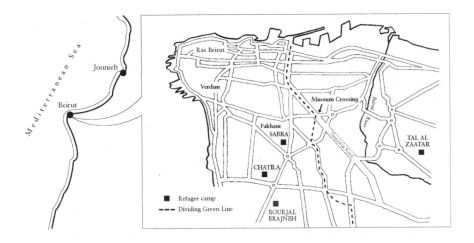

he was a landed aristocrat and principal chieftain of what ordinary Muslims regard as an obscure and heretical religious sect, the Druze.

Jumblatt's political activities and writings gave him an influence well beyond his original power base. They won him the Soviet Union's Order of Lenin, and allowed him to emerge in the early 1970s as uncontested leader of Lebanon's radicals. In this role he set out, in alliance with the forces of the Palestinian resistance, to effect what amounted to a revolution in Lebanon – the abolition of confessional politics, the system that placed power in the hands of the Maronite Christians and Sunni Muslims and constituted an obstacle to the political advancement of other sects. His campaign played a major part in precipitating the civil war of 1975–6, and in the process landed the PLO in deep trouble – both with its Lebanese opponents and with the Syrians.

Arafat had learned to respect Jumblatt in the late 1960s when, as Lebanese Interior Minister, he had had responsibility for implementing the doomed Cairo Agreement; in the ensuing years, the two men had become close friends. Apart from the personal chemistry, Arafat was captivated by Jumblatt's political ideas, a vision of a democratic secular state that was not dissimilar to Arafat's own hazy conception of the future Palestine. In fact, the Druze leader had his own motive for seeking to enlist PLO co-operation: his desire to harness the Palestinians' superior firepower in support of the National Movement's impending struggle for control of Lebanon.

'Jumblatt had quietly tutored the PLO about Lebanon,' said Walid Khalidi. 'Arafat is no fool, but Jumblatt really invested an awful lot of time in giving Arafat and his inner group of lieutenants his version of what is Lebanon. I think Jumblatt very, very shrewdly seized upon the talk of a democratic secular state [in Palestine] and began to weave a scenario which ideologically appealed to Arafat.'[13]

Profiting from the hard lessons he had learned from Jordan and forgetting all the talk of non-interference in Arab countries' affairs, Arafat thus deliberately set out to strengthen the link with Jumblatt and thereby insert the PLO into the fabric of Lebanese society, to a point where the fortunes of the Palestinians and the Lebanese National Movement became inextricably tied together. He also built up links with an increasingly influential Shia Muslim leader, Imam Musa Sadr, offering military training to his supporters and even suggesting a name – Amal, meaning 'Hope' – for his newly founded militia. Amal's slogan – 'arms are the ornament of men' – was also borrowed from the Palestinian movement. Sakher Abu Nizar, the Arafat point man in Lebanon, neatly described the process. 'We tried,' he said, 'to make sure that it was not a case of Palestinians interfering in Lebanese affairs but of our Lebanese allies interfering in their own affairs.'[14]

It was a dangerous illusion. The Lebanese National Movement was a motley crew, composed of mafioso-style thugs as much as of political idealists. In company with such characters, the Palestinians fooled themselves into thinking that they could put down roots in Lebanon. Arafat, for his part, felt he was becoming a power in the land, a patron in a country where patronage reigned supreme, and a political leader with whom the Lebanese chieftains would have to do business.

Beguiled by his new status, he paid little attention to the corruption and indiscipline that were spreading through his entourage. As in many of the newly rich Arab states, the sudden influx of money brought trouble, turning the PLO into a bloated and in parts rotten bureaucracy. Officials, eyeing the prospect of wealth beyond the imaginings of an ordinary Palestinian refugee, freely siphoned off funds for their own use or dabbled in dubious business deals – and as a rule the higher up they were, the more they dabbled.

In those days, Arafat even had time to indulge in romantic dalliance. Colleagues recall that he was a frequent caller at a fashionable salon near the Beirut waterfront belonging to a well-endowed and well-connected Palestinian widow, Nada Yashrouti. Nada's late husband, the wealthy contractor Khaled Yashrouti, had been active in the PLO until he was crushed by falling masonry on a building site in 1970. Nada herself maintained family tradition, serving on occasion as an inter-mediary between Arafat and President Franjieh. So close did she and the PLO leader become that he is said to have asked for her hand in marriage. Nada, so the story goes, gently rebuffed him, saying, 'I love you as a leader, not as an ordinary man.'[15] His relationship with Nada Yashrouti set a pattern for a series of close friendships with women in later years – with his Syrian secretary Umm Nasser for one, and his Egyptian biographer Rashida Mahran for another. Like Nada, they were both amply built mother figures.

As the fateful spring of 1975 approached, events in Lebanon and the wider Middle East were themselves distracting enough. For a start, there were distinct signs that the coalition of Arab states that had united to fight the October War with Israel and to back the PLO's quest for recognition was fraying. Syria's President Assad was making efforts to improve his relations with the Palestinians' enemy, King Hussein. Worse still, Egypt's President Sadat was inching his way, under the guileful tutelage of Henry Kissinger, towards a new disengagement agreement with Israel – an accord that, as Arafat saw it, would be bound to entail further concessions at the Palestinians' expense and to fracture an already fragile Arab consensus. Developments back in Beirut were no less threatening, with Phalange leader Pierre Gemayel making inflammatory speeches accusing the Palestinians of abusing Lebanese hospitality, and calling for a referendum on their continued presence in the country.

*   *   *

The uncomfortable truth was that little more than a year after the October War, mainstream Arab leaders were tiring of the excesses of radical PLO factions and too immersed in domestic preoccupations to bother unduly about the fate of the Palestinians. To countries like Egypt, bent on making peace with Israel and solving its own formidable economic problems, or even Saudi Arabia, grappling with a cornucopia of riches after the quadrupling of oil prices, the PLO's travails in Lebanon had become little more than a sideshow. Arafat's own propaganda had begun to backfire: just as he had argued that the liberation of Palestine had to come before Arab unity, so Arab leaders with states to look after had decided that their domestic affairs were more pressing than some grand Arab design.

Such dismal realities go some way towards explaining why Arafat behaved as he did when war broke out with the retaliatory massacre of a busload of Palestinians that mid-April Sunday morning in 1975. Sensing his political isolation in the Arab world and the utter hostility of the opposing camp, he mistakenly placed his bets on his alliance with Kamal Jumblatt. His organisation's leftist factions – and quite a number of guerrillas from his own Fatah group – were already fighting side by side with Jumblatt's men in any case, and Jumblatt himself went all out for escalation. On 26 April, the Lebanese National Movement responded to the Phalange's apparent involvement in the Ain Rummaneh massacre by demanding the party's removal from the government. When Arafat endorsed the statement, the die was cast: in political if not yet in openly declared military terms, the PLO had taken sides in the Lebanese civil war.

In the next few months, as fighting intensified, ceasefires collapsed and Arab and European negotiators fruitlessly came and went, Arafat redoubled his efforts to mediate between the warring factions and to pretend, despite significant involvement of Palestinian fighters on the Muslim side, that the PLO, and more especially Fatah, had no part in the war. But the conflict between Christian east Beirut and a predominantly Muslim west had developed its own momentum. The Maronite Christians provoked a fresh upsurge of fury among their opponents by starting to talk openly about the partition of Lebanon into separate sectarian enclaves. The Lebanese Muslims, Druze and the Palestinians resolutely opposed Maronite demands that the army be called in to restore order, a move which Arafat, as ever seeking to represent the broadest spectrum of Palestinian opinion, feared would lead to the liquidation of the PLO's extremist factions. The Palestinian leadership's sense of isolation grew sharply in September 1975, when President Sadat signed his second Sinai disengagement agreement with Israel, unilaterally promising in the teeth of PLO and Syrian opposition to resolve the Middle East conflict by peaceful rather than by military means.

Arafat's problems were compounded by the fact that the PLO and even Fatah itself were split, just as they had been in Jordan. Fatah leaders insisted that the conflict was a conspiracy aimed at dividing Lebanon and distracting the Palestinians from their fight against Israel. But they were opposed by a substantial body of opinion among the leftist groups and within Fatah, some of whose most senior military commanders argued with exceedingly dubious logic that the road to liberating Palestine led through the Lebanese Christian port of Jounieh, and that what was at stake was a 'class struggle' between poor oppressed Muslims and rich privileged Maronites.[16]

The confrontation that would tip the balance between these two schools of thought, and dramatically escalate the war, was not long in coming. On 4 January 1976, Maronite militiamen closed in on and laid siege to two Palestinian refugee camps in east Beirut, Tal al-Zaatar and Jisr al-Basha, from where Palestinian leftist forces controlled roads into the city. To the PLO leadership, which demanded the immediate lifting of the blockade and threatened to break it by force if necessary, the move was intolerable. When, on 14 January, Maronite forces besieged and overran the Dbayeh refugee camp on a hilltop north of the capital, butchering many of its Palestinian Christian inhabitants, Arafat and his colleagues concluded that the time for action had arrived. Abandoning all pretence that this was not the PLO's war, they and their Lebanese radical allies vowed to respond with all the force at their disposal.

The chosen location for PLO reprisals was Damour, a small Christian town near the coast south of Beirut. Sitting amid a rolling countryside of mulberry fields and silk factories, Damour occupied a strategic position on the coastal highway linking Beirut with the pro-Palestinian south. It was also the stronghold of a Maronite leader, Camille Chamoun, who was a particular target of Palestinian hatred. From mid-January 1976, columns of Fatah fighters from the southern port city of Sidon converged on Damour under the command of a former Jordanian artillery officer, Mohammed Said Musa Maragha: under his *nom de guerre*, Abu Musa, he would gain notoriety seven years later as one of the leaders of a bloody mutiny against Arafat's leadership. After shelling Damour for eight hours, the combined Palestinian and Lebanese Muslim forces broke through into the town on 20 January. As church bells rang out in east Beirut to signal Christian alarm, an orgy of looting, destruction and murder was unleashed on those inhabitants who had not already fled. Damour was reduced to a ghost town.

The drama that unfolded in the ensuing months caught all the combatants in a tangled web of distrust and deception, whose strands were almost entirely of their own weaving. Above all, it is the story of a battle over Lebanon's future between two ruthless and ambitious leaders, Kamal Jumblatt and Hafez al-Assad of Syria, and of the vacillations of a third man torn between the two, Yasser Arafat.

Under heavy pressure from the Palestinian rank and file, Arafat and his fellow Fatah leaders had crossed a Rubicon. A conflict they had previously insisted was a purely Lebanese affair had become an all-out confrontation between Palestinian and Maronite Lebanese forces, and a full-time distraction from the PLO's, supposed purpose, the struggle against Israel. It was a fight, moreover, in which Lebanon's powerful eastern neighbour, Syria, was taking an increasingly close interest thanks to the urgent appeals for help which Arafat had addressed to President Assad.[17]

The Syrian leader's main preoccupation was to maintain the balance in Lebanon – to prevent the Maronite Christians from crushing their opponents but equally to keep the Lebanese radicals and Palestinians from overturning the existing order. On 19 January, he had fired a warning shot in support of the resistance by despatching units of the Palestine Liberation Army under Syrian command across the border into Lebanon's Bekaa Valley. A day later he sent his foreign minister, Abdel Halim Khaddam, to Beirut at the head of a high-powered mediating team. It swiftly produced what President Franjieh announced on the 22nd as an 'agreement between all the parties towards an overall solution of the Lebanese crisis'.[18] The Syrians promised to co-operate with the Palestinians and the Lebanese in imposing and enforcing an effective ceasefire. The fighting died away: as the Syrian and Lebanese Governments got to work on drafting a programme of political reform, it began to seem as if the civil war might be over.

Nothing, of course, could have been further from the truth. The suspicions ran too deep on all sides for the truce to be any more than temporary, in addition to which both the PLO and Kamal Jumblatt's Lebanese National Movement were now involved in machinations that would lead to a new and even more serious confrontation, this time directly involving the Syrian army.

Jumblatt was deeply wary of Syrian motives in spite of the arms Assad had provided for his movement over the years and the help he had afforded in January. He was also contemptuous of the political reforms the Syrian President was trying to impose on Lebanon – piecemeal change which would give the Muslims more power but would leave intact the system that barred anyone other than a Maronite Christian from becoming President.

In February and March 1976, Lebanon's armed forces began to disintegrate as a breakaway group of Muslim soldiers, calling itself the Lebanese Arab Army, gathered recruits and took control of military barracks in the eastern Bekaa Valley. Then on 11 March, the Muslim commander of the Beirut garrison, a flamboyant officer named Brigadier Aziz Ahdab, seized the capital's radio and television stations, proclaimed himself provisional military governor, and demanded the resignation of President Franjieb within 24 hours.

Both moves bore clear traces of PLO involvement, notwithstanding subsequent denials by the leadership. Khalil al-Wazir, keen to improve his firepower with weapons seized from the Lebanese Army, co-operated with dissident officers to hasten its break-up. Fatah had undeniably provided the coup-making brigadier with a military escort. But the Palestinians and their Lebanese radical allies were playing with fire, for their activities amounted to an intolerable affront not only to the authority of Franjieh, who vowed that 'the only way I'll leave the presidency is in a coffin', but also to that of Assad himself.[19] Arafat and his intelligence chief Salah Khalaf were duly summoned to Damascus to explain themselves.

The meeting, on 16 March, was long even by Assad's windy standards, lasting a full twelve hours. The Syrian President was in a foul temper, calling Arafat and Khalaf 'men who betrayed his confidence while pretending to be his friends'.[20] When Assad was informed by telephone during the discussions that Jumblatt had made a declaration denouncing Syrian meddling in Lebanese affairs, his displeasure deepened. It was only with the greatest difficulty that the Palestinians finally persuaded Assad to make one more attempt to patch things up by receiving Jumblatt in Damascus. Far from reconciling the two men, their meeting eleven days later – against the background of a fresh upsurge of fighting between combined Palestinian and Lebanese radical forces and those of the Maronite Christian right – merely set the seal on their estrangement, prompting Assad to suspend arms deliveries to the Lebanese National Movement.

It had become a personal quarrel of a bitterness unusual even by the standards of the Arab world, based on a curious and unstable chemistry between Assad and Jumblatt, both of whom came from minority sects.

Their feud placed Yasser Arafat on the horns of a most awkward dilemma, for he was now under intense pressure to choose between the two. To alienate Assad, president of the country that had given Fatah its first military bases and the wherewithal to launch its armed struggle, would be foolhardy, to say the least. Yet to do as Assad seemed to be demanding and distance the Palestinian movement from Jumblatt, the man who more than any other served as guarantor of the PLO's freedom of action in Lebanon, could have equally serious consequences. 'In short,' said Khalaf, 'the Palestinian resistance was torn between the need to maintain its good relations with its Syrian ally and the moral obligation to stand by the Lebanese left.'[21]

Unable to decide, Arafat took the course of which he was past master: he temporised. At another meeting with Assad on 16 April, he agreed to a seven-point ceasefire plan. But all the while the fighting sputtered on, with the combined Palestinian–Lebanese forces making perceptible gains at the expense of the Maronites. By the end of April 1976, Jumblatt was able to boast that his National Movement controlled 82 per cent of Lebanese territory.[22]

With the repeated and humiliating collapse of his mediation efforts, Assad was rapidly approaching the end of his tether. He had been willing to support the Palestinians and the Lebanese radicals up to a point as a way of bolstering his influence in Lebanon, but he most emphatically did not want to see the overthrow of the existing Maronite-dominated order. So at the end of May he took one of the most contentious decisions of his controversial career: he sent his army into Lebanon to fight alongside Maronite Christian forces and crush the combined Palestinian–Lebanese offensive. By the end of the first week of June, around 12,000 Syrian troops, accompanied by tanks, were advancing into the country in three separate thrusts.

For the PLO and Jumblatt's radicals, this was a challenge of an altogether more serious order than they had faced hitherto. They swiftly formed a unified military command to confront the invaders, put up fierce resistance in the mountains of central Lebanon and in the outskirts of its three main coastal towns, and retaliated by overrunning the Beirut bases and offices of the Syrian-controlled PLO faction, al-Saiqa.

But from the outset, the Palestinian–Lebanese alliance was caught on the wrong foot by the superior Syrian force. Arafat himself was out of the country on an ill-timed diplomatic round. Unable to return because of the fighting, he appealed for Arab intervention from the Algerian, Libyan and Egyptian capitals but, although Arab foreign ministers responded to his pleas by persuading the Syrians to accept a ceasefire on 9 June, the resulting stalemate was merely the prelude to something much worse than that which had gone before.

In the eyes of the PLO's leaders, the 'international conspiracy' of which they had been warning for well over a year was proved. If any further proof were needed they had only to point to the evident approval with which Syria's move into Lebanon had been greeted in the United States and even in Israel, which assented to the invasion under US-mediated 'red line' agreement. The fact that the instrument for carrying out the plot was a supposedly 'progressive' Arab regime, Syria, merely compounded the PLO's rancour.

In effect, the choice which Arafat had been unwilling to make, between his tactical alliance with Assad and his strategic friendship with Karnal Jumblatt, had been made for him, and his falling out with Syria had lasting consequences. In his relations with the implacable Syrian President, Arafat had passed a point from which there could be no wholehearted return, temporary reconciliations notwithstanding. One chilling conversation he had with Assad during their arguments in 1976 stuck in his mind. 'You do not represent Palestine any more than we do,' the Syrian President told him. 'There is neither a Palestinian people, nor a Palestinian entity, there is only Syria, and you are an inseparable part of the Syrian people and Palestine is an inseparable part of Syria.'[23] Not even the Israeli leader, Golda Meir, who once observed there was no such thing as a Palestinian people, had put it quite so bluntly.

Late in June 1976 the Maronite militias seized their moment to fight back. The site was a cluster of Palestinian and Lebanese Shia Muslim settlements in east Beirut; the name of one of them, the refugee camp of Tal al-Zaatar, was to earn a place of enduring notoriety in Palestinian lore. Tal al-Zaatar, a shanty town constructed from breeze blocks and corrugated iron, had been blockaded since January, its exit roads cut off by gunmen, its inhabitants unable to secure adequate provisions. The PLO leadership had made repeated attempts to lift the siege, whether by military or other means; indeed, at one point Khalif al-Wazir, who was in charge during Arafat's prolonged foreign travels, opened negotiations with the powerful Maronite clergy to buy the land on which the camp was built for four million US dollars. It was a gesture typical of the wheeling-dealing world of Lebanese politics, but it was to no avail.

On 22 June, several hundred Christian militiamen launched a full-scale attack on Tal al-Zaatar as well as the smaller camp of Jisr al-Basha and the nearby Muslim quarter of Nabaa. As mortars and rockets rained down, Tal al-Zaatar's inhabitants took refuge in underground sewage tunnels. Ominously, the Syrian army cut off supply lines to the camp from the mountains behind Beirut. Within six days, Jisr al-Basha had fallen amid accusations of Syrian complicity from Arafat, watching impotently from a succession of Arab capitals.

Without reinforcements. the collapse of Tal al-Zaatar was inevitable. On 6 August the Muslim quarter of Nabaa fell to the Maronite militiamen, and on the 12th, after an artillery bombardment that had stretched over 52 consecutive days, Tal al-Zaatar itself surrendered under an evacuation agreement hammered out by the Arab League. The camp's 30,000 inhabitants had been brought to the brink of famine, and forced to risk their lives in drawing water from their one polluted well. Even in surrender, there was no end to the suffering. As unarmed refugees began to make their way out of the camp, Maronite gunmen opened fire, indiscriminately shooting Palestinians – women, babies and the elderly as well as men of fighting age. In all, during the siege and its bloody aftermath, an estimated 3,000 – most of them civilians – were killed, with at least as many wounded.

This was a catastrophe on a scale unprecedented even in the battered annals of the Palestinian movement. The day after the massacre, Arafat urged Arab leaders to convene a summit meeting with a view to halting carnage evidently abetted by the 'progressive', Arab nationalist, Syrian army. Their replies, trickling in over the next couple of weeks, were noncommittal.

For the Syrians, the PLO's state of shock created an opening. They lost little time in pressing home their advantage, mounting an offensive in late September to dislodge the Palestinian and Lebanese opposition forces from their strategic mountain strongholds. Realising how heavily the odds were stacked against it, the PLO leadership discreetly disengaged itself from a still defiant Jumblatt and withdrew. It was only when the Syrians renewed their attack in mid-October against Palestinian and Lebanese forces dug in at the picturesque summer resort of Bhamdoun above Beirut that Arafat succeeded in obtaining a concrete response to his appeals for Arab help. On 14 October, he got through by telephone to Crown Prince (later King) Fahd of Saudi Arabia and explained the Palestinians' plight. 'I will settle the problem,' said Fahd. 'Give me a few hours.'[24]

Arafat and Khalaf took refuge with the Saudi ambassador in Beirut. Within two days, six of the Arab world's most influential men – the rulers of Kuwait, Egypt and Saudi Arabia as well as those directly involved in the conflict – assembled in the desert city of Riyadh to close this bloody chapter of the Lebanese civil war. As the 'mini-summit' convened, President Assad brought eighteen months of bitter fighting to an end by proclaiming a ceasefire. At a subsequent enlarged meeting in Cairo, the leaders of the Arab world in effect endorsed the establishment of a new order in Lebanon, one dividing the country into separate spheres of influence and giving Syria's military presence – in the thin disguise of an Arab Deterrent Force – a predominant role.

The toll the conflict had taken on the PLO was enormous, with some 5,000 Palestinians killed. To make matters worse, a few short months later the PLO's main Lebanese ally was dead. On 16 March 1977, Kamal Jumblatt was assassinated in his car near a Syrian roadblock in the vicinity of his ancestral home. Nobody was in any doubt whom to blame.

But all was by no means lost for Arafat in the autumn Of 1976. He, too, had effectively been granted his own Lebanese fiefdom under the compromise agreed at Riyadh: a sizeable swathe of territory between the southern Litani river and Beirut itself. The PLO chairman now tried his hand at another new role, as president of something approaching a real state within the state. Like the sheriff of some latter-day Dodge City, he set out from his offices in west Beirut to impose the PLO's rule on the wayward Lebanese, and in the process to win credit in the outside world as a leader of substance.

The PLO's presence in Lebanon was steadily becoming an end in itself, to be defended at all costs. It was a power base that allowed Arafat a measure of independence in facing the machinations of Arab regimes and the undying hostility of Israel. It also appeared to offer him new opportunities to break through the indifference of the Western country he most wanted to talk to: the United States.

9. KNOCKING ON WASHINGTON'S DOOR

'The US holds the key to Israel.' Yasser Arafat in interview with *Time* magazine, 11 November 1974.

Cyrus Vance could tell something was wrong the moment his limousine drew up at the marbled airport in the western hills of Saudi Arabia. Where optimism had radiated the day before, gloom now clouded the hawklike features of the Saudi Foreign Minister who had come to bid the American Secretary of State a formal farewell. As a dejected Prince Saud al-Faisal look him off to the VIP lounge for a final round of talks, Vance braced himself for bad news. 'Arafat has been in touch,' he was told, once they had stepped out of the August heat. 'He said he just didn't have the votes to carry the day. The opportunity has gone.'[1]

In his less demonstrative way, the American diplomat shared the prince's frustration. Twenty-four hours earlier, On 7 August 1977, the two men had thought they were close to achieving a breakthrough. During a flying visit to the Saudi royal family's summer residence in the hill town of Taif, Arafat had promised to persuade his colleagues to recognise Israel's right to exist, a move which might pave the way for full-scale Arab–Israeli negotiations and produce a diplomatic win for the Administration of President Jimmy Carter in its first year. The PLO chairman's failure to do so the previous night in Damascus had put the US, Saudi Arabia and everybody else with an interest in involving the Palestinians in Middle East peace moves back where they started.

Vance left for Israel, the next stop on his second Middle East tour in six months, with a heavy heart. He had gone as far as he could to entice the PLO into breaking down the barrier that prevented it from communicating directly with Washington, and in the process, as good as guaranteed himself a hostile reception from the hardline leadership in Jerusalem.[2]

For Arafat, 850 miles away in Damascus, it was a disappointment of a kind that had become depressingly familiar. Seeking American recognition, he had been sending conciliatory messages to Washington through Saudi, Syrian and Egyptian intermediaries ever since President Carter's inauguration at the beginning of the year. Now his comrades had blocked his manoeuvres. The concession being demanded of the PLO in return for a dialogue with the US – acceptance of a key UN resolution affirming the right of all states in the region to exist in peace – was simply too much to swallow. A political opportunity was slipping away.

The pity of it was that 1977 had begun on an unusually hopeful note. Rescued by the Saudis from disaster in Lebanon, the Palestinians had picked themselves up with remarkable speed, redeploying their forces in the south of the country to resume the fight against Israel. Arafat, the perpetual survivor, bounced back faster than anticipated. In one of those intensely public and almost equally cosmetic reconciliations for which Arab politics are notorious, he even made peace of sorts with President Hafez al-Assad of Syria. Only months after the two leaders had called openly for each other's removal, they were pictured together, beaming from the pages of government-controlled newspapers in Damascus.[3]

Now, freed for a time from the debilitating task of damage limitation, the PLO leader threw himself into a new round of diplomacy. With the inauguration of President Carter, the Arab states were preparing themselves for another US mediation effort in the Middle East, and the PLO was beginning to think again about its political objectives.

In mid-March, the organisation's legislature, the Palestine National Council, convened for an important session in Cairo, and not before time. The Council had last met nearly three years before, and its subsequent inactivity had become a symbol of the Palestinian movement's disarray. As delegates gathered, they rehearsed all that had changed in the intervening years. The Palestinians within the Israeli-occupied territories were becoming steadily more assertive. The people of the West Bank and Gaza had voted overwhelmingly for pro-PLO mayors in municipal elections staged by Israel in 1976, now they were demanding that the exiled leadership take account of their views about the need for a political settlement. The PLO itself had been sobered by its experience in Lebanon, but far from eroding Arafat's control of the organisation, the Lebanese civil war had strengthened his position at the expense of his leftist opponents. George Habash's Popular Front, which had been in the vanguard of events that dragged the Palestinians into the conflict, emerged from it divided, demoralised.

As a result, the Cairo PNC meeting took several steps that would have been inconceivable when participants last gathered there in June 1974. It called explicitly for the establishment of an 'independent national state' on 'national soil'[4] thereby spelling out a goal that had hitherto been shrouded in obfuscation, that of a Palestinian mini-state in the West Bank and Gaza. It signalled the PLO's desire to participate in international peace negotiations on acceptable terms. Even more controversially, it debated the secret contacts that had existed over the previous year between Arafat associates and leftist Israelis.

The meeting's closing statement was a delicately poised victory for those PLO leaders who were keen to insert the Palestinian movement into the peace moves that seemed, in early 1977, to be gathering momentum. For Yasser Arafat, once again taking a mile where his colleagues had given a few inches, it was a cue to embark on a political course as full of promise as it was layered with difficulty: that of reaching out to the United States and its promising new President, Jimmy Carter.

Arafat had long been obsessed with America, and almost equally bewildered by it. There was nothing he wanted more than to make his views heard where it really mattered, in the country on which Israel counted for support. The question was, how?

Arafat had tried sending political messages to President Nixon's National Security Adviser, Henry Kissinger. He had even tried using the rostrum of the United Nations to appeal to American public opinion. 'What, I ask you plainly, is the crime of the people of Palestine against the American people?' he had said plaintively during his November 1974 speech to the UN General Assembly. 'Why do you fight us so?'[5]

But it was to little avail. America's deeply ingrained support for Israel translated into equally deep-seated hostility to the PLO. Fumbling efforts to break down this barrier preoccupied Arafat for much of his career and caused him no end of trouble with his Palestinian critics.

It was against this unpromising background that the newly installed Carter Administration turned its attention to the Middle East in early 1977. For Arafat, the advent of Jimmy Carter had seemed a moderately hopeful development only because it meant the exit from the scene of Kissinger, a man the PLO leader held personally responsible for many of the afflictions that had befallen him since the late 1960s, not least the crushing defeat in Jordan of Black September 1970. But Arafat certainly had no idea that Carter was planning a radical break with the Middle East policies of his predecessors, Nixon and Ford. As the PLO's laconic 'foreign minister', Farouk Kaddoumi, put it in late February when asked about American efforts to convene a peace conference, 'We believe that the United States is going through the motions, not really taking action. We do not expect anything from this operation, because it is an American manoeuvre.'[6]

Only a few days later, in the midst of the Palestine National Council's deliberations on a new political programme in Cairo, Arafat received word of an intriguing presidential statement which prompted him to think again.

On 16 March 1977, in the unlikely setting of a small town meeting in Massachusetts, Jimmy Carter set out his views on the Middle East problem. Dealing with the Palestinian issue was a key requirement for resolving the conflict, he said, going on to voice the hope of inviting all the parties to a reconvened Geneva conference towards the end of the year. 'There has to be a homeland provided for the Palestinian refugees who have suffered for many, many years,' he proclaimed.[7]

Arafat did not know what to make of Carter's apparently off-the-cuff statement, but if it truly reflected the thinking of the US President, something approaching a Copernican revolution in America's attitude to the Palestinians appeared to be under way. No senior US official, still less a president, had ever referred publicly to a Palestinian homeland before, always preferring to treat the problem purely as one of refugees to be handled within the framework of existing Middle Eastern states. Now here was Carter inviting the wrath of Israel to associate himself with an aim that seemed tantalisingly close to that of the Palestinians themselves. As Arafat remarked, 'If this is true, he has touched the core of the problem without which there can be no settlement.'[8] Sending out cautiously positive signals in response, he resolved to try once more to find an opening to Washington.

Carter had realised that he was unlikely to succeed in his ambition of engineering a comprehensive Arab–Israeli peace negotiation without involving the PLO. So, as he and Secretary of State Cyrus Vance embarked on a round of meetings with Arab and Israeli leaders in Washington and the Middle East, they gradually came to focus on the need to bring Yasser Arafat into the picture. Perhaps the PLO leader could be pressed by the Egyptian, Saudi and Syrian Governments, which were all express-ing interest in progress towards peace, to say the magic words that would open the way to direct contact between his organisation and Washington.[9] The problem, on this as on many later occasions, lay in the tough terms Kissinger had attached to a US–PLO dialogue: in particular, the requirement that the Pales-tinians accept the UN's Resolution 242 of 1967, long the subject of almost ritual denunciation by the PLO. To the Palestinians it offered nothing beyond a brief reference to 'just settlement of the refugee problem' and ignored their central demand for the right to determine their own future. It was a pill which Carter was to have the greatest difficulty in sugaring to the PLO's taste.

Arafat, nevertheless, was intrigued by the American overtures but more than a touch wary of the demand by which they were accompanied. In June he responded via Saudi Arabia's Crown Prince Fahd, explaining that the Palestinians were ready to accept Israel but needed their own state in return. Back came the reply: first signal your clear acceptance of the UN resolution, then we will be prepared to do business. It was a case of Catch-242, and rapidly degenerated into a game of semantics as the two sides groped for a form of words which would enable the Palestinians to meet America's terms without compromising their principles. Summer turned to autumn. It became clear that the exercise was doomed.

During Vance's Middle East tour in August, the Saudis sulkily admitted defeat in their mediation effort, blaming Arafat for his failure to deliver the goods. The arguments in Beirut and Damascus intensified, with the PLO leader becoming so agitated during one meeting that he broke a glass table with his fist.[10] By early September 1977, when Carter had one last stab at getting through to the PLO, Arafat was behaving like a man under siege. Carter's personal emissary, a Quaker friend of his wife's named Landrum Bolling, was treated in a series of talks in Beirut between 9 and 11 September to complaints: about contradictory messages Arafat had received from his two principal Arab intermediaries, Egypt and Saudi Arabia; about the 'blackmail' Arafat was under from other Arab states, chiefly Syria, not to accept the US terms; and about the convoluted politics of his own organisation.[11]

In this atmosphere of recrimination and paralysis, America's attempt to foster a dialogue with the PLO came to a halt. Responsibility for the failure was not all on one side. Carter had scarcely eased Palestinian suspicions when he had made what appeared to be contradictory statements, vacillated in the face of Israeli pressure and tightened the restrictions on dealing with the PLO to cover all official contacts.[12] Nor had the PLO's supposed Arab friends helped, when they relayed distorted versions of what the Americans and the Palestinians were trying to say; indeed, Carter was to make the revealing observation two years later that he had 'never met an Arab leader who in private professed the desire for an independent Palestinian state'.[13]

The ultimate problem, however, lay within the Palestinian leadership. Caught between such a host of conflicting pressures, Arafat was in no position to compromise. He, as much as any of his colleagues, feared to concede what the Palestinians saw as one of their very few bargaining cards before they had even got to the negotiating table. Like the merchant's son he was, he also clung to the mistaken idea that he could somehow haggle with the legalistic Americans to improve the terms, whereas in reality there was nothing to bargain about. It was a clash of cultures. Conscious of his weakness, he finally told Bolling that he could only move if Carter would do something equally implausible: guarantee the Palestinians a state.

The President's men concluded that the PLO had fluffed a political opportunity. 'It's too bad, because I think it would have made a big difference if we had been able to cross that bridge at that particular time,' said Vance.[14]

Arafat later called his experience of dealing with the Carter Administration 'a very bad lesson' and claimed that the US had let him down.[15] But in his more reflective moments he is prepared to admit that 'We might have lost an opportunity during the Carter days.'[17]

In spite of his disappointment Arafat continued his efforts to throw himself at the US – to an extent that prompted some of his colleagues to compare him jokingly to an importunate woman. On occasions, Arafat would tell his favoured intermediaries – the Saudis, say, whose oil wealth meant that they commanded considerable attention in Washington – that he was about to come up with a statement that would meet American conditions. But he was invariably promising more than he could deliver, and the result was frustration all round. In any case, the Americans never listened as attentively as they did in 1977 – at least, that is, not until 1988.

'We had messages coming to us from all over the world,' recalled one long-serving State Department official. 'For example, Arafat would plant a message on a visit to Indonesia and, sure enough, along would come a cable from the Indonesian Government saying: "Why don't you understand the PLO? Don't you realise that if you don't support the moderates, the moderates will collapse?" It became sort of like a ritual incantation. But Arafat's problem was that he couldn't deliver.'[17]

Little did Arafat know, as his leadership colleagues continued their deliberations through September and October 1977, that events were in the making that would reduce the whole debate to irrelevance. Within a matter of weeks, the PLO would be confronted with an event as discomforting as any it had encountered before.

Middle East politics was about to take a leap of fate. In Egypt President Anwar Sadat appeared increasingly impatient to move towards peace negotiations with or without his stalling Arab brethren. In Israel, a general election in May had brought a hardline new government to power under a man who had been the stuff of Palestinian mythology since the 1940s, the former Jewish terrorist leader, Menachem Begin.

10. ON THE DEFENSIVE

'If you put a cat in a corner, it will defend itself.' Yasser Arafat, in interview with *Time* magazine, 9 April 1979.

On 8 November 1977, Yasser Arafat was summoned Cairo, where Vice-President Hosm Mubarak relayed to him two requests from his boss, Anwar Sadat. First, Arafat was to travel to Tripoli to mediate in a dispute between Sadat and Libya's maverick leader Colonel Gadaffi. Then, he was invited to attend a session of the Egyptian parliament to bear an important speech by Sadat.

Travelling to Libya and back in a military plane laid on by the Egyptians, Arafat, who had never been invited to the People's Assembly before, wondered what Sadat could be up to. His curiosity mounted when he returned to Cairo to discover that the parliamentary session had been specially delayed to await his arrival, and that Sadat took several opportunities during his speech to shower praises on the 'dear and wonderful' PLO leader's head.[1] Even by his own mercurial standards, the Egyptian President was exuberant as he regaled the assembled deputies and dignitaries with a catalogue of his untiring efforts to achieve a Middle East settlement, but the address seemed to contain little to justify the headline billing Sadat had given it.

Then, departing from his prepared text, the President dropped his bombshell. 'I am willing to go to Geneva, nay, to the end of the world,' he proclaimed. 'In fact I know that Israel will be astounded when I say that I am ready to go to their very home, to the Knesset, to debate with them.'[2]

What seemed to be an impromptu remark left Arafat puzzled, but he found no clue to Sadat's intentions in the faces of the President's deputy or of his prime minister. Witnesses say that when Sadat had finished speaking, the PLO leader even joined in the polite applause, a happenstance that rankled with Arafat's critics within the PLO. The more Arafat thought about Sadat's words, though, the more incredulous he became. After the speech, he collared Ismail Fahmy, Sadat's Foreign Minister. 'What is the meaning of this?' he asked. 'Is Sadat saying this intentionally in my presence? Have you invited me to come to Cairo in order to hear such a thing?'[3] By now, having had time to reflect on what was said, Arafat was seething. If Sadat really did intend to go to Israel the consequences did not bear thinking about: it seemed implausible that he would raise so serious an idea purely as a rhetorical flourish. Worse, by flagging it in the PLO leader's presence, the Egyptian President had created the false impression that Arafat had approved.

In an attempt to cool things, Vice-President Mubarak took Arafat to his villa in Heliopolis, but to no avail. Within a short period, the PLO leader was off to the nearby airport. 'A long time will pass before I come again to Egypt,' he sullenly told aides as he boarded the plane to Damascus en route for Lebanon. It was a prophetic statement. Arafat would not revisit the city of his birth for six long years.[4]

Back in Beirut, Arafat rehearsed his suspicions with his colleagues. Still they could not quite believe that Sadat had meant what he said. Surely the Egyptian leader could not be seriously contemplating such a drastic step, one that would cut him loose from the rest of the Arab world overnight, scupper prospects of a comprehensive Arab–Israeli negotiation and, worst of all, signal his abandonment of the Palestinian cause in pursuit of a separate peace. Perhaps Sadat had been carried away with his own oratory, or was simply playing to the gallery of Western opinion.

The PLO leaders were clutching at straws. On 16 November 1977 Sadat headed for Damascus in a vain attempt to persuade President Assad not to oppose his planned trip to Jerusalem, and three days later the Palestinians found themselves glued to their TV sets as the Egyptian presidential Boeing landed at Tel Aviv airport and Sadat strode down the steps to shake the hands of the enemy. Watching impotently from the offices of his organisation's political department in Beirut, Arafat was furious.[5] Worse was to come the next day, when Sadat travelled to Jerusalem to deliver his historic address to Israel's parliament, the Knesset. It was bad enough for the Palestinians to witness the leader of the most powerful Arab country visiting what they regarded as their occupied capital. But when they heard Sadat's Knesset speech, their feeling of betrayal was complete. Although packed with fulsome references to the Palestinians' desire for a homeland, there was no mention of the PLO itself.

Much as Sadat attempted to reassure the Palestinians in subsequent weeks that he still had their interests at heart, they knew that a rupture had occurred. Although Arafat himself had authorised a dalliance with left-wing Israelis, nobody in the PLO would ever have dreamed of contemplating as direct an approach to the enemy as this. What Sadat had done amounted, in Palestinian eyes, to surrender, and one that risked casting the PLO adrift. No longer could Arafat rely on an Egyptian safety net in his delicate balancing act between the Arab regimes. No longer, with the Arab world rapidly polarising into mutually hostile factions, could there be any pretence of solidarity in defence of the Palestinian cause. From now on, the PLO was on its own, or at best thrown on the not-so-tender mercies of the one frontline state with which it still (just) maintained a working relationship: Syria.

Sadat's move left Arafat in a quandary. To mount, as many of his closest colleagues now demanded, a 'frontal and sustained attack' against the Egyptian leader and any states that supported him would be to risk leaving the PLO dangerously isolated, especially since the peace move enjoyed full American support.

Yet opinion in the movement was so strong that he had no choice but to comply. Three days after Sadat had stood in the Knesset, Arafat was in Damascus issuing a joint call with President Assad for the 'treasonous' Egyptian leader's overthrow. Then, on 2 December, he led a high-powered PLO delegation to a hastily convened summit meeting of leaders hostile to Sadat in the Libyan capital, Tripoli.

By all accounts, it was a stormy affair. With the Palestinians squabbling publicly among themselves and the other leaders at each other's throats, it was only with the greatest difficulty that a common front was patched together to present to the rest of the Arab world.[7] Full of sound and fury, the meeting signified typically little. It certainly did not prevent Arafat from maintaining secret channels of communication to Sadat throughout the ensuing Arab boycott of Egypt. But the hardening of attitudes reflected in the formation of the so-called 'Steadfastness and Confrontation Front' by Syria, Algeria, Libya and South Yemen did foreclose any possibility that the Palestinians might give Sadat's initiative a chance. Angered by the Tripoli meeting's accusations of 'high treason', Sadat severed all relations with the participants. Not surprisingly, when Sadat tried to convene a conference of Israeli, Egyptian and Palestinian officials in December at the Mena House Hotel next to the Pyramids, the PLO refused to attend. It was a fateful decision, for it shut the organisation out of any involvement in Sadat's peacemaking. Had Arafat agreed to send someone to Cairo, he might at least have scored some propaganda points by provoking an Israeli walkout. As it was, the Palestinian flag was pulled down outside the hotel before the talks even began.

On 15 December 1977 the US President who had seemed so full of promise earlier in the year formally placed the Palestinians out in the cold, declaring that 'by its completely negative attitude, the PLO has excluded itself from any immediate prospect of participating in the peace negotiations'. Or, as his National Security Adviser Zbigniew Brezinski put it in an oft-quoted interview with *Paris Match*, 'Bye Bye PLO'.[8]

The valediction infuriated Arafat. Like so many others pronounced on his movement over the years, it proved to be wide of the mark, but as the implications of Sadat's move sank in over the next few months, there was no mistaking the steady build-up of pressure on the PLO. The loss of Egypt as an ally was devastating, which, in addition to removing Sadat once and for all from the Arab–Israeli military equation, left the Palestinians perilously exposed in their 'last refuge' of Lebanon.

After the civil war Of 1975–6, the PLO had lost no time in re-establishing roots in its Lebanese stronghold in the south of the country. Its guerrillas also maintained a considerable presence in the capital and the central Chouf Mountains. Taking advantage of an influx of heavy arms seized from the Lebanese army during the conflict, Arafat had stepped up efforts to reshape his troops into something approximating a regular defensive army. Specialist divisions were set up and a rank structure established. Gradually, the PLO patched together a crude armoury, including sixty obsolete Soviet-built T-34 tanks and an array of firepower from howitzers to anti-aircraft guns and rocket launchers.[9]

The PLO bureaucracy and its increasingly important economic arm, Samed, were also still growing, to a point where Arafat found running them a full-time job in itself. From a body founded by Fatah in Jordan eight years earlier to provide work for the families of guerrillas killed in action, Samed had ballooned into one of Lebanon's major industrial employers. In a network of 36 factories along the Lebanese coast and in the capital, it produced a range of goods from shoes and clothes to furniture and processed food. Ultimate control, in this as in other departments, still rested with Arafat – by now effectively chairman, managing director, treasurer, company secretary and personnel manager of PLO Inc., a complex multinational organisation in which no staff appointment would take place outside his purview.

Nowhere was his dominance more apparent than in his vicelike grip on PLO finances. Arafat personally oversaw the allocation of money from the budget of the Palestine National Fund, the PLO 'finance ministry', and from his own Fatah treasure chest, a juggling act that required, on occasion, some fairly creative accounting since the PNF was regularly in deficit and depended on annual transfers from Arafat's Fatah fund to make up the shortfall. In his control of the purse strings Arafat showed much of the canniness of the small trader but he also wasted a great deal of money in the dispensation of patronage: to corrupt individuals inside and outside the PLO to organisations of dubious value and to impoverished Third World states whose claim to PLO assistance was flimsily based on a single UN vote. Frugal in his personal habits, Arafat liked nevertheless to be seen dispensing largesse in the style of a traditional Arab potentate.

Arafat's management of PLO money had one other almost incalculable advantage as far as his own leadership of the Palestinian national movement is concerned. It put him closely in touch with a class of multimillionaire Palestinian merchants, traders and builders who became one of the pillars on which his authority rested. Arafat took to referring to these mega-rich Palestinians, such as Hassib Sabbagh, the Athens-based construction magnate, as 'my compradours'. It was both a term of endearment and a recognition that, in his efforts to reach out to the broadest cross-section of the Palestinian community and to sometimes antagonistic Arab regimes, he needed the services of well-heeled and obliging go-betweens.

By the late 1970s, the organisation's elaborate Lebanese infrastructure had created a curious and seductive air of permanence, and keeping it ticking over had come to seem almost an end in itself. But as events were to show, the PLO's presence in Lebanon still rested on the shakiest of foundations. In the first place, Arafat could not ignore a military force that was considerably more powerful than his own: the Syrian army, which would not hesitate to rein in the Palestinians in the event of trouble. Nor had the Lebanese exactly subsided into a tranquil state. Following the assassination of Kamal Jumblatt the previous year, the Palestinians' Lebanese allies were leaderless and divided. Their old foes in the Maronite Christian community were more intent than ever on pursuing their struggle against a Palestinian movement that looked as though it was in Lebanon to stay.

Most disturbing of all were the threatening gestures emanating from Israel under Begin's leadership. The Likud-led government was unlike anything that had gone before, both in its determination to hang on to the occupied Arab territories of the West Bank and Gaza and in its opposition to a Palestinian state. As to the PLO, Begin's election platform had been unequivocal: it was 'no national liberation organisation but an organisation of assassins' which Israel would 'strive to eliminate',[10]

No longer having to worry about an Egyptian military threat, the Israelis could now pay much closer attention to Palestinian activities beyond their northern frontier and provide considerable assistance to the Lebanese Maronite Christians. It was only a matter of time before the PLO leadership, looking for a way of asserting itself in the face of Sadat's new 'conspiracy', would provide Israel with an opportunity to strike directly.

In the small hours of 11 March 1978, a group of eleven Fatah commandos, led by a young woman, landed on a beach some fifteen miles south of the Israeli port of Haifa and on the main coastal highway to Tel Aviv hijacked a bus with 63 passengers aboard. Careering through police roadblocks with Israeli security forces in pursuit, the bus ended up in a bloody shoot-out in a northern suburb of Tel Aviv. By the time the firing stopped, 34 Israelis and 9 guerrillas were dead and a total of 84 were wounded.

The response was not long delayed. During the night of 14 March, after an artillery bombardment, an Israeli armoured force eventually comprising up to 28,000 men rolled across the border and launched a frontal attack against PLO bases in southern Lebanon. As other units landed on the coast and the Israeli airforce bombed Palestinian camps as far north as Beirut itself, Israeli spokesmen explained that their aim was to 'liquidate terrorist bases along the border' and to establish a so-called 'security belt' to prevent Palestinian infiltration. By the time the Israelis ordered a ceasefire one week later, at least 200 PLO fighters and 500 Palestinian and Lebanese civilians had been killed for the loss of 20-odd Israeli soldiers; scores of Lebanese villages had been destroyed; and hundreds of thousands of refugees had started pouring northwards to the capital. A new phase in Lebanon's steady disintegration was underway.[11]

For Yasser Arafat, despite his confident declarations about the bravery with which PLO fighters had resisted, this first Israeli invasion of Lebanon served to underline how isolated the Palestinians were. Just as during the Israeli attack on Karameh almost exactly a decade earlier, his forces had been far outnumbered and outgunned, but this time no help was forthcoming from a friendly Arab army and no plaudits were heard for Palestinian bravery against the odds. The Syrians, although the dominant force in Lebanon, kept well out of the way. Sadat, now preoccupied with the next move towards peace with Israel, limited his response to an even-handed condemnation both of the invasion and of the guerrilla raid that had precipitated it. It was only when the UN Security Council called on 19 March for an immediate Israeli withdrawal and the establishment of an international peacekeeping force that serious pressure began to build for an end to the fighting. That was a sign of the times.

Israel's newly aggressive stance was having one mildly positive side effect in Arafat's eyes: in combination with the continuing occupation of territories captured in 1967, it was helping to turn a significant portion of world opinion against the Jewish state.

Such observations were small consolation to Arafat, however, as he contemplated his immediate prospects. In effect, the PLO had been suddenly pitched into a long battle for its existence in Lebanon against a foe more formidable than any it had faced before. Realising the implacable nature of the Israeli threat, Arafat looked for protection. He found it, of all places, in the hastily despatched 'blue berets' of the UN peacekeeping force, known as UNIFIL (United Nations Interim Force in Lebanon). On 28 March in its west Beirut offices, Arafat met UNIFIL commander Emmanuel Erskine, and informed him that the PLO would agree to halt hostilities in the area adjoining the border while Israeli forces withdrew.

This was a major departure. For the first time, Arafat was committing himself to a ceasefire to which Israel was also a party. In the process, while swearing blind that the PLO would resist any attempt to limit its freedom of action in southern Lebanon, he was also casting himself in an unfamiliar role: that of Palestinian policeman with a mandate to rein in the unruly forces under his command. Thus in April 1978, when a group of dissident Fatah officers challenged his decision to accept the ceasefire, he moved with unusual decisiveness, using force to crush the mutiny. On 19 April, 123 of those involved were arrested. Ninety of them were subsequently kicked out of Lebanon, and two of the main participants were shifted to pen-pushing jobs in Beirut.[12] It was a marked contrast to the normal indiscipline of PLO forces; clearly, when he wanted to in those days, Arafat could assert control.

As Arafat saw it, a measure of continuing disaffection in the ranks was a small price to pay for the international prestige he could reap from co-operating with UNIFIL.

But Arafat's manoeuvrings could not disguise the fact that the PLO had by mid-1978 become locked into a defensive posture on all fronts. In Lebanon, its ability to conduct cross-border raids was severely constrained, for although the Israelis had gradually pulled their forces back, they retained control of a strip of territory along the frontier and installed a friendly local militia there to keep up the fight against the Palestinians. Never terribly convincing, the 'armed struggle' now seemed more aimless than ever.

Arafat fared no better in his relations with Arab regimes. Sadat had failed to achieve the psychological breakthrough he had hoped for in Israel but was pressing on regardless with efforts to make peace. The Arab world, still reeling from the shock of the Egyptian President's trip to Jerusalem, was in deepening disarray. As ever, within the Palestinian movement itself, the PLO leader was confronted with smouldering, sometimes violent disputes. A stream of conciliatory statements by Arafat to Western newspapers concerning coexistence between a Palestinian state and Israel continued to provoke great unhappiness within the rank and file. From outside the mainstream, an assassination campaign waged with Iraqi support by the breakaway terrorist group of Sabri al-Banna (Abu Nidal) claimed the lives of several PLO diplomats, including the organisation's representatives in London and Paris, Said Hammami and Ezzeldin Kalak, two men who had worked hard to transmit Arafat's overtures to the West.

Against this background, Arafat made one last effort to convince President Sadat of the error of his ways. In June 1978 he wrote to Sadat pleading with him not to rush into a separate peace with Israel. 'Your position as leader is still strong,' he wrote. 'Don't forget Jerusalem. Don't forget our people who have sacrificed their lives. You can insist on stronger guarantees.'[13]

That letter was Arafat's last direct communication with the Egyptian leader. Three months later, Sadat ensconced himself with Jimmy Carter and Menachem Begin at the US President's Maryland retreat of Camp David. They emerged on 17 September, after twelve days of talks, with a set of agreements committing Egypt and Israel to negotiating a peace treaty and calling for the establishment of what was called a 'self-governing authority' to administer Palestinian affairs in the Israeli-occupied West Bank and Gaza Strip. It was the last straw. The Palestinians had no doubt as to what the plan for self-rule really meant: a perpetuation of Israeli sovereignty in the territories where the PLO was demanding a state of its own. Arafat himself had dismissed the proposal when it was put forward by Begin as 'less than a Bantustan'.[14]

Burying their differences, the faction leaders united in denunci- ation of the Camp David Accords and set out to scupper them by fair means or foul. Arafat, momentarily forgetting his efforts to climb into bed with the United States, began speaking vaguely about striking at American interests in the Middle East.

In the wider Arab world, too, the Egyptian–Israeli accords caused at least a temporary closing of ranks which resulted, on 2 November, in a summit meeting hosted by Iraq. The Baghdad conference, which urged Sadat anew not to make formal peace with Israel while agreeing to punish him with economic and other sanctions if he did, provided Arafat with some reassurance. It showed that no other Arab leader – not even King Hussein of Jordan, who was under heavy pressure from the US to go along with Sadat – was likely to climb aboard the Camp David bandwagon. And it gave the PLO a hefty financial windfall in the form of a pledge from the wealthy Gulf states of 250 million US dollars a year for the next ten years.[15]

In reality, however, such decisions did little to fill the gaping hole Sadat had left in Arab ranks. Refusing even to hear the summit's appeal, the Egyptian President went ahead and signed his peace treaty with Israel in March 1979. The rupture was final.

As if he did not already have enough to worry about, the PLO leader shortly received a shattering personal blow. On 22 January 1979 in Beirut, a remote-controlled bomb detonated by an Israeli woman agent killed the man he regarded as his 'favourite son': Ali Hassan Salameh. Arafat heard the news in Damascus, where a stormy session of the Palestine National Council had just broken up after heavy-handed Syrian and Iraqi efforts to bring the PLO under their control.[16] When he joined the pallbearers a few days later at an emotional funeral attended by tens of thousands of Palestinians, Arafat's spirits were low.

Arafat would not, however, stay down for long. As Salameh's coffin was laid to rest, events far away were already moving rapidly to a climax that would give the PLO leader an unexpected lift.

On the evening Of 31 January 1979 Arafat stood on the balcony of his residence in west Beirut and triumphantly fired his Beretta pistol in the air. It was the first time anyone close to him could remember Arafat using his personal weapon, and he fired not in anger but as part of a crackling chorus of jubilation all over the

Muslim side of the city. That day, an elderly Iranian clergyman named Ruhollah Khomeini had set foot on his country's soil after an exile of fourteen years, to be greeted in Tehran by tumultuous and triumphant demonstrations. The Iranian revolution had prevailed.

The fall of Shah Mohammed Reza Pahlavi, King of Kings, and the rise of Ayatollah Khomeini's Islamic Republic sent shock waves through Western and Arab capitals alike. But to the PLO leadership, the installation of a militant new government in Tehran seemed to offer fresh hope: a bastion of Western influence and friend of Israel had been toppled by a leader who identified himself strongly with the Palestinian cause. More to the point, Khomeini's movement had already developed close ties with the PLO.

The Palestinians' relationship with Iran's Islamic revolutionaries dated back to the mid-1970s, when a close aide to Fatah intelligence chief Salah Khalaf had befriended an Iranian exile, Mohammed Salah al-Husseini, who had joined the Palestinian movement in Lebanon. Through Husseini, the Fatah official had been introduced to Ayatollah Khomeini, living at the time in the Iraqi city of Najaf, and a regular traffic of messages between the Iranian holy man and the PLO leadership began. In time, through these contacts and through his acquaintance with the Lebanese Shi'ite leader Musa Sadr, Arafat got to know many of the future leaders of the Islamic Republic.[17]

His motives went well beyond the Palestinians' customary reasons for maintaining good relations with other liberation movements. As a Fatah intelligence official explained, 'The Shah was an imperial embodiment of everything we loathed, in his close relationship with Israel, in his suppression of democracy and the hatred he inspired among his people, and in his hostility to Arab nationalism.'[18] By contrast, the Ayatollah's heady brew of politics and religion intrigued the Palestinians, who agreed to provide Khomeini supporters with military training in their camps in southern Lebanon and Syria. Under the auspices of Khalil al-Wazir, hundreds of Iranian militants were schooled in terrorism from 1976, devoting special attention to techniques the PLO had developed for maintaining links between the territories under Israeli occupation and the leadership outside.

By late 1978, the Iranians and the Palestinians were still on a political honeymoon in which both sides temporarily forgot the deep cultural and ideological chasm that divided them. When Khomeini was expelled from Iraq in the autumn of that year, Arafat had even offered him a refuge in southern Lebanon, although the Ayatollah chose in the event to settle in Paris, where he had ready access to Western media. The relationship was at its height when the Ayatollah returned in triumph to Tehran. Arafat, in a moment of revenge on the Carter Administration official who had tried to write him off little more than a year earlier, crowed, 'Bye Bye USA.'[19]

'Arafat considered Khomeini's victory a victory for the Palestinian revolution – not because it was religious but simply because a revolution that was pro-Palestinian had come to power,' recalled one of those involved in building the alliance.[20] As euphoria swept the Palestinian refugee camps in Lebanon, posters appeared in the streets of Beirut bearing a large portrait of Ayatollah Khomeini and the slogan: TODAY IRAN! TOMORROW PALESTINE![21] Nor did Iran's new leaders disappoint Arafat during their early days in power, rewarding the PLO for its support by allowing it to set up its first Tehran headquarters in the former Prime Minister's office. On 17 February 1979, Arafat became the first foreign leader to visit the Iranian capital after the revolution. At a Tehran press conference a euphoric Arafat proclaimed, 'I told His Eminence Ayatollah Khomeini that I really saw the walls of Jerusalem when I heard about the Iranian revolution.'[22]

The alliance with Iran showed Arafat at his most mercurial, involving him as it did in an increasingly complex series of political contortions as he tried to balance his new-found friendship with the anti-Western mullahs in Tehran with a continuing effort to secure Western recognition. Once again, the PLO leader was trying to have it several ways. To Iranian sensibilities, Arafat sought to present himself as a militant pursuing an Islamic *jihad*, or holy war, against Israel. But in Western capitals, where he was now involved in a fresh diplomatic offensive to bolster his political standing, he stressed his desire for peace in an independent Palestinian state. In the Middle East, he used his alliance with Iran to threaten any Arab leader who might still be hankering after a political settlement excluding the PLO.

But in truth the relationship with the mullahs could not last. Less than a year after the Iranian revolution, the contradictions began to tell and the alliance with Ayatollah Khomeini, on which the PLO leader had pinned his hopes, started to come unstuck. Indeed the Palestinian resistance and the Iranian revolution had seemed strange bedfellows from the outset – an avowedly secular movement led by conservatively oriented Sunni Muslims in cahoots with a group of radical Shi'ite clerics. The differences between them over strategy were just as fundamental: while Arafat indicated he was striving as a first step for the relatively modest goal of a mini-state in Palestine, Khomeini imagined that his revolution would engulf the region. Predictably it was the PLO chairman's continuing efforts to ingratiate himself with the US – the 'Great Satan' in Iranian parlance – that brought tensions between them to a head.

In early November 1979, Arafat received a most unusual message. It came from US Secretary of State Cyrus Vance, and its import could be summed up in one word: Help! A few days before, amid massive anti-American demonstrations, a group of revolutionary Iranian youths had seized the US embassy in Tehran and taken 52 diplomats and other staff hostage.

Dreaming of the publicity that would greet a PLO-mediated solution and making promises he was not sure he could fulfil, Arafat sent two of his senior aides, his special envoy Hani al-Hassan and military commander Saad Sayel, to try to persuade the Iranians to hand the American diplomats over. They were disappointed. When they met Khomeini's powerful henchman, Ali Akbar Hashemi-Rafsanjani, they were greeted with angry incomprehension.

'The Iranians were infuriated by this interference in their internal affairs,' recalls one of those involved in the initiative. 'They said "this is a dirty game being played by the Great Satan, and you are supposed to be angels; you have no business with this." They completely refused to give the Palestinians a mediating role. They simply couldn't understand why we wanted to win over the US Administration. In fact they thought it was a privilege to be confronting the US.'[23]

In the end, Arafat's mediation effort did little to advance his cause and a certain amount to retard it, since he was later accused by critics within his own organisation of having provided detailed intelligence on the Iranian armed forces to the CIA. Largely unsung in the United States, his effort also took a terrible toll on the PLO's relations with its new-found Iranian allies. Khomeini never forgave the Palestinian leader for seeking to meddle in what he regarded as Iran's heroic confrontation with the Great Satan. From that point on, he took to referring to Arafat contemptuously as 'Al Qazam' – The Dwarf.[24]

Nor did the other benefits from the relationship come up to the PLO's expectations. In the early, honeymoon days of the revolution, the Iranians had given the Palestinians extravagant promises of practical assistance in Lebanon, offering to send thousands of volunteers to help them combat Israel and even to provide them with surface-to-surface missiles to deter another Israeli invasion.[25] Few of the fighters arrived, and the missiles simply did not materialise. The alliance which Arafat had briefly thought would rescue his movement from isolation and exposure turned out to be built on sand. As 1980 progressed, fear of Ayatollah Khomeini was causing renewed disarray in Arab ranks. A new war was looming – this time not against Israel but against a dangerous new adversary to the east.

On 22 September 1980, thousands of Iraqi troops poured across the Iranian border and Iraqi aircraft bombed targets deep inside Iranian territory. The invasion followed months of mounting tensions between the two countries. Arafat knew that it also spelled great danger for the PLO. With two allies (for Iran could still just about be counted as such) now at war and resisting all mediation efforts including his own, he was once again going to have to make a choice, one made no easier by the fact that another state on which the Palestinians depended, Syria, had sided with Iran against Iraq.

Once again the Palestinians risked being caught in a tightening squeeze between squabbling Arabs on the one hand and an increasingly hardline Israel on the other, the latter sparing no effort to suppress pro-PLO sentiment in the occupied territories.

Predictably, as had been the case in 1975 and again in 1978, it was in the PLO's base in Lebanon that its problems came home to roost. The initial signs of trouble involved Syria rather than the PLO. In late April 1981, tension in Lebanon rose sharply when Israel shot down two Syrian helicopters and the Syrians responded by stationing several batteries of SAM-6 anti-aircraft missiles in the country's eastern Bekaa Valley. When Israel threatened to eliminate them by force, a military showdown looked likely. Ronald Reagan, newly installed in the White House, despatched veteran troubleshooter Philip Habib to defuse the crisis.

Well aware of the threat a new flare-up in Lebanon would pose to the PLO, Arafat spent much of May that year jetting around the Gulf and North Africa seeking to energise his distracted Arab brethren. The resistance had been especially exposed to Israeli fire since the previous year, when Syria – wary of becoming involved in a dust-up in Lebanon – had suddenly withdrawn its forces from the coastal areas south of Beirut where Palestinians were concentrated. As Israel compensated for the restraint it was showing over the Syrian missiles by stepping up its attacks on Palestinian positions, the urge grew within the PLO to respond in kind. On 10 July 1981, when the Israeli air force conducted another of its periodic pre-emptive raids in southern Lebanon, the urge became irresistible. The PLO retaliated by shelling a northern Israeli settlement.

The ensuing two-week confrontation became known as the 'War of the Katyushas', after the Soviet-manufactured rockets the PLO had installed in its Lebanese bases. The Palestinians rained rockets and artillery shells down on the towns and villages of Galilee, sending thousands of Israelis fleeing southwards to safety. Israel's air force bombed the Fakhani district of west Beirut where the PLO had its headquarters, leaving 300 dead and 700 wounded. Philip Habib urgently turned his attention to trying to engineer a ceasefire.

It was not something they had exactly planned in advance, but Arafat and his colleagues watched the unfolding escalation from their Beirut operations room in a state of some excitement. To be sure, their forces were taking heavy casualties as a result of the Israeli pounding, but more important in their eyes was the impact their own rocket bombardment was having in Israel itself. Momentarily, they seemed to have put the Jewish state under more pressure than in all the long years of their ineffectual 'armed struggle'. Most significant of all, a senior US emissary was now struggling – through intermediaries, since he was barred from talking directly to Arafat's people – to arrange what would in effect be a ceasefire between Israel and its arch-enemy, the PLO.

The ceasefire demand, passed to Arafat by the UNIFIL commander, General William Callaghan, prompted a spirited debate among the assembled PLO leaders. Some favoured immediate acceptance with a view to regrouping and opening fire again later; others, including Arafat, argued for a slight delay to put further pressure on Israel, then firm compliance.[25] The latter view won the day, and on 24 July Philip Habib announced in Jerusalem that 'as of 1330 local time, all hostile military actions between Lebanese and Israeli territories in either direction will cease.'[26]

In accepting the ceasefire, Arafat had performed a conjuring trick at which he had become quite adept over the years, turning the Palestinians' limited military resources to political advantage. But the agreement also changed the ground rules of the conflict between Israel and the Palestinians, for what Habib had hammered out was a barely disguised understanding between the PLO and a government that had vowed never to negotiate with it. It was an oblique and reluctant form of recognition, and a concession that the Israelis from that point on were determined to annul. 'There is a dialogue through this confrontation. What does this mean?' asked Arafat mischievously in an American TV interview two days after the agreement was concluded.[27]

For Arafat, who knew as well as anyone that the ceasefire was a fragile affair, the unwritten agreement represented both a threat and a potential opportunity. Anxious to preserve the PLO's base in Lebanon at all costs and to project the image of a leader who could honour his side of a bargain, he again kept his troops on a tight rein to prevent ceasefire violations. At the same time, he told himself, the truce might provide the PLO with a useful political opening, either as a prelude to broader negotiations or as a stepping stone towards the cherished goal of American recognition. It was time for a fresh round of diplomatic activity.

That summer, Arafat played a prominent, though unpublicised, role in drafting an eight-point peace plan announced by Crown

Prince Fahd of Saudi Arabia. Calling for the establishment of an independent Palestinian state and affirming that 'all states in the region should be able to live in peace',[28] the plan once again split the PLO leadership and provoked arguments among the Arab states. It was shelved when a hostile President Assad of Syria, more suspicious than ever of Arafat's manoeuvrings and resentful at not having been consulted, boycotted an Arab summit meeting at Fez in November 1981. What only a handful of people knew, as the Arab bickering continued, was that Arafat was also engaged in another, altogether more discreet, diplomatic exercise.

In Beirut on 4 August 1981, Arafat met a young American of his acquaintance named John Edwin Mroz, and asked him to pass a message to the Reagan Administration. It contained a seven-point peace proposal similar to the Fahd plan and suggested talks on 'a possible framework for a US–PLO agreement'.[29] Mroz, a genial 32-year-old, had got to know the PLO leader while researching a book on Middle Eastern security issues. He had excellent connections in the US Administration, and in the influential Jewish community; and at the State Department, where he had already been in touch with officials before travelling to Beirut, he found he was pushing a half-open door. After consultations involving both President Reagan and his Secretary of State, Alexander Haig, Mroz was authorised to pursue discussions with the PLO chairman. The goal: to meet America's terms for a dialogue by recognising Israel's right to exist and renouncing terror.[30]

Over the next nine months, Mroz spent no fewer than 400 hours in 50 separate meetings with Arafat. They met in a bewildering variety of locations, including once in a hospital ward where Arafat had just had an operation for the removal of kidney stones. They discussed the whole panoply of Arab politics and the pressures on the PLO. They exchanged texts phrased in obscure diplomatic jargon in search of a form of words acceptable to Washington for the initiation of a formal dialogue. And the Reagan Administration, using the laborious machinery of the Saudi Government as a 'back channel' to confirm the messages it was hearing through Mroz, made a number of gestures to reassure Arafat that it was acting in good faith. On one occasion, the CIA, which was in regular touch with Mroz, may well have saved

Arafat's life by tipping him off about a Syrian plot to ambush his motorcade.

The problem, as ever, lay in the words Arafat was being asked to pronounce in order to qualify for a dialogue. Just as in 1977, he hesitated to make the concession of recognising Israel. In any case, he was unsure what to make of the renewed American approach. 'He had his moments when he took it very seriously, and he had his moments when it was just another trial balloon,' said Mroz. 'You could really see the way the organisation was being buffeted by external Arab forces. He would constantly tell me: yes, but when the time is right.'[31]

It was the old, familiar balancing act, only on this occasion the forces the PLO leader was balancing looked more menacing than ever. Embarrassingly dependent on Damascus, he was in no position to make peace moves of which the Syrian President disapproved. And if he needed any reminder of the dangers of going it alone in negotiations he had only to look to Cairo where, in October 1981, President Anwar Sadat had been assassinated by Islamic extremists in retribution for his peace treaty with Israel. 'What am I to do, end up like Sadat?' became Arafat's regular refrain when pressed to make concessions.[32]

Most disturbing of all was the atmosphere in Israel, where the hardliner Ariel Sharon was now Defence Minister and making intensive new efforts to suppress Palestinian nationalism in the occupied West Bank and Gaza. Unmistakably, the drums of war were beating. By May 1982, when John Mroz returned to Beirut for one last try, Arafat was still interested in pursuing the dialogue but his attention frequently wandered to the bellicose noises from the south. 'Let them come to Beirut if they want to fight us. We are ready,' he proclaimed to the young American.[33] But the bravado was wafer-thin.

Arafat and Mroz fixed a date for another meeting in mid-June, at which the PLO leader promised he would give his response. But for reasons that remain unclear, Mroz was ordered by Alexander Haig not to return to Beirut. Within less than a month, the Israeli invasion of Lebanon had begun. Not the smallest cause of Arafat's subsequent disappoinment was the feeling that he had been the victim of an elaborate American double-cross.[34]

Part Three

11. INVASION

'Lebanon is easy to eat, but almost impossible to digest.' Bashir
Gemayel, ABC News interview, 27 June 1982.

Yasser Arafat was surprisingly calm. Like a man who has long
since prepared himself for the worst, he quietly sifted the dramatic
news flooding in to his luxury suite in the imposing guest palace
in Riyadh, the desert capital of Saudi Arabia. As he riffled through
the telex traffic that included secret PLO communications and
news agency flashes, his mind was quickly weighing up the latest
drama to befall the Palestinians. After a moment's contemplation,
he turned to his aides and declared, 'This is not a limited war as
the Israelis say, but the all-out war I have been predicting for some
time.'[1]

The date was 6 June 1982. That very morning, Israel had
launched a massive offensive across its northern boundary into
Lebanon. As Arafat studied the latest news from the battlefield,
Israeli troops were driving north in a *blitzkrieg* that would bring
them in a very short time within sight of Beirut itself. He made an
instant decision. He would go straight back to Beirut, cutting short
his participation in a Gulf war mediating mission – a mission that
had brought him, improbably, to the Saudi capital, just as the
winds of Israel's advanced war preparations were gusting northwards towards his Beirut headquarters.

Racing to get home before the Israelis thrust towards the main
road connecting the Lebanese capital with Damascus, thus
endangering his one relatively secure route into Beirut, Arafat did
not contemplate for one second breaking his cardinal rule: he
would not fly direct into Beirut Airport. The risk of an Israeli
interception over Lebanon's unguarded skies was simply too great.
He would, as he normally did, fly to Damascus and then travel the
rest of the way by car through the mountains to Beirut.

Arafat left Riyadh at 5 p.m. on 6 June for the 850-mile flight
north to Damascus. As he boarded his Gulfstream jet, supplied
courtesy of the Saudis, he knew he was a prime target of the Israeli
invasion but he could not have realised then that Israel would go

as far as it did in its efforts to eliminate both him and the top leadership of the PLO.

As his convoy careered along the Beirut–Damascus highway, a road he had traversed hundreds of times before, but rarely with such urgency, Arafat was briefed on the latest developments. The news was bad. PLO resistance in the south had crumbled and Israel's advance towards Beirut showed no sign of slowing. On the contrary, all the indications even at that early stage were that the Israelis were determined to push much further north than they had ever come before. For Arafat, the news signalled the beginning of the most testing phase of his thirteen-year leadership of the guerrilla organisation. It was also a time when he would come face to face, in a battle of nerves and bombs, with the PLO's nemesis.

General Ariel Sharon, the bellicose Israeli Defence Minister had by the summer of 1982 effectively taken command of Israel's foreign policy. Begin proved a willing accomplice until he realised the costs, but by then it was too late. The United States, in the person of General Alexander Haig, would also be duped in its fumbling efforts to manage a crisis to which it had made no small contribution in the first place. When General Sharon requested an appointment with Alexander Haig in the second half of May 1982, the Secretary of State's professional advisers shuddered. They knew only too well what was on Sharon's mind. They understood much better than their volatile boss the dangers of what was being proposed.

In edgy discussions with Haig since his appointment as Defence Minister in the second Begin government, in July 1981, Sharon had made no secret of his ambitions. His impossibly grand design envisaged a quiescent and collaborative population in the occupied territories, a Lebanon totally liberated of the PLO and, ultimately, the fulfilment of an oft-stated dream: that Jordan should become Palestine, Jordan would be the repository of Palestinian aspirations and the Palestinian people, thus relieving pressure on an Israel whose territorial ambitions now stretched well beyond its pre-1967 war frontiers. He did not try to hide his obsessive desire that the US 'understand' the need for what was described repeatedly as a 'limited operation' against the PLO to relieve the pressure on Israel's northern settlements; never mind that the pressure had already been considerably lessened by the US-brokered ceasefire agreement of the previous year.

Even in his early talks with Haig, Sharon was looking beyond the PLO's ouster to a crucial US role in the remaking of Lebanon and indeed of a big slice of the Middle East. In a two-and-a-half-hour discussion on 25 May in Haig's austere suite of offices on the seventh floor of the State Department, Sharon asked, in effect, for the 'green light' to smash the PLO, In the words of one of Haig's advisers, Sharon received a 'qualified red light',[2] but not before there had been a lively discussion about what might constitute a pretext for an Israeli invasion. 'How many Jews,' Sharon had asked acidly, 'have to be killed for it to be clear provocation? One Jew? Two Jews? Five? Six? . . . To us it's obvious.' Haig, whether by design or through an oversight, simply failed to spell out US objections to Sharon's proposals.

The subtleties of Haig's 'qualified red light' hardly matched either the circumstances in Israel at the time or the personalities in power. Haig's own appreciation of Middle East complexities was rated by State Department colleagues as weak and, perhaps even more fatally, they believed his own presidential ambitions conflicted with his role as Secretary of State. 'I respected the man,' concluded Nicholas Veliotes, Assistant Secretary of State responsible for Middle East affairs, 'but I believe that his presidential ambitions ran away with him and literally destroyed his judgement.'[3]

The Israelis apparently came away from the meeting believing that the Secretary of State had accepted their arguments for action. Haig's limp warnings against Israel becoming embroiled in something that was beyond its ability to control, allied with advice that if action was taken it should be swift, was music to the ears of Sharon and his colleagues. General Avraham Tamir, who served as Israel's National Security Adviser, says that Sharon was satisfied that Haig 'understood' his arguments for military action in Lebanon, and this is what he reported to the cabinet in Jerusalem.[4]

Throughout the early months of 1982, Arafat himself was acutely aware of the dangers of an impending storm from the south. At meeting after meeting in his headquarters in west Beirut, he talked of a planned Israeli attack that would link up with the

Christian Lebanese Forces militia in the north in an 'accordion' movement. His men would be trapped in the middle of this pincer exercise. Repeatedly, he warned colleagues,'Sharon is planning to come all the way to Beirut.'[5]

Arafat's own mood during this period swung wildly between unwarranted bravado and jittery concern. Brian Urquhart, the veteran UN official who got to know him well in the Lebanon years, recalls a strange conversation in Beirut in February 1982, in which he was asked to convey messages both to the Americans and to Begin. In his message to the latter there was more than a hint of pleading. 'Tell Begin,' Arafat had said, 'that I don't like war any more than you do. You have to understand that when I propose a Palestinian entity in the West Bank and Gaza Strip it may not seem much to you, but it's tremendously important on our side, because it's a great concession.'[6] Arafat also had a message of a curiously personal nature for Begin. 'I just want Mr Begin to know that I have learned so much from him. I have followed his historical career very closely, and he has taught me many things.'[7] He concluded by asking Urquhart to point out that his successors would not be so accommodating. There would be much less chance of a peace settlement if he were to be removed from the scene. Begin's response to this bizarre communication on the eve of battle was a bemused: 'Oh, really.'[8]

As the long hot summer approached in the eastern Mediterranean, the Palestinians, like so many rabbits frozen into immobility by a car's headlights, were slow to respond to multiplying signals that the Israelis were indeed mobilising for war. Even given the massive differences in firepower between the two sides, Palestinian preparations were puny. Yezid Sayigh, the Palestinian military historian, said that while Arafat himself showed an 'impressive degree of foresight' – he ordered the stockpiling of food and ammunition in Beirut and insisted that additional fortifications be dug – local commanders, especially those in the south, let him down. 'It wasn't enough for him to go and visit them, and brief them. The implementation needed to be overseen,' says Sayigh.[9]

Not for the first time, Arafat found himself in a minority in warning about the dangers of apocalypse. His alarums were supported by his trusted lieutenant, Khalil al-Wazir, and to a lesser degree by Brigadier Saad Sayel, the military commander of the PLO forces, but other members of the leadership took the threat less seriously. After all, wasn't there an American-sponsored ceasefire agreement in place? And even if the Israelis did invade Lebanon, as they had in the so-called Litani operation of 1978, would they dare to trespass so far north that it would bring them into collision with Syrian forces who would almost certainly be obliged to engage them?

By the end of May 1982, Arafat's military advisers were convinced that an Israeli thrust into Lebanon was imminent but they still doubted that Israel would advance on Beirut, and this was the substance of the daily estimates that were presented to Arafat by PLO intelligence. 'The question which I failed to answer, and I made a mistake, was: will they come to Beirut or not? I believed that they would not dare to make war with Syria, and Syria would not allow it to reach that point without clashing with them. What happened was exactly that,' said a senior Arafat adviser.[10]

Arafat had his own reasons for believing, too, that the US would do more to restrain the Israelis, in particular his lengthy and secret negotiations on mutual recognition with the American emissary, John Edwin Mroz. He should have known better. Arafat and his senior colleagues might also have paid closer attention to developments in east Beirut where, by early in 1982, Israel and the Maronites were in the process of cementing an unholy alliance that would end in tears for both of them, and the United States as well.

In the winter of 1981–2, with Israel's invasion plans taking shape, Sharon secured permission from Begin for a highly delicate mission. He would travel by darkened helicopter at nightfall from Tel Aviv north over the sea to the Christian port of Jounieh in east Beirut where he would meet a young man on whom the Israelis had pinned quite unreasonable hopes. The meeting on Lebanese soil between Sharon and Bashir Gemayel, the tough Christian Lebanese militia commander, would be an event of no small significance.

When the helicopter landed on the darkened beach not far from the headland dominated by the twinkling lights of the Casino du Liban, Bashir Gemayel stepped forward to greet his bulky visitor, kissing him on both cheeks in traditional Arab style. Sharon's dreams of a strategic partnership between Jews and Christians in a hostile Islamic sea must have seemed, in his considerable conceit, almost tangible to him then.

Sharon left his Christian hosts in no doubt in discussion over dinner at Gemayel's well-guarded Bikfaiya home in the hills behind Beirut that it was only a matter of time before Israel responded to their pleas for help, but he warned them that there were limits to what the Israelis could do. Israel's army would not enter Beirut, nor would it seek to expel the Syrians. But what he did offer the Christians was a partnership in remaking Lebanon to their mutual advantage.

Flying back to Tel Aviv the following night, Sharon peered silent and thoughtful from the helicopter at the lights of Sidon and Tyre, and the estuaries of the Rivers Awali, Zaharani and Litani. He was studying the landmarks-to-be of Israel's drive north in the first furious days of its invasion of Lebanon less than six months later.

Within hours of Sharon's arrival in east Beirut as an honoured guest of the Gemayels, Arafat had been informed: in Lebanon, there are few secrets that remain secrets for very long. The visit was correctly seen by the PLO leaders as one more emphatic sign of evolving military and political co-operation between Israel and the Phalangists, but not yet taken as conclusive proof that an audacious operation was imminent against the PLO's very nerve centre in Beirut. In any case, Arafat and his colleagues had other seemingly more pressing concerns in an Arab world that had been further weakened and divided by the onset of the Gulf war in September, 1980. The PLO lacked a strong Arab sponsor. Syria was openly hostile. Egypt, engaged in final delicate negotiations on Israel's withdrawal from the Sinai, was firmly out of the picture. Iraq was consumed by its war with Iran. The Gulf states, panicked by the nasty conflict to their north, were in no position to offer more than their usual jittery financial support. The Soviet Union, then in the last days of the Brezhnev era, appeared increasingly uninterested in the plight of the Palestinians.

The world at large was also distracted. In early 1982, Alexander Haig had unsuccessfully sought to stave off the war between Britain and Argentina over the Falkland Islands in the South Atlantic. In Poland, martial law had been declared in response to the agitation of the Solidarity trades union movement under Lech Walesa. And the US now had a President whose knowledge of the Middle East did not extend far beyond the Jewish jokes he had learned on the beefsteak and burgundy circuit. Indeed, in the early months of the Reagan Administration Philip Habib, the special US Middle East envoy, was obliged to give mini-lectures on the region to a President whose first reaction when the word Palestinian was mentioned was to equate it with 'terrorist'.[11]

The man General Sharon chose to execute the first part of his great plan –subduing the occupied territories – was an obscure right-wing professor of Arabic literature named Menachem Milson. On 1 November 1981, Milson had been appointed to head a new civil administration in the territories. It was hardly an inspired choice. Milson had first come to notice after the landslide victory of PLO-supported candidates in the 1976 municipal elections, with his arguments that the Arafatists had triumphed through bribery and intimidation. The trend could be countered, he argued, by cultivating a pliable, indigenous leadership. Needless to say, Milson's views were appropriated by Sharon, receptive as he was to any plan that might put the PLO in its place. When, in early 1982, Israel ousted the pro-PLO mayors of three large Arab towns to help make way for the new order, violence erupted in the territories, leaving 21 Palestinians dead and scores wounded. Soldiers had fired on stone-throwing youths: armed Jewish settlers had joined in as well.

Milson's appointment was merely one indication, however, of the new 'smash the PLO' mood of a xenophobic Israeli Government. Another sign, as far as Arafat was concerned, was Begin's announcement on 14 December that Israel was annexing the Golan Heights, captured from Syria in the 1967 war. What worried the PLO most was not so much Syria's timid reaction – the PLO leadership knew that Syria was in no position to engage Israel by itself – but the lessons to be drawn from Begin's disdain for international censure and limp-wristed US disapproval. The annexation of the Golan was regarded by Arafat as another indication that here was a government prepared to go nearly all the way in pursuit of its aims. But even this event, and others such as the Sharon visit to east Beirut in January, did not dispel the aura of complacency that had settled over many in the PLO leadership in their comfortable west Beirut redoubt.

Not only was the possibility of an Israeli advance to the gates of Beirut discounted but the leadership had become so inured to the almost daily threats of an imminent invasion that it tended to regard each new signal as further blustering and posturing. General Rafael Eitan, Israel's chief-of-staff and one of its more voluble hawks, left no doubt that he was itching for a fight when he told an Israeli newspaper in mid-May that 'since I have built an excellent military machine worth billions of dollars, I must make use of it.'[12]

Sharon, on his return to Israel after his January talks with the Gemayels, had initiated an intense period of military preparation, ordering the redrafting of original war plans significantly to enlarge the proposed military operation. He wanted a much more detailed outline of possible political and military co-operation with the Christians. He was also much preoccupied with Israel's final withdrawal from the Sinai which took place on 26 April amid bitter opposition from right-wing settler groups.

When Israel's Defence Minister presented his expanded battle plan, renamed Operation Pines, to the cabinet on 16 May he was rebuffed, in spite of Begin's support, and told to scale down the operation that would have taken him to the gates of Beirut. He was authorised instead to advance a maximum of 45 kilometres into Lebanon, to destroy PLO bases in southern Lebanon, and to put Israel's northern settlements beyond the range of PLO artillery.

Sharon certainly did not regard this setback as the last word as he prepared to set off for Washington and his 25 May meeting with Haig. Begin and Sharon were, by the end of May, so much ensnared in their plans for war that there would be no turning back.

Throughout May, Arafat was, as usual, constantly on the move. Ahmed Sidki al-Dajani, the Palestinian intellectual and PLO executive committee member, remembered accompanying him to India, Pakistan, Kuwait, Qatar and Saudi Arabia before returning with him to Beirut for a crucial meeting of the Executive Committee on Tuesday, 1 June.

The PLO 'cabinet' concentrated its attention almost exclusively on Israel's war preparations. Much of the talk focused, not surprisingly given the PLO's vastly inferior firepower, on what diplomatic initiatives might be taken to deal with an Israeli invasion. Farouk Kaddoumi, the PLO 'foreign minister', would go to the United Nations accompanied by Dajani; Arafat would continue with his mission to Saudi Arabia in efforts to mediate in the Gulf war which had taken a decided turn for the worse for the Arabs following Iran's recapture of Khorramshahr on 24 May. If Arafat's colleagues were surprised that their commander-in-chief should decide to leave Beirut at that critical moment, they did not remark on it at the time. Arafat's quicksilver movements had long since become a fact of life for those close to him. In any case, a visit to Riyadh now might enable him to stiffen Saudi support for the PLO in its impending ordeal.

Ariel Sharon, meanwhile, travelled in early June to friendly Romania with a small party of aides, including General Avraham Tamir, his national security adviser. The countdown to war was well and truly under way when, on 3 June 1982, the trigger was pulled. Shlomo Argov, Israel's ambassador to the Court of St James, had been critically wounded in an assassination attempt. Sabri al-Banna (Abu Nidal), the Fatah renegade, had struck again although on behalf of whom it remains unclear to this day. Was Iraq, for example, behind the attack? Wasn't Banna then operating from the Iraqi capital, Baghdad? The Iraqis would not have been at all unhappy to see Syria, Iran's ally and to some extent the PLO's, sucked into conflict with Israel in Lebanon. The conspiracy theorists had a field day.

For Tamir and Sharon the question of whether or not it was a conspiracy to bring down the wrath of Israel on Syria and the PLO was immaterial. They both knew on that fateful day, 3 June, that this was the pretext to attack that Israel had been waiting for. 'It was only a question of when the government was going to give the green light,' said Tamir. 'If it had not been Argov, then something else would have come along.'[13] Raphael Eitan, the tough-talking army commander, put Israel's attitude on the Argov shooting more bluntly when the argument was raised that Arafat and the mainstream PLO could not be held responsible for the actions of one of its renegades. 'Abu Nidal, Abu Shmidal,' he had replied. 'We have to strike at the PLO.'[14]

By the time Sharon hastened to Israel from Romania, the Israeli air force had already swept into action to avenge the Argov shooting, striking at targets in southern Lebanon and on the outskirts of Beirut, killing more than 60 people and wounding 200 more. For the PLO leadership it was, to say the least, provocative. Ever since the previous summer, when the 'War of the Katyushas' across Israel's northern border had been ended by a US-mediated ceasefire, PLO guns had been more or less silent. Now they could stay quiet no longer. On the same day as the Israeli air force struck, PLO units retaliated with rocket and artillery attacks on northern Israel and the enclave in southern Lebanon controlled by Israel's puppet, Major Saad Haddad.[15] Sharon and Begin had found their *casus belli*.

Israel's cabinet met on the night of 5 June at the prime minister's residence in the Jerusalem suburb of Rehavia, and approved the invasion forthwith after listening to a presentation from Sharon. Essentially, he went over the details of the limited invasion plan approved at the cabinet meeting on 16 May. The cabinet decision was as brief as it was imprecise. Sharon was not exactly given *carte blanche* in Lebanon, but he would have no trouble stretching the meaning of the four-point decision to fit his own designs.

At 11 a.m. on 6 June, less than twelve hours after the cabinet adjourned, Israeli forces poured across Lebanon's southern boundary, supported by air and naval units which blasted targets further north. Some 40,000 Israeli troops in hundreds of tanks and armoured personnel carriers crossed the border and raced north in three directions: along the coast towards Tyre; in the centre towards Nabatiyeh; in the east towards Hasbaiya. At the same time, naval units landed near the coastal city of Sidon, site of the PLO's southern command.[16] By daybreak next day, the Israeli juggernaut had achieved most of its ostensible, limited war aims: it was on the way to putting Israel's northern settlements beyond rocket and artillery fire from Palestinian strongholds in southern Lebanon; it had thrown the Palestinian military leadership in the south into disarray; and at that early stage it had avoided direct clashes with the Syrians. It was not quite a rout for the PLO resistance in and around what had become known as 'Fatahland', but it was close to it.

International efforts to restrain the Israeli war machine were ineffectual, and the US – the only power that might have stood a faint chance of doing so – seemed confused. The State Department had issued repeated calls for restraint, and on 5 June, Haig had announced that special envoy Philip Habib would return forthwith to the Middle East to restore the July 1981 ceasefire. But President Reagan, in Versailles for a summit of Western leaders, seemed at odds with his advisers: to the surprise of his fellow heads of government he appeared to justify the invasion when he said it stemmed from the constant bombardment of northern Israel from southern Lebanon. Evidently, he was not aware that the front had been quiet for the best part of a year. Against this background, calls for an immediate ceasefire – whether from the Group of Seven leaders or from the UN Security Council – were not going to deflect Begin and Sharon from their war aims.

On the second day, the dominoes continued to fall. Beaufort Castle, the great Crusader landmark with its commanding views towards Galilee, fell; pockets of resistance in Tyre were pacified; Nabatiyeh and Hasbaiya were seized; the noose around Sidon was tightened. The Syrians found themselves under increasing pressure to enter the conflict as Israeli troops brushed aside flimsy resistance in the central Chouf Mountains and raced on towards the Beirut–Damascus highway. But on the morning of the third day it was clear that Begin's talk of a 45-kilometre thrust into Lebanon, followed by a quick withdrawal – an aim he repeated on the floor of the Knesset that very day and in repeated messages to the Americans – was a grand deception. Sharon had been given his head. There would be no stopping him. As General Tamir observed in his memoir, 'What was unfolding on the ground was not the brief limited action which the cabinet had considered at its Saturday night meeting, but Operation Pines, the far more ambitious plan which was meant not only to solve Israel's immediate security problem but also to change the basic situation in Lebanon.'[17]

Under heavy aerial bombardment in Beirut, Arafat and his colleagues prepared to make their last stand. Like their southern commanders, they had been dismayed by the speed of the Israeli advance. Haj Ismail, the military chief in charge of 2,000–3,000 guerrillas in the south, and later accused by some inside the PLO of cowardice, had been caught outside Sidon when it was encircled by Israeli forces. Palestinian fighters notionally under his command had been reduced to a rabble. The Israeli advance in the south swept on more or less unimpeded, although sporadic resistance continued in the large Ein el-Hilweh camp near Sidon until the middle of June. 'The senior command levels turned out to be very poor,' observed the Palestinian military historian Yezid Sayigh. 'Despite all the warnings they were taken very much by surprise, and the level of contingency planning was very poor.'[18]

Holed up in their Beirut bunkers, Arafat and his colleagues scarcely had time to debate the organisation's military failures, but it was clear to all that the organisation had fallen into an elementary trap. It had sought to build a conventional armed presence in southern Lebanon complete with larger artillery pieces and the odd tank, when there was never any possibility that it would be in a position to match Israel. PLO fighters, better suited for guerrilla warfare, were caught trying to fight a static engagement for which they were completely unsuited. The error was due in no small part to Arafat's oft-stated ambition to build a conventional army, complete with naval and air force units.

By the third day of the invasion, Sharon was already getting on with the hitherto less conspicuous elements of his grand design. With Israeli forces moving towards Beirut on several fronts, albeit more slowly, he summoned Bashir Gemayel to Israel's northern military headquarters. It was a difficult encounter. Sharon, the strategic mastermind impatient for quick results, briefed Gemayel on his plans to cut off the Beirut–Damascus highway, and to link up with the Christian forces. Imperiously, Gemayel was told that he should ready his men to push into west Beirut. Without delay, he was to prepare for the formation of a new government committed to re-establishing Lebanon's independence and sovereignty . . . under Israel's tutelage.

Gemayel, with dreams of reuniting Muslims and Christians under his rule, baulked at what he was being asked to do. What had seemed feasible, even desirable, at the candlelit dinner with Shiron at his Bikfaiya home in January, now seemed like a very bad idea indeed. Did he, Bashir Gemayel, wish to emerge from the fires of the Lebanon engagement, branded an Israeli puppet? Even the boisterous Gemayel knew that the chances of surviving such a stain on his reputation were almost nil. So he stalled. It was at that precise moment that Sharon's plan to create a new order in Lebanon, based on Maronite compliance, was shown for what it was: at best, a calculated gamble, at worst a reckless game in which there would be no winners. But having committed 60,000–70,000 men to the battle and having vowed to rid Lebanon of the 'malevolent criminal terrorists', as Begin incessantly called the PLO, there was no turning back.

On 9 June, Israeli jets blasted Syrian SAM missile batteries in the Bekaa valley in eastern Lebanon, the same day downing 29 Syrian MIG jets in a series of one-sided air battles. By the end of the first week, Israeli forces were occupying Damour, they had pushed to within a few miles of the Damascus–Beirut highway. They had destroyed a total of 79 planes, or one quarter of the Syrian air force. On 11 June, Israel declared a unilateral ceasefire which did not apply, in Sharon's words, to the 'terrorists of the PL'. Battered and bruised and with no real desire to fight, the Syrians meekly accepted the ceasefire provided it was 'founded on a total Israeli withdrawal from Lebanon'.[18] These were empty words. Damascus was in no position to set conditions.

The Palestinians were now completely on their own to fight what was described by Walid Khalidi, the Palestinian historian, as the second Israeli–Palestinian war. 'In fact,' Khalidi observed, 'it has been said that Israel fought us in 1948, and forgot about us until 1982, and then in 1982 they decided to go at us again.'[19] Not since Abdel Kader Husseini had led his Palestinian irregulars into an unequal struggle with the Palmach and the Haganah, the forerunners of the modern Israeli army, had the two sides so formally confronted each other. Only, on this second occasion the disparity in firepower, the ability of one side, with a modern arsenal at its disposal, to rain death and destruction on the other on a vast scale, was infinitely greater than on the first.

In their Beirut bomb shelters – at one point the PLO leadership was operating from an underground car park ten floors below street level – Arafat and his colleagues prepared for the siege of Beirut and hoped for a political miracle that would deliver them intact from the storm they were sure was about to engulf them.

On the night of 11 June, and with criticism mounting in Israel itself over the failure of the Christians to enter the war against the PLO 'terrorists', Sharon made a second journey to Jounieh. The atmosphere on this occasion was much less cordial. He had gone to assess on the ground what the Christians might be intending to do to capitalise on the opportunities that had been created for them. The answer was: not very much. Sharon, whose expecta-tions of the Christians had always been wildly unrealistic, came to the dispiriting and belated conclusion that Bashir Gemayel and his commanders were 'not going to be an active ally in the continuing war against the terrorists.'[20]

The next day Israel declared a ceasefire, but like ten others that were to come and go before fighting finally came to a halt two months later, this one had no practical effect. These 'rolling ceasefires' were to be a feature of the war that continued throughout the hot summer months, as Israel endeavoured by all means at its disposal, short of advancing into the crumbling heart of west Beirut itself, to winkle the Palestinians out of their guerrilla strongholds.

When, on 13 June, Ariel Sharon, in full battledress, rode triumphantly, like a latter-day Tamerlane, on top of an armoured personnel carrier into Baabda, the hillside seat of the Lebanese presidency, the PLO's fortunes and morale were at their nadir. Panicky thoughts in the leadership were turning to securing the best terms for evacuation. The Syrians, perhaps the only force that could conceivably have come to Arafat's aid, had been decisively knocked out of the fight. Other Arab governments were sitting by, helpless and in many cases uninterested. Appeals to the UN yielded nothing beyond pious ceasefire resolutions that were totally ignored by Israel.

Worse still was the PLO's position among the Lebanese themselves. In those bleak mid-June days, the PLO had few friends anywhere, and least of all among the Lebanese, many of whom were thoroughly fed up with the years of turbulence that had accompanied the Palestinian guerrilla presence in Lebanon. The arrogant, sometimes criminal, behaviour of local PLO commanders and their troops, especially in the south, had alienated a swathe of the population, as had the conspicuous high living of some senior PLO cadres.

The result, as the Israelis arrived at the gates of Beirut and kept up a relentless bombardment of the city, was mounting pressure on Arafat and his colleagues to withdraw. The message was clear enough on 14 June when Lebanese President Elias Sarkis formed the grandly named Council of National Salvation. It was, in fact, a thinly disguised vehicle to pressure Arafat into removing himself, his headquarters and his fighters from Beirut – and the sooner the better. The question was: how was he to negotiate his way out, and on what terms?

If not downright hostile, the American position was hardly comforting. The US had done little enough to stop the invasion in the first place. Soon after it began, Haig declared that the US would not deny Israel the 'right to legitimate self-defence'.[21] Haig's attitude was certainly no help to Philip Habib who shuttled ineffectually between Beirut, Damascus and Jersualem in an effort to secure the PLO's withdrawal on less than humiliating terms, even as a highly ambivalent US policy undermined his credibility as a broker.

For the first few weeks of the war, confusion reigned in the PLO. Reports of handwringing in the leadership over a possible withdrawal were threatening to sap the morale of fighters in the field. One school, identified with Hani al-Hassan, the close Arafat aide, wanted to negotiate forthwith the best terms for withdrawal. Hassan desired three things in return: a political gain as a quid pro quo for withdrawal, in other words some form of US recognition of a PLO role in any putative peace process; an acknowledgement of the PLO's 'moral victory' resulting from prolonged resistance; and the retention of a PLO political and military presence in Lebanon as one element in a formula to protect Palestinian civilians in Lebanon.[22]

The opposing group, whose most prominent member was Salah Khalaf, wanted to 'hang tough' for as long as possible, in the hope that Israel and the US would tire of attempts to 'negotiate' the PLO infrastructure out of Lebanon. Khalaf and his supporters were determined to give no sign in the first weeks of the war that they accepted the inevitability of PLO withdrawal with the serious effect that would have on rank-and-filed morale. 'Negotiations,' Khalaf would later observe drily, 'were a tactic for some in the leadership, and a strategy for others'.[23]

Arafat himself, predictably enough, wavered between these two approaches – privately signalling his readiness to depart under the right conditions while publicly maintaining a facade of defiance. On 17 June and with the PLO in desperate straits, he made his strongest public statement of the war. In a message to the 'Arab, Lebanese and Palestinian masses . . . and to all the fighters in the field' he railed against Arab timidity and cowardice, and vowed that the forthcoming battle of Beirut would be 'the Stalingrad of the Arabs'.[24]

But even as Arafat authorised those defiant words he knew that time was running out for the PLO's political and military presence in Beirut. He could temporise and delay, tactics which he had honed to near perfection over the years. He would clutch at straws, such as Haig's resignation as American Secretary of State on 25 June, in the hope of stronger US intervention to stop the war. But it would all be in vain.

By early July, Arafat had in any case been obliged, under intense pressure from his Sunni Muslim Lebanese allies, to agree in principle to a PLO withdrawal. The PLO leader knew when he was summoned on 3 July to the grand whitewashed mansion of the former Lebanese Prime Minister, the septuagenerian Saeb Salam, that he was in for a difficult time. Lebanon's elders, members of the Council of National Salvation, made it clear they believed the PLO had outstayed its welcome in Beirut. Whatever their own feelings about the Arab–Israeli dispute, whatever personal friendships they might have with PLO leaders, they could not stand by any longer and see their capital and their country destroyed. The battle, in their view, was over. The PLO had lost.

Accompanied by Hani al-Hassan, a weary Arafat faced men whom he had known as friends since he had established his headquarters in Beirut in the early 1970s. Among all surviving Lebanese leaders, Saeb Salam was perhaps closest to the Palestinians. Arafat counted him not only as a friend, but also as a committed supporter. Now, as discussion droned on throughout a long, steamy July afternoon in the Muslim fasting month of Ramadan, the PLO leader was brought face to face with an unpleasant reality. Even Salam, who had resigned as premier in protest at the failure of the Lebanese army to come to the aid of the Palestinians in the raid on Beirut in 1973 in which three top PLO officials were killed, was telling him to go. Arafat knew in his heart of hearts that Lebanon's tribal elders had every reason to tell him to leave, but this did not make it any easier for him to agree to their demands.

As the afternoon wore on, discussion became more strained with Arafat insisting that there was no way that he and his fighters could leave Beirut in undignified flight. Neither he nor his men could be seen simply to abandon their strongholds under Israeli pressure. They would rather fight to the death and to hell with the consequences for everybody. Warming to his theme, the PLO leader summoned up the ghost of Yousef al-Azmah, the Syrian hero, who had, in spite of impossible odds, defied the French in the battle of Maysaloun near Damascus in 1920. 'I reminded them,' Arafat recalled, 'of when Yousef al-Azmah went out to fight the French; he knew he would lose, yet he went out to defend Damascus, so that it would not be said that an Arab city was subjected to an invasion, and no one defended it.'[25] But even as he regaled his Lebanese listeners with stories of heroic Arab exploits, even as he filibustered through that long afternoon, Arafat understood very well that his time was almost up. Late in the day, after conferring with colleagues, the PLO leader returned to Salam's residence with a handwritten note. Addressed to 'our brother Shafik al-Wazzan', it stated simply and briefly that the Palestinian command had taken a decision to leave Lebanon. Arafat would withdraw, but the timing and conditions for withdrawal were left deliberately vague. Even at that late stage, Arafat and his colleagues were hoping for a change in the situation on the ground: in other words, for a miracle.

In agreeing in principle to go, Arafat calculated that he had bought himself time – and indeed, the pressure did ease somewhat in the ensuing weeks. Through most of July, negotiations continued on terms for an evacuation and for the formation of a multinational force to oversee the exodus of fighters and head-quarters staff. US envoy Habib conferred endlessly with Lebanese politicians and Arab diplomats in Beirut – though he never spoke to the PLO itself; direct American contact with the organisation over political matters was still taboo. In Washington, officials began turning their attention to the practicalities, such as arranging the charter of ships to take the Palestinians away. It was a curious business, not without its farcical moments. The Americans discovered that some PLO officials were as anxious about taking their prized possessions with them as they were about escaping in one piece. 'We got these messages from the PLO containing lists of BMWs and Mercedes that they wanted to get on to the ships,' recalled one White House official who was involved in the evacuation effort. 'They were very concerned to get their fleets of cars on as well as their families. We fell about laughing.'[26]

Arafat, for his part, began to look as if he was enjoying himself. He emerged often to talk to the international press, which had grown steadily more hostile towards Israel over civilian casualties in Beirut. All the while, the clutching at straws continued as Arafat tried to improve the terms of the PLO's eventual departure. He was briefly buoyed by French and Egyptian diplomatic efforts aimed at securing a political gain to the PLO, namely recognition of its role in an international peace effort as the price for its withdrawal. He pinned hope on an Arab League intervention with Reagan. But in the end, the Franco–Egyptian initiative came to nothing, and the Arab League move made no difference. During a visit to Washington, the Saudi and Syrian Foreign Ministers, Prince Saud al-Faisal and Abdel Halim Khaddam, meekly acquies-ced in the plan being proposed by US negotiator Habib for the PLO's removal. Within a few weeks, Israeli pressure would be such that the Habib plan would come to seem the only way out.

In Israel a bitter debate simmered and boiled. Begin and Sharon came under increasing political pressure to justify their decision to go to war at such terrible cost to the civilian population in Lebanon, and to what end? 'I don't believe all this rubbish about smashing the PLO infrastructure,' observed the noted and by no means doveish Israeli historian, Yehoshua Porat. 'It is based not on arms caches or on supply dumps, but in the refugee camps. As long as there is no political solution, the human and ideological foundation for its existence will remain.'[27]

Sharon's dreams of a quick victory, of Israeli troops being welcomed in a 'liberated' Beirut as the saviours of a new, free Lebanon, had evaporated almost as soon as his legions had arrived at the gates of the city in late June. The swift and intoxicating Israeli advance had become a static siege, a nagging war of attrition in which Israeli casualties mounted by the day. Sharon was in political difficulties, and he knew it. As the days turned into weeks through July, he railed at the Americans; he ranted at his Israeli critics; and he chafed at the lack of action on the battlefield. For the impatient bulldozing Sharon, the slow machinations of American diplomacy, seeking not only to move the PLO out of Beirut, but also to prepare the ground for a comprehensive peace in Lebanon, were intolerable. Something had to give.

From 18 July, Begin and Sharon argued bitterly with their cabinet colleagues, some of whom in Sharon's words wanted to 'leave the wagon',[28] about the need for the toughest possible action to break the impasse. On 1 August, Begin and Sharon won the day, in a cabinet exhausted by weeks of argument, by proposing a simple stratagem. They would agree to a ceasefire, but if there was one violation, they would launch massive air strikes against PLO positions. As everyone in the cabinet knew, this was simply a pretext for attack. The cabinet had hardly finished meeting when the Israeli High Command deemed that there had been a violation of the ceasefire. Without delay, Israeli forces attacked from the south and in a fifteen-hour battle took the airport, bringing them perilously close to the PLO refugee camps of Bourj el-Brajneh, Sabra and Shatila, and to the heavily bombed Fakhani area, site of the PLO's headquarters. It was then that Sharon decided to go for the kill.

On 4 August, Israel's Defence Minister ordered the most concerted attacks thus far on PLO strongholds from land, sea and air. The target was Arafat himself, and his senior colleagues. These next few days were ones of maximum personal danger for the PLO leader as he was ferried from one heavily fortified bunker to the next. One of Arafat's senior intelligence aides says that in this period the headquarters staff moved the PLO command centre 'every forty-eight hours . . . We had not one but several alternatives,' he recalled, 'with six telex machines, two international lines and a wireless station. We must have moved as many as ten times between mid-July and mid-August when the bombing stopped.'[29]

With help from agents on the ground and from intercepts of Arafat wireless and telephone communications, Israel was able to pinpoint his whereabouts . . . or so it seemed to the PLO leader. Several bunkers were located in basements in the Hamra district in the business centre of west Beirut. No sooner had he moved to a new fortified location than Israeli jets would zero in on his hideout. It was a deadly game of cat and mouse, and it was being fought with multi-million dollar machines and the most advanced electronic targeting equipment then available in any arsenal in the world. Sharon used his pilots as flying assassination squads in relentless and furious pursuit of his quarry.

On 6 August, Israel came awfully close to nailing its man when its pilots, alerted by an agent with an electronic homing device, literally flattened a seven-storey apartment building near Lebanon's Central Bank with a newfangled 'vacuum bomb', killing or wounding some 200 of those inside. Arafat, who had been using part of the building as his operations room, had left hurriedly moments before. They were nerve-racking times for the commanders of a special unit numbering about 150 Force 17 commandos from Arafat's personal bodyguard, who had been given a very special mission at the onset of the invasion: to make whatever sacrifices were necessary to save Arafat, the symbol of the revolution. Very early in the conflict, said Colonel Mohammed al-Natour, the Force 17 commander, it was decided that the criterion that would be used to judge the success or failure of the Palestinian resistance was whether Arafat himself survived.[30]

The ferocious air, land and sea attacks continued until 12 August when, after eleven consecutive hours of air raids on built-up areas in which Palestinian guerrillas and their leaders had taken refuge, President Reagan finally said: enough. The cumulative effects of growing protests around the world and, more pointedly, the horrible pictures of death and destruction that were appearing on the nightly US television network news, prompted an angry and decisive phone call from the US President to Begin. Reagan expressed 'outrage' over the Israeli actions.[31] He demanded that the bombing stop immediately; otherwise, he warned, he would end US attempts to negotiate the PLO's withdrawal from Beirut.

In an exchange with Begin that must go down in history as one of the sharpest ever to pass between a US president and an Israeli leader, Reagan said grimly, 'Menachem, this is a holocaust.' There was a long pause, before the Polish-born Begin replied frostily, 'Mr President, I'm aware of what a holocaust is.'[32] Six hours later the bombing stopped.

An uneasy calm settled over the smoking ruins of Beirut as Philip Habib began work on the final details of the PLO's withdrawal. For Habib, the task of trying to unravel the mess in Lebanon had proved a dispiriting exercise. Caught between an Israel determined with all force at its disposal to smash the PLO, and Arafat and his men who were fighting for survival, Habib had often been a helpless spectator, his task as a negotiator complicated by his inability to talk directly to the PLO. That task was left to his go-between, Saeb Salam.

One week after Israel ceased its aerial bombardment, Habib's formal 22-point plan for the evacuation of the PLO from Lebanon was presented to the Lebanese Government and to Israel. PLO fighters would be scattered to the four corners of the Arab world. Arafat himself and his headquarters staff would be relocated in Tunis, 2,000 kilometres from the land they called Palestine. The PLO leader had rejected an offer to go to Damascus. The last thing he wanted was to be, in any way, beholden to Hafez al-Assad.

Like most of his colleagues during the long siege of Beirut, Arafat had been disgusted by the lack of Arab support. Beyond pious words, not one Arab state had come to the aid of the PLO. In an Eid al-Fitr message on 20 July, marking the end of Ramadan, the PLO leader had invoked the words of Saladin, the Muslim warrior who had expelled the Crusaders from the Holy Land in the twelfth century, in an effort to remind his brother Arab rulers of their obligations. 'I do not need your prayers, but I need your swords,' he declared. '. . . What then is the explanation for this . . . indifference?'[33] His words were greeted with silence.

As he watched the first of his fighters depart from Beirut port on 21 August, amid emotional scenes, Arafat had mixed feelings. The long and bloody siege of Beirut had lasted from 25 June, but once again he knew that another and perhaps even more difficult struggle was beginning. The organisation had survived; the leadership, through some miracle, had escaped intact; but for the second time in ten years it was being banished to uncertain exile.

By 30 August when Arafat, taking emotional leave of Lebanese notables including Prime Minister Shafik al-Wazzan and Saeb Salam and proclaiming that he was going 'from one exile to another', joined one of the last shiploads of evacuees on board the Greek vessel *Atlantis*, most of the 10,876 Palestinian guerrillas who were to depart Beirut under the Habib plan had gone, along with 2,700 Syrians of the Arab Deterrent Force who had been trapped by the Israeli advance. The PLO fighters left behind a casualty toll that was one of the highest of all Arab–Israeli wars. Some 19,000 people had been killed, according to Lebanese official figures, between the first Israeli bombing raid on 4 June and 31 August. Another 30,000 had been wounded. About half the casualties were civilians. Israel's own death toll was near 400 by the end of the year.[34] The cost of Sharon's grand plan to smash the PLO and create a new Lebanon had been high by any standards, even allowing for the possibility of greatly exaggerated official Lebanese casualty figures.

For the PLO, losing Lebanon was a devastating blow. For more than ten years, despite the travails of civil war, the country had served as a more or less autonomous base for the Palestinians; the only place where they could organise, operate and generate political support with a measure of freedom. Now, the impressive Lebanese infrastructure the PLO had built was shattered, many of its factories destroyed and valuable documents carried off or burned by the Israelis. With its fighters scattered around the Arab world, efforts to continue to pursue 'armed struggle' against Israel would be even more difficult. With Arafat's headquarters shifting to the distant backwater of Tunis, it was going to be hard work keeping world attention on the cause.

As Arafat looked back towards the shore from the deck of the *Atlantis*, he was haunted by a fear about the fate of the Palestinians he was leaving behind. Was there a danger of a repeat of the massacre of Tal al-Zaatar, the refugee camp overrun by Christian militiamen in 1976? Would Palestinian residents of the camps of Sabra, Shatila and Bourj el-Brajneh be safe in the absence of a PLO armed presence? How could he be sure that US security guarantees would be a sufficient safeguard? There were no satisfactory answers to these questions, although Arafat would draw some comfort from the presence of a multinational force from the US, France and Italy.

Arafat's choice of Athens as his first port of call was a pointed rebuff to his fellow Arabs. He would not go to Damascus, home of arch-foe, Assad; he would not go to Amman where differences with Hussein persisted; he would not go to the Gulf where governments' lukewarm support during the siege had been almost more shocking than the failure of others to provide material help; he would not go to Cairo which had been reduced, because of its separate peace with Israel, to diplomatic posturing; he would not go to Baghdad where President Saddam Hussein was continuing to give shelter to Abu Nidal, whose assassins had provided Israel with the pretext to attack in the first place; and he certainly would not go to Tripoli where Gadaffi had urged the PLO to commit collective 'suicide' in Beirut, rather than agree to evacuate the city.

One week before Arafat left Beirut, on 23 August, the 34-year-old Bashir Gemayel had been elected President of Lebanon. The streetfighter had become a warlord and now a national-leader-in-waiting, with pretensions to rule over all of Lebanon. In an Israel still consumed by recriminations over the war, Gemayel's election raised flickering hopes that a Judaeo–Christian axis might yet be established between Jerusalem and east Beirut. On 12 September, Ariel Sharon travelled to Bikfaiya for what would be his 'last supper' with Gemayel. Talk late into the night touched on the difficulty of resolving Lebanon's internal problems . . . and on the negotiation of a peace treaty. The two agreed to another meeting on 15 September, at which Foreign Minister Yitzhak Shamir would be present. But the meeting would never take place.

On 14 September Bashir Gemayel, President-elect of Lebanon, was blown up in the local headquarters of his right-wing Phalange party in east Beirut by a massive bomb presumed to have been planted by a Syrian agent. His corpse was barely recognisable when it was dragged from the rubble. Assad had spoken: any further designs that Israel might have had on the remaking of Lebanon vaporised on the spot.

Gemayel's assassination, apart from putting paid to lingering Israeli ambitions in Lebanon, also unleashed a sequence of tragic events that would reverberate around the world and add two words indelibly to the history books: Sabra and Shatila.

Following Gemayel's death, Israeli troops moved into west Beirut. The PLO leader, visiting Rome for an audience with the Pope, feared the worst when he was told the news by his staff on 15 September. Turning to Afif Safieh, the PLO's leading Catholic layman, Arafat said with deep anxiety in his voice, 'They have entered my office.'[35] A day later he demanded that troops of the multinational force, who had completed their withdrawal from Beirut on 13 September, be returned forthwith. But his call came too late – much too late.

Between early evening on 16 September and the morning of 18 September, Christian militiamen avenging the death of Bashir Gemayel had entered the Sabra and Shatila refugee camps, and had killed and killed repeatedly and indiscriminately . . . men, women and children. Some of the victims were mutilated. Vengeful Phalangist militia had been given permission by the Israelis, who were in control of the area, to enter the run-down shanty towns, their task ostensibly to pursue Palestinian fighters who Sharon alleged were still hiding in the camps. For more than 36 hours, and while Israeli troops ringed the camps, the carnage went on. At the end of it hundreds were dead. The Palestinians say that 1,500 died. The Lebanese Red Cross reported 328 dead and 911 missing. An Israeli commission set up to investigate found that between 700 and 800 had died.[36]

When details of the massacre emerged on 18 September, the first international reaction was one of disbelief. Nowhere was the reaction more vociferous than in Israel itself. Typical was a despatch from Zeev Schiff, the military correspondent of *Haaretz*, who reported on 20 September that: 'A war crime has been committed in the refugee camps of Beirut. The Phalangists executed hundreds or more women, children and old people. What happened was exactly what used to happen in the pogroms against the Jews.'[37]

Speaking for thousands of Israelis, Abba Eban, the former Foreign Minister, observed that 'a hideous pogrom has been perpetuated with fearful death and torment of innocent people in a place where the Israeli Government asserted its responsibility for the maintenance of order and the "avoidance of bloodshed." '[38] Menachem Begin, on the other hand, feigned astonishment at all the fuss. 'Goyim are killing goyim, and the world is trying to hang the Jews for the crime,' he complained to fellow cabinet ministers in what must go down as one of his least sensitive observations.

For Arafat, faced with his demonstrable weakness and isolation, it was one of his bleakest moments. Despairing, he retired to the Hotel Salwa, his temporary headquarters on the waterfront at Hammam Shatt, twenty kilometres southeast of Tunis. According to his adviser, Nabil Shaath, who was with him throughout this period, he went through a process of 'blaming himself, of blaming the Arabs, and the Americans. He felt betrayed.'[39]

12. THE WAR OF INDEPENDENCE

'Mr Arafat, you are *persona non grata*.' A Syrian lieutenant colonel, informing Arafat of his expulsion from Syria, quoted in the *New York Times*, 27 June 1983.

For Brigadier Saad Sayel, better known to his troops as Abu Walid, 27 September 1982 was to be a routine day visiting PLO bases in Lebanon's rich, cannabis-growing Bekaa Valley. The dour, US-trained veteran PLO military chief was traversing a familiar route between the Bekaa's two biggest towns, Zahle and Baalbek, when a fusillade of automatic rifle fire shattered the calm. Sayel's car was riddled with bullets.He was grievously wounded in the femoral artery of his upper thigh. He bled to death in front of distraught comrades.

On the pilgrimage to Mecca, Yasser Arafat was dismayed when he received the news. For him and for Khalil al-Wazir, who was with him, the death of their comrade-in-arms was a particularly sharp personal blow. The three had pledged, during the darkest days of the Israeli siege of Beirut, that if they survived they would make the pilgrimage together.[1] But in the uneasy aftermath of the PLO's ejection from Beirut, Sayel had stayed behind to be with the 8,000 or so PLO fighters still based in the Bekaa.

Ominously, an internal PLO inquiry established that Sayel was gunned down close to a Syrian checkpoint, and that the gunmen had been allowed to escape unchallenged. For the sake of appearances, an official Syrian–Fatah commission put a different complexion on events. Sayel was killed, it found, by members of the Lebanese Sh'ite militia, Amal, operating autonomously. But few in the PLO, least of all Arafat himself, believed this. The pro-Syrian Amal would not have dared to misbehave in Syrian-controlled territory. The conclusion was inescapable: Sayel's death had been a political assassination and, like that of Bashir Gemayel, one instigated by the Syrians.

Arafat's stage-managed departure from Beirut on 30 August 1982 in a blaze of international publicity had been observed from Damascus by a man with hatred in his heart. Hafez al-Assad had

had a wretched Lebanon war. Vilified, unfairly in his view, by PLO commanders for having agreed to a premature ceasefire just five days after the outbreak of the war, he had found himself, in September 1982, close to the lowest point of his twelve-year rule. His air force had suffered a tremendous blow for the second time in ten years. He had felt powerless to relieve a Syrian garrison cooped up in Beirut during the siege. Perhaps most galling of all, he felt he had been duped by the Americans into believing that Israel had had no intention of advancing further than 45 kilometres into Lebanon, hence his hasty decision to agree to a ceasefire. The man he blamed for many of his troubles was Yasser Arafat, who had pointedly thumbed his nose at Syria and the other Arabs on his expulsion from Beirut and sailed off to a hero's welcome in Athens.

Despite his pressing need for allies, Arafat felt justified in holding aloof from Syria. Bitterly, he complained that at the height of the Israeli bombardments Assad had refused even to acknowledge his phone calls. Syria's premature agreement to a ceasefire had been bad enough, but its failure to lift one finger to help the PLO during the worst of the Israeli attacks on Beirut doubled the blow. According to Nabil Shaath, Arafat was convinced 'Assad was out to destroy the PLO and keep it only as a small addendum to his intelligence organisation.'[2]

It was in the immediate aftermath of the war in Lebanon, and at his moment of greatest apparent weakness, that Assad had proved especially dangerous. The 14 September assassination of Bashir Gemayel had been a classically Levantine response to Israeli and US designs in Lebanon; Saad Sayel's death on 27 September was another sign of Syria's determination to fight back. Assad may have been down, but he was certainly not out. For Arafat the form that fight was to take was a full-scale Syrian-backed insurrection in Fatah's own ranks.

Trouble had been brewing for Arafat well before he sailed off to Athens, but the long days of the siege, and the almost constant threat of annihilation, had quietened internal criticism of his leadership; but it was not long resurfacing with recriminations about poor preparation for the Israeli invasion and lax terms for withdrawal. Arafat's obsession with peace stratagems had diverted the guerrilla movement from its core task of confronting Israel. The PLO's disastrous showing in southern Lebanon in the first days of the Israeli invasion was attributable to the poor leadership of Arafat-appointed cronies in key military posts. Arafat was blamed for Sabra and Shatila. In the festering mood of discontent that followed the exodus from Beirut, the list of complaints was endless, and they were made not simply by embittered Fatah dissidents of the pro-Soviet left. Some of Arafat's closest colleagues, including Salah Khalaf, flirted briefly with the opposing faction.

An early sign of the internal troubles came on 9 September at the Arab League summit in Fez when Nimr Saleh, a leftist member of the Fatah Central Committee and the man who would become the dissidents' political commissar, voiced strong opposition to a peace plan adopted by the Arab heads of state.

To Arafat's intense annoyance, Saleh and his hardline colleagues rejected an innocuous-sounding clause in the agreement that called for 'the drawing up by the Security Council of guarantees for peace for all the states of the region, including the independent Palestinian state' – not-so-concealed code language for the implied recognition of Israel and the acceptance of a Palestinian mini-state in the West Bank and Gaza Strip.[3] For the Fatah rejectionists, this formal Arab abandonment of the 'all of Palestine or nothing' stand was anathema; never mind that their Syrian sponsors had themselves endorsed it. Saleh's greatest sin, in Arafat's eyes, was that he had begun to 'consort with the enemy' by holding frequent unauthorised meetings with Assad. Arafat subsequently suspended Saleh from the Fatah Central Committee, a weak response to what amounted to an open challenge to the PLO leader's authority.

Upon his arrival, exhausted, in Athens, Arafat had received an interesting pair of visitors in his large suite in the Grande Bretagne Hotel. Marwan Qasem, Jordan's Foreign Minister, and Ahmed Lawzi, the Speaker of the Jordanian parliament, had been despatched by King Hussein with a message of support for Arafat and, more to the point, an offer of partnership in a new peace initiative.

The opportunistic Hussein had wasted no time in making his pitch for Arafat's co-operation. It came pointedly on 1 September, the very day that President Reagan unveiled his first (and last) serious Middle East peace initiative, calling for a 'fresh start' in efforts to bring about full autonomy for the Palestinians in the West Bank and Gaza Strip. Reagan had proposed a 'freeze' on Israeli settlement activity in the territories and – most important from Hussein's perspective – had emphasised that in the 'firm view of the United States . . . self-government by the Palestinians of the West Bank and Gaza in association with Jordan offers the best chances for a durable, just and lasting peace'.[4] It was a firm re-endorsement of that staple of US Middle East policy, the Jordanian option. As it turned out, Israeli opposition ensured that the 'Reagan autonomy plan', as it was called, had a shelf life of about five minutes.[5] Begin totally rejected it.

After relaying personal greetings from Hussein, Qasem came quickly to the point: 'You are out of Beirut, and we congratulate you on your safety,' he declared. 'This has been a most difficult experience for you. You have depended on many forces you thought would come to your aid and didn't . . . Now, whatever you decide, your decision has to be free from fear, intimidation and old loyalties because you have been let down. Today, what you say ought to represent fully Palestinian interests, whether it coincides with our policy or it conflicts with it.'[6]

Arafat's reply was evasive. He could not give a definitive reply since he had 'just come from the battlefield',[7] but once he had consulted his colleagues he might have a clearer response, both to the Reagan initiative and to Hussein's proposals for a new peace partnership.

Without delay, the king formally invited Arafat to visit Amman where, not many years before, Palestinian and Jordanian had fought in the streets. Now, the two sides were to discuss, as Hussein told the BBC on 13 September, the formation of a federal union on the two banks of the River Jordan and the formulation of a joint Palestinian–Jordanian diplomatic approach.[8] As Hussein saw it, a Palestinian West Bank 'mini-state' would be joined in a mutually beneficial confederation with the Hashemite Kingdom on the East Bank as an interim, and perhaps even permanent, solution to an age-old problem. If this improbable dream could be realised it would serve to answer the incessant harping of the Israeli right on the theme that Jordan, with its preponderance of people of Palestinian origin, was Palestine. What the king was seeking, in effect, was Arafat's blessing to speak on behalf of the Palestinians in American-sponsored negotiations on the future of the Israeli-occupied territories. Loyalties in Jordan were inevitably divided between the Hashemite throne and Palestinian aspirations, imperfectly symbolised by Arafat himself.

When Arafat arrived in Amman in October the Reagan plan was already dead in the water but this did not prevent the two old protagonists conducting an elaborate and not always harmonious six-month *pas de deux* in the hope that something could be salvaged. Hussein spent weeks trying to cajole Arafat into endorsing the Reagan plan and, more particularly, Resolution 242 calling for Israel's withdrawal from territories occupied in the 1967 war, and for all states in the region to 'live in peace within secure and recognised boundaries free from threats or acts of force'.[9] Like his American allies, Hussein had long regarded acceptance of 242 as the essential centrepiece of any Middle East initiative: his difficulties in persuading Arafat to endorse it sorely tested his patience.

Hussein eventually persuaded Arafat to agree to a watered-down peace formula based on the Reagan plan and the Fez Arab League summit resolutions of the previous September, but this was as far as their joint 1983 initiative went.

In early April, after a gruelling eight-hour session with Hussein, Arafat travelled from Amman to Kuwait to try to sell the initiative to the PLO Executive Committee, and to the Central Committee of his own Fatah faction. Acceptance of the formula would, he said, open up the possibility of a US–PLO dialogue – naively regarded by the PLO leader over the years as an end in itself – and would serve to increase pressure on Israel. He got nowhere. The brethren in Kuwait were in no mood to sanction a peace initiative under which the PLO would have to play second fiddle to Jordan. They were unimpressed by its fuzziness as to whether a Palestinian sovereign state would be established before or after confederation with Jordan, or even whether it would be established at all.

Arafat, who had undertaken to hasten back to Amman bearing the consent of his colleagues, did not return to tell Hussein the bad news. He sent an emissary with suggested amendments instead. A furious Hussein rejected these out of hand and in a statement that reflected the pique felt in the palace, the Jordanian cabinet announced on 10 April the abandonment of the joint initiative, and of participation in the Reagan plan.

In the weeks and months after his expulsion from Beirut, Arafat had continued to behave in many ways much as before the Israeli invasion. He travelled widely, consulted Arab heads of state, tried quixotically to mediate in the endless and often highly personal disputes that swirl about the Arab world, received Israeli peace campaigners of dubious relevance at his Tunis headquarters, and generally endeavoured to create the illusion that for the PLO it was business as usual. But even as the PLO leader dabbled and temporised, and dreamed up new stratagems to keep his name in the headlines, the ground was shifting beneath his feet. He appeared not to notice, or even to care, about mutinous noises from some of his erstwhile Fatah colleagues who had, against his wishes, based themselves in Damascus and were now passing their days and nights plotting his downfall. A chilly meeting of the PLO's Central Council came and went in late November without Arafat seeking to force a showdown, but his failure to act was merely storing up trouble. As so often, his tendency to prevaricate made things worse.

The dissident leadership had by then coalesced around four men: Nimr Saleh and Ahmed Kadri, a fellow Fatah Central Committee member, and Colonels Mohammed Said Musa Maragha and Khaled al-Amleh. Of the four, Said Musa, or Abu Musa as he was better known to his colleagues, emerged as the spokesman. A hardened professional soldier who trained in the Jordanian army, he had joined the Palestinian resistance at the height of its conflict with Hussein in 1970. He had fought bravely and had been rewarded with the post of military commander of southern Lebanon when the PLO expanded its bases there after its expulsion from Jordan. A long-standing member of Fatah's 'leftist' tendency, Musa had made no secret of his opposition to the PLO leader's diplomatic machinations.

On 27 January 1983 Musa had made clear the dissidents' objections at a highly charged meeting in Aden of Fatah's Revolutionary Council – the organisation's consultative body. According to one of those present, it was an 'ugly, bitter meeting' that acted as only a temporary safety valve for dissident frustrations.[10] Speaking from a text drafted by his co-conspirators in Damascus, Musa had railed against 'capitulationist' policies under Arafat. He expressed violent opposition to the PLO's diplomatic strategy. He demanded a return to armed struggle as the 'sole road to liberation' in Lebanon, the Israeli-occupied Golan Heights and in the West Bank. Fresh efforts should be made to overthrow the Hashemite regime to enable guerrilla raids on Israel to be conducted from Jordanian territory. An underground war should be declared on American interests in the Middle East, and so on.[11]

Arafat and Fatah leaders listened to Musa in stunned silence. The Aden meeting failed totally in its aim of quieting the voices of dissent. Equally inconclusive was a subsequent meeting of the Palestine National Council, in Algiers in mid-February. The gathering Of 350 Palestinian delegates glossed over contentious issues as much as possible, so as not to exacerbate the PLO's internal divisions, and ended up mouthing platitudes. Cynics dubbed it the lam PNC – a combination of the Arabic words 'no' (la) and 'yes' (nam). In a closed debate on the Reagan plan, Arafat uttered words that could almost be regarded as his signature tune. 'It's true that we are being offered nothing of value, but we can't afford to say no to everything,' he declared. 'We can't say yes to everything either. So we have to learn to say "Yes, but," and "No, but . . ."'[12]

One man who took strong exception to the failure of the Algiers meeting to address substantial issues was Issam Sartawi, Arafat's peace envoy. Denied the right to speak, a disillusioned Sartawi left Algiers observing that, with the PLO's representative body sliding into irrelevance, it might be better to hold its next session in Fiji. But Sartawi, a deeply controversial figure within the PLO because of his daring diplomatic manoeuvres, did not have long to live. On 10 April, the same day that Jordan formally ended its joint initiative with the PLO, he was gunned down by assassins sent by Abu Nidal while attending a meeting of the Socialist International in the Portuguese coastal resort of Albufeira. Among those who were present and who paid tribute was Shinion Peres, the Israeli Labour leader. In Sanaa, the barren high altitude capital of North Yemen, Arafat condemned the killers, describing them as Israeli 'hirelings'. It was not the first time the PLO had hinted at Mossad penetration of Abu Nidal's gang but, on this occasion, the allusion seemed off-beam. The PLO leader was aware that Sabri al-Banna (alias Abu Nidal) had, late in 1982, moved back into Syria's orbit, quietly switching his headquarters from Baghdad to Damascus. It was from there that the statement claiming responsibility for Sartawi's killing had been issued on behalf of Abu Nidal's Fatah Revolutionary Council. Chillingly, it described the heart surgeon and peace campaigner as 'the enemy of our people'.[13]

As Arafat pursued his restless peregrinations the Lebanese time bomb continued to tick. Amid a flurry of diplomatic activity and violence prompted by US and Israeli efforts to construct a new Lebanon from the ashes of the old, the world barely noticed a series of political tremors deep in the Syrian-controlled Bekaa Valley. Early in May 1983, a group of Fatah officers led by the arch-dissident, Colonel Said Musa, commandeered the head-quarters of the PLO's Yarmouk Brigade at Hammara in the Bekaa near the Syrian border. The Fatah mutiny had begun. Its immediate trigger had been Arafat's ill-advised appointment towards the end of April of 51 loyalist officers, several of whom had been accused of cowardice during the Israeli invasion, to command posts in central and northern Lebanon, where thousands of PLO troops had regrouped after the withdrawal from Beirut.

By now thoroughly alarmed by the events in the Bekaa, Arafat had hastened there on 13 May, four days after the mutineers had made their move. From the PLO offices in Damascus, he shuttled back and forth three times in four days and made a series of concessions to the rebels. He agreed to reinstate rebel officers, purge those who had been negligent during the Lebanon invasion and restore Nimr Saleh to the Fatah Central Committee.'[14] He met Assad – their first meeting since Arafat's expulsion from Lebanon – in a half-hearted and ultimately fruitless attempt to iron out their differences; he also felt obliged to echo some of the hardline rhetoric of his opponents, declaring in Damascus on 15 May, 'An effective war is the only way to redraw the map of the Middle East. The way out of this present deadlock is to take a decision to wage war to change the balance of power.'[15]

In early June, open warfare broke out in the Bekaa. Fatah blood was spilled. It would continue to flow for the rest of the year. Breaking off a visit to Romania, Arafat rushed to Algeria and then to Saudi Arabia in a desperate effort to enlist wider Arab support against Syrian and Libyan backing for the mutineers. The fact that his leadership was being challenged by such an array of forces was bad enough. Worse still was the ammunition they were using: all-out criticism of the way he had run the PLO. Rebel leader Said Musa, in an interview with the Arab weekly, *Al-Kifah al-Arabi*, accused Arafat of turning the Palestinian revolution into a 'bureaucracy so rotten that it is worse than the bureaucracy in any underdeveloped country,' adding cruelly, 'Naturally, this institution was not capable of fighting. So when the war [in Lebanon] broke out, the leadership ran away, leaving the rank and file to pay the price.'[16]

On 2 June, Arafat bitterly attacked Libya for its support of the Fatah rebels, but he still stopped short of openly condemning Syria in the hope of preventing any further deterioration in his badly strained relations with Assad. It was not as if he did not have cause for complaint. Damascus was by then making little attempt to hide its backing for the rebels: Syrian troops obstructed and detained Fatah commanders, and several times joined in attacks with heavy weapons on loyalist positions in the Bekaa. 'Arab intervention is no longer limited to material support,' Arafat declared angrily, 'but has been translated into action as well.'[17]

On the evening of 23 June, Intissar al-Wazir, wife of Khalil al-Wazir, telephoned Arafat in Damascus to request an urgent meeting. Once at Arafat's office, she told him she had been informed by a Syrian intelligence source that gunmen were planning to ambush his convoy as it returned later that day to Tripoli in northern Lebanon by way of the Syrian town of Homs. 'He laughed and said he didn't care,' she recalled. 'He really didn't believe me, but he said, "Just repeat your story." So I did, and he said, "OK, I promise I won't go." '[18]

It was a wise decision. The convoy was ambushed outside Damascus. In the shoot-out, one of Arafat's bodyguards was killed and nine others were injured. At dawn, after a sleepless night, a furious Arafat bitterly condemned the Syrian plot to eliminate him, for the first time explicitly charging that Syria was behind the Fatah rebellion.

His criticism drew a quick response. At 8 a.m., he received a curt written ultimatum, signed by General Hikmat Shehabi, Syria's chief of staff, giving him six hours in which to leave the country.[19] The expulsion order amounted to a virtual declaration of war.

Arafat was being kicked out of an Arab capital for the second time in less than a year. But his peremptory expulsion order was nothing compared with the humiliation offered at Damascus Airport as he awaited a flight out of the country. Standing with a group of staff, the PLO leader was approached by a relatively junior officer who sputtered insolently in his face, 'Mr Arafat, you are *persona non grata*.'[20] Arafat was then bundled on to a regular Tunis Air flight to Tunis. On arrival there he declared bitterly that his expulsion was part of a Syrian–Libyan plot against the Palestinian revolution.[21]

On the Syrian side, too, the bitterness was out in the open. Damascus charged that Arafat had been expelled because of his 'continuous slandering . . . against Syria, its sacrifices and its positions of principle'.[22]

Arafat had entered one of his bleakest periods as PLO leader. He had lost the initiative in Lebanon where 10,000 of his best fighters were at the centre of a bloody test of wills with Fatah mutineers supported by other Damascus-based dissident Palestinians. He had worn out his welcome, one way or the other, in the capitals of all the frontline states that share a common border with Israel. Like a cyclist who has to keep peddling to stay upright, an immobile Arafat was in danger of toppling over, obliged to sit impotently in Tunis while his colleagues in Fatah sought to resolve his differences with the rebels.

In his darker moments, Arafat wondered if, after all these years, he might not be on the brink of defeat in his long and bitter struggle to retain freedom of manoeuvre for the Palestinian movement. He was haunted by memories of the fate that had befallen his two predecessors – Haj Amin al-Husseini and Ahmed Shukairy – both of whom had died in lonely exile, and he chafed at the prospect that he might become, in the words of Nabil Shaath, the 'third Palestinian leader to go into oblivion far away from the leadership and decision-making of his people'.[23]

If there was consolation for Arafat it lay in the strong backing he received from the occupied territories. On 26 June, just two days after his expulsion from Damascus, Sheikh Saad al-Din al-Alami, head of the higher Islamic Council, declared melodramatically at a public rally in Jerusalem's al-Aqsa mosque that, 'It is the duty of every Muslim to assassinate the Syrian president for the crimes that he committed against the Palestinian people.'[24] Buoyed by this, Arafat came to the conclusion that he had no other choice but to return to Lebanon to rally his troops and to confront the rebels. The question was when. He would have to await the critical psychological moment.

Late in June, at a seminar in Tunis attended by leading Palestinian intellectuals and businessmen, Arafat was finally persuaded that an audacious step was required. Discussion focused on the idea of declaring an independent Palestinian state in the West Bank and Gaza, and of forming a provisional government exile to replace the PLO.[25] In the midst of all this theorising, Arafat felt quite uncomfortable. What relevance, he asked himself, did discussion of these controversial ideas have to the immediate problems he was facing? Very little, he concluded. What was worse, he saw himself increasingly as a pawn in a game over which he had lost control. He was especially aggrieved that some of his closest allies among wealthy and powerful Palestinians in the Diaspora, the 'compradours' as he called them, were dealing as intermediaries with his bitter foes in Damascus. Besides, enforced inactivity was fraying his nerves.

If Arafat was to break out of this pattern, timing was all. One false move and he would be finished. Syria and the Fatah rebels, not to mention Israel, were waiting to pounce. Ironically, it was the Israelis who unwittingly provided the cue for his dramatic reappearance on the Arab stage.

On 28 August, after months of rising tension, open warfare broke out on the streets of Beirut between the Christian-dominated Lebanese army and the Internal Security Forces on one side, and local leftists and their Syrian-backed Shi'ite Amal militia allies on the other. Amal gunmen clashed with units of the Lebanese Army near the Bourj al-Brajneh quarter in the city's southern suburbs. Fighting quickly spread to west Beirut. For the next 48 hours the anti-government militia forces held sway in the rubble-strewn streets of the predominantly Muslim half of the capital.

For Arafat, the conflagration on the streets of Beirut was a sign that his time was drawing near. But before he made his move, he was momentarily distracted by an announcement from Jerusalem. On 29 August, the 69-year-old Menachem Begin told startled cabinet colleagues that 'I cannot go on any longer.' Two weeks later, the ex-Prime Minister went into dispirited seclusion in his small Jerusalem apartment at No. 1 Zemach Street, from where, as Arafat has since observed, he could look down on Deir Yassin, scene of the massacre of Arab villagers by Begin's Irgun terrorists many years before.[26] The Lebanon misadventure, with its daily toll of Israeli casualties, had simply become too much for the increasingly reclusive and guilt-ridden Begin, burdened by depression following the death of his wife late in 1982. His withdrawal seemed to Arafat like an omen. Bruised and battered as he was, he had at least outlasted the Israeli leader who had set out to destroy him; although he had little time to savour the moment.

In early September, the opportunity arrived for Arafat loyalists, holed up in Lebanon, to seize the initiative. At midnight on 3 September, just a day or so after the fighting had died down in Beirut, the last Israeli units quietly withdrew from their positions in the mountains overlooking Beirut to a new defensive line along the Awali river, well to the south. The fragile power balance in the Chouf Mountains had been dramatically altered. Lebanon was in for another of its convulsions. Into the vacuum created by the Israeli withdrawal stormed the fighters of the youthful Druze warlord, Walid Jumblatt, son of Kamal. They were supported by Arafat loyalists and by units of the Fatah mutineers. In the free-for-all that followed, the Christian Lebanese Forces militia and Christian-dominated Lebanese regular army units were driven back from most of their positions in the commanding heights above Beirut – in spite of aerial support from the Israelis and shelling from US warships offshore. By mid-September, the attackers were on the perimeter of the heavily guarded Christian stronghold of Souq al-Gharb above the presidential palace at Baabda. Indeed, some of the PLO commanders believed the advance might carry them back into Beirut itself, from where they had been so brutally evicted twelve months before.[27]

Fatah loyalists, and Popular and Democratic Front fighters of what was now dubbed the 'loyal opposition' to Arafat, had seized the opportunity of the Chouf War to break the Syrian shackles that had restrained them in the Bekaa. Alarmed at the possibility that they might establish an autonomous base for themselves, Syria took abrupt action on 15 September, instructing the Druze command to insist on the withdrawal of Palestinian guerrillas from the siege of Souq at-Gharb. This had two effects: it took some of the steam out of the assault on the key Christian stronghold and obliged the Palestinians to fall back towards Syrian lines in the Bekaa. But unbeknown to the Syrians – or indeed to the Israelis – the elusive Arafat was already making his move.

Wraithlike, the PLO leader re-emerged in the northern Lebanese city of Tripoli on 16 September. His timing was near-perfect, and he wasted no time in signalling his presence to the outside world. Going straight to the besieged Baddawi and Nahr al-Bared refugee camps, he declared defiantly for the benefit of his opponents in Damascus that the PLO 'is a towering revolution that no one can contain or control . . .'[28] Within days, Arafat's plan, worked out during long days of idleness in Tunis, exhibited signs of achieving its goal: to force Damascus and its rebel Fatah clients to show their hand.

In the last week of September, under concerted Syrian pressure, Fatah loyalist fighters withdrew north from the Bekaa towards Tripoli where Arafat was preparing to fight what many believed would be his last battle. Throughout October, the Syrian-backed Fatah rebels tightened their siege, moving closer to the Baddawi and Nahr al-Bared camps and to Tripoli itself. Offshore, Israeli gunboats ceaselessly patrolled, preventing arms and reinforcements reaching Arafat's beleaguered garrison. It was not the smallest of the ironies that Fatah rebels, themselves committed to the destruction of the Jewish state, were making common cause with the Israeli navy.

As October gave way to November, Arafat found himself besieged for the second time in a little more than a year, this time by the Syrians, dissident Palestinians, Lebanese militia and the Israelis. The enemy camp even contained a contingent of Chadian soldiers reportedly despatched by Libya's Colonel Gadaffi under the mistaken impression they were attacking Tel Aviv. In the face of this bizarre assortment of foes, Arafat's sole local ally was an Islamic fundamentalist party with little more than words to offer in support. Under criticism from his own supporters – the veteran Khaled al-Hassan, for one, wondered why it had been necessary for him to go to Tripoli in the first place 'without a collective decision' – Arafat felt he had no choice. His aim was to confront his enemies and to bring into the open the dimensions of the Syrian involvement in the mutiny. Fighting for his political survival, he had decided to make Tripoli his last stand, if necessary. 'In Tripoli we forced the plotters to expose all of their cards,' he said. 'We disproved the claims that the problem was merely an internal Palestinian conflict.'[29]

As the bitter conflict continued into November, with Palestinian ranged against Palestinian, Arafat and his supporters were relentlessly pushed back, first from the Nahr al-Bared camp, and then from al-Baddawi. Before hastily withdrawing from the latter, Arafat accused Damascus of seeking to turn the PLO into a Syrian 'puppet'. 'They want to end the PLO, to end the independent Palestinian decision,' he said. 'They want to create an alternative PLO that will be a puppet in their hands. But I tell them, I will only bow to God and to the will of my people. I will fight and die here with my people but I will never compromise on my people's dignity, independence or rights.'[30]

Arafat charged that the Syrians had massed up to 25,000 men, 170 tanks and 180 artillery pieces around the refugee camps. Such was the carnage in and around Tripoli in those November days that hospitals ran out of morgue space. These were truly desperate moments with the PLO leader and 4,000 of his best fighters cooped up under heavy shellfire in an area scarcely larger than one square mile. He was faced, it seemed, with the choice between humiliating surrender and a complete rout of his beleaguered forces.

But again fate intervened. When Arafat's forces were expelled from their last military stronghold in the al-Baddawi camp on 17 November alarm spread across a hitherto complacent Arab world. Nowhere was the unease greater than in Saudi Arabia, where the hereditary rulers were filled with horror at the thought of a completely destabilised and vengeful Palestinian movement. Crown Prince Abdullah bin Abdel Aziz, on a visit to Kuwait on 21 November, denounced the rebellion as a 'military coup against Arafat's legitimate leadership'.[31]

Having decided that 'enough was enough', the Saudis wasted no time in exerting pressure on Syria to cease its onslaught against Arafat's last crumbling redoubt in Lebanon. Prince Saud al-Faisal, the Saudi Foreign Minister, was despatched to Damascus to negotiate terms for Arafat's orderly withdrawal from Tripoli, but strangely absent from all the discussions was Hafez al-Assad. Complaining of chest pains and exhaustion, Syria's leader had been secretly admitted to hospital on 12 November at the very height of the onslaught against Arafat's strongholds. Assad's confinement to a sick bed at this critical moment was by no means the least fortuitous development in Arafat's precarious career.

After four days of discussion, on 25 November the Saudi–Syrian agreement on the Fatah loyalist withdrawal from Tripoli was announced. Arafat was to be completely banished from Lebanon but, to balance that, Syria had failed to supplant him as the leader of the revolution. The joint agreement was immediately accepted. With his back to the wall, Arafat had no other choice and neither did the Fatah mutineers. Said Musa and his men did what they were told by Damascus.

On the eve of the truce, Arafat pulled off something of a propaganda coup with the announcement that six Israeli prisoners-of-war with the beleaguered Fatah forces in Tripoli had been exchanged for 4,500 Palestinian and Lebanese prisoners held by Israel. The event projected Arafat's smiling face on to the front pages of the world's press within days of the leader writers having penned another batch of political obituaries: 'Already crippled by Israel, Yasser Arafat has been finished off by Syria,' commented the *New York Times*. '. . . Such is the bizarre ending of a movement that, for all its daring, never found a political vision.'[32]

Negotiations on Arafat's evacuation from Tripoli dragged on for three weeks with the PLO leader, as ever, seeking to make the best of yet another historic setback. Not least of Arafat's concerns was the threat posed by the Israelis to plans for an orderly evacuation of PLO fighters under the United Nations flag, thus guaranteeing their safe conduct. Ariel Sharon, for one, said that Arafat 'should not be allowed to leave Tripoli alive'.[33] Israeli gunboats also kept up the pressure, blasting PLO guerrilla bases around Tripoli in the first weeks of December, further delaying his departure. All this tended to play into Arafat's hands in any case, since he was in no hurry to relinquish his last toehold in Lebanon.

Eventually, on 20 December a convoy of five Greek ships flying the UN flag entered the harbour in Tripoli to ferry the Fatah loyalists to camps scattered about the Arab world. But the way for Arafat's evacuation was not cleared until the US had urged Israel to stop its attacks on PLO positions. Arafat's second exodus from Lebanon was less dramatic than the first but in a way more poignant. He was leaving his last base in Lebanon. His movement was badly fractured. In front of him lay, at best, a deeply uncertain future and, at worst, political oblivion. As he arrived at the quayside in a white Range Rover, he tried to put the best face on things. 'The struggle is not over,' he declared. 'We will continue until we reach Jerusalem, the capital of our Palestinian state.'[34] In the demonstrable weakness and disarray into which the PLO had fallen, it was hardly a credible call to arms.

As his vessel, the *Odysseus Elytis*, prepared to set sail under French naval escort, Arafat appeared on the upper deck to be greeted with the ritual discharge of automatic rifles by PLO and Lebanese fighters. Arafat's aides said he was bound for Tunis but it was very soon apparent that this was a ruse. Arafat had another card up his sleeve.

13. CLIMBING BACK

'We should realise that this is not the time to strive for the resolution of the Palestinian issue, but rather to concentrate on its preservation, lest it become extinct.' Nabil Shaath, *Al-Siyassa*, 15 April 1985.

As Yasser Arafat sailed away from Lebanon, he proclaimed defiantly that he was heading 'from one outpost of struggle to another outpost of struggle'.[1] In fact, he was bound for the land of his birth. Forty-eight hours before he set sail from Tripoli, Arafat had quietly informed Sadat's successor as Egyptian President, Hosni Mubarak, that he would welcome the opportunity for a meeting provided by his passage through the Suez Canal. Aware of likely opposition to his plan – Egypt had been ostracised by the Arab world for more than six years since Sadat's visit to Israel – he did not even share his secret with Khalil al-Wazir, his most trusted lieutenant, who had battled with him in Tripoli to the end. 'I went to Cairo,' he said, 'to convey a message to the world . . . that if they thought that they were able to get rid of us, they were very wrong . . . in addition I felt there was a need for a big step which would overturn the table, and by going to Egypt I overturned the table.'[2]

That Arafat was willing to risk further fragmenting his movement at this time was a measure of his desperate need for new friends and supporters. It was also an indication of the importance he had always attached to Egypt as the Arab world's leading power. Was it not an Egyptian President, Nasser, who had made it possible for him to take over the PLO in the first place? Had Nasser not, as his final act, rescued the movement from destruction in the Jordanian civil war? Had his successor, Sadat, not helped Arafat towards recognition as representative of the Palestinians? Now it was time to make a fresh start. If, by 'overturning the table', he risked further enraging his critics then so be it. Things could hardly get worse.

Arafat was met, when his vessel docked at Port Said, by Mohammed Sobhieh, a long-time loyalist and Cairo resident who was Secretary General of the Palestine National Council. It was hardly a red-carpet reception but Arafat's pulse quickened, nevertheless, at coming back to Egypt after a frustrating six-year absence. 'He was very tired, and full of pain,' recalled Sobhieh, 'But he was also 4looking forward to renewing personal contacts with the Egyptian leadership.'[3]

As Arafat sailed down the Suez Canal to Ismailia to a formal welcome, he was briefed by Sobhieh, and by Nabil Shaath, both of whom had liaised closely with Egyptian officials throughout the Tripoli affair. Appalled by the Syrian-backed onslaught against the organisation's leadership, Egypt would do what it could to assist the PLO mainstream to get back on its feet.

In Ismailia, Arafat was greeted by a bevy of top Egyptian officials before being flown by military helicopter the hundred or so kilometres to President Mubarak's administrative headquarters in Heliopolis. It was in every sense a homecoming, for Arafat flew over the street where he had lived. Rendered homeless twice in the previous fifteen months by Israeli and Arab antagonists, he could barely contain his elation.

The return to Cairo had been carefully calculated. Arafat, the conciliator, had never been one to allow any estrangement to become final. Indeed, his desire to keep lines open to the widest range of contacts had given rise to wry jokes among his colleagues. In one of them, Arafat is on the *haj*, the Muslim pilgrimage to Mecca. Arriving in the valley of Mina for the ritual stoning of the images of the devil, he does not throw his full allotment of seven stones. Asked why, he replies: 'I don't think we should close the door to anybody.'[4]

In this vein, even at the height of the public acrimony between the PLO and Egypt over Sadat's peace treaty with Israel, Arafat had maintained secret contacts through trusted aides like Sobhieh. When Sadat was assassinated, he had discreetly telephoned the new president to congratulate him on his succession. Mubarak, for his part, had shown support for the PLO since the Israeli invasion of Lebanon and during the encirclement of Beirut had angered the Israelis by collaborating with France in a diplomatic initiative calling for PLO participation in peace talks. Now he might reap some reward in the Arab world by extending a welcome to Arafat. Simultaneously, he might quieten criticism within Egypt that the government was not doing enough for the Palestinians.

No sooner had Arafat's helicopter come to rest in the grounds of Kubbeh Palace – where a succession of rulers held court before the overthrow of the monarchy in 1952 – than the Egyptian president stepped forward to greet him. As the television cameras zeroed in, Mubarak clasped Arafat in a bear hug before taking him off for two hours of private talks in his study. There were no illusions on either side about the problems the visit would cause. Sourly, the Israelis, anxiously observing this dalliance between their newfound 'friends' in Cairo and their No. 1 enemy, condemned the Mubarak–Arafat talks as a 'severe blow to the peace process in the Middle East'.[5]

The meeting had, however, served the two leaders' purposes tolerably well. For Arafat, it was a public relations coup. He emerged from the talks to declare theatrically that he had invited the Egyptian president to join him in prayer at the al-Aqsa mosque in Jerusalem. Mubarak simply told reporters that the Arafat visit showed that 'Egypt has been vindicated', and 'It was right all along'.[6]

Within the Palestinian movement such blunt words only served to enrage Arafat's critics. As he was whisked back to the *Odysseus Elytis*, a tempest broke. From Damascus, a host of factions condemned Arafat's 'treasonous' behaviour. Even Arafat's closest friends had found his latest manoeuvre inexplicable. It reduced Khalil al-Wazir to near-impotent rage. One of the least demonstrative of Palestinian leaders, Wazir fell back on what had become a familiar rebuke at moments of extreme frustration with his old friend: 'How could you do this to us, brother?'[7]

To men like Wazir, Arafat seemed to be cutting himself adrift. He had not deigned to consult them before his Egyptian stopover, and he stayed out of touch as his ship continued its voyage down the Red Sea. Even the ship seemed to have lost its way, for its captain was having difficulty in locating Arafat's destination: the North Yemen port of Hodeida. Instead of making straight for the eastern shore of the Red Sea, the Greek vessel – running low on water and with its air conditioning turned off – sailed mistakenly westward towards Port Sudan. Confusion reigned for a few hours. The *Odysseus* seemed a fitting symbol for the state of the PLO itself – wandering aimless and demoralised after the 'war of independence', with a captain whose navigational skills were questionable.

But whatever his colleagues thought, Arafat had not lost his bearings entirely. More to the point, his visit to Cairo had drawn strong support from an increasingly important constituency: Palestinian leaders in the Israeli-occupied West Bank and Gaza Strip. Throughout Arafat's travails, they were the one group who had stood by him constantly. They were also becoming a force to be reckoned with in their own right. It was time for the PLO leader to harness their influence in rebuilding his shattered organisation and his own prestige.

Briefing a reporter on board the *Odysseus*, Arafat declared that the organisation would now focus its attention much more on the West Bank and Gaza Strip and mused vaguely about renewing his joint peace efforts with King Hussein of Jordan.[8]

In Sanaa, capital of North Yemen, Arafat paused briefly to rally his dispirited troops, then headed back to Tunis and an icy reception from senior Fatah colleagues. He was neither surprised nor unduly concerned. The only way for the PLO to break out of its dangerous isolation, Arafat believed, was to take risks. Meeting in Tunis in the first week of 1984, the ten-member Fatah Central Committee meekly declared that Arafat's Cairo visit had been a breach of the principle of collective leadership, and sought to limit his freedom of manoeuvre. It was a weak response to a move that had, after all, left official PLO policy concerning Egypt in tatters. Deep down Arafat's colleagues knew that he was no more likely to heed their strictures now than on the many occasions in the past when they had tried and failed to rein him in.

The more important decision taken that week dealt with a quite different subject: Jordan. Arafat and King Hussein had not been speaking since the breakdown of their negotiations the previous year. Now the Central Committee gave the PLO leader the mandate he wanted to resume contacts with his old sparring partner. Admittedly, it laid down important conditions, rejecting the Reagan plan of 1 September 1982, which called for an autonomous Palestinian homeland in confederation with Jordan, and insisting that any agreement with Jordan must provide, without qualification, for the establishment of an independent

Palestinian state in the occupied territories. But such caveats were of little moment to Arafat. What mattered was that the top leadership of Fatah had given him the go-ahead to rebuild the troubled marriage between Jordan and the Palestinians, essential if he was to stand any chance of reviving his demoralised movement and involving it in Middle East peace moves. The pro-Western Hussein was Arafat's ticket to respectability and even, perhaps, to recognition by the United States.

Sensing that another opportunity had presented itself for him to court Arafat, King Hussein on 16 January reconvened his parliament after a ten-year suspension and in a speech to the opening session called on the PLO to agree on a 'practical formula'[9] for Middle East peace negotiations, leaving no doubt as to what he thought that formula should be. In the gossip-prone Jordanian capital, a fresh appearance by Arafat seemed inevitable.

But before mending the breach with Jordan, Arafat's most pressing task was to revive the demoralised PLO. Shaken to its core by the 'war of independence', the splintered organisation could hardly have been in worse shape to confront its many challenges. Arafat also knew that an exceptional effort was required to shore up his own position as leader. To this end he had begun working from the day of his removal from Tripoli on convening a meeting of the Palestinian 'parliament', the Palestine National Council. But it was to take him most of the year to drag his squabbling and depleted ranks to Amman for such a gathering.

That January, the dogged Khalil al-Wazir persuaded Arafat to sanction an all-out effort to unify PLO ranks in the face of concerted Syrian and Libyan attempts to create an alternative leadership. Always intensely sceptical of Arafat's high-wire diplomacy, Wazir argued that unless the organisation put its house in order it would be in no position to address the challenges of the day. Somehow the lie had to be given to Syria's argument that Arafat had forsaken the Palestinian consensus. Logically, that would entail trying to achieve a reconciliation at least with the two main Damascus-based splinters – the Popular and Democratic Fronts for the Liberation of Palestine.

Given the depth of animosity, reconciliation effort, in which both Algeria and South Yemen acted as mediators, moved fast.

Early in July, Arafat was able to announce, in a message marking the end of Ramadan, that he was back on speaking terms with George Habash and Nayef Hawatmeh of the Popular and Democratic Fronts.

The fragile consensus was enshrined in a set of agreements, announced on 13 July and named the Aden–Algiers Accords. These laid down ground rules for the future conduct of the PLO's component factions and contained numerous clauses aimed at ensuring that Arafat would henceforth toe the party line on such vexed issues as relations with Egypt and Jordan.[10] That, at least, was the theory. In practice, not many months would pass before Arafat was bending and stretching the agreement to an extent which rendered it virtually meaningless.

The Algiers–Aden agreements were significant in another respect: in their sharp focus on the occupied territories.

Article 1 dealt at length with the need to pour maximum resources into confronting the Israeli occupation, urging 'every kind of support to the struggle of our people in the occupied territories against Israeli occupation, its repressive terroristic measures, and escalating attempts to expropriate the land, to build settlements and expel the population in preparation for annexing the occupied territories'.[11] During the years in Jordan and Lebanon, the leadership had paid insufficient attention to the problems of the Palestinians under occupation. Distracted by delusions of power and involvement in two civil wars, Arafat and his fellow faction leaders had only sporadically worked on building grassroots support and stiffening resistance to Israeli rule in the territories but, when the PLO had come under increasing pressure in Lebanon and the armed struggle looked ever more forlorn and aimless, the occupied territories had begun to seem the most promising battleground.

None of the PLO factions had been more successful on this front than Arafat's Fatah. As the largest grouping in the organisation it had much greater resources to devote to the territories than the others, and also had a determined organiser, in the person of Khalil al-Wazir. After 1981, Wazir, commander of the so-called Western Sector of PLO operations that specifically included the West Bank and the Gaza Strip, had devoted more and more of his time to the occupied territories. His mission was, in his words, to create a 'parallel authority [to the Israelis] reaching from the kindergarten to the grave'.[12]

With Arafat's approval, he had maintained a network of contacts. He had built a detailed personal archive of thousands of individuals throughout the West Bank and Gaza and kept in touch with Palestinian prisoners inside Israeli jails, even devising ways to establish communications between the prisons themselves. After the PLO's expulsion from Lebanon in 1982, he had quietly rented a house in Amman, from where he was in virtual daily contact with his agents across the Jordan river. With his guidance, Fatah had penetrated many of the institutions that had formed in Palestinian society under Israeli rule: it dominated the student organisations, the unions, the press and the women's groups.

Arafat had long viewed Israel's policy of establishing Jewish settlements in the territories as a serious threat, understanding very well that the Israeli right was intent on creating a colonial *fait accompli*, in open defiance of the Americans with a view to establishing permanent control. Hadn't the publication in the spring of 1984 of an authoritative Israel study of the territories confirmed the worst fears of the Tunis leadership? Funded by liberal American institutions, the report had reached the conclusion that Israeli settlement activity had passed the point of no return, and that Israel's 'creeping annexation' of the territories was becoming irreversible.[13]

In the months after his expulsion from Tripoli, Arafat was once again in perpetual motion. By mid-year, he had helped Egypt return to the Islamic Conference Organisation, the umbrella grouping for Islamic countries worldwide. He had quixotically offered to mediate again in the Gulf war, then at its fiercest, although he had long since ceased to be a welcome guest in Iran. But the appearance of frenetic activity was deceptive, In reality, Arafat was simply marking time, waiting for the moment to relaunch his peace duet with King Hussein, and anxiously watching developments in Israel where early opinion polls indicated that elections to be held in July would be won by the Labour Party led by Shimon Peres.

The PLO leader was in no doubt the poll would have direct bearing on chances for peace negotiations which he badly wanted to join. A Labour victory under the relatively conciliatory Peres promised progress; a win by Likud under the hardline Yitzhak Shamir would spell deadlock. Neither occurred. After weeks of haggling over the formation of a coalition government following a deadlocked election, Peres and Shamir uneasily joined forces in a 'Government of National Unity'. It was hardly the most propitious development for two Arab leaders intent on another burst of peacemaking. By the autumn of 1984 Arafat and Hussein, for better or worse, were set on a new tryst, to be followed by an uneasy wedding, and ultimately by a messy divorce.

For Arafat, a nagging question remained: how was he to bring his movement along with him to the altar? What he needed was a meeting of the PLO 'parliament'. What he seemed to lack was a venue for the proposed session, and a quorum of delegates. Plenty of people were set on preventing a conference that might serve to shore up Arafat's battered leadership: none was more determined than his old foe, President Hafez al-Assad of Syria. If he could not unseat Arafat by fomenting insurrection in his own ranks, then he had other cards to play. In September 1984, Assad took the unusual step of leaving his Damascus stronghold and flying to Algeria to urge President Chadli Benjedid not to host Arafat's proposed parliamentary session. Benjedid acquiesced.

From that point on, the Arab world indulged in overheated speculation about the venue for the PLO meeting. Arafat's ability to convene the PNC with the necessary quorum of two-thirds of the body's 384 members – without the attendance of the Damascus-based groups – was rapidly coming to be seen as a gauge of his leadership. Jokingly, Arafat began to tell anyone who would listen that he would hold the session 'on board a ship' in the Mediterranean if all else failed. That would not be necessary, as Arafat was fully aware. He had long since decided where he wanted to hold the PNC: in the Jordanian capital, Amman.

Presiding over a public meeting in Amman would give him access to a potential daily television audience of more than two million Palestinians in the occupied territories and in Israel itself. Such an event would have a galvanising effect in what had become his most prized constituency. By seeking to deny him other venues for the meeting, Arafat's enemies were playing into his hands.

So the stage was set for the theatrical Arafat ably supported by that other noted Arab thespian Hussein bin Talal. Broadcasting from Aden on 12 November, the Voice of Palestine radio station proclaimed: 'The leadership has defined with courage, clarity and finality, that 22 November will be the final date for the convocation of the PNC, and that Amman will be the capital in which the PNC's seventeenth session will be held.'[14]

On the evening of 22 November, in a sports complex on the rocky hills of Amman, King Hussein officially opened the first large-scale PLO gathering to be held in the Jordanian capital in fourteen years. An extraordinary spectacle greeted the select few journalists and diplomats who witnessed the opening session. Seated in the audience was a gaggle of ageing revolutionaries whose bloodcurdling threats against King Hussein's life following Black September of 1970 had seemed to preclude any prospect of reconciliation. And yet here they were, back in Amman, listening attentively to a man many of them, including Arafat himself, had dubbed the 'butcher'.

Speaking with force and resonance for thirty minutes but never once raising his voice, Hussein called on the PLO to abandon 'stagnation'. More pointedly, he urged the Palestinians to embrace Security Council Resolution 242 'as a basis for a just and peaceful settlement'.[15] The king could not be accused of failing to address the most difficult issue head-on.

For Hussein, acceptance of Resolution 242, with its implied recognition of Israel's right to exist behind pre-1967 war boundaries, was the *sine qua non* for solving the Arab–Israeli conflict. But for many among his audience, the Resolution's rightful place was in the charnber of conspiracies against Palestinian rights; along with the Balfour Declaration, the Sykes–Picot Agreement, the UN Partition Plan of 1947 and the Camp David Accords.

Arafat had his own role to play, and he played it for all it was worth: to his immediate audience in Amman; to his enemies in Damascus; and, most important, to the people in the next important theatre of PLO operations – the West Bank and the Gaza Strip. 'We are only some kilometres away from our

Palestine,' he declared[16] – all too well aware that while this might be literally true, the PLO was still far away from sitting down at the same table and negotiating with Israel and further still from reclaiming one inch of territory.

Never mind: Arafat had his own very specific aims. He wanted to prepare for a new peace initiative whose immediate aim was to secure American recognition of Palestinian rights and a clear acknowledgement of the PLO's status as the spokesman of the Palestinians. He wanted to bolster his working relationship with Hussein and Jordan, partly as a cover for the PLO's growing links with, the neighbouring occupied territories. Above all, he wanted to shore up his own position as leader in the face of continuing threats from Damascus, and of rumbling criticism of his autocratic leadership style from within the ranks. He chose a characteristically melodramatic means of doing so.

Following some harsh words at a late session about his refusal to consult colleagues, he theatrically tended his resignation. It was not the first time Arafat had threatened to quit in order to get his way, but he added an additional note of drama to the occasion by inviting his colleagues to 'change this donkey'.[17] It was about as close as Arafat would come to apparently serious self-criticism.

To increase the drama, he left his resignation on the table throughout the night and into the next day. When the session resumed, Arafat sat quietly in the third row of the audience, fiddling distractedly with his black and white chequered head-dress. He would not be moved, or so he pretended. Selim Zaanoun, an old student friend and deputy speaker of the PNC, was obliged to abandon the session's formal agenda to implore him to withdraw his resignation. 'You do not own yourself,' Zaanoun declared. 'You belong to the Palestinian people.'[18]

Milking the occasion for more than it was worth, Arafat would consider withdrawing his resignation, but only because the 'conspiracy' mounted by Syria and the Fatah mutineers was directed not only against himself but against the whole PLO. 'You are the only people who can ask me to stay or leave,' he declared. 'Not this or that Arab regime.'[19]

Standing before his brethren Arafat declared, 'You, the members of the Palestine National Council who represent the legitimacy of the Palestinian people, you are the ones who can decide: you can say Abu Ammar go, or Abu Ammar stay.'[20] It was, of course, the cue for a choreographed chorus of 'Abu Ammar stay, Abu Ammar stay'.

In Damascus, the show of support for Arafat caused extreme irritation. Syria's attempts to block the parliamentary session had failed, and so, too, had its half-baked efforts to mount a rival television show to the one being beamed daily via Jordan Television to the Palestinians in the territories. Particularly infuriating was the fact that many of the 250,000 or so Palestinians living in Syria itself spent their days glued to Jordanian broadcasts. If the 1984 PNC, boycotted by all the Damascus-based groups, was one more *coup de theatre* in the long internal struggle over Arafat's stewardship of the Palestinian movement, its most visible external manifestation was the 'battle of the airwaves'.

While Syria wheeled forward a shadowy bunch of mutineers to denounce a 'traitorous Arafat', the PLO's mainstream leadership was appearing in Palestinian living rooms all over the region, seen to be engaged, for the most part, in constructive debate. Typical of reaction in the territories was this simple observation from a young man in Dheisheh refugee camp outside Jerusalem: 'I touched this [Palestinian] democracy through television,' he told reporters.[21] In predictable counterpoint, Israel's Foreign Minister Yitzhak Shamir sourly observed that the performance had brought closer the 'voice of the PLO terrorist organisation'.[22]

Arafat himself ended the week's deliberations on a defiant note. Speaking at a final press conference before flying off to Saudi Arabia to brief King Fahd on the results of the meeting, he sharply criticised Syria and the Palestinian mutineers. 'We are determined,' he declared, 'that this faciscm will not drive us from our democratic ideals. We will preserve our ideals in this jungle of guns.'[23]

Before the year was out, Arafat and his lieutenants were to be reminded yet again that the 'jungle of guns' still had the power to disrupt and intimidate. On 29 December, Fahd Kawasmeh, the deported former mayor of Hebron in the West Bank, and one of the new members of the PLO's Executive Committee, was gunned down in Amman. Khalil al-Wazir immediately charged that the killing had been directed from Damascus. It was a quick and bloody riposte from Arafat's enemies, which punctured the euphoria that had accompanied his theatrical 're-election'.

But the Amman meeting had served its purpose nonetheless. As Arafat saw it, the way was now clear for a joint peace initiative with King Hussein that might bring him closer to his long-cherished goal: a direct and open dialogue with the United States. Their efforts to agree on a new peace formula took on particular urgency, as King Fahd was due to visit Washington in the second week of February 1985. Both Arafat and Hussein had resolved – naively, as it turned out – that the Saudi monarch was the man to present their peace proposal to the Americans.

Fahd was well aware of the PLO–Jordanian efforts to agree on a new peace initiative. He had been kept separately informed by both sides of stuttering attempts to draft an agreement. He was also intensely sceptical about the likelihood of the two coming up with a form of words that would satisfy the Palestinian consensus, the Jordanians and the Americans. He was proved right, but not before Hussein and Arafat, on the very day he was due to have his fireside chat with Reagan, took a clumsy stab at drafting a formula acceptable to all.

14. THE ODD COUPLE

'After two long attempts, I and the government of the Kingdom of Jordan hereby announce that we are unable to co-ordinate politically with the PLO leadership until such a time as their word becomes their bond, characterised by commitment, credibility and constancy.' King Hussein, address to the nation, 19 February 1986.

It was mid-morning on a sunny winter's day. Yasser Arafat, in his bulletproof limousine, swept through the heavily guarded entrance to al-Nadwa palace overlooking the old city of Amman. It was a route Arafat had traversed more times than he cared to remember in his long, fractious relationship with the Jordanian monarch. Many of his visits to the palace had simply been courtesy calls but this occasion, he had no doubt, would be strictly business. Hussein expected agreement on a new peace initiative to flow from their deliberations that day. Arafat, too, was anxious to reach an understanding. It was 11 February 1985.

Hussein greeted Arafat cordially in the embrace Arab etiquette demanded. The two men exchanged pleasantries before adjourning with their advisers for a round of discussions. Talk continued at a good-humoured lunch in which Hussein and Arafat, flanked by their aides, sat facing one another. Underlying all the civilities was a sense of urgency. It was the day of King Fahd's visit to Washington. Both men were possessed of the need to come up with something he could pass on to Reagan and after more than two months of talks, they knew they were little closer to their goal than when they started.

Debate had focused on the same old troublesome issue: Resolution 242 and an independent Palestinian state. The Jordanians, seeking to meet American demands, would probe for acceptance of 242 and the PLO would resist. The Palestinians would try to include the words 'independent state' and 'self-determination', and Jordan would refuse. The two sides also haggled about the terms of a confederation between the Kingdom of Jordan and a theoretical Palestinian government in the West Bank and Gaza.

As the jockeying between Hussein and Arafat continued that February day Hussein reached for a menu and scribbled down some points in Arabic. He handed the menu across the table to Arafat who, reading it quickly, declared, 'This is excellent.' Thus, at the eleventh hour they agreed on a compromise formula that would seek to be all things to all men. They need not have bothered. When King Fahd called on President Reagan in Washington later in the day, he did not even mention the agreement. As the Saudis subsequently explained, much to the consternation of the Palestinians and the Jordanians, Fahd was 'not going to embarrass himself again with a US President' with a document signed by Arafat alone and not endorsed by the Executive Committee of the PLO. He had been let down by the PLO leader before.[1]

In Amman, public confusion reigned about what Hussein and Arafat had actually agreed and it continued for several days, the time it took to translate the king's Arabic scrawl on the lunch menu into a publishable document. When Arafat's colleagues were apprised of the details, they were horrified. To their dismay, there was no specific reference to an 'independent Palestinian state' either within or outside a Palestinian–Jordanian confederation. Instead, the issue was obscured in a tangle of verbiage.

Hussein's skills as a legal draftsman certainly did not match his ability as an orator. The key section of the five-point accord – Article 2 – was gobbledegook that really did read as though it had been scribbled on the back of a menu: 'Palestinians will exercise their inalienable right of self-determination when Jordanians and Palestinians will be able to do so within the context of the formation of the proposed confederated Arab states of Jordan and Palestine.'[2] In agreeing to this, as on so many occasions in the past, the equivocating Arafat had sought to reinterpret PLO policy to his own ends.

After several difficult sessions with his colleagues in Tunis, who had all along been opposed to the exercise, an exasperated Arafat despatched Salah Khalaf and Mahmoud Abbas (Abu Mazen), a senior Fatah cadre, back to Amman in March to discuss amendments with the king. A secret codicil was agreed that would make a clear distinction between 'two states of Jordan and Palestine' within a wider *dawlati*, or confederation.

The inauspicious birth of their joint initiative did not deter Hussein and Arafat from seeking to market it far and wide. Arafat led a delegation to China. Hussein visited Washington in an attempt to interest the Americans, whose reaction had been, to say the least, lukewarm.

Deprived of their land bases in Lebanon, Khalil al-Wazir and the PLO leadership were still anxious to keep up their attacks on Israel. In the circumstances they concluded they had no choice but to give more attention to seaborne operations. So it was that at the end of the second week of April 1985, Wazir gave a final briefing to Fatah naval units aboard the *Atavarius*, a PLO-owned vessel at a naval base outside Algiers.

What was planned was one of the PLO's most audacious missions. The commandos, who had received extensive training in Algiers, were to attack the General Staff Headquarters of the Israeli army in Tel Aviv, to take hostages and demand the release of Fatah prisoners in Israeli jails.

The PLO's top leadership had its own special reasons for wanting a spectacular success. It was hoping to neutralise the heavy criticism it was under from inside Fatah and from radical splinters who were accusing it of meekly abandoning armed struggle. But dreams of a major coup to silence the critics were in vain.

On the night of 20–1 April, the *Atavarius* was blasted out of the water after an exchange of gunfire with an Israeli naval vessel. Of the 28 on board, only eight survived and were taken prisoner after an Israeli ship-to-ship missile literally tore the *Atavarius* apart.

Even before the blood was spilled, the Amman accord was heading for the rocks. During April, Arafat had received the unwelcome news from Jordan that Hussein had replaced his prime minister with a man whose history reeked of antagonism towards the PLO. Perhaps assuming that his joint initiative with Arafat was doomed, Hussein brought back his childhood friend, Zeid al-Rifai. The ostensible reason for replacing the traditionalist Ahmed Obeidat was that he had shown little enthusiasm for the Amman accord and that this was affecting US support. A more plausible explanation was to be found in *realpolitik*. In the deadly game of musical chairs that passes for diplomacy in the Arab world, Hussein had decided to improve his shaky relations with his northern neighbour, Syria. Rifai was close to Syria. If the Jordanian reconciliation with Damascus was at the expense of Arafat's PLO, then so be it.

Assad was as set as ever on undermining Arafat. Opposition to the Amman accord among radical Palestinian groups provided him with additional ammunition. In late March, Damascus had acted as midwife to the formation of a new Palestinian body, grouping six of the factions under its umbrella in a new anti-Arafat Palestine National Salvation Front. The inclusion of George Habash's Popular Front, which had remained, for the most part, on the sidelines during the Fatah mutiny of 1983, gave the new group a veneer of credibility.

But Syria's relations with even its most obedient Palestinian clients came under tremendous strain in late May and early June when what became known as the 'Camps War' in Lebanon erupted. In a sickening spectacle, the Syrian-backed Shi'ite Amal militia, aided by Shi'ite units of the Lebanese army, laid siege to the Palestinian refugee camps of Sabra and Shatila, and Bourj el-Brajneh. Less than three years after the massacres of Sabra and Shatila, the inhabitants of these ill-fated shanty settlements again came under assault, only this time the assailants were using heavy weapons and tanks.

The immediate target of the attack was Arafat's fighters who had slipped back into Lebanon after their expulsion by the Israelis in 1982. But for Assad, it was another opportunity to get at Arafat himself. Hundreds, including women and children, died in the bloody siege.

Arafat's bitterness towards Assad knew no bounds. 'The plot . . . has been aimed at the Palestinian existence in Lebanon,' he told the Kuwaiti daily *Al-Qabas* early in June. 'To control the Palestinian gun, they must expel Palestinians from Beirut and southern Lebanon.'[3] In the long run, far from serving Syria's interests, the attacks unified Palestinian ranks.

Dreadful as the scenes in Beirut were, the Arab world paid little attention. Arab leaders had other preoccupations. Hussein, for one, was still absorbed in his attempts to engage a reluctant US Administration in a renewed peace drive, but he got little encouragement. Earlier in May, Secretary of State George Shultz had toured the Middle East in an effort to find 'safe' non-PLO Palestinians to join a Jordanian team in negotiations with Israel. But it was a fruitless process that came more and more to resemble a child's game of pinning the tail on the donkey.

In Peking, Arafat used one of his well-worn metaphors to decry Shultz's insipid diplomacy. 'They are still trying to hide the sun with their finger,' he declared, 'neglecting realities and facts in the area.'[4]

Hussein's Washington visit did produce a minor flurry when he declared at a press conference in the White House Rose Garden on 29 May that the PLO had agreed that the peace talks be conducted under the 'umbrella' of an international conference and on the basis of 'pertinent UN resolutions, including Security Council Resolutions 242 and 338'.[5] In US diplomat-speak, Hussein's intervention became known as the 'Rose Garden' statement, as if the location added fresh fragrance to tired words. In Tunis, Arafat's colleagues were more than a little surprised that Hussein had presumed to make such a bald statement on their behalf, indicating acceptance of 242 and 338; but for the moment, and uncharacteristically, they kept their counsel.

American diplomacy was briefly energised after the Hussein visit, and so, too, was Israeli Labour leader Shimon Peres in his desire to initiate a process that would help to reduce Israel's post-1982 isolation in international forums. But by the autumn, and in the absence of a strong American push, it was clear there was very little of substance behind all the diplomatic to-ing and fro-ing. Commitment was simply lacking at the top.

Arafat and Hussein had, in any case, long since got the message that there was very little Arab support for their joint initiative. An emergency Arab summit in Casablanca in the autumn, boycotted by Syria and Libya, among others, had pointedly not endorsed the Amman accord.

Khalil al-Wazir and his Western Sector commanders, together with those of Force 17, Arafat's praetorian guard, had become increasingly agitated as the months passed in 1985 over Israel's repeated successes in interdicting PLO seaborne traffic in the eastern Mediterranean. The failure of the *Atavarius* mission in April was one example, but there were others that had affected both Western Sector missions planned for Israel itself and efforts by the two interlocking organisations to ferry men and weapons into Lebanon. This latter task had been made infinitely more urgent by the savage militia onslaught against Palestinian refugee camps in Beirut and in southern Lebanon: the need to bolster guerrilla strongholds in Lebanon was now paramount.

Fatah's dismal relations with Syria, which controlled the only feasible land route into Lebanon, made it absolutely essential to maintain a sea link. In this, the island of Cyprus, less than half a day's sailing from the Lebanese coast, was a vital way-station. It was also a place where the eyes and ears of myriad intelligence services – Western, East Bloc, Arab and Israel – ceaselessly monitored comings and goings by air and by sea. Long a murky crossroads, Cyprus, in the last week of September, witnessed a cold-blooded slaying with fateful consequences.

On 25 September, Yom Kippur, the Jewish Day of Atonement, three gunmen of Arafat's Force 17 – two Arabs and a blond Briton – stormed an Israeli yacht lying at anchor in the crowded marina at Larnaca, a resort town on Cyprus's south coast. The gunmen shot a woman passenger and subsequently two men on board. The PLO claimed that they were Israeli agents spying on ship movements in the Mediterranean, but Israel denied the charge, and threatened vengeance. It was not long in coming.

Ahmed Abdel Rahman, the PLO's official spokesman, was shaving when the phone rang just before 10 a.m. on 1 October in his comfortable villa near the Tunis seashore. It was Arafat on the phone, calling from one of his safe houses elsewhere in the city. Arafat wanted to review his day's schedule. But just as the two men were concluding their phone conversation they heard, simultaneously, a series of huge explosions from the direction of the PLO headquarters at Hammam Shatt, twenty kilometres southeast of the city on the Gulf of Tunis. They slammed down the phones and raced for their cars.

When Arafat arrived at what was left of his administrative headquarters he was appalled. Three buildings used by the PLO, including his own offices, had been reduced to rubble by a clutch of attacking aircraft with the Star of David insignia on their tails. Dozens of people, including Palestinians and Tunisians – the final toll was 73 dead – had been killed and injured.[6]

In Washington, Ronald Reagan praised Israeli 'intelligence capabilities', a remark that scarcely dampened PLO accusations of US complicity in what had manifestly been an attempt to kill Arafat himself.

President Mubarak of Egypt, who had just returned to Cairo from Washington, described the bombing as a 'horrible criminal operation'[7] that aimed a major blow at peace efforts. The Security Council condemned the raid 14–0 with one abstention: the US. 'Israel,' a shaken Arafat declared as he peered into one of the craters left by a bomb, 'has bombed the peace process.'[8]

Angry protests over the Israeli raid swirled about the Arab world for several days, only to be submerged by one of the messiest and most senseless acts in the long and bloody history of the Palestinian struggle. On 1 October, the same day the Israelis bombed Tunis, an Italian cruise liner, the 23,629-ton *Achille Lauro*, sailed from Genoa on a leisurely voyage around the Mediterranean. Among planned ports of call were Alexandria and the Israeli port city of Ashdod. Many different nationalities had joined the cruise, including a party of American Jews. Also on board were four desperate young men of the Palestine Liberation Front splinter group associated closely with Arafat's Fatah. Their suicide mission, as it later emerged, was to steal ashore in Ashdod and blow up oil storage tanks. They had also been instructed to seize hostages to be traded for the release of Palestinians in Israeli jails. But in the time between the sailing of the *Achille Lauro* from Alexandria and its arrival off Port Said things fell apart.

While the *Achille Lauro* was off the coast of Egypt on 7 October, the four PLF gunmen rushed into the dining room, discharging their weapons. They then stormed the bridge and ordered Captain Gerardo de Rosa to sail north towards Syria. The episode was scarcely believable. Four young men, barely out of their teens, were holding hostage 427 passengers and 80 crew on board a large cruise liner steaming the Mediterranean. The world was transfixed. This was piracy on a grand scale. In Tunis, PLO leaders watched in amazement, and in growing dismay, as the seajacking unfolded amid rumours that at least one of the passengers had been killed.

Within a few hours of the story breaking, Mohammed Zaidan, better known as Abul Abbas, the Palestine Liberation Front leader and PLO Executive Committee member, was despatched to Egypt to sort out the mess. Zaidan wasted no time in summoning his men back from further disaster, instructing them to return forthwith to the waters off Port Said while negotiations continued on their safe passage out of Egypt. International opinion was outraged. Egypt was outraged. Arafat himself, who was in Senegal in West Africa, was under heavy pressure to intervene. On 8 October, he met the ambassadors of Egypt, France and Italy in Dakar. Ahmed Abdel Rahman, Arafat's spokesman, recalls that in a sometimes fraught and confused four-way discussion conducted in French, Italian, Arabic and English, the PLO leader agreed, as a way of defusing the crisis, to accept responsibility for the hijackers, and to 'discipline' them. At that moment, Rahman insists, neither he nor Arafat was aware that one of the passengers had been killed.[9] It was a situation Arafat had confronted many times before in his long stewardship of the fractious Palestinian movement. He handled it little differently from other such terror episodes, denying advance knowledge and equally refusing to condemn.

When the *Achille Lauro* anchored off Port Said on 9 October, and American officials were able to go on board, the truth emerged. Leon Klinghoffer, a 69-year-old American Jew confined to a wheelchair, had been shot in cold blood and thrown overboard off the Syrian coast. So outraged was Nicholas Veliotes, the American ambassador, when he discovered what had happened that in a ship-to-shore conversation with his colleagues, he demanded that the hijackers, who had been spirited away, be brought to justice. 'You tell the foreign ministry that we demand they prosecute those sons of bitches,' he shouted down the phone.[10]

Infuriated by what it regarded as impertinence by a serving ambassador, Egypt had made arrangements to get the four hijackers and Zaidan himself out of the country as quickly as possible. The last thing the Cairo Government needed or wanted at a time when it was seeking to re-establish its Arab credentials was to come under pressure to put on trial a bunch of Palestinian desperadoes. But there were unaccountable delays. One story had it that Tunis was slow in giving clearance for an EgyptAir plane carrying the hijackers to land; another said that they had been refused passage through Jordan on their way to sanctuary in Iraq. Whatever the reason, the delays enabled the US to put in train an audacious plan which would cause dismay in Cairo and jubilation in the White House.

In what must rank as one of the more bizarre actions ever authorised by an American head of state, President Reagan ordered that a civilian plane belonging to a friendly country be forced down. F-14 fighters from the *USS Saratoga* of the US Mediterranean Sixth Fleet were scrambled aloft. Guided by US Hawkeye radar aircraft, they made contact with the EgyptAir Boeing as it cruised westward in the darkness, south of Crete, forcing it to land at Sigonella airbase in Sicily, and there the four hijackers and Zaidan were taken into custody by the Italian *Carabinieri*. At the White House, Reagan could scarcely contain his glee. 'They can run, but they can't hide,' said the President of the United States.[11]

Some of the American euphoria dissipated in the cold light of day when Washington realised the extent to which its unorthodox action had angered and humiliated its main Arab ally – President Mubarak accused the US of 'air piracy'.[12] And the Americans, who had begun attempts to extradite Zaidan, failed to get their man. To Washington's consternation, the Italians allowed him to slip quietly away to Yugoslavia.

Seeking to widen his options and in the wake of the *Achille Lauro* affair which had put paid to any peacemaking involving the Americans and the PLO for the time being, Hussein reached out to the Israelis. In mid-October, he travelled to Paris for secret talks with the Israeli Premier, Shimon Peres, one of many clandestine meetings between the two men over the years. The talks produced quick results: later that month, Peres presented the UN General Assembly with an offer of a peace partnership with Jordan. The result was a flurry of Israeli–Jordanian contacts, in which the two sides came close to establishing a 'condominium of interests' in the occupied territories. But even in the midst of his latest dalliance with Israel Hussein's real preoccupation was Syria.

On 10 November, the Jordanian press published an extraordinary letter from the king to his prime minister. Even by Hussein's own melodramatic standards, it was a curious document. In it he admitted Jordan's errors in dealing with Syria – not least the assistance it had provided to the underground *Ikhwan* in its struggle to overthrow President Assad's regime. Hussein's *mea culpa* was the price of reconciliation with Damascus. The king, sensing that his initiative with Arafat was all but dead, had decided to cut his losses. He had also concluded that if there was to be any prospect of a Middle East peace process, Syria could not continue to be ignored.

For Arafat, who had taken refuge in Baghdad after the Tunis bombing, Hussein's declaration was bad news. With the Jordanian monarch reaching out to Assad, the PLO leader was reminded once again of the fickleness of Arab friends.

To make matters worse, Arafat was in trouble in Egypt over the *Achille Lauro* affair. Angry as Cairo had been with Washington, it was also furious with the PLO leadership for not exercising stricter discipline over its people. The last thing cash-starved Egypt needed was any episode that might cut the flow of tourists or aid money. At the end of the first week of November, the Egyptians forced Arafat to read out a statement, in the presence of President Mubarak, in which he denounced and condemned terrorist attacks against 'unarmed civilians in any place'.[13] It was a largely meaningless statement, since it had long been PLO policy to eschew armed operations outside Israel and the occupied territories, but at least it provided the Egyptians with a piece of paper to wave at Washington.

As autumn gave way to winter, Hussein and Arafat continued to make a pretence of co-operating, but there was precious little goodwill between them. Matters came to a head on 29 January at a tense meeting in the Prime Minister's office and chaired by Hussein himself. Arafat informed the king that he could not accept Resolution 242 unless the Americans agreed in writing to recognise Palestinian rights to self-determination, to which

Hussein replied, 'They cannot do more, and we cannot ask for more.'[14] Arafat then said that he would need to consult the Palestinian leadership and left the king alone with his advisers. An exasperated Hussein turned to his courtiers, and said, '*Khalast*. That's it.'[15] Arafat remained in Amman for another week, seeking to mend fences and to offer fresh formulas, but it was in vain.

In his anger and disappointment, Hussein instructed his adviser Adnan Abu Odeh to draft a lengthy speech detailing why his joint initiative with Arafat had failed. For the record, he wanted to review the various twists and turns in his two failed peace efforts with the PLO leader, as if he were trying to purge himself of an unpleasant memory.

On 19 February, Hussein appeared on television and spoke for three hours about his troubled relations with the PLO. He had penned the last angst-ridden words himself, and in them he came very close to calling Arafat a liar. 'After two long attempts, I and the government of the Hashemite Kingdom of Jordan hereby announce that we are unable to continue to co-ordinate with the PLO leadership until such time as their word becomes their bond, characterised by commitment, credibility and constancy,' he said.[16]

In the weeks after his address, Hussein continued his offensive against the PLO leadership. In private, he railed against Arafat's duplicity. In public, he began a blatant campaign to encourage the growth of an alternative pro-Jordanian leadership in the Israeli-occupied territories. He abandoned all restraint, it seemed, in his bitter criticism of Arafat and his colleagues in Tunis. At the end of February he told the editor of the conservative Kuwaiti daily, *Al-Siyassa*, that the PLO had 'lost credibility and the Palestinians inside and outside the occupied territories will have to choose another leadership, or reconsider their political representation'.[17]

Not since the bleak days of the Jordanian civil war had relations reached quite such a low, and they would not improve for many months as the king and his Prime Minister, Zeid al-Rifai, sought by all means to whittle away Arafat's position inside and outside the territories. But before their campaign got off the ground an event occurred that should have given them pause.

In early March, Zafir al-Masri, the recently appointed mayor of the West Bank town of Nablus, had been shot in broad daylight as he walked to work, by a member of George Habash's Damascus-based Popular Front. Masri's sin, in the view of the PLO radicals, was his willingness to serve under the Israeli Civil Administration in the territories. In other words, they thought he was a stooge of both the Israelis and the Jordanians. They were wrong; he was in fact a popular man, a member of one of Nablus's leading families, and a known supporter of Fatah. Hussein's calls for a new PLO leadership inside and outside the territories had almost certainly hastened his death. Predictably, Fatah cadres turned Masri's funeral into a mass demonstration of support for Yasser Arafat and the PLO, and a mass denunciation of Hussein, a message that Hussein and his Prime Minister ignored to their cost.

Arafat had reacted with restraint to the king's 19 February diatribe. Even after Hussein had performed the last rites on the Amman accord, the PLO leader still insisted, rather lamely, that he was bound by it. But the pretence could not last. Hussein was now committed to a political and diplomatic war with the PLO. Once set on a course of action, the stubborn king was not easily deflected.

Goaded on by Rifai, he sanctioned a crackdown on pro-PLO journalists in Amman; gave support to feeble attempts to promote Atallah Atallah, a discredited former senior PLO official, as an alternative to Arafat; initiated a West Bank economic development plan in a thinly disguised and unsuccessful attempt to 'buy' support in the territories. He also ordered the closure of some 25 PLO offices, including the headquarters of the Palestine National Fund, and the expulsion of dozens of PLO officials, among them Khalil al-Wazir.

For the moment, however, there was nothing for Arafat and his senior lieutenants to do but to turn their attention back to putting the rickety PLO house in order. Khalil al-Wazir told the Lebanese weekly *Al-Ousbou al-Arabi* that the PLO had formed a 'reconciliation committee', and that it was being helped to resolve its internal differences through Algerian and Soviet mediation.[18]

Arafat was back in the Arab political bazaar, clinging to the hope that time would act as a healer. Precedent certainly suggested it would. As Khaled al-Hassan observed in a radio interview in late 1984, 'I do not believe Arab history has ever known a final estrangement. Our Arab history is full of agreements and differences. When we differ and then grow tired of differing, we agree. When we grow tired of agreeing, we differ, and so on. After every agreement or difference we pass through a time that changes things . . . this is the Arab nature.'[19]

On 20 April 1987, Arafat convened the eighteenth session of the Palestinian 'parliament', the Palestine National Council, in a marbled conference centre thirty kilometres west of Algiers on the Mediterranean coast. It was a time for 'agreeing' after a fashion. Once again, Arafat was able to elicit an endorsement of his leadership and, since this was the purpose of the exercise, to appear shakily in harmony with some of his erstwhile foes. George Habash's Popular Front returned to the fold, as did Nayef Hawatmeh's Democratic Front. The price Arafat paid for this facade of togetherness was to bury the Amman accord once and for all. It was hardly a high price. Arafat's equivocation and Hussein's impatience had long since rendered it null and void.

The hardly memorable Algiers PNC produced one jarring moment when Egypt reacted angrily to criticism of its peace treaty with Israel. Arafat had fought to prevent any such criticism, but was forced to give way in the end. Infuriated, Mubarak ordered the closure of all PLO offices in Egypt, except those functioning as diplomatic premises.

Momentarily out in the cold with yet another Arab regime, Arafat had re-unified his battered PLO at a very small personal cost. He had also, to his immense satisfaction, further isolated the Fatah mutineers in Damascus. Sourly, Syria tried to prevent Popular and Democratic Front delegates travelling to Algiers, but its efforts to disrupt the gathering lacked conviction. Paradoxically, Arafat had reasons to be grateful to the Syrians. The vicious attacks on Palestinian refugee camps in Lebanon by the Syrian-backed Shi'ite militia since 1985 – and a siege that had continued off and on for nearly two years – had acted as a catalyst for unity. As one delegate in Algiers put it, 'The blood from our martyrs has healed our divisions.'[20]

Once again, Middle Eastern politics had reverted to a familiar holding pattern. If Arafat was to preserve the new-found unity of his organisation, he would have to play it safe. Now was not the time for adventurous diplomacy. And in any case the opportunities were simply not there.

In Israel, the two main blocs – Labour and Likud – continued to work in opposite directions and to cancel each other out. Labour leader Shimon Peres pursued his secret dalliance with King Hussein. In the same month that the Palestinians gathered in Algiers, the two men held another of their clandestine meetings – this time in Britain – and signed what became known as the 'London document', calling for an international peace conference as a cover for direct negotiations between Israel and its Arab enemies, including a joint Jordanian–Palestinian delegation.[28] The Likud leader, Yitzhak Shamir, determined to hang on to the occupied territories in perpetuity, described his coalition partner's plan as a 'perverse and criminal idea' that must be 'wiped off' the cabinet table.[21]

Not the least of Arafat's worries were Hussein's continuing efforts to confine him to the sidelines. Nowhere was this campaign more evident than at a summit meeting of Arab leaders that convened in Amman in November 1987. It was an occasion on which Arafat was rendered apoplectic by what he believed were deliberate slights administered to him by Hussein and his aides.

When Arafat flew in, Hussein, who had greeted all the other visiting kings, emirs and presidents in person, was not at the airport to meet him. Instead, he sent Zeid al-Rifai, the PLO's number-one enemy in the Jordanian Government, and the man who had masterminded efforts to undermine Arafat's position in the territories. Arafat boycotted a Hussein-hosted banquet in protest. Ever protocol-conscious, the leader-without-a-state smouldered and sulked through the summit deliberations, his mood not improved by the fact that the Palestinian issue was virtually ignored. Arab leaders were much more preoccupied about events in the Gulf.

Arafat spent much of his time in his Regency Hotel suite complaining about the perfidy of Hussein and Syria's Hafez al-Assad. His staff, accustomed to Arafat's volcanic moods, could scarcely remember a time when he was more irascible. He believed, quite rightly, that Hussein and Assad were attempting to cut his movement down to size. The issue came to a head when

Jordan and Syria, entrusted, along with the PLO, with responsibility for drafting the resolution on the Palestine question, sought to exclude specific reference to the PLO's participation in a proposed international conference. Eventually, after much delay and not a little acrimony, the resolution was reworded to take account of PLO objections. The words 'including the Palestine Liberation Organisation, on an equal footing' were added to the communiqué.[22] But that was not the end of, the story.

Arafat's sour mood did not improve as he watched, on television in his hotel suite, Hussein's performance at his post-summit press conference. Asked at one point whether the PLO would be invited to participate in an international peace conference, the king gave an unctuous smile and said: 'Hopefully'.[32] This was bad enough, but Arafat was rendered almost speechless when he discovered that the English version of the summit's final communiqué omitted the one standard phrase that represented what he saw as the most tangible symbol of his achievements in all his years as PLO leader. Whether by design or accident the English text did not include the words 'sole, legitimate representative of the Palestinian people', when referring to the PLO. Arafat naturally assumed the worst. Hussein, he believed, had engineered the omission; the king had often enough made clear his displeasure at the decision of Arab leaders thirteen years earlier at the Rabat summit to block his own ambitions by vesting Arafat's PLO with sole responsibility for the Palestinians.

For a man accustomed to a position at centre stage, it was a bad experience indeed, but one that would soon fade. Jordan's attempts, wilful or otherwise, to downgrade the PLO in full view of a large and politically aware Palestinian television audience in the West Bank and Gaza backfired. As the king bade his summit guests farewell, resentment was bubbling in the shanty settlements of the occupied territories, one of the main factors being the perceived efforts on the part of Hussein and Assad to belittle the role of the Palestine Liberation Organization. The king would have reason to regret his point-scoring at Arafat's expense.

Part Four

15. *INTIFADA*

'With stones in their hands they defy the world and come to us like good tidings. They burst with anger and love, and they fall.' Nizar Kabbani, 'Children Bearing Rocks', December 1987.

When Shlomo Sakal, a 45-year-old Israeli merchant, was stabbed in the neck in Gaza's seedy Palestine Square on 6 December 1987, it barely rated a mention in the international press. Sporadic violence between Arab and Jew was hardly big news. Sakal's death was just another statistic in a ceaseless battle. But within a very short time, it proved to be much more than that.

Two days after Sakal's death, in an apparently unrelated incident, an Israeli truck cannoned into a line of oncoming vehicles near the Erez security checkpoint at the northern entrance to the Gaza Strip. Four Palestinian workers died and seven were injured in the accident, which looked to many of the dozens of horrified Palestinian witnesses like a deliberate act. It did not help that three of those who died were from the Jabaliya refugee camp, whose 50,000 residents were among the most militant in the whole of the festering Gaza Strip. Rumours spread that the Israeli driver was avenging the stabbing of Sakal.

Outraged, 10,000 of Jabaliya's inhabitants turned the funerals of those killed into a huge demonstration against Israeli military rule. They thronged its narrow streets, chanting nationalist slogans and waving the green, red, white and black Palestinian flag. Late into the night they poured out their anger in demands for vengeance. The stage was set for what was to become known as the *intifada* or, literally, 'shaking'. The West, from days of repetition, was about to add an Arabic word to its vocabulary.

Just after 8 a.m on 9 December, an Israeli army patrol entered the Jabaliya camp on a routine mission, but the reception it got was anything but routine. Still agitated from the night before, Jabaliya youths pelted the soldiers in their jeep with stones. The Israelis gave chase on foot, setting a pattern that was to become familiar in the years ahead. When they returned to their vehicle they found it surrounded by an angry mob. Suddenly, out of nowhere, two flaming petrol bombs were thrown. In the panic that ensued the soldiers opened fire on the crowd and a 15-year-old youth named Hatem Sissi died almost instantly of a bullet wound in the heart. The *intifada* had claimed the first of many hundreds of victims. By next day, much of the Gaza Strip was in turmoil. Trouble broke out in Khan Younis, another large refugee camp. Black smoke from burning tyres hung in the air. Rioting youths, their faces masked by *keffiyehs*, set up rudimentary roadblocks, using rocks and anything else they could lay their hands on. Agitation continued in Jabaliya. Thousands demonstrated outside Shifa Hospital in Gaza as the casualties began to mount. Disturbances, like a bushfire in a high wind, spread to West Bank camps near Jerusalem and Nablus, and many other centres besides. A spontaneous rebellion had begun. Palestinian anger and resentment were boiling over and no one, least of all the PLO leadership in distant Tunis and Baghdad, could be sure where it would lead.

As Arafat studied the first intelligence and wire service reports coming in from the 'battlefront', he was as unsure as his colleagues what it all meant. Was this the start of something big or was it simply another tremor, albeit a bigger one than normal? He consulted Khalil al-Wazir, the godfather of resistance in the territories. Was this planned? 'No, it was not,' Wazir told him, although he couldn't help adding that 'the PLO's underground organisation was in much better shape to sustain a rebellion than it had ever been before.'[1]

Arafat, who as a child in Jerusalem had witnessed some of the ferment in Palestine in the first *intifada* against British rule and Jewish immigration in 1936, understood the challenges better than most of his colleagues. Among his immediate concerns was whether the leadership outside could maintain control in the event of a full-scale uprising. Hadn't the national leadership in exile under Haj Amin al-Husseini failed in this regard in the late 1930s? Hadn't local commanders behaved like warlords, taking matters into their own hands and dissipating the energies of the rebellion in senseless acts of violence? Hadn't Arabs killed Arabs in their scores as the uprising turned in upon itself? Hadn't the divisions of the 1930s sapped the resolve of the nationalist movement for more than a generation? Hadn't the failures of the 1930s contributed to the catastrophe of 1948? All this and more went through Arafat's mind as he contemplated the implications of the rioting. Yet he also sensed that here was something different, more profound: that even if it had wanted to, the outside leadership could not turn off the tap. Arafat was, in any case, in a mood for risk-taking. What had he to lose?

He was still smouldering after the indignities he had suffered at the hands of King Hussein at the Amman summit in November. He had watched with dismay Hussein's reconciliation with President Hafez al-Assad of Syria. He had sensed that fellow Arab rulers were losing interest in Palestine in light of their many other problems. The Soviets, whom he had counted on for support, were making friendly gestures towards Israel. Most frustrating of all for the hyperactive leader of a scattered people, he had lost the thread in his efforts to advance their cause politically. Arafat in the early winter of 1987–8 was, in short, at something of a dead end. Might not the violence of 9–10 December offer a way out?

On the night of 10 December, PLO Radio, broadcasting from Baghdad, carried the staccato voice of Yasser Arafat exhorting his people to step up the 'uprising'.[2] His use of that all-embracing word, 'uprising', was significant at that early stage: although he could not possibly have appreciated all the implications then, Arafat had given his imprimatur to a revolt against Israeli rule. He had found a new cause and he would exploit it for all it was worth, pretending that the PLO had initiated the uprising and was in full command of events.

But, like all his veteran colleagues in Tunis, Arafat was privately just as perplexed as they were about the chemistry that had produced the mass revolt. How had it spread so quickly throughout the territories? What force was driving the rebellion? They all remembered other, similar events in the past that had fizzled out after a few days. Hardened politicians all, they reserved judgement. In a characteristically sober assessment, Salah Khalaf said that 'Nobody had been calculating on such an *intifada*, with its force and power. The one who was most in touch with the occupied territories was Abu Jihad [Khalil al-Wazir], but even he didn't expect it to be like that.'[3]

As the days of violence turned into weeks, Israeli reaction ranged from bloodthirsty demands for a tougher crackdown – General Sharon told anyone who would listen that he would finish the *intifada* in days – to handwringing among the Israeli doves.

Throughout December and January, amid insistent TV images of *keffiyeh*-clad youths battling helmeted Israeli soldiers in rock-strewn streets, Israel's Defence Minister Yitzhak Rabin and his military commanders desperately sought a formula to put down the uprising. Curfews, mass arrests, deportations and the use of live ammunition, accompanied by melodramatic threats to apply the 'iron fist', made little impact, The days of rage continued, Rabin's 'might, power and beatings' policy, announced on 19 January, brought censure from some of Israel's most committed US supporters; the then liberal *Jerusalem Post* decried the minister's 'jarringly brutal language'.

Arafat and the Tunis leadership debated how to hitch themselves to the spontaneous uprising, while Israelis and Palestinians alike sifted through possible reasons for the eruption.

Had the legions of wise men in rarefied Jerusalem been taking more careful note, they might have been been alerted by a particularly bloody episode in the Gaza Strip that October. Agents of the Israeli Shin Bet security apparatus engaged in a shoot-out with a group of heavily armed Palestinians after a high-speed car chase through the streets of Gaza City, four Palestinians and one Shin Bet agent dying in the gangland-style exchanges. At least two of the dead Palestinians had been members of the militant Islamic Jihad (Holy War) Organisation, growing stronger by the day in Gaza's shanty towns and in the old quarter of Gaza City itself. The strengthening Islamic trend reflected developments elsewhere in the Arab world. Festering, overcrowded and impoverished Gaza was a perfect breeding ground for the spread of a new, more militant Islam.

By New Year 1988, when it had become clear that the *intifada* was much more than a passing violent spasm, the first cooler assessments were being made about its causes. Quite simply, the 1.7 million residents of Gaza and the West Bank, fed up with twenty years of increasingly tiresome occupation and with the perceived indifference of the Arab world, had taken matters into their own hands.

To many Arab intellectuals, however, the troubles signified something deeper: an outburst of frustration and disgust on the part of Arabs with their rulers and politicians. As Nizar Kabbani, the well-known Syrian poet, put it in his verse praising the 'Children Bearing Rocks':

Like mussels we sit in cafes
one hunts for a business venture
one for another billion
and breasts polished by civilisation

One stalks London for a lofty mansion
One traffics in arms
one seeks revenge in nightclubs
one plots for a throne, a private army, and a princedom.

Ah, generation of betrayal
of surrogate indecent men,
generation of leftovers,
we'll be swept away
– never mind the slow pace of history – by children bearing
    rocks.[4]

As the *intifada* took on the dimensions of a mass popular uprising, Arafat and the Tunis leadership found it a struggle to stay abreast of events. The PLO's co-ordinating committee for the territories, established after the April 1987 Palestine National Council in Algiers, met repeatedly in Tunis and Baghdad in late 1987 and early 1988. According to Suleiman Najab, a veteran communist and member of the committee, the 'aim was to give the *intifada* full support without giving specific instructions; we considered that those on the battlefield knew better what specific steps to take'.[5] This tentative approach reflected continuing deep uncertainties in Tunis and growing concern that the young activists in the territories might be establishing a rival leadership. This was one of Arafat's recurring nightmares. It was not something he could or would tolerate.

Nothing caused quite as much soul-searching in Tunis as the autonomous decision early in 1988 by those steering the uprising to form a unified leadership, grouping the main PLO factions. Nervously, Tunis gave its approval. Not all would be plain sailing, however, for the Unified National Leadership, whose main components were Fatah, the Popular and Democratic Fronts, and the Communists. The Fatah-dominated secularists were repeatedly reminded of the growing strength of the Islamic groups which would often go their own way, calling independent strike days and bitterly taking issue on occasion with the PLO's political strategy. The emergence in mid-year of the militant Hamas, a word that means zeal and is also an acronym for the Movement of the Islamic Resistance, was widely seen as a challenge to the mainstream.

Watching from the outside, Arafat did not always agree with his own people inside – he was against their decision early in 1988 to force the resignation of Arab municipal councils, for example – but was obliged to go along with them. PLO leaders worried that economic pressures would abort the uprising. Khaled al-Hassan told the Lebanese newspaper *Al-Sayyad* early in January that the riots could not attain the dimensions of a civil revolt because of the economic difficulties that would ensue.[6]

But Hassan and the other sceptics within the exiled Palestinian leadership were about as wrong as they could be. In short, the stone-throwers and their underground leadership had hit on the most effective form of protest in more than twenty years of Israeli occupation. If the Palestinians under occupation had taken matters into their own hands, they were also demanding action from the PLO outside. What was needed was a political initiative to match the practical sacrifices being made on the ground, already generating waves of international sympathy.

Arafat was quicker than most to draw the logical conclusion. In an interview with Jonathan Randal of the Washington Post in early January, he dropped hints of where his thoughts were leading. The PLO, he said, should form a government in exile: code phrase for a respectable body that could take responsibility for the people under occupation. 'No doubt,' he added, such a move would be accompanied by 'a major new political platform'.[7]

The question was: how? To come up with a fresh initiative, Arafat would have to reopen all the tired old controversies that had dogged the Palestinian movement since the early 1970s and, above all, he would have to persuade the PLO to formulate a clear statement of its willingness to coexist with Israel in a Palestinian 'mini-state' in the West Bank and Gaza. It was far from clear that he could prevail now where he had failed so many times in the past.

Like their colleagues outside, traditional leaders inside the territories – the so-called Palestinian notables – were also desperately searching for a formula that would give political form and substance to the demands of the street activists. On 14 January, the group had convened at East Jerusalem's National Palace Hotel, hoping to find a means of harnessing the agitation and to lay down principles for a dialogue with Israel. They issued a fourteen-point document. 'Real peace cannot be achieved except through the recognition of Palestinian national rights, including the rights of self-determination and the establishment of an independent Palestinian state on Palestinian national soil,' it warned. 'Should these rights not be recognised, then the continuation of Israeli occupation will lead to further violence and bloodshed, and the further deepening of hatred.'[8]

The appeal was ignored in an Israel consumed throughout 1988 by preparations for elections in November, and by internal and external pressure to combat the uprising at all costs. Israel was not finding the going easy in the early days of the *intifada*, and predictably began blaming the messenger. Officials accused reporters of anti-Israel bias and in some cases of anti-semitism. It was not long before Israel's hard-pressed military began declaring wide swathes of the West Bank and Gaza closed to the press, and more particularly to television crews. For Israel's propagandists, the unpleasant story told through the unblinking eye of the television camera was difficult to counter, and nowhere was television making a bigger impact than in the all-important court of American opinion.

Two episodes seemed particularly shocking. In one, Israeli soldiers attempted on 5 February to bury alive four Palestinian youths in the village of Salem near the large Arab West Bank town of Nablus. In the other, late in February, the American CBS network filmed four soldiers brutally beating two Arab youths in

Nablus itself in a long sequence that discomforted even the most hardened observers of violence in the territories.

What surprised Israel and even Palestinians themselves was the speed with which the resistance organised itself into a mass movement, and into popular committees in almost every town and hamlet, giving the uprising the strength to weather mass arrests of thousands of activists and the deportation of some of its leaders. At the core of this activism was the pro-Fatah al-Shabibeh, or youth movement, which had become deeply entrenched in the universities. Scores of its leaders had received their political education in Israeli jails: a generation of Palestinian youth referred to prison experience as 'revolutionary school'. 'It was excellent experience. Given that we were well organised in jail, it helped us to organise ourselves outside,' declared a hardened activist and one of the founders of the youth movement in 1977.[9]

Ever so slowly, after the 1974 Palestine National Council had called for a 'national authority' in the West Bank and Gaza, the territories had come into focus as the next theatre of the Arab–Israeli conflict. The scaling down of the quixotic dream of liberating all of Palestine had obliged the PLO to examine what might be achieved underground, and later above ground in the occupied territories. All factions – Fatah, the Democratic and Popular Fronts, the Communists and, with increasing strength, Islamic groups – were engaged in institution-building, and often in conflict with one another.

But it was not until after the PLO's bloody defeat in Lebanon in 1982 that its leaders, and in particular Khalil al-Wazir, the PLO's military chief, really focused their energies on the West Bank and Gaza. 'The PLO took a long time to realise the possibilities of mass organisation in the occupied territories,' observed a Palestinian activist from the territories. 'They had their own infrastructure and fighters in Lebanon; they were a power there; they were part of the game of Arab politics.'[10]

Heightened PLO activism in the territories had coincided with the opening of universities in the West Bank and the Gaza Strip. Bir Zeit College became a university in 1976; An-Najah, Bethlehem and Gaza opened in 1977. 'Ironically, the Israelis had fuelled the nationalist spirit they were trying to crush by allowing the universities to open. They thought that educating Palestinians to be professionals would cause them to forget about Palestinian nationalism. They thought we could be Americanised – that Bir Zeit would become one big disco. We had the choice between working underground or becoming an open, mass organisation, and we chose the latter. The Israelis couldn't arrest 40,000 people, after all,' recalled one student leader.[11]

'In spring 1981, we had a meeting of students at Bir Zeit and founded the Palestinian Youth Organisation of Social Work. The goals were social: cleaning streets and camps; helping the mayors and their employees; instituting special days in the camps and villages such as medical day, folklore day, volunteers day; supporting poor families and martyrs' families. We decided we didn't need money at the start; we wanted to be independent.'[12]

By the time Ariel Sharon sent the tanks into Lebanon in June 1982, a political reawakening in the West Bank and Gaza was already well under way. The Sabra and Shatila massacres, the expulsion of Fatah from Lebanon in 1983 and a realisation in the territories that there was little prospect of an end to occupation unless the residents themselves took matters into their own hands fuelled the resurgence.

For Faisal al-Husseini, then Arafat's senior Fatah representative in the territories, the idea of 'non-violent demonstrations' had begun to take shape on the first anniversary of Sabra and Shatila in September 1983 when he organised a protest in Jerusalem. In his view the peaceful protest, which attracted fewer than one hundred people, was disappointing: 'But the aggressive way the Israeli police attacked us gave me the feeling that if they were so afraid of such a thing, maybe this was the way. When I saw an officer hitting my daughter who was in those days nine years old, it was obvious they wanted to cut the roots of such a movement from the beginning.'[13]

Husseini continued to assert himself quietly as a figure of authority in the territories. The heir to a Palestinian dynasty, the son of the martyr Abdel Kader was slowly emerging as a natural leader, filling a vacuum that had existed for a very long time. The Israelis recognised the danger signs, which is why they repeatedly detained him. Husseini's Arab Studies Society – founded with the blessing if not the direct financial support of Tunis – gave him a platform from which to operate. More to the point, he was becoming a bridge between the 'street' activists and the notables who frequented East Jerusalem's quaint American Colony Hotel, briefing diplomats, journalists and earnest fact-finding delegations from the US and Europe. He demonstrated his increasing authority in the late summer of 1986, when he successfully opposed plans by the salon Palestinians to meet George Bush. The then vice-president and presidential aspirant was making an obligatory pre-election swing through the Middle East to be photographed in the smiling company of Israel's leaders: the American Jewish vote beckoned.

Husseini appeared on Salahadin Street, Arab East Jerusalem's main thoroughfare, urging a boycott of Bush to protest at the lack of American support for the Palestinians. In the end a compromise was struck. The East Jerusalem newspaper editor, Hanna Seniora, handed the US president-to-be a letter outlining Palestinian grievances. The episode would prove, in the words of one Palestinian observer, a 'last hurrah' for established spokesmen such as Seniora and Elias Freij, the Bethlehem mayor.[14] The power of the 'street' was beginning to make itself felt.

The episode did not go unnoticed in Tunis, but even the most percipient observer could hardly have judged this mini-struggle to represent the authentic voice of the Palestinians as a signpost to the *intifada*. Arafat himself believed that the reaction in the West Bank and Gaza to the long, drawn-out and bloody 1985–6 'Camps War' in Lebanon between the PLO and the Syrian-backed Amal militia together with angry demonstrations protesting over the first phase of the war in mid-1985 were signs of a closer identification between younger militants inside and their brothers and sisters outside.[15]

Throughout 1987, attitudes in the territories hardened. Frustration with the Americans, in particular, was building. When George Shultz, the US Secretary of State, visited the Middle East in the third week of October, pressure from the 'street' forced Palestinian notables to boycott a meeting with him: leaflets and graffiti scrawled on walls expressed contempt at continuing US attempts to exclude the PLO from the peace process. The tired old American dream of having King Hussein represent the Palestinians didn't match reality. As the lugubrious Shultz waited in vain in his room on the eighteenth floor of Jerusalem's Hilton Hotel for eight secretly invited Palestinians to attend for consultations, his advisers at last began to realise that. Richard Murphy, Shultz's senior Middle East aide, later described the mission as the 'end, not the beginning' and 'the bottom of the barrel'.[16]

In a Washington that had engaged for the most part in some mild and largely meaningless criticism of its Middle East ally, there was increasing alarm at the way things were going in the territories. The power of television was making itself felt and liberal American Jews were by no means the least outspoken among those demanding action. In late January George Shultz reluctantly began to make preparations for a return to the Middle East on his second mission in less than six months, but he despatched Richard Murphy to the region first, to sound out opinion before committing himself. In the event, his visit was viewed cynically by the Arabs as a limp attempt to reduce pressure on Israel.

Their shaky confidence in American intentions was hardly strengthened by the leaking late in February, as Shultz was on his way to the Middle East, of an unhelpful intervention from Henry Kissinger. At a breakfast meeting with American Jewish leaders early in February, the former Secretary of State had urged that the Palestinian uprising be 'brutally and rapidly' suppressed.[17] and that television cameras be banned from the territories. According to a four-page memo summarising his remarks, Kissinger argued that the 'insurrection must be quelled immediately, and the first step should be to throw out television, *à la* South Africa. To be sure, there will be criticism . . . but it will dissipate in short order. There are no rewards for losing with moderation.'[18]

Shultz arrived in Israel on the first stage of a long and fairly aimless series of peace shuttles that would continue until June, the last desultory attempt by the Reagan Administration to improve its indifferent record in the Middle East. Shamir had already despatched Ehud Olmert, one of the young 'princes' of Israel's rightist Likud bloc, to Washington to tell the Administration that

Israel would not be party to any plan that involved exchanging 'land for peace'. Like an overweight bloodhound who has lost the scent, Shultz visited Jerusalem, Amman, Damascus and Cairo in a fruitless search for a common denominator. Only in Egypt, dependent as it was on US largesse, did he receive any real encouragement. In Jerusalem, a familiar pattern repeated itself. Shultz received a second snub in less than six months from Palestinian notables, some of whom were referring to themselves deprecatingly as the 'Mickey Mouse leadership'.[19]

Arafat, who was by then anxiously casting around for ways to capitalise politically on the *intifada* before it ran out of steam, was at first prepared to sanction discussions between pro-PLO notables and Shultz. But he changed his mind when he became aware of the opposition in the territories. 'The Palestinian people in revolt reject the Israeli–American conspiracy that some Arab elements are trying to help further,' said the underground leadership in a leaflet. 'They are trying to force it on our people in a hopeless attempt to abort the uprising.'[20] Tunis got the message. It quickly denied that it was planning to approve an encounter with Shultz inside the territories.

Instead, in an episode highly revealing of the evolving power relationship between the 'street' activists and Tunis, the inventive Arafat proposed a meeting involving a joint delegation of Palestinian representatives from inside and outside the territories to take place in a neighbouring country, possibly Egypt. There was never any possibility that the cautious Shultz would meet a PLO-sanctioned delegation in these circumstances, and plans for a direct dialogue between him and representative Palestinians collapsed.

Nevertheless, in a postscript, the dogged Shultz turned up at the American Colony Hotel in the heart of Arab East Jerusalem on a grey winter's day in late February to read a brief statement in lieu of his meeting with Palestinian notables. In it, he talked about the need to respect Palestinian 'political and economic rights' – a slight advance on previous American positions. But there was no mention of self-determination. Among the few 'real' Palestinians who witnessed the performance were members of the hotel's largely Palestinian staff.

Shultz travelled next to London early in March for a meeting with King Hussein before returning to the Middle East to continue his efforts. But on 4 March when he belatedly unveiled a peace plan that called for an accelerated process of negotiations on Palestinian autonomy under the auspices of an international conference, his initiative was dead.[21] Israeli intransigence and Arab suspicion – not least Hussein's – had seen to that.

Clearly judging Shultz's peregrinations to be irrelevant, Israeli leaders had taken a decision that amounted to an act of war against the PLO. In early March, Israel's military and intelligence chiefs, and the so-called 'club of Prime Ministers' – Yitzhak Shamir, Shimon Peres and Yitzhak Rabin – decided in principle to assassinate Khalil al-Wazir, the 'godfather' of the uprising. Israel, they reasoned, needed a military success to balance domestic disappointment at the army's failure to curb the troubles. What would better serve their purposes, they asked themselves, than the slaying of one of the PLO's top leaders?

Wazir was the logical target. Hadn't he helped build the resistance in the territories? Wasn't he by far the single most important figure in the PLO when it came to directing hostilities in the West Bank and the Gaza Strip? Hadn't he stepped up efforts to infiltrate guerrillas across Israel's borders to carry out terrorist actions? And to make matters worse, wasn't he audaciously communicating directly with his men inside the territories by telephone calls and fax messages routed through Europe and Cyprus? Israel would not have long to wait for a pretext.

On 7 March, three Fatah guerrillas seized a bus in the southern Negev desert not far from Israel's Dimona nuclear facility. Their objective was to attack Dimona but they never got that far. They were killed in a shoot-out with security forces that also left three Israelis dead. Wazir had authorised the suicide mission and he also personally wrote the communiqué in the name of al-Asifa, Fatah's military wing, hailing their sacrifice. Israel's 'club of Prime Ministers' had found an excuse to put its assassination plan into action.

When Khalil al-Wazir returned in the early hours of 16 April to his villa in the Tunis suburb of Sidi Bou Said, a contingent of

Israeli commandos supported by agents of Mossad was lurking in the darkness. Soon after 1.30 a.m. they made their move, breaking into the house, killing a driver and two guards in the process. Wazir was at work upstairs – on a message, as chance would have it, to the underground leadership of the uprising. He would never finish it. Disturbed by the commotion, he grabbed a pistol and, with his wife Intissar following close, made for the door of their bedroom. Emerging into the corridor, he had time to fire just one round at figures ascending the stairs before he was cut down. Trained assassins, the Israeli commandos calmly poured dozens of shots into him. So intense were the bursts of gunfire that his pistol hand was near severed from his wrist, his body riddled with more than sixty bullets from head to toe. Peering from an upstairs window Intissar al-Wazir saw some two dozen dark figures running away from the house. She had no doubt they were Israelis.[22]

Hearing the news, a distraught Arafat rushed back to Tunis from the Gulf. The loss of Wazir was a devastating blow. He and Arafat had been close friends for more than thirty years, and comrades in arms for well over twenty. He had been a pillar of the PLO and of Fatah, his dogged, calm personality complementing Arafat's volatile temperament. He had saved Arafat from his own miscalculations on numerous occasions. The two men were so close that Arafat said of him, 'We were one spirit in two bodies.'[23]

In the first rush of grief, Arafat vowed vengeance. 'Those who think the assassination of Abu Jihad will smother the Palestinian uprising are deluding themselves,' he declared. 'His death will give new life to this heroic revolt. The blood of Abu Jihad will be dearly paid for.'[24] Blood did flow, but it was not Israeli. A dozen Palestinians died in protests that swept the territories on the day of the assassination, the *intifada's* worst single day of violence. Seven of those killed by Israeli bullets were from the Gaza Strip – the breeding ground for Wazir's own early resistance activities.

George Shultz and his aides recognised that the slaying of Arafat's right-hand man would hardly improve the climate for conciliation in the Middle East, but he pursued nevertheless his proposal for an international peace conference on yet another shuttle mission to the Middle East in May. He left Israel early in June after failing again to budge Israeli Premier Shamir. Exas-

Above and below The guerrilla leader: Arafat visits Ramtha, Jordan, in October 1970. *(Popperfoto)*

Above Arafat addresses the UN General Assembly on 13 November 1974. Note the empty chairs (*far left*) normally occupied by the Israeli delegation. *(Popperfoto)*

Below Arafat with the Ayatollah Khomeini (*left*) and Ahmed Khomeini. *(Popperfoto)*

Right Keeper of the flame: Arafat helps to carry a torch during a rally to commemorate the eighth anniversary of the battle of Karameh, 20 March 1976. *(Popperfoto)*

Below Arafat's handshake with Yitzhak Rabin, after the signature of their historic agreement on Palestinian autonomy in the occupied territories, 13 September 1993. *(Popperfoto)*

Left Arafat kisses the ground on arrival in Palestinian-controlled Gaza after twenty-seven years of exile, 1 July 1994. *(Popperfoto)*

Below Entering Gaza City after crossing into Gaza at the Rafah border point, 1 July 1994. *(Popperfoto)*

Above Posing with Shimon Peres *(middle)* and Yitzhak Rabin *(right)* in Oslo, Norway, having received the Nobel Peace Prize, on 10 December 1994. *(Popperfoto)*

Above The White House, 28 September 1995: President Clinton and Hosni Mubarak, President of Egypt (*far left*) look on as Arafat and Yitzhak Rabin sign an accord expanding Palestinian control in the West Bank. *(Popperfoto)*

Left 22 October 1995: Arafat addresses a United Nations special session marking the fiftieth anniversary of the organisation. *(Popperfoto)*

Left Washington, 2 October 1996: Arafat and Benjamin Netanyahu shake hands as they leave a White House news conference, having agreed to resume peace talks. President Clinton and Jordan's King Hussein (hidden by Arafat's kaffiyeh) look on. *(Popperfoto)*

Right Arafat speaks at Elnajah University, 5 April 1996. *(Popperfoto)*

Left Some 25,000 supporters turn out to greet Arafat as he arrives in Hebron on 19 January 1997. The limousine in which he is standing is invisible. *(Popperfoto)*

Above Arafat gives a double victory sign after a speech on 19 January 1997 from the former Israeli army headquarters in Hebron, a symbol of occupation there for thirty years. In his speech, Arafat sought to reassure the Jewish settlers who remained in the largely PLO-controlled city of his desire for peace. *(Popperfoto)*

Above Arafat waves to the crowd in Ramallah, 14 May 1998, during a demonstration to mark *al-Nakba* ('the catastrophe') which Arabs say befell them with the proclamation of Israel's creation fifty years before. Arafat said that Jerusalem will remain 'our eternal capital'. *(Popperfoto)*

Top left 19 January 1997: President Arafat reaches out to shake a supporter's hand in Hebron. *(Popperfoto)*

Bottom left Rafah border, Gaza Strip. Arafat returns from talks in Washington on 27 February 1998. The Egyptian government newspaper *al-Jumhuriya* had reported that he planned to step down as President of the Palestinian Authority on health grounds – the report drew a swift denial from Ahmed abdel Rahman, General Secretary of the PA cabinet. *(Popperfoto)*

Above Arafat kisses the forehead of Jordan's Crown Prince Hassan on arrival at the Royal Palace in Amman, 31 August 1998. *(Popperfoto)*

Below Arriving in Hebron on 4 September 1998 for the weekly Palestinian cabinet meeting. *(Popperfoto)*

Above An evening summit meeting on 22 October 1998 with (*from left to right*) President Clinton, Nabil Abu Rudineh, translator Gamal Halel, Nabil Shaath, Chairman Arafat, Danny Naveh and Israeli Prime Minister Benjamin Netanyahu at the Wye River Conference Center in Maryland. Israeli and Palestinian officials said that they were close to a deal in their marathon US-brokered summit, but US officials urged strong caution until an agreement was reached. *(Popperfoto)*

Right 23 October 1998: Arafat kisses President Clinton prior to the formal signing of the land-for-security deal, which included the release of hundreds of Palestinian prisoners from Israeli jails. US Secretary of State Madeleine Albright watches in the background. *(Popperfoto)*

Above An exhausted Arafat waves upon his arrival in the Gaza Strip, 28 October 1998, following the Wye Plantation summit. *(Popperfoto)*

Below 30 November 1998: In Washington to appeal for aid at a one-day international donors' conference to be held at the US State Department, Arafat shakes hands with President Clinton. *(Popperfoto)*

Above 14 December 1998: Yasser Arafat and US President Bill Clinton applaud as members of the Palestinian Council in Gaza City vote to cancel anti-Israeli clauses in the Palestinian National Charter. Clinton was on a three-day trip to Israel and the Palestinian territories. *(Popperfoto)*

Left Arafat acknowledges his supporters from in front of his Gaza Strip office, 2 August 2000. *(Popperfoto)* perated, Shultz issued what was, for him, an unusually blunt statement: 'The continued occupation of the West Bank and the Gaza Strip, and the frustration of Palestinian rights, is a dead-end street,' he declared. 'The belief that this can continue is an illusion.'[25]

As Shultz shuffled off the Middle East stage, Arab leaders assembled for a summit meeting in a dowdy hotel in Algiers to debate a development that filled them all with unease: the six-month-old Palestinian uprising. The central player was a man whom many of the same leaders had done their best to ignore at their last meeting in Amman the previous November. Yasser Arafat was back at centre stage, demanding Arab endorsement for the struggle in the occupied territories and a fresh injection of Arab money for the PLO. He had been agitating for the summit for months, but the initial answer from Arab leaders, worried lest the sight of Palestinian youths engaging in spontaneous protests should prove contagious at home, had hardly been enthusiastic. Now, they yielded. Arafat was determined to use the occasion as a means of consolidating the revival of his political fortunes.

He was not disappointed. However fervently many of the assembled leaders may have wished the PLO and Arafat would melt away, they buried their misgivings in praise of the 'heroic' uprising against Israeli rule and promised (falsely, as it turned out) to increase their donations to PLO coffers, and to reinvigorate their diplomatic efforts in defence of the Palestinian cause. Even King Hussein, who had been trying over the preceding two years to preserve a role for himself as representing the Palestinians, felt obliged to defer to his old rival. In a melancholy speech, he complained that Jordanian intentions had all too frequently been misunderstood and promised to bow out of efforts to represent the Palestinians if the Arab states so wished. Behind his magnanimity, however, lay disappointment and worry lest the *intifada* spill over the Jordan river into his own kingdom. Indeed, he was dismayed that the Palestinians of the occupied territories seemed to be spurning him as much as they were rejecting the Israelis.

Never one to advance on only one front, Arafat was also engaged in another of his Byzantine efforts to push the Palestinian movement towards more conciliatory policies. The means chosen was an anonymous article distributed to journalists while Arafat was being insincerely feted in the conference room. It purported to set out the PLO's view of the prospects for an Israeli–Palestinian peace settlement and represented another Arafat trial balloon, albeit one floated so discreetly that it could almost have passed unnoticed.

Those who did pick it up, however, were struck by a quite unusual tone. 'We believe that all peoples – the Jewish and the Palestinians included – have the right to run their own affairs, expecting from their neighbours not only non-belligerence but the kind of political and economic co-operation without which no state can be truly secure,' the article said. 'The Palestinians want that kind of lasting peace and security for themselves and the Israelis because no one can build his own future on the ruins of another's.'[26]

What was most intriguing was the article's provenance, for the author was Bassam Abu Sharif, an Arafat aide and former chief spokesman for the hardline Popular Front for the Liberation of Palestine. Abu Sharif had convincing 'revolutionary' credentials having been mutilated by an Israeli parcel bomb delivered in a book with a cover depicting Che Guevara. But since 1987, when he was expelled from the PFLP Central Committee for refusing to toe the party line, he had moved close to Arafat. Now here he was putting his name to an article with language as conciliatory as any produced by the PLO in more than two decades.

Abu Sharif claimed that the piece was his own handiwork. 'I started thinking about writing such an article in March 1988,' he said. 'The idea was mainly that our *intifada* should have a political programme that is realistic, achievable and accepted internationally . . . I wanted to tell the world that the Palestinians, after years and years of struggle for one democratic state called Palestine, have realised that the only realistic solution is a two-state solution.'[27]

On this occasion, the gesture set off political waves, both within the PLO and in the outside world. The Abu Sharif document attracted particularly keen attention in Washington, where the US Administration was already beginning to cast around for new approaches to the Arab–Israeli conflict following the failure of George Shultz's last peace mission. Says a former senior Shultz aide, 'We heard that and we thought, Jesus, they're being sensitive to Israeli security concerns. Now that's the way to make an impact. It was the tone as much as anything – the language that said: believe me, we understand your Israeli concerns, we've got the same concerns. They just had not gotten that across as sensitively before as they did in that single document.'[28]

An influential section of the American Jewish community was also roused to something like enthusiasm. After Abu Sharif's article was reproduced in the American press, he received a letter expressing interest from New York lawyer Rita Hauser. She was to play an important role in the US effort to institute a dialogue with the PLO later that year.

Inside the PLO, by contrast, people were underwhelmed. 'There were a lot of questions,' Abu Sharif recalled. 'There were different reactions from support to criticism of the language to criticism of the timing to criticism of the idea.'[29] The overwhelming verdict – even from within Fatah, whose members were piqued that someone from outside the mainstream had been used to convey Arafat's latest signal – was negative.

Recriminations were continuing when, nearly two months later, the PLO received an unanticipated jolt from Amman. King Hussein had not forgotten the snub administered to him by the Arab summit which had vested the PLO with sole authority to distribute the new allocation of funds in the territories (previously Jordan had shared this task). Ruminating over the outcome with his advisers on the plane home from Algiers, he had concluded reluctantly that any dreams he may have entertained of a role for Jordan with the Palestinians in a joint peace effort were unrealistic.[30] A decision was taking shape in his mind that would change the ground rules of the Middle East conflict.

16. INDEPENDENCE

'The State of Palestine is the state of Palestinians wherever they may be . . . It will join with all states and peoples in order to assure a permanent peace based on justice.' Yasser Arafat, proclamation of an independent Palestinian state, Algiers, 15 November 1988.

In the early evening of 31 July 1988, the citizens of Jordan saw a familiar face peering out from their television sets. 'In the name of God, the compassionate, the merciful,' intoned the gloomy monarch.

King Hussein had gone on television to announce the end of a dream: the idea that he could one day restore his dynasty's rule over the Palestinians of the West Bank. For 21 years, since the Israelis had captured the half of his kingdom that lay across the Jordan river in the Six-Day War, he had clung to the belief that he would one day get it back. Despite endless statements from the Arab world that the PLO, not Jordan, represented the Palestinians of the West Bank, he had retained close ties with the Arabs under Israeli rule. Now, seated before a large portrait of his grandfather King Abdullah, who had annexed the West Bank in 1950, he was preparing to break with his ancestor's legacy.

'Since there is a general conviction that the struggle to liberate the occupied Palestinian land could be enhanced by dismantling the legal and administrative links between the two banks, we have to fulfil our duty, and do what is required of us,' he said. 'Jordan is not Palestine. And the independent Palestinian state will be established on the occupied land after its liberation, God willing.'[1]

Hussein's move was a gesture both of resignation and of hurt. Deeply preoccupied with the surge of Palestinian nationalism that had found its voice in the *intifada*, he wanted to slap the Palestinians for rejecting him, and to show that they would make no progress towards their goal without him. In the process, he also dealt a lethal blow to American-sponsored Middle East peace moves which had, to that point, hinged on the idea that the West Bank should maintain a close association with Jordan after an eventual Israeli withdrawal. If the US Administration had been gradually reaching the conclusion that its previous Middle East policy was bankrupt, Hussein's announcement delivered the *coup de grace*.

The one person who stood to gain or lose most from Hussein's announcement was Yasser Arafat. For twenty years as PLO chairman he had claimed to represent the Palestinians of the West Bank but had been shielded by Jordan from having to exercise direct responsibility for them. Now the PLO and the Palestinians under occupation were being brought face to face. Sooner or later, the latter were bound to ask the former what it was doing to relieve their plight.

On the face of it, the Jordanian move did not bode well. Hussein had not deigned to consult Arafat before making his announcement and it looked very much as if he was up to his old machinations against the PLO. Unlike Hussein, who had developed a co-operative relationship with Israel over the years, the PLO was simply in no position to assume responsibility for the occupied territories. Unless Arafat moved fast, a dangerous political vacuum might arise.

As Salah Khalaf put it, 'We knew that the king had not made his decision for the benefit of the cause. I believe personally that the king was betting that the PLO would not be capable of making an initiative. The bet was that either there would be a failure to take a decision, or a failure to implement it, and that in either case the PLO would have to go back to him again.'[2] But what if Hussein had miscalculated? What if Arafat and his colleagues were able to defy the sceptics and mount a new diplomatic initiative? This time, in the absence of Jordan from the equation, the world would have to listen. 'The main argument of the Americans and the Israelis about the Jordanian option had been eliminated,' said Khalaf. 'It confronted them with the fact that they would have to deal with the PLO.'[3] The more Arafat thought about it, the more tantalising this prospect became.

After several days of debate, the Baghdad meeting concluded that the king's decision presented an opportunity which the PLO could not afford to pass up. A special committee was set up to consider a response. It was agreed that an emergency meeting of the organisation's main decision-making body, the Palestine

National Council, should be convened within weeks. There could be no mistaking the pressures on the PLO leadership. In the occupied territories, influential voices were calling openly for a unilateral declaration of independence for the West Bank and Gaza, to give form to the struggle for a state. One man who was emphatically of this view was Faisal al-Husseini. When the Israeli authorities arrested Husseini yet again at the beginning of August, they even found a draft of such a declaration in his files. Prime Minister Shamir termed it 'a crazy idea, since there is no chance whatsoever that it will be realised.'[4]

Crazy or not, the idea of declaring independence was laden with historical significance for Arafat and his colleagues. It would entail formal acceptance of something that the previous generation of Palestinian leaders had unequivocally rejected more than forty years before: the United Nations proposal to partition Palestine into two states, one Jewish, one Arab. It would involve, in effect, recognising UN General Assembly Resolution 181, the vote that had served as a birth certificate for the state of Israel.

This was precisely the idea for which Arafat set out to muster support during August. Palestinian experts in international law got to work on an independence formula. Leaders of the various PLO factions huddled in Tunis and elsewhere, testily debating the politics of the move.

Arafat himself clocked up thousands of air miles jetting between Arab and other capitals in an effort to build a consensus for an independent Palestinian state, and ferried a diverse cast of outside advisers to see him in a plane placed at his disposal by Palestinian millionaire Hassib Sabbagh. It was an unusually delicate task, for what Arafat was proposing was more than a simple independence declaration. He was also anxious for the PLO to adopt a new and realistic political programme that would break with the taboos of the previous twenty years. Specifically, he wanted acceptance of UN Security Council Resolution 242 of 1967, setting out Israel's right to exist in peace and security.

Such a decision, as Arafat saw it, could pave the way for increased recognition for the PLO at a time when rapid change in the international climate had raised hopes for the settlement of regional conflicts, as it had contributed to a ceasefire in the

Iran–Iraq war that summer. With relations between the super-powers thawing, it might even win him a prize that had eluded his grasp for the past fifteen years: dialogue with the United States. For although Arafat's colleagues did not realise it, he was once again making overtures to Washington, and in return was receiving indications of serious American interest in talking to the PLO.

Arafat's chosen intermediary for this most tentative and clandestine of courtships was a Washington-based Palestinian, Mohammed Rabieh. In early August, Rabieh showed up in the office of William Quandt, a former US official who retained influential contacts with the State Department's Arabists. His message was simple: the PLO was ready to accept Resolution 242 in return for American agreement to open a dialogue and recognition of Palestinian 'political rights'. Together, the two men drafted a statement which Quandt then took to the State Department. What would the Administration's response be if this became PLO policy? Considering the contempt in which Secretary of State George Shultz was known to hold Arafat, the answer was surprisingly positive. Quandt was told that if the PLO would meet long-standing US conditions, a dialogue could begin within 24 hours.[5]

The fact was that the Americans had been wrong-footed by Hussein's disengagement from the West Bank. If they were to retain credibility as a peace-broker in the Middle East, they badly needed to come up with a fresh approach. Not that there could be any question of parlaying openly with the Palestinians at this stage, even through intermediaries. The whole idea was far too sensitive in American political terms for that. It all had to be at more than arm's length, top secret and, above all, deniable. Fortunately for Shultz and for Arafat, there were third parties on hand to provide the necessary 'cover' for their diplomatic manoeuvring.

Principal among them was the Swedish politician Sten Andersson. Andersson was a veteran leader of Sweden's Social Democratic Party, and a long-time confidant of the country's late premier, Olof Palme. In the post of Foreign Minister since 1986, he had inherited Palme's sense of mission as an international peacemaker and was anxious to continue his country's long tradition of mediation in the Middle East. Haunted by what he had seen on a visit to the region in March 1988, he had turned his attention to the Arab–Israeli conflict. Could Sweden's good offices now be turned to useful effect in breaking down the obstacles to a dialogue between Israel and the Palestinians?

On one side at least, the circumstances did not seem all that encouraging. Andersson had concluded during his Middle Eastern tour that the Israelis were in a bind of their own making: they were 'not capable of taking any peace initiative themselves'.[6] But he had been told privately by Shimon Peres, the Israeli Labour leader and Foreign Minister: 'If you get the PLO to renounce terrorism and recognise Israel, I would respect them.'[7]

Unsure what that remark might mean, Andersson resolved to test it out and did so a couple of weeks after returning from the Middle East when he discussed the issue with George Shultz during a visit to Washington.

During a lunch in the State Department banqueting room, Andersson and Shultz repaired to the balcony for fifteen minutes' private chat. What if Sweden were to try to arrange a meeting between a group of prominent American Jews and the PLO as a first step towards breaking the ice? Shultz's reaction was typically Delphic. According to Andersson's aides, he 'neither supported nor opposed'[8] the suggestion, but that was enough for Andersson. In the ensuing weeks, he established regular contact with Arafat advisers and with suitable American Jews – people who would be both respectable enough to give his effort credibility and sympathetic enough to his aims not to run off and inform the Israelis. During a visit to Moscow, he informed the Soviets in 'very general terms' of his plans. The last thing he wanted was for the PLO's allies in the Kremlin to play a spoiling role.[9]

Before anything else could happen, however, the PLO had to be encouraged to move. How was Arafat to persuade the movement to adopt a conciliatory statement without provoking something that had happened on so many previous occasions: a walkout by the rejectionists, notably George Habash?

Arafat spent much time that autumn wooing the Marxist leader. Outsiders Arafat had drafted in to join the debate were despatched one by one to present their views to Habash, and they were all asked to handle him with kid gloves.

As the debate wore on, many observers began to wonder whether Arafat's plans for a new political initiative were in trouble. The promised meeting of the Palestine National Council was repeatedly put off and all manner of contradictory statements continued to emanate front the PLO leadership. Arafat, however, true to his oft-repeated maxim that 'politics is the art of timing', was playing a clever hand. Unbeknown to his colleagues, he had received a secret promise from Shultz that the US would respond positively to any PLO peace gestures, and that it would give its answer after the American presidential elections. Meantime Arafat was waiting for the right moment to convene the troops, and using the delay to wear his opponents down.

In November the moment arrived. With elections in Israel as well as the United States safely out of the way, the Palestinian 'parliament' was preparing to meet in Algiers.

Late one night at the beginning of the month, the PLO faction leaders gathered in a hall in a Tunis suburb for one last discussion of the agenda. It was a solemn occasion, in keeping with the importance of the issues. 'I have attended all sorts of organisational meetings and debates over the last 21 years,' said Salah Khalaf. 'It was the first time that there had been a responsible and serious discussion among all the factions.'[10]

The meeting did not resolve differences between supporters and opponents of a conciliatory political programme but it did take a decision that was in effect just as important. Participants agreed that the factions would be free to express their opinions for and against at the forthcoming National Council session but that nobody would have a veto and nobody would walk out. The *intifada*, in whose name the session was being convened, had forced a new unity on the fractious PLO. What Khalaf called 'the etiquette of the *intifada*' had arrived.[11]

Ten days later, 380 Palestinian worthies assembled, as they had before, at the Club des Pins conference centre 30 kilometres west of Algiers. It was an appropriate venue for such a meeting: Algeria, though far from Palestine, had provided inspiration for Arafat's Fatah movement in the early 1960s and been its first and most consistent supporter. With anti-aircraft batteries outside guarding against aerial attack and a Soviet warship anchored offshore, the delegates assembled in the circular conference hall decked with red, green, white and black Palestinian flags. This assortment of dignitaries, activists and ageing revolutionaries was the essence of the Palestinian movement Arafat had led for twenty years, the parliament of a people without a country. It was an extraordinary talking shop, in which Palestinian doctors rubbed shoulders with American university professors, trades unionists with terrorists, socialist revolutionaries with capitalist plutocrats, Christian intellectuals with Islamic fundamentalists. It was a travelling stage, a forum for the exercise of Arafat's histrionic talents.

Only this time, there was a difference. The change was obvious from the start. The old chants about 'revenge' and 'revolution until victory' came out with less gusto than before. Intermingled with them were new slogans in support of the *intifada*. When 'the great fighter Yasser Arafat' was cheered to the podium, it was to audiences well beyond the hall, rather than to the battered strugglers in exile, that he addressed his speech: to the 'people of the glorious blessed *intifada*' and, astonishingly, to the president-elect of the United States, George Bush. 'I appeal to President Bush to adopt a new policy, not one simply aligned with Israel,' he said. 'We are not asking for the impossible.'[12]

The tone was set, and so was the target. In the face of Arafat's determination to push through a new political platform, the rejectionists were in retreat. Try as he might during three days of arduous debate to win delegates over to his side, George Habash found himself outmanoeuvred. Instead of distributing the text of the controversial declaration, Arafat insisted on having it read out loud, thus handing an instant advantage to those on his side who already knew what it contained.

At the climax of the debate Arafat left it to his deputy Salah Khalaf, who had always been a much better public speaker, to clinch the argument. Khalaf received a big ovation. As he sat down, a bemused Habash remarked, 'What's all this? You're speaking about treason, and they're clapping you?'[13]

In the small hours of 15 November 1988, the Palestinian flag was raised in the conference centre to the sound of a blustering brass band. Yasser Arafat read out a solemn declaration. 'The Palestine National Council, in the name of God and in the name of the Palestinian Arab people, hereby proclaims the establishment of the State of Palestine on our Palestinian territory with its capital Holy Jerusalem,' he declaimed. 'Now at last the curtain has been dropped around a whole epoch of prevarication and negation.'[14]

There was a certain unconscious irony in the latter statement, for although Arafat was referring to the changes in attitudes to the Palestinian cause that had been wrought by the 'heroic' uprising in the occupied territories, he might just as well have been talking about the PLO's own position. For years, in hope more than expectation, his movement had clung to extravagantly unrealistic visions of what it could achieve. Now, with a political statement issued alongside the independence declaration, it spelled out in clearer terms than ever before that its goal, for international consumption at least, was the establishment of a state living in peace alongside Israel.

The PLO's new programme was not without flaws. As the Israelis and other critics hastened to point out, the phrasing was obscure and circumlocutory, bearing all the hallmarks of a document written by committee. Neither it nor the independence declaration signalled the definitive abandonment of the PLO's dream: the replacement of Israel with a single democratic state for Arab and Jew. But the members of the Palestine National Council were in no doubt about what they had done. Four decades after the Jewish nationalist movement had accepted partition and declared independence, the Palestinians had steeled themselves to do the same, settling for a state in less than a quarter of the land called Palestine.[15]

Small wonder that the declaration was a subdued affair. All present in the conference hall knew, too, that even the modest state they had proclaimed did not exist, except on paper. Many felt that in agreeing to confine their demands for sovereignty to the West Bank and Gaza, they had signed away part of their birthright. In the Israeli-occupied territories, festivities were muffled by a curfew restricting all Palestinians to their homes for 24 hours. At its very inception, the plan for statehood was overshadowed by the grim reality of Israeli rule.

If Arafat was disturbed by such thoughts, he certainly did not show it. Armed with his movement's conciliatory programme, he was bent on using it to win new international respectability and an opportunity to address the United Nations for the first time since 1974.

On 6 December 1988, Arafat and a group of aides strode down the steps of his private jet at Stockholm airport. By helicopter they were transferred to the Haga Palace, the nineteenth-century residence of the kings of Sweden. Snow lay on the ground. Arafat and his entourage shivered in their thin cotton clothes against the cold. But if the climate caught them unawares, they were even less prepared for what they were about to hear in their discussions with the Swedish Government.

In the three weeks since the declaration of independence, things had not entirely gone Arafat's way. To be sure, many nations around the world had granted his symbolic Palestinian state formal diplomatic recognition and the countries of Western Europe had warmly welcomed the PLO's new political pro-gramme. But the government he was most anxious to address, the one in Washington, had been at best lukewarm. Although the White House had murmured faint praise about 'positive elements' in the Algiers declaration, both Reagan and President-elect George Bush agreed that it was not sufficiently clear to meet America's conditions for dealing with the PLO. To add insult to injury, George Shultz had just refused Arafat a visa to visit New York for his planned address to the UN General Assembly. Arafat, Shultz had proclaimed to a chorus of indignation from around the world, was an 'accessory to terrorism', and as such represented a threat to US national security.[16]

But all was by no means lost. If the Americans were still unimpressed and the Israelis resolutely refused to see anything new in what the PLO was now saying, many other countries were determined not to let slip this opportunity to present Arafat the peacemaker to the widest possible public. The UN General Assembly, outraged by Shultz's move, resolved to transfer its deliberations across the Atlantic to Geneva for a day on 13 December, in order to hear the PLO leader.

Against this backdrop, Arafat's visit on 6 December 1988 to

Stockholm, a capital that had long been friendly to the Palestinian cause, was not just a routine diplomatic stop. He was there to meet a group of influential American Jews seeking to encourage PLO 'moderation'. Although Arafat had met American Jews before, just as he had held talks with Israeli peace campaigners, this group was different from those he had encountered in the past. It included Republican lawyer Rita Hauser, a wealthy liberal called Stanley Scheinbaum, and a professor and Holocaust survivor, Menachem Rosensaft. It carried credibility and political clout and its members were anxious to facilitate an official dialogue between the PLO and the US.

Just a fortnight before, also in Stockholm and in conditions of great secrecy, Hauser and Scheinbaum had held talks with Arafat's veteran foreign policy adviser Khaled al-Hassan, and elicited from hint after a feisty discussion a statement clarifying the PLO peace platform. Now, summoned back to Sweden with a cryptic message from its embassy in Washington saying that 'the big man' was coming, they were after an endorsement of the same words from Arafat himself. Getting it would involve pushing him beyond what was said at Algiers, to a crystal clear recognition of Israel and a formal renunciation of terror, the two main conditions that Washington had long set. 'The problem with the Algiers declaration was that it was not a legally drafted document,' said Hauser. 'It was repetitive, inconsistent and incoherent. It was really a very confusing document.'[17]

As the two sides sat down to talk in the Haga Palace, Arafat was in convivial mood. He and Hauser, whose New York law practice was active in the Middle East, notably in Lebanon, discovered that they had friends in common. What Arafat did not realise, as the haggling got under way, was that another diplomatic game was about to commence. For his hosts had a surprise up their sleeve: an unexpected missive from the highest echelon of the US Administration. In his quiet, methodical way, Sten Andersson had been working on the Americans since the Algiers meeting, keeping Washington informed of the latest nuances in PLO policy. A week earlier, he had sent word to Secretary Shultz of Arafat's imminent arrival, and he had asked Shultz, gently, whether he might have anything to tell the PLO leader.

The result outstripped the Swedes' expectations. At almost exactly the same time as Shultz was deciding to deny Arafat a visa to go to the UN, he wrote a confidential letter to the Swedish Government holding out the prospect of an American dialogue with the PLO provided the latter would clearly recognise Israel and renounce terrorism. The letter was considered so sensitive that Shultz even kept its contents from some of his own staff, and the Swedes had it carried back from Washington by hand.[18] No wonder, for it appeared to presage a breakthrough of major proportions: in effect, Shultz was writing the precise lines that Arafat would have to speak to qualify for recognition by Washington, and telling him in advance what the Americans would say in return. While one half of the Secretary of State's legalistic mind was excoriating Arafat as a terrorist, the other was admitting that the PLO could not forever be excluded from Middle East peacemaking.

When Arafat was privately shown the Shultz letter, he was astonished. Here, on the American Secretary of State's personal stationery, was the clearest and most formal overture he had yet received from Washington. Throughout the evening of 6 December, the faxes flew across the Atlantic carrying suggested amendments to the US wording. Most of the PLO's proposals were accepted. The stage was set for what the Swedes hoped would be a dramatic declaration by Arafat in Stockholm the very next day and an even more dramatic American answer, but they were reckoning without Arafat's innate caution. Now that he was so close to what had been his obsessive goal, he was gripped by a sudden anxiety. This was too big a decision for him to make on his own. The PLO had long regarded formal, as opposed to implicit, recognition of Israel as its last bargaining card; to play it, he had to have clearance from other members of the PLO Executive Committee. To get it, he spent the entire night phoning round the world. The Swedes, who were both paying the bill and listening in, found his conversations not without interest.[19]

Even on the threshold of success, Arafat was hesitant. Perhaps Stockholm was not the place to do the deed after all. Perhaps the Americans were setting him up for a fall. Perhaps anything he said would be eclipsed by news from the Reagan–Gorbachev summit due to take place in New York the same day. Better, after all, to wait for a wider, safer stage before committing himself to America's arms. To the frustration of the Swedes, he told them that he would give his final answer after consulting yet again with the Executive Committee. After signing the less contentious statement proposed by the American Jews, he headed back to Tunis.[20]

For five days there was silence. Then came the answer, carried to Stockholm on 12 December by Arafat's aide, the Palestinian poet Mahmoud Darwish. Yes, he said, the Executive Committee had accepted the American conditions and Arafat would incorporate statements to that effect in his address to the UN General Assembly in Geneva the next day. The champagne was uncorked.

Less than 24 hours later, Yasser Arafat marched into a packed UN conference chamber. Not since his previous UN appearance in New York fourteen years before had he been the subject of so much diplomatic fuss. As then, ministers and senior emissaries had flown in from around the world to acclaim him. Television cameras and reporters' notebooks were poised to record his words. The Swiss had surrounded the Palais des Nations, an Art-Deco edifice on the snowy banks of Lake Geneva, with security almost as tight as New Yorkers had seen in 1974.

Only this time, it was a different Arafat standing behind the lectern. What was left of his hair and his beard were grey. Instead of ill-fitting jacket and baggy trousers, he wore a neatly pressed suit of green military fatigues together with chequered *keffiyeh*. As he donned a pair of brown-rimmed spectacles to read out the prepared text in Arabic it was clear that he had new lines to speak and a new objective in mind.

'I come to you in the name of my people, offering my hand so that we can make true peace, peace based on justice,' he proclaimed. 'I ask the leaders of Israel to come here under the sponsorship of the United Nations ... Come, let us make peace. Cast away fear and intimidation. Leave behind the spectre of the wars that have raged continuously for the past forty years.'[21]

The tone was reasonable, the words emollient, but there was one man in the audience who listened to Arafat's speech with a mounting sense of unease: this was supposed to be the consummation of the deal which Sten Andersson had worked so hard to broker between Arafat and the Americans. Yet where were the magic phrases that the PLO leader had promised to pronounce? Where was the explicit recognition of Israel and renunciation of terror?

Andersson's alarm was shared by at least one of Arafat's advisers, who prefers to remain anonymous.[22] Forty-eight hours earlier, on a miserable rainswept day in Tunis, he had helped the PLO leader put the finishing touches to an address containing all the right words that would unlock the door to negotiations with the US. But at the last minute, the unpredictable Arafat had changed his speech.

Four thousand miles away in Washington DC, a group of US officials huddled in front of a television set in a small private room on the seventh floor of the State Department. George Shultz and his top aides had no illusions about the performance they were watching live. They had seen something similar so many times before. One of those present had wagered a dollar that Arafat would fluff his lines. He won the bet. Once again, in the eyes of the American Administration, Arafat had sidled towards a diplomatic breakthrough but baulked at the final hurdle. Praising the 'interesting and positive developments' in the address, the State Department swiftly affirmed that it did not meet US conditions for a dialogue with the PLO. Worse still for Arafat, President-elect Bush chipped in with a statement of his own to the same effect. Much as the PLO's Arab allies – men like President Hosni Mubarak of Egypt – sought to salvage the situation with calls to President Reagan, Washington would not budge. All the painstaking negotiations of the preceding two months had come to little.

Arafat, resting back in his top floor suite at the Intercontinental Hotel, digested the news. Surely he had done what he was asked to do, he insisted. Maybe he had not spoken the words in the exact sequence demanded by Washington, but the peaceable sentiments were all there: the call for an international peace conference on the basis of UN Security Council Resolution 242, the pursuit of a 'comprehensive settlement' including Israel. Why were the Americans letting him down again?

But he had only himself to blame. In changing the speech, he had been trying to engage in one last piece of haggling, trying to say things in his own way. The legalistic Americans were bound to think he was up to his old tricks. 'He probably thought, being the wily politician that he is, that he would be able to get away with it,' said an Arafat adviser. 'Well, he didn't. He simply didn't understand the way the US system works – the fact that there were teams of State Department lawyers combing through his speech looking at every last comma.'[23]

As the implications of the blunder sank in, gloom descended on Arafat's hotel suite. His advisers debated what to do. PLO 'foreign minister' Farouk Kaddoumi, who had been deeply unhappy about the concessions Arafat had agreed to in any case, thought the matter was at an end. 'We've done all we can, and there's no point even in holding a press conference now,' he said.[24]

'What are you saying?' shot back businessman Hassib Sabbagh, who had played a behind-the-scenes role in steering the PLO leader to Geneva. 'That we've moved the entire UN General Assembly across the Atlantic for nothing? That this opportunity is simply to be thrown away? And what are we to tell the hundreds of journalists waiting out there?'

'Tell them to go away,' was Kaddoumi's dour reply.[25]

In this vein the conversation droned on into the small hours. There the affair might well have rested, had it not been for the determination of two of the PLO leader's associates, Sabbagh and fellow businessman Bassel Akel, to try again. Perhaps, they reasoned, Arafat could read a new text to his press conference later in the day, clearly recognising Israel and renouncing terror in US-approved language. Perhaps, after all, the Americans might be persuaded to listen if he came out with the right words at the second attempt. Heading back to the Intercontinental, they found Arafat already awake and alert and put it to him. It was, he agreed, worth one more push.

There followed hours of juggling. The PLO leader's press conference was postponed from midday to 7 p.m. while his aides drafted and redrafted formulations for formal recognition of Israel. At the same time, Sabbagh went into action. As the Washington day began, he got on the phone to Richard Murphy, the US Assistant Secretary of State and, while Arafat was sitting in the room, read over the proposed new statement. Murphy said he would consult his boss Shultz, President Reagan and President-elect Bush. and get back with Washington's response. Within a couple of hours, and after a couple of minor amendments, the statement was approved. Sten Andersson, who had himself been in touch with Washington to try to salvage the situation, confirmed that the deal was once more on. Arafat's advisers, nervous in any case about his imperfect English, set about rehearsing him in his lines.

In such strange ways is history made. At 8.30 p.m. on 14 December 1988, Yasser Arafat began to read a prepared statement in halting English. 'Between Algiers and Geneva,' he intoned, 'we have made our position crystal clear.'[26] But with his aides hovering at his elbow, prompting him in an audible whisper, he went on to make it even clearer. He accepted 'the right of all parties in the Middle East conflict to exist in peace and security.'[27] With redoubled emphasis, he added, 'I repeat for the record that we totally and absolutely renounce all forms of terrorism'[28] – his stage fright was such that the word came out sounding like 'tourism'.

Finally, in a blunt aside to his unseen listeners in Washington, he warned them against expecting any more concessions.

'Enough is enough. Enough is enough. Enough is enough,' he proclaimed with a mixture of fatigue and defiance. 'What do you want? Do you want me to striptease? It would be unseemly.'

Minutes later, the message, taped and transmitted by phone across the Atlantic, was being dissected by State Department bureaucrats in Washington DC. Following a brief discussion, George Shultz picked up the handset. 'We're agreed that he did it,' he told the White House. Within another two and a half hours, scores of Palestinians gathered around their hotel television sets in Geneva to watch the Secretary of State's impassive face as he announced that the United States was prepared to open a 'substantive dialogue with PLO representatives'.

It was a dramatic moment for the Palestinian leader. The years of equivocation and hesitation were at an end. Arafat had played the PLO's 'last card'.

But there was to be no curtain call. By the time the news filtered through to snowy, staid Geneva, the elusive Yasser Arafat was airborne again, on his way to another performance of his perpetual balancing act in what was then still the Cold War capital of East Berlin.

Strapped into his seat for the brief flight across the Iron Curtain, Arafat had reason to reflect on the latest twist in his fortunes. By cajoling his movement into accepting the idea of peaceful coexistence with Israel, and by stating that goal unambiguously in Geneva, he had secured unprecedented world recognition as leader of the Palestinians. Now, more than ever, he felt he had ensured that the PLO could not be ignored in any settlement of the Middle East conflict.

There was one major problem. As far as Israel was concerned, the independent Palestinian state that Arafat had proclaimed was simply a figment of everybody else's imagination. He had no guarantee that his decision to pursue the struggle principally by political means would bring him any closer to turning his dream into a reality, as he had admitted in Algiers when he promised that if the diplomatic tack did not work the Palestinians could always think again. Who was to say that within a year or two, he would not find himself doing what his opponents had predicted: admitting that, since diplomacy had failed, other means of struggle – including violence – would have to be reactivated?

17. THE WRONG HORSE

'When I have only two options, I cannot sleep because I want a third.'
Saying frequently attributed to Yasser Arafat.

It was a brilliant sun-filled morning on Israel's Mediterranean coast. The beach club of Nizzanim, a resort eighteen miles south of Tel Aviv, was packed. As they did every year at this time, Israelis were enjoying the Shavuot, the Jewish holiday that marks the handing down of the Ten Commandments and the beginning of high summer. The date was 30 May, 1990. Suddenly, the holidaymaking was disturbed by the clatter of machine-gun fire and the whirr of rotor blades. As the noise grew nearer a small speedboat roared into view, pursued closely by Israeli air force attack helicopters. The craft had eleven men aboard. It sliced across the bay, coming at one point within 200 yards of the beach, then weaved off to the south in a hail of bullets. As police sirens wailed, the stunned holiday-makers were herded away from the shore, and the beach was sealed off.[1]

What they had just witnessed was the abortive outcome of an attempted guerrilla raid on Israel by the Palestine Liberation Front, a faction of Yasser Arafat's PLO. It was designed to be one of the most audacious Palestinian attacks on the Jewish state for many years. Three days previously, a Libyan merchant ship had sailed from the port of Benghazi carrying six Libyan-made fibreglass speedboats and perhaps several dozen commandos, some of whom had been training in Libya for up to two years. The mother ship had deposited the boats named after a string of famous Arab battles in the Mediterranean some 120 miles off the Israeli coast. According to the PLF leader, Mohammed Zaidan (Abul Abbas) – who had achieved earlier notoriety for the hijacking of the cruise liner *Achille Lauro* in 1985 – 'Operation Jerusalem' was aimed at a private Tel Aviv bathing resort for senior army officers, a 'legitimate' military target. According to the Israelis, its goal was to kill and maim indiscriminately in the hotel area of downtown Tel Aviv.[2] Not much went according to plan. Three of the Palestinian boats broke down on the way to Israel, and a fourth – a fuel supply vessel – sank. Of the two that managed the full voyage, one was intercepted by an Israeli naval patrol boat near a kibbutz to the north of the metropolis; the other was pursued to Nizzanim, where seven of its crew surrendered and the other four were killed in a gun battle. No Israelis were harmed.[3]

The raid did, however, exact serious political casualties – principal among them Yasser Arafat, who was then wrapping up a meeting of Arab leaders in the Iraqi capital Baghdad. For the PLO leader, the attack could scarcely have come at a worse time. For months he had been struggling to keep alive the hopes he had invested in the dialogue his organisation had secured with the United States in December 1989. For months he had been arguing with colleagues that it was worth persevering with the PLO's peace initiative, despite the barely perceptible progress it had yielded towards winning recognition for Palestinian rights. Now, with the political climate in the Middle East deteriorating with a rapidity no one could have foreseen, his attempt to garner kudos for the PLO in the West had reached a dead end. Instinctively Arafat knew that he would not be able to escape being called to account by the American Government over the raid. The Israelis, who had been conducting a rearguard action against the US–PLO dialogue from the very first, held Arafat personally responsible for the attack, saying that it proved that the PLO had not, as Arafat had pledged, abandoned terrorism.[4] The Americans were demanding that, in order to demonstrate the contrary, he condemn it and punish those responsible.

The problem was that in this case 'those responsible' included some powerful friends – allies he could hardly afford to alienate. They included a man with whom Arafat's fortunes had by now become fatefully entangled: Iraq's President Saddam Hussein, principal sponsor of the Abul Abbas group. Arafat was beginning to realise that his latest dalliance might carry a price.[5]

In the eighteen months since his fumbling 'breakthrough' to talks with the American superpower Arafat had been on a revealing journey. It started amid extravagant Palestinian hopes that, in finally agreeing to a dialogue with the PLO after more than a decade's cold shoulder, the US had at least implicitly endorsed the Palestinians' right to a state of their own. It continued through forlorn expectations that Washington would use its undoubted leverage over Israel to prod it into meaningful peace negotiations. It ended – with the Jewish state refusing to budge and welcoming a new tide of immigrants – in a despairing sense that the Americans were content to acquiesce in the final obliteration of the Palestinians' quest for a homeland.

Part of the problem lay in the utterly divergent assumptions with which the two sides had approached the talks. As far as Arafat was concerned, a dialogue with the US in itself promised to take him three-quarters of the way to a settlement of the Palestinian problem. He had always told himself, as he remarked back in 1974, that 'the US holds the key to Israel'.[6] As he saw it, US 'recognition' of the PLO would automatically entail pressure on Israel to do likewise – and if it failed to comply it would have to face the consequences. For the Americans, agreeing to talk to the PLO was never more than a small part of the means to an end. The dialogue was to be restricted in scope and confined to one diplomatic channel, involving the American ambassador in Tunis, Robert Pelletreau, and a middle-level PLO negotiating team. In the meantime, the PLO was to be pressed to the hilt to abide by the letter and spirit of Arafat's latest commitments – especially his pledge to renounce terrorism.[7]

As the dialogue got under way in early 1989 in a Tunisian Government guesthouse near the ruins of Carthage, testing questions remained – not least concerning how terrorism was to be defined. In his first formal meeting with the three-man PLO team, Pelletreau spent much of the time urging his interlocutors to order a halt to Palestinian cross-border raids into Israel. Arafat was troubled, for he thought it had been understood that the PLO reserved the right to persist with 'legitimate acts of resistance' against the Israeli occupation of Palestinian land; although his own Fatah forces had quietly stopped cross-border activities some weeks before in what was tantamount to a truce, he knew it would be impossible to persuade the more militant factions within the PLO to do likewise.[8]

Notwithstanding the desire of the newly installed US President, George Bush, to make progress on the Middle East conflict, the history of their arm's length dealings with Arafat had taught the

Americans to be wary negotiators. If Washington still harboured doubts, the Israelis, who had been shocked when the dialogue with the PLO started, were determined to amplify them. Scarcely a week went by when Israeli propaganda did not find an opportunity to cast aspersions on the image of a peace-loving PLO. In February, government sources claimed that Arafat's Fatah faction had set up an underground 'Popular Army' in the occupied territories with the aim of assassinating Israelis as well as Palestinians accused of collaborating with the Israeli authorities.[9] On other occasions, PLO leaders themselves provided their detractors with ammunition by uttering bloodcurdling threats against Israel or suggesting to their constituents that the organisation's 'two-state' peace plan was merely a stage on the road to the recovery of all of Palestine. Arafat was no more willing or able to rein in his intemperate colleagues than he had been in the past. Over time, the Israelis were able to use the continuation of such rhetoric to sow mounting disquiet among sympathisers in the US Congress.

Nevertheless, the PLO's new line was beginning to bring other sorts of dividend. Capitalising on the PLO's unilateral declaration of an independent state the previous November, Arafat trotted the Arab, socialist and non-aligned parts of the globe, raising the Palestinian flag outside newly renamed PLO 'embassies'. The organisation stepped up its long-standing campaign to win full membership of United Nations agencies, focusing its efforts, much to the annoyance of the US and other Western countries, on the hitherto non-political World Health Organisation and on Unesco. Arafat himself – ever a stickler for protocol – began to demand a formal enhancement of his status.

On 2 April, PLO headquarters in Tunis announced that the movement's Central Council had unanimously elected him President of the still putative State of Palestine. He would retain the job, said his spokesman, until democratic elections could take place there. The timing of the move baffled even Arafat's closest colleagues. The idea of 'promoting' him had been a debating point for at least six months, but those who had considered it thought they had decided it could await progress towards formation of a provisional government for the state. Was their leader now intent on giving himself more than the usual airs?[10] The explanation was that Arafat was about to embark on his first meetings with some of the most important Western leaders and wanted to be able to communicate with them on an equal footing. Even if they did not recognise his state, the governments of France, Italy and Japan would have to give him presidential treatment.

His Paris visit, in May 1989, was a high point. From his heavily guarded suite in the Hotel Crillon, he watched with relish as Jewish demonstrators protested outside in the Place de la Concorde; was received by President Mitterrand; banqueted with government ministers; and gave an address (impromptu, because an aide had forgotten to bring his prepared speech) to the cream of the French intelligentsia.[11]

It was an act that was going to be difficult to sustain. Arafat was still under pressure from his Western interlocutors to offer further concessions to Israel – for example, by getting the PLO formally to scrap its National Covenant, which called for the liberation of all Palestine through armed struggle and declared the establishment of Israel 'fundamentally null and void'. His response, as usual, was to indulge in wordplay. When in Paris he took up a suggestion from French Foreign Minister Roland Dumas and declared the Covenant *caduc* – a French legal term whose approximate meaning can be translated as 'lapsed' or 'superseded'.[12] Arafat had certainly never heard the word before; asked by an Arab journalist why he had used a French term, he said with no conscious irony that French was 'a universal language which is a treasure of legal terms such as *persona non grata*'.[13]

Symbolically important as they were, all Arafat's diplomatic gains could not disguise the fact that there was precious little evidence of progress towards the goal he had set himself: the convening of an international Middle East peace conference, under UN sponsorship, to bring Israel, the PLO and Arab states together and force Israeli withdrawal from the occupied territories. Israel's coalition government, dominated by hard-line Prime Minister Yitzhak Shamir and his Likud party, had other ideas. As adamantly opposed to an international conference as they were to the idea of talking to Arafat's PLO, the Likud and Labour coalition partners were cooking up a plan designed to launch a different kind of 'peace process' and to deflect external pressure on them to concede territory. The proposal, originally devised by the Labour Defence Minister, Yitzhak Rabin, and touted by Shamir during a visit to Washington in April, was to hold elections among the 1.7 million inhabitants of the West Bank and Gaza Strip with a view to selecting a delegation for talks with Israel. While the final status of the territories would be left indeterminate, the initial objective would be to set up a limited form of Palestinian self-rule for a transitional period lasting up to five years. The plan, in emphasising democracy, was calculated to appeal to the Bush Administration. But in ruling out any role for the PLO, and indeed implying that alternatives to the organisation might be found were the Palestinians of the territories to be allowed to vote free from 'intimidation', it was bound to be viewed by Arafat with scepticism to say the least.

This was the proposal that Bush and his Secretary of State, James Baker, picked up and set about trying to sell to the PLO. It was, they reasoned, about the best opening bid that could be expected from Israel's divided government. But it might just, with suitable modification, be turned into a basis for Israeli–Palestinian talks – what one Baker adviser described as 'a journey of a thousand steps'.[14]

So began a protracted bout of shadow-boxing between Shamir, Defence Minister Rabin and Arafat, with Washington as timid referee and amid persistent heckling from Israeli and Palestinian opponents on the sidelines.

The common ground was tenuous, to put it mildly. Neither Shamir nor the PLO viewed the process with anything other than distaste, but neither wanted to be blamed for bringing it to a halt; each saw his essential task as being to lure the other into a political trap. That was certainly the argument that Palestinians in the occupied territories were putting to Arafat as a justification for not saying no to elections. By playing along, they said, you stand a chance of forcing Shamir to implement a plan in which he himself does not actually believe. If you reject elections, as Shamir fully expects, you will be 'tainted as using "terror" rather than politics'.[15]

For the first few months, Arafat seemed to be winning something of a victory on points. He was heartened by some unusually robust criticism from the Bush Administration of Israel's policies on the occupied territories, and further encouraged by the evident signs of discomfort in the Israeli Government. In talks with the Americans, his representatives remained suspicious but noncommittal, seeking to encourage the US to flesh out Israel's ideas. 'Who can be against elections?' he exclaimed. 'But they have to be part of a whole plan from A to Z.'[16]

After the Shamir Government reached agreement on the plan in May, the PLO demanded assurances that elections would form part of a process that might lead to the establishment of a Palestinian state; it queried whether Palestinians from East Jerusalem would be allowed to take part (a controversial issue because Israel had annexed the Arab eastern half of the city and regarded it as part of its eternal and indivisible capital); it sought to ensure that in any pre-election negotiations with the Israelis, the PLO would be properly represented through the presence of Palestinian spokesmen from outside as well as inside the Israeli occupied territories; it repeatedly made the rather ridiculous suggestion that Israel withdraw from the territories *before* elections, as South Africa had done from Namibia. But it did not, as some in the Israeli Government undoubtedly hoped it would, reject the idea out of hand. As he later hinted, Arafat even received what amounted to personal messages about the plan from Rabin, carried by an Arab member of the Israeli Knesset, Abdelwahab Darousha.[17]

For once, the PLO was handling its side of the argument skilfully. Indeed, Arafat's behaviour was sensible enough to alarm the Israeli Likud. Acting out of a mixture of personal ambition and ideological concern, hawks on the right of the party – principal among them the architect of the 1982 Lebanon invasion, Ariel Sharon – challenged Shamir. The Prime Minister, they said, was doing the unthinkable: negotiating by proxy with Yasser Arafat. His election plan, they claimed, was the first step down a slippery slope that could lead all the way to the establishment of a Palestinian state. The process had to stop.

The stratagem settled on by Sharon and his cohorts was to attempt to tie Shamir's hands by forcing him to attach conditions to the election plan that would in effect kill it. Their campaign came to a head at a raucous Likud central committee meeting in Tel Aviv on the evening of 5 July: Shamir gave in to their demands. 'There could be no elections,' he stated, 'until the Palestinian *intifada* had been extinguished; East Jerusalem Arabs would be excluded from the process; Jewish settlement of the occupied territories would continue; and there could be no question of a Palestinian state emerging at the end.'[18]

It was a serious blow to American hopes of getting negotiations moving. But within little more than twelve hours it was eclipsed by a terrible bus accident on the Tel Aviv–Jerusalem highway, caused by a Palestinian extremist. With the bus nine miles west of Jerusalem, a bearded Arab man rushed up the aisle shouting '*Allahu Akbar*' (God is great), grabbed the steering wheel, and sent the vehicle plunging into a ravine. Fourteen Israelis were killed and 27 injured.[19]

There was no obvious link between the political setback and the act of violence. Yet somehow, as so often in the Middle East, they seemed like two segments of the same taut piece of piano wire.

The pressures on Arafat, from within and outside the PLO, were by now considerable. With the *intifada* in its twentieth month, there was little to suggest that the considerable sacrifices made by the inhabitants of the occupied territories had yielded progress towards a peace settlement. Moreover, Arafat was having great difficulty persuading the Arab states to live up to their pledges of financial support. At their summit in Algiers the previous year, Arab leaders had agreed to stump up 43 million dollars a month for the *intifada*, but only one country, Iraq, was maintaining a regular flow of funds. So difficult had the financial position become that Arafat was forced to institute a sweeping austerity programme. It was a consideration which was to weigh heavily on Arafat's mind as he reviewed his options in the coming months.[20]

In short, their hopes having been raised excessively high the previous winter, all that the Palestinians could now see was Arafat apparently making concession after concession, Israel digging in its heels, and the US Administration, along with the moderate Arab states which ostensibly supported the PLO initiative, sitting helplessly by. More than that, the Americans seemed to Arafat to be conspiring to make things more difficult for him. They were repeatedly raising problems over visas for PLO officials wanting to visit the US to put across the Palestinian case; they had refused frequent requests to upgrade or broaden the dialogue or to allow the PLO office in Washington to reopen; they were continuing to veto resolutions in the UN Security Council that they considered hostile to Israel; and they were always raising concerns about the multiplicity of apparently threatening PLO statements. Some of these slights may seem trivial, but to Arafat, for whom the diplomatic niceties are akin to matters of substance, they were a serious rebuff. 'We kept receiving letters saying our deputy representative in Djibouti had been overheard in a bar saying aggressive things about Israel,' recalled Nabil Shaath.[21]

The steam building up within the movement was evident at a closed-door meeting of the 1,290-member Fatah congress, Arafat's main power base, in Tunis in early August 1989. This was the first gathering in nine years of the guerrilla fighters and others who formed the core of Fatah. The message it delivered could not have been clearer. There were complaints about Arafat's leadership: his autocratic style, the concessions he had offered the US and Israel without getting anything in return, and Fatah's apparent abandonment of the 'armed struggle' across Israel's northern border. The final resolution called for a 'continuation and escalation of armed struggle . . . to end Israeli occupation of our occupied Palestinian land', a hint that, in the absence of eventual progress in the PLO peace initiative, the pressure would continue building for a return to arms. For good measure, the meeting rejected several of Arafat's nominees for key Fatah posts. Top of the poll came PLO 'foreign minister' Farouk Kaddoumi, noted for his uncompromising views.[22]

With lines thus hardening on both the Israeli and Palestinian sides, and Arafat warning periodically that he might consider calling for an all-out campaign of civil disobedience in the occupied territories or even the use of firearms, time was slipping away for American peace efforts. Secretary Baker struggled to keep the momentum up in the next few months, enlisting Egypt's President Hosni Mubarak in a fresh bid to set up an acceptable Israeli–Palestinian negotiating framework. But nobody's heart was in it: all the exchanges produced was an arcane collection of procedural documents, ranging from a ten-point initiative from Mubarak to a five-point plan from Baker. The ideas involved meetings of Egyptian, Israeli and American Government officials and the selection of 'acceptable' Palestinian negotiating partners. But no proposal could bridge the fundamental divide between Shamir's refusal to have anything to do with the PLO and Arafat's insistence on preserving at least a symbolic role in the process. As the PLO leader never tired of pointing out, it was probably the first time in history that one party to a negotiation was insisting on choosing the opposing team. All Baker could do to signal his impatience with the Israelis was threaten to drop the mediation effort once and for all.

By December, Arafat's frustration had welled up. He was fed up with the US attempts to appease Israel by whittling away the PLO's role to invisibility. He had received no reply to a direct message he had sent President Bush the previous month demanding 'a more aggressive attitude by the United States towards Israel'.[23] Moreover, he was becoming seriously irritated by the role of Egypt, whose diplomats had all but taken the place of the US–PLO dialogue as America's principal channel of communication with the organisation and were beginning to apply what he saw as crude pressure on him to accept the American plan. Arafat could not accept Egypt – financially and politically beholden as it was to the US – as an intermediary.

It was the end of the road; events in the wider world had become too momentous and too alarming for these desultory peace efforts to have much relevance. The Soviet Union, traditional ally of the Arabs, was near collapse. The PLO's other friends in what used to be communist eastern Europe – Husak in Czechoslovakia, Honecker in East Germany and Ceaucescu in Romania – were falling like dominoes to democratic revolutions. Worst of all for the Palestinians, a swelling flood of Jewish emigrants was being allowed to leave the Soviet Union and, thanks to a recent tightening in immigration rules in the US, first choice of destination for many of them, they were heading in their thousands to Israel. As Arafat watched this latest drama unfold he concluded the current strategy had run out of steam. It was time to explore other options with other friends.

President Saddam Hussein marched down the steps of his plane and on to the red carpet spread out on the tarmac. It was 23 February 1990. The Iraqi leader had arrived in Amman to take part in a summit meeting to mark the first anniversary of the Arab Co-operation Council, a grouping of four Arab states – Iraq, Jordan, Yemen and Egypt – that he had been instrumental in setting up. For Saddam this was an occasion of some importance, for he planned to deliver a speech that would send ripples through the Arab world and beyond.

When the other leaders gathered at Amman's sports centre the next day – as King Hussein remarked, the 'glorious and dear occasion' of the Prophet Mohammed's ascension – the Iraqi President did not mince words. The world, he said, was changing in dramatic and, for the Arabs, potentially disturbing ways. The collapse of the Soviet Union had left the United States paramount, and the Arabs dangerously exposed to American and Israeli might. 'Given that the influence of the Zionist lobby on US policies is as powerful as ever,' he went on, 'the Arabs must take into account that there is a real possibility that Israel might embark on new stupidities within the next five years. This might take place as a result of direct or tacit US encouragement.'[25] Saddam spoke of the challenge to Arab security posed by the continuing presence of US warships in the Gulf – conveniently forgetting that this presence had been one of the factors that had helped Iraq stave off defeat at the hands of Iran only two years before. He denounced America's encouragement for an 'unprecedented exodus of Soviet Jews to Palestinian territory', and its 'increasing support for the Zionist entity's strategic arms stockpiles'. He issued a call for the Arabs to close ranks to confront the now unchallenged super-power. 'There is no place among the ranks of good Arabs for the faint-hearted who would argue that, as a superpower, the United States will be the decisive factor and others have no choice but to submit,' he said.[26]

One of his listeners, Egypt's President Hosni Mubarak, was dismayed. As a close ally of Washington and recipient of more than two billion dollars a year in US aid, he could not but take Saddam's statement as personal criticism. The speech, however, was aimed at a wider audience than that in the conference chamber.

Transmitted live on Jordanian TV, it was watched by hundreds of thousands of Palestinians in Jordan itself and in the Israeli-occupied territories: among them it had an electrifying effect. Saddam, possessor of the largest and most powerful army of any Arab state, hardened by eight years of war with Iran, had in effect made the first public move in a bid for Iraqi leadership of the Arab world, and he was mounting his campaign in the time-honoured way by posing as the true guardian of the Palestinian cause. It was a bid that was calculated to build support for him among Palestinians throughout the Diaspora. It was also already having curious effects on the behaviour of King Hussein of Jordan, whose kingdom contained more Palestinians than any other Arab country and who, throwing his hitherto moderate image to the winds, had started making similarly militant speeches of his own. 'That speech caught the attention of every Palestinian,' said Arafat's adviser Nabil Shaath. 'In standing up to the US and Israel in these terms, he was uttering words that had not been heard in the Arab world for a very long time.'[27]

Arafat was likewise attracted by what he had heard. Saddam had brought the litany of Palestinian complaints into the open. More than that, he had presented the Arabs with a possible course of action to redress the situation. Saddam, he reasoned, might well have the strength to force the Americans to take the PLO seriously. So began the most dangerous alliance of Arafat's career: an open alliance with a man who was already unwittingly on course for collision with a powerful array of Western nations and half the Arab world; a man, moreover, whose real aims only tangentially coincided with those of the PLO.

The PLO leader had not always been on good terms with Saddam Hussein. Indeed, they had exchanged words back in 1970, when Iraqi forces stationed in Jordan had failed to come to the aid of the Palestinians in the Black September civil war. And throughout the second half of the 1970s Iraq's militant ruling Baath Party had conducted a violent campaign to undermine Arafat's leadership through the agency of a Palestinian splinter group, the Fatah Revolutionary Council, led by Sabri al-Banna (Abu Nidal). It was Saddam who had facilitated Banna's break with Arafat in 1974. So deep was the enmity between the two faction chiefs that a Fatah court sentenced Banna to death in absentia in 1975.

PLO–Iraqi relations began to thaw as Iraq, under pressure in the Iran–Iraq war, sought to return to the mainstream of Arab politics in the early 1980s. Baghdad became the PLO's main military base after its evacuation from Beirut in 1982 and, following the Israeli bombing of his political headquarters in Tunis in October 1985, Arafat spent weeks on end in the Iraqi capital. As his feelings of insecurity grew – notably after the murder of his deputy Khalil al-Wazir in April 1988 – he came to rely more and more on Saddam's security forces for protection. 'Arafat felt at personal risk after the assassination of Wazir; the only place he felt secure was his office in Baghdad,' said an aide.[28]

The Iraqis helped in other ways, not least in supporting the *intifada*. In the very earliest days of the Palestinian uprising, the PLO was stunned to receive a lump sum payment of 50 million dollars from Baghdad. 'It was the largest single sum the PLO had ever received from any body,' an Arafat confidant recalled. 'And this at a time when Iraq was virtually alone in paying. Arafat went through very difficult times in 1988–9 keeping the *intifada* going. Gadaffi, for example, would pay up one month, then get angry again with the PLO for three months. But all the while, Iraq was paying systematically, regularly, four million dollars a month to the *intifada* right from the beginning.'[29] In 1989, Saddam went further still, by according the family of every 'martyr' of the uprising a sum of money equivalent to a martyr's pension from the Iraqi army. Just as important, he provided Arafat with much needed political backing when he was struggling to sustain his attempt to initiate peace talks. In the face of mounting criticism of Arafat's concessions from Libya and Syria, the Iraqi leader reportedly told him at one point, 'God bless you. Go ahead with your peace initiative.'[30]

It was a seductive mix, especially when contrasted with the perceived parsimony of the other Arab states. By early 1990 Arafat had become increasingly preoccupied with the lack of financial and political support he was receiving from elsewhere in the Arab world. On the one hand, he was under pressure from the Egyptians for failing to comply with American demands over the peace process – pressure that increased sharply in early February after a grenade attack by Palestinian extremists on an Israeli tourist bus near the Egyptian town of Ismailiya, in which ten people were killed. On the other, the traditional Arab monarchies of the Gulf – main source of his funding over the previous 25 years – had drastically reduced their contributions to the PLO's and Fatah's coffers.

Arafat was aware that the Saudis and the Kuwaitis, while still collecting money for the *intifada*, were using other conduits than the PLO to funnel it into the occupied territories.

Funds, from both Kuwait and Saudi Arabia, were passed directly to Hamas, the Islamic fundamentalist group that was gaining increasing support in the territories, especially in Gaza, in competition with the mainstream PLO factions. While the Gulf sheikhs were probably responding to domestic fundamentalist pressures in their redirection of funds, Arafat smelled conspiracy to bolster Hamas and weaken the PLO. He took to criticising Gulf rulers, contrasting the amounts they had given the Palestinian movement with the lavish sums spent, in co-operation with the US, on supporting the Afghan resistance.

'The Arab governments spent in Afghanistan in a single year more than they have provided to the PLO in the past 25 years,' he claimed in a February newspaper interview. 'Is it not a shame that the Arabs should be so miserly towards the *intifada*?' In an aside, he suggested that Jerusalem – 'al-Quds' in Arabic – should be given the Afghan-sounding name 'Qudsabad' to persuade the Arabs to support its liberation.[31]

Against this background, it is not entirely surprising that Arafat found himself lurching towards Baghdad in the spring of 1990. The storm clouds over the Middle East were large enough to warrant an urgent search for shelter. The US-sponsored peace process had died its lingering death: the coffin was slammed shut on 13 March when the Israeli Government collapsed in disagreement over the plan for Palestinian elections; its successor seemed likely to be a coalition of the hard right, led by a Shamir still less likely to make concessions. The *intifada*, main engine of the revolution these past 28 months, appeared to be losing momentum, degenerating into intra-Palestinian feuds which had already claimed the lives of more than 200 Arabs.

Deepening the gloom was the continuing flow of émigrés from the Soviet Union to Israel. In the early months of the 1990s as Soviet Jews took advantage of Moscow's newly relaxed emigration rules, several planeloads were arriving every day at Tel Aviv's Ben Gurion Airport. During 1990 alone, Israel was expecting up to 100,000 to come by way of various European centres, and as many as 500,000 by 1995. For Arafat and every other Palestinian, this new influx to the promised land was disastrous. It gave a fresh infusion to the Jewish state and eroded the demographic arguments predicting that, thanks to their higher birth rate, Palestinians would outnumber Jews in Palestine in a few decades' time. In short, it reawakened memories of previous Palestinian disasters: the exodus during Israel's War of Independence in 1948 and the Six-Day War in 1967.

Arafat felt these calamitous events demanded action. In April he embarked on a tour of the Arab world. His goal: to arrange an emergency summit meeting of heads of state that would consider a unified Arab approach to the challenges facing the Palestinians. The summit would be held in the one capital which seemed to appreciate the need to confront the problem – Saddam Hussein's Baghdad.

Saddam had his own pressing reasons for wanting to host a summit. The mixture of paranoia and hubris that had given rise to his February speech in Amman had merely intensified in the intervening weeks, fuelled by threatening noises from Israel, increasing economic hardship at home, and what he took to be signs of a Western conspiracy against him. Britain and the US, in particular, had been leading an international crackdown on Iraqi efforts to augment its military arsenal with weapons of mass destruction. In March, Saddam's regime gave ammunition to its Western detractors by hanging a British-based journalist, Farzad Bazoft, on unproven charges of spying for Israel. On 2 April, in a speech broadcast on Baghdad radio, Saddam warned Israel not to attempt a pre-emptive strike against Iraq, as they had done nine years before in bombing an Iraqi nuclear reactor. Anyone threatening Iraq with nuclear weapons would be met with a chemical attack, he said. 'I swear to God that we will let our fire eat half of Israel if it tries to wage anything against Iraq.'[32] A summit meeting would be a means of rallying the rest of the Arab world behind him in the developing confrontation, and thereby further enhancing his status, in much the same way as Gamal Abdel Nasser had done in the 1960s.

At this stage, the PLO leader was still trying to preserve the fiction that he could continue to straddle the rapidly deepening divide at the centre of Arab politics. An alliance with both Egypt and Iraq, he told his aides, would enable him to maintain channels to the US in pursuit of his peace initiative, while at the same time demonstrating that the PLO had other options. It was a strange and self-deluding variation on the theme of 'peace through strength', as explained later by Afif Safieh, the PLO's representative in London: 'We hoped to remain equidistant between Cairo and Baghdad, to use Iraq's military power to improve our bargaining position.'[33]

In reality, Arafat was already more deeply in cahoots with Saddam than he cared to admit. In late April, the PLO Executive Committee convened in Baghdad and issued a fawning statement of support for 'His Excellency the Knight President Saddam Hussein'.[34] A few days later, reports emerged that Arafat had ordered 3,000 guerrilla fighters from Jordan and Yemen to regroup in Iraq by the middle of May. Their purpose was to train and 'to protect Iraq against a possible Israeli assault', said a PLO spokesman.[35]

By no means all of the Palestinian movement was in sympathy with Arafat's shift. Senior PLO officials regarded their enforced sojourns in Baghdad with distaste; they found the atmosphere oppressive, the communications erratic, the hotels unpleasant. Many in the PLO wondered uneasily what sort of *quid pro quo* the Iraqi leader might demand.

Arafat brushed aside such doubts. 'He would say we are not being asked by the Iraqis to do anything,' one PLO official later recalled. 'He could not see what this would cost or what the Iraqis would require of him.'[36]

In the early morning of 20 May 1990, about fifty Palestinian men from the Gaza towns of Rafah and Khan Younis gathered at the intersection of two main roads in Rishon Le-Zion, a suburb just south of Tel Aviv. Casual construction labourers, they were waiting to be picked up for the day's work when an Israeli dressed in army uniform appeared. Brandishing a rifle, he ordered the Arabs to sit on the ground in three rows. Then he started to shoot at them. Indiscriminately and repeatedly he fired at the small crowd, stopped to reload, fired again, and drove off. Seven Palestinians died and eleven were wounded.[37]

With the Arab world already working itself up into a rhetorical frenzy over Soviet immigration to Israel, this senseless incident, perpetrated by a man the Israeli authorities described as 'deranged', prompted some of the worst riots since the intifada had begun. At a meeting of the UN Security Council, specially convened in Geneva because the US Administration, as in 1988, had refused him a visa to visit UN headquarters in New York, Arafat demanded measures to protect the Palestinians. Behind the scenes, the Americans indicated that they would be prepared to back a major UN fact-finding mission to the occupied territories. There was no need, therefore, for the PLO to press for a fully-fledged resolution on the issue just yet. Somewhat mollified, Arafat left again for Tunis, only to discover that the Americans were having second thoughts. Nabil Shaath would report later, 'Arafat was enraged; he felt defeated; he felt tricked; he felt ambushed. He really felt at the end of the rope with the Americans reneging on everything, even a small fact-finding party.'[38] It was to be the last gasp in Arafat's faltering diplomatic attempt to engage the attention of the West.

It was also an ominous backdrop for the summit meeting of Arab leaders about to convene in Baghdad. What had happened on Black Sunday in Israel and thereafter at the UN added fuel to Saddam Hussein's argument that, since Israel was bent on crushing the Palestinians and the US Government was not to be trusted to stop it, the Arab states had better get ready to act in defence of the cause themselves.

As the leaders gathered on 28 May in the glass and marble conference centre across the road from Baghdad's Al-Rashid Hotel for their inappropriately named 'summit of hope and necessity', they knew they were about to participate in a battle for the soul of the Arab world, a struggle between advocates of confrontation and of conciliation. It had to be said that, as had been the case before the war of 1967, events were moving rapidly in the confrontationists' direction. Arafat, having persuaded Saddam to put this particular stage at his disposal, took to it with a slide projector and maps, seeking to illustrate the Zionists' plan to establish a 'Greater Israel from the Nile to the Euphrates'.[39] Saddam himself (the name means 'one who confronts') emerged triumphant, confirmed in the eyes of many observers as paramount leader of the Arab world and protector of the oppressed, his standing with the PLO enhanced by another cash injection of 25 million dollars.

What outsiders did not realise as the deliberations ended was that Saddam had also privately placed his own, quite different agenda on the table, and that some of those he was confronting had been right there in the conference chamber. At a closed summit session with only the other Arab leaders present, Saddam complained bitterly about overproduction of oil by the pro-American states of the Gulf, which he said was driving prices down and depriving Iraq of sorely needed income. Looking pointedly at the Emir of Kuwait and the President of the United Arab Emirates, he proclaimed, 'You're virtually waging an economic war against my country.'[40] It was, as the other Arab states became uncomfortably aware in the next few weeks, the first shot in Saddam's real war – a campaign to intimidate his Gulf neighbours, push oil prices up and thereby bail out his bankrupt economy, a campaign in which the support of the PLO, as representative of the 'struggling Palestinian masses', was to be a vital ingredient.

Barely was the ink dry on the summit's final communiqué when Saddam sent another unmistakable message, in the form of the 30 May speedboat raid on the beaches of Tel Aviv by guerrillas of the Palestine Liberation Front. That the Iraqi leader was behind the attack could not seriously be in doubt. PLF leader Abul Abbas had long been based in Baghdad and was frequently to be seen in Saddam's company. Moreover, the raid and its consequences dovetailed neatly with Saddam's grand strategy – to undermine pro-Western Arab leaders and create an atmosphere of violent uncertainty across the Middle East.

For Arafat, it should have been warning enough that his alignment with Iraq was going to carry a cost. One PLO insider recalled, 'It really put him in an impossible position. The Abul Abbas incident had been calculated by Saddam as a grand finale for the summit – not to embarrass him as such but to show other Arab leaders that the way to liberation was through arms not conciliation. The Egyptians certainly felt it was aimed at them and their moderate line.'[41]

Whatever the intention, its main effect was to further undermine the dialogue with the US as Arafat came under insistent pressure from Washington to condemn the raid and discipline Abul Abbas. But his displeasure with the US over its handling of the recent UN debate – expressed the day after the raid in an American veto of a fact-finding mission to the occupied territories – and his cosy relationship with Saddam meant that he was neither willing nor able to comply. Action against Abbas, he felt, would anger the Iraqis as well as his Palestinian constituents, at a time when he was in any case wondering whether the US dialogue was actually worth saving. On 20 June an exasperated President Bush announced he was suspending talks. In effect, the US and its moderate Arab allies were giving up on Arafat who was sinking ever deeper into Saddam's embrace.

Growing tensions in the Arab world were evident at a meeting of Arab foreign ministers in Tunis in mid-July. Moderate Egypt did not even bother to attend. Arafat joined forces with Iraqi Foreign Minister Tariq Aziz in barely-disguised criticism of President Mubarak. In one of those arcane historical disputes that often cause rows of baffling toxicity in the Arab world, Arafat touched nerves with a slighting reference to a pre-revolutionary Egyptian prime minister, Mustafa Nahhas Pasha, who he said had urged the Palestinians to hand the Wailing Wall over to the Jews.[42] Cairo responded in kind, with bitter personal attacks in the press and recrimination from Mubarak himself. Egypt, he said, had worked hard to keep the US–PLO talks alive at Arafat's request. Yet his reward had been Palestinian abuse.[43]

With the Arab players who had been most keen to co-operate with American peace moves now squabbling openly, the scene was set for Saddam the confrontationist to make his big power play.

'I came when I
Emir on the Sund
shore. 'I worked
your country. I a
sincere when I te
Hussein . . . Pay I
you can lease him
only solution to s

'Do you mean
distractedly, 'I dor

Jaber persisted:
use force.'

'Maybe Presider
But the Emir v
could hardly be n
was proposing am
him aside, Sheikh
what Arafat was o
The Kuwaitis see
storm.[49]

On the morning of 17 July, Aziz arrived at the office of Arab League Secretary-General Chedli Klibi and handed him a piece of paper. A memorandum from Saddam Hussein, it amounted to a virtual declaration of war on Kuwait. The letter accused Kuwait and the UAE of deliberately undermining the Iraqi economy by exceeding their OPEC oil production quotas. It charged Kuwait with violating the Iraqi border to steal Iraqi oil reserves; with committing aggression by building military installations on Iraqi territory; and it demanded that the billions of dollars the Gulf states had lent Iraq during its war with Iran should be written off.[44] Saddam was demanding money with menaces. Implicitly, he was also reviving a long-standing dispute over the Iraq–Kuwait frontier and the status of two small Kuwaiti islands, Bubiyan and Warbah, and reawakening memories of attempts by Iraq in the past to swallow its tiny neighbour whole. This was the conflict for which Saddam had been preparing all these months, and the reason why he had been anxious to secure political support from the Palestinians. By imposing his will on Kuwait, Saddam calculated that he would be well on the way to a dominant position in the entire Gulf region, capable of extorting more funds from his neighbours and of dictating their policies on oil production and prices, and bolstered in his determination to lead the Arab world in standing up to the US and Israel.

Klibi immediately set off for Kuwait to try to defuse the row, followed by a procession of other would-be mediators, including Mubarak. The Egyptian President secured what he thought was a promise from Saddam not to use force and an agreement between the Iraqi leader and Sheikh Jaber-al-Sabah, the Emir of Kuwait, to hold talks in the Saudi Arabian port of Jeddah. But even as these diplomatic efforts were set in train the Iraqis were stepping up their demand for an immediate cash payment of more than 2.4 billion dollars in compensation for oil allegedly stolen by Kuwait from the Rumailah oilfield and at the same time were massing tens of thousands of troops on the Kuwaiti frontier.[45]

Enter Yasser Arafat. The PLO leader had been feeling increasingly isolated as the war of words between Iraq and Kuwait intensified, flitting between his lonely Baghdad redoubt and his political headquarters in Tunis. The May Arab summit had

resolved none
none of the A
nobody was e
in the 'Middle
might have ha
talks moving
mid-July with
Community,
conveyed a de
cans were prej
much anybod
Arafat soug
mediation effe
which he had
when the Iraq
the emirate in
bout of bully
Thursday 26
Kuwait, Awni
He planned t
settlement he
for signs of fl
for hope. Befo
Kuwaiti Crow
Abdullah al-Sa
convey to Araf
Flying south
jet, Arafat felt
conversation v
Iraqi leader me
give him what
would grab the
Arafat was awa
the place whe
colleagues had
Palestinian rev
Saad and his c
from themselve

18. ENGULFED

'Iraq and Palestine represent a common will. We will be together side by side and after the great battle, God willing, we will pray together in Jerusalem.' Arafat to a rally in Baghdad on 7 January 1990.

It was just before dawn on 2 August when Awni Battash, the PLO's long-serving ambassador to Kuwait, was awakened by the insistent ringing of the telephone beside his bed. A friend was on the phone with startling news. Iraq had invaded its tiny neighbour at 2 a.m., two hours before, sweeping aside flimsy Kuwaiti resistance in the process. Thousands of Iraqi troops, many of them from Saddam Hussein's Republican Guard, had poured across the frontier in tanks and armoured personnel carriers and were heading for the centre of Kuwait City itself.

As Battash shook himself awake and tuned in to Kuwait Radio, he knew that his most urgent task was to make contact with Tunis. Within seconds he had a familiar voice on the line. It was 2 a.m. at the other end of the Arab world. Yasser Arafat was surprised to hear from his ambassador at such an early hour. Listening to Battash's breathless report that Iraq had invaded Kuwait, and that its troops were swarming into the centre of the city, Arafat was at first sceptical. At the most, he had expected the Iraqis to occupy the frontier zone around the disputed Rumailah oilfield, and perhaps seize Bubiyan and Warbah islands. But he had certainly not anticipated that his ally in Baghdad would grab the lot. Battash had some difficulty persuading Arafat that the Iraqis had come all the way into Kuwait and were in fact in the street outside his house. At one point in their seven-minute conversation he was obliged to hold the phone to the Kuwait Radio broadcast so that Arafat could hear for himself news of the invasion. So stunned was Arafat by developments, recalled Battash, that he took refuge in an appeal to the Almighty with the words: 'Nothing can be done: only by God the powerful'.[1]

Arafat got no sleep that night. Anxiously, he conferred with his lieutenants while keeping in constant touch with Battash in

Kuwait. Among those summoned from their beds in the early hours of 2 August was Salah Khalaf. Together they assessed where Iraq's audacious land-grab might leave the PLO. Khalaf felt the dangers much more acutely than his boss. The PLO Number Two worried about the fate of the more than 400,000 Palestinians in Kuwait, the largest and most important Palestinian community in the Gulf, among them his own wife and children. He feared that the crisis would further deflect the Arab world's flickering attention from the Palestine issue. And perhaps most important, he sensed with his keen analytical mind that Saddam Hussein's gamble would confront the PLO with one of its most agonising choices. In short, he felt a foreboding, for he had never shared Arafat's enthusiasm for the tilt towards Baghdad. Khalaf was an infrequent visitor to the Iraqi capital. He found the atmosphere there oppressive. He was not persuaded that Saddam, with his ambitions to lead the Arab world towards a new dawn, was the answer to the Palestinians' dreams.[2]

Arafat, on the other hand, saw it from a rather different perspective. His first reaction was that here was an opportunity to engage in one of his favourite pastimes – mediating among members of the squabbling Arab family. As so often in the past, the Iran–Iraq conflict being just one example, he found himself fluttering, like a moth to a flame, towards the role of go-between. If he could build on his pre-invasion mediating efforts he would put the Arab world in his debt. For a leader without a country and almost totally reliant on the largesse of others it was a tantalising prospect, never mind the risks of offending one side or the other in what was to prove one of the great Arab watersheds. In his near obsession with his self-proclaimed role as mediator Arafat was to commit an historic blunder, one that would place him seriously at odds with his Gulf benefactors and with Egypt, and do his shaky reputation in the West no good at all, since in Western eyes he would come to be seen as Saddam's lackey. But in those first hours after the invasion he simply did not foresee the risks. In any case he had, by foolishly putting himself so much in Saddarn's thrall, severely limited his room for manoeuvre.

Throughout 2 August, the day of the invasion, Arafat, Khalaf and others in the Palestinian leadership obsessively monitored developments in Kuwait and in the wider Arab world. Arafat was constantly on the telephone: to Arab governments; to leading Palestinians throughout the Diaspora; to members of his own Executive Committee scattered about the Arab world, most especially Farouk Kaddoumi, the PLO 'foreign minister' who was chairing an emergency session of the Arab League Council in Cairo, it being Palestine's turn to chair such gatherings. The question Arafat was asking himself and others was what sort of deal would entice Saddam into disgorging most of Kuwait except perhaps for the Rumailah oilfield and Warbah and Bubiyan islands.[3] To the PLO leader at that very early stage the issue was not one of principle, that is the inadmissibility of the seizure of territory by force, the very issue used by the PLO to assail Israel all these years, but of what bargain could be struck in the great Arab bazaar. He was not alone in this. King Hussein of Jordan was another who, having lurched into Saddam's embrace, would have immense difficulty distancing himself from the man he would describe in an interview with American television two days after the invasion as an 'Arab patriot' – a phrase that would rebound against him as he engaged in increasingly futile mediation efforts.[4]

On that first day, as Arafat plotted his mediation moves, events were proceeding with bewildering speed. Against a background of ferocious world condemnation including an unprecedented joint US–Soviet statement, Iraq's ruling Revolutionary Command Council announced that Iraqi forces had entered Kuwait at the request of the Kuwaiti opposition, the so-called 'Interim Government of Free Kuwait'.[5] It was a sham. In the days that followed no Kuwaiti oppositionist stepped forward to provide any cover at all for Baghdad's crude lunge against its tiny neighbour. Kuwait's Emir, Sheikh Jaber al-Ahmed al-Sabah, and his cousin, Crown Prince Saad, had, meanwhile, fled to Saudi Arabia just ahead of the invading Iraqis who laid siege to the Emir's Dasman palace.

As Arafat prepared to set off on his travels, continuing the mediating role he had sought to play between Iraq and Kuwait before the invasion, powerful Arab figures were entering the fray. Arafat's efforts would seem puny by comparison. Syria's President Hafez al-Assad, in telephone conversations with Saudi Arabia's King Fahd and Egypt's President Hosni Mubarak on the day of the invasion, called for an emergency summit of 21 Arab heads of state to condemn the Iraqi aggression. President Bush, for his part, ordered the aircraft carrier *USS Independence* to leave its station forthwith in the Indian Ocean for the Gulf region. 'We are not ruling anything in or out,' said an American official grimly, as the Pentagon hastily dusted off its plans for military intervention to keep oil flowing from the Gulf.[6]

In fetid midsummer Cairo, Arab foreign ministers gathered in emergency session in the conference room of the Semiramis Intercontinental Hotel on the banks of the Nile. It was an acrimonious affair. After two days of sharp exchanges, the Arab League Council voted by 14–6 (the six included the PLO and Jordan) to 'condemn' the invasion and 'call for an Arab summit'.[7] Farouk Kaddoumi, in the chair, was hard-put to keep control and came under attack from both sides. The Egyptians accused the PLO official of trying to prevent the resolution coming to a vote, while the Iraqis in the person of Saadoun Hammadi, the Deputy Prime Minister, accused him of being part of the 'conspiracy' against Iraq, to which Kaddoumi replied within earshot of other foreign ministers, 'You know how much I support Iraq, and yet you accuse me.'[8] It was not the most judicious remark in the circumstances and would be counted as one more strike against the PLO's claims to even-handedness.

Arafat himself had set off from Tunis on the morning of 3 August at the start of an ill-fated odyssey in search of an 'Arab solution'. Travelling by one of the Iraqi jets he had on more or less permanent loan from Baghdad, he went to Libya where he cooked up the first of a number of peace plans of dubious relevance. Basically, it involved frontier concessions plus the payment of money by Kuwait in exchange for an Iraqi agreement to withdraw – much the same deal as he had outlined to the Emir at his meeting with him just days before the invasion. Arafat took his 'peace plan' to Egypt on Saturday 4 August, before going on to Baghdad the next day. When he returned to Egypt on Monday 6 August for a meeting with Mubarak at the Egyptian leader's summer residence near Alexandria, criticism was spreading like a virus in Arab capitals of the PLO's failure to condemn the invasion and unequivocally to call for Iraq's withdrawal. The best the organisation could do at that early stage was to issue a limp Executive Committee statement, urging Arab leaders to end the conflict.[9]

Throughout his post-invasion manoeuvres Arafat had kept in close touch with King Hussein who, no less than the PLO leader himself, was obsessed with the search for an 'Arab solution' – a solution that seemed increasingly to Arab states opposed to the invasion like a recipe for the appeasement of Iraq. The king claimed that he had elicited Saddam's agreement to attend a mini-summit in Jeddah on Sunday 5 August, with King Fahd and other heads of state, but this had all come unstuck after the Arab League Council in Cairo condemned Iraq. Hussein was to complain with increasing bitterness that his mediation efforts had been torpedoed by Mubarak and Fahd who had allowed the Arab League Council resolution to go forward.[10]

Arafat was hardly faring any better than Hussein in his efforts to promote an Arab solution. When he arrived in Jeddah on Monday 6 August to be greeted by a low-ranking member of the Saudi Royal Family it was already becoming clear that his manoeuvrings in the Arab arena were beginning to cause grave offence among those states most bitterly opposed to Iraq's seizure of Kuwait. Pointedly, the PLO chairman was kept waiting for six hours at the palace to see King Fahd on the Tuesday and then was received for a mere half-hour, hardly time for him to outline his peace plan. The king and his courtiers were not much impressed with the bill of goods Arafat was trying to peddle, and in any case the Saudis were even then heavily engaged in discussions with the visiting US Defence Secretary, Dick Cheney, on the deployment of foreign forces. 'We think Arafat would do much better for himself if he left us alone and devoted his efforts to solving the Palestinian question,' was a Saudi official's caustic observation.[11]

Still, like a man possessed, Arafat shuttled on, going back to Baghdad to be photographed yet again in Saddam's fond embrace – an image replayed endlessly on Western television that did more than perhaps anything else to reinforce suspicions that he was somehow colluding with the Iraqi leader. PLO propaganda continually railed against the prospect of foreign intervention, while skating over the causes of the crisis, namely Iraq's invasion of Kuwait. 'The objective of the United States is the continuation of its hegemony over the oil-producing countries in the Arab Gulf,' charged the Voice of Palestine, broadcasting from Algiers. 'Iraq's invasion of Kuwait . . . constitutes a challenge to the United States and its policy in the area.'[12]

Cairo in midsummer is not the most comfortable of places, but when President Mubarak on 8 August, at the very height of the hot season, pleaded with Arab heads of state to hasten to the Egyptian capital for an emergency summit, most answered his call, with the notable exception of Saddam Hussein himself. 'It must not be an Arab summit at which we trade accusations and curses or tear each other apart,' Mubarak declared in a nationwide broadcast. 'It must be a summit for resolving the problem within the Arab framework which is more dignified for the Arab nation.'[13] If Yasser Arafat heard these words, there was no sign that he heeded them. Indeed, the Cairo summit of 9–10 August was a debacle for the hot-headed Arafat, and one for which he was to pay dearly in the weeks and months ahead.

The portents were not good when the PLO leader arrived at Cairo Airport for the summit, in an Iraqi Airlines plane with its distinctive green markings, to be greeted curtly by an unsmiling Mubarak. Arafat's use of an Iraqi jet was hardly politic. So, it was a grim-faced Arafat who arrived in the late morning of 10 August at the conference hall set aside for the emergency summit in Cairo's Nasr City, not far from the district where he had spent his youth.

The Cairo summit was marked by angry exchanges between members of the Iraqi delegation, led by the first Deputy Prime Minister Taha Yassin Ramadan, and the Kuwaitis. Watching from the sidelines Arafat was in no mood to see it all for what it was – low-grade farce. He was determined to have his say and, more to the point, advance his latest mediating ploy which was to recommend that a five-man delegation of Arab heads of state depart immediately for Baghdad to negotiate with Saddam. He, Yasser Arafat, was to be a member of this group that would also include Mubarak of Egypt, Hussein of Jordan, Benjedid of Algeria and Ali Abdullah Saleh of Yemen. But unbeknown to Arafat, at the precise moment he was suggesting, improbably, that leaders like Mubarak should wait on Saddam in his Baghdad citadel, a most damaging transcript was circulating among summit delegates. The Iraqi leader had chosen that day to launch his most intemperate attack on Arab leaders, calling on the 'Arab masses' to rise up against them. 'Oh Arabs, oh Moslems and the faithful everywhere, this is your day to rise and defend Mecca which is captured by the spears of the Americans and the Zionists,' urged Saddam. 'Revolt against oppression, corruption, treachery and backstabbing . . . revolt against the oil emirs who accept to push the Arab women into whoredom.'[16]

Any possibility that Arafat's proposal might be taken at all seriously vanished on the spot, but still the PLO leader pressed on, raising points of order, challenging Mubarak's rulings as summit chairman to the intense annoyance of the dour Egyptian President. As one of Arafat's senior advisers observed, 'While Mubarak might have understood the word "order" there was no sign that he appreciated what was meant by "point of order".'[17]

For Arafat and the PLO, the Cairo summit was a disaster and any slim chance the organisation had of carving out a respectable role midway between the two Arab camps – as, say, the Algerians were able to do – went out of the window. In the words of a close Arafat aide, 'He was obsessed with the idea of sending a delegation. He thought it was the only solution to prevent the whole thing escalating into absurdity. He was so obsessed that he could not recognise that no one was willing to support him; that in the final analysis he was just being an irritant to the others.'[18] Arafat's protestations continued up to the last minute and even involved challenging the legality of the summit resolution which was carried by a thin majority of just twelve votes out of the twenty states present, with the PLO together with Iraq and Libya initially being recorded as having voted against.[19] In all the confusion, it took several days for PLO headquarters in Tunis to issue a clarification of the PLO position. The organisation had not voted against the summit resolution, which legitimised the commitment of foreign forces to Saudi Arabia, but, like Jordan, it had expressed reservations. Explaining the confusion over the PLO's voting position, a spokesman in Tunis observed that the vote had taken place in 'indescribable disorder'.[20] Not least of those responsible for the chaos was Arafat himself.

A reflective Arafat later told Nabil Shaath that he had erred in suggesting a delegation go to Baghdad in the light of Saddam's unrestrained attack on Mubarak, Fahd and others. Whatever the circumstances, it was one of his most lamentable performances, and marked the beginning of 'open season' for increasingly virulent criticism of Arafat and the PLO throughout the Arab world, with the Egyptian press leading the way. A few days after the emergency summit a cartoon in Egypt's leading newspaper, *al-Ahram*, depicted the PLO chairman as a pair of identical Siamese twins facing in opposite directions – one twin was following a sign that read 'occupied Kuwait', the other a sign that said 'occupied Jerusalem'. Each of the Arafats was carrying a placard. One read 'Up with taking territory by force', and the other 'Down with taking territory by force'. *Al-Ahram*, it might be said, had gone for the jugular.[22]

Arafat withdrew in disarray from the city of his birth in a dark mood reminiscent of his departure in November 1977 after President Sadat made his surprise announcement that he was prepared to go to Jerusalem. Belatedly he was beginning to understand the dimension of the problems confronting the PLO in its growing isolation. But as he headed back to Tunis for a meeting of the enlarged PLO leadership – including members of the Executive Committee and the Fatah Central Committee – he was buoyed by an announcement from Baghdad. Taking his cue from the Security Council resolutions that were raining down almost daily upon Iraq, Saddam announced on 12 August that 'all issues of occupation, or those projected as occupation, in the whole area, should be resolved on the same basis and principles as put forward by the Security Council.'[23]

Thus Saddam called for 'an immediate and unconditional Israeli pull-out from the Arab occupied territories in Palestine, Syria and Lebanon, the withdrawal of Syria from Lebanon and withdrawal between Iraq and Iran, in addition to laying down arrangements for the case of Kuwait.' An implementation of this withdrawal programme should begin with the occupation that took place first, he added, 'and subsequently . . . related to all these cases until we reach the last one (Iraq's occupation of Kuwait),'[24] So the word 'linkage' entered the Gulf War vocabulary, the idea that the issues of Palestine and Kuwait could be resolved in tandem. PLO leaders clung to this notion in the hope that it would somehow provide a respectable escape from their growing isolation in a divided Arab world. It was an illusion, since even most Arab states themselves saw it for what it was – a cynical and belated attempt by Saddam to find a less than dishonourable way out of his predicament.[25]

When the Palestinian leadership assembled in Tunis on the night of 14 August at their customary meeting place in a large villa near the city's sports stadium, the mood was resentful. The PLO position on the Gulf crisis was being misrepresented, the leadership believed. There was much gloomy talk about a 'conspiracy' against the organisation. Arafat, for his part, was coming to understand his predicament. According to Nabil Shaath, 'Arafat was feeling very, very lonely. He was beginning to comprehend the great risk he had taken. He was really quite worried about the Iraqi gamble. He felt it might destroy everything.'[26]

Arafat also confided details at this time to close associates of a conversation he had held with Saddam in the first week of August in which the Iraqi leader, tiring of warnings of the dangers of continuing to occupy Kuwait, had accused the PLO chairman of 'trying to instil doomsday in my heart'. Saddam had added, recalling something Arafat had told him about his own preparations for martyrdom during the siege of Beirut, 'Abu Ammar, am I not to smell the fragrance of paradise as you did? Should I be denied the privilege you talked about? So let it be, I'm not afraid of the challenge.'[27]

As discussion droned on among Palestinian leaders throughout that mid-August period, often into the early hours of the morning, it was clear that the leadership itself was far from united on how to assess and respond to the latest catastrophe to befall the Arab world. There were those, like veteran cadres Hail Abdul-Hamid, Sakher Abu Nizar and Abbas Zeki, who, while not in favour of the Iraqi takeover of Kuwait, saw in it an intriguing challenge to the status quo in the region – in the words of one of those present, 'a rippling storm in a stale pond'.[28]

The other main trend, led by Salah Khalaf and the long-standing Executive Committee member Mahmoud Abbas, was very sceptical about the Kuwaiti adventure and, in private, extremely critical. However, they muted their criticism in public, partly because of fevered support for Saddam among many Palestinians in the occupied territories and throughout the Diaspora, most notably in Jordan, and partly because Arafat's own ill-advised closeness to Baghdad had fatally compromised the organisation.[29]

Arafat had his own difficulties in discussions with senior comrades in those mid-August days. Under fire over the public presentation of the PLO position, he even offered to resign – a tactic he had employed so often in the past when criticised by his peers.

Out of the leadership meetings between 14–18 August came a new PLO peace plan, masterminded in part by Nabil Shaath in close consultation with Arafat. It was to prove the basis of the PLO's faltering diplomatic efforts that would continue right up to the Security Council 15 January deadline for Iraq's withdrawal from Kuwait. Its salient points included a proposal for the withdrawal of Iraqi forces in stages from Kuwait matched by a similar staged US pull-back from the Gulf to coincide with fresh attempts to arrive at an 'Arab solution' to the Kuwait crisis. While the plan was stillborn, since hardly anyone was of a mind to listen to the Palestinians as the region slid inexorably towards war, it did have the merit of being somewhat more principled than Arafat's first effort which had effectively required Kuwait to accede to Iraq's bullying demands for money and territory.

As Arafat resumed his vain attempts to sell a PLO peace plan to the few who would listen – his movements throughout the Arab world were by now severely restricted since he was *persona non grata* in the Gulf, in Egypt and in Syria – the news for his organisation from the Gulf itself went from bad to worse. Incensed by Arafat's stand on the crisis, Kuwaiti leaders vowed retribution against the 400,000-strong Palestinian community in Kuwait, accusing Palestinians of collaborating with the Iraqi occupiers. Most damagingly, Gulf states terminated their financial contributions to the PLO. Such was the ire of the Gulf sheikhs, and the rulers of Saudi Arabia in particular, that his aircraft was even banned from crossing Saudi airspace. Just as bad from his own point of view, Arafat was the target of some of the most vicious personal attacks ever levelled against an Arab leader.

One particular broadside stood out, not just because of the language used, but also because of its provenance. Ghazi al-Qosaibi, Saudi Arabia's ambassador to Bahrain, a respected former minister and sometime poet, lambasted Arafat as a 'sad clown' who had betrayed his friends and let down his people. 'This sad clown is now trying to snuff out the last candle left flickering in the long, dark tunnel – the Palestinian people's relationship with the Gulf . . .' charged Qosaibi in response to a Palestinian statement accusing Kuwaiti officials of killing and raping Palestinians in Kuwait. 'This sad clown – when will he stop howling and check into the Home for Aged Sad Clowns?'[30]

Energised, nevertheless, by the formulation of the new PLO peace plan, Arafat redoubled his peacemaking efforts, shuttling between Baghdad, Amman, Tripoli, Tunis and Rabat. But it was to no avail. The fissures in the Arab world were too deep to facilitate any co-ordinated effort to end the crisis. When Chedli Klibi, the Arab League's long-serving Secretary General, resigned on 3 September, just a few days after presiding over an Arab League foreign ministers' meeting in Cairo, boycotted by the PLO among eight absentees, it merely emphasised the depth of the divisions between the anti-Iraq majority led by Egypt and the rest.[31]

In mid-September, Arafat was briefly distracted from the Gulf crisis itself by events in Lebanon where fighters of his Fatah mainstream faction expelled guerrillas of the Abu Nidal-led renegade Fatah Revolutionary Council (FRC) from the large Ain al-Hilweh refugee camp near the city of Sidon in a three-day battle. The crushing victory by the Arafat forces, which consolidated Fatah's influence throughout Lebanon, gave the PLO leader one of his few causes for celebration in many months. The episode showed, if nothing else, that even in the midst of a wider Middle East crisis Lebanon continued to be a focus of tension, for the fractious Palestinian movement and Arafat could not ignore threats to his Fatah powerbase there.[32]

*   *   *

As talk of war swirled about the Arab world and the US continued the inexorable build-up of forces in the Gulf region, one of those shocking events that are so typical of the Middle East intervened. On this occasion, and in the extremely tense circumstances that prevailed, the slaying on 8 October of eighteen Palestinians on Jerusalem's Temple Mount by Israeli border police firing indiscriminately symbolised all the unresolved problems of the region, all the hatred, all the bitterness.

According to the Palestinians the incident occurred when rumours spread that Jewish zealots were advancing on the Haram al-Sharif or the Noble Sanctuary, home of the two most important Muslim shrines outside Mecca and Medina, to press their claims for the rebuilding of the Jewish temple on the site where it had stood nearly 2,000 years ago. In the disturbances that ensued Israeli policemen had gone berserk and gunned down Palestinians. According to the Israeli version, Palestinian demonstrators had begun raining rocks, sticks and pieces of masonry on hundreds of Jews, including many from abroad, worshipping below at the Western 'Wailing' Wall on the Festival of the Tabernacles, one of the Jews' holiest occasions. Under extreme provocation, the police had intervened.

Whatever the truth, the episode diverted attention, momentarily, from the Gulf crisis itself and, to the acute discomfort of the US in particular, enabled Arafat and the Iraqis to press demands for 'linkage' between a settlement of the Palestine and Kuwait questions. In the hard, cruel world of Middle East politics, the Temple Mount killings could hardly have come at a more favourable moment for Arafat, languishing in his isolation and in danger of being consigned permanently to the sidelines. The episode was, in the callous language of a Palestinian journalist in Jerusalem, 'like manna from heaven for the PLO'.[33]

Pressing for a Security Council resolution with 'teeth' that would both condemn Israel and provide for the immediate despatch of a high-level fact-finding mission to the territories, the PLO convened an emergency session in Tunis of its 'mini-parliament', the Central Council, to debate the bloodiest episode in Jerusalem since the 1967 war. In an opening address Arafat assailed the United States which he claimed was providing an umbrella for Israel 'to commit odious crimes' in the occupied territories.[34] Saddam Hussein himself had greeted the grim news from Jerusalem with a warning that Israel was coming 'closer to the abyss'. He also used the occasion to announce that Iraq had acquired a powerful new missile which would strike at Israel 'when the time of reckoning comes'.[35]

After four days of debate and much to-ing and fro-ing behind the scenes, the Security Council eventually approved unanimously a resolution that condemned the 'violence' of the Israeli police, and also instructed the UN Secretary General to send a representative to the Israeli-occupied territories with a brief to report back by the end of October – a much lower level mission than the PLO had demanded.[36] It was the first time the US had actually sponsored a resolution condemning the Jewish state. The Jerusalem slayings and their aftermath were to be the last serious diversion from events in the Gulf before the end of the war itself. As October gave way to November, war drums were beating ever more insistently.

Still, Arafat pressed on with his forlorn peace efforts and was briefly encouraged by a call from King Hassan of Morocco in mid-November for a 'last ditch' Arab summit to resolve the Gulf crisis. In vain the PLO leader tried to promote the summit, shuttling between Amman for talks with King Hussein and Baghdad where he met Saddam for the umpteenth time since the crisis broke. But there was simply no support for the summit proposal in the wider Arab world. The powerful Saudi–Egyptian–Syrian axis said a meeting of Arab heads of state would be 'useless' unless Saddam agreed in advance to get out of Kuwait. Egypt's President Mubarak observed that such a gathering would simply turn into a 'shouting match'.

All the time, the US continued to pour troops, planes and warships into the Gulf region as the Security Council moved ever closer to authorising the use of force to remove Iraq from Kuwait. A resolution to this effect came on 29 November by a vote of 12–2, with Yemen and Cuba opposing and China abstaining. Iraq was given until 15 January to withdraw. In the meantime, President Bush had authorised the despatch of an additional 100,000 troops to the Gulf in a clear sign that the US meant to go to war if all diplomatic efforts to dislodge Iraq from Kuwait failed. A day after the UN 'war resolution' was passed Bush invited Iraqi Foreign Minister Aziz to Washington for talks and offered to send the US Secretary of State, James Baker, to Baghdad. Iraq accepted Bush's offer, but insisted that it wanted to broaden the discussions to include other Middle East issues, including Palestine. In the battle of deadlines, ultimatums, brinkmanship and sheer Iraqi bloody-mindedness that ensued, the stuttering attempts to arrange the 'last gasp' Baker–Aziz meeting merely proved to be one more signpost on the road to war.

In the first week of December, Arafat was briefly buoyed by his inclusion in a 'quadripartite' meeting in Baghdad, presided over by Saddam, with King Hussein and the Yemeni Vice-President, Salim al-Bidh. The Iraqi leader used the occasion to announce the release on 6 December of all foreign hostages. Arafat was to claim tangential credit for the hostage release, but in truth the gesture had more to do with a realisation in Baghdad that the hostages would not prove a deterrent to war, and were, in fact, fuelling foreign hostility.

As the countdown to war gathered pace, Arafat continued his fruitless peace efforts, even travelling in the third week of December to Africa for improbable meetings in the midst of the deepening Gulf crisis with Presidents Museveni of Uganda, Mwinyi of Tanzania and Mugabe of Zimbabwe.[37] With much of the Arab world closed to him, not to mention Europe, a visit to Black Africa offered one of the few opportunities for him to be photographed in the embrace of fellow 'heads of state'.

While Arafat continued throughout the first days of the New Year to insist that war in the Gulf could be averted, alarm was growing in the PLO leadership. Nabil Shaath, for one, felt that the Iraqis and the Americans were on a 'collision course' and that war had become all but inevitable.[38] But Arafat insisted, against all the evidence, there would be 'no war', as he kept telling reporters.

Arafat's own hopes and those of his colleagues were raised by the 9 January Baker–Aziz meeting in Geneva. Here, they thought, was an opportunity for a disaster to be averted. Here was also a chance for the PLO to score points if it could be seen to help facilitate some sort of last-minute breakthrough. So Arafat sent his 'foreign minister' Farouk Kaddoumi to Geneva to liaise with Tariq Aziz. The PLO leader was still hoping that 'linkage' could somehow be established between a settlement of the Palestine and Kuwait questions.

But in Geneva the Palestinians were again to be disappointed. It was becoming clearer by the day that Saddam was intent on carrying brinkmanship beyond all reasonable bounds. At Arafat's urging Kaddoumi proposed, after the failure of the Aziz–Baker talks,[39] that the Iraqi Foreign Minister, in an effort to find a way out of the impasse, meet his twelve EC counterparts, either in Tunis or in Algiers. Hopes flickered briefly at PLO headquarters in Tunis that such an encounter could be arranged, but they died almost immediately when Aziz said he was not prepared to meet the EC Foreign Ministers before the 15 January 'deadline', but rather on 17 January, two days later. Said an Arafat adviser deeply involved in those negotiations: 'We felt that would be disastrous. The attempt to flout the deadline looked disastrous. Yasser Arafat was appalled.'[40]

As the moments slipped away towards the 15 January deadline, Arafat was almost constantly in Baghdad, conferring frequently with Saddam, receiving journalists in his heavily guarded residence and dreaming up last-minute peace stratagems, in consultation with such unlikely figures as the former President of Nicaragua, Daniel Ortega. He was also on hand for the arrival in the Iraqi capital of the UN Secretary General, Javier Perez de Cuellar, who, after cooling his heels for much of Sunday 13 January, eventually saw Saddam late in the day for an aimless discussion that conveyed none of the urgency that might have been expected at that late stage. Surprisingly, Perez de Cuellar did not advance any new ideas, and Saddam himself engaged for the most part in a fruitless description of the origins of Iraq's dispute with Kuwait. It seemed that he had set his face against making what he regarded as any further concessions. 'To utter the word withdrawal while there is still a chance for war means that we would be creating the psychological conditions for enemy victory over us,' Saddam told Perez de Cuellar.[41] The Secretary General left Baghdad on his UN jet, confiding to staff that what Saddam needed was not a mediator but a 'psychiatrist'.[42]

Arafat himself was briefed by Saddam on the morning of 14 January about his talks with Perez de Cuellar the evening before. The Iraqi leader claimed he had indicated a willingness to withdraw, although a transcript of his conversation with the UN official does not support such a contention. Intriguingly, Arafat has since confided to senior aides that Saddam Hussein told him at their last meeting before the war: 'Wait till 17–18 January and Baker will come to Baghdad and Bush will chicken out, and there will be no war.'[43] This, then, was the Iraqi leader's game. He was convinced that even after the 15 January deadline, the US President would go the 'extra mile' to avert war and initiate negotiations. Could it be, asks a senior PLO official privy to those last-minute discussions, that 'Saddam deliberately destroyed the Perez de Cuellar and European peace missions in the hope of bringing the Americans into the negotiations? He believed they were the only worthwhile negotiating partners.'[44]

The failure of the Perez de Cuellar mission and the quick slide to war sank the last of the PLO's myriad peace stratagems. Arafat, who had been busily telling journalists all week there would be 'no war, no war, no war'[45] left for Amman soon after his meeting with Saddam on 14 January to confer with King Hussein even as the war clouds darkened. Arafat had also observed in bantering discussions with reporters at his Baghdad residence that the only significance about the date 15 January was that it was the 73rd anniversary of late Egyptian President Gamal Abdel Nasser's birthday.

The time in Tunis was just before 11 p.m. on 14 January. Salah Khalaf had completed a simple meal in the downstairs reception room of the house in the beachside suburb of Carthage of his friend Hail Abdul-Hamid, better known in PLO circles as Abu Houl, the organisation's internal security chief. Also present was Fakhri al-Omari, one of Khalaf's most trusted aides. Conversation, not surprisingly, with only hours to go before the 15 January deadline, had focused obsessively on fading prospects of peace and the increasing likelihood of war. Khalaf took little notice when one of his host's bodyguards, a young man named Hamza Abu Zaid, wandered into the room carrying his Kalashnikov rifle.

Absent-mindedly, Abdul-Hamid told his guard to help himself to some of the leftover food, but at that very moment Abu Zaid pivoted towards the small gathering and at close range let fly with a burst of automatic rifle fire. His main target was Khalaf himself who died instantly after four bullets ripped into his chest and another thudded into his head.[46]

For the PLO, the slaying of the 57-year-old Salah Khalaf was a sickening development at a time when the organisation was at a near-historic low in relations with much of the Arab world, and on the eve of what was to prove a catastrophic war. Like the death in Tunis of the PLO's military commander, Khalif al-Wazir, three years before at the hands of Israeli assassins, Khalaf's demise was a reminder of how vulnerable the PLO was to predators from inside and outside the organisation. His loss to the PLO and more particularly to Yasser Arafat himself was incalculable. Their lives had been intertwined for more than thirty years, first as student politicians together in Cairo, then as founders of Fatah and comrades-in-arms through many ups and downs, and latterly as members of the PLO's dwindling band of veteran cadres. Khalaf's toughness, his keen intellect mixed with a ruthless pragmatism, his wry sense of humour, had made him indispensable in an organisation conspicuously short on talent. Perhaps most import-ant, he had provided a foil in the later years, especially since al-Wazir's death, for the mercurial Arafat – one of very few PLO officials who had the authority to curb some of their leader's excesses. Now, he was gone, and with his death Arafat was left almost alone among those who formed what had become known as the PLO's historic leadership.

When Arafat was dragged from his bed in Baghdad on the morning of 15 January, the day of the UN deadline, to be told the grim news he wasted no time returning to Tunis. As so often in the past Arafat found himself rushing back to his base to pay condolences to the families of fallen comrades. As his Iraqi jet lifted off from Saddam Airport en route to Tunis, nagging questions were already being asked about just who gave the order for Khalaf to be killed. It had been quickly established that Hamza Abu Zaid, the assassin, was a member of Abu Nidal's Fatah Revolutionary Council, the terrorist group that had shed so much

PLO blood over the years. What was not immediately clear was on whose behalf the renegade gang was acting on this occasion. But in the minds of top PLO officials a chilling thought occurred. Hadn't Abu Nidal recently moved back into Baghdad's orbit after an absence of some years? Was it not just possible that Saddam Hussein himself may have ordered the slaying as a warning to the PLO to stay the course with him in his looming confrontation with the Americans?

Such a possibility hardly bore thinking about, but it was well known that Salah Khalaf had been among the least enthusiastic PLO leaders about the tilt towards Baghdad; not only that, he had argued vigorously with Saddam at several meetings in an effort to persuade him to withdraw from Kuwait. On one occasion the Iraqi leader had sought to exclude Khalaf from a session he was to have with Arafat. Arafat had insisted that his deputy attend and Saddam had reluctantly agreed, but Khalaf himself demurred and left Baghdad without delay. Arafat advisers suspected Saddam's involvement. 'There is strong reason to believe that Saddam Hussein was behind the assassination of Abu Iyad; he was being too outspoken at a time when Saddam was not allowing anyone to take exception to his views,' said one.[47]

As Arafat set about making his condolence rounds in Tunis on the afternoon of 15 January, it was clear that the latest catastrophe to have befallen his organisation had very seriously affected him. Attending a gathering for the family and friends of the deceased at the al-Quds (Jerusalem) primary school in suburban Tunis, he threw himself, sobbing, into the arms of a PLO comrade. Arafat may have understood then that his ill-judged tilt towards Baghdad had ensnared Khalaf.

It was well after midnight in Baghdad. The well-lit streets were deserted. The date was 17 January and the time 2.35 a.m. (22.35 GMT, 16 January), less than nineteen hours after the deadline had expired for Iraq's withdrawal from Kuwait. There had been a certain tension in the air throughout the day, but no sign of panic in the Iraqi capital. At the Al-Rashid Hotel foreign reporters were on alert. The White House had been sending cryptic messages to the US networks, warning them that an attack against Iraq was imminent. When the aerial blitz came it was swift, brutal and quite devastating. Within hours, Iraq's air force was disabled, its Soviet-supplied electronic system crippled and its military installations coming under a withering bombardment. In an address from the White House, announcing the beginning of the 'air war', George Bush declared that the allies were 'targeting Saddam's military arsenal'.[48]

In far-off Tunis Arafat digested the war news as he prepared for Salah Khalaf's funeral. In the previous 24 hours he had reluctantly accepted that war was imminent, and that chances of a successful last-minute peace initiative, in which the PLO might usefully play a role, had disappeared. On the eve of the battle and in the expectation that the region was about to enter a period of heightened tension and instability, he had advised fellow members of the leadership to disperse. In the words of one of his closest colleagues he feared that the 'Israelis might use the war to conduct another wave of assassinations'.[49]

Arafat's fears proved groundless, but in the early stages of the conflict Israel was sorely provoked when Saddam Hussein made good his threat to launch missiles into the heart of Tel Aviv, although, for the most part, these attacks did only limited damage and caused few casualties. Much more damage was rendered to the fragile process that Arafat himself had sponsored over the years towards building confidence between the PLO and liberal Israelis. Sickened by the organisation's support for Iraq and appalled by the spectacle of Iraqi-flag-waving Palestinians in the territories appearing on their rooftops to cheer on the Scud missile attacks, Israeli peace campaigners vowed never again to trust the PLO.

As the allied air war ground mercilessly on, day by day, reducing Iraq's military assets to rubble, Arafat's was a small voice on the sidelines; alternately calling on Western leaders to 'put an end to the war which risks spreading to the entire region'[50] and at the same time issuing increasingly ludicrous forecasts about Iraq's ability to withstand the pressure. In a Radio Monte Carlo interview two weeks into the air war he described Iraq as a mountain that 'cannot be shaken by the wind', and declared, 'If we held out for three months (against the Israelis) in Beirut, then Iraq and its army and people can resist for three years.'[51]

In those late January and early February days, Arafat was having some trouble himself resisting pressure from Baghdad which was beginning to ask why the Palestinians, after all their talk about being in the 'same trench' as the Iraqis, were not doing more to put their words into action. A close Arafat aide said that tensions with Saddam grew at this time, since the PLO leader would not sanction terrorism and also steadfastly refused to move units of the Palestine Liberation Army in support of Iraq during the war.[52] An episode late in January tends to give some credence to claims Arafat was indeed resisting pressure from Baghdad, not that anything the PLO could have done militarily would have made one iota of difference to the course of events. After two days of PLO Katyusha rocket attacks from Lebanon into Israel's northern security zone, and amid Israeli charges that the organisation was seeking to open a new front on behalf of Iraq, PLO headquarters in Tunis denied Arafat had sanctioned any such move and said that the officer in command of PLO forces in Lebanon, Colonel Zeid Wehbe, had been reprimanded.[53]

When Arafat returned to Baghdad in the wake of the 13 February US bombing of what Iraq claimed was a civilian bomb shelter, his first and last visit to the Iraqi capital during the war itself, renewed Soviet attempts to stave off a devastating land war were getting under way in the person of special envoy Yevgeny Primakov who had seen Saddam on 12 February. A former Middle East correspondent of the Soviet Communist Party newspaper, Pravda, the personable Primakov had managed to elicit an agreement from the Iraqi leader to co-operate with Soviet peace moves.[54] Three days later on the eve of a visit to Moscow by Foreign Minister Tariq Aziz, Saddam acknowledged his readiness to pull out of Kuwait under the terms of Security Council Resolution 660, provided withdrawal was linked with a settlement of other Middle East issues such as the Palestine question. President Bush immediately dismissed the offer as a 'cruel hoax' and preparations for the allied 'knockout blow' against Iraq continued apace. It was the last time the Iraqis seriously raised the issue of 'linkage' as a precondition for withdrawal, a development that tended to confirm the suspicions of PLO sceptics that it was a cynical ploy in the first place. Lamely, Arafat said the Iraqi offer merited a 'positive response'.[55]

Undeterred, the Soviets pressed on with their peace efforts, even as the allies remorselessly continued with their bombing campaign, but Moscow's efforts would be in vain. By the time Foreign Minister Aziz announced on 23 February that Iraq had agreed to the immediate and unconditional withdrawal of its forces from Kuwait, provided Security Council resolutions passed after Resolution 660 were shelved, it was too late. An allied deadline expired that day and Bush, after consulting his main Gulf War allies, launched the long-awaited land war that, within 24 hours, devastated Iraq's defences in and around Kuwait. By 26 February, Saddam Hussein had had enough, announcing that all Iraqi troops were being withdrawn and that the emirate was no longer part of Iraq.[56] But this latest Iraqi offer was not sufficient for the allies who, intent on demolishing as much of the Iraqi military as possible before world disquiet forced an end to the carnage, continued the war for two more days. It was during this time that thousands of fleeing Iraqis perished on the road north from Kuwait to Basra in what one US pilot described, laconically, as a 'turkey shoot'.

Announcing the suspension of hostilities on 28 February, a triumphant President Bush said he was sending Secretary Baker to the Middle East forthwith to begin fashioning a durable peace. 'This war is now behind us,' Bush declared. 'Ahead of us is the difficult task of securing a potentially historic peace.'[57] Arafat, who had been rendered virtually speechless by the destruction of the Iraqi military within a few hours against all his predictions, may well have taken some comfort from those words, but he also must have known that the road back for both himself and PLO would be long and difficult: not least of the problems he faced was getting back on speaking terms with leaders of the Gulf and in Egypt. He had committed, in word if not in deed, a grave mistake. There would surely be costs.[58]

Part Five

19. IN THE WILDERNESS

'There is no forgiveness or forgetting. The crime, the sin is too big.'
Abdullah Bishara, Secretary-General, Gulf Co-operation Council,
March 1991.

In the spring of 1991, as he surveyed the wreckage war had
strewn around the Middle East, Yasser Arafat felt time and history
weighing heavily. It was not only Iraq that was in ruins, having
been pummelled into submission by the allied coalition. Ravaged,
too, was much of what he, Arafat, had striven for in the last two
decades: the PLO's carefully constructed network of support from
Arab states; its fragile credibility with the West, and with at least
a segment of Israeli opinion; its diplomatic initiative aimed at
securing a Palestinian homeland alongside Israel; the flow of Arab
money that had kept the organisation afloat and had enhanced his
power over the years. Thanks to his alliance with Saddam
Hussein, Arafat's leadership was being called into question by
some in the West, in the Arab world and even among Palestinians
in the Israeli-occupied territories.

If nothing else, the war between Iraq and an allied coalition,
including all Gulf states plus the Egyptians, Syrians and Moroc-
cans, also confirmed that a much-weakened Soviet Union under
the liberalising Mikhail Gorbachev no longer had either the will
or the inclination to provide a counterweight to America in the
Middle East. Moscow's limp last-minute diplomatic manoeuvres to
get Saddam off the hook had come to naught. In any case, the
Soviets had given solid support at the UN to a series of resolutions
that not only provided the legal justification for the liberation of
Kuwait, but also a framework for punitive post-war sanctions
against Iraq.

In the immediate aftermath of the war a battered Arafat retired
to his Tunis headquarters to ponder an uncertain future: bereft of
friends and support among traditional allies in the Gulf; unwelcome in Egypt, the land of his birth; ridiculed in the West where
television stations had endlessly replayed film from Baghdad,
taken at the height of the Gulf crisis, of his embrace of Saddam

Hussein – like a slow-motion soccer replay. Arafat would continue in his efforts to justify his ill-starred alliance with Saddam, but his words sounded empty. How, he asked repeatedly, could the anti-imperialist revolutionary have accepted the presence of Western military forces on Arab land? 'We are writing this [history] for the generations, regardless of the results of this battle . . . The PLO cannot but be in the trenches against Israel and the champions of Israel,' he would say to those who questioned his judgement.[1]

As Arafat licked his wounds in Tunis in those first days and weeks after Saddam's legions were put to flight in Desert Storm, there was one other issue which continued to bear down upon him. The flow of Soviet Jews to Israel persisted in full flood. While the nationalist government of Yitzhak Shamir denied that it was channelling the new arrivals into the occupied territories, there was also no doubt that population pressures and, more to the point, pressure on housing in Israel itself, was creating a ripple effect which was spreading to East Jerusalem, where Jewish residents had come to outnumber Arabs, and to the West Bank. But with his credibility in shreds Arafat was scarcely in a position to make his voice heard.

So began one of those bleak, down periods for the PLO leader, reminiscent of other moments during his long stewardship of the fractious guerrilla movement, such as the dog days after his retreat from Lebanon in 1982. Consigned to a Middle East Coventry by his Arab brethren, most of whom either were not speaking to him or, worse, were continuing to vilify him, Arafat was left talking forlornly about his place in history as the 'leader of one of the few liberation movements left in the world', engaged in a continuing struggle for national rights and self-nation. 'There is something here that the West seems incapable of understanding or absorbing, that the dynamism of our people is not a passing thing; the dynamism of our people is deeply rooted in history,' he told an Arab interviewer at the height of the Gulf War. 'Ours is an epic people. It has been struggling since 1917, from the Balfour declaration until today. That is 73 or 74 years, five generations . . . As chairman of this organisation and leader of this people, I do not seek wealth. If I were seeking wealth, I would go to the wealthy. I seek a place in history.'[2] He would also seek to put the best gloss on a bad situation by claiming that Iraqi defiance had 'created new facts on the strategic level that serve our cause and national struggle', as he told a meeting called to mark the fortieth month of the *intifada*.[3]

Arafat's rush to embrace Saddam prompted continuing murmurings of discontent among his lieutenants, a number of whom were convinced that Iraq had been behind the killing of Salah Khalaf.

But in the midst of the gloom there were glimmers of promise for Arafat, whose determined optimism, even at the bleakest moments, has always been one of his strengths. When a triumphant George Bush, at the very zenith of his power and popularity, addressed a joint session of Congress on 6 March, less than a week after the end of Gulf War hostilities, his words provided some encouragement to the leader of a movement close to the nadir of its fortunes.

'All of us know the depth of bitterness that has made the dispute between Israel and its neighbours so painful and intractable,' Bush said. 'We must do all we can to close the gap between Israel and the Arab states and between Israelis and Palestinians. The tactics of terror lead nowhere. There can be no substitute for diplomacy ... A comprehensive peace must be grounded in United Nations Security Council Resolutions 242 and 338 and the principle of territory for peace,' he continued. 'This principle must be elaborated to provide for Israel's security and recognition, and at the same time for legitimate Palestinian political rights. Anything else would fail the twin tests of fairness and security.'[4]

The words and sentiments were hardly new, but here was an American President, with enhanced credibility in the Middle East theatre, declaring unequivocally that territorial compromise was the only way forward, along with acceptance of Palestinian 'national rights' – diplomatic code language for a process that might lead to self-determination. Bush was also preparing to put words into action by despatching James Baker, the Secretary of State, back to the Middle East to start what would prove to be a protracted series of diplomatic shuttles that before the year was out would yield a remarkable diplomatic achievement.

In Tunis, a beleaguered Arafat seized on Bush's remarks as the first good news he had heard in months. Interviewed by the Spanish daily *El Pais*, he said, 'It's the first time that a US President has spoken with total clarity in assuring that there must be peace in exchange for territory and justice in exchange for security.' Describing Bush's remarks as a 'decisive step', Arafat observed: 'He also supported the implementation of United Nations Security Council Resolutions 242 and 338, and for solutions to be worked out under the auspices of the UN and in accordance with the legitimate political rights of the Palestinian people.'[5] In the same interview Arafat also repeated his defence of his alliance with Saddam, and his own position as leader of a movement that many of his critics believed was living on borrowed time. 'I have been chosen to be where I am by the Palestinian people,' he said. 'I didn't arrive here in a tank, nor by any foreign mandate. I was elected in a democratic fashion – or does the West not trust democracy when it occurs in the Third World?'[6]

These moments of promise were few and far between in those difficult post-war days. Arafat had plenty of time to reflect upon the past, and to wonder whether time might not be running out for him in his ceaseless quest for what he calls Palestine. As if his problems of loss of credibility and criticism from within the Palestinian movement were not enough, Arafat was also obliged in early 1991 to come to terms with the severing of a financial lifeline that had helped keep his movement alive through its many ups and downs, and, more to the point, had underpinned his own domination of PLO institutions right from the moment he was elected Chairman of the Executive Committee in 1969. Early benefactors such as Saudi Arabia and Kuwait simply stopped paying, furious as they were at Arafat's alignment with Saddam. Indeed, all states of the Saudi-dominated Gulf Co-operation Council froze their donations. Iraq itself, which had become the PLO's most reliable paymaster from 1988, was in no position to maintain the flow. Arafat estimated that, as a result of the crisis, the PLO had lost approximately 120 million dollars in annual contributions from Saudi Arabia, Kuwait and Iraq alone. Loss of income and money lodged in Kuwaiti banks took the overall amount forfeited by the Palestinians as a direct result of the crisis well above 10 billion dollars, he said.[7]

It would be several years before the Gulf states resumed contributions, albeit on a much reduced scale. Such was the continuing rage of Gulf rulers that Abdullah Bishara, secretary-general of the Gulf Cooperation Council, vowed at the time there could be 'no forgiveness, no forgetting . . . There is no forgiveness for this. It is not a romance where lovers quarrel. The crime is too big to forgive. Mr Arafat took a very reckless course of action and will have to bear the consequences.'[8]

Grimly aware that his predecessors Husseini and Shukairy lost their hold over the Palestinian movement in part because they ran out of money, Arafat had no choice but to order swingeing cuts in PLO expenditure. Funds were slashed for the PLO's diplomatic network, and expenditures for the PLO's 14,000 strong military, including a tiny 'air force' and 'navy', were cut to the bone. Contributions to hospitals and social welfare institutions across the region were much reduced, and pensions to the families of the estimated 18,000 Palestinian 'martyrs' of the Arab–Israeli conflict were pared back, or stopped altogether.[9]

Nor did the consequences stop there. During the Iraqi occupation and in its aftermath, tens of thousands of Palestinians had to leave Kuwait – one of the most important bases for the Diaspora – as Kuwaitis exacted their revenge for alleged Palestinian co-operation with the occupiers. More were expelled by Saudi Arabia and the other Gulf states. Arafat himself was scarcely best placed to plead their cause, having been declared *persona non grata* in about half the countries of the Arab world.

In running the expensive and unwieldy PLO apparatus, Arafat had always been reliant on wealthy friends. The organisation had long had its own fundraising network in the Palestinian Diaspora – involving Palestinians in the Gulf, who were obliged to contribute between five and seven per cent of their gross salaries to the cause, thus raising around 40 million dollars a year, as well as the big Palestinian business magnates to whom Arafat had always been close. Separately, Arafat had seen fit to build up a treasure chest for his own Fatah movement, including for the most part prudent investments worth more than 2 billion dollars in equities, bonds and other securities, from which he would periodically bail out the PLO's treasury, the Palestine National Fund. But right from the start, the main source of funds was Arafat's Arab benefactors: Saudi Arabia, the most important of them, contributing about 85 million dollars annually to the PLO and an unspecified, though almost certainly greater, amount to Fatah; the United Arab Emirates and Kuwait, which stumped up lesser amounts; and Libya and Iraq, which gave sporadically.

Hardly had the echoes from George Bush's imprecations before Congress concerning the need for a concerted new effort to deal with the Arab–Israel issue died down than James Baker was on his way to the Middle East on a long march that would come to be regarded as a textbook example of American diplomacy at its best and most persistent. Baker began his journey in the second week of March with impressive credentials, and, perhaps more import-ant, with the full backing of a president who not only understood Middle East complexities, but was prepared to risk the ire of the powerful American Jewish lobby. He would need all the backing he could get in what was to become a public test of wills with the obstinate Yitzhak Shamir who had little interest in seeing the peace process advance beyond the word 'go'.

To the task of manoeuvring the various Middle East players towards a common goal, the patrician James Baker III brought the instincts of a river-boat gambler and the singlemindedness of someone unused to failure, not to mention invaluable experience gained from a previous abortive attempt that had merely sharp-ened his determination to succeed this time. The contrast with the flaccid efforts at Middle East peacemaking of his predecessor, the plodding George Shultz, could scarcely have been greater. Baker had given some clue to the tactics he might employ in a revealing interview with *Time* magazine early in 1989, as he was preparing to assume responsibility as Secretary of State. Musing on the relationship between turkey shooting, one of his favourite pas-times, and the task ahead in the Middle East, he observed that the most important thing was 'getting them where you want them on your terms. Then you control the situation, not them. You have the options. Pull the trigger or don't. It doesn't matter once you've got them where you want them. The important thing is knowing that it's in your hands, that you can do whatever you determine is in your interests to do.'[15]

Stalking his prey on his return to the Middle East in March – the first of eight such visits to the region in 1991 – Baker did a good deal of listening, without revealing his hand; although Shamir and those around him could have been under few illusions that they were up against anything other than a formidable individual who had already bared his teeth in some of the most forthright criticism of the Jewish state uttered by an American official in many years. In a speech soon after becoming Secretary of State to the American Israel Public Affairs Committee (AIPAC), the principal Jewish lobby group in the US, Baker had said: 'For Israel, now is the time to lay aside, once and for all, the unrealistic vision of a Greater Israel . . . Forswear annexation; stop settlement activity; allow schools to reopen; reach out to the Palestinians as neighbours who deserve political rights.'[11]

A year later, having failed to persuade the Israelis to abandon their dream of a Greater Israel, let alone sit down and talk to a 'sanitised' group of Palestinians who were prepared to disguise their PLO links, Mr Baker's patience deserted him. Testifying before Congress on lack of progress in Middle East peacemaking, he blamed Shamir. In remarks that brought squeals from Israel and its supporters, he gave the State Department telephone number as a contact if the Israelis wished to pursue discussions about peace. 'Everybody over there should know that the telephone number is 1-202-456-1414. When you're serious about peace, call us.'[12]

As Baker shuttled back and forth to the Middle East – he visited the region once in March, and then twice in April – he prompted yet again the old arguments among Palestinians about whether they should meet this harbinger of peace masquerading, in the eyes of some, as the handmaiden of Israeli designs. Baker did his best on these early visits to enlist the co-operation of Palestinians inside the territories, spending hours talking to their representatives in East Jerusalem, assuring them that he had their interests at heart.

Invariably, much of the conversation at these sessions would encompass the role of the PLO in any proposed peace conference with the Palestinians of the territories, while appearing to enjoy more freedom of manoeuvre from Tunis in the post-Gulf War era, insisting, nevertheless, that they could not be separated from their 'national leadership' outside.

Watching Baker's comings and going from his Tunis isolation, Arafat was alternatively tantalised and apprehensive about what the Americans might be up to. He saw in the Baker shuttles promise of progress towards an international Middle East peace conference under UN auspices; but at the same time he worried that Washington might be using the PLO's manifest weakness after the Gulf War to cut it out of the game completely. He gave voice to these concerns after a meeting in April with Algerian President Chadli Bendjedid – one of the few Arab leaders prepared to receive him at the time – when he said, 'The establishment of a new security order in the Arab world and the normalisation of Arab–Israeli relations . . . are manoeuvres aimed at liquidating the Palestinian question and depriving the Palestinians of their legitimate rights.'[13] Later in April, however, Arafat appeared to be warming to proposals being floated by Baker for a regional conference between Israel and the so-called Arab 'frontline' states – Jordan, Syria and Lebanon – under the sponsorship of the United States and Soviet Union. After meeting Arafat in Libya, France's Foreign Minister Roland Dumas told reporters that 'Mr Arafat seemed to me to be open to the suggestion made by the US Secretary of State, but he is anxious that the core subjects not be ignored'.[14] Dumas identified among these 'core subjects' the issue of the 'authentic representation' of Palestinians in the negotiations.

From a personal standpoint, an isolated Arafat had reason to be grateful to the French. His meeting with Dumas was his first encounter with a senior Western official since the Gulf War, and encouraged him to believe that his days of international solitude might be coming to an end. Arafat was also buoyed when an apparently determined President Bush made it clear that the US was digging in its heels over an Israeli request for American loan guarantees to cover 10 billion dollars in borrowing over five years to settle the hundreds of thousands of Jews who had arrived from the Soviet Union. Bush told the Israelis they could not expect to receive the guarantees that would enable them to borrow internationally at more favourable rates of interest while they continued their headlong rush to build settlements in territory seized in the 1967 war. Settlement building, he declared, was an 'obstacle to peace'.[15]

So the stage was set for a bruising encounter between Israel and its guardian superpower that would drag on for months, bring relations to historic lows, and in the end serve the useful purpose of helping to educate the Israeli public that its representatives could not continue to shun international pressure and expect to avoid penalty. Bush and Baker had begun sowing the seeds of Yitzhak Shamir's downfall at elections due in mid-1992, but in the meantime they had also inveigled him into agreeing in principle to Israel's participation at a proposed peace gathering scheduled for later in the year. By early in June when Bush despatched letters to regional leaders outlining Washington's 'ideas' for a regional peace conference, James Baker's 'turkey shoot' was coming into focus.

As always, the vexed issue of Palestinian representation hovered in the background, with Shamir adamant that Israel would not sit down with Palestinians tainted by overt connection with the PLO. Nor would he countenance negotiations with Palestinians from East Jerusalem, since the Jewish state regarded the whole of Jerusalem, Arab and Jewish, as its undivided capital in perpetuity.

Thus began the circulation of 'lists' of Palestinians who might be acceptable, a process that was to continue, with Tunis's involvement. Arafat himself was, by the middle of June, fully engaged in discussions on the issue of participation, and was being persuaded that his own, and the PLO's, best hope of ending their isolation was to appear to co-operate in the convening of a peace conference; although the trick was to try to ensure that the organisation would not be further marginalised by agreeing to remain out of sight.

Throughout the long, hot months of a Mediterranean summer Arafat, with his eyes firmly on Palestinian militants who were certain to oppose any concessions over PLO representation, continued to decry attempts to exclude the organisation from the conference, but all the time he plotted with trusted aides how best to secure Palestinian endorsement for a move that he knew provided the only realistic avenue forward. Typical of his public comments at the time were those to reporters in Amman in mid-July, after his first visit to Baghdad since the Gulf War, when he said, 'America's efforts are not aimed at achieving peace in the region, they are a bluff. They [US and Israel] want time for land, not land for peace.'[16]

By now, planning was well under way for a special session of the Palestine National Council as a means of providing Arafat with the institutional cover for approving Palestinian participation in the forthcoming peace gathering. But towards the end of August an event would occur that would distract the PLO chief momentarily from his preparations for the PNC. Like much of the rest of the world the Palestinian leadership, cloistered in its sun-drenched villas in some of Tunis's classier suburbs, watched obsessively on Cable News Network the dramatic events in Moscow between 19–23 August when hardliners moved abortively against Mikhail Gorbachev, and in the process hastened the collapse of the Soviet Union. Some PLO stalwarts, who had been angered by Moscow's abandonment under Gorbachev of support for national liberation movements, applauded his apparent downfall, but for once Arafat stayed quiet. After Gorbachev re-emerged, the PLO leader congratulated him on his 'triumphant victory' and expressed the hope that he would continue to support Palestinian self-determination.[17]

Arafat's main preoccupation, however, was not international developments but preparations for the PNC to be held in Algiers in the last week of September. As always, he planned meticulously for the event to ensure that he would get exactly what he wanted: in this case the right to sanction Palestinian participation in a Middle East peace conference without direct PLO involvement.

Among the secrets of Arafat's control of his sometimes chaotic movement has been his mastery of quasi-representative institutions such as its parliament-in-exile, which has invariably bowed to his wishes while at times providing a safety valve for his opponents, such as the Popular Front of George Habash, to let off steam.

Interestingly, in his attempts to ensure that the forthcoming PNC would prove reasonably representative of Palestinian aspirations, Arafat travelled to Khartoum in the first week of September for a meeting with Ibrahim Ghosheh, spokesman for Hamas, the Islamic resistance movement, which had its strongest roots in the Gaza Strip, and which had emerged as a powerful and militant counterweight to Fatah. For some time, Arafat had been attempting to draw Hamas into the broad PLO church. As in the past, the discussions with Hamas went nowhere, since its conditions for engagement in the PNC were outrageous. It wanted 40 per cent of the seats to reflect what it said was its popularity in the territories.[18]

So the stage was set for the Algiers PNC of 1991, the twentieth in the PLO's chequered history, and the sixteenth over which Arafat himself had presided since his election in 1969 as chairman of the organisation's Executive Committee. This time, as the more than 300 delegates gathered in the by now familiar circular conference chamber of the Club de Pins, half an hour's drive west of Algiers, their deliberations would be less momentous than their independence declaration three years previously. But their acquiescence in Arafat's careful steps towards endorsing Palestinian participation at the forthcoming US–Soviet sponsored peace conference would yield more immediate benefits.

'We renew our readiness to work with all international parties to make the peace conference succeed to fulfil what the people of the region are striving for in terms of a just peace, security and stability . . . and we renew our readiness to co-operate so that the remaining obstacles on the road to convening it can be removed,' Arafat told the opening session.[19]

But in debate on the chamber floor, in discussions in smoke-filled anterooms of the conference centre, and in talk into the early-morning hours in Arafat's villa on the shores of the Mediterranean, the PLO leader was not yet ready to ask his colleagues for a clear-cut endorsement of Palestinian participation in the peace conference. Rather, he wanted something fuzzier that would give him room for manoeuvre until the last minute before the conference convened late in October. 'You are not required to say yes, but we cannot say no. You have to find a formula,' he advised delegates.[20]

In the end, the PNC, after a spirited debate involving Arafat loyalists on one side and the 'loyal opposition' of George Habash's

Popular Front on the other, endorsed a document outlining the terms of Palestinian participation in the peace conference. The vote in favour of allowing 'non-PLO' Palestinians to negotiate directly with the Israelis was 256 to 68: a second vote on a 'declaration of principles' to guide the discussions was carried by 313 votes to 18. 'We want a peace of the brave, not capitulations. We will not make any obstacles to peace, but we reject the Israeli conditions,' Arafat told reporters at the end of the PNC.[21] In fact, in his pragmatic decision to sanction Palestinian involvement without the overt participation of the PLO, Arafat was falling into line with Israeli demands that excluded the PLO and representatives from East Jerusalem. An important footnote to the twentieth PNC was the appearance at a closed session late one night – journalists were ushered from the chamber – of Faisal Husseini, Arafat's chief representative in the territories, and Hanan Ashrawi, the West Bank academic whose calm, articulate description of the Palestinian predicament was gaining widespread notice internationally. In defiance of Israeli law banning contacts with the PLO, the two mingled with conference delegates and made a persuasive case for Palestinian involvement in the forthcoming peace conference. Ashrawi, who had attended a number of meetings with James Baker, said she believed the Americans had a greater appreciation of the Palestinian viewpoint, and were indeed prepared to do something about trying to slow Israel's settlement drive in the occupied territories.[22] Back in Israel, hardliners urged that Husseini and Ashrawi be arrested on their return for fraternising with the enemy, but apart from a summons for questioning by the police the issue was not pursued. Even in Shamir's Israel taboos against the PLO were crumbling.

As the date for the opening of the Middle East peace conference at the end of October approached, Arafat had one further hurdle to overcome: he convened a session in Tunis of the ninety-member Central Council, the Palestinian 'mini-parliament', to approve the names of seven Palestinians in a joint Jordanian–Palestinian delegation. This endorsement was duly secured, and Arafat departed for consultations in Damascus and Cairo, thus ending a protracted period of diplomatic isolation following his Gulf War folly. His visit to Egypt on 21 October, his first in fourteen months, in which he held ninety minutes of talks with President Hosm Mubarak, was low-key. The meeting was held in Mubarak's house, and press and television were barred.

At this time, as preparations gathered speed for the first ever formal face-to-face meeting between Israel and its Arab foes, James Baker dispatched a letter of assurance to the Palestinians. It was more generous to Palestinian aspirations than any other official American pronouncement in the last thirty years. Importantly, it said nothing that would preclude the direct participation of the Palestinian leadership outside the territories in the process at a later date.[23]

As delegations to the Middle East peace conference began arriving at the end of October in a Madrid bathed in autumnal colours, it was clear that a diplomatic event of more than usual significance was in the offing. But few could have predicted then that within less than two years it would yield at least the appearance of progress towards the beginning of a resolution of the near century-long conflict between Arab and Jew in the narrow crescent bounded by the Mediterranean and the River Jordan; or, for that matter, that by sharpening the appetite in Israel itself for progress towards peace it would prove to be so crucial in hastening the electoral downfall of Shamir and his nationalist camp.

Vowing that never again would the Middle East dispute bring the world to the brink of war, Messrs Bush and Gorbachev opened proceedings on 30 October in the majestic Hall of Columns in Madrid's Royal Palace, before a worldwide television audience and in the presence of 4,665 journalists from 54 countries who had converged on the Spanish capital. Bush's speech was low-key, but it also left no doubt that the Americans believed that, for there to be progress towards peace, Israel would have to show much greater flexibility. 'Israel now has an opportunity to demonstrate that it is willing to enter into a new relationship with its Palestinian neighbours . . . we believe territorial compromise is essential to peace,' he declared pointedly.[24]

Proceedings over the next 36 hours of the latest and, as it turned out, most productive American effort to bring peace to the Middle East were notable for their theatrical moments.

The spectacle of the Israelis sitting at a T-shaped table facing their most bitter Arab foes – the Syrians, Lebanese, and a joint Jordanian–Palestinian delegation – was made all the more remarkable by the fact that those participating were not the doves of the centre and left, but the hardliners of the nationalist right.

Watching events in Madrid obsessively from his Tunis headquarters, Arafat could not but have experienced twinges of disappointment, but there was consolation in the way things turned out. Not only had the public presentation of the Palestinian position been handled skilfully by Hanan Ashrawi and others, but Arafat himself had clearly not been out of mind during the proceedings. He had ensured that the PLO presence in Madrid, spearheaded by his trusted aide, Nabil Shaath, would be noticed and for it to be made plain that his lieutenants were co-ordinating the efforts of the Palestinian delegation, and that he (Arafat) was in effective command from Tunis, like Tiberius on the end of a telephone.

Indeed, Arafat representatives in Madrid made no attempt to disguise their contact with Tunis. Nabil Shaath, who manned round the clock what he described as an 'operations room', told reporters who swarmed around him, 'We are here to make sure the Palestinian delegation is fully equipped and supported by the best Palestinian brains, expertise and the right political position. That involves doing everything except sitting at the negotiating table,' he said.[32] After labouring for years to achieve a modicum of recognition and fearing above all else the loss of control, Arafat was not going to allow a group of Palestinians from the territories to get ideas above their station.

The Madrid conference, which ended on an upbeat note with the beginning of discussions between Israel and its neighbours, raised hopes that real advances might be made towards a resolution of outstanding problems. These bilateral talks involving the Palestinians, Jordanians, Syrians and Lebanese would have mixed consequences: success for Jordan and Lebanon, qualified progress for the Palestinians, and disappointment in the case of Syria; although it is also true that the process was important in educating all sides about what might be possible. Similarly, parallel multilateral talks involving arms control, economic development, water, refugees, and the environment were useful – up to a point – in defining issues.

But progress of the faltering bilateral talks in Washington, under the watchful eyes of State Department officials, would prove to be painfully slow. They were particularly frustrating for the Palestinians whose expectations, after years of setbacks, were more acute than other participants.'

With the Madrid conference out of the way, Yasser Arafat sprang one of his biggest surprises. In November 1991, at the age of 62, and having proclaimed for as long as anyone could remember that he was betrothed to the revolution, he took a wife 34 years his junior. His choice of companion was intriguing. Suha, a 28-year-old Palestinian Christian, was the daughter of Raymonda Tawil, a long-standing Palestinian activist and journalist. Sorbonne-educated and fluent in English, French and Arabic, she had gone to work as Arafat's secretary in 1989. She had become a constant companion, travelling with him on his frequent missions across the Arab world. Her PLO connections were impeccable: two of her sisters were married to PLO officials, one of them to Ibrahim Souss, the organisation's Paris representative.

Domestic issues only briefly diverted attention, however. With Israel in the throes of preparations for its forthcoming elections, as Middle East politicking entered a lull, there was a rather less pleasurable distraction.

On 8 April, while on a flight from Khartoum to Tunis, Arafat's plane, a Russian AN-26, went down in the desert near the Libya–Sudan border after being caught in a sandstorm. When news of the crash emerged, few believed the PLO leader had survived. In Tunis, something approaching panic gripped colleagues, who were roused from their beds to be told that the 'Old Man' was missing in the Libyan desert. Not least of their concerns was whether the secretive Arafat had entrusted anyone with details of the PLO's billions. 'Where's the notebook?' was one of the first questions anxious PLO officials asked each other, a reference to the accounting records of the organisation's investments and bank accounts.[35] Hours were to pass before confirmation was received that Arafat had indeed miraculously emerged from the aircraft wreck in which three crewmen, including pilot and co-pilot, had died.

In all his years of living dangerously, Arafat had not experienced a closer call. In the days after the crash, Arafat could not be accused of avoiding an opportunity to bolster the myth of invincibility, and to add some deft political touches to the story of a remarkable escape. In one interview, he claimed that he had shouted 'Abu Jihad, I am coming' as his plane hurtled towards the desert.'[27] This was a reference to his deceased comrade-in-arms, Khalil al-Wazir, who was assassinated by the Israelis in 1988. It was not the smallest of ironies that, within a fairly short time, Arafat would be doing business with the man who, as Israeli Defence Minister, had ordered his friend's execution.

20. THE RECKONING

'You, the Palestinians in the territories . . . Take our peace proposal seriously, give it the seriousness it deserves to spare yourselves yet more suffering and bereavement. Enough of tears and blood!' Yitzhak Rabin, Knesset speech, 13 July 1992.

For a man who had spent his life cultivating a halting, laconic style, Yitzhak Rabin spoke with unusual eloquence. Standing on the speaker's podium in Israel's parliament, he addressed his words to the people who had just delivered him an emphatic election victory and to the Arab leaders from whom he as Israel's army chief of staff had seized swathes of territory during the Six-Day War exactly 25 years before. It was time, he declared, for Israelis to 'overcome the sense of isolation that has held us in its thrall for almost half a century' and join 'the international movement toward peace, reconciliation and co-operation'. It was time, too, for Israel's Arab neighbours: 'I invite the King of Jordan and the Presidents of Syria and Lebanon to this rostrum in Israel's Knesset, here in Jerusalem, for the purpose of talking peace.' If they were not prepared to come to him, he would go to them: 'In the service of peace, I am prepared to travel to Amman, Damascus and Beirut today, tomorrow. For there is no greater victory than the victory of peace. Wars have their victors and vanquished, but everyone is a victor in peace.'[1]

For the Palestinians of the occupied territories, Rabin – taking office as premier on 14 July 1992, for the second time in twenty years – had a message of a rather more ambiguous kind. He was out to negotiate a means of rapidly giving them control over their own affairs, and they should talk if necessary, in continuous negotiations rather than the fits and starts that had characterised the peace process so far. But if they persisted in 'terror and violence', then his government would use 'every possible means' to crush them.[2]

It was a familiar theme, one that the 70-year-old Rabin had played to great effect during the election campaign in which he had just trounced Yitzhak Shamir's Likud party, mixing a hard-headed readiness to make concessions for peace with the toughest of responses to perceived security threats. This theme was calculated to appeal to mainstream Israeli voters tired of war but worried about the consequences of showing weakness in negotiations – people who could be persuaded to trust the former general who first captured the territories in 1967 to extricate Israel from the moral and political quagmire into which it had been plunged.

Rabin's words found a receptive audience elsewhere. In faraway Tunis, Yasser Arafat was listening intently, hoping that the new prime minister was planning a bold departure towards the Palestinians, fantasising that he might even be prepared to break the long established Israeli taboo and talk direct to the enemy as Arafat himself had suggested. But for public consumption the PLO fell back on the familiar complaints and accusations. 'Mr Rabin failed to show courage and take the necessary step to react to Mr Arafat's proposal that the two men should sit down to negotiate a political solution. He totally forgot the Palestinians' representative. What we need is a willingness to deal with issues seriously, to undo the bad taste left by Shamir,' said an Arafat spokesman.[3]

In private, Arafat harboured other hopes. His political instincts – and, as important, his colleagues in the occupied territories, whom he consulted with increasing frequency concerning Israeli affairs – told him that the Israeli election of 23 June 1992 had been of potentially momentous significance, perhaps the most important in the history of the Jewish state.[4] After fifteen years of governments dominated by a party (Likud) determined to hang on to all the occupied territories and irredeemably hostile to Palestinian political rights, Israelis had voted for a change. They had elected a government that said it favoured a rapid move towards interim Palestinian self-rule. The extent of the change this represented would become clear as the months wore on.

In his more upbeat moments, the PLO leader was prepared to admit that the election had indeed broken new ground. 'They voted against Shamir: that is a vote for peace,' he told an interviewer on 1 July.[5] As he rebuilt his strength after the travails of the past few months, Arafat was exploring new ways of inserting himself back into the Middle East negotiating game – this time as direct interlocutor of the Israeli Government.

His point of departure, as on so many previous occasions, was in next-door Jordan. Confined to Amman following surgery in the first week of June to remove a blood clot near his brain caused by his plane crash, Arafat seized the opportunity to make a gesture towards Israel and more particularly the peace camp. On the eve of the poll, he invited the Palestinian negotiators from Madrid led by Faisal al-Husseini to Amman. There, having made sure TV cameras were on hand, he hugged and kissed his representatives from the territories who had come to the Jordanian capital to congratulate the President of Palestine on his recovery.

This was a theatrical episode of some subtlety – at least in comparison with previous ham-fisted attempts to sway past Israeli elections. Although the Palestinian negotiators had met Arafat on many previous occasions in private, it was the first time they had done so – deliberately – publicly. In the process, the PLO leader blew to pieces the fiction at the heart of the serving Israeli government's Palestinian policy.

Prime Minister Shamir, true to form, had been fighting the election on a platform of implacable opposition to dealing with the PLO. The Palestinian delegates with whom he had sat at Madrid and with whom his officials had subsequently negotiated in Washington were, he insisted, representatives of the West Bank and Gaza Arabs and had no direct link with Arafat's terror organisation.

Rabin's campaign was much more straightforward in this regard. He said he intended to negotiate with the West Bank and Gaza Palestinians. He did not care with whom their representatives conferred. Charged with secretly planning to deal with the PLO, he countered that this was what Shamir was doing already. 'Despite the Likud declarations and despite the fact it is sticking its head in the sand, this government has ongoing direct negotiations with the PLO,' said a Labour statement after the Amman meeting.[6] Beyond threatening to arrest the Palestinian negotiators on their return from Jordan – a move that would almost certainly have killed the peace process and led to an estrangement with the US – Shamir's ministers were stumped for a coherent reply. Thus was the die cast for election of a government that, on paper at least, seemed more amenable to tackling the core of the Palestinian problem than any of its predecessors.

Arafat, for his part, while clear enough concerning what Israelis had voted against, was less sure what they had voted *for*. His views about Rabin in particular were ambivalent. He heard the overtures concerning a rapid push for Palestinian autonomy in the territories, but remained sceptical of the new Prime Minister's sincerity. His scepticism was prompted by what he knew of Rabin's history. Was he not the man who, after conquering the West Bank from Jordan and Gaza from Egypt, set out to implant Jewish settlements on Arab land? Was it not he who, as Defence Minister under Shamir in 1988, proclaimed a policy of 'might, force and beatings' to suppress the Palestinian *intifada*? Had he not ordered the assassination of Arafat's friend and right-hand man Khalif al-Wazir? These were themes that Arafat's left-wing rivals such as George Habash harped on in the weeks following Rabin's election – and which Arafat occasionally echoed, when he was not issuing calls on Rabin to meet him in person and strike a 'peace of the brave' or to 'join the tide of history'.[7]

'I don't see Rabin as different from Shamir,' he said in Cairo as Rabin prepared to take office. 'Unfortunately, some of our Arab brothers have slipped and welcomed him. Rabin broke the bones of our brothers. He set up the early settlements in the occupied lands.'[8]

The rancour was predictable, and mutual. What Arafat failed fully to comprehend was that, in Rabin, toughness and conciliation were two sides of the same coin. The only native-born Israeli to have served as Prime Minister to that point and a man whose distinguished military record dating back to the 1948 War of Independence won him widespread public trust, Rabin often talked of a strategy of 'marching with both feet' – the military and political. His coalition contained a party – Meretz, allied with the Peace Now movement – that openly favoured direct contacts with the PLO. Moreover, his Foreign Minister – Shimon Peres – was inclined to a similar view. The government was already talking of curbing the growth of Jewish settlements in the territories. Before it had been in office a month, it dangled before Arafat's eyes the carrot of an end to the ban on contacts between

Israeli citizens and the PLO – while still ruling out negotiating with the organisation itself.

With these blandishments, Arafat girded for business. In Tunis, he called a top-level strategy meeting to assess the implications of the new Israeli Government. Separately, in the occupied territories, his chief lieutenant Faisal al-Husseini began to contemplate adopting a more co-operative stance towards the occupation forces. But the Palestinians under occupation were realists.

If Rabin was true to form he would combine conciliatory gestures in negotiation with an iron fist in the territories.

The first test of the Palestinians' new approach was not long in coming. On 15 August, four weeks after Rabin took office, Israeli troops moved in and surrounded Al-Najah University in the West Bank town of Nablus – in search, the Israelis said, of a group of armed Palestinians who had infiltrated the campus in the midst of a fiercely contested student election. There followed a tense stand-off, in which troops kept several thousand students bottled up inside the university without food or water, demanding they surrender the gunmen. On such occasions in the past, the result had almost always been bloodshed and spreading protest. This time, a Palestinian team led by Husseini managed to negotiate a settlement with the Israeli Administration, working under the direct control of Rabin: six radicals were deported to Jordan and the Israelis agreed to take no further action against the university. Husseini told startled reporters he did the deal to preserve the peace process and prevent further violence and then went on to pay an unusual tribute to Rabin himself: 'He is a man who is ready to play the game.'[9]

It was perhaps the most striking example yet of the Palestinian leaders in the territories acting to their own script, rather than to one written in Tunis. Arafat's reaction to the university siege differed both in tone and substance from that of his men on the ground. While Husseini was locked in talks with the Israelis, he spent his time faxing out statements lambasting Rabin's 'authoritarian policies' and 'escalating repression' against the students, and calling on the US to intervene.

The 'game' to which Husseini had referred was the Washington negotiations, for which Arafat's hopes were building ahead of another foray into the region by US Secretary of State James Baker. He was soon to discover that his hopes were premature. Rabin was in no hurry to move, and President Bush and Secretary Baker were certainly not going to exert immediate pressure on a Prime Minister so much more to their liking than Shamir. Instead, in August Bush invited Rabin to his holiday retreat in Kennebunk-port, Maine, welcoming him with great warmth and a promise to release the 10 billion dollars in US loan guarantees, which had been held up because of Administration displeasure with Shamir.

Adding to Arafat's frustrations at this point was the fact the Middle East peace process was once again falling victim to the US electoral cycle. President Bush's re-election campaign was in trouble. In an attempt to save it he called Baker back from State to the White House. Baker's recall deprived the negotiations of what little momentum they had had. To Arafat's greater, though probably unjustified, disappointment his place was taken by his deputy, Lawrence Eagleburger – a man who, as the PLO leader observed, had been a 'pupil' of his old nemesis Henry Kissinger and had 'in the past shown public bias towards Israel'.[10] 'Baker's departure is bound to reflect negatively on the peace process,' said Arafat as he headed for talks in Khartoum with the Islamic fundamentalist rulers of Sudan. 'We simply have to wait and see how much.'[11]

Arafat's judgement was correct. As the Bush Administration spent its energies in a forlorn election fight, the Washington negotiations sank into the doldrums – and the occupied territories, as was customary when peace moves were becalmed, were gripped by violence. This time, though, there was a twist as ominous for Arafat as for the Israelis. The more extreme of the violent acts were being carried out by a Palestinian group that was deeply hostile to his ideas of coexistence beside Israel in a Palestinian mini-state. The organisation was called the Islamic Resistance Movement, or Hamas (Zeal). In the Gaza Strip it had become the biggest challenge to the PLO since Arafat became chairman.

On the morning of 13 December 1992, a 29-year-old Israeli border policeman named Nissim Toledano was walking to work through the streets of his home town, Lod, a nondescript extension of Tel Aviv's urban sprawl. Suddenly, he was set upon by masked assailants and manhandled into a car. He was not seen alive again. That night, two similarly masked Palestinians marched into a Red Cross office in the West Bank town of El-Bireh and presented an ultimatum for the release of the Hamas spiritual leader, Sheikh Ahmed Yassin, who was serving a life sentence for manslaughter. If the Israeli authorities refused to comply, Sergeant Toledano would be killed. The statement was accompanied by a police ID card in Toledano's name, and signed by Hamas's 'military wing', the Izzedine Al-Qassam Battalion.

Rabin's response was characteristically direct. Within two days of the discovery of Toledano's body pitted with stab wounds, Israel rounded up 1,600 Palestinians suspected of Hamas connections. Then, after a hurried legal wrangle in its constitutional court, it proceeded to bus a quarter of them in blindfolds across its northern border and dump them in freezing rain and fog on a Lebanese hillside. By pushing some 400 alleged activists, by far the largest group to be expelled at one time in the 25 years since Israel had conquered the West Bank and Gaza, into no-man's-land, Rabin had escalated Israel's struggle with its reluctant Arab subjects to new heights.

It thus seemed all the more puzzling that he insisted his actions were in the cause of peace. 'Today there is before us a chance for making progress towards peace,' he told TV viewers at the height of the crisis. 'As we advance, those who oppose it will try to increase their terror. I therefore call on the public to believe in the army and in the security services, to believe in the chance for peace. You shall see, we shall achieve it.'[12]

The man who liked to deflect hecklers at political rallies by boasting of the number of Arabs he had expelled was still 'marching with both feet'. His message was addressed squarely to his Palestinian adversaries as much as to the Israelis themselves. Co-operate and negotiate, he was telling the majority of Palestinians who supported the PLO rather than the extremists of Hamas. By working together, we could combat the fundamentalist menace.

The message was not lost on Yasser Arafat in Tunis. For some time he had been expressing concern at the growing influence of

Hamas, born out of the worsening economic misery in the territories. He was getting intelligence that the fundamentalists had received substantial financial aid from Iran and Saudi Arabia – according to one report, the Islamic Republic had provided 30 million dollars – for use in building their own network of schools, hospitals and other social facilities. This was galling enough for the PLO leader at a time when his own funding from former Arab benefactors had slowed to a trickle, and his ability to influence events in the territories had shrunk correspondingly. Worse, Hamas's spiralling attacks on Israeli targets and on other Palestinian groups such as his own Fatah movement ran the risk of further destabilising a rocky PLO. In a revealing aside, Arafat accused the Islamists of 'fighting other Palestinians on Tehran's orders'.[13] On the fifth anniversary of the *intifada* in early December, he issued a call for 'effective national unity between all groups and forces fighting the Israeli occupation'.[14]

Arafat's first reaction to the mass deportation was in a similar vein: while urging escalation of the uprising against the 'fascist Israelis', he called on Hamas to join forces and invited its leaders to a meeting. His aim was not to hitch the PLO to some new armed struggle against the Jewish state, but to co-opt the Islamic movement into at least tacitly supporting his diplomacy. 'We have to put our differences aside,' said close aide Yasser Abed Rabbo. 'We are not asking Hamas to change its policies, but we have to deal with this situation in a realistic way.'[15] Nobody was surprised when Arafat's overtures to Hamas ended without agreement: there was a world of difference between the PLO's hard-won mandate for negotiations with Israel and Hamas's demand that it pull out of the Washington talks and declare a *jihad*, or holy war.

Arafat, now in his 64th year, married and at the end of most of his nine lives, was aware of the ironies of his predicament. Indeed, the dilemma had been implicit in all his manoeuvrings of recent years, in all his attempts to move the Palestinian movement away from 'armed struggle' and towards the negotiating table. Now Hamas had adopted the classic guerrilla tactics with which Arafat had made his name thirty years before, and was challenging the established Palestinian leadership as Fatah young Turks had done in the 1960s. The danger was that, if this continued, his control in the territories would slide away – and with it the claim to lead the drive for Palestinian statehood. The alternatives were stark. To align himself with the fundamentalists and other radicals would be to risk losing everything for which he had fought. Yet to rein them in, he simply did not possess the means. Not, that is, unless Israel and the PLO could somehow overcome barriers to direct negotiations.

Such were the calculations beginning to take shape in Arafat's restless mind as he assessed the fallout from the deportations and watched the world gearing up for one of its periodic bursts of manufactured outrage. He would have to tread delicately, seeking to secure international condemnation of Israel's action but doing nothing that might seriously upset the peace talks. His nephew and UN mission chief, Nasser al-Qudwa, was detailed to rail against Israel in the ensuing Security Council debate, and Palestinian participation in the Washington Arab–Israeli negoti- ations was 'suspended', ostensibly until a solution could be found to the issue of the deportees. But that was a holding pattern. *Sotto voce*, the PLO chairman was sending signals that the deportees were a side issue. 'The case of the deportees is important, but we consider the basic issue to be that of Jerusalem,' he told one interviewer. 'It is not a matter of the deportees alone, it is a matter of the Palestinian cause as a whole.'[16] The peace convoy, in other words, must be made to move on, preferably with Arafat himself at the wheel.

The question was: how? The Washington negotiations would scarcely be a promising avenue even when they resumed. In the eight rounds to date, they had done little more than mark time, with Israel proposing five years of limited self-rule in the territories pending agreement on their final status, and the Palestinians constantly seeking assurances on what shape such a final settlement might take. It was a recipe for deadlock. Nor could the US be expected to lend much of a hand: President Bill Clinton, elected the previous November, though committed to persevering with the process set in motion by his predecessor, was a novice.

In Arafat's mind, the Washington talks had another serious flaw: under the negotiating format initiated at the 1991 Madrid peace conference, they did not directly involve him. True, the

Palestinian delegation was careful to refer every topic back to Tunis. Arafat's adviser Nabil Shaath was omnipresent in the wings, so he was able to claim control over the process. But communications were often garbled, delayed or distorted by distance. As Arafat complained, the 'Madrid formula' – devised to spare the embarrassment of an Israeli government not yet prepared to admit it was dealing with the PLO – had become more of a hindrance than a help. To begin to make peace, Arafat needed to talk more directly to his enemies – and vice versa.

So began the saga of Yasser Arafat's secret dealings with Yitzhak Rabin. Like other cases where political enemies have tentatively joined hands, it was founded in a sense of shared self-interest between two old fighters in their twilight years – an Israeli Prime Minister elected on a promise to deliver peace on the one hand, a PLO leader desperate to secure progress of any kind on the other.

In Israel, the genesis itself was a complex affair, requiring unprecedented co-operation between two men – Rabin and Foreign Minister Peres – whose long rivalry for the Labour leadership had scarred their relationship.

Israeli attitudes to Arafat were in any case thawing. Confronted with the alternative of Islamic extremism, Israelis were coming round to the idea that they preferred the devil they knew, but Arafat contributed to the change by becoming somewhat more successful in his efforts to reach out to Israeli public opinion – something he had often attempted but mishandled in the past. After years spent concentrating on the battle for American support, he was beginning to play to a gallery that mattered, inviting leading Israeli journalists for interviews in Tunis and endeavouring to keep his fatal tendency to say different things to different audiences in check.

Arafat saw other indications suggesting a more accommodating Israeli attitude once Rabin took office.

One was the increasing frequency of his (Arafat's) contacts with the Arab members of the Israeli Knesset, sometimes purporting to be conveying messages from the Prime Minister himself. Another emerged in the multilateral talks between Israel and the Arabs, on such practical issues as economic co-operation, that had been set up under the Madrid process to complement the bilateral negotiations in Washington in 1991. For a whole year, the Israelis had adamantly refused to negotiate with any Palestinian from outside the occupied territories, for fear of encouraging discussion of issues they had no intention of addressing, such as the refugee question. Then, in October 1992, Rabin and Peres quietly dropped the condition, permitting 'outsiders' – including senior figures from the PLO – to attend the talks as advisers to the Palestinian delegates.

Though largely unheralded at the time, this was an important step. It materialised at a meeting of the multilateral talks in Paris in October 1992 – appropriately enough in the conference centre where US and Vietnamese officials tried to negotiate an end to the Vietnam War. Israel was coming closer to dealing directly with acknowledged representatives of the PLO. What is more the two sides were talking about basic, practical issues such as how to build confidence and improve economic conditions in the occupied territories. And to assist matters further, the negotiations were being boycotted by Syria and Lebanon, leaving room for the Israelis and Palestinians to make headway without 'spoiling' from other Arab states.

The leader of the PLO negotiating team – pulling the strings from a hotel near the Paris conference centre – was a balding Palestinian banker who, though little used to the limelight of international diplomacy or media attention, had worked for years in the nerve centre of Arafat's organisation. His name was Ahmed Kora'i, his *nom de guerre* Abu Ala'a, and his official title economic adviser to the chairman. In reality, he was the financial czar of 'PLO Inc.' – controller of the investment assets that Arafat had gathered for his Fatah movement over the years. Now, assuming progress could be achieved in negotiations with Israel, Arafat had asked Kora'i to produce an investment plan aimed at effecting a rapid improvement in economic conditions in the occupied territories, and preventing further slippage in his influence there. Kora'i's presence in Paris intrigued the Israelis. A paper he had produced on economic co-operation in the Middle East in the event of peace bore similarities to the vision often rehearsed by Foreign Minister Peres. More to the point, he seemed to have command over what was happening in the negotiations: that could only mean he was speaking with his master's voice. 'Everything had to be passed to Abu Ala'a in a nearby hotel for agreement,' said an Israeli negotiator. 'We had the impression that nothing could move without the PLO.'[17]

Kora'i's role was central for another reason. The PLO's need for funds, already acute after the cut-off of Arab assistance in the Gulf War, was now getting desperate – so much so that in January 1993 Arafat dispatched one of his chief lieutenants, Mahmoud Abbas (Abu Mazen), to Saudi Arabia and the other Gulf states to make a public apology for having supported Saddam Hussein two years before. The response was cool, and in financial terms certainly not adequate to begin to meet the unfulfilled demands piling up in Tunis, not least from the occupied territories themselves. All over the West Bank and Gaza, institutions such as universities, schools, hospitals and newspapers that had previously relied on PLO funding – and generated support for Arafat – were feeling the pinch. Welfare payments to families of refugees and 'martyrs' had become erratic and in many cases stopped altogether.

So deep was the disenchantment seeping through the Palestinian movement that Arafat's financial as well as political management was questioned. Dissident voices at the highest levels of the organisation – men and women who had not taken much interest in the PLO's finances during the preceding quarter-century – demanded that he reverse the cuts.

Small wonder that Arafat was so anxious to find a new political approach in that bleak midwinter of 1992–3. The PLO leader found himself contemplating the real possibility that large parts of the organisation he had spent his life constructing would simply wither for lack of financial sustenance. His best chance of salvaging something from the wreckage lay in the West Bank and Gaza. As Kora'i worked on his development programme for the territories, an extraordinary meeting of minds with Israel began to take shape. In truth, Kora'i's economic modelling was incidental to a wider game.

21. ACCORD

'[Israel and the PLO] agree that it is time to put an end to decades of confrontation and conflict, recognise their mutual legitimate and political rights . . . and achieve a just, lasting and comprehensive peace settlement.' Oslo Accord, September 13, 1993

The catalyst of the Process was a young Norwegian social scientist, Terje Rod Larsen, whose Oslo research institute was likewise examining economic conditions in the territories. He had got to know a number of senior PLO officials including Ahmed Kora'i, and, in Israel, a doveish Labour politician named Yossi Beilin. In the Rabin government that took power in July 1992, Beilin became Deputy Foreign Minister, and soon afterwards Larsen came calling with a proposal from PLO headquarters. He was in a position, he said, to put the new government in contact with senior Palestinians who wanted to discuss a peace agreement with Israel. Beilin was intrigued but sceptical. The government was not yet ready to plunge into direct talks with the PLO. But he suggested that Larsen stay in touch with a history professor friend of his, Yair Hirschfeld of Haifa University, who would keep him informed. Then, on September 1992, Larsen came calling again, this time in the company of a senior Norwegian diplomat, State Secretary Jan Egeland. Sitting with Beilin and Hirschfeld at the Tel Aviv Hilton, they amplified the proposal: Norway could act as a 'facilitator' for talks between Israeli and PLO representatives, in secret, away from the bright lights and rhetoric of the Washington negotiations. Beilin, still operating at arm's length, suggested that Hirschfeld give it a try.[1]

One morning in December Hirschfeld met Larsen for breakfast at a hotel in London's West End. After a brief exchange, Larsen departed. Into his place slipped Yasser Arafat's personal representative, Ahmed Kora'i. Strictly speaking, Hirschfeld was breaking the law. Israel's ban on contacts with the PLO was still in place, though the Knesset was already debating its repeal.

This was the moment at which the two sides began to do serious business. The breakfast meeting broke the logjam. On 19

January 1993, the Knesset finally rolled back the taboo on contacts with the PLO. The next day, Hirschfeld and Kora'i gathered with Larsen and Norwegian Foreign Minister Johan Joergen Holst – a man who had developed a cordial relationship with Arafat in the late 1970s in Lebanon – on a secluded country estate sixty miles east of Oslo. The 'Norway channel' was formally open.

Yasser Arafat, through his point man Kora'i, was back in the game of Middle East peacemaking, though none but his closest advisers knew it at the time. This explained his ebullience when, on the second day of the Norwegian talks, he made an extraordinary 'live' intervention by phone on an Israeli TV programme. 'I repeat my call to Mr Rabin and his government to convene a meeting of the brave to forge a peace of the brave,' he proclaimed from Tunis. That countryside meeting was the first of fourteen Israel–Palestinian sessions in Norway over the ensuing months. They took place in an ever-changing variety of secret locations and in unusually intimate circumstances, surrounded by the Norwegian facilitators' families and lubricated by food and drink. Participants used code names for their superiors: Peres and Holst were 'the fathers'; Beilin 'the son'; and Arafat and Rabin, appropriately enough, 'the grandfathers'. Unbeknownst to the official negotiators on both sides, they were making dramatic progress on an outline plan for Palestinian self-rule in the West Bank and Gaza. By April, they had drawn up a 'Declaration of Principles' which the Israelis deemed solid enough to be taken to Foreign Minister Peres and Prime Minister Rabin. Though the latter remained sceptical, the Israeli elders agreed to signal their seriousness by sending a senior official, Foreign Ministry director Uri Savir, to join the talks.[2]

It was the breakthrough Arafat had been looking for ever since he had cajoled the PLO into recognising Israel and accepting a 'two-state solution', back in 1988. For four years, he had been signalling his readiness to engage in dialogue with the Israelis, only to be repeatedly rebuffed by the Shamir government's determination to keep him sidelined.

Now at last he had found a substantial partner to talk to, and a feasible plan to talk about: proposed arrangements for Palestinian autonomy in – and Israeli withdrawal from – parts of the occupied territories, starting with the Gaza Strip and a patch of land around the Jordan Valley town of Jericho. In itself this plan was nothing startlingly new. It built on several blueprints for self-rule that had been advanced in the past, ideas that Arafat had often derided as likely to create South African-style 'Bantustans', reduce Palestinian rights to those of North America's Indians, or even create a territorial map resembling a Swiss cheese. Israel's initial suggestion in the Norway talks had been that it start by withdrawing just from Gaza – an idea calculated to be of greater appeal to an Israeli public opinion tired of ruling over Gaza's violence and squalor than to the PLO. Now, however, Israel was indicating a readiness to talk about pulling out of parts of the West Bank too. Arafat and the closed circle of advisers in Tunis who knew what was afoot worked to build this into a proposal for Israeli withdrawal from West Bank population centres known as 'the leopard spot plan'.[3] So the ideas bounced back and forth between Tunis, Jerusalem and the Norwegian woods and finally came to rest on Gaza and Jericho.

In agreeing to this proposed 'interim arrangement' for five years, Arafat knew he was taking a gamble. Although he had often said over the past two decades that he would be prepared to run up the Palestinian flag on any inch of Palestine, even just the city of Jericho, he was now faced with turning rhetoric into reality. He could scarcely be sure that the Norway channel would lead either to the goal he craved – Israeli recognition of the PLO as a negotiating partner – or, ultimately, to some assurance that the Palestinians would be permitted to pursue their independent state, though he could legitimately argue that the agreement might bring statehood a big step closer. Indeed, the outline Norway deal involved another large concession that he was going to find extremely difficult to sell to his colleagues: for the first two years at least of interim self-rule, it removed the perennially thorny issue of Jerusalem from the negotiating table. In accepting Jericho but leaving Jerusalem to one side for now, Arafat left himself vulnerable to accusations of sellout.

Such sensitivities were among the host of reasons for preserving a shroud of secrecy around the Norway talks. For fear of leaks, Arafat, already deprived of his two most capable and long-serving lieutenants, Khalil al-Wazir and Salah Khalaf, by assassins' bullets in the past five years, kept what was going on from his negotiating team in Washington and even from the PLO's long-serving 'foreign minister', Farouk Kaddoumi. One influential figure who was in the loop and who had been with Arafat in Fatah from the early days was Mahmoud Abbas, alias Abu Mazen, head of the PLO's Arab and international affairs department. Self-effacing, Abbas had been a key player in Arafat's secret overtures to left-wing Israelis over the years, as well as helping to nurture Arafat's Soviet connection; in the late 1970s he completed a doctorate on Israeli affairs at Moscow University. Since Khalaf's death, Arafat had come to rely increasingly on his political advice. Otherwise, though, the chairman retreated further into the company of a small band of like-minded counsellors, several of whom – men like Bassam Abu Sharif and Yasser Abed Rabbo, from the Popular and Democratic Fronts – had joined his team relatively recently and at the expense of breaking with their political roots. Arafat was not the only one who found himself on unsteady terrain.

In the West Bank and Gaza, conditions were hardly propitious for another round of peacemaking. At the end of March, the Israeli authorities – reacting to continuing attacks on Jews – sealed off the territories, barring 120,000 Palestinian labourers indefinitely from going to work in Israel. In retrospect, this, too, was something of a psychological turning point. Once again, Rabin was resorting to extreme measures to stamp on unrest and reassure Israelis on the security front, as well as putting the economic squeeze on an Arab population already suffering considerable hardship from the curtailment of PLO funds. But in a curious way he was also laying the groundwork for the political breakthrough that was to follow. In preventing Palestinians from leaving the territories for a prolonged period, he both provided a vivid demonstration of their dependence on Israel and subtly reinstated the 'green line' that had separated Jews and Arabs before the 1967 war and which had been gradually eroding ever since. Rabin himself was in no doubt that his springtime clampdown was the vital precursor to reaching agreement with the PLO. 'Without it I couldn't have gone where we are going,' he said the following September.[4]

If Rabin's intention had been to send a message to Tunis, he succeeded. By May, Arafat was ready to begin the endgame. That month saw another round of negotiations in Washington between the official Palestinian and Israeli delegations. This round was even more fruitless than its predecessors. The Israelis realised instantly what was going on: Arafat himself had brought things to a halt to force some sort of closure through the Norway channel. 'By the tenth round, everything was completely blocked,' said one official. 'And we knew exactly who was behind it.'[5]

The failure of that meeting finally convinced Rabin of a truth that Arafat had been energetically trying to convey to him for nearly a year: the 'Madrid formula' keeping the PLO away from the negotiating table was past its sell-by date. 'We tried negotiating with the Palestinians from the occupied territories and we found more and more that they were just messengers,' he observed later. 'They had no influence at all in what they said in the meetings.'[6] That discovery left Rabin facing a choice: 'We came to the conclusion that among the Palestinians we can either talk to the PLO and its supporters who favour an agreement, or to Hamas, which opposes one, or remain in the current situation because there is no other partner.'[7] The conclusion was obvious.

Days later, Arafat put his own spin on the state of play. He summoned European ambassadors to his headquarters, complained he was under pressure to discuss a US–Israeli blueprint for autonomy, and warned that the peace talks were in jeopardy because of 'Israeli intransigence and American bias'.[8] What he did not tell them was that, through his secret Norwegian talks, he was doing just what the Israelis wanted.

Many of the building blocks were in place. The edifice, however, was still far from secure. It was in danger of being toppled by premature publicity and nearly did, when word of the Norway channel leaked to an Israeli newspaper in mid-July. Caught unawares, Arafat initially appeared to confirm its existence only to retract his statement the next day.[9] The danger could only grow as both sides broadened their contacts in order to check that what was being said in Norway corresponded to their leaders' true positions. Over the next two months, there were at least three such meetings in Cairo and Jerusalem between Israeli officials and cabinet ministers on the one hand and top Arafat advisers on the other. Then there were still sizeable problems of substance. Who, for example, would control the Allenby Bridge across the Jordan River once Israeli troops had withdrawn from Jericho? And precisely how were the two Palestinian enclaves in Gaza and the West Bank to be linked? The talks nearly collapsed in July over the latter question, with Arafat demanding the establishment of what he quaintly called a 'kissing point' between the two. Finally, there lay ahead the thorny but for Arafat most vital question of all: the agreement he desired on mutual recognition between Israel and the PLO.

By the end of the month, most details of the autonomy deal had been ironed out. Arafat was ready to break cover. He did so with characteristic sleight of hand. During a visit to the region by US Secretary of State Warren Christopher in early August, the PLO leader suddenly intervened over the heads of his own negotiators. An hour before they were due to meet the American, he faxed them a document with instructions to hand it on. As they read it through, the negotiators were astonished to see that it bore little resemblance to the PLO position that they had steadfastly been defending for months in the Washington talks, but contained major concessions to Israel on the issue of Jerusalem and the scope of Palestinian self-rule, and suggested that the Gaza Strip and Jericho would be a useful starting point for implementation of any agreement. What they were reading was the deal cooked up by Arafat's men and the Israelis in the Norway channel.[10]

The events that followed can only be described as political pantomime as the three top Palestinian negotiators trooped off to Tunis, purportedly threatening to resign over the concessions Arafat had offered behind their backs. For days they were locked in meetings with Arafat and his colleagues. The world's press indulged in a surfeit of speculation about alleged splits between the Palestinians in the occupied territories and the PLO outside. Such comment was wide of the mark. Arafat may have acted without their knowledge, his concessions may have been hard to stomach, but there was no doubt that the negotiators, chief among them Faisal al-Husseini, would toe the line, and return to sell the deal in the territories. At the end of it, they emerged as fully fledged members of the PLO leadership. Significantly, Israel raised no objection and, with that, Arafat was on the home straight to securing what he had been after in return for the autonomy deal: Israeli recognition as a negotiating partner.

On 19 August 1993, Shimon Peres turned up in Oslo for what was billed as a routine official visit. After dinner that night, he was whisked to a government guesthouse. Waiting for him there were Ahmed Kora'i and a document setting out the autonomy agreement reached through the Norway channel. In Peres's presence, Kora'i and Israeli Foreign Ministry Chief Uri Savir sat down to sign.

The deal, still ostensibly secret, did not remain so for long. Already talk of Arafat's concessions was spreading dismay in the PLO's upper echelons. Scarcely was the ink dry in Oslo when a succession of important figures in the organisation from Arafat's favourite poet, Executive Committee member Mahmoud Darwish, to the veteran PLO representative in Lebanon, Shafik al-Hout, tendered their resignations, while in the Syrian capital Damascus, home of Arafat's left-wing rivals, criticism was spreading like the plague.

To Arafat's opponents, even for supporters, it looked like the final capitulation. 'Ever since the negotiations started, all they have gained so far is God knows how many people killed, how many people wounded, how many homes demolished, how many new settlements established and how many people deported,' complained Shafik al-Hout from Beirut. 'The perception of the people is: "The leadership is giving concessions, so where's the reward?" '[11] Arafat, said Darwish, was 'taking uncalculated political risks. I don't want to be a witness and a collaborator in this downfall.'[12] In Damascus, George Habash and Nayef Hawatmeh forecast that the deal would fail, and that Arafat and his acolytes would pay the price.[13]

The atmosphere was not improved by the state of decay in which the PLO found itself. Staff were being laid off in their thousands (in one celebrated example, Arafat had sent hundreds of white-collar workers off to cool their heels in a Libyan military camp); guerrilla fighters stationed in the Arab countries had not been paid their salaries for seven months; education and health services in the refugee camps faltered; and, in August, four of the PLO's most important departments, those dealing with information, culture, social affairs and 'returnees', were simply closed down.[14]

By the time the PLO Executive Committee gathered in Tunis to review the draft accord with Israel on the night of 26 August, criticism was in full spate, with influential voices calling for a full debate in the PLO's parliament, the Palestine National Council. But Arafat played his cards skilfully. He knew that the financial crisis, which may not have been quite as grave in reality as he was allowing everybody else to say, would concentrate minds on the serious business in hand, and that the PNC could not convene for lack of a suitable Arab venue. He also knew, as even many of his critics were prepared in their hearts to concede, that there was little alternative to the course of action he proposed. It was this awareness, coupled with the fact that his opponents were themselves divided, that deprived the ensuing ritual demands for his resignation of much of their bite. There were dangers, to be sure: not least the threat from splinter groups in Damascus that the PLO chairman would be assassinated. But in political argument, Arafat held the ace: the prediction that, whatever the Israelis might say about the deal at this stage, it stood a chance of marking a concrete step on the road to a Palestinian state. The critics, he declared loftily, were trying 'to belittle this historic achievement'. The PLO and Israel would reach a 'just and comprehensive peace that will take account of the Palestinian people's political rights.'[15] Before long the Palestinian flag would be fluttering from the minarets of Jerusalem.

Armed with such arguments and with the backing of his Fatah movement's Central Committee, Arafat took off on a tour of Arab capitals to enlist support for the deal.

In his wilderness years, shunned in so many parts of the Arab world, he had been prevented from indulging his penchant for diplomacy. Now he took to it again with gusto: he beamed his way through frosty audiences with Hafez al-Assad of Syria and Jordan's King Hussein, both fuming at the fact that Arafat had not deigned to consult them on his separate deal with Israel; he returned to Cairo and to the embrace of President Hosni Mubarak; he inveigled his way back to the Gulf, asking Oman's Sultan Qaboos to secure forgiveness for the PLO and funding to underpin his Palestinian proto-state.

All the while, the back channel with Israel was churning away in Norway and in Paris, where the French Government, miffed at its exclusion from the action so far, was anxious to put its seal on proceedings – to put the final touches to a mutual recognition accord. For Arafat, this was the most important barrier to surmount and, to do so, he was going to have to get his Executive Committee to meet apparently unthinkable Israeli demands: that it agree to suspend large chunks of the PLO's precious founding charter and call on Palestinians in the occupied territories to end the *intifada*.

By 5 p.m. on 8 September 1993, as Savir and Kora'i continued to haggle in a Parisian hotel over the wording in which Israel and the PLO were to proclaim peace (at least for the moment), Arafat was back in Tunis and ready to leap the final hurdle. He had not slept in two nights, but was euphoric as he bantered with Israeli journalists and with his wife Suha, before speeding off to join bleary-eyed colleagues in the flat-roofed concrete villa where they had been awaiting his arrival. Events were moving fast. Johan Joergen Holst, the Norwegian Foreign Minister, was coming to witness Arafat's signing of a historic letter recognising Israel. In Washington, preparations were under way for a full-dress ceremony on the White House lawn at which the Prime Minister of Israel and chairman of the PLO would meet for the first time.

What remained was for Arafat to secure the backing of his Executive Committee, and this was not a done deal. Five members of the eighteen-strong Executive Committee were missing, having either resigned or decided to boycott the meeting. Five more, principal among them Kaddoumi, the 'foreign minister', were bitterly opposed. For eight hours, with a telephone line open to Kora'i in Paris, Arafat kept his colleagues at the conference table, chipping away at the resistance of the floating voters in their midst. As debate wore through the night and into the next day, the 'No' camp resisted. How could Arafat call for suspension of the *intifada* and revision of the charter? complained Kaddoumi. It was tantamount to abandoning the PLO's 'basic commitment' to keep up the struggle until Palestine was liberated. So what alternative did Kaddoumi propose? countered Arafat. The Israelis might not be offering much but if the PLO did not accept, it would get nothing at all and the offer might be gone for good.

That was the clincher. The chairman got his way, though by a finer margin than he might have wished – a vote of eight to four with one abstention was scarcely unanimous, as the critics pointed out in ensuing months. Satisfied nonetheless, he hurried off to meet Holst, who was waiting to carry a letter to Jerusalem and to receive a separate document pledging to urge Palestinians in the West Bank and Gaza to cease violence. At a quarter to midnight on 9 September, an elated Arafat emerged to meet the world's press. 'I have signed. I have signed the letter,' he exclaimed.

The next morning, 2,000 kilometres across the Mediterranean, Holst extracted the letter from his briefcase and handed it to Yitzhak Rabin. At a ceremony in his office, the Israeli Prime Minister carefully read the four pages, took out a plastic pen, and signed his reply. The deed was done. Arafat and Rabin were bound for Washington. The following Monday, 13 September 1993, the two men stood alone with President Bill Clinton in the Blue Room of the White House. They looked each other in the eye, and Rabin broke the silence. 'You know, we are going to have to work very hard to make this work,' he said in a low growl. 'I know,' replied Arafat. 'And I am prepared to do my part.' Neither of them in that euphoric moment, whatever their individual misgivings, could have anticipated the difficulties involved, or in Rabin's case the price he would obliged to pay.

22. BODY-BLOW

'Violence is undermining the very foundations of Israeli democracy. It must be condemned, denounced and isolated.' Yitzhak Rabin, Peace Rally, Tel Aviv, 4 November 1995.

The time in Tel Aviv when Yitzhak Rabin finished speaking was around 9 p.m. and a good-natured overflowing crowd in the city's central Malkhei Yisrael square showed its appreciation by chanting his name, and that of his Foreign Minister Shimon Peres. But within a very short time those chants turned to anguished screams. At 9.47 p.m. on 4 November, Yigal Amir, a young man infected by hatred of peace efforts with the Palestinians, fired three shots at Rabin in the back from a silenced pistol, wounding him fatally, and in the process dealing what was to prove a body-blow to overall efforts to achieve peace and build confidence between Israelis and Palestinians. It may not have been clear at the time, but Rabin's death was to prove devastating for the peace camp on both sides. A motley political alignment, from the remnants of the fanatical Kach movement of the late Rabbi Meir Kahane to ultra-nationalist supporters of Likud leader Benjamin Netanyahu, had reaped their reward after weeks and months of agitation in which Rabin was accused of being a traitor, and even lampooned on a poster in an SS uniform at a rally at which Netanyahu spoke. Little wonder that Rabin's widow Leah could barely bring herself to acknowledge Netanyahu at her late husband's funeral.[1]

In the Gaza Strip, Yasser Arafat, who had been entertaining the visiting Portuguese President Mario Soares, first heard the news that Rabin had been shot (although at that early stage it was not known how seriously) as he was accompanying Soares to a guest-house the Palestinians were using for visiting dignitaries. Marwan Kanafani, Arafat's press spokesman who was with the chairman, said that while Soares retired to bed upstairs Arafat was constantly on the phone seeking details of what happened. When he finally learned of Rabin's demise he wept.[2] Arafat then returned to his office to call Shimon Peres to express his condolences, but even then at that early stage and in spite of Peres' commitment to peace

Arafat was beginning to understand the dimensions of the tragedy. Rabin was irreplaceable. As Kanafani observed, 'Rabin changed a lot as he gained a better understanding of our position and problems. He had a much better rapport with Arafat towards the end.'[3] For safety reasons, the Palestinian leader was not invited to the funeral, attended by US President Bill Clinton and many other world leaders – Ahmed Kora'i, the architect of Oslo, led the Palestinian delegation – but he did visit Rabin's widow at the end of the seven days of mourning. Arafat was pictured, bald-headed without his *keffiyeh* sitting with Mrs Rabin in the couple's Tel Aviv apartment. It was one of the sadder images of an intensely emotional period which had followed a roller-coaster two years since September 1993 during which the two sides sought to put flesh on the bones of Oslo.

Just two weeks after the signing of the Oslo Declaration of Principles on 13 September 1993 Nabil Shaath, Arafat's trusted adviser, found himself in the Egyptian resort town of Taba across the border from the Israeli holiday playground of Eilat sitting opposite Israeli Defence Forces Deputy Chief of Staff Amnon Shahak, who had been chosen by Rabin to head the Israeli negotiating team. The choice of Shahak, a veteran military commander and close associate of Rabin himself, underlined at that early stage Israel's main preoccupation: security. Shaath found himself in the awkward position of both facing a man across the table who had Palestinian blood on his hands (Shahak had been one of commandos who had killed Palestinian leaders including Shaath's friend Kamal Adwan in the vengeance raid on Beirut in 1973 for the Munich Olympic Games massacre) and also – not being entirely comfortable with the brief he had been handed – turned the Oslo-negotiated Declaration of Principles into an agreement, in other words 'Oslo 1'. But Shaath, in spite of reservations, particularly on such issues as settlements (there was no undertaking to dismantle them even in Gaza), and with no guarantees about Jerusalem in the interim period, threw himself into the negotiations. As he put it, quoting Arafat: 'It was the least of all evils. While there might have been a million reasons to reject the agreement there was one compelling reason to accept it, and that was that it gave us a chance to head back home and build a state in Palestine and not in Lebanon.'[4] Arafat meanwhile had set off on his perambulations around the Arab world, visiting Jordan (twice) in an effort to enlist the support of King Hussein who was complaining privately that what the PLO had agreed to in Oslo was less than he had achieved in his private understandings in secret meetings with Israeli leaders over the year, including Rabin himself. Arafat also went to Syria where Syrian President Hafez al-Assad was making no secret of his displeasure. Indeed, in a long demarche on 1 October he gave voice to his irritation, reflecting long years of frustration with Arafat and Palestinians. 'The PLO was the Arab party pressing most for co-ordination among Arab parties. We have also stood for co-ordination, because we thought intra-Arab co-ordination could propel the peace process forwards towards its objective and firm up the steps leading in that direction . . . Thus, the Arabs moved in tandem towards a common objective. All of a sudden, we hear that a secret agreement was reached between some PLO members and Israel. It turns out that the agreement was worked out in many months of secret negotiations when, meanwhile, Arab states were meeting at levels I have noted. The Palestinian side was engaged in talks with Israel, without the co-ordination it had pressed for. To my mind, this is not the best option, nor the best route to the establishment of peace. Yet, we decided not to obstruct the agreement. We said this is up to the Palestinian people and their organisations. However, no one should expect us to wax enthusiastic over a secret agreement concluded behind our backs.'[5]

While Hafez al-Assad may not have campaigned overtly against the agreement sanctioned by Arafat, there were plenty of others who did, including dissident Palestinian groups in Damascus and in Lebanon (the home of the bulk of the refugees who feared they would be disenfranchised) to what was probably more immediately worrisome – the Islamists in the West Bank and Gaza who were flying a number of different flags, including Hamas, Hezbollah and Islamic Jihad. Apart from the poet Mahmoud Darwish, Arafat loyalists like the veteran Hani al-Hassan voiced their objections, speaking on behalf of the '1948 exiles'.

In an interview with *Mideast Mirror* on 9 October, just three weeks after Washington, al-Hassan described the agreement as tantamount to striking the refugee issue off the agenda once and for all. 'That is why we, the 1948 exiles, categorically reject what is happening. The PLO leaders who concluded the deal with Israel have all but buried the refugees' right of return.' He added, 'It is true that we will get a handful of billions of dollars and that we will build power stations in Gaza and a sewage system on the West Bank. But this is not what the PLO is about.'[6]

To these dissident voices from the broader Palestinian Diaspora, leaders from the inside, from the West Bank and Gaza Strip, added their thoughts in what was to prove a prophetic but ultimately futile attempt to persuade Arafat and his Tunis-exile leadership clique of the pitfalls ahead. After all, the internal leadership, as they were known, had lived with the grinding reality of Israeli occupation for the previous 26 years day in, day out, and some of them such as Faisal Husseini, Arafat's man in Jerusalem, had spent time in jail. But if Arafat and his cronies were predisposed to listen there was little sign of it, intoxicated as they were by dreams of raising the flag of Palestine over Jerusalem within a few short months, ignoring realities on the ground. In November 1993, Palestinian notables from Jerusalem, the West Bank and Gaza made what was to prove one of their last gestures as a group, to explain these realities before the Arafatists. Like a plague of locusts, they returned to the Gaza Strip and Jericho in mid-1994 under the terms of the Cairo Accord, in effect Oslo 1, which was signed on 4 May 1994 in the Egyptian capital. The document, forwarded to Arafat and members of the PLO Executive Committee just two months after the signing of the Declaration of Principles on the White House lawn, bears exposure because, in light of all the disasters which were to ensue, including the shambolic nature of the administration over which Arafat would preside as the first head of what was to become known as the Palestinian Authority, it was extraordinarily prophetic.

In an acidic memorandum, the internal leadership made four very specific complaints, and a list of nine demands, most of which were subsequently honoured in the breach. Complaint number one proved especially prescient in view of what happened subsequently. 'We are not satisfied with the political leadership's method of work at this stage ... the political leadership is practising its role in a manner that is close to improvisation.' Complaints and demands continued in this vein, making clear the deep and, as it turned out, entirely justified scepticism harboured by Palestinians in the occupied territories about the quality, or lack of it, of the so-called leadership which was about to descend upon them.

But if Arafat was fazed by these sorts of criticisms, or the fact that negotiations aimed at consolidating ideas incorporated in the Oslo Declaration of Principles were floundering, he did not show it, as he continued a dizzy round of largely meaningless consultations with supporters and critics of Oslo alike. He did begin a series of meetings with Israeli leaders, including Rabin and Peres, aimed as much at building confidence as breaking the log jams that inevitably arose in the difficult negotiations upon which Shaath had embarked in Taba with Amnon Shahak on 13 October. Arafat had met Rabin in Cairo on 6 October as a prelude to the beginning of the Taba negotiations during which the Israeli leader emphasised – and re-emphasised – the security issue as the key test for the Palestinians in the first of many lectures on the subject. Not surprisingly, the Taba negotiations were bogged down on issues of security for the enclaves of Gaza and Jericho over which the Palestinians were about to assume control under Oslo, with the Palestinian side demanding autonomy and the Israelis insisting on retaining a presence in Gaza itself to protect Jewish settlements there. Sharp and fundamental differences also quickly emerged on control of border passages from Gaza to Egypt and from the Jericho enclave to Jordan, prompting Arafat to voice one of his well-worn complaints that Israel's obsessions about security would lead to the creation of Palestinian Bantustans, a reference to the tribal enclaves of the former Apartheid regime in South Africa.[9]

A low point was a meeting with Rabin in Cairo on 13 December when the two men were left alone for the first time by Egyptian President Hosni Mubarak, the convener of the gathering. A gulf quickly developed over security issues, which were left unresolved, principally on the question of which side would control the border crossings, something that was non-negotiable as far as Rabin was concerned.[10] Meanwhile, discussions between the Palestinian and Israeli negotiating teams staggered on with political pressures on the two sides pulling them apart. One memorable exchange between Shaath and Shahak summed up the divergence. 'Amnon, you see everything only in terms of immediate need and never consider the long-term ramifications,' said Shaath. 'Nabil, if there is terrorism, there won't be any long-term to worry about,' Shahak responded.[11] This was the tone of the discussions which continued until 20 January when Arafat and Rabin held several meetings in Oslo, where they were attending the funeral of former Norwegian Foreign Minister Johan Jorgen Holst who had played such a key role in laying the groundwork for Israel's recognition of the PLO less than six months before. These discussions, which helped to define areas of agreement and disagreement, paved the way for much more productive negotiations on 28 and 29 January in Davos, at the fringes of the World Economic Forum; and in Cairo between 7 and 9 February when a preliminary agreement on border security was initialled. The stage was being set for one of Arafat's more theatrical performances, namely the signing in Cairo on 4 May of the Cairo Accord.

But even as this difficult *pas de deux* continued between Arafat and Rabin, Israelis and Palestinians, events were taking place in the wider context of Arab–Israel relations which should have set alarm bells ringing among the Palestinians. For even as Rabin, ever the strategist marching with both feet, was seeking to press forwards with his negotiations with the Palestinians he was also exploring a parallel track with the Syrians – with American help. In truth, Rabin regarded a breakthrough with the Syrians, with their arsenal of short-range missiles aimed at Israeli population centres, as almost more pressing than agreement with the Palestinians themselves. Thus, in his inaugural address to the Knesset on 13 July 1992 on being elected Prime Minister, Rabin had referred to uttered these words: 'I call on the leaders of the Arab countries to follow in the footsteps of Egypt and its presidents, to make the move that will bring peace to us and them. I invite the King of Jordan and the Syrian and Lebanese Presidents to come here to this podium, here in Israel's Knesset in Jerusalem, and talk peace. I am willing to travel today, tomorrow, to Amman, Damascus, Beirut on behalf of peace, because there is no greater triumph than the triumph of peace.' Syrian leader Hafez Al-Assad's response to this sort of blandishment was his standard demand that Israel return the Golan Heights in their entirety and dismantle settlements there. In exchange he would end the 'state of war'. And so there the matter rested until President Bill Clinton met Assad in Geneva on 16 January to seek to tease from the canny Syrian leader some sense of what gestures might be possible towards an agreement which might mirror that between Israel and Egypt in Camp David 1. In the event, Clinton got little from Assad beyond an agreement to engage in serious exploration of possibilities based on cautious public indications from Rabin that a return of the Golan Heights might be possible under certain conditions aimed at ensuring Israeli security. It was on the basis of these winks and nods that US Secretary of State Warren Christopher, following the Clinton–Assad Geneva summit, shuttled between Israel and Damascus from 18–21 July, and again in August and October, the latter in preparation for a visit by Clinton himself to Damascus on 27 October following the signing of the Jordan–Israel peace treaty the previous day. This presaged further intense diplomacy, including visits by Rabin to Washington and Christopher to Damascus before the end of 1994, during which discussions began to focus on what security arrangements might apply in the event of a possible framework agreement.[13]

But in fact the Syrian track, as it was known, proved a serious distraction from attempts to flesh out Oslo, absorbing American diplomatic energy and distracting Rabin from what should have been the main game – corraling the Palestinians into workable arrangements for a lasting peace and not allowing too much time to elapse before the rot set in within territories under Arafat's control, as inevitably would be the case, with corruption, mismanagement and malfeasance taking root. All this against a background of continued fundamentalist insurgency, only barely – and temporarily – suppressed by the new facts on the ground. The Palestinians themselves were slow to recognise the dangers of the Syrian distraction, but Shaath observed that energy dissipated by US and Israeli efforts on the Damascus connection throughout 1994 had been unhelpful, especially since it underlined Rabin's own hesitations about peace with the Palestinians. 'It was like Rabin was trying to have a bet each way, not sure about us and hoping at the same time to use the Syrian track to forge a more comprehensive Middle East peace, which was always his aim,' said Shaath.[14]

Two weeks after the Palestinians and Israelis initialled their preliminary agreement on security arrangements for Gaza and the Jericho enclave, a terrible event would take place which would throw into the starkest possible relief all the problems, all the hatreds, all the toxic prejudice that stood at the heart of the conflict between Arab and Jew, like a boil waiting to be lanced. On the morning of 25 February, Baruch Goldstein, a medical doctor born and raised in Brooklyn, a member of late Rabbi Kahane's extremist Kach movement and resident of Kiryat Arba, the Jewish settlement overlooking Hebron, slunk into the Ibrahimi mosque in the city centre while the faithful were performing their dawn prayers and began firing into the crowd, methodically reloading his automatic weapon, until 29 of the worshippers were dead. Goldstein himself was set upon and killed by an enraged mob, but not before his action had further stained in the most dramatic way possible an already bloody tableau. Needless to say, the Hebron massacre formed a sickening punctuation mark to delicate peace negotiations in which security from terrorism for Israelis was a constant sticking point. Instead it was Palestinians who had been massacred by an Israeli terrorist operating in a secure area which was supposedly under the guard of Israel's defence forces. In hindsight, the slaughter might be regarded as the moment when the real challenge to both leaderships became apparent. It might also have been the occasion when chances of failure in the joint peace enterprise outweighed the possibility of success. Arafat, in Tunis, expressed his anguish and refused to receive phone calls from Rabin, saying, 'I will not speak to him, not while my people are being massacred.'[15] But in reality, Arafat's options were limited. While the PLO's Executive Committee resolved on 1 March to suspend the peace negotiations, this was largely a symbolic protest. The Palestinians managed to get the UN Security Council to condemn the massacre in Resolution 904 which also called for the stationing of unarmed UN observers in Hebron – a small step towards what had always been a Palestinian aim of getting the UN more involved in the occupied territories. The US abstained, after initially threatening to veto the resolution unless Arafat agreed to return to peace talks. There followed what can only be described as a dance of several veils as Israeli delegations of increasing seniority were despatched to Tunis to persuade Arafat to return to the negotiating table, during which the Israelis were treated to the chairman's theatrical repertoire, from hurt and apoplexy to rage. At one point Arafat outdid himself when the Israelis suggested an enlargement of Red Cross units on the ground in Hebron to guard against a repeat of what had happened. 'The Red Cross! The Red Cross! What do you want to do? Bring in nurses to give people injections? I can't be hearing this right. They're burning my portrait in the streets of Hebron, and the Israelis are talking about injections . . . Unbelievable!'[16] In truth, these histrionics were a diversion: Arafat wanted to get back to the table to complete negotiations on Gaza and Jericho as soon as possible to show that he had something tangible for his people for the concessions made in Oslo. Swelling frustration among Palestinians was underscored by two very early suicide bombings – on 6 April when a bomber blew up a bus near Afula, south of Tel Aviv, killing eight people, and then on 13 April when six people were killed in a blast in Tel Aviv. Both events were a portent of much worse to come.

The mood was expectant when on 3 May Arafat, Rabin, Peres, US Secretary of State Christopher, Egyptian Foreign Minister Amr Moussa, Dennis Ross, the US special envoy to the Middle East, and heads of the respective negotiating teams, Shaath and Shahak, gathered in the commodious Cairo office of Egyptian President Hosni Mubarak to put the finishing touches to the Gaza–Jericho accord, or Oslo 1. Shaath recalls that haggling continued through the night with Mubarak offering fowl and falafel sandwiches with local pickles in a coarse Egyptian bread to the the participants. The buttoned-up Christopher was a particular target for Mubarak's homespun hospitality with frequent encouragement to eat more peasant Egyptian food.[17] Close to exhaustion, the negotiators concluded their work at 4 a.m. with Rabin allowing the Jericho enclave to be increased by six square kilometres and agreeing to an extension of Arafat's civil control in Gaza, but he would not budge on a demand that Palestinian policemen be allowed to stand on the Allenby Bridge, the historic crossing point between the West Bank and Jordan. So, the stage was set for what was to prove one of Arafat's more combustible performances, and one that would not endear him to his host Mubarak or to other participants, including those on his own side. At the signing ceremony in a convention centre in an Egyptian suburb, Arafat balked at initialling maps which confirmed agreements reached about territory to be transferred to Palestinian control and other details worked out in months of painstaking discussion. Arafat claimed he had not seen the maps and was therefore not going to initial them. What he was doing, of course, for the benefit of a television audience, was seeking to appear to be obdurate to the end in the interest of the Palestinians, but his theatricality simply did not wash with those who were with him on the stage. A furious Mubarak corraled Arafat in a corner and demanded that he sign, pointing out that he had indeed agreed to the maps in discussions which had dragged on until the early hours of the morning. Reluctantly, like a virgin playing hard to get, Arafat signed, but not before his behaviour had left a nasty taste in the mouths of participants, including Shaath himself who was deeply hurt, not for the first time, or the last, by his leader's pyrotechnics.[18]

In speeches to the many dignitaries present, plus representatives of the Palestinian, Israeli and international media, Arafat and Rabin invoked the Almighty, not surprisingly given the importance of the occasion. In retrospect, their words make what has happened since seem all the more disappointing. 'One hundred years of the Palestinian–Israeli conflict and millions of people who want to live are watching us. May God be with us,' said Rabin. 'O God, you are peace, peace comes from you, and peace is for you. Blessed are you, God, full of majesty, bounty and honour. Glory to God in the highest, peace on earth and goodwill towards men. Peace be with you,' said Arafat.[19]

What the Cairo Accord achieved, practically speaking, apart from its symbolic importance, was that it both gave nuts and bolts expression to the Oslo Declaration of Principles and, perhaps more important, started the clock ticking on a five-year transitional period leading to talks on the final status of a Palestinian entity which were to begin no later than May 1996, with May 1999 envisaged as the end of the transitional period.[20] The accord also opened the way for Arafat to return to Palestinian territory, after an absence of 27 years, as chairman of the Palestinian Interim Authority, until elections could be held and the establishment of the Palestinian Authority proper. Arafat was about to find a stage, in the full glare of international publicity, commensurate with his theatrical tendencies. He was not to know this would mark something of a high point in his stewardship of the Palestinian movement.

Preparations for Arafat's return to Gaza and the Jericho enclave on 1 July 1994 began almost as soon as the ink was dry on the Cairo Accord, presided over by trusted lieutenants like Shaath who recalls that on 19 May, a 'euphoric day', he entered Gaza from El Arish on the Egyptian side of the border by way of the Rafa checkpoint. Like an Arab Santa Claus, the rotund Shaath was carrying half a million US dollars in two 'huge bags' which he distributed to Palestinian workers.[21] It must have seemed to the destitute of Gaza that the Palestinian leadership, momentarily, represented some sort of cargo cult. Arafat, meanwhile, had travelled to South Africa where he gave a speech in Arabic in a mosque calling for a *Jihad*, or holy war, to reclaim Jerusalem as capital of a Palestinian state. Not for the first time this tendency to say different things to different audiences, speaking out of both sides of the mouth, breathing lies, as his detractors would say, was to get him into hot water with the Israelis and do nothing to engender confidence that he might in the new circumstances be capable of rising to the occasion in a statesman-like manner.

But as a foetid summer settled over the Gaza Strip, finishing touches to arrangements for Arafat's return to a small corner of Palestine went ahead. He travelled on a plane supplied by the president of Tunis to Cairo from where, accompanied by Egyptian President Hosni Mubarak, he flew to El Arish on the Mediterranean, adjacent to Gaza. With Mubarak, Arafat walked to the border crossing at Rafa and was ushered through the gate as Israeli border guards stood aside. At that moment, as the Palestinian leader made the journey from Rafa, past cheering crowds of Palestinians waving the Palestinian ensign and brandishing his picture, it seemed that indeed it would not be long before he was worshipping in the Al Aqsa mosque in Jerusalem, as he had promised Mubarak in an aside as he was farewelled at the border. According to press spokesman Marwan Kanafani, who was with the leader, it took Arafat four hours to traverse the 35 kilometres from Rafa to Gaza City where a makeshift stand had been set up near the main square for his historic address to his people and to a worldwide audience of millions tuned in live via CNN. It was significant that even in those first unscripted words Arafat sought to reach out to the sceptics, principally the Islamic fundamentalists, whose movement had taken deep root in Gaza and who were bitterly opposed to what they regarded as the Oslo 'sellout'. Addressing the families of Palestinian 'martyrs' and those who were prisoners, including 'my brother Ahmed Yassin' (Yassin, the spiritual leader of Hamas, was serving a life sentence for incitement to kill Israelis), Arafat vowed: 'We have promised our martyrs that we will pray in Jerusalem.' He also did not neglect to remind his Palestinian audience that 'we have a big mission ahead of us; a big mission to build this homeland; to build our institutions, and to rebuild the institutions that Israeli occupation destroyed.'[22] It was not clear, however, whether Arafat himself understood the dimensions of the task ahead of him, still less recognised his own limitations. But within a week or so of his historic address in Gaza City Arafat was to be reminded brutally of the difficulties ahead. Kanafani recalls travelling with Arafat by Egyptian-supplied helicopter from Gaza to Jericho in early July on a flight path which took them north towards Tel Aviv and then east towards the Jericho enclave. It was Arafat's opportunity to study from the air what he had to that point only been made aware of in one-dimensional maps, namely settlements. According to Kanafani, Arafat was 'astonished' by what he saw from his vantage point above the ground, including the Jewish settlements ringing Jerusalem, which appeared to him more like 'fortresses and castles' clinging to hilltops than housing clusters.[23] At that moment, it is reasonable to speculate that the Palestinian leader may have regretted not insisting in the Oslo process on tougher wording restricting the spread or 'thickening' of settlements, and the creation of new outposts. Apart from the settlements issue, Arafat at that early stage was also becoming aware of the challenges he faced in persuading a sceptical donor community, including his brother Arabs who had still not forgiven him for his support of Saddam Hussein, to provide the wherewithal for his putative Palestinian state. After a symbolic meeting in Gaza on 2 July of the executive of the Palestinian Interim Authority, Arafat complained of donors' miserly attitude which he described as just 'promises, promises, promises'.[24]

After the euphoria engendered by Arafat's return to Taba under the terms of the Cairo Accord subsided, the Palestinians and Israel took a breather – although the need to maintain the momentum of peace efforts was never really absent from the minds of senior Israelis and Palestinians. But in truth the cautious Rabin wanted to see how the Palestinians handled their new responsibilities for actually beginning to administer territory under their control, as opposed to mouthing slogans at a distance. The first weeks and months, after Arafat's return, were not particularly encouraging for the Israelis who could not help noticing that, in spite of undertakings by Arafat himself and senior colleagues to rein in the Islamic fundamentalists and assert control, little or nothing effective was done to that end despite a presence on the ground of some 9,000 Palestinian 'policemen'. It was also during this time that security services, actually militias, began to proliferate in a worrying echo of what had happened in Beirut in the 1970s. Human rights abuses also became commonplace in an early sign that the so-called rule of law would be honoured in the breach, more often than not. People like the prominent Gaza psychiatrist Eyad el Serraj, who had been co-opted as a human rights ombudsman, found very quickly that heavy-handed security measures were the norm, rather than the exception. El Serraj himself was subjected to mistreatment by the security apparatus after pursuing cases of abuse. Embittered now by his experience, he, like many other professionals in Gaza and the West Bank, withdrew from active engagement in the Palestinian enterprise and is one among many whose criticism of Arafat himself is toxic. 'It was as if they [the Tunis leadership] learned nothing in all their years of exile,' he said.[25] Rabin himself, in a 10 August meeting with Arafat on the boundary between Gaza and Israel proper, issued one of many warnings about the risks of failing to deal forcefully with Islamic extremists. 'This is your test,' Rabin said. To all intents and purposes it fell on deaf ears.

But as the year drew to a close and Palestinian and Israeli negotiators led by Shaath and Shahak continued their painstaking task of negotiating an agreement dealing with the West Bank, infinitely more complex than that relating to Gaza and Jericho, a formal peace agreement was reached between Israel and Jordan which involved some minor territorial adjustments. The signing took place on 27 October at the new crossing point between the Red Sea towns of Aqaba and Eilat. Rabin and King Hussein initialled the document with President Bill Clinton looking on. It ran to just twenty articles, a reflection of the relatively straightforward nature of the issues involved.[26] Arafat was not present. As Uri Savir, then head of the Israeli Foreign Ministry, commented, 'Yasser Arafat had not been invited to attend the occasion because of Rabin's and Hussein's personal aversion to him, though it was absolutely clear that the peace being celebrated at the Aqaba crossing would not have been signed had it not been for the Oslo breakthrough.'[27]

Before the year was out Arafat, Rabin and Peres would be buoyed with the news they had been awarded, jointly, the Nobel Peace Prize. They were on hand to receive the award and in separate speeches made eloquent statements about the need to complete unfinished business. 'We have covered only a short distance. We should have the courage and move as fast as possible to cover the greater distance based on just and comprehensive peace and to absorb the strength of creativity which is contained in the deeper lesson of peace,' said Arafat.[28] The awarding of the Nobel to Arafat was criticised at the time as being premature, and so it proved.

As the inevitable teething troubles spread and deepened in Gaza, Arafat would receive a gift on a personal level that many had not believed likely. In June, Suha Arafat gave birth to a daughter in Paris who was named Zahwa, after her paternal grandmother who had died young in Cairo. Arafat was certainly not a conventional father. In any case he and Suha had begun drifting apart before Zahwa was born. His nomadic life, and his obsessive-ness with the detail of running the Palestinian movement, simply left no time for family. He had many things on his mind as the humid summer deepened in Gaza, not least the need to complete negotiations on the West Bank agreement before the year was out: indeed, by a notional deadline of 13 September, the anniversary of the signing of the Oslo Declaration of Principles, just a giddy two years before. On 10 August, Arafat, who had involved himself more deeply in Oslo 2 than Oslo 1 in secret communication with Peres outside the formal negotiating channel, met Israel's Foreign Minister in Taba in an effort to settle outstanding differences, especially over the timing of Israel's withdrawl from most of the West Bank. Naturally, the Palestinians wanted it sooner rather than later. Hebron, with its decades of festering animosity, with its religious sites, sacred to Muslim and Arabs, with its toxic recent memory of the massacre of Palestinians at worship, was the main sticking point. A compromise was proposed under which the Palestinians would maintain a police station in Hebron pending completion of a separate agreement on an Israeli withdrawal. It was 2 a.m. in the morning of 11 August when the two sides resolved that sticking point, but there were others over a whole range of issues, from the size of the Palestinian Legislative Council (the Israelis wanted a bigger council to broaden democratic institutions – and lessen Arafat's control) to the Palestinians' insistence that settlers be removed from Hebron under any conceivable arrangement. The 13 September deadline came and went before negotiations on the final phase began on 17 September at the Hilton Hotel in Taba, on the Egyptian side of the Gulf of Aqaba border. These continued over a full week, and included, apart from territory and pace of withdrawal, vexed questions dealing with water and the release of Palestinian prisoners in Israeli jails, including women. Eventually, after days of the most intense discussion, involving Arafat and Peres themselves, documents and maps were initialled prior to a signing ceremony in Washington on 28 September in Clinton's pres-ence.[29] In all, the Interim Agreement on the West Bank and Gaza Strip ran to 410 pages and included eight maps. Under the terms of what became known as Oslo 2, the West Bank and Gaza were divided into three zones. About three per cent, including all of the major towns, would be under full Palestinian control. Another 24 per cent, mostly surrounding the towns and including many villages, would be under Palestinian civilian control, while leaving Israel responsible for security. Settlements would remain under exclusive Israeli control. Israel would withdraw from some 27 per cent of the West Bank, including major towns (except Hebron) and all 465 villages, within three months. That would be followed by elections in early 1996 for a President and Legislative Council. Permanent status negotiations would begin no later than 4 May 1996.[30] Unlike the signing on the White House lawn of the Oslo Declaration of Principles on 13 September, there was no euphoria this time as Clinton, Egyptian President Hosni Mubarak and King Hussein bore silent witness. All understood that such was the complexity of Oslo 2, and so testing were the issues left unresolved – refugees and Jerusalem, to name but two – that it would be a miracle if the agreement proved anything but a bastard child. However, none of those present in Washington on that autumn day could possibly have anticipated in less than two months that the peace process would be deprived of its most critical element: Yizhak Rabin himself.

23. DOLDRUMS

'You have lost a partner. You can count on me to be your partner in peace.' President Bill Clinton to Shimon Peres in a private discussion after Yitzhak Rabin's funeral.[1]

Well may Clinton have declared that Rabin is dead, long live the peace, because at that early stage it seemed that in spite of the disaster sufficient momentum had been generated for the process to continue to move forwards. Widespread disgust in the Israeli electorate at the circumstances surrounding Rabin's death, including the failure in the weeks and months beforehand by the nationalist right, notably its leader Benjamin Netanyahu, to condemn violent criticism of his peacemaking by extremists, provided a boost to the peace camp. As 1995 gave way to 1996, it seemed that Shimon Peres, leading comfortably in the polls, was on course for election in his own right as Prime Minister after several failed attempts. But the Palestinian leadership in their Gaza beachfront apartments were apprehensive. Arafat, in particular, was coming to the stunned realisation that Rabin's death was much more of a body-blow to Palestinian aspirations than even his worst initial fears had suggested. Part of the problem, as far as the Palestinians were concerned, was Peres himself. While they acknowledged his contribution to attempts to advance the peace, including his role in Oslo, they worried about his ability to carry the Israeli electorate with him. As Marwan Kanafani, Arafat's press spokesman at the time and sometime confidant, observed of an early meeting with Peres: 'We realised the size of the catastrophe when we met Peres for the first time (after Rabin's death) and came to the conclusion he did not have the leadership qualities to go forward.'[2]

But in the first weeks Peres pushed ahead determinedly with the peace schedule under the terms of the interim agreement on the West Bank and Gaza, authorising the withdrawal of the Israeli Defence Forces from the West Bank towns of Tulkarm, Kalkilya, Nablus, Ramallah and Bethlehem.[3] He also authorised his assistant, Yossi Beilin, to begin secret talks with Mahmoud Abbas,

Arafat's deputy, on the possible outline of a permanent settlement under 'final status' talks that were to get under way on 4 May 1996, according to the interim agreement, or Oslo 2, signed in Cairo the previous September. Beilin and Abbas made remarkable progress, although details of their secret discussions did not emerge until after the failure of Camp David 2 in late 2000. Israel would recognise a demilitarised Palestinian state with all the attributes of sovereignty. The vexed issue of the larger settlements around Jerusalem would be dealt with by allowing Israel to annex a portion of the West Bank in exchange for territory ceded along the Gaza Strip. Israeli settlers not annexed to Israel would have the option of compensation or living in the Palestinian state, with special security arrangements in place. Palestinian refugees would not have the 'right of return' to Israel proper, but there would be no limit on immigration to the Palestinian state. The highly contentious issue of Jerusalem would be dealt with under a formula by which the Palestinians would recognise Israeli sovereignty in West Jerusalem. Israel would recognise Palestinian sovereignty in its Palestinian capital, al-Quds, in an area to the west of the Old City. East Jerusalem, including the Old City, would remain disputed territory under de facto Israeli sovereignty with the Palestinians being accorded extraterritorial authority over the Haram al-Sharif, or Temple Mount, as it is known to Israelis. Jerusalem would be divided into boroughs, according to religiosity and ethnicity of the inhabitants of each area, under a 'roof municipality'. Arab residents within Israel's borders could be citizens of the Palestinian state. Indeed, the package was not all that different from the ideas discussed – and rejected – at Camp David, four years later.

These behind-the-scenes diplomatic machinations coincided on the Palestinian side with stuttering efforts to build a civil society under Palestinian control, first in the Gaza Strip and Jericho under Oslo 1, and then in the West Bank under Oslo 2. After the euphoria surrounding Arafat's return to Gaza, to Palestine itself, on 1 July 1994 after an absence of 27 years, unpleasant realities had fairly quickly asserted themselves. Indeed, many of the worst fears of Palestinians from the territories were realised. Control was highly centralised in the hands of Arafat and a small group of

Tunis cronies in a twenty-member 'executive'; human rights abuses began to proliferate including the first deaths in custody of dissidents; press freedoms began to be trampled on; and corrupt practices in the disbursement of money began to assert themselves almost as soon as the Palestinian National Authority – the interim government – was proclaimed in July 1994. Part of the problem lay with the flawed framework agreements – the Declaration of Principles leading to Oslo 1 – under which Arafat returned to the territories. While the PNA, under the Basic Law, or interim Palestinian constitution until a state was formed, had nominal authority, control ultimately still rested with the Israeli military. Further complicating the issue was the anomalous role of the Palestine Liberation Organisation itself which retained absolute powers over the PNA under the terms of the Basic Law and, worse, entrenched Arafat's own authority in such a way that he was virtually beyond challenge legally. Thus, Arafat, as Chairman of the PLO Executive Committee, the source of real power in the Palestinian movement, was given virtually carte blanche by the Basic Law to interpret his role in whichever way he chose. The operative words of the law were those which allowed the president as 'Chairman of the PLO Executive Committee [to exercise powers] prescribed for him in the Basic Laws of the PLO, the resolutions of the PNC, the Central Council of the PLO and the Executive Committee of the PLO'.[5]

Even if he was predisposed to accept the principle of legal constraints, or show any real appreciation of what was implied by the need to build a civil society, based on the rule of law, Arafat demonstrated very quickly that in the transtion from guerrilla chieftain to leader of a state-in-waiting he was not about to change his spots. Indeed, what began to emerge in Gaza was an institution which mirrored some of the worst characteristics of corrupt Arab regimes, tribal in its personal affiliations and riddled with nepotism. Partly this reflected Arafat's own inability to change the habits of a lifetime in the sense that highly centralised control, and thus patronage, was the only method familiar to him as a leader, and partly it was a consequence of the difficulties involved in building new administrative structures from the ground up, where none existed before. But even allowing for those difficulties, the results for Palestinians who might have hoped for better were, to put it bluntly, dismaying. As Dr Mahdi Abdul Hadi, founder of the Palestinian Academic Society for the Study of International Affairs, one of the early Palestinian attempts to encourage a constructive dialogue about the future, observed of the PNA: 'It was just another Arab regime. Arafat himself will tell you, "I'm the sheikh, I'm the father". He likens Fatah to a political tribe, the tribe of Fatah. But the real shock for me was the corruption, the copying of Arab regimes. That was a real shock.'

In one important respect the 'copying of Arab regimes' was raised under Arafat's PNA to a fairly advanced stage, namely in the creation of a security apparatus whose mission was aimed more at protecting the regime than at guaranteeing public order itself. Thus, within a fairly short space of time, a plethora of security power centres had emerged in the Gaza Strip and West Bank, reflecting Arafat's own obsession with avoiding the concentration of authority in too few hands, lest any one individual becomes too powerful, especially if that individual has a security function. By some counts security services under the PNA numbered at least nine within a year or so, including Arafat's Force 17 praetorian guard. The 9,000-man Palestine 'police force', established under the terms of the Oslo agreements, most of its members recruited from Palestine Liberation Army forces dotted around the Arab world, included: a civil defence force responsible for normal policing; a national guard responsible for joint security with the Israeli military; an emergency force responsible for public order, in other words riot control; and an intelligence service known as the Preventive Security Apparatus responsible for internal security.

It was this intelligence service, in keeping with practices elsewhere in the Arab world, to which Arafat devoted most attention. Almost immediately, under Arafat's aegis, the so-called Preventive Security Apparatus (PSA) masticised into five separate fiefdoms, each with its own chief. Loyalty to Fatah was the most important qualification for preferment. Most prominent among Arafat's security cadre was Mohammed Dahalan, head of the PSA in Gaza, and Jibril Rajoub, the security boss in the West Bank, although the influence of both these Fatah stalwarts ebbs and flows depending on the boss's whims. In essence, what Arafat re-created in short order was a system of security militias like those which helped transform the Lebanese capital Beirut into a haven for marauding gangs during the PLO's ascendancy there in the 1970s, and which contributed in no small way to an intensification of the Lebanese civil war. Bringing this hydra-headed monster under control will not be the least of the challenges facing Arafat's successors. One example of the pervasiveness of the new security apparat was the pressure applied to the local press to avoid criticism of the leadership, and Arafat in particular. Thus, the PSA's Moral Guidance Division issued an edict after the closure in July 1994 of the pro-Jordanian Al-Nahar, which could just as easily have been concocted in Baghdad or Damascus, warning Palestinians not to be taken in by 'Western schools of thought . . . which justify antagonistic policies towards the Third World, by bringing up freedom of opinion, democracy and human rights'.

Then there was the issue of money. Since Arafat's PLO was nearly broke, after disgusted Arab states scaled back their contributions following the Gulf War, funding was an obsession for the PLO leader, and its lack a source of some of his greatest frustrations. Disappointment set in early. The Palestinians in the aftermath of the the signing of the Oslo Declaration of Principles in September 1993 had estimated reconstruction needs in the Gaza and West Bank at 11 billion dollars over seven years. In the event, a conference in October 1993 of 22 donors held under the auspices of the World Bank pledged just 2.1 billion dollars over the anticipated five-year interim period. Arafat regarded this as derisory, but he made matters worse by interfering in the disbursement of funds in such a way that the process of releasing money for so-called 'immediate-impact projects' became log jammed. The World Bank had established the Palestinian Economic Council for Development and Reconstruction (PECDAR) to oversee urgent renewal projects under an independent structure but, jealous of any sign of autonomy in the disbursement of money, which equated to patronage in Arafat's mind, he passed a decree in November 1993 stating that PECDAR would be accountable to him and that he would be its chairman. As a UN official said at the time, 'Arafat has made himself accountable to

Arafat.'⁹ This episode, early in the formative life of the PNA, may have been the single most telling moment in the authority's slide under Arafat's stewardship. It was certainly ominous. Indeed, the critics' worst fears came to be realised with widespread corruption seeping into many levels of Arafat's chaotic administration, and while the President himself may not have been directly involved it was impossible to believe that he was not aware of the irregular behaviour of some of his closest confidants. As early as October, 1994, not long after Arafat's triumphant return to the Gaza Strip/Jericho enclave, Farouk Kaddoumi, head of the PLO's Political Department, nominally the Palestinian 'Foreign Minister', wrote disparagingly to Arab donor countries about the Palestinian Authority's 'slow progress' in establishing acceptable standards for aid, and the 'lack of clear lines of authority and communication among the various ministries and institutions.' In other words, Kaddoumi, who had opposed Oslo and had refused to return to Gaza with the other Tunis PLO luminaries, was sounding an early alarm about pervasive malfeasance at the most senior levels. But while his warnings may have been heeded in the wider Arab world among states which had pledged assistance, there was no sign they made an impact on Arafat himself beyond his irritation at Kaddoumi breaking ranks on such a sensitive issue. The securing, control and disbursement of funds was the one prerogative which Arafat would have tremendous difficulty yielding over the next several years at tremendous cost to his own reputation, and thatof his ramshackle administration. Matters had become so bad by 1997 that the Palestinian Legislative Council, the largely toothless legislature, recommended in a report on corruption that Arafat sack his entire cabinet and initiate legal action against certain ministers; although it was careful not to cast aspersions on Arafat himself. 'This is the first important report done by the Council to investigate issues of corruption. We hope that the executive authority will respond positively to this report in our national interest. Not responding would mean sinking deeper and deeper into a sea of corruption,' said Hatem Abdul Qader, a member of PLC's investigating committee. But in the event while some heads did roll, the committee's warnings were largely ignored, coming on top, as they did, of an earlier report by the PA's comptroller that the mismanagement and misuse of funds in 1996 had cost the Palestinians $326 million. Among the more conspicuous symbols of the misappropriation of funds were the luxury cars widely distributed among members of the leadership and their families, and the construction of showy villas. Incipient corruption in the Palestinian Authority under Arafat's control was not least of the reasons foreign aid donors, including the United States and Europe, proved increasingly reluctant to release funds to the Palestinians. Incompetence in the utilisation of funds available, largely the consequence of a shambolic bureaucracy, was also cause for donor tardiness in providing assistance. In fact, it was not until mid-2001 with the appointment of Salam Fayad, a former International Monetary Fund official, as Finance Minister that real controls began to be exercised over the disbursement of funds, a long overdue whittling away of Arafat's hold on the purse strings.

By early 1996, preparations for elections to be held on 20 January in Gaza and the West Bank were in full swing under the Oslo formula, which guaranteed 'direct, free and general political elections . . . [which] will constitute a significant interim preparatory step towards the legitimate rights of the Palestinian people and their just requirements.' (See Article III of Declaration of Principles on Interim Self Government Arrangements, the so-called Oslo Agreement.)[10] Elections were duly conducted and were pronounced by observers, including former US President Jimmy Carter, as 'free and fair', but this rather ignored the fact that the PNA had used its authority fairly ruthlessly to ensure that voter registration would favour Fatah candidates, a number from the Tunis PLO, dominated the poll. Arafat himself was elected as the first president of the PNA against a sole opponent, Samiha Khalil of the Palestinian Women's Movement, who got around twelve per cent of the vote among the approximately one million Palestinians who went to the polls. Arafat himself refrained from campaigning on the grounds that as the 'father' of the Palestinian movement it would have been unseemly for him to be seen to engage in politicking on such an occasion, never mind that the man lived and breathed politics 24 hours a day. Fatah candidates with 30 per cent of the vote secured an overwhelming plurality in the Legislative Council, winning more than 50 seats in the 88-member chamber. Architect of Oslo Ahmed Kora'i was elected speaker in a move aimed at ensuring Fatah's control of the PLC's agenda. But it would not be long before Arafat would be expressing significant displeasure at the council's predisposition to question some of his decisions, and to raise doubts about the probity of many of his lieutenants who were widely seen to be profiting personally from their positions. Incensed at such impertinence during an early session held in Bethlehem, Arafat walked out, berating the elected representatives of Palestine as 'dogs and sons of bitches!', even though the council is virtually toothless since it has no real powers to change anything. It was not clear at that early stage whether the Palestinian leader grasped what was involved in participatory democracy. This, in spite of the fact that in all the years of presiding over the Palestine National Council, the Palestinian 'parliament-in-exile', one of his mantras was to refer to 'our Palestinian democracy', as if this distinguished the Palestinians from the other Arabs. Ziad Abu Amr, a US-educated social scientist, head of the council's Political Committee and a member, in his words, of the 'loyal opposition', expressed a common frustration when he said that Arafat simply did not – or would not – understand the purpose of such an institution. 'Arafat's argument is that we can't have a democratic representative system because of the difficulties we are facing as a nation, including most especially the confrontation with Israel.'[11]

But the unsteady progress of Palestinian democracy was to take a back seat to dramatic events which began unfolding in early 1996 and which led by the middle of the year to crippling backsliding in progress towards peace, including the shock defeat of the Israel peace camp in May elections. The trigger came early in the year when Israeli security on 5 January killed Yehiya Ayash, a Hamas terrorist known as 'the Engineer' because of his bomb-making abilities. In the sort of payback which is almost beyond irony in the Middle East Israel's Shin Bet used a cellular phone rigged to explode when answered to kill the bomber whom the Israelis claimed had taken the lives of more than fifty of their own. Within a few short months Ayash's death would be avenged many times over to the point where it left confidence between an Israeli public and the Palestinians in tatters, and dashed Peres' hopes of finally being the popularly elected Prime Minister of Israel.

On 25 February, in the first of a series of suicide bombings, a bomber blew himself up on a bus in Jerusalem, killing 24 people, including the son of Nahum Barnea, one of Israel's leading journalists. This was followed over the next several weeks by another three major suicide bombings, including most shockingly one outside the Dizengoff Centre, a large shopping mall in Tel Aviv, which left thirteen dead and many others wounded. In all 58 people had been killed and 200 wounded in the worst outbreak of violence inside Israel's borders since the founding of the state. In the space of a few weeks Peres' prime ministership was doomed. Peace between Israel and the Palestinians hung by a thread. Not even an unprecedented meeting in Sharm el-Sheikh, dubbed the 'Conference of Peace Makers', orchestrated by President Clinton and attended by thirty national leaders committed to Middle East peace, including Peres and Arafat, could restore equilibrium. It was at that moment that it became clear that Arafat's attempts to co-opt the Islamists had failed. The genie was well and truly out of the bottle, and their target was as much Arafat's authority as it was Israel itself. Attempts by Israel and the Palestinians to strengthen their own security co-operation in the weeks after suicide war was declared produced some interesting initiatives, but did not really change festering circumstances on the ground.[12]

But for a brief moment, Arafat contrived to buoy the peace camp in Israel when on 24 April, Israel's Independence Day, he presided over a session of the Palestine National Council in Gaza which voted to change the Palestinian Covenant denying Israel's right to exist. By a margin of 504 out of the PNC's 572 members the 21st PNC voted to replace the Covenant with a new one based on the Oslo accords, the PNC's 1988 Declaration of Independence and political statement (which explicitly recognised the state of Israel) and those UN resolutions pertinent to the Palestinian question, especially 242 and 338 which call for a resolution of the Arab–Israeli conflict on the principle of land for peace.[13] Arafat, who had also authorised a belated sweep against Islamic extremists, arresting hundreds of activists, putting mosques under the control of his authority and raiding Palestinian institutions, was doing his best for Peres, but the tide had turned.

On 29 May, Israelis went to the polls after a campaign completely dominated by security in the shadow of graphic images of blood- and body-part-spattered buses and streets of Jerusalem and Tel Aviv. Polls had shown the two candidates, Peres and the Likud's Benjamin Netanyahu, running neck and neck. Exit polls on the night indicated initially that Peres had scored the narrowest of victories, but as counting continued into the early hours of the morning support for Peres ebbed away to the point where it became clear that Netanyahu, 'Mr Security' in his own words, the American-educated former Israeli ambassador to the UN and a man for whom the Palestinians had contempt, would be the next Prime Minister of Israel by a margin of 51–49 per cent (55 per cent of the Jewish vote). In Gaza, the nocturnal Arafat, who had satisfied himself that he would still have a peace partner in Peres before he went to bed around midnight, awakened to find that his expectations had been turned upside down. Marwan Kanafani woke the Palestinian leader with the bad news at seven a.m. Arafat was stunned by the realisation that for the second time in less than six months an Israeli peace partner, however imperfect in the case of the latter, had been cut down, first by an assassin's bullet, and now by the Israeli electorate itself. As Kanafani observed, 'With Rabin's death and Peres' defeat at the polls, we never regained the atmosphere of trust and understanding with the Israelis which had prevailed before.'[14]

Nabil Shaath, Arafat's trusted adviser and on-again, off-again chief negotiator with the Israelis over many years depending on his boss's whims, was himself in Gaza on the night of election and recalls 'rejoicing past midnight with a group of Americans, Israelis and Palestinians'.[15] But these celebrations had turned to ashes by morning, as the Palestinian brains trust absorbed the consequences. Netanyahu, they concluded, would be at best a reluctant partner, at worst, in their terms, a disaster. In the event their worst fears were realised. As Shaath observed: 'It is true that negotiations were never easy with the Israelis over issues such as security, settlements and water, but generally speaking we were able to find a way forward. After Netanyahu came in, it was a completely different ball-game. Three years of Netanyahu were a disaster.'[16] Ahmed Kora'i, speaker of the Palestinian 'parliament' and architect of Oslo, came to the same reluctant conclusion: 'Ideologically, Netanyahu was against Palestinian national rights,' he observed.[17]

Palestinian misgivings were reinforced by Netanyahu's campaign rhetoric, by his Likud Party's own policy platform for the election, and by the new Israeli Prime Minister's inaugural speech to the Knesset which left no doubt about his priorities. 'We will be the ones who will defend ourselves. The Oslo concept has failed. Yasser Arafat cannot and does not want to protect us. We must put our defence back in our hands and give our security forces the freedom to hit where and when they deem right,' was a typical refrain in the weeks before polling day.[18] The Likud platform was unequivocal: 'no' to a Palestinian state in the West Bank, no shared sovereignty in Jerusalem, no return of Palestinian refugees (either to Israel or to the occupied territories), and no halt to Jewish settlement, whether in the 'Galilee and Negev', or in 'Judea, Samaria' (the biblical name used by the Israeli settler movement for the West Bank), Gaza and the Golan Heights.[19] In his Knesset speech following the formation of a rightist government on 18 June, Netanyahu expanded on these themes, epousing the contradictory aims of continuing settlement construction while pushing forward with peace efforts, even though he had declared the Oslo concept, on which they were based, a 'failure'.

Watching this from Washington, the Clinton administration realised that Netanyahu's election would create difficulties, but it resolved to deal with the new realities as best it could. In July, Clinton, who had been a vigorous 'facilitator' of Middle East peace efforts, more than any other president since Jimmy Carter, had his first meeting with the new Israeli leader in the White House. The US interest was to keep peace efforts more or less on track. To this end the Americans encouraged both Egyptian President Hosni Mubarak and Jordan's King Hussein to engage Netanyahu, against both their deep misgivings for a man whom they regarded, correctly as it turned out, as a threat to the whole peace enterprise. An early indication of the difficulties ahead was Netanyahu's steadfast refusal, unlike his predecessor's, to engage Arafat directly. It was not until October (in a meeting in Washington brokered by Clinton), more than four months after his election, that Netanyahu had the first of several invariably unsatisfactory face-to-face encounters with the Palestinian leader whose temper had been aroused early in August by an Israeli decision to 'unfreeze' settlement construction and by the closure of Palestinian offices in East Jerusalem affiliated with the PNA. Matters were made much worse by Netanyahu's subsequent decision on 23 September, without reference to his own security advisers, to open an ancient 488-metre archaeological tunnel in the Old City which would allow people to go from the Western ('Wailing') Wall to one of the entrances of the Dome of Rock mosque in the Muslim quarter of Jerusalem, inflaming religious sensitivities. In days of rioting which followed, Jerusalem itself, the West Bank and Gaza witnessed the worst violence in the 29 years of Israeli occupation since 1967. By the end of September, nearly one hundred people had been killed, most of them Palestinians, more than a thousand wounded. In an ominous sign of things to come Palestinian police fired back at Israeli troops, adding significantly to the mayhem and level of fatalities. The first steps were taken towards the 'weaponisation' of the conflict.[20]

Watching this disaster unfold, Clinton stepped in with an invitation to both Netanyahu and Arafat to come to the White House with King Hussein (Egypt's Mubarak was unwilling to participate because of his distaste for Netanyahu). Clinton and Hussein left Arafat and Netanyahu alone after their lunch to resolve their differences. A positive result, one of very few for the Palestinians in the Netanyahu years, was agreement to resume discussions on Israel's withdrawal from Hebron. For the moment the two sides had been dragged back from the brink. However, even more than in the past Palestinian destiny was in the hands of the Americans, and a President who was about to face re-election, never mind the year-long distraction that would follow of embarrassing questions about his relationship with Monica Lewinsky, a White House intern. The Netanyahu period, with the exception of the agreement for a withdrawal from much of Hebron in January 1997, and the Wye River Accords of October 1998 aimed at energising sluggish peace efforts, were doldrums years, marked by bad feeling and ill temper on both sides. Nabil Shaath, for one, blames Netanyahu for the failure of Camp David 2 in July 2000 because a negotiating pattern, albeit built on shaky foundations, was broken, never to be re-established with any degree of sincerity. 'Netanyahu set up the situation for the disappointments of the next stage,' said Shaath.[21]

Palestinian spirits were buoyed by Clinton's re-election in November and the reasonable expectation that in his second term he would prepared to take additional risks for peace, including being prepared to exert pressure on Israel if and when it was needed. Shaath for one had invested significant hopes in Clinton whom he described as 'America's most forward-looking President' in the chequered Palestinian experience.[23] Clinton's inauguration for a second term did coincide with perhaps the most positive (from the Palestinians' perspective) development of all the Netanyahu years. On 15 January 1997, Israel and the Palestinian Authority signed the Hebron Accords, the smaller missing piece in the jigsaw puzzle left over from the Interim Agreement on the West Bank and Gaza Strip, signed in September 1995, a little more than a month before Rabin's assassination. The much larger absent element of the puzzle was, of course, the failure to persist with talks on the permanent status of the Palestinian entity in the West Bank and Gaza, in other words statehood. Under the terms of Oslo 2 these were meant to get under way by 4 May 1996 and to be completed within three years (actually they began in March that year), but the defeat of Peres and the election of Netanyahu meant this process was stillborn.

Under the terms of the Hebron Agreement, which differed from arrangements governing other West Bank towns from which Israel had withdrawn under Oslo 2, the Israelis were to maintain a security presence in the town to protect between 400 and 500 Jewish settlers who had attached themselves limpet-like to the Tomb of Patriarchs in the centre of Hebron. Thus, the Palestinians would control 80 per cent of the town with Israel in charge of security in the remainder. Significantly, there was no commitment by Israel to further withdrawals under the terms of Oslo 2. A reluctant Netanyahu had not put his name directly to the document. Instead, Dennis Ross, the US Middle East envoy, had included a 'Note for the Record' which described Israel's commitment to the process based on 'reciprocity'.

The word 'reciprocity' had become a favourite of Netanyahu's, since assessment of reciprocal gestures on the part of the Palestinians could amount to an entirely subjective judgement on his part. US acquiescence in this device was confirmation in the Palestinian view of a definite US tilt towards Israel and the start of festering misgivings about the even-handedness of Clinton's Middle East team which would only intensify in the years ahead.[24] The Ross 'note' dealt with such issues as a further redeployment of Israeli forces from parts of the West Bank from early 1997; prisoner releases; negotiations on an airport and seaport for Gaza; and the resumption of 'final status' talks in March 1997; but, most significantly, in the Ross 'note', and in a subsequent letter from US Secretary of State Warren Christopher to Netanyahu, there was no reference to a commitment on Israel's part to adhere to a timetable for further withdrawals under the terms of Oslo 2, beyond a reference to the desirability that these be completed 'not later than mid-1998'.[25] In one other respect, Christopher's communication with the Israeli leader was significant in that he appeared to reinterpret – to Israel's advantage – established understandings of the language of UN Security Council Resolution 242. Christopher referred to 'secure and defensible borders' while the language of the 1967 UN resolution quite clearly calls for a return to 'secure and recognised' borders.[26]

In spite of these disturbing indications, Arafat himself sought to put the best face on things when, less than a week after the signing of the Hebron Accord, he addressed a crowd of 20,000 from the balcony of the new Palestinian police headquarters. 'They told us it would be Gaza/Jericho first and last,' he said. 'But we got Nablus, Ramallah and Bethlehem, and now Hebron and, God willing, onto Jerusalem as the capital of our independent Palestinian state'.[27] However, virtually no sooner were these words uttered, empty as they sounded in the circumstances, than Netanyahu pulled the rug from any lingering sense of expectation from the signing of the Hebron Accords by approving the building of 6,500 new housing units on disputed land in East Jerusalem in an area called Har Homa by the Israelis, but known to the Palestinians as Jabal Abu Ghneim. Coming on the heels of Hebron this was like a red rag to the Palestinians and led to days of rioting and weeks and months of tension, all but putting paid to further meaningful progress between Israeli and Palestinian peace negotiators. Palestinian confidence in US good intentions was hardly enhanced by a US veto on 21 March of a Security Council resolution critical of Israeli construction at Har Homa. Arafat was beginning to understand that a second Clinton administration may not be as prospective as he had hoped, especially one where the President was increasingly preoccupied with the gathering storm that would break in 1998 around allegations of a relationship with a White House intern, something he denied publicly and was then forced to recant. The Palestinians were also obliged to accomodate themselves to a new Secretary of State. Their initial impressions were not encouraging.

While Clinton kept much of his Middle East team in place, led by Dennis Ross, he appointed a new Secretary of State, Madeleine Albright, to replace Christopher. Whatever Christopher's shortcomings might have been in the eyes of the Palestinians, including his somewhat colourless personality, his replacement would represent a colossal disappointment. Albright made it clear when she was sworn in that she would take her time turning her attention to the Middle East and that is how it turned out. It would be be more than six months before she made her first trip to the region, on 10 September 1997, and this proved little more than a listening tour; although she said some of the right things as far as the Palestinians were concerned, expressing concern about their 'suffering', and reaffirming US support for the 'land for peace' formula as a basis for any settlement.[28] Nabil Shaath said it was clear from an early stage that Albright would be a reluctant participant in Middle East peacemaking. The Palestinians began describing her as 'Dennis Ross's parrot'.[29]

By the second half of 1997, Middle East peacemaking had entered the doldrums, punctuated by flickering moments of promise such as the meeting on 8 October, at the Erez checkpoint dividing Gaza from Israel proper, between Arafat and Netanyahu, their first face-to-face encounter in eight months. This prompted a resumption of half-hearted peace negotiations, but it was becoming clearer by the month that much of the energy had been leached from the process. A meeting in Europe in November between Arafat and Netanyahu, brokered by Albright, ended unsatisfactorily on the twin issues of further Israeli withdrawals and a freeze on settlement construction. Clinton himself, in the gathering storm surrounding his private life, summoned Arafat and Netanyahu to Washington in January in an attempt to energise the process, advancing US ideas for a further Israeli withdrawal from 13 per cent of the West Bank in exchange for an improved Palestinian performance on security. Arafat balked initially at the Clinton proposal since it represented much less than the Palestinians had anticipated under Oslo, leaving aside the collapse of a timetable for 'final status' negotiations, but by the time the Palestinian leader met Albright in London in early May he assented reluctantly. Netanyahu, however, resisted on the grounds that the Palestinians were not keeping their 'reciprocal' side of the bargain as far as security was concerned. The US considered an ultimatum to the Israeli side, but thought better of it. In the long summer of Clinton's embarrassment over Lewinsky – on 17 August he admitted having lied publicly about the affair – the Administration simply did not seem to have the time or energy to devote to Middle East peacemaking. That would prove the case until autumn when the president re-engaged in spite of the pressure exerted by a looming – and prolonged – impeachment process that would drag on into the early months of 1999. One result of this spasmodic re-engagement by Clinton was his insistence, following his meetings with Arafat and Netanyahu in Washington in late September, on a summit meeting at the Wye River Plantation in East Maryland aimed at breaking the log jam in Middle East peacemaking.[30]

In early October, Albright travelled to the Middle East for meetings both with Arafat, whom she saw in Jericho, and with Netanyahu, in Jerusalem, to prepare for Wye. Her discussions with the two protagonists enabled her to announce at the end of her talks they had agreed to an intensive three-way summit with President Clinton to begin on 15 October.[30] It was not the smallest of ironies that one of those present at the Wye summit in a negotiating role would be Ariel Sharon, who replaced David Levy as Israel's Foreign Minister on 9 October. Absorbing this development Arafat and his advisers wondered who might be worse from their point of view, a Netanyahu who conspicuously failed to live up to undertakings, or a Sharon who never made any secret of his antipathy towards them and their cause. 'At least with Sharon you knew where you stood,' said Nabil Shaath.[31]

When the Palestinians and Israelis gathered in Wye in mid-October for what was to prove a fractious nine days of negotiations, goodwill was virtually absent. But for Clinton's personal involvement, including his hyperactive participation in an all-night negotiating session on 22–3 October, there would have been no agreement. The aim of Wye was to get the peace process, battered by the frustrations of the Netanyahu years, back on track to provide a foundation for final status talks which were meant to be concluded by May 1999 under the terms of Oslo. In the event, Wye's five articles laid heavier emphasis on demands that Palestinians do more to enhance security than they did on providing a road-map for the way forward. The agreement – signed by Arafat and Netanyahu in Clinton's presence – under which Israel undertook to withdraw from a further thirteen per cent of the West Bank, was honoured in the breach as another wasted year drew to a close during which Palestinian extremism continued to deepen its roots.[32] Wye was notable, however, for one cameo performance, that of King Hussein, suffering lymphoma and terminally ill, who, in one of his last public appearances, joined the talks as a facilitator. His eloquence, in brief remarks, could hardly have contrasted more starkly with the sour atmosphere which prevailed, including an almost complete lack of empathy between Clinton and Netanyahu. 'We have no right to dictate through irresponsible action or narrow-mindedness the future of our children and their children's children', he said. 'There has been enough destruction. Enough death. Enough waste ... It's time that, together, we occupy a place beyond ourselves, our peoples, that is worthy of them under the sun, the descendants of the children of Abraham'.[33] The King may as well have been talking to himself.

In any case, he would soon depart the stage. Hussein bin Talal died on 7 February 1999 at 11.50 a.m. local time in Amman,

Jordan, at the age of 63, having succumbed quickly in the end to a cancer which the best medical treatment in the world could not arrest. Arafat, who was visiting the United States at the time for meetings with, among others, Clinton himself, suffered mixed emotions. Arafat and Hussein had been joined since the 1960s like two Chinese dolls in a relationship which had run the full gamut from bloody conflict during Black September 1970 to later stuttering peace partnerships, and ultimately to the two going their separate ways. Each had sought to gain the upper hand in diplomatic manoeuvrings around the Arab world, much of it related in their case throughout the 1970s and 1980s to a titanic struggle to be the authentic voice of the Palestinians. Jealousies and tensions engendered by this contest had brought both to moments of speechless rage and frustration, each with the other, but as Arafat surveyed a landscape without Hussein, it seemed lonelier. One by one Arab rulers of Arafat's generation were passing from the scene. A fairly pro-forma statement of condolence issued by the Palestinian Authority in Arafat's name hardly did justice to the circumstances, but Arafat knew there were many among his coterie who were not all that unhappy to see the end of Hussein: after all some had been involved in plots over the years to assassinate him. 'President Yasser Arafat and the Palestinian people and leadership received with great sorrow and pain the news [of King Hussein's death],' said the PA, in an official statement.[34]

Out of Wye came one windfall for Arafat, although it was certainly not the energisation of the peace process itself, since almost before the ink was dry on the Wye memorandum progress had stalled. Arafat's major achievement was to elicit from Clinton an agreement to visit Gaza by the end of the year to address a session of the Palestine National Council, its 'parliament-in-exile' (before a state is formed) which represented both the Palestinians of the Diaspora and those of the inside. The presence of an American president in impoverished Gaza represented something of an apotheosis for Arafat, who had devoted enormous effort over many years to engaging America, which he had assumed naively was all that was required to deliver Palestine to the Palestinians. That illusion may have been dispelled, but Arafat was buoyed, nevertheless, by the honour he felt had been conferred on him as the the leader of the stateless Palestinians by the presence in Palestine of the leader of the free world, the representative of the sole remaining superpower. Ostensibly, Clinton was in Gaza to bear witness to the PNC formally revoking in full the 1968 PLO Charter denying Israel's right to exist, sections of which had been amended in 1996, but more than that, the US President had his eyes on a bigger push for peace in the last years of his presidency – and his place in history. 'Surely, to goodness, after five years of this peace process, and decades of suffering, and after you have come here today and done what you have done, we can say enough of this gnashing of teeth, let us join hands and proudly go forward together,' Clinton concluded in front of a grinning Arafat, Arafat's wife Suha, Hillary Clinton and applauding PNC delegates.[35]

But these words could not disguise the slough into which relations between Arafat and Netanyahu, Palestinians and Israelis had slid in early 1999. In any case, elections in Israel beckoned following the unravelling of a Likud-led constellation of nationalist and ultra-nationalist, religious and ultra-religious factions in a government which was paralysed by discussion about even the smallest concessions for peace. Netanyahu's own popularity was sliding, and thus his ability to keep a fractious house in order. The 4 May end of the interim period of Oslo during which the 'final status' of the Palestinians was to have been resolved had come and gone with threats from Arafat to declare statehood and counter-threats from Netanyahu to annex Israeli-controlled areas of the West Bank. This crisis was averted with a letter from Clinton to Arafat on the eve of Israel's 17 May poll promising that the US and the Clinton himself would use their good offices to do all they could to push for a final status agreement – in other words a concerted effort towards peace would be made during the last two years of the Clinton presidency. It was enough to stay Arafat's hand, pending the Israeli elections.

In the event, the election result, in which Labour's Ehud Barak crushed Netanyahu, securing 56 per cent of the vote, matched Palestinian hopes for a changing of the guard. However, while Palestinian leaders in their Gaza redoubt were quietly satisfied that they had seen the back for the moment of Netanyahu whom they had come to despise, there were few illusions about Barak, an unknown quantity politically. Arafat and his colleagues could also not put out of their minds that it was Barak, the military man, who had led elite Israeli commandos on a raid of Beirut in 1973, to avenge the Munich Olympic Games massacre, in which a troika of the PLO's most promising cadres were assassinated. Hopes for the new period were mixed with trepidation, but as Nabil Shaath observed, 'Anything was better than Netanyahu.'[36]

24. DISAPPOINTMENT

'Now it is our duty to complete the mission, and establish a comprehensive peace in the Middle East which has known so much war.' Ehud Barak speech to the Knesset on the presentation of his government, 6 July 1999.[1]

Newly-elected Prime Minister Ehud Barak's words, in his first major speech after forming what turned out to be a fragile coalition of seven disparate – in some cases mutually antagonistic – factions, might have come from the late Yitzhak Rabin's songbook. Indeed, Barak saw himself very much in Rabin's mould, having served in many of the same military positions occupied by Rabin himself, including army Chief of Staff. The Palestinians themselves and Arafat in particular invested significant, certainly unrealistic, hopes in Barak, although he was relatively unknown as a peacemaker. The Palestinian assessment at that early stage, according to Arafat confidant Nabil Shaath, was that Barak would represent a substantial improvement on Netanyahu, but there were reservations not least on account of Barak's relative lack of political experience – he was a relative newcomer to elected office – and thus his ability to navigate through the dangerous shoals of Israeli politics: so it proved.[2] If Palestinian hopes were buoyed, so were those of President Bill Clinton who had concluded that it was unlikely anything further could be achieved in Middle East peacemaking while Netanyahu remained Prime Minister. Indeed, relations between the White House and the Likud leader had reached something of a nadir in the last months of his prime ministership. It was against this background that Arafat and Barak, with Clinton as an enthusiastic facilitator in the final eighteen months of his presidency, began a concentrated effort towards forging peace between Israel and the Palestinians. It was a process which promised much, but ultimately ended in frustration and rancour. Failure left a bitter aftertaste. Lingering disappointment of having come relatively close to an agreement and then sliding back contributed in no small part to the violence which followed the collapse of the Camp David process.

But in the summer of 1999, much seemed possible. Clinton, who had shrugged off the threat of impeachment, wasted little time, following the Israeli elections, in seeking to energise the peace process. On 15 July, he met Barak in the White House to discuss the way ahead. It was at that meeting and subsequent encounters over the next several days that the bare bones of a new peace strategy were discussed, with Barak, in his soliderly way, telling Clinton that the incrementalism of Oslo had outlived its usefulness. Barak had never had much time for what he regarded as the slow-moving Oslo process, which would always be prey to sudden shifts in the political cycle in Israel itself, and in the United States where windows of peacemaking opportunity would open and close depending on whether a presidential election was in the offing. In an early encounter with Terje Roed Larsen, the UN's special representative in the occupied territories and one of the instigators of the Oslo process, Barak had likened Oslo to 'a very ugly dog': 'The tail is not ugly, the head is ugly, but you don't chop the head, you chop the tail, but not a bit every day,' Barak told Larsen.[3] In other words, take the good bits of Oslo and discard the rest. Larsen was not convinced that Barak was right, believing that he fractured the Rabin–Peres strategy of gradualism which had delivered Oslos 1 and 2, leading subsequently to the pull-out from Hebron and the Wye River agreement. Dan Yatom, a former head of Mossad, later Barak's chief of staff during his prime ministership, said Barak's view was 'let's jump into the water and start dealing with the tough issues now – Jerusalem, borders, refugees, settlements'.[4] That was the strategy which evolved; although in the early days of Barak it was not clear where the priorities would lie.

Watching all this unfold the Palestinians were alarmed by Barak's apparent initial enthusiasm for the 'Syrian track', recalling that Rabin himself had been diverted in the early days of his prime ministership by the false promise of progress towards a settlement with Syria. Much time and energy had been wasted, in the Palestinian view, by Rabin and the Americans on Syria when these energies might more productively have been utilised in dealing with the Palestinian dimension. But Barak, like Rabin and for the same reasons – both military men feared Syria's capacity to harm

Israel more than they did the Palestinians – wanted to test Syrian possibilities. Clinton, who had immersed himself in the first round back in 1996, meeting Syrian leader Hafez al-Assad on several occasions, did not need much convincing that a 'two-track' approach to Middle East peacemaking – Syria and Palestine in tandem – was desirable. Barak's own view was that each track would complement the other, and nothing would be lost by a parallel approach.[5] Thus began another feint towards Damascus, involving Clinton himself in an inconclusive meeting with Assad in Geneva on 26 March 2000 which faltered on the non-negotiable issue of complete Israeli withdrawal from the Golan Heights, or what was known as a return to the 4 June (1967) line. Withdrawal to this pre-1967 Six-Day War boundary was a *sine qua non* for the Syrian leader, which makes all the more remarkable the assumption that appears to have informed the American and Israeli positions in early 2000 that somehow the immovable Lion of Damascus could be budged from this position by whatever creative formulas might have been floating around, including gradual withdrawal accompanied by US guarantees of a special force to patrol the Golan Heights. The issue was simply non-negotiable. That would be the end of the Syrian track for the foreseeable future, not least because Assad himself passed away not long after his meeting with Clinton, on 10 June, apparently of a heart attack. Arafat himself ritually lamented Assad's passing, saying that he mourned the 'loss to the Syrian people and Arab nation', but privately the Palestinian leader drew grim satisfaction from having outlived his nemesis who had more than once tried to liquidate both his leadership and his movement. Assad's death also left Arafat as one of a dwindling clutch of long-serving Arab leaders, including Gaddafi of Libya, Saddam Hussein of Iraq, Fahd of Saudi Arabia and Qaboos of Oman. Hassan II of Morocco had died in July 1999.

The Israeli–US divergence over Syria did not preclude the beginning of a process of regular exchanges between Arafat and Barak which were aimed at restoring some of the personal goodwill between the Palestinians and Israelis which had evaporated under Netanyahu. But if the Palestinian leader was hoping for a return to the 'good old days' which had prevailed, at least in the

Palestinian imagination, in the months before Rabin's assassination, he would be disappointed. Barak, with his military background, may on the surface have had much in common with Rabin, but they were poles apart in other respects, not least in their respective political experience and self-confidence. Rabin had been conditioned over several decades in the piranha tank of Israeli politics, including an earlier bruising stint as Prime Minister when he had been obliged to step aside over questions regarding his wife's personal financial arrangements. By comparison Barak was a neophyte. He also had the sort of personality which meant that right from the beginning he kept his own counsel, which made it difficult, from the Palestinian perspective, to engage him. Ahmed Kora'i, chief negotiator for the Oslo Declaration of Principles and speaker of the Palestinian Legislative Council, described Barak as a 'closed man'. 'You never knew what he wanted,' said Kora'i.[6] This was a common complaint of Palestinians obliged to deal with Barak before, during and after Camp David.

In their first working session on 27 July following Barak's swearing in, Arafat and Israel's new Prime Minister, with US encouragement, focused on getting what was left of the battered Oslo process back on track, and more particularly agreements reached at the Wye summit the previous October. These provided for a further Israeli withdrawal from 13 per cent of the West Bank. This agreement had fallen victim to the last days of Netanyahu rule and with it the timetable for 'final status' talks which were meant to have been completed under the Oslo formula by May 1999. In the event, after gruelling negotiations, which indicated to the Palestinians that a Barak administration would be as vexatious as any which they had dealt with in the past, the two sides reconfirmed understandings reached at Wye and also, more significantly, set the stage for the beginning of 'final status' talks – although Barak himself was formulating other plans which would make any such 'final status' discussions redundant. On 3 September, Arafat and Barak travelled to Sharm-el-Sheikh where, in the presence of US Secretary of State Madeleine Albright, they signed understandings which laid out a timetable for further Israeli withdrawals from the West Bank, thus reconfirming Wye. But the going would be tough in late 1999 and early 2000. In October, for example, talks stalled over the Palestinians' right of free passage between the Gaza Strip and the West Bank, with Israel wanting to retain full control of security arrangements. By March 2000, painstaking negotiations had produced an Israeli agreement to a further withdrawal from a sliver of Palestinian territory, but it was clear to the Palestinians in those early months of 2000 that Israel was not fully engaged in the process. The Syrian diversion was one explanation for the apparent Israeli reluctance to engage fully, another was that Barak was preparing himself for a 'big bang' effort at breaking the log jam in Israeli–Palestinian peacemaking, so that the process, as he told associates, would not always be at risk of 'dying the death of a thousand cuts'.[7] Whether Barak spelled out his intentions with such clarity in his conversations with US peace envoys is not clear – he certainly didn't take Arafat into his confidence – but in his tactical and strategic calculations he was labouring under the pressure of knowing that by mid-2000 Clinton had just six months left in the White House. He was also dealing with the unravelling of his own coalition where there was at best a fractured consensus on steps towards peace, and more particularly on concessions to the Palestinians. It was against this background that Israel's cabinet decided on 5 March to remove Israeli troops from Lebanon by July, thus bringing to an end an eighteen-year occupation of a southern portion of that country. Unsurprisingly, Hezbollah and its allies hailed Israel's decision to withdraw unilaterally as a triumph for the resistance. It was, Hezbollah leaders averred, the first time Israel had been 'defeated'. Watching this from their offices and apartments in Gaza, the Palestinian leadership drew mild ecouragement from the an-nouncement, but they knew that such were the complexities of their own situation vis-à-vis the Israelis that Lebanon may as well have been another world.[8]

Less than a week after Hafez al-Assad's death, Arafat found himself sitting in the Oval office with Clinton in what would prove the start of an extraordinary episode in modern Middle Eastern diplomacy, and one which would ultimately epitomise all the frustrations, all the misunderstandings, all the prejudices, all the accumulated victimhood of participants in attempts to resolve

perhaps the most intractable – certainly one of the bloodiest –
conflicts left on the international agenda. In the end the casualties
would not only include the Palestinians and Israelis, and the peace
process itself, but the reputations of some of those involved on the
American side, including members of Clinton's own Middle East
team. But in the weeks leading up to Camp David 2, as it came to
be known, there was expectancy, although those intimately
involved on the Palestinian side were pessimistic about a breakthrough.[9] Clinton's own involvement in the last months of his
presidency, the need for Barak to gain something to show the
Israeli electorate that progress towards peace was at hand, and the
sense that the Palestinians, in their weakened state, could be
dragged kicking and screaming to an accommodation encouraged
a belief, naive as it turned out, that progress might be made.

On 5 July, Clinton announced that Israeli and Palestinian
leaders would meet at Camp David six days later, leaving
unspecific the time which they would be given to ironing out their
differences. But even before the respective negotiating teams got
to the presidential retreat in Maryland, yawning gaps in each camp
were apparent. On the eve of Camp David, Barak, whose Foreign
Minister David Levy was rebelling over mooted concessions to the
Palestinians, narrowly survived a no-confidence motion in the
Knesset, only after promising to place any peace deal before
Israel's voters in a referendum. On the Palestinian side, differences
were less visible, but Arafat's senior lieutenants, including Mahmoud Abbas, nominally his number two, and Ahmed Kora'i, one
of the chief proponents of adventurous peacemaking, were barely
speaking to each other. Abbas, according to Shaath, thought the
whole process was 'useless'.[9] Arafat himself – unforgivably –
played a passive role in the lead-up, as if he was frightened of
having his name associated with any concessions which might
advance the issues involved. In truth, according to his lieutenants,
he had little confidence in Barak delivering on his undertakings
because of Israel's fractured domestic political situation, therefore
why should he, with the Islamists breathing down his neck, take
risks for peace when the other side might not be a position to
reciprocate?[10] This distractedness on Arafat's part plus serious
dislocation among his lieutenants meant that preparations for

Camp David were quite inadequate, indeed almost moribund. This was not the least of the reasons for the failure, but there were others of consequence, including Barak's own singular negotiating style which meant that he kept his cards close to his chest until it was too late. Barak's great phobia, according to Chief of Staff Dan Yatom, was that Arafat would simply pocket any concessions offered as a means of extracting the maximum from Israel while giving nothing in return, such was the poor level of trust between them.[12]

In any case, the two sides went to Camp David with their formal negotiating positions far apart – and seemingly unbridgeable. As William B. Quandt summarised in his book *Peace Process: American Diplomacy and the Arab–Israel Conflict since 1967*, 'Arafat insisted on full Israeli withdrawal from all occupied territory, including East Jerusalem; the establishment of a Palestinian state with East Jerusalem as its capital; and the right of Palestinian refugees to return to their homes, or compensation. Barak maintained that there would be no withdrawal to the 1967 lines, no recognition of a right of return for Palestinian refugees, no removal of all the settlements beyond the 1967 line, no re-militarisation of the West Bank and Gaza, and no relinquishment of the parts of Jerusalem taken in the 1967 war.'[13] In other words, formal differences between the two sides could hardly have been wider on the fundamental issues. But far beyond these divergent negotiating positions was the contrast in the personalities of the two main players, Arafat and Barak.

In a game of cat and mouse, in which Barak was the cat and Arafat the mouse, neither the cat nor the mouse was predisposed to play. Hussein Agha and Robert Malley in their description in the *New York Review of Books* of what went wrong at Camp David reported, 'The Palestinians' overall behaviour, when coupled with Barak's conviction that Arafat merely wanted to extract Israeli concessions, led to disastrous results. The mutual and, by then, deeply entrenched suspicion meant that Barak would conceal his final proposals, the "endgame", until Arafat had moved, and that Arafat would not move until he could see the endgame. Barak's strategy was predicated on the idea that his firmness would lead to some Palestinian flexibility, which in turn would justify Israel's making further concessions. Instead, Barak's piecemeal negotiating style, combined with Arafat's unwillingness to budge, produced a paradoxical result. By presenting early positions as bottom lines, the Israelis provoked the Palestinians' mistrust; by subsequently shifting them, they whetted the Palestinians' appetite. By the end of the process, it was hard to tell which bottom lines were for real, and which were not.'[14]

In an atmosphere of high drama and low farce, in which Clinton alternately pleaded with and cajoled the players to engage with each other, there was stuttering progress, but no sign of a breakthrough. After two weeks, during which Clinton left for several days to attend the G-8 summit in Okinawa, Japan, an exasperated US President said to Arafat, 'If the Israelis can make compromises and you can't, I should go home. You have been here fourteen days and said no to everything. These things have consequences; failure will mean the end of the peace process . . . Let's let hell break loose and live with the consequences.'[15] Clinton wasn't to know how prophetic his words would prove to be for both Arafat and for the peace process itself, for the failure of Camp David 2 with all that implied would be followed by some of the worst – and most sustained – violence in the bloodstained history of the Palestinian–Israeli dispute. But while Clinton reserved his most scornful remarks for the Palestinians both publicly and privately, he was also frustrated with the Israelis. At one point, realising, apparently, that Barak had precious little idea – even less inclination – how to reach out to the Palestinians, Clinton offered this advice: 'You are smarter and more experienced that I am in war. But I am older in politics. And I have learned by my mistakes.'[16]

Much blame has been attached to the Palestinians for Camp David's failure, not least by Clinton himself, who barely contained his irritation when announcing at midnight on Tuesday, 25 July 2000, that the summit had ended. 'Prime Minister Barak showed particular courage and vision, and an understanding of the historical importance of this moment. Chairman Arafat made it clear that he, too, remains committed to the path of peace,' said Clinton, leaving no doubt whom he held accountable.[17] But the Palestinians themselves, understandably, demurred; although they proved incapable of countering the general impression that it was their intransigence, and their intransigence alone, which derailed the enterprise. What is the case, contrary to misinformation spread at the time, is that the Palestinians were not offered 95 per cent of what they asked for, or anything like it, at Camp David. This simplistic spin on the washup of the failed enterprise, promoted most notably by Clinton's Middle East team, who themselves were far from blameless, was parroted endlessly by commentators in the US mainstream press. They might have been less credulous. As Agha and Malley (the latter participated in the summit as a Special Assistant to Clinton for Arab–Israeli affairs) attest, there were serious errors on both sides. Even Barak's own chief of staff, Dan Yatom, had pleaded with his boss at a critical moment to reach out to Arafat (extraordinarily, Barak, apart from a brief moment, spent no time alone with the Palestinian leader), saying, 'Ehud, you will have to sit and talk with Arafat because this is the essence of Camp David,' but Barak was immovable.[18]

Finally, it was not as though Camp David was without any redeeming features. Progress was made on issues like: boundaries of a Palestinian state which would take account of settlements near Jerusalem (the Palestinians were prepared to consider an exchange of Israeli land to compensate for territory); the vexed right of Palestinians to return to their homes in what had been mandated Palestine (the Palestinians were prepared to agree to limit numbers in exchange for compensation for those unable to return); even Jerusalem, where the Palestinians were willing to entertain the idea of a division of East Jerusalem under a formula which would enable Israel to retain sovereignty over Jewish areas such as the Jewish Quarter of the Old City and the Western (Wailing) Wall. But because of the fuzziness of the negotiations, the lack of clarity in ideas advanced and not responded to, and the almost complete lack of trust between the respective leaders, some promising initiatives remained just that – initiatives. The Palestinian perspective, several years on from Camp David, is not without humour. Referring to what the Palestinians believed was a convoluted formula advanced by Barak for resolution of the Jerusalem conundrum, under which there would be all sorts of complications, including the idea of 'vertical sovereignty' to take account of the Haram al-Sharif, third most sacred site to Muslims after Mecca and Medina, from where the Prophet is believed to have ascended to heaven, and below it, the ruins of the Second Temple, most sacred to Jews, Nabil Shaath observed, 'You would have needed a GPS navigational system in your shoes to negotiate Barak's Jerusalem.'[19] Whatever the rights and wrongs of Camp David 2, few involved would have disagreed with Shaath who described it as a 'Greek tragedy'. 'It had to happen and it had to fail,' he said.[20]

In the aftermath of Camp David's failure – and to this day – the Palestinians remain highly critical of Clinton's advisers, in particular senior Middle East envoy Dennis Ross, whom they regarded as irredeemably biased towards Israel. If there is a villain of the piece, as far as the Palestinians are concerned, it is Ross whom they blame for sins of omission and commission, including poor preparation for Camp David itself. 'All he was interested in was keeping the process going, and not in the end result. He had tried to delay the inevitable until it was not inevitable at all,' said Shaath.[21] Ross himself has strenuously rebutted such criticism, most notably in a response to the Agha–Malley assessment of Camp David, saying he was 'dismayed' by their account which had confused tactical mistakes with strategic errors. 'Did Prime Minister Barak make mistakes in his tactics, his negotiating priorities, and his treatment of Arafat? Absolutely. Did the American side make mistakes in its packaging and presentation of ideas? Absolutely. Are Prime Minister Barak and President Clinton responsible for the failure to conclude a deal? Absolutely not. Both Barak and Clinton were prepared to do what was necessary to reach agreement. Both were up to the challenge. Neither shied away from the risks inherent in confronting history and mythology. Can one say the same about Arafat? Unfortunately not . . .' wrote Ross.[22]

Hardly had the dust settled on Camp David 2, with recriminations still hanging heavy in the air between the Palestinians, Americans and Israelis, than Arafat found himself in New York in the first week of September for the UN Millenium summit, at which an indefatigable Clinton again made an effort, futile as it proved, to bridge the gap between the two sides. These discussions took place against the background of Arafat's threats to declare statehood unilaterally on 13 September (the PLO's Central

Committee postponed an announcement indefinitely on 10 September under pressure from the US). That week in New York also witnessed what must surely go down in history as one of the more bizarre exchanges involving Arafat, buffeted by weeks of negative publicity after the failure of Camp David, unfairly in his view, and a senior American official. The scene was the Waldorf Astoria on Park Avenue, and the participants included Arafat himself, Nabil Shaath and US Secretary of State Madeleine Albright.

The groups were waiting to see Clinton and, while they were cooling their heels, Albright, according to Shaath, asked Arafat, 'What are you going to tell the President of the United States about the Temple Mount?'

Arafat: 'What I tell the President of the United States is none of your business. By the way, it is not the Temple Mount, it is the Haram al-Sharif.'

Albright: 'I know it as the Temple Mount.'

Arafat: 'It's the Haram al-Sharif.'

Albright: 'OK, it's the Temple Mount/Haram al-Sharif.'

Arafat: 'No, it's the Haram al-Sharif.'

Albright: 'OK, call it what you wish. Are you going to accept the proposal made by the President of the United States about shared sovereignty [for the holy places]?'

At that moment, an enraged Arafat walked out, saying, 'You know nothing about the history of the place . . . You are delaying the meeting with the President of the United States.'

As if Clinton was not having enough difficulty mediating between fractious Israelis and Palestinians he was now obliged to make peace between a furious Arafat and a bruised Albright.

After a thirty-minute private meeting with Arafat and Shaath, Clinton asked if he could summon Madeleine who was 'hurt'. When she entered the room, according to Shaath, Arafat kissed her on the forehead.[23] In such strange ways did relations between US officials and the Palestinians move after the intensity and anticlimax of the Camp David process which had brought them closer together personally, and yet left them far apart on issues of substance. Shaath tells revealing stories about private conversations with Clinton during the two weeks the Israelis, Palestinians and Americans were closeted at the presidential retreat. 'Clinton kept dreaming all the time. "Nabil, I can see myself raising the Palestinian flag over Jerusalem on the day you declare your state." . . . "Nabil, I dream of that moment when I help you raise the Palestinian flag over your capital in Jerusalem." He had a biblical view of things. He really taught himself the ABC of the Arab–Israel dispute. He had the zeal and passion for it. He could not have done more to achieve a settlement.'[24] In the end one of the real tragedies of Camp David 2, and one of the greatest disappoint- ments, was Clinton's own failure to bring the parties together. This was partly as a result of being let down by poor staff work, but perhaps of equal consequence was that expectations were raised unreasonably because of Clinton's own unrealistic – oversold – view of his abilities to close a deal by the sheer force of his personality, to bridge the chasm that existed.

If Arafat was not up to confronting, in Dennis Ross's words, history and mythology, he was about to get a reality check in the person of his arch-nemesis, Ariel Sharon, newly selected as head of the Likud, leader of Israel's opposition, who, in typically confrontational fashion, contrived to inflame the Palestinians in a way which scarcely could have been more provocative. On 28 September, Sharon, guarded by a phalanx of Israeli policemen, visited the Haram al-Sharif/Temple Mount (of vexatious discussion between Arafat and Albright in New York earlier in the month). Here was the architect of the Lebanon invasion to rid Lebanon of the PLO; here was the man censured by an Israeli commission of inquiry for being neglectful of the risks involved to Palestinians in the refugee camps of Sabra and Shatila who were subjected in 1982 to a pogrom at the hands of Israel's militia allies, the Phalange; here was the godfather of the Israeli settler movement treading upon a sacred Islamic site, albeit that beneath the ground on which Sharon stepped were the ruins of the Second Temple. Two days before Sharon's fateful – intentionally provocative – act, Arafat, at a private dinner with Barak outside Tel Aviv, had pleaded with Israel's leader to ban the visit, arguing that it would be like 'putting gasoline on the fire'.[24] But Barak, in his political weakness, was not prepared to intervene and the visit went ahead with incendiary consequences.

On 29 September, the eve of Rosh Hoshana, the Jewish New Year, when a larger number of Jews than usual were worshipping at the Western (Wailing) Wall, Palestinians retaliated by hurling stones and rocks from the Haram al-Sharif compound on the worshippers below. Panicked, the police opened fire, killing a number of Palestinians and wounding dozens of others. While a Palestinian earthquake may have been on the cards, even planned, after the failure of Camp David, there is also no doubt that Sharon's calculated provocation was aimed at inflaming passions for political advantage, to demonstrate to his own supporters on the nationalist right that he was prepared to enter the lion's den, and at the same time expose his opponent's weakness. If that was the aim, tactically it worked. But Sharon's gambit also contributed to the start of what became known as *Intifada II*. Blood shed in the next weeks, months and years would stain what was left of the peace process itself, further debilitate a weakened peace camp in Israel and, worse from Arafat's standpoint, lay the Palestinian leader open to the charge that he instigated the uprising, or at the very least made only limp efforts to stop it. Supporters claimed that frustration over lack of progress towards peace, allied with disappointment at worsening economic circumstances on the ground in the West Bank and Gaza, made such an explosion inevitable.[26] But in the whole of Arafat's tumultuous reign there was perhaps no other episode which ended up being quite as damaging. And worse, he had only himself to blame, since, by any reasonable judgement, his equivocation, his lack of leadership, his prevarication, his demonstrable ineffectiveness contributed to the mess which followed – and to his own lengthy isolation, his credibility in shreds. The genie of atavistic violence between Palestinians and Israelis, Arabs and Jews was well and truly out of the bottle.

As September gave way to October, a mini war had broken out in which Israel deployed helicopter gunships and tanks against Palestinian gunmen and stone-throwers. In those first days, as serious rioting engulfed the West Bank and Gaza, the world was to get an inkling of a new stage in an age-old conflict, one in which Palestinians began making greater use of firearms, thereby inviting more extreme forms of retaliation: the cycle of violence deepened. Suicide bombing entrenched itself as a weapon-of-choice for the more extreme groups. So concerned was the White House about the rapid deterioration that CIA chief George Tenet was sent to the region to set up high-level security talks between Israelis and Palestinians. But he was greeted on arrival by one of the more barbaric episodes in the entire history of the conflict. On 12 October, a Palestinian mob invaded a Palestinian police station in the West Bank town of Ramallah and murdered two Israeli soldiers who were being held after having lost their way. One of the bodies was desecrated and paraded through the streets of Ramallah. Ghoulish Palestinian murderers held up hands covered in Israeli blood for the television cameras, an image that would be very difficult to erase.

Four days later on 16 October, Clinton hurried to the Egyptian Sinai resort of Sharm el-Sheikh to mediate between Arafat and Barak, now barely on speaking terms, winning grudging agreement, after 24 hours of arm-twisting, from both to lend their voices to an end to the violence. But this was to little avail as fierce fighting across the West Bank saw casualties mount on both sides. On 22 October, the same day as an Arab League summit condemned Israeli 'atrocities',[27] Barak announced he was suspending the peace process, a largely meaningless gesture since it was virtually defunct in any case. But Clinton himself, as the US prepared for elections in the second week of November, was not giving up. He had simply invested too much time and effort, both physical and intellectual, in trying to close the gap. Even Barak's decision, on 28 November, to call elections after his government had all but collapsed, did not stay Clinton's hand.

With casualties mounting by the day (by the end of the year close to four hundred people had perished, most of them Palestinians) Clinton, now in the final 'lame duck' stages of his presidency, summoned Palestinian and Israeli negotiators to the White House on 23 December to receive what became known as the 'Clinton plan'. It was a skimpy document that sought to draw on positive elements of Camp David 2 in an offer which involved giving the Palestinians 94–6 per cent of the West Bank and Gaza. Compared with the complexities of Oslo 1 and 2, the Clinton plan was simplicity itself. It dealt with four headline issues: territory; security; Jerusalem; and refugees, plus a short – and wildly presumptuous – statement on 'The End of Conflict'.[28] So began, not the permanent status discussions which Oslo had envisaged, but a last-ditch attempt to strike a deal with Palestinian and Israeli negotiators meeting in the Red Sea resort of Taba, even as Clinton was packing his bags to leave the White House to make way for George W. Bush.

At the core of the Clinton plan were propositions aimed at addressing what had defined themselves as the main sticking points in all the weeks, months and years of difficult negotiations since the Oslo Declaration of Principles in September 1993 was initialled: Jerusalem and refugees. What Clinton proposed in those last days before leaving office was a trade-off between the two. If the Palestinians would give way on the 'right of return' for all refugees to their ancestral homes in Israel proper, Israel might be persuaded to give ground on Jerusalem under Clinton's 'shared sovereignty' formula. As summarised by William B. Quandt, Clinton's plan 'would give Arab neighborhoods to the Palestinians, including the Muslim and Christian parts of the Old City, and most importantly the Haram al-Sharif compound. Israel would retain the Jewish quarter and a passageway through the Armenian quarter and would retain control over the Western Wall and Temple Mount beneath Haram al-Sharif.'[29]

Palestinian and Israeli negotiators began meeting in Taba in the first week of 2001 after Barak had persuaded his cabinet to accept in principle the Clinton plan, and Arafat, reluctantly, concurred, after having his arm twisted at a final meeting with Clinton at the White House on 2 January. According to Shaath, who headed the Palestinian negotiating team in Taba, Arafat had little confidence in the process and in Barak who was then in his death throes politically with Israeli elections beckoning on 6 February, but he went along with the idea of a last gasp attempt because, as much as anything, he felt he owed it to Clinton.[30] If the truth be known Arafat was still smarting from all the opprobrium which had been heaped on his head for the failure of Camp David 2. But in light of all their misgivings the Palestinians certainly did not go to Taba without registering their strong reservations with the Clinton plan.

On 2 January, the same day Arafat met Clinton at the White House, the Palestinians issued a statement in which they noted that the plan 'failed to satisfy the conditions required for a permanent peace'. Palestinian objections were as follows. It would: (1) divide a Palestinian state into three separate cantons connected and divided by Jewish-only and Arab-only roads and jeopardise the Palestinian state's viability; (2) divide Palestinian Jerusalem into a number of unconnected islands separate from each other and from the rest of Palestine; and (3) force Palestinians to surrender the right of return of Palestinian refugees. It also fails to provide workable security arrangements between Palestine and Israel, and to address a number of other issues of importance to the Palestinian people. The United States proposal seems to respond to Israeli demands while neglecting the basic Palestinian need: a viable state.[31]

So began the last stuttering attempt to bridge the gap, even as the last grains of sand were trickling from a Middle East hourglass. What the Palestinians and Israelis found at Taba was that Camp David 2 had been quite cathartic in the sense that issues like Jerusalem and refugees had been discussed more candidly, if not constructively, than previously. Indeed, at Taba the two sides made more progress in a few days than in a few weeks at Camp David, but, of course, these were phoney negotiations, as everyone knew, in the shadow of a Clinton departure from the White House and the impending defeat of Barak at the polls. In the words of Shaath, it was all too little and too late, certainly to help Barak across the line in the forthcoming election, which was one of Clinton's principle aims.[32] The discussions continued desultorily until 28 January when Barak brought them to a halt until after the elections. This was to be the last serious negotiation, if it could be described as such, between Palestinians and Israelis for at least several years. It was also a prelude to possibly the most difficult, ultimately damaging, period in Arafat's long stewardship of the Palestinian movement.

25. BESIEGED

'Peace requires a new and different Palestinian leadership, so that a Palestinian state can be born. I call on the Palestinian people to elect new leaders, leaders not compromised by terror.' President George W. Bush, Middle East speech, White House, 24 June 2002.[1]

As Arafat, in the second week of February 2001, surveyed what was left of the peace process, and what little trust remained between Palestinians and Israelis, he could not have anticipated, even at his most pessimistic, just how dire his situation would become in the months ahead. He had reacted to Sharon's expected landslide victory in the 6 February poll by saying he hoped that peace efforts would continue under a new Israeli administration. But he was keenly aware that in Sharon he was facing the man who had sought to kill him during the siege of Beirut in 1982 by using the Israeli air force as flying assassination squads. According to Shaath, Arafat's calculations in early 2001 were not altogether different from those in early to mid-1982 when Israel's war plans for Lebanon were being hatched by then Defence Minister Sharon.[2] Sharon would seek to crush the resistance by military means, while seeking to persuade a new US administration (President George W. Bush, inexperienced in foreign policy, was sworn in on 20 January) that the Palestinians, and Arafat in particular, were culpable for any failures to advance peace, indeed that the other side was vandalising the process. When Sharon formally took office on 7 March at the head of a so-called national unity government with Shimon Peres as foreign minister, the Palestinians were not encouraged. They knew that tensions within Sharon's seven-faction coalition would weigh heavily on any sustainable efforts at peace, and so it proved. Arafat confidant Bassam Abu Sharif sought to put the best face on the Palestinian predicament in those early days, describing the situation as a 'battle of patience';[3] but Arafat would not have needed reminding that, at the age of 72 and in indifferent health, time 'in this battle of patience' was not necessarily on his side.

As spring gave way to summer, the Palestinians' worst fears were realised. Not only was the peace process virtually frozen, but the Israelis, as Arafat had anticipated, began employing more extreme military measures, including targeted assassinations of suspected militants, using Apache helicopter gunships. The Israeli army also reoccupied territory, notably in Gaza, controlled by the Palestinians and which had been vacated under the various agreements negotiated after 1993. Suicide bombings became more common. The slide to violence continued, like a dripping tap, day in and day out. For a beleaguered Palestinian leadership there were a few brief moments of encouragement such as publication in April of a report which had been commissioned the previous October at the Sharm el-Sheikh peace talks presided over by Clinton. The Mitchell report of 30 April, chaired by former US Senator George Mitchell, whose origins were partly Lebanese, decisively called for an end to the violence, a resumption of peace talks and, perhaps most importantly from the Palestinian perspective, a freeze on settlements.[4] But predictably Sharon dismissed Mitchell out of hand, describing settlements as 'a vital national enterprise'.[5]

Against this bleak background, Palestine would lose one of its favourite sons, and someone who just might have been an alternative to Arafat himself as leader of the Palestinians – if he had been given a chance. On 31 May Faisal Husseini, the 'father' of the Palestinians in Jerusalem, died suddenly of a heart attack while on a visit to Kuwait. He was 61. Another potential rival to Arafat had fallen by the wayside, for it was no secret that Arafat and Husseini, if not estranged, had drifted far apart since the former's return to Palestine in mid-1994. Ever jealous of his dominance, Arafat had effectively marginalised Husseini, member of an aristocratic Palestinian family and son of the Palestinians' most celebrated 'martyr', Abdel Kader who had died in 1948 commanding the Palestinian forces in defence of Jerusalem against Israel's Palmach. Husseini's supporters in Jerusalem might have been tempted to observe that he died of a broken heart at the mistakes and missed opportunities which had befallen the Palestinians in the six years since Arafat's return to Palestine. In Brussels, Arafat described Husseini's death as a 'great loss for the Palestinian people'. Personally he escorted the coffin from Amman to the West Bank (but not Jerusalem for burial). Another old soldier of the Palestinian struggle had fallen by the wayside, leaving Arafat, in the midst of one of his most challenging periods, increasingly bereft of experienced cadres who commanded even a modicum of respect across Palestinian factions.

As the Mitchell plan lay virtually dormant on the table, another document surfaced which also quickly took on all the characteristics of a bombed out piece of wartime ordnance rusting in the desert. The Palestinian-Israeli Security Work plan, known as the 'Tenet plan' after CIA chief George Tenet, who had been dispatched to the Middle East in mid-2001 to calm things down, spelled out a programme of enhanced security co-operation between Palestinians and Israelis, but the plan's laudable aims of a 'mutual, comprehensive cease-fire applying to all violent activities' were not even honoured in the breach.[6] As these desultory efforts towards securing a Middle East calm on behalf of a disengaged Bush administration were proceeding, violence took even deeper roots in the territories with Arafat's ability to rein in the militants lessening by the day, even if he had wanted to. It was in this doldrums period before 11 September changed the world that sometimes rancorous debate ebbed and flowed in Israel's cabinet, split between hawks and doves, on whether to strike militarily at Arafat himself in retaliation for further escalations of the *Intifada* or whether a better option might be to expel him. This unresolved debate sputtered on throughout the Sharon government's first term with Sharon himself content to allow the issue to remain stalemated, since he knew that expulsion of the elected leader of the Palestinians would be hard to sell internationally, even to his new best friend George W. Bush in Washington.

Still the targeted assassinations and suicide bombings continued in a remorseless cycle. On 9 August a Hamas bomber blew himself up in a crowed pizza parlour in Jerusalem, killing 15 people and wounding 90 in one of the worst episodes, and one which seemed more than others to embody all the toxicity of the Palestine-Israel conflict. Israel retaliated by rocketing the Palestinian police headquarters in Ramallah, not far from Arafat's own HQ. Ritualistically, the Palestinian leader condemned the Jerusalem bombing, but his remarks seemed to underscore his impotence, since no one seemed to be taking the slightest bit of notice. Arafat's inability –

or unwillingness – to rein in the suicide bombers allowed ample scope for Israel to claim that rather than trying to stop them he was complicit since an offshoot of his own Fatah faction – the al-Aqsa Martyrs Brigades – had become deeply involved in suicide bombing, beginning in November, 2000. In fact, the Martyrs Brigades which came into being and were so named after Sharon's September, 2000 visit to the Haram al-Sharif, the site of the Aqsa mosque, were responsible for more suicide attacks on Israel in the following year than Islamic extremists themselves who had pioneered the terror weapon. In its attempts to pin ultimate responsibility for the activities of the suicide bombers on Arafat himself, Israel by early 2002 had collected truckloads of documents – fifty thousand by one account – which it claimed included damaging material which did indeed make the link. While the mass of paperwork seized in Israeli raids on Palestinian Authority offices in the West Bank did indicate that a number of Arafat's close aides were involved in activities which might be described as incompatible with their status as non-combatant servants of the Palestinian administration, there was no smoking gun as such as far as Arafat was concerned. However, on the face of it – and allowing for inevitable distortions, wilful or otherwise, in Israel's interpretation and presentation of the material seized – what can be said is that for whatever reason Arafat's apparent inability to assert control over a group associated with his own faction, leaving aside the Islamists – Hamas and Islamic Jihad – was revealing and very damaging. The Bush administration appeared by mid-2002 to have bought Israel's contention that Arafat was complicit in terrorist activities, if not an actual instigator, and this more than anything resulted in calls for 'regime change' in the Palestinian leadership. By the autumn of 2002 it was not only Washington which had come down on Arafat like a ton of bricks on the issue of terrorism. In a highly damaging 170-page report, the respected US-based Human Rights Watch accused Arafat of not doing nearly enough to prevent the suicide bombings which it condemned as a crime against humanity. While the group found no evidence to support Israel's claim that Arafat orchestrated the attacks, his Palestinian Authority was at fault for failing to rein in and punish the militants behind the bombings. 'Arafat and the Palestinian Authority bear a high degree of political responsibility for the atrocities that occurred,' said Kenneth Roth, the rights group's executive director. Roth described individuals who carried out the bombings as 'war criminals'.

In the days before 11 September, the ground was continuing to shift for the Palestinian leadership. But the tremors of 2001, violent though they may have seemed in leadership redoubts in Gaza and West Bank towns, were nothing compared with the shocking events in New York of the second week of September. When Arafat, in his Gaza headquarters, watched the unfolding drama of passenger jets slamming into the World Trade Centre and the Pentagon, he was left virtually speechless, muttering to himself in Arabic that it was 'unbelievable', according to those present. But 'unbelievable' though it may have seemed to someone who had involved himself in more than his share of terrorist acts over the years, and might have dreamed of capturing world attention in such a dramatic way, Arafat knew that in his demonstrable vulnerability he could not delay for a second in voicing his condemnation. At 5.56 p.m. Gaza time, two hours after American Airlines Flight 11 slammed into the World Trade Centre, Arafat made a public statement before a media scrum outside his offices: 'I send my condolences, and the condolences of the Palestinian people to American President Bush and his government and to the American people for this terrible act,' said Arafat.[7] He was not alone among world leaders whose words seemed quite inadequate for the occasion, like the sound of a tin whistle.

But whatever trauma the events of 11 September might have caused for Americans themselves, the event was very quickly transformed, in the shared self-centred world of victimhood of Palestinians and Israelis, into an issue of particular relevance for them. As the US sought to steady itself after the crushing body blow it had suffered, its officials, including Secretary of State Colin Powell, busied themselves on the phone to Middle East leaders in an effort to shore up support, and persuade the Arab and Israeli parties to return to negotiations. For if 11 September had demonstrated one thing to a US administration whose main players had a fairly simplistic view of the world, and Middle East issues in particular, it was that a region shorn of hope was much more dangerous than one where hope at least sprang eternal. But Sharon demurred unless the Palestinians ceased all 'terrorist' activities. Unhelpfully, he referred to Arafat as the 'bin Laden of the Middle East'.[8] In his attempts to manipulate 11 September to Israel's advantage – and Palestinian disadvantage – Sharon would, not for the first time, nor the last, overstep the mark. His refusal to re-engage immediately in cease-fire talks with the Palestinians, including a meeting with Arafat himself, drew an irritated response from Washington. But he was steadfast. In an interview with the Jerusalem Post he was adamant – no return to negotiations. 'I have made it clear to the administration as well as to a list of countries in Europe, that while stability in the Middle East is important to them, and is very important to Israel. We will not pay the price for that stability. We will simply not pay it.'[9] As Sharon was digging in his heels, Palestinian gunman struck at the heart of his government, killing ultra-nationalist Tourism Minister Rehavam Zeevi in a Jerusalem hotel. The death of Zeevi, a former military comrade-in-arms of Sharon's, was a prelude to Arafat being put under virtual house arrest in Ramallah as the Palestinian leadership resisted pressure to hand over the suspected killers from the Popular Front for the Liberation of Palestine.

Three weeks after 11 September, Arafat was encouraged briefly by remarks from the White House when President Bush spoke for the first time in favour of a Palestinian 'state'. These ideas were further fleshed out in a blueprint for the Middle East released on 11 October, exactly one month after the dramatic events in New York and Washington. The plan incorporated Clinton's 'shared sovereignty' of Jerusalem proposals, but Arafat would have been much less sanguine if he had been privy to some of the discussions which surrounded the US initiative, for powerful figures in the administration were convinced that peace would remain elusive as long as he remained leader of the Palestinians. In summary he was regarded as 'part of the problem and not part of the solution.' When Secretary of State Powell got to his feet for a major speech on the Middle East at the University of Louisville,

Kentucky, on 19 November, the administration's thinking had evolved to the point where he was in a position to lay out a fairly clear – and even-handed – position. 'Both sides will need to face up to some plain truths about where the process is heading . . . Palestinians must eliminate any doubt, once and for all, that they accept the legitimacy of Israel as a Jewish state . . . The Palestinian leadership must end violence, stop incitement and prepare their people for the hard choices ahead . . . Israel must be willing to end its occupation, consistent with the principle embodied in Security Council Resolutions 242 and 338, and accept a Palestinian State in which Palestinians can determine their own future on their own land and live in dignity and security. They too will have to make some hard compromises.'[10] Powell also announced that Retired Marine Corps General Anthony Zinni was being sent back to the Middle East for what proved to be months of futile activity in an attempt to put in place what the Secretary of State called a 'durable cease-fire'.[11]

What Zeevi's death on 17 October ensured was that Israeli military violence, above all else, would escalate throughout the latter months of 2001 as Sharon attempted to suppress the Palestinian resistance – and demonstrate to hard-liners in his own cabinet that he was not prepared to flinch. In early December, with Arafat cloistered in Ramallah, under siege by a cordon of tanks, Israeli jets and helicopters blasted targets in the West Bank and Gaza Strip, including Arafat's own Gaza beachfront home. Targeted assassinations of militant leaders became more commonplace than suicide bombings. The aim of this offensive was to pressure Arafat to do more to rein in Islamic militants, but it was fairly clear as 2001 gave way to 2002 that there was precious little a weakened Palestinian leader could do about the situation beyond issuing anaemic statements calling for restraint. In any case, Arafat had fallen back on a tried and true formula in circumstances like this: survival as a tactic and a strategy and an end in itself. As Bassam Abu Sharif put it at the time: 'Survival is the formula. He has to survive.'[12] It was not the first time Arafat, like a hunted animal who has gone to ground, would seek to wait out a storm.

The storm would continue to break for days, weeks and months throughout 2002 as Arafat, deathly pale from lack of exposure to the elements, lived like a hermit crab in his Ramallah compound as Israeli tank shells and rockets gradually reduced his living space to two rooms surrounded by rubble. A joke doing the round in early 2003 was that when Arafat made his customary 'V' for victory sign by holding up two fingers what he was really doing was advising people that he had just two rooms left. But even as Arafat fought for survival during what Palestinians began to describing as a 'war of attrition' events elsewhere in the wider Middle East and the world itself did not stop. Arafat was able to draw some satisfaction on 24 January 2002 from the death of Lebanese militia warlord Elie Hobeika who was blown up in a massive car bomb outside his house. It was Hobeika who had commanded the Phalange militia units which were responsible for the 1982 massacres at Sabra and Shatila. No culprit for Hobeika's elimination was identified but one intriguing possibility suggested itself: the Lebanese warlord would have been a material witness at the possible trial of Ariel Sharon in a Belgian war crimes case over the Sabra and Shatila massacres. Now he had been silenced.

But if Arafat drew momentary satisfaction from Hobeika's demise he would not have drawn much comfort from the State of the Union address given several days later by George W. Bush in which he lambasted what he described, in perhaps the most memorable phrase of the post-cold war era, as an 'axis of evil' – Iraq, North Korea and Iran. Pointedly, he also made reference to these countries' 'terrorist allies'. So, the foundations were laid for the new Bush doctrine of 'regime change' whose hot breath would, by early 2003, be threatening Arafat's own survival as leader of the Palestinians. 'States like these (Iraq, North Korea and Iran), and their terrorist allies, constitute an axis of evil, arming to threaten the peace of the world. By seeking weapons of mass destruction, these regimes pose a grave and growing danger. They could provide these arms to terrorists, giving them the means to match their hatred. They could attack our allies or attempt to blackmail the United States. In any of these cases, the price of indifference would be catastrophic,' Bush said.[13] It was not overlooked at the time that just three weeks before Bush spoke a shipment of arms for the Palestinians from the one of these axis of evil states – Iran – had been intercepted by Israel. Arafat denied knowledge of the

50-tonne shipment, which included anti-tank missiles and katyusha rockets, but his denials lacked credibility. Around this time Sharon, in an interview with the Israeli newspaper *Maariv*, said he regretted not having 'eliminated' Arafat during the invasion of Lebanon.[14] This observation was ingenuous, since the elimination of Arafat was not for lack of trying on occasions, including the use of the Israeli air force to blast the Palestinian leader from his Beirut strongholds.

But all this would prove to be sideshow for a further dramatic escalation of violence throughout the month of March, including, on 8 March, the deadliest day of fighting in the entire *Intifada II* in which 40 Palestinians were killed in the West Bank and Gaza. Four days later, 20,000 troops invaded refugee camps in the Gaza Strip and reoccupied Ramallah where Arafat had been cooped up for months. Alarmed by the downward spiral of violence in territories occupied by Israel, the UN Security Council on 12 March for the first time endorsed a Palestinian state (Resolution 1397 affirmed a 'vision of the region where two States, Israel and Palestine, live side by side within secure and recognised boundaries). Secretary General Kofi Annan denounced Israel's 'illegal occupation' of Palestinian land. Even a lackadaisical, as far as the Palestinians were concerned, Bush administration seemed worried. General Zinni returned to the Middle East on 14 March for another – futile, as it turned out – attempt at peacemaking. The result was the 'Zinni Paper' of 26 March which traversed much the same route as the Tenet Plan whose core demand was a comprehensive and durable cease-fire.[15] Nothing was more unlikely in the climate of the times. Equally ineffectual was Security Council resolution 1402 which expressed 'grave concern'.[16] Vice President Dick Cheney's arrival in the region on 18 March, ostensibly to build support for a war against Iraq, did not help either. Indeed, it begged the question what an administration hawk, known for his antipathy towards the Palestinians and Arafat in particular, was doing in the region in any case. After all, Cheney and Defence Secretary Donald Rumsfeld had argued in January that the administration should sever all ties with Arafat.[17]

In the midst of all this coming and going, including unremitting violence, the 22-member Arab League met in Beirut to consider the crisis in the Palestinian areas. Arafat was not an attendee, having decided that the risks of leaving his perch in Ramallah outweighed the benefits. Pressed by the Americans to allow Arafat to travel, Sharon had threatened 'permanent exile' if there were more terrorist attacks while he was in Beirut. In an atmosphere of high drama and low farce which tend to characterise these events, with the Palestinians more often than not at the centre of things, the Palestinian delegation walked out after a misunderstanding with the Lebanese hosts regarding whether 'Chairman Arafat' would be permitted to address the gathering by satellite. In the end he did, treating his audience to a scorching account of the predicament in which the Palestinian found themselves, and, as always, using the occasion to extend the begging bowl for more financial assistance. One concrete achievement of the 14th 'Ordinary Session' of the Arab League, if it could be described as an achievement, was the form and shape given to a peace plan advanced by Crown Prince Abdullah of Saudi Arabia which offered Israel 'peace and security' in exchange for its withdrawal to 1967 boundaries according to Security Council resolutions 242 and 338.[18] So yet another peace plan was born to gather dust in some forgotten pigeonhole.

With Israeli army bulldozers demolishing Arafat's compound and with the Palestinian leader having taken refuge in the basement, Bush made his sternest intervention, telling both sides 'enough is enough', and announcing that he was sending Secretary of State Powell to the region to separate the combatants. Pointedly, Bush put Arafat himself on notice that American patience with the continuing violence, including suicide bombings, had all but run out. In his most pointed criticism to date of Arafat himself, and in a sign that those arguing within the administration for 'regime change' among the Palestinians were winning, Bush observed: 'The situation in which (Arafat) finds himself today is largely of his own making . . . He's missed his opportunities and thereby betrayed the hopes of the people he's supposed to lead.'[19] In Ramallah, where Arafat was preparing to come up for air to meet General Zinni, Bush's criticism was noted, but the Palestinian leader had other things on his mind – like survival. Secretary of State Colin Powell's visit to the region, including an inexplicable detour to Morocco, where he was rebuked by the youthful Moroccan King Mohammed IV, elicited from Arafat on 13 April a statement condemning terrorism, but when Powell left the region four days later there was little to show for his efforts, either in the form of a cease-fire or any sign of progress towards a resumption of peace negotiations.

Secretary of State Powell's brief visit to the Middle East left behind a slew of unresolved problems, not least where next in the dance of death between the Palestinians and Israel, but in May Arafat did gain a reprieve from his lengthy incarceration. After five months, his house arrest was effectively lifted following an agreement to hand over six culprits for the murder of Tourism Minister Zeevi to Anglo-American custody – Israel agreed reluctantly to the assassins being held in Palestinian jails only if they were under the supervision of international jailers – under a deal partly brokered by Powell. Arafat's liberation from custody was hardly a ticket to freedom, however. He remained in Ramallah, eschewing movement outside the country because of concerns that he would not be allowed back. In any case, there were few places, either in the Arab world or in the wider international community, where he was particularly welcome. These were dog days for the Palestinian leader. Among the sops offered by Powell on his visit to try to persuade Arafat and the Palestinian leadership to do more to calm the violence was an undertaking that by mid-year the administration would unveil a new Middle East peace plan. Arafat's expectations about this new American initiative were modest, to say the least. But Powell had certainly not led him to expect that President Bush's most important foray to that point into Middle East peacemaking would include a blunt demand for 'regime change' in the Palestinian leadership. Powell and the State Department had lost, Cheney and Rumsfeld had won.

On 24 June Bush, with Powell on his right and Rumsfeld on his left, delivered the latest American offering. In the event, apart from his re-endorsement of Palestinian statehood, the speech was bitterly disappointing for the Palestinians and Arafat in particular. If there was any doubt about Bush's abiding hostility towards the Palestinian leader it was dispelled in remarks which left no room for misunderstanding. 'When the Palestinian people have new leaders, new institutions and new security arrangements with their neighbours, the United States of America will support the creation of a Palestinian state,' Bush said.[20] Almost as bad, from Arafat's standpoint, was Bush's demand for his removal, as the fact that in the entire speech there was no reference to the 'land for peace' Security Council resolutions 242 and 338, the *sine qua non* of any Middle East arrangement, nor was there a word about the need for Israel to stop settlement building immediately. Bush came no closer to admonishment of Israel than his observation: 'Permanent occupation threatens Israel's identity and democracy'.[21] Reviewing Bush's 'non-plan' brought home to the Palestinian leadership the odds they were up against with an administration increasingly preoccupied with Iraq, and apparently not predisposed to put Israel under any real pressure to re-engage in peace efforts. 'Not unless there is a real commitment by the Americans will anything push that kind of government (Sharon's) to go back to real negotiations leading to peace. It is not impossible, but highly improbable,'[22] was Nabil Shaath's conclusion as the dismal year (for the Palestinians) drew to a close and Israeli elections beckoned.

In the months between Bush's Rose Garden statement and Israel's elections on 28 January 2003, the next moment of reckoning in the troubled history of the Palestinians, the US administration was almost completely preoccupied with its preparations for war against Iraq. Huge diplomatic resources were being thrown at the problem, and a problem it was since White House hawks were having great difficulty persuading a sceptical international community of the need for war. As a consequence, the Palestinian-Israeli issue slid down the US list of priorities; although there were those in senior councils of the Palestinian movement who were prepared to believe that, contrary to conventional wisdom, defeat for the Iraqi regime may not necessarily be a bad thing for the Palestinians. 'What is worse: a stagnant pond or one where the waters have been rippled?' was one view expressed.[23] The Palestinians were also being told that British Prime Minister Tony Blair and his Foreign Secretary Jack Straw had elicited undertakings from Bush and Powell that a genuine effort would be made, post-Saddam, to deal with the Palestinian issue once and for all, 'provided the Palestinians put their house in order'.[24] But the Palestinians were sceptical about these assurances, especially as regards the Americans.

At the same time, the Palestinian leadership, and Arafat in particular, harboured genuine concerns that Sharon would use the cover of war for even more extreme action on the ground – and possibly as a pretext for Arafat's own expulsion from the territories. Some in the Palestinian leadership did take to heart Bush's criticisms of appallingly low standards of corporate governance inside the Palestinian Authority. Nabil Shaath, for one, worked through 2002, overseeing the drafting of a new Palestinian constitution for any future Palestinian state. Pending that outcome, the document would seek to clarify the respective roles of the President of a state-in-waiting (Arafat) and a Prime Minister of such a state. Arafat, of course, wanted his pre-eminence preserved under any circumstances in a way which would have reduced the role of a Prime Minister of a state-in-waiting to that of cipher. But UN and EU representatives, such as the UN envoy to the Middle East Terje Roed Larsen and his EU counterpart Miguel Moratinos made it clear that anything which entrenched Arafat's authority in such a way as would enable him to continue his arbitrary and dictatorial governance was unacceptable internationally. In his demonstrable weakness – and isolation – Arafat had little choice but to pretend to go along with the pressures that were being brought to bear.

It would be wrong, however, to characterise this period as completely unproductive for the Palestinians. Arafat himself, under extreme pressure, was forced to give some ground both to those inside the Palestinian authority who were arguing for greater accountability and to the international community which was demanding reform of his ramshackle enterprise. In a statement on 16 May, he promised reform and fresh presidential elections within six months. In June, he removed some – far from all – cabinet ministers in the Palestinian Authority who were under a cloud for corruption or just plain incompetence, or both. That same month, he indicated to the Israeli newspaper *Ha'aretz*[25] that he was now prepared to accept the Clinton plan of January 2001, which made all the more absurd his prevarication at the time. But, as everyone knew, this was all about playing for time and attempting to appear relevant in the face of irrelevance. In other words, survival.

The European response to the Bush 'non-plan' for the Middle East of 24 June was to push harder for an initiative that would bring together the views of the main international Players – the Quartet of the US, EU, UN and Russian Federation. Representatives, including UN Secretary General .Kofi Annan, Russian Foreign Minister Igor Ivanov, US Secretary of State Powell, Danish Foreign Minister Per Stig Moeller, High Representative for European Common Foreign and Security Policy Javier Solana and European Commissioner for External Affairs Chris Patten, met in New York on 16–17 July to discuss an 'action plan, with appropriate benchmarks' for Palestinian reform leading to the establishment of a Palestinian state. This prompted the drafting and re-drafting of what became known as the 'roadmap', or to give it its working title *Elements of a Performance-Based Road Map to a Permanent Two-State Solution to the Israeli-Palestinian Conflict.*[26] This document sets out a highly ambitious three-phase process towards Palestinian statehood by 2005, beginning with internal reform of the Palestinian Authority including an 'empowered Prime Minister'. The second stage would involve a newly elected Palestine Legislative Council approving a new constitution for a 'democratic, independent Palestinian state', and the third phase would lead to statehood and normalisation of relations with Israel. Israel itself would be obliged to meet 'performance based' criteria under the three-phase formula, including dismantling outlying settlements in the first phase.

While the bigger drama of a looming war with Iraq unfolded, nasty business continued more or less as normal in the West Bank and Gaza Strip where remorseless conflict between Israel and the Palestinian resistance infected the atmosphere at every level and deepened ruin in the local economy. In a report for the year ending 30 September 2001, the Office of the United Nations Special Co-ordinator estimated the impact on the Palestinian economy of confrontation, border closures and mobility restrictions had caused total income losses of between US$2.4–3.2 billion in that year alone, leaving aside the impact on trade and investment, not to mention property damage whose cost was incalculable. More than half the population in the West Bank and Gaza were surviving on US$2 a day or less.[27] In the eighteen months since, the situation has only got worse. On 9 September Arafat appeared for the first time in eighteen months before the Palestine Legislative Council. He used the occasion to condemn 'every act of terror against Israeli civilians', but he stopped short of calling for an end specifically to suicide bombings.[28] Two days later, in a sign that his authority was continuing to weaken, his government was forced to resign to avoid a parliamentary vote of no confidence.

Before the month was out Arafat was to get another reminder of the pressures he was under, both from within his own ranks, and from his Israeli enemies. On 20 September, Israeli tanks and bulldozers smashed their way into his Ramallah compound, leaving him even more besieged than ever in a partly ruined structure at the core of the compound, like a jagged tooth. Arafat, among the ruins of his partially destroyed headquarters, under the guns of Israeli tanks, was not the least compelling metaphor for the circumstances in which he found himself in the winter of 2002–2003. In Israel itself the ground was also shifting politically. On 30 October Israel's coalition government collapsed when Labour leader Binyamin Ben-Eliezer led his troops out of the cabinet leaving Sharon at the head of a narrow right-wing government in the thrall of ultra-nationalists and the religious right. In place of Ben-Eliezer as Defence Minister Sharon appointed General Shaul Mofaz, a man of his own stripe, who had never made any secret of his view that Arafat should be expelled. In Ramallah and Gaza, the Palestinian leadership fastened its safety belts, hopeful, but far from certain, that US interest in avoiding upheaval across the Arab world as war came nearer meant that Israel would be pressured to show some restraint in the next period.

Israeli elections on 28 January provided an expected result when Sharon prevailed easily over his Labour challenger, Amram Mitzna. But the immediate aftermath of the election, with Israel constrained by its usual slow-moving process of coalition building, was not without promise for the Palestinians. Sharon tentatively engaged in discussions with senior Palestinians, including the number two, Mahmoud Abbas, about renewed peace efforts. The Israeli leader indicated he would accept an invitation from Egyptian President Hosni Mubarak to visit Egypt for talks – the first such meeting between the two since Sharon became Prime Minister in 2001. But over and above everything else in this phase it was talk of war, and preparation for war, that dominated all considerations in early 2003. As was the case in 1991, Middle East fortunes, and those of the Palestinians in particular, were hostage to war – and a post-war scenario. If Arafat had a sliver of optimism in the midst of all the uncertainty, and his own bleak circumstances, it was that 1991 might repeat itself when, paradoxically, the post-war period brought with it gains for the Palestinians, notably at the Madrid peace conference. The problem for Arafat, though, is that in 1991, people, in spite of deep reservations, were then prepared to give him the benefit of the doubt. In 2003, the margin of tolerance among people who matter internationally is much diminished.

EPILOGUE

'He walks around his table for hours, long into the night. He goes around and around and around.' Nabil Shaath on Arafat, New York Times, 12 January 2003.

Nabil Shaath, Arafat's long-time confidant and loyal servant, was not meaning to be cruel, but the image of Yasser Arafat, virtually alone in his bombed out Ramallah compound, circling his desk like a wounded animal waiting for the end evoked a pathetic image of a leader whose time is ebbing. Deserted by much of the international community, his moral authority weakened among his people by the incompetence and corruption of his own administration, under constant threat of exile by a nationalist Israeli government, Arafat at 73 in the winter of 2002–03 was close to the nadir. Revising a book about Arafat in these circumstances is a bit like composing an epitaph: it is difficult to imagine the battered leader of the Palestinians will emerge Houdini-like from the present trap into which he has fallen in anything but a symbolic role, if that.

In truth, as the world grappled with the prospect of upheaval in the Middle East and an unpredictable aftermath, the outlook for the Palestinians and for Arafat was about as bleak as it could be. Just as the region is at a dangerous juncture historically, so too are the Palestinians. Now, it is conceivable that Arafat will re-emerge from a post-Iraq scenario as some sort of figurehead – if the Americans, pushed by the Europeans, re-focus their attention on the Arab-Israel issue. After all, Arafat's supporters would argue: who else is there to engage among possible alternatives on the Palestinian side? While that is true, it is also the case that Arafat's ability to participate credibly in any sort of meaningful peace effort is much diminished, even if circumstances were favourable. Under almost any likely scenario Arafat would have great difficulty persuading his interlocutors that he was capable of delivering his side of any bargain, even assuming he were given the chance. Of course, the possibility cannot be excluded that Arafat may surprise again, as he has many times in the past. Whatever else might be said about this perverse and deeply-flawed individual, he has demonstrated survival skills far beyond the ordinary: in fact in the realm of the supernatural on occasions. The Americans in their absolutist way, and the Israelis out of self interest, have repeatedly written off the Palestinian leader only to find that he has survived to fight another day. Arab regimes, including most notably the Syrians, have also consigned Arafat to whatever receptacle of history seemed appropriate at the time, but in spite of the most unpromising circumstances he regained his balance, like one of those oriental dolls which are impossible to knock over.

After the first Gulf War, his historic miscalculation in supporting Saddam Hussein rendered him persona non grata across much of the Arab world. Europe and the United States were predisposed to dimiss him from their calculations, and yet the Madrid peace process gave him a new lease which he exploited to the full. But that was more than a decade ago. Time has not been kind to the Palestinians or to Arafat. Close aides say that concerns about his health are exaggerated. They attribute his trembling lips and hands, not to a degenerative illness, but to his plane crash in the Libyan desert which required neuro-surgery to remove a blood clot from his brain. But there is also no doubt that Arafat's physical capabilities are diminished, his mental sharpness dulled, his boundless energy ebbing. Quite simply, even in the event he has not passed the end of his shelf life as leader of the Palestinians, he looks like a man on a downward slide physically. What is left is his importance as a symbol, not necessarily the only symbol, but a symbol nevertheless, of the Palestinian struggle, and even that has been compromised by his lamentable performance as the putative leader of a state-in-waiting.

The problem for the Palestinians, in common with many Third World countries, is how to bring to an end constitutionally the rule of someone like Arafat who has no nominated successor, and who shows no inclination to go. Plans for Palestinian elections in January 2003 were shelved because it would have been impossible under Israel's security dragnet to have conducted any sort of representative poll. Arafat himself cannot have been displeased that an excuse was found to defer the election because there was no guarantee that he and his once dominant Fatah faction would have prevailed in a free and fair contest. Indeed, latest opinion polling in the West Bank and Gaza shows that his popularity is at its lowest ebb since he returned to Gaza and the West Bank in 1994 and established his ramshackle Palestinian Authority. Arafat goes through the motions of being in charge, issuing statements and calling meetings in his Ramallah headquarters, sections of which have been demolished by Israeli earth-moving equipment even as Arafat was cloistered inside. But there is an element of farce in all of this since edicts and orders from the 'old man' are largely ignored, especially by Islamic militants who have all but hijacked the Palestinian struggle, rendering calls for moderation by the tired men of Arafat's generation increasingly irrelevant. Arafat would also be aware that as his authority ebbs and questions become more pervasive about his mental capabilities, rivals and would-be successors manoeuvre.

If there is a half-logical alternative to Arafat it might be Mahmoud Abbas (Abu Mazen), the recently nominated Prime Minister and signatory – with Shimon Peres – to the Oslo Declaration of Principles in Washington in September, 1993. Interestingly, in a speech given in the Gaza Strip in late 2002, Abbas, the Palestinians' chief negotiator post Oslo, criticised the 'weaponisation' of the *intifada* as a 'mistake', in language that made it clear he was calling Arafat himself to account and therefore positioning himself as a possible alternative. But even if Arafat fell under the proverbial bus tomorrow and Abbas succeeded him, it is doubtful he would be anything more than a stopgap. Arafat's closest advisers fear chaos if he goes, as well they might, since anger among the Palestinians is barely contained. Internecine conflict, a Palestinian civil war even, could not be excluded if and when Arafat passes from the scene, and possibly even while he is still nominally in place if his capacities continue to weaken. Conventional wisdom has it that Arafat's departure would prompt a contest between heads of the various Palestinian security apparatuses and the Islamists who would certainly seek to fill any leadership void. In such circumstances, it is unlikely there would be any clearcut winners, apart from a deluded Israeli right which might regard such turmoil among Palestinians as a godsend since it would have the effect – momentarily – of reducing pressures for engagement in a renewed peace effort. But such attitudes would be short-sighted as a further step-down into anarchy would inevitably have spill-over consequences for Israel itself. Further radicalisation of the Palestinians is not in anyone's interests – with or without Arafat in the picture.

So what was going through Arafat's mind as he circled his desk in his ruined Ramallah compound? According to confidants such as Shaath and Bassam Abu Sharif, and members of the 'loyal opposition' like Hanan Ashrawy, the Palestinian leader is full of anger against the Americans whom be blames for many of his ills, including his present marginalisation. He is incensed that the George W. Bush mantra of 'regime change' extends to the Palestinians. He is deeply resentful that he received most of the blame for the failure of Camp David when he believes that inadequate preparation by the Americans and a cheeseparing attitude by Ehud Barak made these other parties at least as culpable. He rails, as he has many times before, against Arab regimes who have turned their backs because of their own internal problems, not least in the provision of funds which has left the Palestinian Authority near-destitute. His own deepening frustration is also being fed by the certain knowledge that his ability to manipulate and control Palestinian institutions and individuals who were previously dependent on him for their survival is weakening by the day. His own Fatah treasure trove is drying up, further limiting his options. Political impotence in the face of all these pressures is the source of enormous frustration. Worst of all is the sense that he is losing relevance, for relevance is the one attribute he has craved most throughout his career – first as the convener of an embryonic Palestinian faction back in Kuwait in the 1950s, then as Chairman of the Palestine Liberation Organisation from 1969, and more recently as head of the Palestinian Authority. Relevance has been his lifeblood, and that is clearly ebbing.

However, Arafat has always been an optimist; although that quality is being tested as never before. But if there are flickers of hope in the gloom it is that the exigencies of a Middle East re-made by a second war with Iraq will bring him back into the picture. In the fevered breast hope springs eternal: Arafat would argue that since the Palestinian cause is just and he remains its symbol then whether the Americans and their European allies like it or not, it will be difficult to exclude him completely. Among various peace plans which might yet rescue Arafat from history's scrapheap is one being formulated by the so-called Quartet – the United States, Russia, the European Union and the United Nations – which has the virtue of setting a definite goal of Palestinian statehood by 2005, thus overcoming one of the weaknesses of Oslo which left final-status issues prey to endemic political uncertainty. President George W. Bush's reluctant agreement to publication of the so-called 'road map' holds a flickering promise for the Palestinians post-Iraq. The possibility that Arafat, who has used up more than his nine lives, might yet be rescued by those who are predisposed to write him off as he was at Madrid, assumes a lot, and probably much more than is reasonable, but the Palestinian leader has no choice but to watch and wait – and circle his desk. Events in the winter of his deepest discontent had moved far beyond his control.

APPENDIX

ELEMENTS OF A PERFORMANCE-BASED ROAD MAP TO A
PERMANENT TWO-STATE SOLUTION TO THE
ISRAELI-PALESTINIAN CONFLICT – DRAFT, 15 OCTOBER
2002
The following are elements of a performance-based plan, under the
supervision of the Quartet, with clear phases and benchmarks
leading to a final and comprehensive settlement of the Israeli-
Palestinian conflict by 2005, as presented in President Bush's speech
of 24 June, and welcomed by the EU, Russia and the UN in the 16
July and 17 September Quartet Ministerial statements. Such a
settlement, negotiated between the parties, will result in the
emergence of an independent democratic Palestinian state living side
by side in peace and security with Israel and its other neighbors. The
settlement will end the occupation that began in 1967, based on the
Madrid Conference terms of reference and the principle of land for
peace UNSCRs 242, 338 and 1397, agreements previously reached
by the parties, and the Arab initiative proposed by Saudi Crown
Prince Abdullah and endorsed by the Arab summit in Beirut.

PHASE I: OCTOBER 2002–MAY 2003 (TRANSFORMATION/
ELECTIONS)
FIRST STAGE: OCTOBER–DECEMBER, 2002
- Quartet develops detailed roadmap, in consultation with the
  parties, to be adopted at December Quartet/AHLC meeting.
- Appointment of new Palestinian cabinet, establishment of
  empowered Prime Minister, including any necessary Palestinian
  legal reforms for this purpose.
- PLC appoints Commission charged with drafting of Palestinian
  constitution for Palestinian statehood.
- PA establishes independent Election Commission. PLC reviews
  and revises election law.
- AHLC Ministerial launches major donor assistance effort.
- Palestinian leadership issues unequivocal statement reiterating
  Israel's right to exist in peace and security and calling for an

immediate end to the armed Intifada and all acts of violence against Israelis anywhere. All Palestinian institutions and incitement against Israel.

- In coordination with Quartet, implementation of U.S. rebuilding, training and resumed security cooperation plan in collaboration with outside oversight boards (U.S. – Egypt – Jordan).
  – Palestinian security organizations are consolidated into three services reporting to an empowered Interior Minister.
  – Restructured/retrained Palestinian security forces and IDF counterparts begin phased resumption of security cooperation and other undertakings as agreed in the Tenet work plan, including regular senior-level meetings, with the participation of U.S. security officials.
- GOI facilitates travel of Palestinian officials for PLC sessions, internationally supervised security retraining, and other PA business without restriction.
- GOI implements recommendations of the Berlini report to improve humanitarian conditions, including lifting curfews and easing movement between Palestinian areas.
- GOI ends actions undermining trust, including attacks in civilian areas, and confiscation/demolition of Palestinian homes/property, deportations, as a punitive measure or to facilitate Israeli construction.
- GOI immediately resumes monthly revenue clearance process in accordance with agreed transparency monitoring mechanism. GOI transfers all arrears of withheld revenues to Palestinian Ministry of Finance by end of December 2002, according to specific timeline.
- Arab states move decisively to cut off public/private funding of extremist groups, channel financial support for Palestinians through Palestinian Ministry of Finance.
- GOI dismantles settlement outposts erected since establishment of the present Israeli government and in contravention of current Israeli government guidelines.

SECOND STAGE: JANUARY–MAY 2003

- Continued Palestinian political reform to ensure powers of PLC, Prime Minister, and Cabinet.

- Independent Commission circulates draft Palestinian constitution, based on strong parliamentary democracy, for public comment/debate.
- Devolution of power to local authorities through revised Municipalities Law.
- Quartet monitoring mechanism established.
- Palestinian performance on agreed judicial, administrative, and economic benchmarks, as determined by Task Force.
- As comprehensive security performance moves forward, IDF withdraws progressively from areas occupied since 28 September 2000. Withdrawal to be completed before holding of Palestinian elections. Palestinian security forces redeploy to areas vacated by IDF.
- GOI facilitates Task Force election assistance, registration of voters, movement of candidates and voting officials.
- GOI reopens East Jerusalem Chamber of Commerce and other closed Palestinian economic institutions in East Jerusalem.
- Constitution drafting Commission proposes draft document for submission after elections to new PLC for approval.
- Palestinians and Israelis conclude a new security agreement building upon Tenet work plan, including an effective security mechanism and an end to violence, terrorism, and incitement implemented through a restructured and effective Palestinian security service.
- GOI freezes all settlement activity consistent with the Mitchell report, including natural growth of settlements.
- Palestinians hold free, open, and fair elections for PLC.
- Regional support: Upon completion of security steps and IDF withdrawal to 28 September 2000 positions, Egypt and Jordan return ambassadors to Israel.

PHASE II: JUNE 2003–DECEMBER 2003 (TRANSITION)
- Progress unto Phase II will be based upon the judgment of the Quartet, facilitated by establishment of a permanent monitoring mechanism on the ground, whether consultations are appropriate to move on – taking into account performance of all parties and Quartet monitoring. Phase II starts after Palestinian elec-

tions and ends with possible creation of a Palestinian state with provisional borders by end of 2003.

- International Conference: Convened by the Quartet, in agreement with the parties, immediately after the successful conclusion of Palestinian elections to support Palestinian economic recovery and launch negotiations between Israelis and Palestinians on the possibility of a state with provisional borders.
- Such a meeting would be inclusive, based on the goal of a comprehensive Middle East peace (including between Israel and Syria, and Israel and Lebanon), and based on the principles described in the preamble to this document.
- Other pre-Intifada Arab links to Israel restored (trade offices, etc.).
- Revival of 'multilateral talks' (regional water, environmental, economic development, refugee, arms control issues).
- Newly elected PLC finalizes and approves new constitution for democratic, independent Palestinian state.
- Continued implementation of security cooperation, complete collection of illegal weapons, disarm militant groups, according to Phase I security agreement.
- Israeli-Palestinian negotiations aimed at creation of a state with provisional borders. Implementation of prior agreements, to enhance maximum territorial contiguity.
- Conclusion of transitional understanding and creation of state with provisional borders by end of 2003. Enhanced international role in monitoring transition.
- Further action on settlements simultaneous with establishment of Palestinian state with provisional borders.

PHASE III: 2004–2005 (STATEHOOD)

- Progress into Phase III, based on judgment of Quartet, taking into account actions of all parties and Quartet monitoring.
- Second International Conference: Convened by the Quartet, with agreement of the parties, at beginning of 2004 to endorse agreement reached on state with provisional borders and to launch negotiations between Israel and Palestine toward a final, permanent status resolution in 2005, including on borders,

Jerusalem, refugees and settlements; and, to support progress toward a comprehensive Middle East settlement between Israel and Lebanon and Syria, to be achieved as soon as possible.

- Continued comprehensive, effective progress on the reform agenda laid out the Task Force in preparation for final status agreement.
- Continued sustained, effective security cooperation based on security agreements reached by end of Phase I and other prior agreements.

Arab state acceptance of normal relations with Israel and security for all the states of the region, consistent with Beirut Arab summit initiative.

NOTES

PROLOGUE
1. *News.Com International*, 11 September 2001.

CHAPTER 1
1. *Fiches du Monde Arabe*, 6 August 1975, quoting UN Relief and Works Agency figures, No. 347.
2. Article in the *Observer*, 3 September 1967.
3. Abu Iyad, *My Home, My Land*, New York, 1981, p. 3.
4. Benny Morris, *The Birth of the Palestinian Refugee Problem, 1947–49*, Cambridge, 1987, pp. 113–15.
5. Menachem Begin, *Revolt: Story of the Irgun*, Jerusalem, 1951, p. 164.
6. Morris, op. cit., p. 207.
7. *Fiches du Monde Arabe*, No. 347.
8. George Habash interview, Damascus, November 1989.
9. Yasser Arafat interview, Tunis, June 1989.
10. Yasser Arafat interview, Baghdad, January 1990.
11. Yasser Arafat interview, Tunis, June 1989.
12. Interview with the authors, Jerusalem, June 1989. Name withheld on request.
13. Ibid.
14. Ibid.
15. Ibid.
16. Khaled al-Hassan interview, Kuwait, April 1989.
17. Yasser Arafat interview, Tunis, June 1989.
18. Ibid.
19. Ibid.
20. R. Mitchell, *The Society of the Muslim Brothers*, London, p. 59.
21. Walid Khalidi interview, Cambridge, Massachussetts, November 1989.
22. Zoheir al-Alami interview, Sharjah, September 1989.
23. Faisal al-Husseini interview, Jerusalem, May 1989.
24. Husam Abu Shaaban interview, Kuwait, September 1989.

25. Interview with the authors, Cairo, April 1989. Name withheld on request.
26. Derek Hopwood, *Egypt: Politics and Society, 1945–1981*, London, 1982, p. 30.
27. Salah Khalaf interview, Tunis, June 1989.
28. George Habash interview, Damascus, November 1989.
29. Ibid.
30. Hopwood, op. cit., p. 32.
31. Yasser Arafat interview, Tunis, June 1989.
32. Bashir Barghouti interview, Jerusalem, September 1989.
33. Salah Khalaf interview, Tunis, May 1989.
34. Gamal Sourani interview, Cairo, September 1989.
35. *See* Khalil al-Wazir, *Bidayat (Beginnings)*, limited edition published by PLO Western Sector.
36. Mohammed Hamza interview, Tunis, August 1989. Hamza is Wazir's biographer.
37. Zoheir al-Alami interview, Sharjah, September 1989.
38. Yasser Arafat interview, Tunis, June 1989.
39. Zoheir al-Alami interview, Sharjah, September 1989.
40. Zoheir al-Alami interview, Sharjah, September 1989.
41. Peter Ruehmkorf, *Die Jahre die Ihr Kennt*, Hamburg, 1972, pp. 86–7.
42. Ibid.
43. Hopwood, op. cit., p. 55.
44. Yasser Arafat interview, Tunis, June 1989.
45. Ibid.
46. Ibid.
47. Ibid.

CHAPTER 2

1. Khalil al-Wazir, *Bidayat (Beginnings)*, limited edition published by PLO Western Sector.
2. Farouk Kaddoumi interview, Tunis, September 1989.
3. *See* Khalil al-Wazir, op. cit.
4. Ismail Shammout interview, Kuwait, April 1989. Shammout was the illustrator for *Filastinuna*.
5. Khalil al-Wazir, op. cit.

6. Interviews with Khaled al-Hussan, Amin al-Agha, Kuwait, April 1989.
7. Salah Khalaf interview, Tunis, June 1989.
8. Ibid.
9. Fatah internal statutes, unpublished.
10. Interviews with Palestinian contemporaries, Kuwait, April 1989. Names withheld on request.
11. *Playboy* magazine, August 1988, p. 62.
12. *Time* magazine, 7 November 1988, p. 34.
13. Rafik al-Natshe interview, Tunis, August 1989.
14. Abu Nabil interview, Tunis, June 1989.
15. Hani al-Hassan interview, Tunis, August 1989; *also* Abdullah Franji interview, Bonn, July 1989; *also* discussion with German intelligence official, November 1989.
16. Zoheir al-Alami interview, Sharjah, September 1989.
17. Yasser Arafat interview, Tunis, December 1989.
18. Mohammed Abu Mayzar interview, Paris, August 1989.
19. Mohammed Hamza interview, Tunis, August 1989; *also* Intissar al-Wazir interview, Amman, June 1989.
20. Mohammed Abu Mayzar interview, Paris, August 1989.
21. Ahmed Sidki al-Dajani interview, Cairo, November 1989.
22. Khaled al-Fahoum interview, Damascus, May 1989. Fahoum was a founder member of the PLO Executive Committee and later served as speaker of the Palestine National Council; he is now an Arafat opponent in Damascus.
23. Salah Khalaf interview, Tunis, June 1989.
24. Yasser Arafat interview, Tunis, December 1989.
25. Ibid.
26. Selim Zaanoun (Abul Adeeb) interview, Kuwait, April 1989. Zaanoun is now Fatah's chief representative in the Gulf.
27. Zoheir al-Alami interview, Sharjah, September 1989.
28. Farouk Kaddoumi, quoted in John Amos, *Palestinian Resistance*, New York, 1980, p. 57.
29. *Al-Rai al-Am*, 7 January 1965, quoted in Amos, op. cit., p. 293.
30. General Aharon Yariv interview, Tel Aviv, November 1989.
31. Interview with former Fatah official, name withheld on request.

32. Al-Anwar, Beirut, 2 January 1965.
33. Fathi al-Dib, quoted in *Al-Gumhuriah*, Cairo, August 1966. Al-Dib was head of the Arab affairs department in the Arab Socialist Union.
34. Text of Fatah Central Committee report, 2 May 1966 (unpublished).
35. Ahmed Shukairy, quoted in David Hirts, *The Gun and the Olive Branch*, London 1977, p. 289.

CHAPTER 3

1. Nasser's resignation broadcast, Cairo Radio, 9 June 1967, reproduced in Laqueur and Rubin (Eds.), *The Israel–Arab Reader*, London 1984, pp. 189–94.
2. Salah Khalaf interview, Tunis, June 1989.
3. Nabil Shaath interview, Cairo, March 1989.
4. Hani al-Hassan interview, Tunis, August 1989; *also* Mohammed Abu Mayzar interview, Paris, September 1989; *also* Farouk Kaddoumi interview, Tunis, September 1989.
5. Hani al-Hassan interview, Tunis, August 1989.
6. Ibid.
7. Yasser Arafat interview, Tunis, December 1989.
8. Faisal al-Husseini interview, Jerusalem, May 1989.
9. Ibid.
10. Yasser Arafat interview, Tunis, December 1989.
11. Ibid.
12. *Fiches du Monde Arabe*, No. 959.
13. Yasser Arafat, quoted in *The Middle East* magazine, March 1988, p. 22.
14. Abdullah Franji interview, Bonn, July 1989.
15. George Habash interview, Damascus, October 1989.
16. Reported in *Time* magazine, 13 December 1968, p. 35.
17. Abdulmajeed Shoman interview, Amman, September 1989; *also* Ibrahim Bakr interview, Amman, September 1989. Bakr was the PLO's first and only deputy chairman under Arafat and has since left the movement.
18. General Aharon Yariv interview, Tel Aviv, November 1989.
19. Yasser Arafat interview, Tunis, December 1989.
20. Ibid.

21. Ibid.
22. Interviews with participants; *also* Filastin al-Thawra; *see also* Uri Milstein, *A History of the Israeli Paratroopers*, Tel Aviv, 1985, Vol. III, pp. 1276–80.
23. Yasser Arafat interview, Tunis, December 1989.
24. Mashour Haditha al-Jazy interview, Amman, June 1989.
25. General Aharon Yariv interview, Tel Aviv, November 1989.
26. Ihsan Bakr interview, Cairo, October 1989.
27. Salah Khalaf interview, Tunis, June 1989.
28. Mohammed Abu Mayzar interview, Paris, August 1989.
29. Michael Bar-Zohar and Eitan Haber, *The Quest for the Red Prince*, New York, 1983, p. 99.
30. Mohammed Hassanein Heikal interview, Cairo, May 1989.
31. Ibid.
32. Ibid.
33. Tahseen Bashir interview, Cairo, October 1989. Bashir was Nasser's spokesman.
34. Edgar O'Ballance, *Arab Guerrilla Power, 1967–72*, London, 1974, p. 59.
35. Mohammed Hassanein Heikal interview, Cairo, May 1989.
36. Yasser Arafat, quoted in *Al-Sayyad*, Beirut, 23 January 1969.
37. Abu Iyad, *My Home, My Land*, New York, 1981, p. 139.
38. Essay by Zvi Elpeleg in *Jerusalem Quarterly* No. 50, spring 1989.
39. Nabil Shaath, quoted in Alain Gresh, *The PLO: The Struggle Within*, London, 1985, p. 37.
40. Salah Khalaf interview, Tunis, June 1989.
41. Programme of February 1969 Palestine National Council, quoted in Gresh, op. cit., p. 18.
42. Nabil Shaath interview, Cairo, March 1989.
43. Khaled al-Fahoum interview, Damascus, May 1989. Al-Fahoum was a member of the PLO Executive Committee at the time.
44. Yehoshafat Harkabi, *The Palestinian Covenant and its Meaning*, London and New York, 1979, p. 61.
45. Abu Daoud interview, Tunis, November 1989.
46. *Al-Ahram*, Cairo, 4 February 1969.
47. Nabil Shaath interview, Cairo, December 1989.

48. Khaled al-Hassan interview, Kuwait, April 1989.

CHAPTER 4

1. John Cooley, *Green March, Black September*, London, 1973, pp. 103–4; *also Fiches du Monde Arabe*, 11 January 1978, No. 850; and interviews with Arafat aides.
2. Moshe Shemesh, *The Palestinian Entity, 1959–74*, London, 1988, p. 130.
3. Yasser Arafat interview, Tunis, December 1989.
4. King Hussein, quoted in *Le Monde*, 23 March 1968.
5. Khalil al-Wazir, August 1972, quoted in Shemesh, op. cit., p. 133.
6. Zeid al-Rifai interview, Amman, June 1989. Rifai was Jordanian Prime Minister in the mid-1970s and again in the late 1980s, and a friend of King Hussein from childhood.
7. Asad Abdelrahman, *History of the PLO* (in Arabic), Cyprus, 1989, p. 178.
8. Yasser Arafat, quoted in *Time* magazine, 13 December 1968, p. 32.
9. Zeid al-Rifai interview, Amman, June 1989.
10. Abu Daoud interview, Tunis, November 1989.
11. Salah Khalaf interview, Tunis, August 1989.
12. William Quandt, *Decade of Decisions*, Los Angeles and London, 1977, p. 91.
13. *Fiches du Monde Arabe*, 18 January 1978, No. 885; *also* Edgar O'Ballance, *Arab Guerrilla Power, 1969–74*, London, 1974, pp. 120ff; *also* Shemesh, op. cit., p. 138.
14. Mashour Haditha al-Jazy interview, Amman, June 1989.
15. Ibrahim Bakr interview, Amman, September 1989.
16. Yasser Arafat, quoted in *Al-Hayat*, London, 1 January 1990.
17. See O'Ballance, op. cit., pp. 128–9; *also* James Lunt, *Hussein of Jordan*, London, 1989, p. 12.
18. Yasser Arafat, quoted in *Al-Hayat*, London, 1 January 1990.
19. General Aharon Yariv interview, Tel Aviv, November 1989.
20. Henry Kissinger, *White House Years*, New York and London, 1979, pp. 341, 344, 362 and 558 passim.
21. Shemesh, op. cit., p. 109.
22. Ibrahim Bakr interview, Amman, September 1989.

23. Ahmed Baha el-Dine interview, Cairo, October 1989. El-Dine was a prominent Egyptian journalist and confidant of Nasser.
24. Zoheir al-Alami interview, Sharjah, September 1989.
25. Ibrahim Bakr interview, Amman, September 1989.
26. Zeid al-Rifai interview, Amman, June 1989.
27. Yasser Arafat interview, Tunis, December 1989.
28. Abu Daoud interview, Tunis, November 1989.
29. Ibid.
30. Yasser Arafat interview, Tunis, December 1989.
31. Tahseen Bashir interview, Cairo, October 1989. Bashir was Nasser's spokesman.
32. Ibid.
33. *See* Mohammed Hassanein Heikal, *The Cairo Documents*, London, 1972, p. 17.
33. William Quandt, Fuad Jabber and Ann Mosely Lesch, *The Politics of Palestinian Nationalism*, Los Angeles and London, 1973, p. 128.
35. Shemesh, op. cit., p. 146.
36. Ibrahim Bakr interview, Amman, September 1989.
37. Munib al-Masri interview, London, August 1989.
38. Ibid.
39. General Aharon Yariv interview, Tel Aviv, November 1989.
40. Abu Iyad, op. cit., pp. 92–3.

CHAPTER 5

1. Information from West European intelligence official. Name withheld on request.
2. US Foreign Broadcast Information Service, *Middle East Monitor*, Vol. 3, No. 8, 15 April 1973, pp. 7–8.
3. Abu Daoud interview, Tunis, November 1989.
4. Yasser Abed Rabbo interview, Tunis, August 1989.
5. Interview with Arafat adviser, Tunis, November 1989. Name withheld on request.
6. *An-Nahar Arab Report*, Beirut, 6 December 1971, quoted in John Cooley, *Green March, Black September*, London, 1973.
7. Abu Iyad, *My Home, My Land*, New York, 1981, p. 96.
8. Ibid., p. 97.

9. Yasser Arafat, quoted in *Journal of Palestine Studies*, Washington and Kuwait, winter 1973, p. 174.
10. Abu Iyad, op. cit., p. 95.
11. Ibid., p. 98.
12. BBC Summary of World Broadcasts, Amman domestic radio, 17 December 1971.
13. Lester Sobel (Ed.), *Palestinian Impasse: Arab Guerillas and International Terror*, New York, 1977.
14. Interview with West German intelligence official, Germany, July 1989. Name withheld on request.
15. General Aharon Yariv interview, Tel Aviv, November 1989.
16. Western intelligence report on planning and preparation of Olympic attack, November 1972 (unpublished).
17. Interview with a colleague of Zamir, Tel Aviv, December 1989. Name withheld on request.
18. Abu Iyad, op. cit., pp. 112–13.
19. Sobel, op. cit., p. 123.
20. Ibid., p. 121.
21. Mahmoud Darwish, 'Going to the World: A Stranger to the World', from *The Complete Works of Mahmoud Darwish*, Beirut, 1979.
22. Sobel, op. cit., p. 123.
23. General Aharon Yariv interview, Tel Aviv, November 1989.
24. Ibid.
25. Interview with Israeli official, Jerusalem, December 1989. Name withheld on request.
26. Interview with PLO intelligence official, Cairo, May 1989. Name withheld on request.
27. Sobel, op. cit., p. 129.
28. Interview with Israeli intelligence official, Jerusalem, December 1989. Name withheld on request.
29. Sobel, op. cit., pp. 126–7.
30. *Washington Post*, 4 March 1973.
31. BBC Summary of World Broadcasts, Khartoum radio, 6 March 1973.
32. *Washington Post*, 13 February 1986.
33. Interview with US intelligence official, Washington, November 1989. Name withheld on request.

34. US State Department cable 039764, 7 March 1973, released under the Freedom of Information Act.
35. Abu Iyad, op. cit., p. 102.
36. Interview with Nimeiri adviser, Cairo, December 1989. Name withheld on request.
37. Yasser Arafat, quoted in Sobel, op. cit.

CHAPTER 6

1. General Vernon Walters interview, Bonn, November 1989.
2. Ibid.
3. *See* Yehoshafat Harkabi, *Fedayeen Action and Arab Strategy*, International Institute for Strategic Studies, Adelphi Paper No. 53, London, December 1968.
4. Mehdi Abdel-Hadi interview, Jerusalem, June 1989. Abdel-Hadi is director of Passia, a Palestinian study institute in the West Bank.
5. Yasser Arafat on PLO Radio, quoted in Moshe Shemesh, *The Palestinian Entity 1959–74*, London, 1988, p. 161.
6. Salah Khalaf interview, Tunis, June 1989.
7. Alain Gresh, *The PLO: The Struggle Within*, London, 1985, p. 105.
8. Moshe Ma'oz, *Palestinian Leadership in the West Bank*, London, 1984.
9. *Washington Post*, 29 September 1972.
10. Gresh, op. cit., p. 112.
11. Salah Khalaf, quoted by Eric Rouleau in *Foreign Affairs*, Washington, spring 1975.
12. Gresh, op. cit., pp. 88–9.
13. Shemesh, op. cit., p. 259.
14. Yasser Arafat, quoted in *Filastin al-Thawra*, 1 January 1973, reprinted in *Journal of Palestine Studies*, Vol. II, No. 3, spring 1973.
15. Nayef Hawatmeh interview, Damascus, May 1989.
16. Salah Khalaf interview, Tunis, August 1989.
17. Ibid.
18. For accusation against Khalaf, *see* Sadat, quoted in John Amos, *Palestinian Resistance: Organisation of a Nationalist Movement*, New York, 1980, p. 414.

19. Salah Khalaf interview, Tunis, August 1989.
20. Abu Iyad, *My Home, My Land*, New York, 1981, p. 129.
21. Mohammed Abu Mayzar interview, Paris, August 1989.
22. Yasser Arafat, quoted in *Journal of Palestine Studies*, Vol. IV, No. 2, winter 1974–5.
23. William Quandt, *Decade of Decisions*, Los Angeles and London, 1977, p. 160.
24. Henry Kissinger, *Years of Upheaval*, London and New York, 1982, pp. 626–7.
25. Ibid., pp. 503, 626–7.
26. Alfred (Roy) Atherton interview, Washington, November 1989.
27. General Vernon Walters interview, Bonn, November 1989.
28. Kissinger, op. cit., pp. 628–9.
29. Interview with the authors, Washington, November 1989. Name withheld on request.
30. Nabil Shaath interview, Cairo, December 1989.
31. Abu Iyad, op. cit., pp. 135–6.
32. Ibid.
33. George Habash, quoted in *Journal of Palestine Studies*, Vol. III, No. 3, spring 1974.
34. Programme of 12th PNC, broadcast on Voice of Palestine, Cairo, 8 June 1974, quoted from BBC Summary of World Broadcasts, 11 June 1974.
35. Shlomo Avineri interview, London, October 1989.

CHAPTER 7
1. Harris Schoenberg, *A Mandate for Terror: the United Nations and the PLO*, New York, 1989, pp. 1–40.
2. Ibid.
3. Ibid.
4. Ibid.
5. *Fiches du Monde Arabe*, 15 November 1978, No. 1113.
6. Nabil Shaath interview, Cairo, December 1989.
7. Abu Iyad, *My Home, My Land*, New York, 1981, pp. 144–9.
8. Ibid.
9. Ismail Fahmy, *Negotiating for Peace in the Middle East*, London, 1983, p. 98.

10. Farouk Kaddoumi interview, Tunis, September 1989.
11. Quoted in *Akhbar al-Yom*, Cairo, 2 November 1974, pp. 3–4.
12. Mahmoud Riad interview, Cairo, May 1989.
13. Walter Laqueur and Barry Rubin (Eds.), *The Israel–Arab Reader*, London, 1984, p. 518.
14. Lester Sobel (Ed.), *Palestinian Impasse: Arab Guerrillas and International Terror*, New York, 1977, p. 204.
15. Yasser Arafat, quoted in *Journal of Palestine Studies*, Vol. IV, No. 2, winter 1975.
16. *Time* magazine, 11 November 1974, p. 31.
17. Ibid.
18. Nabil Shaath interview, Cairo, December 1989.
19. Yasser Arafat, quoted in *Journal of Palestine Studies*, winter 1982. Arafat was reflecting in an interview on what he had said at the time.
20. Ibid.
21. Yasser Arafat, quoted in Laqueur and Rubin, op. cit., pp. 504–18.
22. Ibid.
23. Stephen Day interview, Tunis, August 1989. Day served as press attaché in the UK mission to the UN and later as British ambassador to Tunis.
24. Nabil Shaath interview, Cairo, December 1989.
25. *New York Times*, 14 November 1974.
26. Schoenberg, op. cit., pp. 40ff.
27. Ibid.
28. Farouk Kaddoumi interview, Tunis, September 1989.
29. Yasser Arafat interview, Tunis, December 1989.
30. Fahmy, op. cit., p. 211.
31. Yasser Arafat interview, Tunis, December 1989.
32. Ilan Halevy interview, Paris, August 1989. Halevy is PLO representative to the Socialist International.
33. Ibid.
34. Ibid.
35. *The Times*, 16 November and 17 December 1973.
36. Uri Avnery interview, Tel Aviv, November 1989.
37. Ibid. *See also* Uri Avnery, *My Friend, The Enemy*, London, 1986.

CHAPTER 8

1. Salah Khalaf interview, Tunis, August 1989.
2. Suleiman Franjieh's speech to the UN, reproduced in *Journal of Palestine Studies*, Vol. IV, No. 2, winter 1975.
3. Kemal Salibi, *Crossroads to Civil War: Lebanon 1958–76*, London, 1976, p. 98.
4. Quoted in Walid Khalidi, *Conflict and Violence in Lebanon: Confrontation in the Middle East*, Cambridge, Massachussetts, 1979, p. 185.
5. Mahmoud Riad interview, Cairo, May 1989. Riad was Egyptian foreign minister at the time and later Secretary-General of the Arab League.
6. Walid Khalidi interview, Cambridge, Massachussetts, November 1989.
7. Mamdouh Nofal interview, Tunis, August 1989.
8. Sakher Abu Nizar interview, Tunis, September 1989.
9. Yasser Abed Rabbo interview, Tunis, August 1989.
10. Walid Khalidi interview, London, October 1989.
11. Salah Khalaf interview, Tunis, August 1989.
12. Interview with the authors, London, November 1989. Name withheld on request.
13. Walid Khalidi interview, London, October 1989.
14. Sakher Abu Nizar interview, Tunis, September 1989.
15. A widely circulated piece of PLO folklore.
16. Interview with senior Fatah intelligence official, Cairo, May 1989. Name withheld on request.
17. Adeed Dawisha, *Syria and the Lebanese Crisis*, London, 1980.
18. Khalidi, op. cit., p. 52.
19. *Fiches du Monde Arabe*, 18 October 1978, No. 1093.
20. Abu Iyad, op. cit., p. 184.
21. Ibid., p. 181.
22. *Fiches du Monde Arabe*, 21 January 1981, No. 1798.
23. Kamal Jumblatt, *This Is My Legacy*, Paris, 1978, p. 105.
24. Abu Iyad, op. cit., p. 196.

CHAPTER 9

1. Cyrus Vance interview, New York, November 1989.
2. Ibid.

3. *New York Times*, 15 December 1976.
4. Programme of 13th PNC, quoted in Helena Cobban, *The Palestinian Liberation Organisation*, Cambridge, 1984, p. 85.
5. Yasser Arafat's UN speech, reproduced in *Journal of Palestine Studies*, Vol. IV, No. 2.
6. Yasser Arafat interview, Tunis, December 1989.
7. William Quandt, *Camp David: Peacemaking and Politics*, Washington, 1986.
8. Yasser Arafat, quoted in David Hirst and Irene Beeson, *Sadat*, London, 1981, p. 257.
9. Quandt, op. cit., pp. 40–57.
10. Cobban, op. cit., p. 89.
11. Quandt, op. cit., pp. 101–2.
12. Interviews with former State Department officials, Washington, November 1989. Names withheld on request.
13. Jimmy Carter, quoted in *New York Times*, 1 September 1979.
14. Cyrus Vance interview, New York, November 1989.
15. Yasser Arafat, quoted in *New York Times*, 9 March 1984.
16. Yasser Arafat, quoted in *Al-Hayat*, 1 January 1990.
17. Interview with the authors, London, April 1989. Name withheld on request.

CHAPTER 10
1. Quoted in David Hirst and Irene Beeson, *Sadat*, London, 1981, p. 255.
2. Mahmoud Riad, *The Struggle for Peace in the Middle East*, London, 1981.
3. Ismail Fahmy, *Negotiating for Peace in the Middle East*, London, 1983.
4. Mohammed Sobhieh interview, Cairo, November 1989. Sobhieh is Secretary-General of the Palestine National Council, and resides in Cairo.
5. Abdel Latif Abu Hijleh (Abu Jaafar) interview, Tunis, August 1989.
7. Abu Iyad, *My Home, My Land*, New York, 1981, pp. 210–2.
8. Jimmy Carter, quoted in *New York Times*, 16 December 1977. *Fiches du Monde Arabe*, 23 January 1980, No. 1486.

9. Mamdouh Nofal interview, Tunis, August 1989. Nofal is a senior DFLP commander in Lebanon.
10. Likud coalition platform, quoted in Walter Laqueur and Barry Rubin (Eds.), *The Israel–Arab Reader*, London, 1984, pp. 591–3.
11. Ibid., Nos 945–6.
12. *Middle East Reporter*, Beirut, 12 August 1978.
13. Mohammed Sobhieh interview, Cairo, November 1989.
14. Yasser Arafat, quoted in *New York Times*, 2 May 1978.
15. *Fiches du Monde Arabe*, 15 November 1978, No. 1118.
16. *Middle East Reporter*, 27 January 1979.
17. Yasser Arafat, quoted in *Al-Hayat*, 1 January 1990.
18. Interview with the authors, Tunis, June 1989. Name withheld on request.
19. Ibid.
20. Ibid.
21. Helena Cobban, *The Palestinian Liberation Organisation*, Cambridge, 1984, p. 104.
22. Aaron David Miller, 'The PLO' in *The Middle East Since Camp David*, ed. Robert Freedman, Boulder, Colorado, 1984.
23. Interview with Fatah intelligence official, Tunis, June 1989. Name withheld on request.
24. Yasser Arafat quoted in *Time* magazine, 9 April 1979.
25. Cobban, op. cit., p. 107.
26. Cyrus Vance interview, New York, November 1989; *also* Edward Said interview, New York, November 1989.
27. Interview with Fatah intelligence official, Tunis, June 1989. Name withheld on request.
28. Interview with Arafat opponent, Damascus, May 1989. Name withheld on request.
29. Fatah intelligence official, Tunis, June 1989. Name withheld on request.
30. Emad Shakur interview, Tunis, June 1989. Shakur is Arafat's adviser on Israeli affairs.
31. Cobban, op. cit., pp. 111–12.
32. *Washington Post*, 27 July 1981.
33. Fahd plan quoted in Walter Laqueur and Barry Rubin (Eds.), *The Israel–Arab Reader*, London, 1984, pp. 623–4.

34. John Edwin Mroz interview, New York, November 1989.
35. Ibid.; *also* Nicholas Veliotes interview, Washington, November 1989; and *New York Times*, 19 February 1984. Nicholas Veliotes is a former Assistant Secretary of State and later served as US ambassador to Egypt.
36. John Edwin Mroz interview, New York, November 1989.
37. Ibid.
38. Ibid.
39. Ibid.

CHAPTER 11

1. Interview with Arafat aide, London, June 1989. Name withheld on request.
2. Nicholas Veliotes interview, Washington, November 1989.
3. Nicholas Veliotes interview, Washington, November 1989.
4. General Avraham Tamir interview, Tel Aviv, November 1989.
5. Interview with Arafat adviser, Tunis, September 1989. Name withheld on request.
6. Brian Urquhart interview, London, May 1989.
7. Ibid.
8. Ibid.
9. Yezid Sayigh interview, Oxford, October 1989.
10. Interview with the authors, Cairo, October 1989. Name withheld on request.
11. Nicholas Veliotes interview, Washington, November 1989.
12. *Yediot Ahronoth*, 14 May 1982.
13. General Avraham Tamir interview, Tel Aviv, December 1985.
14. Ze'ev Schiff and Ehud Ya'ari, *Israel's Lebanon War*, New York, 1984, p. 98.
15. *Fiches du Monde Arabe*, 19 February 1986, No. 2521.
16. Ibid.
17. Avraham Tamir, *A Soldier in Search of Peace*, London, 1988, p. 128.
18. *Fiches du Monde Arabe*, 19 February 1986, No. 2521.
19. Walid Khalidi interview, Cambridge, Massachussetts, December 1989.
20. Sharon, op. cit., p. 472.

21. *Journal of Palestine Studies*, Vol. XI, No. 4, 'The War in Lebanon', summer/autumn 1982.
22. Rashid Khalidi, *Under Siege: PLO Decisionmaking during the 1982 War*, New York, 1986, p. 110.
23. Ibid., p. 113.
24. WAFA report, quoted in Khalidi, op. cit., p. 118, WAFA is the official PLO news agency.
25. Yasser Arafat interview, Tunis, December 1989.
26. Interview with the authors, London, February 1990. Name withheld on request.
27. Ibid., 3 July 1982.
28. Sharon, op. cit., p. 486.
29. Interview with the authors, Cairo, October 1989. Name withheld on request.
30. Colonel Mohammed al-Natour interview, Tunis, May 1989.
31. Interview with former White House staffer, London, February 1990. Name withheld on request.
32. Ibid.
33. WAFA report, reprinted in *Journal of Palestine Studies*, Vol. XI, No. 4, summer/autumn 1982.
34. *Fiches du Monde Arabe*, 5 March 1986, No. 2540.
35. Afif Safieh interview, the Hague, July 1989. Safieh was the PLO representative in the Netherlands, and an Arafat confidant.
36. *Fiches du Monde Arabe*, 4 December 1985, No. 2537.
37. *Haaretz*, 20 September 1982.
38. *Jerusalem Post*, 24 September 1982.
39. Nabil Shaath interview, Cairo, December 1989.

CHAPTER 12
1. Yasser Arafat interview, Baghdad, January 1990.
2. Nabil Shaath interview, Cairo, December 1989.
3. Walter Laqueur and Barry Rubin (Eds.), *The Israel–Arab Reader*, London, 1984, p. 664.
4. Ibid., pp. 656–63.
5. Ibid.
6. Marwan Qasem interview, Amman, November 1989.
7. Ibid.

8. Emile Sahliyeh, *The PLO after the Lebanon War*, Boulder, Colorado, 1986.

9. Laqueur and Rubin, op. cit., p. 365.

10. Nabil Shaath interview, Cairo, December 1989.

11. Eric Rouleau, 'The PLO After Lebanon' in *Foreign Affairs*, Washington, autumn 1983, p. 143.

12. Ibid., p. 150.

13. *International Herald Tribune*, 11 April 1983.

14. Yezid Sayigh interview, Oxford, October 1989.

15. WAFA report from Damascus, 15 May 1983.

16. *International Herald Tribune*, 5 June 1983.

17. Ibid., 21 June 1983.

18. Intissar al-Wazir interview, Amman, June 1989.

19. *Washington Post*, 25 June 1983.

20. *New York Times*, 27 June 1983.

21. *International Herald Tribune*, 25 June 1983.

22. Ibid., quoting Syrian news agency SANA.

23. Nabil Shaath interview, Cairo, December 1989.

24. Abdullah Hourani interview, Tunis, June 1989.

25. Ibid., p. 148.

26. Yasser Arafat interview, Tunis, December 1989.

27. Yezid Sayigh, *Quest for a Homeland: Palestinian Military History, 1949–88* (working title, unpublished).

28. Ibid.

29. Yasser Arafat interview, Tunis, December 1989.

30. Associated Press, 5 November 1983.

31. Kuwaiti news agency Kuna, 21 November 1983, quoted in Sahliyeh, op. cit., p. 171.

32. *New York Times* editorial in the *International Herald Tribune*, 18 November 1983.

33. Associated Press, 8 December 1983.

34. Yasser Arafat quoted in *Washington Post*, 25 December 1983.

CHAPTER 13

1. *Middle East Reporter*, 24 December 1983.

2. Yasser Arafat interview, Tunis, December 1989.

3. Mohammed Sobhieh interview, Cairo, November 1989.

4. Widely circulated PLO joke.

5. *New York Times*, 23 December 1983.
6. *Washington Post*, 23 December 1983.
7. Yasser Arafat interview, Tunis, December 1989.
8. *Washington Post*, 27 December 1983.
9. *New York Times*, 17 January 1984.
10. Accords published in *Democratic Front for the Liberation of Palestine Bulletin*, No. 84/85, July 1984.
11. Ibid.
12. Mohammed Hamza interview, Tunis, August 1989. Hamza is Wazir's biographer.
13. West Bank Data Base project: A survey of Israel's Policies, American Enterprise Institute, Washington, 1984.
14. PLO radio recorded by US Foreign Broadcast Information Service, 14 November 1983.
15. *Middle East Reporter*, 1 December 1984.
16. Ibid.
17. *Guardian*, 29 November 1984.
18. Ibid.
19. *Daily Telegraph*, 29 November 1984.
20. Ibid.
21. *Washington Post*, 28 November 1984.
22. *Washington Post*, 28 November 1984.
23. *New York Times*, 30 November 1984.

CHAPTER 14
1. Taher al-Masri interview, Amman, December 1989.
2. *New York Times*, 24 February 1984.
3. *Al-Qabas*, 6 June 1985.
4. *Washington Post*, 13 May 1985.
5. *New York Times*, 30 May 1985.
6. Ahmed Abdel Rahman interview, Tunis, September 1989.
7. *New York Times*, 2 October 1985.
8. *Newsweek* magazine, 14 October 1985.
9. Ahmed Abdel Rahman interview, Tunis, June 1989.
10. Ibid.
11. Interviews with Egyptian officials, Cairo, October 1985.
12. *Financial Times*, 13 October 1985.
13. *New York Times*, 8 November 1985.

14. Hussein aide interview, Amman, September 1989. Name withheld on request.
15. Ibid.
16. *Financial Times*, 20 February 1986.
17. *Middle East Reporter*, 3 March 1986.
18. *Middle East Reporter*, 3 March 1986.
19. US Foreign Broadcast Information Service, 11 December 1984.
20. *Middle East International*, 1 May 1987.
21. William Quandt (Ed.), *The Middle East Ten Years After Camp David*, Washington, 1988, appendix G, p. 475.
22. *New York Times*, 13 May 1987.
23. Taher al-Masri interview, Amman, November 1989.
24. Author's note on press conference.

CHAPTER 15

1. Interview with Arafat adviser, Tunis, September 1989. Name withheld on request.
2. *Middle East Reporter*: Contemporary Mideast Backgrounder, No. 244, December 1987.
3. Salah Khalaf interview, Tunis, June 1989.
4. Zachary Lockman and Joel Beinin (Eds.), *Intifada*, Washington, 1989, p. 100.
5. Suleiman Najab interview, Tunis, June 1989.
6. *Al-Sayyad*, 8 January 1988.
7. *Washington Post*, 4 January 1988.
8. *See* William Quandt (Ed.), *The Middle East Ten Years After Camp David*, Washington, 1989, p. 485.
9. Interview with the authors, Jerusalem, June 1989. Name withheld on request.
10. Ibid.
11. Ibid.
12. Ibid.
13. Faisal al-Husseini interview, Jerusalem, May 1989.
14. Daoud Kuttab interview, Jerusalem, October 1989. Kuttab is a Palestinian journalist.
15. Yasser Arafat interview, Tunis, June 1989.
16. Richard Murphy interview, London, April 1989.

17. *Washington Post*, 28 February 1988.
18. Ibid.
19. Interview with Palestinian insider, Jerusalem, November 1989. Name withheld on request.
20. *Washington Post*, 26 February 1988.
21. See 'The Shultz Initiative, 4 March 1988' in Quandt, op. cit., appendix K, p. 488.
22. Intissar al-Wazir interview, Amman, June 1989.
23. Yasser Arafat interview, Baghdad, January 1990.
24. *Financial Times*, 19 April 1988.
25. *Washington Post*, 6 June 1988.
26. PLO brochure distributed to press at Algiers summit, June 1988.
27. Bassam Abu Sharif interview, Tunis, August 1989.
28. Interview with the authors, London, April 1989. Name withheld on request.
29. Bassam Abu Sharif interview, Tunis, August 1989.
30. Interview with Hussein aide, Amman, December 1989. Name withheld on request.

CHAPTER 16

1. Text issued by the royal palace, Amman, 31 July 1988.
2. Salah Khalaf interview, Tunis, June 1989.
3. Ibid.
4. *New York Times*, 15 August 1988.
5. William Quandt interview, Jerusalem, June 1989.
6. Interview with Swedish foreign ministry official, Stockholm, July 1989. Name withheld on request.
7. Ibid.
8. Ibid.
9. Ibid.
10. Salah Khalaf interview, Tunis, June 1989.
11. Ibid.
12. Text of speech distributed by PLO, 15 November 1988.
13. Salah Khalaf interview, Tunis, August 1989.
14. Text of declaration distributed by PLO, 15 November 1988.
15. *See* declaration in Zachary Lockman and Joel Beinin (Eds.), *Intifada*, Boston, 1989, pp. 395–9.

16. *New York Times*, 28 November 1988.
17. Rita Hauser interview, London, April 1989.
18. Interview with Swedish official, Stockholm, July 1989. Name withheld on request.
19. Ibid.
20. Interview with Arafat aide, Tunis, August 1989. Name withheld on request.
21. *New York Times*, 14 December 1988.
22. Interview with the authors, London, October 1989. Name withheld on request.
23. Ibid.
24. Ibid.
25. Ibid.
26. *New York Times*, 15 December 1988.
27. Ibid.
28. Ibid.

CHAPTER 17
1. *Washington Post*, 31 May 1990.
2. *Al-Siyassa*, Kuwait, 4 June 1990; *Mideast Mirror*, 6 June 1990.
3. *Washington Post*, 31 May 1990.
4. Ibid.
5. Interview with Arafat aide, London, February 1991. Name withheld on request.
6. *Time* magazine, 11 November 1974.
7. *New York Times*, 15 December 1988.
8. *Washington Post*, 3 January 1989.
9. *Washington Post*, 2 February 1989.
10. Interviews with PLO officials, Tunis, April 1989. Names withheld on request.
11. Leila Shaheed interview, Paris, 29 May 1989.
12. Arafat on French television, BBC Summary of World Broadcasts, 4 May 1989.
13. Radio Monte Carlo, BBC SWB, 5 May 1989.
14. Dennis Ross interview, Washington, November 1989.
15. *See* article by Daoud Kuttab, *Washington Post*, 16 April 1989.
16. *Washington Post*, 18 May 1989.

17. Interviews with PLO officials, Tunis, June 1989. Names withheld on request.
18. *Financial Times*, 7 July 1989.
19. Ibid.
20. Bassel Akel interview, London, April 1991.
21. Nabil Shaath interview, London, February 1991.
22. Accounts of Fatah meeting from Fatah officials, Tunis, August 1989.
23. *Washington Post*, 23 November 1989.
24. *Washington Post*, 4 December 1989.
25. BBC SWB, 26 February 1990.
26. Ibid.
27. Nabil Shaath interview, Cairo, April 1991.
28. Interview with Arafat adviser, London, February 1991. Name withheld on request.
29. Bassel Akel interview, London, April 1991.
30. Mohammed Milhem interview, Amman, March 1991.
31. Quoted in *Mideast Mirror*, 12 February 1990.
32. *Mideast Mirror*, 2 April 1990.
33. Afif Safieh interview, London, April 1991.
34. BBC SWB, 23 April 1990.
35. *Middle East Reporter*, 12 May 1990.
36. Interview with PLO official, Amman, March 1991. Name withheld on request.
37. *Washington Post*, 21 May 1990.
38. Nabil Shaath interview, Cairo, April 1991.
39. BBC SWB, 30 May 1990.
40. Iraqi account of summit session, quoted in Pierre Salinger, Secret Dossier, London, 1991, p. 31.
41. Interview with PLO official, Amman, March 1991. Name withheld on request.
42. *Mideast Mirror*, 23 July 1990.
43. Ibid.
44. *Financial Times*, 19 July 1990.
45. *Financial Times*, 25–6 July 1990.
46. Nabil Shaath interview, London, February 1991.
47. Awni Battash interview, Amman, March 1991.

48. Account of conversation from Gamal Sourani interview, Cairo, April 1991.
49. Awni Battash interview, Amman, March 1991.

CHAPTER 18
1. Awni Battash interview, Amman, March 1991.
2. Interview with Khalaf confidant, Amman, March 1991. Name withheld on request.
3. Bassel Akel interview, London, April 1991.
4. *Mideast Mirror*, 6 August 1990.
5. *Middle East Reporter*, 4 August 1990.
6. Ibid.
7. Ibid.
8. Interview with PLO official, Amman, March 1991. Name withheld on request.
9. Associated Press, 7 August 1990.
10. *Mideast Mirror*, 6 August 1990.
11. Associated Press, 7 August 1990.
12. BBC Summary of World Broadcasts, 5 August 1990.
13. BBC SWB, 10 August 1990.
14. *Akhbar al-Yom*, Cairo, 9 March 1991.
15. Interview with PLO official, Cairo, April 1991. Name withheld on request.
16. *Middle East Reporter*, 11 August 1990.
17. Interview with Arafat adviser, Cairo, April 1991. Name withheld on request.
18. Interview with Arafat aide, Amman, March 1991. Name withheld on request.
19. *Middle East Reporter*, 11 August 1990.
20. *Financial Times*, 21 August 1990.
21. Nabil Shaath interview, Cairo, April 1991.
22. *Financial Times*, 21 August 1990.
23. *Middle East Reporter*, 18 August 1990.
24. Ibid.
25. Bassel Akel interview, London, April 1991.
26. Nabil Shaath interview, Cairo, April 1991.
27. Interview with Arafat associate, Amman, March 1991. Name withheld on request.

28. Interview with PLO official, name withheld, Amman, March 1991.
29. Ibid.
30. *Mideast Mirror*, 21 September 1990.
31. *Middle East Reporter*, 6 October 1990.
32. *Mideast Mirror*, 11 September 1990.
33. *Financial Times*, 20 October 1990.
34. Associated Press, 11 October 1990.
35. Reuters, 9 October 1990.
36. *Middle East Reporter*, 17 October 1990.
37. Associated Press, 19 December 1990.
38. Nabil Shaath interview, Cairo, April 1991.
39. *Middle East Reporter*, 12 January 1991.
40. Interview with Arafat adviser, London, April 1991. Name withheld on request.
41. For transcript, see the *Independent*, 14 January 1991.
42. Interview with Western official, Amman, January 1991. Name withheld on request.
43. Interview with Arafat aide, Amman, March 1991. Name withheld on request.
44. Interview with PLO official, Cairo, April 1991. Name withheld on request.
45. Reuters, 13 January 1991.
46. Interview with PLO official, Amman, March 1991. Name withheld on request. Also see *Vanity Fair*, April 1991.
47. Interview with Arafat adviser, London, April 1991. Name withheld on request.
48. *Middle East International*, 25 January 1991.
49. Interview with PLO official, Amman, March 1991. Name withheld on request.
50. WAFA despatch, Algeria, 24 January 1991.
51. BBC SWB, 1 February 1991.
52. Interview with Arafat aide, Cairo, April 1991. Name withheld on request.
53. *International Herald Tribune*, 31 January 1991.
54. *Time* magazine, 4 March and 11 March 1991.
55. Associated Press, 16 February 1991.
56. *Middle East Reporter*, 2 March 1991.

57. Ibid.
58. Nabil Shaath interview, Cairo, April 1991.

CHAPTER 19
1. *Mideast Mirror*, 11 February 1991.
2. Ibid.
3. Associated Press, 9 March 1991.
4. *Washington Post*, 7 March 1991.
5. *El Pais*, 11 March 1991.
6. Ibid.
7. *New York Times*, 16 March 1991.
8. *Washington Post*, 1 A[ril 1991.
9. *See* Walid Khalidi, *At a Critical Juncture: the United States and the Palestinian People*, Washington DC, 1989, pp. 23–8.
10. *Time* magazine, 13 February 1989.
11. United States Information Service Bulletin, 23 May 1989.
12. *Washington Post*, 13 March 1991.
13. Associated Press, 7 April 1991.
14. Associated Press, 23 April 1991.
15. *New York Times*, 24 May 1991.
16. Associated Press, 14 July 1991.
17. WAFA report, 23 August 1991.
18. Associated Press, 8 September 1991.
19. *Washington Post*, 25 September 1991.
20. Associated Press, 26 September 1991.
21. Associated Press, 28 September 1991.
22. *See Washington Post*, 27 September 1991.
23. *See* William Quandt, *Peace Process: American Diplomacy and the Arab–Israeli Conflict since 1967*, Washington, 1993, Appendix M, pp. 497–501.
24. Ibid., pp. 504–5.
25. Associated Press, 31 October 1991.
26. *Washington Post*, 5 June 1992.
27. *Guardian*, 20 April 1992.

CHAPTER 20
1. Reuters, 13 July 1992.
2. Ibid.

3. Reuters, 14 July 1992.
4. Reuters, 30 June 1992.
5. Reuters, 1 July 1992.
6. Reuters, 19 June 1992.
7. Reuters, 28 June 1992.
8. Reuters, 11 July 1992.
9. *Washington Post*, 16 August 1992.
10. Associated Press, 16 August 1992.
11. Ibid.
12. Associated Press, 14 December 1992.
13. *Guardian*, 21 December 1991.
14. Associated Press, 8 December 1992.
15. Associated Press, 18 December 1992.
16. Associated Press, 6 March 1992.
17. Interview with Freddy Zach, Israeli co-ordinator in multilateral talks, Jerusalem, September 1993.

CHAPTER 21
1. *New York Times*, 5 September 1993.
2. Ibid.
3. *Washington Post*, 6 September 1993.
4. Interview with the authors, Jerusalem, September 1993.
5. Ibid.
6. Ibid.
7. *Washington Post*, 9 September 1993.
8. Associated Press, 26 May 1993.
9. Associated Press, 13 May 1993.
10. Interview with Freddy Zach, Jerusalem, September 1993.
11. Associated Press, 12–13 July 1993.
12. Associated Press, 8 August 1993.
13. *Middle East Reporter*, 28 August 1993.
14. Associated Press, 20 August 1993.
15. *Middle East Reporter*, 28 August 1993.

CHAPTER 22
1. Uri Savir, *The Process*, Chapter 8, Peace and Violence, pp. 247–64.

2. Kanafani interview with the authors, Gaza, January 2002.
3. Ibid.
4. Interview with the authors, Gaza, January 2002.
5. *The Israel–Arab Reader*, pp. 433–5.
6. Ibid., pp. 435–6.
7. Ibid., pp. 436–9.
8. Ibid., p. 437.
9. Uri Savir, *The Process*, pp. 103–4.
10. Ibid., p. 105.
11. Ibid., p. 110.
12. *The Israel–Arab Reader*, p. 407.
13. William B. Quandt, *Peace Process: American Diplomacy and the Arab–Israeli Conflict 1967*, pp. 328–32.
14. Interview with the authors, Gaza, January 2002.
15. Said K. Aburish, *Arafat: from Defender to Dictator*, p. 270.
16. Uri Savir, *The Process*, p. 131.
17. Interview with the authors, January 2002.
18. Ibid.
19. *The Israel–Arab Reader*, pp. 455–9.
20. William B. Quandt, *Peace Process: American Diplomacy and the Arab–Israeli Conflict since 1967*, p. 330.
21. Interview with the authors, January 2002.
22. The *New York Times*, 2 July 1994.
23. Interview with the authors, Gaza, January 2002.
24. *Agence France Presse*, 2 July 1994.
25. Interview with the authors, Gaza, January 2002.
26. *The Israel–Arab Reader*, pp. 477–86.
27. Uri Savir, *The Process*.
28. *The Israel–Arab Reader*, p. 494.
29. Uri Savir, *The Process*, pp. 228–39.
30. William B. Quandt, *Peace Process: American Diplomacy and the Arab–Israeli Conflict since 1967*, p. 335, and Uri Savir, *The Process*, pp. 240–2.

CHAPTER 23

1. Uri Savir, *The Process*, p. 262.
2. Interview with the authors, Gaza, January 2002.
3. Uri Savir, *The Process*, p. 262.

4. William B. Quandt, *Peace Process: American Diplomacy and the Arab–Israeli Conflict since 1967*, pp. 336–7.
5. Graham Usher, *Palestine in Crisis: The Struggle for Peace and Political Independence after Oslo*, pp. 44–6.
6. Interview with the authors, Jerusalem, January 2002.
7. Graham Usher, *Palestine in Crisis: The Struggle for Peace and Political Independence after Oslo*, pp. 65–7.
8. Ibid., p. 68.
9. Ibid., p. 63.
10. *The Israel–Arab Reader*, p. 414.
11. Interview with the authors, Gaza, January 2002.
12. Uri Savir, *The Process*, pp. 292–8.
13. Graham Usher, *Palestine in Crisis: The Struggle for Peace and Political Independence after Oslo*, p. 84.
14. Interview with the authors, Gaza, January 2002.
15. Ibid.
16. Ibid.
17. Interview with the authors, Ramallah, January 2002.
18. Graham Usher, *Palestine in Crisis: The Struggle for Peace and Political Independence after Oslo*, p. 89.
19. Ibid., p. 85.
20. William B. Quandt, *Peace Process: American Diplomacy and the Arab–Israeli Conflict since 1967*, p. 343.
21. Interview with the authors, Gaza, January 2002.
22. Uri Savir, *The Process*, p. 299.
23. William B. Quandt, *Peace Process: American Diplomacy and the Arab–Israeli Conflict since 1967*, p. 345.
24. Shaath, interview with the authors, Gaza, January 2002.
25. *The Israel–Arab Reader*, pp. 523–4.
26. William B. Quandt, *Peace Process: American Diplomacy and the Arab–Israeli Conflict since 1967*, p. 347.
27. Graham Usher, *Palestine in Crisis: The Struggle for Peace and Political Independence after Oslo*, p. 91.
28. *PASSIA Summary of 1998*, p. 268.
29. Interview with the authors, Gaza, January 2002.
30. *PASSIA Chronology 1998*, p. 295.
31. Interview with the authors, Gaza, January 2002.
32. *The Israel–Arab Reader*, p. 534.

33. Ibid., p. 534.
34. Ibid., pp. 535–41.
35. William B. Quandt, *Peace Process: American Diplomacy and the Arab–Israeli Conflict since 1967*, p. 357.
36. Interview with the authors, Gaza, January 2002.

CHAPTER 24

1. *The Israel–Arab Reader*, pp. 541–3.
2. Nabil Shaath, interview with the authors, Gaza, January 2002.
3. Larsen, interview with the authors, Jerusalem, January 2002.
4. Yatom, interview with the authors, Tel Aviv, January 2002.
5. Ibid.
6. Interview with the authors, Ramallah, January 2002.
7. Yatom, interview with the authors, Tel Aviv, January 2002.
8. Shaath, interview with the authors, Gaza, January 2002.
9. Ibid.
10. Ibid.
11. Ibid.
12. Yatom, interview with the authors, Tel Aviv, January 2002.
13. Quandt, pp. 363–4.
14. The *New York Review of Books*, 9 August, 2001.
15. Ibid.
16. Ibid.
17. *The Israel–Arab Reader*, pp. 551–4.
18. Interview with the authors, Tel Aviv, January, 2002.
19. Interview with the authors, Gaza, January, 2002.
20. Ibid.
21. Ibid.
22. The *New York Review of Books*, 20 September 2001.
23. Shaath, interview with the authors, Gaza, January 2002.
24. Ibid.
25. Ibid.
26. Ibid.
27. Arafat speech to the Summit, 21 October, *The Israeli–Arab Reader*, pp. 556–60.
28. *The Israel–Arab Reader*, pp 562–4.
29. William B. Quandt, Peace Process: American Diplomacy and the Arab-Israel Conflict since 1967, p. 371.

30. Shaath, interview with the authors, Gaza, January, 2002.
31. The Israel–Arab Reader, pp. 567–73.
32. Shaath, interview with the authors, January 2002.

CHAPTER 25
1. bitterlemons.org website documents.
2. Shaath, interview with authors, Gaza, January 2002.
3. Interview with authors, January, 2002.
4. bitterlemons.org website documents, 30 April 2001.
5. Guardian Unlimited Special Reports 2001
6. bitterlemons.org website documents, June 2001
7. News.Com international website, 11 September 2001
8. *The Guardian*, 19 September 2001
9. *Jerusalem Post*, 17 September 2001
10. bittlerlemons.org website document, 17 November 2001
11. Powell Kentucky speech, 17 November 2001
12. Interview with the authors, Ramallah, January 2002
13. State of the Union Address, White House website, 29 January 2002
14. *Maariv*, 1 February 2002
15. bitterlemons.org
16. Ibid.
17. *Time* magazine, 25 March 2002, p. 29
18. bitterlemons.org
19. *New York Post*, 5 April, p. 3
20. bitterlemons.org
21. Ibid.
22. bitterlemons.org interview, 16 December 2002
23. Name withheld, interview with the authors, Ramallah, January 2003
24. Ibid.
25. *Ha'aretz*, 21 June
26. bitterlemons.org
27. UNSCO report I October 2000–30 September 2001
28. Guardian Unlimited website, Middle East timeline, July–October 2002 Epilogue

BIBLIOGRAPHY

BOOKS

Adams, J. *The Financing of Terror*, London, 1986.

Amos, John W. *Palestinian Resistance: Organisation of a Nationalist Movement*, New York, 1980.

Arian, A. *Politics in Israel: The Second Generation*, London, 1985.

Attayib, Abu, *Flash Back: Beirut 1982*, Nicosia, 1985.

Avnery, U. *My Friend, The Enemy*, London, 1986.

Bakhash, S. *The Reign of the Ayatollahs: Iran and the Islamic Revolution*, London, 1985.

Ball, George W. *Error and Betrayal in Lebanon: An analysis of Israel's invasion of Lebanon and the implications for US–Israeli relations*, Washington, 1984.

Bar Zohar, M. and Harber, E. *The Quest for the Red Prince*, New York, 1982.

Becker, J. *Hitler's Children: The Story of The Baader–Meinhof Gang*, London, 1977.

—— *The PLO: The Rise and Fall of the Palestine Liberation Organisation*, London, 1984.

Begin, M. *The Revolt: Story of the Irgun*, Jerusalem, 1951.

Behbehani, H. *China's Foreign Policy in the Arab World 1955–75*, London, 1981.

Blechman, B. and Kaplan, S. *Force without War: US Armed Forces as a Political Instrument*, The Brookings Institution, Washington.

Brand, L. *Palestinians in the Arab World: Institution Building and The Search for State*, New York, 1988.

Brzezinski, Z. *Power and Principle*, New York, 1985.

Bulloch, J. *Death of a Country: The Civil War in Lebanon*, London, 1977.

Carter J. *The Blood of Abraham: Insights into the Middle East*, Boston, 1985.

Chapman, C. *Whose Promised Land?*, London, 1983.

Chomsky, N. *The Fateful Triangle: The United States, Israel and the Palestinians*. London and Sydney, 1983.

Christopher, W. and others. *American Hostages in Iran: The Conduct of a Crisis*, New Haven and London, 1985.

Cobban, H. *The Palestinian Liberation Organisation: People, Power and Politics*, Cambridge, 1984.

Collins, L. and Lapierre, D. *O Jerusalem*, London, 1972.

Cooley, J. *Green March, Black September*, London 1973.

Curtis, M. (Ed.), *The Palestinians: People, History, Politics*, New Brunswich, New Jersey, 1975.

Darwish, M. *The Complete Works of Mahmoud Darwish*, Beirut, 1979.

Dawisha, A. *Syria and the Lebanese Crisis*, London, 1980.

Day, A. *East Bank/West Bank: Jordan and the Prospects for Peace*, New York, 1986.

Dayan, M. *Story of My Life*, London, 1976.

Deacon, R. *The Israeli Secret Service*, London, 1977.

Dobson, C. and Payne, R. *The Never-Ending War: Terrorism in the 80s*, New York, 1987.

Eisenberg, D. *The Mossad: Inside Stories*, New York, 1978.

Fahmy, I. *Negotiating for Peace in the Middle East*, London, 1983.

Fallaci, O. *Interview with History*, Boston, 1976.

Franji, A. *The PLO and Palestine*, London, 1983.

Freedman, R. *The Middle East since Camp David*, Boulder, Colorado, 1984.

Friedman, T. *From Beirut to Jerusalem*, New York, 1989.

Ghabra, S. *Palestinians in Kuwait: The Family and the Politics of Survival*, Boulder, Colorado, 1987.

Gibb, H. and Kramers, J. *Shorter Encyclopaedia of Islam*, Leiden, 1974.

Gilbert, M. *The Arab–Israeli Conflict: Its History in Maps*, London, 1988.

Gilmour, D. *Dispossessed: The Ordeal of the Palestinians 1917–1980*, London, 1980.

Goldschmidt, A. *A Concise History of the Middle East*, Boulder, Colorado, 1979.

Gordon, D. *The Republic of Lebanon: Nation in Jeopardy*, Boulder, Colorado, 1983.

Gresh, A. *The PLO: The Struggle Within*, London, 1985.

Harkabi, Y. *Israel's Fateful Decisions*, London, 1988 (first publication in Hebrew in 1986).

—— *The Palestinian Covenant and its Meaning*, London and New York, 1979.

Hart, A. *Arafat: Terrorist or Peacemaker?* London, 1984.

Heikal, M. *The Sphinx and the Commissar: The Rise and Fall of Soviet Influence in the Middle East*, New York, 1978.

—— *Cutting The Lion's Tail: Suez Through Egyptian Eyes*, London, 1986.

—— *Nasser: The Cairo Documents*, London, 1972.

—— *The Road to Ramadan*, London, 1975.

—— *Autumn of Fury: The Assassination of Sadat*, London, 1983.

Herzog, C. *The Arab–Israeli Wars: War and Peace in the Middle East from the War of Independence to Lebanon*, London, 1982.

Hiro, D. *Inside The Middle East*, London, 1982.

Hirst, D. *The Gun and The Olive Branch: The Roots of Violence in the Middle East*, London, 1977.

Hirst, D. and Beeson, I. *Sadat*, London, 1981.

Hopwood, D. *Egypt: Politics and Society, 1945–1981*, London, 1982.

Horne, A. *A Savage War of Peace*, London, 1977.

Jumblatt, K. *This is My Legacy*, Paris, 1978.

Ignatius, D. *Agents of Innocence*, New York, 1987.

Israeli, R. (Ed.), *PLO in Lebanon: Selected Documents*, London, 1983.

Iyad, Abu (with Eric Rouleau), *My Home, My Land: A Narrative of the Palestinian Struggle*, New York, 1981.

Kamel, M. *The Camp David Accords*, London, 1986.

Keppel, G. *The Prophet and Pharaoh*, London, 1985.

Khalidi, R. *Under Siege: PLO Decisionmaking During the 1982 War*, New York, 1986.

Khalidi, W. *Conflict and Violence in Lebanon: Confrontation in the Middle East*, Cambridge, Massachusetts, 1979.

Kiernan, T. *Yasir Arafat: The Man and the Myth*, New York, 1975.

Kirisci, K. *The PLO and World Politics: A Study of the Mobilisation of Support for the Palestinian Cause*, London, 1986.

Kissinger, H. *White House Years*, New York and London, 1979.

—— *Years of Upheaval*, New York and London, 1982.

Laqueur, W. and Rubin, B. (Eds.), *The Israel–Arab Reader: A Documentary History of the Middle East Conflict*, London, 1984.

Lockman, Z. and Beinin, J. (Eds.), *Intifada: The Palestinian Uprising Against Israeli Occupation*, Boston, 1989.

Lunt, J. *Hussein of Jordan: Searching for Just and Lasting Peace*, London, 1989.

McDowall, D. *Palestine and Israel: The Uprising and Beyond*, London, 1989.

Ma'oz, M. *Palestinian Leadership on the West Bank*, London, 1984.

—— *Asad: The Sphinx of Damascus*, New York, 1988.

Mansfield, P. *The Arabs*, London, 1982.

Martin, D. and Walcott, J. *Best Laid Plans: The Inside Story of America's War against Terrorism*, New York, 1988.

Meir, G. *My Life*, London, 1975.

Melman, Y. *The Master Terrorist: The True Story Behind Abu Nidal*, New York, 1986.

Melman, Y. and Raviv, D. *The Imperfect Spies: The History of Israeli Intelligence*, London, 1989.

Midkadi, L. *Surviving the Siege of Beirut: a personal account*, London, 1983.

Milstein, U. *A History of the Israeli Paratroopers*, Tel Aviv, 1985 (in Hebrew).

Mishal, S. *The PLO Under Arafat: Between Gun and Olive Branch*, New Haven and London, 1986.

Mitchell, R. *The Society of the Muslim Brothers*, London, 1969.

Morris, B. *The Birth of the Palestinian Refugee Problem, 1947–49*, Cambridge, 1987.

O'Ballance, E. *Arab Guerrilla Power, 1967–72*, London, 1974.

Odeh, B. *Lebanon: Dynamics of Conflict*, London, 1985.

Owen, R. (Ed.), *Essays on the Crisis in Lebanon*, London, 1976.

Palumbo, M. *The Palestinian Catastrophe: The 1948 Expulsion of a People from their Homeland*, London, 1987.

Perlmutter, A. *Two Minutes Over Baghdad*, London, 1982.

Plascov, A. *The Palestinian Refugees in Jordan 1948–57*, London, 1981.

Quandt, W. *Camp David: Peacemaking and Politics*, Washington, 1986.

—— *Decade of Decisions: American Policy Toward the Arab–Israeli Conflict, 1967–1976*, Los Angeles and London, 1977.

—— *Peace Process: American Diplomacy and the Arab–Israeli Conflict since 1967*, Los Angeles, 2001.

—— (Ed.), *The Middle East: Ten Years after Camp David*, Washington, 1988.

Quandt, W., Jabber, F. and Moseley Lesch, A. *The Politics of Palestinian Nationalism*, Los Angeles and London, 1973.

Randal, J. *The Tragedy of Lebanon: Christian Warlords, Israeli Adventurers and American Bunglers*, London, 1983.

Rhodes, James, R. *Anthony Eden*, London, 1986.

Riad, M. *The Struggle for Peace in the Middle East*, London, 1981.

Rodinson, M. *Israel: A Colonial–Settler State?* Paris, 1973.

—— *Israel and the Arabs*, London, 1968.

—— *Mohammed*, London, 1983.

Rosie, G. *The Directory of International Terrorism*, Edinburgh, 1986.

Roth, S. (Ed.), *The Impact of the Six-Day War: A Twenty-Year Assessment*, London, 1988.

Rubenberg, C. *Israel And The American National Interest: A Critical Examination*, Chicago, 1986.

Ruekmkorf, P. *Die Jahre die Ilr Kennt*, Hamburg, 1972 (in German).

Sadat, A. *In Search of Identity*, London, 1978.

Sahliyeh, E. *The PLO After the Lebanon War*, Boulder, Colorado, 1986.

—— *In Search of Leadership: West Bank Politics since 1967*, Washington, 1988.

Said, E. *The Question of Palestine*, New York, 1979.

Salibi, K. *Crossroads to Civil War: Lebanon, 1958–1976*, London, 1976.

Savir, U. *The Process: 1,100 Days that Changed the Middle East*, New York, 1999.

Sayigh, R. *Palestinians: From Peasants to Revolutionaries*, London, 1979.

Sayigh, Y. *Quest for a Homeland: Palestinian military history 1949–88* (working title, unpublished).

Schiff, Z. and Rothstein, R. *Fedayeen: The Story of the Palestinian Guerrillas*, London, 1972.

Schiff, Z. and Ya'ari, E. *Israel's Lebanon War*, New York, 1984.

Schoenberg, H. *A Mandate for Terror: The United Nations and the PLO*, New York, 1989.

Seale, P. *Asad of Syria: The Struggle for the Middle East*, London, 1988.

Segal, J. *Creating the Palestinian State*, Chicago, 1989.

Sharon, A. *Warrior*, New York, 1989.

Shemesh, *The Palestinian Entity, 1959–1974: Arab Politics and the PLO*, London, 1988.

Shimoni, Y. *Political Dictionary of the Arab World*, London, 1987.

Shipler, D. *Arab and Jew: Wounded Spirits in a Promised Land*, New York, 1986.

Shoman, A. *The Indomitable Arab: The Life and Times of Abdulhameed Shoman, Founder of the Arab Bank*, London, 1984.

Silver, E. *Begin: A Biography*, London, 1984.

Sobel, L. (Ed.), *Palestinian Impasse: Arab Guerrillas and International Terror*, New York, 1977.

Sterling, C. *The Terror Network: The Secret War of International Terrorism*, London, 1981.

Stephens, R. *Nasser: A Political Biography*, London, 1971.

Steven, S. *The Spymasters of Israel*, New York, 1982.

Tamir, A. *A Soldier in Search of Peace*, London, 1988.

Timerman, J. *The Longest War*, London, 1982.

Urquhart, B. *A Life in Peace and War*, New York, 1987.

Usher, G. *Palestine in Crisis: The Struggle for Peace and Political Independence after Oslo*, London, 1997.

Vatikiotis, P. J. *The History of Egypt: From Muhammad Ali to Mubarak*, London, 1985.

Venn-Brown, J. (Ed.), *For a Palestinian: A memorial to Wael Zuwaiter*, London, 1984.

Woodward, R. *Veil: The Secret Wars of the CIA 1981–1987*, London, 1987.

Wright, R. *Sacred Rage: The Wrath of Militant Islam*, London, 1986.

Yodfat, Y. and Arnon-Ohanna, Y. *PLO: Strategy and Tactics*, London, 1981.

MONOGRAPHS, DOCUMENTS AND PERIODICALS

Arab Studies Society, 'Uprising in Palestine: The First Year' (Documentation on Human Rights and Palestinian Uprising), Chicago, 1989.

Benvenisti, M. 'Demographic economic, legal, social and political developments in the West Bank', The West Bank Data Base Project, Jerusalem, 1987.

Dodd, P. and Barakat, H. 'River Without Bridges: A Study of the Exodus of the 1967 Palestinian Arab Refugees', Institute for Palestine Studies, Beirut, 1968.

Fiches du Monde Arabe, Beirut.

Financial Times, London.

Foreign Affairs, Washington.

Foreign Policy, Washington.

Guardian, London.

Haddad, W. 'Lebanon: The Politics of Revolving Doors', The Washington Papers, New York, 1985.

International Affairs, London, spring, 1989.

'Israel in Lebanon': The Report of the International Commission to inquire into reported violations of International Law by Israel during its invasion of the Lebanon, London, 1983.

Jaffee Centre for Strategic Studies, 'International Terrorism in 1988', Tel Aviv, 1989.

Jaffee Centre, 'The West Bank and Gaza: Israel's Options for Peace', Tel Aviv, 1989.

Jaffee Centre, 'The International Dimension of Palestinian Terrorism', Tel Aviv, 1986.

Journal of Palestine Studies, Washington and Kuwait.

The Jerusalem Quarterly, Nos 47–9, 1988.

The Jerusalem Journal of International Relations, June, 1989.

Khalidi, W. 'At A Critical Juncture: The United States and the Palestinian People', Washington, March, 1989.

McDowall, D. 'The Palestinians: The Minority Rights Group Report', No. 24, London, 1987.

Miller, A. D. 'The Arab States and the Palestinian Question: Between Ideology and Self-Interest', The Washington Papers, New York, 1986.
—— 'The PLO and the Politics of Survival', published with the Centre for Strategic and International Studies, Georgetown University, Washington, DC, 1983.
Middle East International, London.
The Middle East Journal, autumn, 1988.
Mussalam, S. 'The PLO: The Palestine Liberation Organization', Brattleboro, Vermont, 1988.
New York Times, New York.
Playboy magazine, New York.
Roy, S. 'The Gaza Strip Survey', The West Bank Data Base Project, Jerusalem, 1986.
Safieh, A. 'One People Too Many?', Nijmegen, 1987.
Time magazine, New York.
The Tower Commission Report, *New York Times*, New York, 1987.
The Washington Institute's Presidential Study Group, 'Building for Peace: An American Strategy for the Middle East', Washington, 1988.
Washington Post, Washington.
Ziad, Abu-Amr, 'The Origins of Political Movement in the Gaza Strip (1948–67)', Bir Zeit University, West Bank.

INDEX